Internet-Based Workflow Management

Internet-Based Workflow Management

Toward a Semantic Web

Dan C. Marinescu

A JOHN WILEY & SONS, INC., PUBLICATION

Copyright © 2002 by John Wiley & Sons, Inc., New York. All rights reserved.

Published simultaneously in Canada.

For ordering and customer service, call 1-800-CALL WILEY.

Library of Congress Cataloging-in-Publication Data:

Marinescu, Dan C.
 Internet-based workflow management: Toward a semantic web/
 Dan C. Marinescu.
  p. cm.
  Includes bibliographical references and index.
  ISBN 0-471-43962-2 (cloth: alk. paper)

Printed in the United States of America

10 9 8 7 6 5 4 3 2 1

To Magda and Andrei

Contents

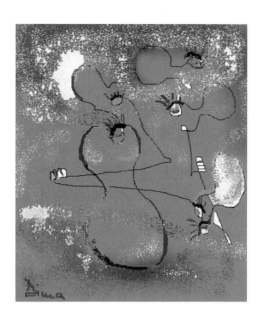

Preface

The term *workflow* means the coordinated execution of multiple tasks or activities. Handling a loan application, an insurance claim, or an application for a passport follow well-established procedures called *processes* and rely on humans and computers to carry out individual tasks.

At this time, workflows have numerous applications in office automation, business processes, and manufacturing. Similar concepts can be extended to virtually all aspects of human activities. The collection and analysis of experimental data in a scientific experiment, battlefield management, logistics support for the merger of two companies, and health care management are all examples of complex activities described by workflows.

There is little doubt that the Internet will gradually evolve into a globally distributed computing system. In this vision, a network access device, be it a a hand-held device such as a palmtop, or a portable phone, a laptop, or a desktop, will provide an access point to the information grid and allow end users to share computing resources and information.

Though the cost/performance factors of the main hardware components of a network access device, microprocessors, memory chips, secondary storage devices, and displays continue to improve, their rate of improvement will most likely be exceeded by the demands of computer applications. Thus, local resources available on the network access device will be less and less adequate to carry out user-initiated tasks.

At the same time, the demand for shared services and shared data will grow continuously. Many applications will need access to large databases available only through network access and to services provided by specialized servers distributed throughout the network. Applications will demand permanent access to shared as well as private data. Storing private data on a laptop connected intermittently to the network limits access to that data; thus, a persistent storage service would be one of several societal services provided in this globally-shared environment.

New computing models such as nomadic, network-centric, and network-aware computing will help transform this vision into reality. We will gradually build a semantic Web, a more sophisticated infrastructure similar to a power grid called an information grid, that favors resource sharing. Service grids will support sharing of services, computational and data grids will support collaborative efforts of large groups scattered around the world.

Information grids are likely to require sophisticated mechanisms for coordination of complex activities. Service composition in service grids and metacomputing in computational grids are two different applications of the workflow concept that look at the Internet as a large virtual machine with abundant resources.

Even today many business processes depend on the Internet. E-commerce and Business-to-Business are probably the most notable examples of Internet-centric applications requiring some form of workflow management.

There are two aspects of workflow management: one covers the understanding of the underlying process, identification of the individual activities involved, the relationships among them, and, ultimately, the generation of a formal description of the process; the other aspect covers the infrastructure for handling individual cases. The first problem is typically addressed by domain experts, individuals trained in business, science, engineering, health care, and so on. The second problem can only be handled by individuals who have some understanding of computer science; they need to map the formal description of processes into network-aware algorithms, write complex software systems to implement the algorithms, and optimize them.

This book is concerned with the infrastructure of Internet-based workflows and attempts to provide the necessary background for research and development in this area to domain experts. More and more businesspeople, scientists, engineers, and other individuals without formal training in computer science are involved in the development of computing systems and computer software and they do need a clear understanding of the concepts and principles of the field.

This book introduces basic concepts in the area of workflow management, distributed systems, modeling of distributed systems and workflows, networking, quality of service, open systems, software agents, knowledge management, and planning. The book presents elements of the process coordination infrastructure.

The software necessary to glue together various components of a distributed system is called middleware. The middleware allows a layperson to request services in human terms rather than become acquainted with the intricacies of complex systems that the experts themselves have troubles fully comprehending.

The last chapter of this book provides some insights into a mobile agent system used for workflow management. A link to the supplementary software files for this book is provided through the Wiley catalog at www.wiley.com on Electrical Engineering page's Software Supplements section. The files can be accessed directly on the Wiley public ftp area at the address: `ftp://ftp.wiley.com/public/sci_tech_med` `/internet_workflow/index.html`

The author has developed some of the material covered in this book for several courses taught in the Computer Sciences Department at Purdue University: the undergraduate and graduate courses in Computer Networks; a graduate course in Distributed Systems; and a graduate seminar in Network-Centric Computing. Many thanks are due to the students who have used several chapters of this book for their class work and have provided many sensible comments.

Howard Jay (H.J.) Siegel and his students have participated in the graduate seminar and have initiated very fruitful discussions. Ladislau (Lotzi) Bölöni, Kyungkoo Jun, and Ruibing Hao have made significant contributions to the development of the system presented in Chapter 8.

Several colleagues have read the manuscript. Octavian Carbunar has spent a considerable amount of time going through the entire book with a fine tooth comb and has made excellent suggestions. Chuang Lin from Tsinghua University in Bejing, China, has read carefully Chapter 3 and helped clarify some subtle aspects of Petri net modeling. Wojciech Szpankowski has provided constant encouragement throughout the entire duration of the project.

I would also like to thank my coauthors I have worked with over the past 20 years: Mike Atallah, Timothy Baker, Tom Cassavant, Chuang Lin, Robert Lynch, Vernon Rego, John Rice, Michael Rossmann, Howard Jay Siegel, Wojciech Szpankowski, Helmut Waldschmidt, Andrew Whinston, Franz Busch, A. Chaudhury, Hagen Hultzsch, Jim Lumpp, Jurgen Lowsky, Mathias Richter, and Emanuel Vavalis.

I extend my thanks to my former students and post-doctoral fellows who have stimulated my thinking with their inquisitiveness: Ladislau Bölöni, Marius Cornea-Hasegan, Jin Dong, Kyungkoo Jun, Ruibing Hao, Yongchang Ji, Akihiro Kawabata, Christina Lock, Ioana Martin, Mihai Sirbu, K.C. vanZandt, Zhonghyun Zhang, Bernard Waltsburger, Kuei Yu Wang.

Philippe Jacquet from INRIA Rocquancourt has been a very gracious host during the summer months for the past few years; in Paris, far from the tumultuous life of West Lafayette, Indiana, I was able to concentrate on this book. Erol Gelenbe and the administration of the University of Central Florida have created the conditions I needed to finish the book.

I would like to acknowledge the support I had over the years from funding agencies including ARO, DOE, and NASA. I am especially grateful to the National Science Foundation for numerous grants supporting my research in computational biology, software agents, and workflow management.

I am indebted to my good friend George Dima who has created the drawings for the cover and for each chapter of this book. George is an accomplished artist, a fine violinist, member of the Bucharest Philharmonic Orchestra. I knew for a long time that he is a very talented painter, but only recently I came across his computer-generated drawings. I was mesmerized by their fine humor, keen sense of observation, and sensibility. You may enjoy his drawings more than my book, but it is worth it for me to take the chance!

Last but not least, I want to express my gratitude to my wife, Magdalena, who has surrounded us with a stimulating intellectual environment; her support and dedication have motivated me more than anything else and her calm and patience have scattered many real and imaginary clouds.

I should not forget Hector Boticelli, our precious "dingo", who spent many hours sound asleep in my office, "guarding" the manuscript.

DAN C. MARINESCU

March 1, 2002
Orlando, Florida

Acronyms

ABR	available bit rate
ACL	agent communication language
ACS	agent control subprotocol
ADSL	asymmetric data service line
AF	assured forwarding
AIMD	additive increase multiplicative decrease
AMS	agent management system
API	application program interface
ARP	address resolution protocol
ARQ	automatic repeat request
AS	autonomous system
ATM	asynchronous transmission mode
BDI	belif-desire-intentions
BEF	best-effort
BNF	Backhus Naur Form
BPA	basic process algebra
CAD	computer-aided design
CBR	constant bit rate
CCD	charged coupled device
CIDR	classless interdomain routing
CL	controlled load

CORBA   Common Object Request Broker Architecture
CRA   collision resolution algorithm
CSMA/CD carrier sense multiple access with collision detection
CSP   communicating sequential processes
CU   control unit

DBMS   database management systems
DCOM   distributed component object model
DCT   discrete cosine transform
DFT   discrete Fourier transform
DHCP   dynamic host reconfiguration protocol
DNS   domain name server
DRR   deficit round robin
DV   distance vector routing algorithm

ECN   explicit congestion notification
EF   expedited forwarding
ER   entity relationship

FCFS   first come first serve
FDA   Food and Drug Administration
FDDI   fiber distributed data interface
FDM   frequency division multiplexing
FIFO   first in first out
FIPA   Foundation for Intelligent Physical Agents
FTP   file transfer protocol

GIF   graphics interchange format
GPE   global predicate evaluation
GPS   generalized processor sharing
GS   guaranteed services
GUI   graphics user interface

HFC   hybrid fiber coaxial cable
HLPN   high-level Petri net
HTML   hypertext markup language
HTTP   hypertext transfer protocol

IANA   Internet Assigned Numbers Authority
ICMP   Internet control message protocol
IDL   Interface definition Language
IETF   Internet Engineering Task Force
iff   if and only if
IMAP   Internet mail access protocol
IP   Internet protocol
ISDN   integrated services data network

ISO	International Standards Organization
ISP	Internet service provider
IT	information technology
JNI	Java native interface
JPEG	Joint Photographic Experts Group
Jess	Java expert system shell
KB	knowledge base
Kbps	kilobits per second
KQML	Knowledge Querry and Manipulation Language
LAN	local area network
LCFS	last come first serve
LDAP	lighweight directory access protocol
LIFO	last in first out
LS	link state routing algorithm
MAC	medium access control (networking)
MAC	message authorization code (security)
Mbps	megabits per second
MIME	multipurpose Internet mail extension
MPEG	Motion Picture Expert Group
MPLS	multi protocol label switch
MSS	maximum segment size
MTU	maximum transport unit
NAP	network access point
NC	no consensus
OKBC	open knowledge base connectivity
OMG	Object Management Group
OS	operating system
OSPF	open shortest path first
PD	program director
PDA	personal digital assistant
PDE	partial differential equations
PDU	protocol data unit
PHP	per-hop behavior
PS	processor sharing
P/T	place/transition net
QoS	quality of service
RDF	resource description format
RED	random early detection
RIO	random early detection with in and out classes
RIP	routing information protocol

RMA	random multiple access
RMI	remote method invocation
RPC	remote procedure call
RR	round robin
RSVP	resource reservation protocol
RTCP	real-time control protocol
RTP	real-time protocol
RTSP	real-time streaming protocol
RTT	round trip time
SF	sender faulty
SGML	Standard Generalized Markup Language
SHLPN	stochatic high-level Petri net
SMTP	simple mail transfer protocol
SPN	stochastic Petri net
SQL	structured query language
SR	selective repeat
TCB	trusted computer base
TCP	transport control protocol
TDM	time division multiplexing
TDU	transport data unit
ToS	type of service
TRB	terminating reliable broadcast
TTL	time to live
UDP	user datagram protocol
URL	uniform resource locator
UTP	unshielded twisted pairs
VBR	variable bit rate
VC	virtual circuit
VKB	virtual knowledge beliefs
VLSI	very large scale integration
VMTP	versatile message transaction protocol
WAN	wide area network
WfMC	Workflow Management Coalition
WFDL	workflow definition language
WFMS	workflow management system
WFQ	weighted fair queuing
WRED	weighted random early detection
WRR	weighted round robin
XML	Extended Markup Language

Internet-Based
Workflow Management

1

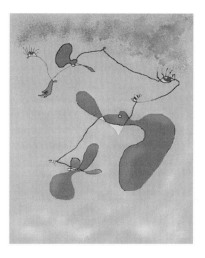

Internet-Based Workflows

1.1 WORKFLOWS AND THE INTERNET

Nowadays it is very difficult to identify any activity that does not use computers to
store and process information. Education, commerce, financial services, health care,
entertainment, defense, law enforcement, science and engineering are critical areas
of human activity profoundly dependent upon access to computers. Without leaving
her desk, within the time span of a few hours, a scholar could gather the most recent
research reports on wireless communication, order a new computer, visit the library
of rare manuscripts at the Vatican, examine images sent from Mars by a space probe,
trade stocks, make travel arrangements for the next scientific meeting, and take a
tour of the new Tate gallery in London. All these are possible because computers are
linked together by the worldwide computer network called the Internet.

Yet, we would like to use the resource-rich environment supported by the Internet
to carry out more complex tasks. Consider, for example, a distributed healthcare
support system consisting of a very large number of sensors and wearable computers
connected via wireless channels to home computers, connected in turn to the Internet
via high-speed links. The system would be used to monitor outpatients, check their
vital signs, and determine if they are taking the prescribed medicine; it would allow a

patient to schedule a physical appointment with a doctor, or a doctor to pay a virtual visit to the patient. The same system would enable the Food and Drug Administration (FDA) to collect data about the trial of an experimental drug and speed-up the drug approval process; it would also enable public health officials to have instant access to data regarding epidemics and prevent the spreading of diseases.

Imagine that your business requires you to relocate to a new city. The list of tasks that will consume your time and energy seems infinite: buy a new home, sell the old one, find good schools for your children, make the necessary arrangements with a moving company, contact utilities to have electricity, gas, phone, cable services installed, locate a physician and transfer the medical records of the family, and on and on. While this process cannot be completely automated, one can imagine an intelligent system that could assist you in coordinating this activity. First, the system learns the parameters of problems, e.g., the time frame for the move, the location and price for the home, and so on. Then, every evening the system informs you of the progress made; for example, it provides virtual tours of several homes that meet your criteria, a list of moving companies and a fair comparison among them, and so on. Once you have made a decision, the system works toward achieving the specific goal and makes sure that all possible conflicts are either resolved or you are made aware of them, and you will have to adjust your goal accordingly.

In each of these cases we have a large system with many data collection points, services, and computers that organize the data into knowledge and help humans coordinate the execution of complex tasks; we need sophisticated workflow management systems.

This chapter introduces Internet-based workflows. First, we provide a historic perspective and review enabling technologies; we discuss sensors and data intensive applications, and present nomadic, network-centric, and network-aware computing. Then, we introduce workflows; we start with an informal discussion and provide several examples to illustrate the power of the concept and the challenges encountered. We examine the workflow reference model, discuss the relationship between workflows and database management systems, present Internet workflow models, and cover workflow coordination. Then, we introduce several workflow patterns and workflow enactment models and conclude the chapter with a discussion of challenges posed by dynamic workflows.

1.1.1 Historic Perspective

Historically, very little has happened in the area of computer networks and workflows since the fall of the Roman Empire in 476 A.D. until the 1940s.

The first operational computer, the ENIAC, was built by J. Presper Eckert and John Mauchly at the Moore School of the University of Pennsylvania in the early 1940s and was publicly disclosed in 1946; the first commercial computer, UNIVAC I, capable of performing some 1900 additions/second was introduced in 1951; the first supercomputer, the CDC 6600, designed by Seymour Cray, was announced in 1963; IBM launched System/360 in 1964; a year later DEC unveiled the first commercial minicomputer, the PDP 8, capable of performing some $330,000$ additions/second; in

1977 the first personal computer, the Apple II was marketed and the IBM PC, rated at about $240,000$ additions/sec, was introduced 4 years later, in 1981.

In the half century since the introduction of the first commercial computer, the price performance of computers has increased dramatically while the power consumption and the size have decreased at an astonishing rate. In the summer of 2001 a laptop with 1 GHz Pentium III processor has an adjusted price/performance ratio of roughly 2.4×10^6 compared to UNIVAC I; the power consumption has decreased by three to four orders of magnitude, and the size by almost three orders of magnitude.

In December 1969, a network with four nodes connected by 56 kilobits per second (Kbps) communication channels became operational. The network was funded by the Advanced Research Project Agency (ARPA) and it was called the ARPANET. The National Science Foundation initiated the development of the NSFNET in 1985. The NSFNET was decommissioned in 1995 and the modern Internet was born.

Over the last two decades of the 20th century, the Internet had experienced an exponential, or nearly exponential growth in the number of networks, computers, and users. We witnessed a 12-fold increase in the number of computers connected to the Internet over a period of 5 years, from 5 million in 1995 to close to 60 million in 2000. At the same time, the speed of the networks has increased dramatically.

The rate of progress is astonishing. It took the telephone 70 years to be installed in 50 million homes in the United States; the radio needed 30 years and television 13 years to reach the same milestone; the Internet needed only 4 years. Our increasing dependency on computers in all forms of human activities implies that more individuals will use the Internet and we need to rethink the computer access paradigms, models, languages, and tools.

1.1.2   Enabling Technologies

During the 1900s we witnessed an increasingly deeper integration of computer and communication technologies into human activities. Some of us carry a laptop or a wireless palmtop computer at all times; computers connected to the Internet are installed in offices, in schools and libraries and in cafes. At the time of this writing a large segment of the households in the Unites States , about 25%, have two or more computers and this figure continues to increase, and many homes have a high-speed Internet connection.

Significant technological advances will alter profoundly the information landscape. While the 1980s was the decade of microprocessors and the 1990s the decade of optical technologies for data communication and data storage, the first decade of the new millennium will most likely see an explosive development of sensors and wireless communication, see Fig. 1.1.

Thus, most of the critical elements of the information society will be in place: large amounts of data will be generated by sensors, transmitted via wireless channels to ground stations, then moved through fast optical channels, processed by fast processors, and stored using high-capacity optical technology. The only missing piece is a software infrastructure facilitating a seamless composition of services in a semantic Web. In this new world, the network becomes a critical component of the

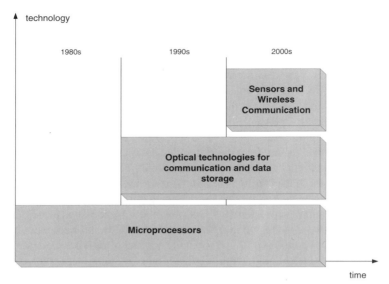

technology

1980s   1990s   2000s

Sensors and
Wireless
Communication

Optical technologies for
communication and data
storage

Microprocessors

time

Fig. 1.1   Driving forces in the information technology area.

social infrastructure and workflow management a very important element of the new economy.

The unprecedented growth of the Internet and the technological feasibility of Internet-based workflows are due to advances in communication, very large system integration (VLSI), storage technologies, and sensor technologies.

Advances in communication technologies. Very high-speed networks and wireless communication will dominate the communication landscape. In the following examples the bandwidth is measured in million bits per second (Mbps), and the volume of data transferred in billions of bytes per hour (GB/hour). Today T3 and OC-3 communication channels with bandwidth of 45 Mbps and 155 Mbps, respectively, are wide-spread. The amount of data transferred using these links are approximately 20 and 70 GB/hour, respectively. Faster channels, OC-12, OC-48, and OC-192 with a bandwidth of 622 Mbps, 2488 Mbps, and 9952 Mbps allow a considerable increase of the volume of data transferred to about 280 GB/hour, 1120 GB/hour, and 4480 GB/hour, respectively.

Advances in VLSI and storage technologies. Changes in the VLSI technologies and computer architecture will lead to a 10-fold increase in computational capabilities over the next 5 years and 100-fold increase over the next 10 years. Changes in storage technology will provide the capacity to store huge amounts of information.

In 2001 a high-end PC had a 1.5 GHz CPU, 256 MB of memory, an 80 GB disk, and a 100 Mbps network connection. In 2003 the same PC is projected to have an 8 GHz processor, a 1 GB memory, a 128 GB disk, and a 1 Gbps network connection. For 2010 the CPU speed is projected to be 64 GHz, the main memory to increase to 16 GB, the disk to 2, 000 GB, and the network connection speed to 10 Gbps.

In 2002 the minimum feature size will be 0.15 μm and it is expected to decrease to 0.005 μm in 2011. As a result, during this period the density of memory bits will

Table 1.1 Projected evolution of VLSI technology.

Year	2002	2005	2008	2011
Minimum feature size (μm, 10^{-6} meter)	0.13	0.10	0.07	0.05
Memory Bits per chip (billions, 10^9)	4	16	64	256
Logic Transistors per cm^2 (millions, 10^6)	18	44	108	260

increase 64- fold and the cost per memory bit will decrease 5-fold. It is projected that during this period the density of transistors will increase 7-fold, the density of bits in logic circuits will increase 15-fold, and the cost per transistor will decrease 20-fold, see Table 1.1.

Hand-held network access devices and smart appliances using wireless communication are likely to be a common fixture of the next decades.

Advances in sensor technologies. The impact of the sensors coupled with wireless technology cannot be underestimated. Already, emergency services are alerted instantly when air bags deploy after a traffic accident. In the future, sensors will provide up-to-date information about air and terrestrial traffic and will allow computers to direct the traffic to avoid congestion, to minimize air pollution, and to avoid extreme weather. Individual sensors built into home appliances will monitor their operation and send requests for service directly to the company maintaining a system when the working parameters of the system are off. Sensors will monitor the vital signs of patients after they are released from a hospital and will signal when a patient fails to take prescription medication.

1.1.3 Nomadic, Network-Centric, and Network-Aware Computing

The Internet will gradually evolve into a globally distributed computing system. In this vision, a network access device, be it a a hand-held device such as a palmtop, or a portable phone, a laptop, or a desktop, will provide an access point to the information grid and allow end users to share computing resources and information.

Though the cost/performance factors of the main hardware components of a network access device, microprocessors, memory chips, storage devices, and displays continue to improve, their rate of improvement will most likely be exceeded by the demands of computer applications. Thus, local resources available on the network access device will be less and less adequate to carry out the user tasks.

At the same time, the demand for shared services and data will grow continuously. Many applications will need access to large databases available only through network access and to services provided by specialized servers distributed throughout the network. Applications will demand permanent access to shared as well as private data. Storing private data on a laptop connected intermittently to the network limits access to that data, thus, a persistent storage service would be one of several societal services provided in this globally shared environment.

New models such as nomadic, network-centric, and network-aware computing will help transform this vision into reality. The definitions given below are informal and the requirements of the models discussed below often overlap.

Nomadic computing allows seamless access to information regardless of the physical location of the end user and the device used to access the Internet.

Network-centric computing requires minimal local resources and a high degree of connectivity to heterogeneous computational platforms geographically distributed, independently operated, and linked together into a structure similar with a power grid.

Network-aware computing views an expanded Internet as a collection of services and agents capable of locating resources and accessing remote data and services on behalf of end users.

Traditional distributed applications consist of entities statically bound to an execution environment and cooperating with other entities in a *network-unaware* manner. A network- unaware application behaves identically whether it runs on a 100 Gflops supercomputer connected to the Internet via a 145 Mbps link or on a palmtop PC connected to the Internet by a 9600 bps channel. This dogma is challenged by mobile, network-aware applications, capable of reconfiguring themselves depending on their current environment and able of utilizing the rich pool of remote resources accessible via the Internet.

Nomadic, network-centric, and network-aware computing are a necessity for a modern society; they are technologically feasible and provide distinctive economical advantages over other paradigms.

The needs for computing resources of many individuals and organizations occur in bursts of variable intensity and duration. Dedicated computing facilities are often idle for long periods of time. The new computing models are best suited for *demand-driven computing*.

The widespread use of sensors will lead to many data-intensive, naturally distributed applications. We say that the applications are *data intensive* because the sensors will generate a vast amount of data that has to be structured into some form of knowledge; the applications are distributed because the sensors, the actuators, the services, and the humans involved will be scattered over wide geographic areas.

1.1.4 Information Grids; the Semantic Web

The World Wide Web, or simply the Web, was first introduced by T. Berners-Lee and his co-workers as an environment allowing groups involved in high-energy physics experiments at the European Center for Nuclear Research (CERN) in Geneva, Switzerland, to collaborate and share their results.

The Web is the "killer application" that has made the Internet enormously popular and triggered its exponential growth. Introduced in the 1990s, the Web is widely regarded as a revolution in communication technology with a social and economic impact similar to the one caused by the introduction of the telephone in the 1870s and of broadcast radio and television of the 1920s and 1930s. In 1998 more than 75% of the Internet traffic was Web related.

While the Web as we know it today allows individuals to search and retrieve information, there is a need for more sophisticated means to gather, retrieve, process, and filter information distributed over a wide-area network. A very significant challenge is to structure the vast amount of information available on the Internet into knowledge. A related challenge is to design information grids, to look at the Internet as a large virtual machine capable of providing a wide variety of societal services, or, in other words, to create a semantic Web.

Information grids allow individual users to perform computational tasks on remote systems and request services offered by autonomous service providers. Service and computational grids are collections of autonomous computers connected to the Internet; they are presented in Chapter 5. Here, we only introduce them informally. A service grid is an ensemble of autonomous service providers. A computational grid consists of a set of nodes, each node has several computers, operates under a different administrative authority, and the autonomous administrative domain have agreed to cooperate with one another.

Workflows benefit from the resource-rich environment provided by the information grids but, at the same time, resource management is considerably more difficult in information grids because the solution space could be extraordinarily large. Multiple flavors of the same service may coexist and workflow management requires choices based on timing, policy constraints, quality, and cost. Moreover, we have to address the problem of scheduling dependent tasks on autonomous systems; we have the choice of anticipatory scheduling and resource reservation policies versus bidding for resources on spot markets at the time when resources are actually needed.

Service composition in service grids and metacomputing in computational grids are two different applications of the workflow concept that look at the Internet as a large virtual machine with abundant resources. While research in computational grids has made some progress in recent years, the rate of progress could be significantly accelerated by the infusion of interest and capital from those interested in E-commerce, Business-to-Business, and other high economic impact applications of service grids. Let us remember that though initially developed for military research and academia, the Internet witnessed its explosive growth only after it became widely used for business, industrial, and commercial applications. We believe that now is the right time to examine closely the similarities between these two applications of workflows and build an infrastructure capable of supporting both of them at the same time, rather than two separate ones.

1.1.5 Workflow Management in a Semantic Web

Originally, workflow management was considered a discipline confined to the automation of business processes [41]. Today most business processes depend on the Internet and workflow management has evolved into a network-centric discipline.

The scope of workflow management has broadened. The basic ideas and technologies for automation of business processes can be extended to virtually all areas of human endeavor from science and engineering to entertainment. Process coordination provides the means to improve the quality of service, increase flexibility, allow more choices, and support more complex services offered by independent service providers in an information grid.

Production, administrative, collaborative, and ad hoc workflows require that documents, information, or tasks be passed from one participant to another for action, according to a set of procedural rules. Production workflows manage a large number of similar tasks with the explicit goal of optimizing productivity. Administrative workflows define processes, while collaborative workflows focus on teams working toward common goals. Workflow activities emerged in the 1980s and have evolved since into a multibillion dollar industry.

E-commerce and Business-to-Business are probably the most notable examples of Internet-centric applications requiring some form of workflow management. E-commerce has flourished in recent years; many businesses encourage their customers to order their products online and some, including PC makers, only build their products on demand. Various Business-to-Business models help companies reduce their inventories and outsource major components.

A number of technological developments have changed the economics of workflow management. The computing infrastructure has become more affordable; the Internet allows low-cost workflow deployment and short development cycles.

In the general case, the actors involved in a workflow are geographically scattered and communicate via the Internet. In such cases, reaching consensus among various actors involved is considerably more difficult. The additional complexity due to unreliable communication channels and unbounded communication delays makes workflow management more difficult. Sophisticated protocols need to be developed to ensure security, fault tolerance, and reliable communication.

The answers to basic questions regarding workflow management in information grids require insights into several areas including distributed systems, networking, database systems, modeling and analysis, knowledge engineering, software agent, software engineering, and information theory, as shown in Figure 1.2.

1.2 INFORMAL INTRODUCTION TO WORKFLOWS

Workflows are pervasive in virtually all areas of human endeavor. Processing of an invoice or of an insurance claim, the procedures followed in case of a natural disaster, the protocol for data acquisition and analysis in an experimental science, a script describing the execution of a group of programs using a set of computers interconnected with one another, the composition of services advertised by autonomous service providers connected to the Internet, and the procedure followed by a pilot to land an airplane could all be viewed as workflows.

Yet, there are substantial differences between these examples. The first example covers rather static activities where unexpected events seldom occur that trigger the

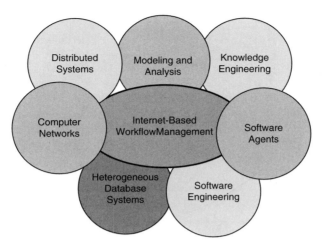

Fig. 1.2   Internet-based workflow management is a discipline at the intersection of several areas including distributed systems, networking, databases, modeling and analysis, knowledge engineering, software agents, and software engineering.

need to modify the workflow. All the other examples require dynamic decisions during the enactment of a case: the magnitude of the natural disaster, a new effect that requires rethinking of the experiment, unavailability of some resources during the execution of the script, and a severe storm during landing require dynamic changes in the workflow for a particular case. For example, the pilot may divert the airplane to a nearby airport, or the scientist may request the advice of a colleague.

Another trait of the second group of workflows is their complexity. These workflows typically involve a significant number of actors: humans, sensors, actuators, computers, and possibly other man-made devices that provide input for decisions, modify the environment, or participate in the decision-making process. In some cases, the actors involved are colocated; then the delay experienced by communication messages is bounded, the communication is reliable, and the workflow management can focus only on the process aspect of the workflow.

In this section we introduce the concept of workflow by means of examples.

1.2.1   Assembly of a Laptop

We pointed out earlier that several companies manufacture PCs and laptops on demand, according to specific requirements of each customer. A customer fills out a Web-based order form, the orders are processed on a first come, first served basis and the assembly process starts in a matter of hours or days. The assembly process must be well defined to ensure high productivity, rapid turnaround time, and little room for error.

We now investigate the detailed specification of the assembly process of a computer using an example inspired by Casati et al. [13].

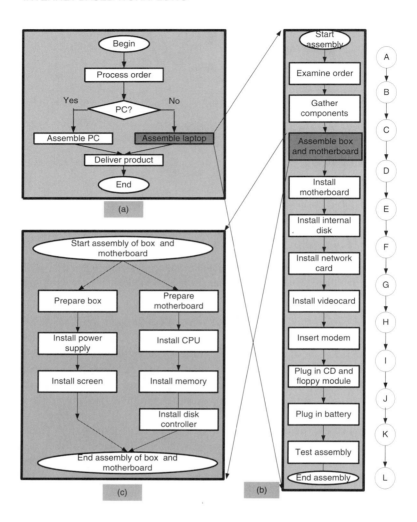

Fig. 1.3 The process of assembly of a PC or a laptop. (a) The process describing the handling of an order. (b) The laptop assembly process as a sequence of tasks. On the right the states traversed by the process. In state A the task `Examine order` is ready to start execution and as a result of its execution the system moves to state B when the task `Gather components` is ready for execution. (c) The process describing the assembly of the box and motherboard.

The entire process is triggered by an order from a customer, as shown by the process description in Figure 1.3(a). We have the choice to order a PC or a laptop. Once we determine that the order is for a laptop, we trigger the laptop assembly process. The laptop assembly starts with an analysis of customer's order, see Figure 1.3(b). First, we identify the model and the components needed for that particular model. After collecting the necessary components, we start to assemble the laptop box and the motherboard; then we install the motherboard into the box, install the hard disk followed by the network and the video cards, install the modem, plug in the module containing the CD and the floppy disk, mount the battery, and finally test the assembly.

Some of the tasks are more complex than the others. In Figure 1.3(c) we show the detailed description of the task called *assemble laptop box and motherboard*. This task consists of two independent subtasks:

(i) prepare the box and install the power supply and the screen;

(ii) prepare the motherboard, install the CPU, the memory, and the disk controller.

Task execution obeys causal relationships, the tasks in a process description such as the ones in Figure 1.3 are executed in a specific order. The "cause" triggering the execution of a task is called an *event*. In turn, events can be causally related to one another or may be unrelated. A more formal discussion of causality and events is deferred until Chapter 2. Here we only introduce the concept of an event.

A first observation based on the examples in Figure 1.3 is that a process description consists of tasks, events triggering task activation, and control structures. The tasks are shown explicitly while events are implicit. Events are generated by the completion of a task or by a decision made by a control structure and, in turn, they trigger the activation of tasks or control structures. For example, the task "assemble laptop" is triggered by the event "NO" generated by the control structure "PC?"; the task "install internal disk" in the process description of the laptop assembly is triggered by the event signaling the completion of the previous task "install motherboard."

The process descriptions in Figure 1.3 are generic blueprints for the actions necessary to assemble any PC or laptop model. Once we have an actual order, we talk about a *case* or an instance of the workflow. While a process description is a static entity, a case is a dynamic entity, i.e., a process in execution. The traditional term for the execution of a case is *workflow enactment*.

A process description usually includes some choices. In our example the customer has the choice of ordering a PC or a laptop as shown in the process description in Figure 1.3(a). Yet, a process description contains no hints of how to resolve the choices present in the process description. The enactment of a case is triggered by the generation of a *case activation record* that contains the attributes necessary to resolve some choices at workflow enactment time. In our example the information necessary to make decisions is provided by the customer's order. The order is either for a PC or for a laptop; it specifies the model, e.g., Dell Inspirion 8000; it gives the customer's choices, e.g., a 1.5 GHz Pentium IV processor, 512 MB of memory, a 40 GB hard drive.

1.2.2 Computer Scripts

Scripting languages provide the means to build flexible applications from a set of existing components. In the Unix environment the Bourne shell allows a user to compose several commands, or *filters*, using a set of connectors. The connectors include the *pipe* operator "|" and re-direction symbols ">" and "<".

Let us now examine a simple script. The `last` shell command displays login and logout information about users and the terminals they used to connect to a system; the `sort` command sorts the input lines and writes the result on the standard output.

The following script lists all users of a system, sorts the list alphabetically, and writes it to file "users":

```
last | sort -u > users
```

Often, a complex computational task requires the coordinated execution of several programs. Consider the following example: We have a file containing the electron microscope images of a virus. The virus has two components, a large structure with icosahedral symmetry connected to a much smaller structure with unknown symmetry.

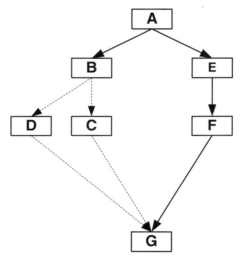

Fig. 1.4 The process described by the Pearl-like script. Dotted lines correspond to choices; either D or C are executed.

We have a program A that processes individual images and isolates images of each of the two structures, a program B capable of determining the orientation of each projection of a symmetric particle, and two versions of a program to perform a three-dimensional reconstruction of a symmetric particle from two-dimensional projections. One of the two versions, D, allows interactive visualization during the reconstruction and the other one, C, does not, see Figure 1.4.

We also have a program E able to determine the orientation of an asymmetric particle, a program F to perform a three-dimensional reconstruction of an asymmetric particle from two-dimensional projections and, finally, a program G able to combine the two three-dimensional representations of the symmetric and asymmetric particles.

The graph in Figure 1.4 shows the dependencies and the data flow between the seven programs. The execution of program A produces results needed for the execution of programs B and E that can be executed concurrently. Program F is executed sequentially after E. The dotted lines connecting B with C and D mean that there is a choice and either C or D will be executed but not both. Concurrent tasks must be *synchronized* at some point in time. In our example, program G can only be executed after B followed by either C or D *and* E followed by F have terminated.

Scripting languages such as Pearl could be used to describe such a complex computational task. The following Pearl-like script involves the execution of the seven programs on some system:

```
#!/usr/bin/perl

# Start program A # arg1, arg2 are arguments if any.
open(PROGA, "progA arg1 arag2 |") or die "cannot start \n";
                                # Program A returns the
                                # program ids, pids of
                                #  its children, B and E
$pidofB = <PROGA>;
$pidofE = <PROGA>;
 waitpid $pidofB;               # wait until B ends
if ($ARGV[0] eq "-display")     # do we want to display?
   {
   @arg = ("C", "arg1", "arg2"); # start program C;
   system(@arg)                 # wait until C ends
   }
else
   {
   @arg = ("D", "arg1", "arg2"); # start program D;
   system(@arg)                 # wait until D ends
   }
waitpid $pidofE;                # wait until E ends
@arg = ("F", "arg1", "arg2");   # start program F
system(@arg);                   # wait until F ends
@arg = ("G", "arg1", "arg2");   # start program G
system(@arg);
```

The directed graph in Figure 1.4 is a process description where each task corresponds to the execution of a program. The directed links reflect producer-consumer relationships, one program produces results used as input by the other. The *precursor* of a program P in the activity graph is the program generating the data P needs for execution. The *preconditions* of P are all the conditions necessary for the activation of P, including computing resources and data. Examples of resources are primary and secondary storage, specialized hardware such as video cards, software libraries, and so on.

1.2.3 A Metacomputing Example

Let us now examine a different scenario. Instead of being forced to execute the set of programs in the previous example on a single system we have access to a computational grid. Each program can be executed on a subset of grid nodes. This paradigm is known as metacomputing.

Consider a grid $\mathcal{G} = (\mathcal{N}, \mathcal{L})$ with $\mathcal{N} = \{N_i\}, i \in (1, q)$, the set of nodes and $\mathcal{L} = \{L_j\}, j \in (1, r)$, the set of communication links.

Now the enactment of a case is slightly more complex. Call $\mathcal{P} = \{P_k\}, k \in (1, p)$ the set of programs involved in the metacomputing exercise. For every member of the set $\forall P \in \mathcal{P}$ call $\mathcal{R}(P) \subset \mathcal{N}$ the set of nodes of the grid where P could run. To execute a program $P \in \mathcal{P}$ we need to go through the following steps:

(i) Identify $\mathcal{R}(P)$ in the activation record of the case, or contact a resource broker capable of locating the subset of grid nodes where P may run. A resource broker maintains information about resources available on a grid. It acts as a matchmaker between clients and servers.

(ii) Select one member of the set $N_i \in \mathcal{R}(P)$ to minimize a cost function and/or to satisfy a policy requirement. For example, we may select N_i to minimize the execution time and/or the communication costs. A policy requirement could be to avoid a node N_j under some conditions.

(iii) Ensure that the preconditions of P are satisfied on node N_i. For example, we need to make sure that the data produced by the precursor of program P in the activity graph is available on node N_i. The precursor may have been allocated to node N_k, thus, we have to migrate the data needed as input by P from N_k to N_i. To minimize communication costs we may need to compress the data on N_k before transmission and then uncompress it on N_i.

(iv) Start P, monitor its execution, and generate an event signaling its completion.

Figure 1.5 illustrates the additional complexity encountered in the enactment of a process on a grid and identifies three aspects of a workflow:

1. the process dimension,

2. the resource allocation dimension, and

3. the communication dimension.

The three dimensions cover the abstract definition of the process, the interactions between the workflow and the computational grid, and, last but not least, the communication between various entities involved. The communication plane consists of activities such as data staging from the producer of the data to the consumer of it, data compression and uncompression, data encryption and decryption, format transformations.

Even in this case we may be able to write a Pearl script to perform these computations, but the script would be rather complex. From this example we see that metacomputing requires a middleware layer performing functions similar to the ones provided by the operating system of a computer. This topic is addressed in Chapter 5.

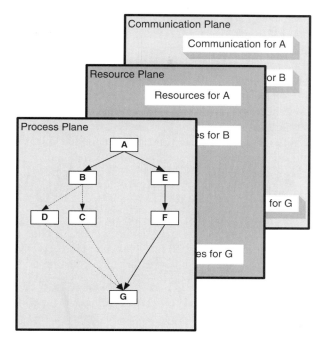

Fig. 1.5 Workflow planes: (i) the process description plane; (ii) the resource plane; (iii) the communication plane.

1.2.4 Automatic Monitoring and Benchmarking of Web Services

Let us now consider an E-commerce application. The Web technology is discussed in depth in Chapter 5. Here, we only assume that the reader is a casual user of Web services and at some point or another in time has experienced the frustration of waiting to make an online airline reservation, access her brokerage account, or buy a product online.

We assume that company X intends to rely on a cluster of Web servers to provide its services over the Internet and it is very concerned with the response time, the time it takes a client to carry out a transaction. Clearly the response time depends on the load placed on the servers and also on the communication time.

Company X decides to employ company Y to benchmark its cluster of servers before making them available to the general public. Benchmarking means evaluating the performance of a system using an artificial workload similar to the one encountered during the normal use of the system.

Company Y uses commercially available benchmarking software as well as proprietary products for Web benchmarking. Company Y has several sites around the world and attempts to determine the response time as seen by a local user under different loads placed on the server.

The first step undertaken by company Y is to download the benchmarking software and the files containing the access patterns for the Web server cluster of company X at each site selected to carry out the measurements. The access patterns describe the actual object requested from the servers, as well as the timing of the request. Once the software and the access description files are installed at each site, the measurements are carried out for a period of several weeks at different instances during the day and measurement data are collected.

The next phase is data analysis. Data from all the measurement sites as well as the logs maintained by the Web server are collected at the site where the analysis tools are installed. During this phase, a statistical analysis reveals the distribution of the response time as a function of the time of the day and the load placed on the server. Finally, the results are reported to company X.

Company X then reacts to the results by adding more systems to the server, redistributing the objects on the servers, and by establishing a relationship with content-delivery services such as Akamai, see Section 5.8.2. The content delivery services replicate the objects on servers located closer to the point of consumption and reduce both the load placed on the company servers and the communication delays.

The process described above is a workflow consisting of several activities: software installation, measurements, and data analysis that have to be properly coordinated. An actual implementation of a benchmarking system for a Web server is presented in Chapter 8.

1.2.5 Lessons Learned

We identified two components of a workflow:

1. A static component, the process description. The primitives concepts necessary to describe a process are tasks, events, and control structures.

2. Dynamic components, cases. The enactment of a case is triggered by the generation of an activation record.

We also observed that a workflow may involve primitive tasks, as well as complex tasks that can be decomposed into a set of primitive tasks. Both workflow description and workflow enactment should support hierarchical decomposition and aggregation. Process descriptions must have provisions to specify *sequential tasks*, *concurrent tasks*, and *choice*.

In our first example we examined a workflow where the individual tasks necessary to assemble a laptop are carried out by humans. In our second example all tasks are handled by computers interconnected by communication networks. The humans trigger only the execution of a case.

Our third example covered process coordination on a grid. The enactment on a grid raises two important questions: (i) how to coordinate the process execution and (ii) how to monitor and control each individual task. This subject is discussed in depth in Section 1.5. Here we note only that we need several agents, one to coordinate the enactment of a case and individual agents to control the execution of each task.

1.3 WORKFLOW REFERENCE MODEL

We now turn our attention to the common elements of the workflows presented earlier and describe an abstraction, a model, for workflow management proposed by the Workflow Management Coalition (WfMC), see Figure 1.6. From our examples it is clear that we need an environment to define the process, one to control its execution, and one to monitor different phases of the execution.

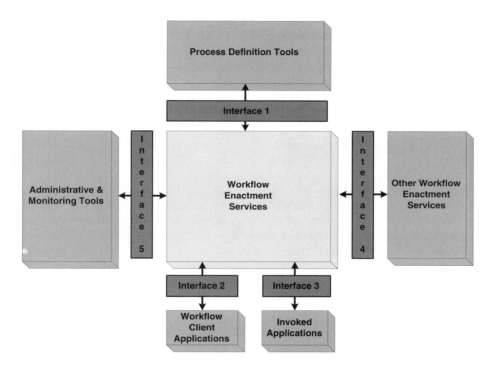

Fig. 1.6 The workflow reference model

The model in Figure 1.6 describes the architecture of a system supporting workflow management. Once we are able to identify the tasks required and their relationships, we need some language and a set of tools to define the process. The next phase is the *workflow enactment* phase, when an engine takes as input the description of the process and instantiates individual tasks. The workflow enactment engine interacts with several components; some provide feedback regarding the execution, others support auxiliary services, allow the engine to interact with legacy applications, or provide results to various clients. Several interfaces link the workflow enactment engine to the other components of the system.

Monitoring and control tools report partial results, perform consistency checks, monitor the quality of service, inform the engine about the completion of individual tasks, and so on. Legacy applications like database systems are often involved in workflow management. Auxiliary components are used for functions such as data staging, security management, and data compression.

Though we are only interested in computer-assisted workflow management, the model discussed in this section is general; the process could be described in a natural language, the role of the workflow enactment engine could be played by an individual, monitoring could be done by humans and/or electronic or mechanical devices.

1.4 WORKFLOWS AND DATABASE MANAGEMENT SYSTEMS

Early workflow management systems were based exclusively on a transactional model and were implemented on top of database management systems (DBMS). The database literature identifies three types of workflows:

(i) human-oriented,

(ii) system-oriented, and

(iii) transactional.

Transactional workflows consist of a mix of tasks, some performed by humans, others by computers, and support selective use of the transactional properties for individual activities or for the entire workflow [28]. In the transactional models a task is carried out by a transaction.

1.4.1 Database Transactions

We now take a closer look at transactions in database systems to understand some of the subtle differences between a database transaction and a generic task. In database systems queries translate into transactions. *Transactions* are computations that transform a database through a sequence of read and write operations.

The concept of a transaction was introduced by Jim Gray. In his seminal work [21] he reflects on the concept of a transaction in contract law and points out that two parties negotiate before making a deal and then the deal is made binding by the joint signature of a document; if the parties are suspicious of one another they appoint an intermediary to coordinate the commitment of the transaction.

This perspective outlines the permanent and unambiguous effects of a transaction in contract law. A database transaction inherits these properties from the business transaction; it is a unit of consistent and reliable computation. A transaction operates on a database and generates a state transition, leaving the database in a different state. A database transaction consists of a sequence of read and write operations on the database together with some computations.

The consistency and reliability characteristics of a database transaction are a consequence of the ACID properties; this acronym results from concatenating the initials of individual properties:

Atomicity: the transaction is an atomic unit of work and it is either successful and *committed* or fails and is *aborted*.

Consistency: a transaction leaves a database in a consistent state. The database may be in an inconsistent state on a temporary basis during the execution of the transaction.

Isolation: concurrent transactions do not introduce inconsistencies in the database, a transaction does not expose partial results of its execution.

Durability: the effects of a committed transaction are permanent.

Transactions are classified based on several criteria, one of them being their lifetime. *Short* transactions are executed in a matter of seconds while *long* transactions like the ones involving image processing or complex computations could take hours or even days. *Flat* transactions have single starting and termination points. *Nested* transactions contain embedded subtransactions.

1.4.2 Workflow Products

Several database workflow products designed to automate the business process are available. According to Special Report on Workflow Products [39], these products address three application areas:

1. Processing of transactions such as credit approval and insurance claims. The processing is highly repetitive and structured and the volume of transactions is usually very high and involves many participants.

2. Administrative processing such as monthly expense reports. The volume of transactions and the number of participants is lower. Some changes are possible.

3. Ad hoc and collaborative processing such as creating, routing, and tracking office documents. The workflow is usually low throughput and involves few participants.

According to the Workflow Management Coalition, a nonprofit organization of workflow vendors, users, analysts, and research groups [41], the key benefits of using workflow products are:

(i) Improved efficiency – automation of many business processes results in the elimination of many unnecessary steps.

(ii) Better process control – improved management of business processes achieved through standardizing working methods and the availability of audit trails.

(iii) Improved customer service – consistency in the processes leads to greater predictability in levels of response to customers.

(iv) Flexibility – software control over processes enables their redesign in line with changing business needs.

(v) Business process improvement – focus on business processes leads to their streamlining and simplification.

Workflow systems include a number of standard components: a design utility for constructing a workflow map; a rules engine for defining and executing the process; a client interface; and administrative and run-time management utilities.

Workflow products were offered in the 1980s: the first vendor was File-NET with *Workflo*, followed by IBM with *Flowmark*, and Bull with *FlowPath*. There are several hundred workflow products offered today and the workflow industry is experiencing a growth rate of 20% to 30% per year.

We now list some of the most significant features of several workflow products.

FlowMark. The design of this IBM product is based on an object-oriented database. It consists of four components:

1. the application server;

2. the database server, either Object Store or DB2;

3. a run-time client;

4. a built run-time client.

The system is scalable; it uses service brokers to connect to different operating environments. The enactment engine uses several services such as notification, navigation, distribution, audit trail, and so on.

InConcert.   This product of InConcert company is a client-server system supporting Oracle, Sybase, or Informix databases. The system allows dynamic workflow modifications.

JetForm.   This product of JetForm company is based on three-tier client server architecture and supports any relational database including Oracle and Sybase. The system has a Web browser interface.

Workflow. The system produced by Eastman Software is designed for distributed workflows. The system is scalable, consists of a network of workflow servers and supports load balancing and a "failsoft" fault tolerance model. The security support is limited and the system does not allow the use of time as a variable in the decision-making process.

WorkFlo. The WorkFlo system produced by Panagon is designed for distributed workflows. The system is scalable, consists of a network of workflow servers, and has adequate security support. The system is compliant with the WfMC specifications.

1.5   INTERNET WORKFLOW MODELS

Workflow models are abstractions revealing the most important properties of the entities participating in a workflow management system. When the activities invoked by a process require Internet services, we talk about Internet workflows. The Internet services could be limited to transport services or may cover societal services such as directory, event, brokerage, and so on. The activities of an Internet workflow are carried out by autonomous service providers and the workflow management requires *service composition*.

1.5.1   Basic Concepts

We now provide several definitions necessary for the models presented in this section.

Definition. *Tasks* are units of work to be performed by the agents, humans, computers, sensors, and other man-made devices involved in the workflow enactment. A task is characterized by:

(i) Name – a string of characters uniquely identifying the task.

(ii) Description – a natural language description of the task.

(iii) Actions – an action is a modification of the environment caused by the execution of the task.

(iv) Preconditions – boolean expressions that must be true before the action(s) of the task can take place.

(v) Postconditions – boolean expressions that must be true after the action(s) of the task do take place.

(vi) Attributes – provide indications of the type and quantity of resources necessary for the execution of the task, the actors in charge of the tasks, the security requirements, whether the task is reversible or not, and other task characteristics.

(vii) Exceptions – provide information on how to handle abnormal events. The exceptions supported by a task consist of a list of pairs: (event, action). The exceptions included in the task exception list are called *anticipated exceptions*, as opposed to unanticipated exceptions. In our model, events not included in the exception list trigger replanning. *Replanning* means restructuring of a process, redefinition of the relationship among various tasks.

A *composite task* is a structure describing a subset of tasks and the order of their execution. A *primitive task* is one that cannot be decomposed into simpler tasks. A composite task inherits some properties from workflows, it consists of tasks, has one start, and possibly several end symbols. At the same time, a composite task inherits some properties from tasks, it has a name, preconditions, and postconditions. There are no actions and exceptions associated with a supertask.

Definition. A *routing task* is a special-purpose task connecting two tasks in a workflow description. The task that has just completed execution is called the *predecessor* task, the one to be initiated next is called the *successor* task. A routing task could trigger the sequential, concurrent, or iterative execution. We distinguish several types of routing tasks:

A *fork routing task* triggers execution of several successor tasks. Several semantics for this construct are possible:

(i) all successor tasks are enabled,

(ii) each successor task is associated with a condition and these conditions are evaluated and only the tasks with a `true` condition are enabled,

(iii) same as (ii) but the conditions are mutually exclusive and only one condition may be `true`, thus, only one task is enabled, and

(iv) nondeterministic, k out of $n > k$ successors are selected at random to be enabled.

A *join routing task* waits for completion of its predecessor tasks. There are several semantics for the join routing task:

(i) the successor is enabled after all predecessors end,

(ii) the successor is enabled after k out of $n > k$ predecessors end, and

(iii) iterative – the tasks between the fork and the join are executed repeatedly.

Routing tasks and workflow patterns are discussed in Section 1.7.

Definition. A *process description*, also called a workflow schema, is a structure describing the *tasks* or *activities* to be executed and the order of their execution. A process description contains one start and one end symbol.

A process description can be provided in a *workflow definition language (WFDL)*, supporting constructs for choice; concurrent execution, the classical `fork`, `join` constructs iterative execution. An alternative description of a workflow can be provided by a transition system describing the possible paths from the current state to a goal state.

Sometimes, instead of providing a process description, we may specify only the goal state and expect the system to generate a workflow description that could lead to that state through a set of actions. In this case, the new workflow description is generated automatically, knowing a set of tasks and the preconditions and postconditions of each one of them. In Artificial Intelligence this activity is known as *planning*.

Definition. A *case* is an instance of a process description.

The start and the stop symbols in the workflow description enable the creation and the termination of a case.

Definition. An *enactment model* describes the steps taken to process a case.

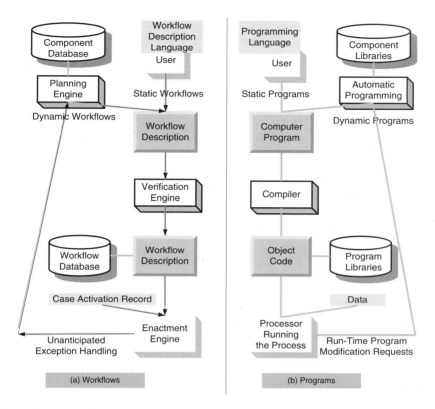

Fig. 1.7 (a) The life cycle of a workflow. (b) The life cycle of a computer program. The workflow definition is analogous to writing a program; planning is analogous to automatic program generation; verification corresponds to syntactic verification of a program; and workflow enactment mirrors the execution of the compiled program.

When all tasks required by a workflow are executed by a computer or by humans required to report the results to a computer, the enactment can be performed by a computer program called an *enactment engine*.

1.5.2 The Life Cycle of a Workflow

The phases in the life cycle of a workflow are creation, definition, verification and enactment. There is a striking similarity between the life cycle of a workflow and that of a traditional computer program, namely, creation, compilation, and execution, see Figure 1.7.

The workflow specification by means of a workflow description language is analogous to writing a program. Planning is equivalent to automatic program generation. Workflow verification corresponds to syntactic verification of a program, and workflow enactment mirrors the execution of a compiled program.

Static workflows are typically used by traditional workflow management applications such as office automation, whereas Internet applications are likely to require dynamic workflows.

There is some interest in automatic program generation, some Problem Solving Environments allow a user to select a particular processing path and then assemble the modules capable of performing the desired actions, compiling them, and producing a custom object code.

1.5.3   States, Events, and Transition Systems

To monitor the progress of a case, we need to introduce the concept of state. The state of a process is defined as a vector of events, the last one for each chain of causally related events. The *state space of a process* is the set of states a process may reach. The *state of a case* at time t is defined in terms of tasks already completed at that time. Events cause transitions between states.

Identifying the states of a process consisting of concurrent activities is considerably more difficult than the identification of the states of a strictly sequential process. Indeed, when several activities could proceed concurrently, the state has to reflect the progress made on each independent activity.

In the simple case described by the process in Figure 1.3(b), we can easily identify the states of the process and label them as

$$A, B, C, D, E, F, G, H, I, J, K, L$$

We say that the system is in state D if the last event witnessed is the completion of the assembly of the laptop box and of the motherboard; it is in state H if we have installed the video card, and so on.

We now introduce several types of graphs describing the states and the transitions between states. First, we provide a formal definition of a transition system.

Definition. A *transition system* is a directed graph. The nodes of the graph correspond to the states of the system and the edges denote the events in the system. A transition system has two distinguished states, an *initial* state with no incoming edge and a *goal* or *termination* state with no outgoing edge. All the other states of the system are called *internal* states.

In Figure 1.8 we concentrate on the assembly of the box and motherboard and show both the tasks and the events. Here the events are labeled independently. For example, (3) is the event generated when the installation of the power supply was completed, (1) is the event triggering the assembly of the box and motherboard, and (9) is the event signaling that the laptop box and the motherboard are ready.

In a transition system such as the one in Figure 1.9 all states can be reached from the initial state. We say that a state can be reached from the initial state if there is a sequence of events and states leading to that state. We are only interested in transition systems where all states are reachable from the initial state.

The transition system in Figure 1.9 shows that the process has 21 states labeled $S1, S2, S3, \ldots S20, S21$. The numbers in parenthesis on the left of each state indicate

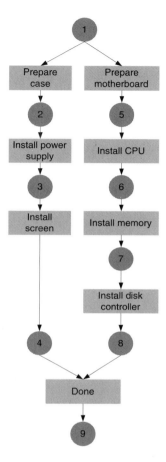

Fig. 1.8 The tasks and the events in the assembly of the box and motherboard. The circles with a number inside show the events. For example (3) is the event generated after we have completed the installation of the power supply.

the last events generated before the system reached that state. This labeling strategy allows a simple binary encoding of a state as a 9-bit integer, each bit indicating the events that could cause the system to enter the state. For example, the state $S5$, with label $(2, 5)$, is encoded as 010010000, bits two and five from the left are set to one.

The transitions between states are labeled by the event(s) causing that transition. The events are shown in parenthesis. For example in state $S5$, the label $(2, 5)$ indicates that we have completed tasks 2 and 5. There are three ways to reach this state: (i) from state $S2$ when the event 5 occurs; (ii) from state $S3$ when the event 2 occurs; (iii) from the initial state $S1$ if both events 2 and 5 occur at the same time. Recall that this process consists of two independent "tracks", one to assemble the box and the other to assemble the motherboard, thus, two events may occur at the same time.

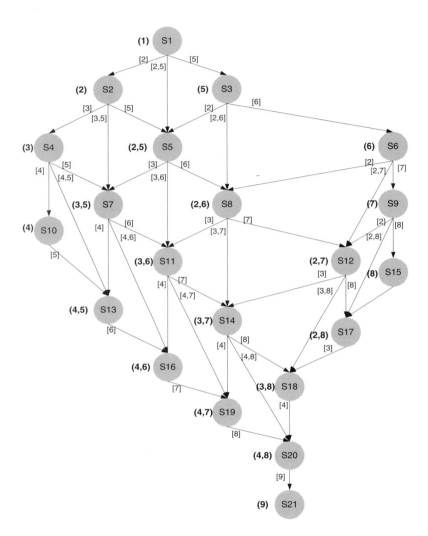

Fig. 1.9 The transitions system for the process describing the assembly of the laptop box and motherboard. States are labeled by the last events generated before the system reached that state. Each transition is labeled by the event(s) causing that transition. For example, in state $S5$, the label $(2, 5)$ indicates that we have completed tasks 2 and 5. There are three ways to reach this state: (i) from state $S2$ when event 5 occurs; (ii) from state $S3$ when the event 2 occurs; (iii) from the initial state $S1$ if both events 2 and 5 occur at the same time. Once in state $S5$, there are three transitions out of it: (i) event 3 occurs and we reach state $S7$; (ii) event 6 occurs and we reach state $S8$; (iii) events 3 and 6 occur at the same time and we reach state $S11$.

There is a one-to-one mapping between the process description in Figure 1.3(c) and the transition system in Figure 1.9. Given one of them we can construct the other. We now discuss the algorithms to map a process description and a transition system into each other.

Given the process description, we take the following four steps to construct the transition system:

1. Construct the set E of individual events. In our example $E = \{1, 2, 3, 4, 5, 6, 7, 8, 9\}$. There are nine individual events.

2. Split E into equivalence classes based on the causality relationship. In our example, we have two classes $E_1 = \{1, 2, 3, 4, 9\}$ and $E_2 = \{1, 5, 6, 7, 8, 9\}$. In each class the events are causally related and event 8 may occur only after 7.

3. Add to E all feasible combinations of events. A feasible combination contains at most one event from each class. For example $[2, 5]$ and $[3, 5]$ are feasible events, while $[2, 3]$ is not.

4. Construct the set of states S. Initially $S = \{s_{intial}\}$. Construct the subset $E_{intial} \in E$ of all events feasible in that state. For each event $e_{init,q} \in E_{initial}$ label the state reached after the occurrence of that event as s_q where q is the next available index and add s_q to S. Repeat the process for every new state until S includes the goal state s_{goal}.

The mapping in the other direction is trivial. In the transition system we keep only those states and transitions labeled by a single event. The resulting graph is the process description because states are labeled by the events leading to that state and, in turn, individual events are labeled by the task whose completion triggered the event.

The internal states of a transition system are distinguishable from one another only by the events that may occur in that state and by the states reached when the transitions caused by the corresponding events occur.

This means that we can group the states into equivalence classes; all states that are indistinguishable from one another because they allow the same events and the corresponding transitions lead to the same states belong to the same class.

To identify classes of states we may use a coloring algorithm. We start with three colors, one for the initial state, one for the terminal state, and one for internal states. If two states with the same initial color have an edge labeled with the same event and leading to states with different colors, then one of them receives a new color. The process starts from the terminal state and is repeated until all states have different colors or states with the same color are indistinguishable.

Figure 1.10 illustrates the concept of bisimilarity of transition systems. Instead of coloring, we label the states by the color. For example, the states leading to the terminal state 0 are labeled differently, 1 and 2 because the events leading to state 0 are a and b, respectively.

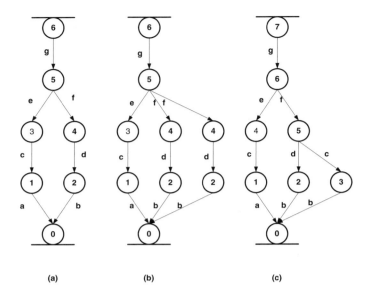

Fig. 1.10   Bisimilarity of transition systems. The transition systems in (a) and (b) are bisimilar, while the ones in (a) and (c), or (b) and (c) are not.

Bisimilarity is an equivalence relationship; two transition systems are bisimilar if they have the same equivalence classes or if they use the same set of colors. The transition systems in Figures 1.10(a) and (b) are bisimilar, while the ones in Figures 1.10(a) and (c), or the ones in Figures 1.10(b) and (c) are not.

In this section we presented several directed graphs describing the same process. In the first graph, the one in Figure 1.3(c), we only show the tasks and their dependencies, in the second, Figure 1.8, we see both the tasks and the events triggering task execution, and in the third, Figure 1.9, we see the transition system describing the process. Bipartite graphs like the one in Figure 1.8 are presented in detail in Chapter 3 where we analyze the static and dynamic properties of Petri nets. Here we concentrate on the properties of transition systems.

1.5.4   Safe and Live Processes

In the previous section we introduced the concept of a state of a process. The state space of a process includes one initial and one goal state. The transition system identifies all possible paths from the initial to the goal state. A case corresponds to a particular path in the transition system. The state of a case tracks the progress made during the enactment of that case.

Now we turn our attention to the correctness of a process description and discuss methods to detect anomalies in the process description. For example, consider the process description in Figure 1.11; the only difference is the effect of the event triggered by completion of C. This process description presents an anomaly that becomes apparent for only some cases.

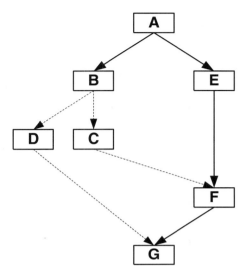

Fig. 1.11 A version of the process in Figure 1.4 that is not live.

Among the most desirable properties of a process description are the *safety* and *liveness* of the process. Informally, safety means that nothing "bad" ever happens and liveness means that something "good" will eventually take place, should a case based on the process be enacted.

Not all processes are safe and live. For example, the process description in Figure 1.11 violates the liveness requirement. As long as program C is chosen after completion of B, the process will terminate. But if D is chosen, then F will never be instantiated because it requires the completion of both C and E. The process will never terminate because G requires completion of both D and F.

An important observation is that we need a process description language that is unambiguous and allows a verification of the process description before the enactment of a case. It is entirely possible that a process description may be enacted correctly in many cases but fail for others. Such enactment failures may be very costly and should be prevented by a thorough verification at the process definition time.

To avoid enactment errors, we need to verify process description and check for desirable properties such as safety and liveness. Some process description methods are more suitable for verification than others.

A note of caution: although the original description of a process could be live, the actual enactment of a case may be affected by deadlocks due to resource allocation. To illustrate this situation consider two tasks, A and B, running concurrently; each of them needs exclusive access to resources r and q for a period of time. Two scenarios are possible:

(1) either A or B acquires both resources and then releases them, and allows the other task to do the same;

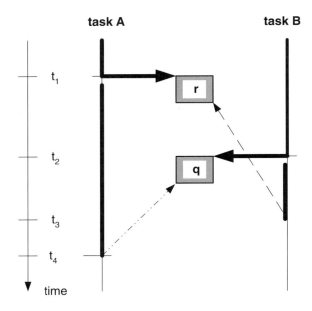

Fig. 1.12   Deadlock may occur during the enactment of a case. Tasks A and B need exclusive access to two resources r and q. At time t_1 task A acquires r, at time t_2 task B acquires q and continues to run. Then at time t_3 task B attempts to acquire r and it blocks because r is under the control of A. Task A continues to run and at time t_4 attempts to acquire q and it blocks because q is under the control of B.

(2) we face the undesirable situation in Figure 1.12 when at time t_1 task A acquires r and continues its execution; then at time t_2 task B acquires q and continues to run. Then at time t_3 task B attempts to acquire r and it blocks because r is under the control of A. Task A continues to run and at time t_4 attempts to acquire q and it blocks because q is under the control of B.

The deadlock illustrated in Figure 1.12 can be avoided by requesting each task to acquire all resources at the same time; the price to pay is underutilization of resources. Indeed, the idle time of each resource increases under this scheme.

1.6   TRANSACTIONAL VERSUS INTERNET-BASED WORKFLOWS

There are similarities and some differences between database transactions and Internet workflows. The similarities are mostly at the modeling level, whereas the differences affect the mechanisms used to implement workflow management systems.

Some of the more subtle differences between database transactions and Internet workflows are:

(i) The emphasis in a transactional model is placed on the contractual aspect of a transaction. In an Internet workflow the enactment of a case is sometimes based on a "best-effort model" where the agents involved will do their best to attain the goal state but there is no guarantee of success.

(ii) A critical aspect of a database transactional model is to maintain a consistent state of the database. A grid is an open system, thus, the state of a grid is considerably more difficult to define than the state of a database.

(iii) The database transactions are typically short-lived. The tasks of a workflow could be long lasting.

(iv) A database transaction consists of a set of well-defined actions that are unlikely to be altered during the execution of the transaction. However, the process description for an Internet workflow may change during the lifetime of a case. After a change, the enactment of case may continue based on the older process description, while in other cases it may be based on the newer process description.

(v) The individual tasks of a grid workflow may not exhibit the traditional properties of database transactions. Consider, for example, durability; at any instance of time before reaching the goal state a workflow may roll back to some previously encountered state and continue from there on an entirely different path. A task of a grid workflow could be either reversible or irreversible. Sometimes, paying a penalty for reversing an action is more profitable in the long run than continuing on a wrong path.

(vi) Resource allocation is a critical aspect of the workflow enactment on a grid without an immediate correspondent for database transactions.

(vii) Mobility of various agents involved in the enactment of a case is important for Internet workflows. The agents may relocate to the proximity of the sites where tasks are executed to reduce communication costs and latency. Again, there is no correspondent for database transactions.

During the 1990s we witnessed efforts to extend the transactional model. The problem of long lasting transactions was first addressed in early 1990s [18]. The subject of workflow changes became popular in mid-1990s and several database research groups reported results in this area. Proper and his coworkers [29] proposed a general theory of evolution for application models, Casati and his group [13, 14] examined workflow models that support evolution, others looked at workflow exception handling [11].

1.7 WORKFLOW PATTERNS

A process requires the activation of multiple tasks. The term workflow pattern refers to the temporal relationship among the tasks of a process. The workflow description languages and the mechanisms to control the enactment of a case must have provisions to support these temporal relationships.

A collection of workflow patterns is available at [8]; the patterns are analyzed by van der Aalst et al. [1], and evaluated by Zaph and Heinzl [35]. These patterns are classified in several categories: basic, advanced branching and synchronization, structural, state-based, cancellation, and patterns involving multiple instances.

We now review several workflow patterns identified by van der Aalst et al. available from **http://tmitwww.tm.tue.nl/research/patterns**, see Figure 1.13:

(a) The *sequence* pattern occurs when several tasks have to be scheduled one after the completion of the other. In our example, task B can only be started after A has completed its execution and, in turn, B has to finish before task C can be activated.

(b) The *AND split* pattern requires several tasks to be executed concurrently. Both tasks B and C are activated when task A terminates. In case of an *explicit AND split* the activity graph has a routing node and all activities connected to the routing node are activated as soon as the flow of control reaches the routing node. In the case of an *implicit AND split,* activities are connected directly and conditions can be associated with branches linking an activity with the next ones. Only when the conditions associated with a branch are true are the tasks activated.

(c) The *synchronization* pattern require several concurrent activities to terminate before an activity can start; in our example, task C can only start after both tasks A and B terminate.

(d) The *XOR split* requires a decision; after the completion of task A, either B or C can be activated.

(e) The *XOR join* occurs when several alternatives are merged into one; in our example C is enabled when either A or B terminates.

(f) The *OR split* pattern is a construct to choose multiple alternatives out of a set. In our example, after completion of A, one could activate either B or C, or both.

(g) The *multiple merge* construct allows multiple activation of a task and does not require synchronization after the execution of concurrent tasks. Once A terminates, tasks B and C execute concurrently. When the first of them, say B, terminates, then task D is activated; then when C terminates, D is activated again.

(h) The *discriminator* pattern waits for a number of incoming branches to complete before activating the subsequent activity; then it waits for the remaining branches to finish without taking any action until all of them have terminated. Then it resets itself.

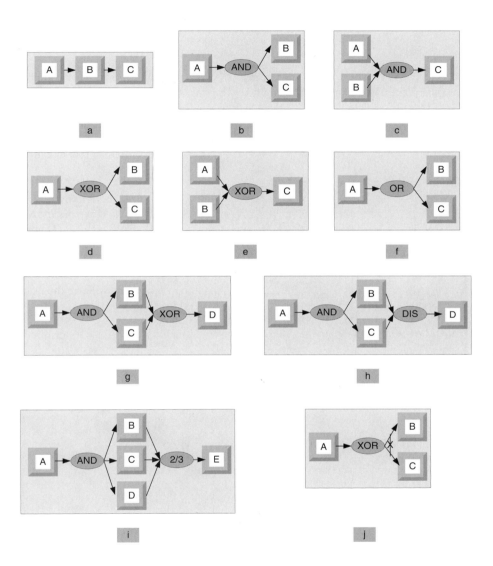

Fig. 1.13 Basic workflow patterns. (a) Sequence; (b) AND split; (c) Synchronization; (d) XOR split; (e) XOR merge; (f) OR split; (g) Multiple Merge; (h) Discriminator; (i) N out of M join; (j) Deferred Choice.

(i) The *N out of M join* construct provides a barrier synchronization. Assuming that $M > N$ tasks run concurrently, N of them have to reach the barrier before the next task is enabled. In our example, any two out of the three tasks A, B, and C have to finish before E is enabled.

(j) The *deferred choice* pattern is similar to the XOR split but this time the choice is not made explicitly and the run-time environment decides what branch to take.

1.8 WORKFLOW ENACTMENT

1.8.1 Task Activation and States

Once we have defined a process we are able to handle individual cases, see Figure 1.14. The enactment represents the active phase in the life cycle of a workflow; individual tasks are activated, carry out their function and at some point in time terminate.

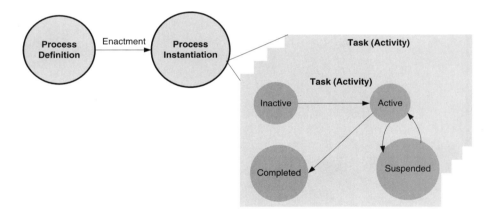

Fig. 1.14 Processes are enacted for individual cases. Each task may be in one of several states: inactive, active, suspended, or completed.

Each task evolves in time and traverses several states. A task waiting for its precondition is in an *inactive* state; once the preconditions are satisfied the task enters an *active* state. A task my be *suspended* for some periods of time waiting for some condition to occur, for example, some of the resources needed for the completion of a task may become temporarily unavailable. Eventually each task of a process enacted for a particular case reaches a *completion* state.

An enactment engine controlling the enactment of a case keeps track of the state of each activity and ensures the seamless transition from one activity to the next.

1.8.2 Workflow Enactment Models

A workflow enactment model describes the control environment and the mechanisms used to ensure a seamless transition from one activity to the next. In the following discussion, an agent is a program performing a control function.

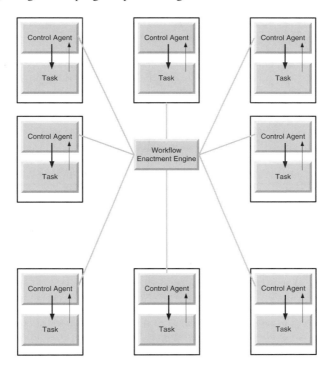

Fig. 1.15 The agents involved in workflow enactment. The coordination and resource allocation is provided by the workflow enactment engine and agents colocated with each task control its life cycle. In this snapshot only the tasks and control agents active at a time t are shown.

Figure 1.15 illustrates an enactment model where: (i) the workflow enactment engine is an agent responsible for coordinating the workflow enactment, and (ii) each individual task is executed under the supervision of a *control agent*. The coordination aspect of the workflow enactment covers both the process and resource dimension. The enactment model presented in Figure 1.15 delegates the task-specific functions to the control agents colocated with the task. This strategy keeps the network traffic to a minimum since task-specific decisions are made locally, and reduces the time for the completion of local tasks.

The model facilitates the design of generic workflow enactment engines and encourages a hierarchical workflow enactment with multiple engines coordinating different aspects of the workflow.

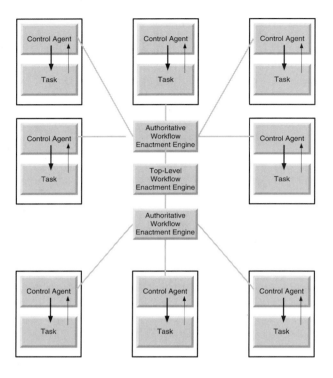

Fig. 1.16 A hierarchical workflow enactment model. Authoritative workflow enactment engines coordinate execution of sets of related tasks. The top-level workflow enactment engine supports the overall coordination among sets of tasks.

A hierarchical workflow enactment, see Figure 1.16, is more scalable, the decentralized decision-making process limits the traffic and shortens the time to decision. In this model the top-level workflow enactment engine provides the overall process coordination and cooperates with authoritative enactment engine for resource allocation.

We discuss only two-level hierarchies consisting of one top-level workflow enactment engine and several authoritative enactment engines that coordinate the execution of a subset of tasks. For very complex workflows multilayer hierarchies could be considered.

Figure 1.17 shows the life span of the agents involved in a hierarchical workflow enactment model for a case involving five tasks, A, B, C, D, E, two authoritative enactment engines, AB and CDE, and a top-level enactment engine. The top-level workflow enactment engine is activated by the arrival of the case activation record at time t_0 and, in turn, it triggers the activation of the two authoritative enactment engines at times t_1 and t_4, in response to an activation event for the first task in each group. The two authoritative enactment engines are deactivated by the top-level

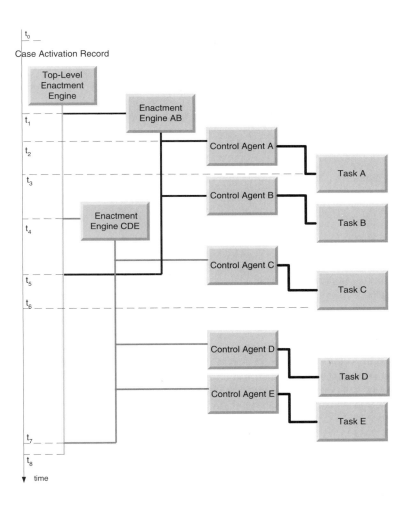

Fig. 1.17 The life span of agents in a hierarchical workflow enactment. The top-level workflow enactment engine is activated at time t_0 and the case is concluded at time t_8. The top-level enactment engine triggers the activation of the two authoritative enactment engines at times t_1 and t_4. The two authoritative enactment engines are deactivated at times t_5 and t_7 respectively. The control agent for task A is activated at time t_2 and terminates at time t_3.

enactment engine when the entire set of tasks has finished its execution, at times t_5 and t_7 respectively.

1.9 WORKFLOW COORDINATION

Given:

(i) A system Σ, an initial state of the system, $\sigma_{initial}$ and a final state, σ_{final}.

(ii) A process group, $\mathcal{P} = \{p_1, p_2, \ldots p_n\}$. Each process p_i in the process group, is characterized by a set of preconditions, $pre(p_i)$, postconditions, $post(p_i)$, and attributes, $atr(p_i)$.

(iii) A workflow described by a directed activity graph $\mathcal{A}$ or by a procedure Π capable to construct $\mathcal{A}$ given the tuple $< \mathcal{P}, \sigma_{initial}, \sigma_{final} >$. The nodes of $\mathcal{A}$ are processes in $\mathcal{P}$ and edges define precedence relations among processes. $P_i \rightarrow P_j$ implies that $pre(p_j) \subset post(p_i)$.

(iv) A set of constraints, $\mathcal{C} = \{C_1, C_2, \ldots C_m\}$.

The coordination problem for system Σ is to reach state σ_{final} given that the system is in state $\sigma_{initial}$, as a result of postconditions of some process $P_{final} \in \mathcal{P}$ subject to constraints $C_i \in \mathcal{C}$. Here $\sigma_{initial}$ enables the preconditions of some process $P_{initial} \in \mathcal{P}$.

Generally, the preconditions of a process are the conditions and/or the events that trigger the execution of the process, or the data the process expects as input; the postconditions are the results produced by the process. The attributes of a process describe special requirements or properties of the process.

The *cost* is an example of an attribute of a process. The cost reflects the resources needed for process execution. An example of a binary attribute of a process is *reversibility*.

A *reversible process* is one whose postconditions are not permanent and can be reversed. For example, a contract between two agents may have a provision to be annulled at the request of one of them. Signing such a contract is an example of a reversible process while signing a contract without an annulling clause is an example of an irreversible process.

A wide range of constraints can be encountered. For example, the pricing model may specify limits for the total cost of all processes in the activity graph. Another type of constraint is the ability to dynamically alter the activity graph.

Some workflows are static, the activity graph does not change during the enactment of a case. *Dynamic workflows* are those that allow the activity graph to be modified during the enactment of a case. Dynamic workflows are very important for workflows that combine computer and human activities.

Let us define the *life span* of a workflow described by an activity graph, $\tau(\mathcal{A})$, as the time elapsed from the activation of process p_{intial} until the completion of

p_{final}. The life span of a workflow enactment can be rather long, weeks, months, or even years. During this time the environment may change and create the need to dynamically alter the activity graph. For example, a workflow involving a legal service may need to be altered due to changes in legislation.

Let us now address the mechanics of workflow enactment. We propose to distinguish two basic models:

1. *Strong coordination models* where the process group $\mathcal{P}$ executes under the supervision of a coordinator process or processes. A coordinator process acts as an enactment engine and ensures a seamless transition from one process to another in the activity graph.

2. *Weak coordination models* where there is no supervisory process.

In the first case we may deploy a *hierarchical coordination scheme* with several levels of coordinators. A supervisor at level i in a hierarchical scheme with $i + 1$ levels coordinates a subset of processes in the process group. A supervisor at level $i - 1$ coordinates a number of supervisors at level i and the root provides global coordination. Such a hierarchical coordination scheme may be used to reduce the communication overhead, a coordinator and the processes it supervises may be co-located.

The most important feature of this coordination model is the ability to support dynamic workflows. The coordinator or the global coordinator may respond to a request to modify the workflow by first stopping all the threads of control in a consistent state, then investigate the feasibility of the requested changes, and finally implement feasible changes.

Weak coordination models are based on peer-to-peer communication between processes in the process group by means of a societal service such as a *tuple space*. Once a process $p_i \in \mathcal{P}$ finishes, it deposits a token including possibly a subset of its post-conditions, $post(p_i)$ in a tuple space. Tuple spaces are discussed in Chapter 5. The consumer process p_j is expected to visit at some point in time the tuple space, examine the tokens left by its ancestors in the activity graph and, if its preconditions, $pre(p_j)$ are satisfied, commence the execution. This approach requires individual processes to either have a copy of the activity graph or some timetable to visit the tuple space. An alternative approach is to use an *active space*, a tuple space augmented with the ability to generate an event awakening the consumer of a token.

In some cases it may be useful to have hybrid coordination models with a coordinator agent and a tuple space service. Such a strategy is reported by Jun [24] for a system of automatic benchmarking of Web servers.

1.10 CHALLENGES OF DYNAMIC WORKFLOWS

The real advantage of looking at complex activities as workflows comes from the possibility of automatic control of the process. The enactment of a case is controlled by an enactment engine that interacts with other agents monitoring individual tasks and ensures a seamless transition from one task to the next until the goal state is reached. While this is a relatively uncomplicated endeavor for static workflows, the problem becomes considerably more difficult for dynamic Internet workflows.

Some of the more difficult questions encountered in dynamic Internet workflow management are:

(i) How to integrate workflow and resource management and guarantee optimality or near optimality of cost functions for individual cases.

(ii) How to guarantee consistency after a change in a workflow.

(iii) How to create a dynamic workflow. Static workflows could be described in some language, e.g., Petri nets or the workflow definition language (WFDL), but dynamic workflows need a more flexible approach. A static workflow description can be assimilated with a program for the enactment engine, but a dynamic workflow would need to modify the program at run time, a proposition widely considered a heresy in computer science.

(iv) How to accommodate the case-by-case changes of a basic workflow. Unless we are able to relate a set of workflows with common traits with each other, we will witness an explosion of the workflow definition space. Moreover, we would need to repeat for every change in the process description, the workflow verification procedures necessary to detect possible anomalies, e.g., deadlock.

(v) How to actually build a "magic" workflow enactment engine that supports dynamic changes and integrates resource management with workflow management.

1.11   FURTHER READING

The Workflow Management Coalition (WfMC) is a nonprofit organization of workflow vendors, users, analysts, and university/research groups whose mission is to promote the establishment of standards for software terminology, interoperability and connectivity between workflow products. WfMC has put out several publications that describe terminology [43], process definition [40], the workflow reference model [41], and the effect of the Internet upon workflow management [42]. The handbook published by WfMC [20] contains useful information.

Models and techniques for business process management are presented in several papers in the book edited by W. M. P. van der Aalst, J. Desel, and A. Oberweis, [7]; the book by Jablonski and Busser is a good introduction to workflow modeling and architecture, [23]. Workflow modeling techniques are also addressed by several references [17, 25, 32].

The group at the Eindhoven University of Technology has contributed to workflow verification [2, 3, 5, 22], to interorganizational workflows [4], to workflow inheritance [6], and to worlflow patterns [1]. Workflow patterns are evaluated in [35]; a collection of workflow patterns is available from [8].

Scientific workflow systems are discussed in [33]. Several reports discuss the limitation of traditional workflow systems and the architecture of distributed workflow systems [9, 10].

AI techniques and application of agents to workflow management are presented in [12, 15, 26, 27]. Workflow models that support evolution are discussed in [13, 14, 19, 29, 30, 36]. Workflow exception handling is covered in [11].

A survey of existing workflow products and an introduction to workflows are available [16, 39]. There is a vast literature on workflow management systems including [31, 34, 37, 38].

1.12 EXERCISES AND PROBLEMS

Problem 1. Generate an informal description of the workflow for processing a home loan application.

Problem 2. Download a copy of the workflow definition language and create a formal description of the process for a home loan application. List the workflow patterns required by this process description.

Problem 3. Generate a formal description of the automatic Web benchmarking process described in Section 1.2.4.

List the workflow patterns required by this process description.

Identify the events triggering each task and construct a diagram similar to the one in Figure 1.9.

Problem 4. Augment the process description in Problem 3 with a monitoring component that takes into account the network latency of different clients. For example, if we wish the server to face a workload of 10,000 requests/second and this workload is generated by three different clients with network latency of 20, 40, and 80 milliseconds, then each client has to adjust its request pattern accordingly.

Problem 5. Federal research funding agencies such as NSF, NIH, or DARPA use a peer review process to make the awards. Each program within an agency periodically sends calls for proposals. Information regarding the areas of interest, criteria for evaluating the proposals, the deadline for proposal submission, the name of those who can provide additional information about the program, and so on is disseminated via Web sites or through direct mail to the institutions of potential grantees.

To assess the technical merits of each proposal the Program Director (PD) has the choice to organize a panel or to request reviews from individuals considered experts in the field. The experts may recuse themselves in case of a conflict of interest.

In the first case, each expert is assigned a subset of proposals and he or she is asked to prepare the reviews for these proposals and be familiar with all the proposals. Then, the experts meet face to face, each proposal is discussed, and ranked based on the the grades assigned to it by the reviewers. In this process, a reviewer may alter her original evaluation and lower or increase her grade. The panel has to agree on the wording of a summary of the discussion of each proposal and must reach a consensus regarding the relative ranking of all proposals. Then, after the meeting, the PD makes the awards based upon the amount of funding available to her program, taking into account the ranking produced by the panel.

If the PD chooses the second alternative, no face-to-face meeting takes place, but the experts send their individual reviews to the PD and she produces a conclusion regarding each proposal.

  (i) Transform the informal and incomplete description of the proposal evaluation process into a formal workflow description for the panel review and for the mail review case.

  Add missing activities, such as travel arrangments for pannelists, and exception handling, for example, handling of the situation when the panel cannot agree on the ranking of the proposal. Consider the solution adopted by the Vatican in the Middle Ages; the cardinals are sequestered in a room, without any contact with the outside world; white smoke coming from the chimney signals the election of a new Pope. This may not work in the third millennium, in Washington D.C.

 (ii) Identify the events triggering each task and construct a diagram similar to the one in Figure 1.9 for the two workflows.

(iii) Combine the two workflows into one.

(iv) Investigate the concept of workflow inheritance to relate the two workflows.

Problem 6. Consider the process of employee relocation.

  (i) List the tasks involved, e.g., selling a home, buying a home, contracting with a moving company, changing license plates, communicating the new address to credit card companies, and so forth.

 (ii) Generate a WFDL description of several processes involved in relocation.

(iii) Identify synchronization points in these process descriptions.

(iv) Study the issue of backtracking and identify points when backtracking is possible in some of the processes involved.

REFERENCES

1. W. M. P. van der Aalst and A. H. ter Hofstede and B. Kiepuszewski and A.P. Barros. Workflow Patterns. Technical Report, Eindhoven University of Technology, 2000.

2. W. M. P. van der Aalst. Verification of Workflow Nets. In G. Balbo P. Anzéma, editor, *Application and Theory of Petri Nets. Lecture Notes in Computer Science*, volume 1248, pages 407–426. Springer–Verlag, Heidelberg, 1997.

3. W. M. P. van der Aalst. The Application of Petri Nets to Workflow Management. *The Journal of Circuits, Systems and Computers*, 8(1):21–66, 1998.

4. W. M. P. van der Aalst. Interorganizational Workflows. An Approach Based on Message Sequence Charts and Petri Nets. Technical Report, Eindhoven Institute of Technology, 1999.

5. W. M. P. van der Aalst. Workflow Verification: Finding Control Flow Errors Using Petri-Net-Based Techniques. In W. M. P. van der Aalst, J. Desel, and A. Oberweis, editors, *Business Process Management. Lecture Notes on Computer Science*, volume 1806, pages 161–183, Springer–Verlag, Heidelberg, 2000.

6. W. M. P. van der Aalst and T. Basten. Inheritance of Workflows. An Approach to Tackling Problems Related to Change. Technical Report, Eindhoven Institute of Technology, 1999.

7. W. M. P. van der Aalst, J. Desel, and A. Oberweis, editors, *Business Process Management, Lecture Notes on Computer Science*, volume 1806. Springer–Verlag, Heidelberg, 2000.

8. W. M. P. van der Aalst, A. H. ter Hofstede, B. Kiepuszewski, and A.P. Barros. Workflow Patterns. URL http://tmitwww.tm.tue.nl/research/patterns/.

9. G. Alonzo. Exotica/FMQM: A Persistent Message-Based Architecture for Distributed Workflow Management. In *Proc IFIP Working Conf. on Information Systems for Decentralized Organizations*, August 1995.

10. G. Alonzo, D. Agrawal, A. El-Abbadi, and C. Mohan. Functionality and Limitations of Current Workflow Management Systems. Technical Report, IBM Almaden Research Center, 1997.

11. A. Borgida and T. Murata. Tolerating Exceptions in Workflows: a Unified Framework for Data and Processes. In D. Georgakopoulos, W. Prinz, and A. L. Wolf, editors, *Proc. Int. Joint Conference on Work Activities, Coordination and Collaboration (WAC-99)*, pages 59–68, ACM Press, New York, 1999.

12. T. Cai, P. A. Gloor, and S. Nog. DartFlow: A Workflow Management System on the Web using Transportable Agents. Technical Report PCS-TR96-283, Dartmouth College, Computer Science, Hanover, New Hempshire, May 1996.

13. F. Casati, S. Ceri, B. Pernici, and G. Pozzi. Conceptual Modeling of Workflows. *Lecture Notes in Computer Science*, volume 1021, pages 341–355, Springer–Verlag, Heidelberg, 1995.

14. F. Casati, S. Ceri, B. Pernici, and G. Pozzi. Workflow Evolution. *IEEE Trans. on Data and Knowledge Engineering*, 24(3):211–238, 1998.

15. J. W. Chang and C. T. Scott. Agent–based Workflow: TRP Support Environment (TSE). *Computer Networks and ISDN Systems*, 28(7-11):1501-1511, 1996.

16. A. Cichocki, A. Helal, M. Rusinkiewicz, and D. Woelk. *Workflow and Process Automation; Concepts and Technology.* Kluwer Academic Publishers, Boston, 1998.

17. D. Lee D, T. Nishimura, and S. Kumagai. Structural and Behavioral Analysis of State Machine Allocatable Nets Based on Net Decomposition. *IEICE Trans. Fundamentals*, E79-A(3):399–408, 1993.

18. U. Dayal, M. Hsu, and R. Ladin. Organizing Long-running Activities with Triggers and Transactions. *SIGMOD Record (ACM Special Interest Group on Management of Data)*, 19(2):204–214, 1990.

19. C. A. Ellis and K. Keddara. A Workflow Change is a Workflow. In W. M. P. van der Aalst, J. Desel, and A. Oberweis, editors, *Business Process Management. Lecture Notes on Computer Science*, volume 1806, pages 201–217, Springer-Verlag, Heidelberg, 2000.

20. L. Fisher, editor. Workflow Handbook 2001. Future Strategies Inc., Book Division, Lighthouse Point, 2001.

21. J. Gray. The Transaction Concept: Virtues and Limitations. In *Proc. 7th Int. Conf. on Very Large Data Bases*, pages 144–154, 1981.

22. D. Hauschildt, H. M. W. Verbreek, and W. M. P. van der Aalst. WOFLAN: a Petri-net-based Workflow Analyzer. Technical Report 97/12, Eindhoven University of Technology, 1997.

23. S. Jablonski and C. Busser. *Workflow Management: Modeling Concepts, Architecture, and Implementation.* Int. Thompson Computer Press, London, 1995.

24. K. Jun. Monitoring and Control of Networked Systems with Mobile Agents: Algorithms and Applications. Ph.D. Thesis, Purdue University, 2001.

25. K. M. Kavi, B. P. Buckles, and U. N. Bhat. Isomorphisms Between Petri Nets and Dataflow Graphs. *IEEE Transactions on Software Engineering*, 13(10):1127-1134, 1987.

26. K. L. Myers and P. M. Berry. At the Boundary of Workflow and AI. In *Proc. AAAI-99 Workshop on Agent-Based Systems in the Business Context*, 1999.

27. P. D. O'Brien and M. E. Wiegand. Agent-based Process Management: Applying Intelligent Agents to Workflow. *Knowledge Engineering Review*, 13(2):161–174, 1998.

28. M. T. Oezsy and P. Valduriez. *Principles of Distributed Database Systems*, second edition. Prentice Hall, Englewood Cliffs, 1999.

29. H. A. Proper and Th. P. van der Weide. A General Theory for the Evolution of Application Models. *IEEE Trans. on Knowledge and Data Engineering*, 7(6):984-996, 1995.

30. M. Reichert and P. Dadam. ADEPTflex - Supporting Dynamic Changes of Workflows Without Losing Control. *Journal of Intelligent Information Systems*, 10(2):93–129, 1998.

31. H. Schuster, S. Jablonski, T. Kirsche, and C. Bussler. A Client/Server Architecture for Distributed Workflow Management Systems . In *Parallel and Distributed Information Systems Conference*, Austin, TX, 1994.

32. M. Voorhoeve. Compositional Modeling and Verification of Workflow Processes. In W. van der Aalst, J. Desel, and A., editors, *Business Process Management*, *Lecture Notes in Computer Science*, volume 1806, pages 184–200. Springer–Verlag, Heidelberg, 1995, 2000.

33. J. Wainer, M. Weske, G. Vossen, and C. B. Medeiros. Scientific Workflow Systems. In *NSF Workshop on Workflow and Process Automation: State of the Art and Future Directions*, May 1996.

34. D. Wodtke, J. Weissenfels, G. Weikum, and A. K. Dittrich. The Mentor Project: Steps Towards Enterprise–Wide Workflow Management. In *Proc. 12th Int. Conf. on Data Engineering*, pages 556–565, IEEE Press, Piscataway, New Jersey, 1997.

35. M. Zapf and A. Heinzl. Evaluation of Process Design Patterns: An Experimental Study. In W. M. P. van der Aalst, J. Desel, and A. Oberweis, editors, *Business Process Management*, *Lecture Notes on Computer Science*, volume 1806, pages 83–98, Springer–Verlag, Heidelberg, 2000.

36. D. M. Zimmerman. A Preliminary Investigation into Dynamic Distributed Workflow. M.S. Thesis, California Institute of Technology, 1998.

37. OMG. BODTF RFP #2 Submission Workflow Management Facility. Technical Report, OMG, 7 1998.

38. Software-LEY. *COSA Workflow 2.0 Product Specification*, 1998. http://www.cosa.de / eng/products/workflow/wfpbeng/ HTTOC.HTM.

39. *Special Report on Workflow Products*, second edition. Doculabs, Englewood Cliffs, 1998.

40. Workflow Management Coalition. Interface 1: Process Definition Interchange Process Model. URL `http://www.wfmc.com`, 11 1998.

41. Workflow Management Coalition. Worfklow Reference Model. URL `http://www.wfmc.com`, 1998.

42. Workflow Management Coalition. Workflow and Internet: Catalysts for Radical Change. Technical Report, Workflow Management Coalition, 1998.

43. Workflow Managment Coalition. Workflow Managment Coalition Terminology and Glossary. Technical Report WFMC-TC-1011, Workflow Managment Coalition, 1996.

2

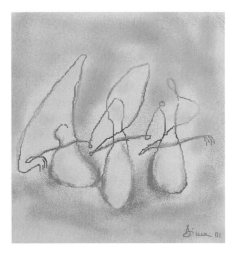

Basic Concepts and Models

This chapter provides the basic concepts and models necessary for understanding large-scale distributed systems consisting of autonomous processing elements interconnected by communication channels. Such systems are inherently very complex and their components, the computers and the communication channels, evolve at a very rapid pace. Understanding the behavior of an ensemble of autonomous systems is a more difficult task than understanding the behavior of its individual components in isolation. Thus, the need for abstractions and simple models.

The two basic abstractions needed for the specification, design, and analysis of any distributed system are *processes*, entities that carry out the computations specified by an algorithm, and *communication channels* or abbreviated, channels, entities that enable processes to communicate with one another by exchanging *messages* [31], see Figure 2.1.

This chapter introduces functional, reliability, performance, and security models for processes and communication channels and it is organized as follows. Section 2.1 presents system models and attributes and outlines the major concerns in the design of distributed systems. Section 2.2 covers basic concepts from information theory, presents models for communication channels, and introduces the reader to information encoding and error detection and correction. Processes, events, local and global

Fig. 2.1 Processes and communication channels. Communication primitives such as *send* and *receive* are used by processes to communicate with one another.

state, causal relationships, and a brief introduction to process algebra are the subjects of Section 2.3. Synchronous and asynchronous system models are presented in Section 2.4. In Section 2.5 we address several topics related to monitoring distributed computations such as causal history, consistent states, and intrusion. Section 2.6 presents failure and fault models and reliable collective communication. Resource sharing, process scheduling, and performance models are covered in Section 2.7 and security models are surveyed in Section 2.8. Finally, in Section 2.9 we review the two pervasive problems in distributed system design, concurrency and mobility.

2.1 INTRODUCTION

2.1.1 System Models

Models help us understand what attributes of the physical components involved in a distributed system are important and what classes of problems can be solved based on a certain set of assumptions. A model is a collection of attributes describing a system and a set of rules indicating how these attributes interact with one another [33].

A *model* is an abstraction that retains only those properties of a system pertinent to a particular type of analysis and ignores attributes that are either irrelevant or have little influence on the analysis we are conducting. A model is *accurate* if the analysis of the model leads to discovery of properties of the system being modeled and it is *tractable* if the analysis is possible. Multiple accurate and tractable models of a system exist. A model must be *validated* once the actual system is implemented.

For example, the computer model of an airplane wing is based on the known equations of fluid dynamics and ignores the color of the wing if the model is used to analyze the liftoff properties of the wing. The model can be validated by building several wings and measuring their liftoff properties in a wind tunnel and comparing them with the ones predicted by the model before actually building the airplane. However, if we want to construct a model describing the thermal properties of the wing or to determine the temperature of the fuel tanks housed by the wing, then the color of the wing may be important.

A distributed system consists of computers interconnected by communication links and is often modeled as a directed graph with computers as nodes and communication channels as links.

Communicating entities are modeled as *processes*, instances of running programs. Each program executes an algorithm and, in turn, each algorithm can be analyzed and modeled separately. Turing machines are powerful models for understanding basic properties of algorithms and the limits of computability.

A communication channel can be modeled as a binary pipe connecting a source and a destination. The bit pipe may be noisy or noiseless. The noise affects the functionality of the channel, the output of a noisy channel may differ from its input, whereas for a noiseless channel the output is identical with its input. The simple models discussed in Section 2.2 allow us to draw important conclusions on how to deal with channel errors.

Models can be classified according to the type of analysis they support; a non-exhaustive list includes functional, reliability, performance, security models, and cost models. A functional model of a system is used to establish whether the system is capable of performing correctly the functions it was designed for. For example, in Chapter 3 we discuss net models of concurrent systems. Such models allow us to establish if a system is subject to synchronization anomalies, e.g., if deadlock is possible; the net models support also reachability analysis used to determine if the system can reach certain states. Another functional model of concurrent systems is provided by process algebra (see Section 2.3.8); this model allows us to partition the set of states a system may find itself in, in equivalence classes and to introduce the branching bisimilarity relationship among processes.

The development of systems can be based only on accurate models of the interactions between different system components. Oftentimes, a complex system has a supervisory subsystem whose task it is to adapt to changes in the environment caused by the the failure of individual components, by new customers joining the systems, or by other events. A type of interaction of particular interest is monitoring of individual components by the supervisory system. Thus, we need to develop models of the interactions between a monitoring system and the system being monitored [28], as discussed in Section 2.5.

Resource sharing is an enduring problem in complex systems and queuing models provide insight into performance tradeoffs. Scheduling dependent activities on autonomous systems is another example of a complex problem that requires carefully crafted models [1].

Performance models of computing systems and communication channels are based on quantitative performance measures such as *CPU*, *memory*, and *I/O bandwidth*, the peak rate for executing instructions, transferring data to/from the memory, and I/O devices, respectively. The *channel bandwidth* is the maximum rate information can be pushed into a channel by the sender and retrieved from the channel by the receiver. The *channel latency* is the time needed to deliver the information to the receiver.

We discuss objective functions such as *resource utilization* and *response time* and argue that tradeoffs are pervasive in the system design. For example, a high level of resource utilization invariably leads to long response time. The *throughput*, or the rate the customers complete their service and leave the system, provides a good measure of the quantity of service, while the *time in system*, the interval elapsed since a customer arrives and the instance it leaves the system, is a good indication of the quality of service.

Different aspects of system design are deeply intertwined. The tradeoffs between the quantity and the quality of service can only be based on a joint analysis of functional, performance, and cost models. One could design a very secure system, but the performance penalty for supporting a high level of security is almost certain to have a very severe negative effect on the system performance.

Two very important facets that cut across all models discussed above are the effect of underlying technologies on one hand, and the demands of the applications on the other hand. The relative merits of models and the importance of problems they solve change in time, driven by these two aspects.

Let us first discuss the effect of the technology substrate. Recall that in early days of integrated system design, a very important facet of logic design was circuit minimization. The importance of circuit minimization has diminished nowadays when microprocessors with 100×10^6 transistors may soon be available. It is more important to build a circuit using a smaller number of different components than to minimize the total number of components.

It is very likely that communication protocols would be impacted by new switching technologies. For example, optical switches may force us to rethink the error control, flow control, and congestion control models. Active networks may become feasible and new security models could be developed for such networks.

However, applications influence the solutions we adopt. For example, the error control mechanisms supported by many communication protocols are now based on error detection and retransmission of packets in error; error correction was considered an exotic solution. With multimedia and other time-sensitive applications, when retransmission is no longer a viable solution, mechanisms such as forward error correction are necessary.

2.1.2   Functional and Dependability Attributes

Any man-made system must satisfy *functionality, performance*, and *cost* require-ments. Functionality requires the system to carry out the functions it was designed for. For example, a Web server should be able to deliver to its clients information stored locally. Performance requires the system to deliver its services subject to a set of predefined requirements, e.g., the response time of the server should be lower than the maximum response time acceptable. Cost is also a major concern; systems that are functional and have good performance may not survive in a competitive environment if their cost is too high.

A system must also exhibit a set of nonfunctional attributes related to the quality of service it delivers, attributes collectively defining the *dependability*. The most important dependability attributes are:

Reliability, measured by the probability $R(t)$ that the system delivers its expected service over the entire interval $[0,t]$.

Availability, measured by the probability $A(t)$ that the system is ready to provide the service at time t.

Maintainability, measured by the probability $M(t)$ that a system that failed at time $t = 0$ is functioning correctly at time t.

Safety, measured by the probability $S(t)$ that no catastrophic failures occur in the interval $[0,t]$.

2.1.3 Major Concerns in the Design of a Distributed System

The design of a system consisting of autonomous computers connected with each other by means of communication channels has to take into account several fundamental problems.

First, we have to address the problem of *unreliable communication*. Messages could be lost, distorted, duplicated, and may arrive in a different order than they were sent in. Due to these communication artifacts the results of activities that require coordination among several nodes cannot be predicted. Communication protocols are designed to solve this problem. A *communication protocol* is a set of rules known and followed by all parties involved that guarantees that all participants get all the messages addressed to them and that transmission errors are handled properly. Once we construct a communication protocol that guarantees message delivery we have to address the second problem, transmission errors. The problem of transmission errors is addressed by the coding theory. Shannon's theorem says that it is possible to transform a noisy channel into an asymptotically noiseless one by *encoding* a message.

Second, we have to deal with *independent failures of communication links and computing nodes*. Each component may fail, communication links may be disconnected or cut, computing nodes may be powered off or may experience hardware failures. The computing nodes and the communication links and the routers of a distributed computing system are autonomous entities. Autonomy means that they are independently owned and operated, each administrative domain has its own policies and rules and may decide to shut down a component for maintenance or to restrict its use.

Third, we need to understand the effects of the *discrepancy among communication and computing bandwidth and latency*. Such discrepancies affect the functionality as well as the performance of a distributed system. Physical limitations restrict the amount of data a computing node can store, or the time it takes to carry out an operation. The processing rate expressed by the number of operations per unit of time is called the *bandwidth* of the component. The *latency* is the time elapsed from the instance an operation is initiated to the instance it terminates. The mismatch between the bandwidth of the components of a distributed systems affect its ability to function properly. For example, if a communication channel delivers data to a computing node at a rate higher than the maximum rate the node is able to process, the system is unstable, and the queue of messages waiting to be processed has an unbounded growth.

Last but not least, we have to address the problem of *insecure communication*. The access to information transmitted through the communication channels must be restricted to authorized individuals. Since this information typically traverses several administrative domains, measures must be taken to protect it from unauthorized access. Nowadays, network security is a major concern because computing networks, and the Internet in particular, are critical to the economic, social, political, and defense infrastructure.

2.2 INFORMATION TRANSMISSION AND COMMUNICATION CHANNEL MODELS

A communication channel is used to transmit information from a source to a destination. The information can be in *analog* or *digital* format. In this chapter we are only concerned with digital information.

The information is transported through a physical channel by a *carrier* such as electromagnetic or light waves. The process of inscribing the information on a physical carrier is called *modulation*; the process of extracting the information from the carrier is called *demodulation*. The analog information from an ordinary microphone is a time-continuous and amplitude-continuous function provided by an electric signal modulated by the sound reaching the microphone. The digital information obtained from a digital still camera consists of a set of numbers, the intensity of the pixels captured by a charged coupled device (CCD) at the time when the picture was recorded.

Sampling is the process of transforming continuous-time information into a discrete one and *quantization* is the process of transforming a continuous-amplitude function into a discrete one. Analog to digital conversion is the process of transforming a continuous-time, continuous-amplitude signal into a digital one and requires both sampling and quantization. Quantization introduces *quantization errors*, unavoidable when one wishes to express a continuous-amplitude function as a digital value with a finite number of digits. Nyquist criteria provide a necessary condition for reconstructing a time-continuous function from a set of samples. Chapter 5 provides more details on this subject, in conjunction with a discussion on multimedia communication.

In the case of digital information, the source and the destination use a finite alphabet; the source constructs *messages* using symbols from this alphabet and sends messages through the channel.

2.2.1 Channel Bandwidth and Latency

A communication channel can be modeled as a bit pipe characterized by several parameters. The most important ones are:

(i) the *bandwidth, B,* the number of bits that can be pushed by the source into the bit pipe per unit of time.

(ii) the *latency of a message*, the time elapsed from the instance a message was generated until it is received.

Figure 2.2 illustrates the relation between the latency of a message and the channel bandwidth. The message latency has two components, the propagation delay and the transmission time. The *propagation delay*, the time it takes a bit to travel from the input of the channel to its output, depends on the length of the channel and the propagation velocity. The *transmission time* depends on the bandwidth and the number of bits in the message.

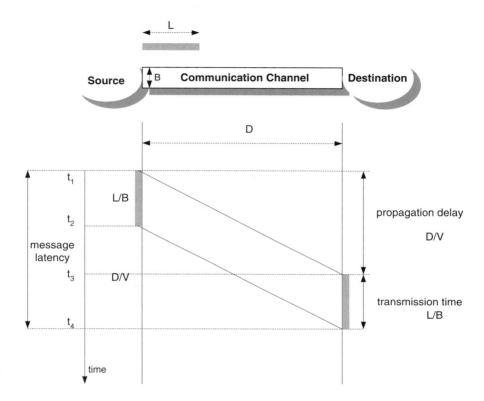

Fig. 2.2 A binary communication channel is characterized by (i) the *bandwidth*, B, the number of bits that can be pushed by the source into the bit pipe per unit of time, (ii) the length of the bit pipe, D, and (iii) the propagation velocity, V. The latency of a message of length L consists of propagation delay, $\frac{D}{V}$ and transmission time, $\frac{L}{B}$. The message transmission starts at time t_1, the last bit of the message is sent at time t_2, the first bit of the message reaches the destination at time t_3, and the last bit of the message arrives at the destination at time t_4.

Example. A T3 optical link has a bandwidth of about 45 Mbps. This means that a sender with a 4.5 Gbit file needs about 100 seconds to transmit the file.

The propagation velocity is close to the speed of light, $c = 3 \times 10^{10}$ cm/second. Thus the propagation delay over a 3000 Km segment of a fiber optic channel is about 10×10^{-6} seconds or 10 μs. The notation μs stands for microsecond; 1 $\mu s = 10^{-6}$ seconds.

If the bandwidth increases by a factor of 100, to 4.5 Gbps, then the transmission time becomes one second, but the propagation delay stays the same. The technological advances in the last few years have pushed the bandwidth to the hundreds of Gbps, but the laws of physics limit the propagation delays.

This observation has profound implications for the design of protocols for high-speed communication. Such protocols depend on feedback from the receiver and/or the network for flow control, congestion control, and error control, mechanisms discussed in depth in the later sections of this chapter and in Chapters 4 and 5. For a fast channel the transmission time is so brief that neither the network nor the receiver have time to react and to slow down the sender.

Observation. The time to send a file of a given size in the previous example is not computed exactly. The bandwidth of a channel is measured in *bits per second (bps)* or multiples of it, $1\ Kbps = 10^3$ bps, $1\ Mbps = 10^6$ bps, $1\ Gbps = 10^9$ bps, and so on. The amount of data in the secondary storage or in the memory of computer is measured in *bits* or bytes and their multiples, $1\ Kbit = 1,024$ bits, $1\ Mbit = 1,024^2$ bits, $1\ Gbit = 1,024^3$ bits, and so on.

2.2.2 Entropy and Mutual Information

A random event provides information about the outcome of an experiment. In the case of a communication channel the experiment is to select a symbol from the input alphabet of the channel, to transmit the symbol, and to observe the output of the channel. The output of a communication channel depends statistically on its input.

To define the capacity of a communication channel we need a measure for the quantity of information; we introduce the concepts of entropy and mutual information [15].

Entropy is a measure of the uncertainty of a single random variable X before it is observed, or the average uncertainty removed by observing it. This quantity is called entropy due to its similarity with the thermodynamic entropy.

Definition. The *entropy* of a random variable X with a probability mass function $p(x)$ is:

$$H(X) = -\sum p(x) \times log_2 p(x).$$

The entropy of a binary random variable is measured in bits.

Example. Consider a binary random variable X and let $p = prob_X(1)$, the probability that the random variable X takes the value 1. Then the entropy of X is:

$$H(X) = -p \times log_2(p) - (1 - p) \times log_2(1 - p).$$

Figure 2.3 shows H(X) function of p. The entropy has a maximum of 1 bit when $p = \frac{1}{2}$ and goes to zero when $p = 0$ or $p = 1$. Intuitively, we expect the entropy to be zero when the outcome is certain and reach its maximum when both outcomes are equally likely.

Example. The same group of eight horses takes part in several horse races. The probabilities of winning for each of the eight horses are respectively:

$$\frac{1}{2},\ \frac{1}{4},\ \frac{1}{8},\ \frac{1}{16},\ \frac{1}{64},\ \frac{1}{64},\ \frac{1}{64},\ \frac{1}{64}.$$

The entropy of the random variable X indicating the winner after one of the races is:

$$H(X) = -\frac{1}{2} \times log_2 \frac{1}{2} - \frac{1}{4} \times log_2 \frac{1}{4} - \frac{1}{8} \times log_2 \frac{1}{8} - \frac{1}{16} \times log_2 \frac{1}{16} - \frac{4}{64} \times log_2 \frac{1}{64} = 2\,bits.$$

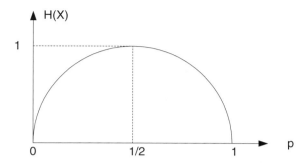

Fig. 2.3 The entropy of a binary random variable function of the probability of an outcome.

If we want to send a binary message to reveal the winner of a particular race, we could encode the horse name in several ways. The techniques discussed in Chapter 5 regarding data compression can be used to show that the following bit strings provide an optimal encoding. An optimal encoding means that the average number of bits transmitted is minimal:

$$0, 10, 110, 1110, 111100, 111101, 111110, 111111$$

The probabilities of winning the race are: $\frac{1}{2}$ for the horse encoded as 0; $\frac{1}{4}$ for 10, and so on. The average length of the string, $\bar{l}$, we have to send to communicate the winner is:

$$\bar{l} = 1 \times \frac{1}{2} + 2 \times \frac{1}{4} + 3 \times \frac{1}{8} + 4 \times \frac{1}{16} + 4 \times (6 \times \frac{1}{64}) = 2 \; bits.$$

The average length of the string identifying the outcome of a race for this particular encoding scheme is equal with the entropy. This example shows that indeed the entropy provides the average information obtained by observing an outcome, or the average uncertainty removed by observing X.

Definition. The *joint entropy of two random variables* X and Y with the joint probability density function $p(x, y)$ is:

$$H(X, Y) \;=\; -\sum_{x \in X} \sum_{y \in Y} p(x, y) \times log_2 p(x, y).$$

Definition. The *conditional entropy of random variable Y given X* is:

$$H(Y|X) \;=\; -\sum_{(x \in X} p(X = x) \times H(Y|X = x).$$

The *conditional entropy of random variable Y given X* is:

$$H(X|Y) \;=\; -\sum_{y \in Y} p(Y = y) \times H(X|Y = y).$$

Table 2.1 The joint probability distribution matrix of random variables X and Y in the conditional entropy example.

Y|X	a	b	c	d
a	1/8	1/16	1/32	1/32
b	1/16	1/8	1/32	1/32
c	1/16	1/16	1/16	1/16
d	1/4	0	0	0

Example. This example is based on one given by Cover and Thomas [15]. Consider two random variables X and Y. Each of them takes values over a four-letter alphabet consisting of the symbols a, b, c, d. The joint distribution of the two random variables is given in Table 2.1.

The marginal distribution of X is $(\frac{1}{2}, \frac{1}{4}, \frac{1}{8}, \frac{1}{8})$, gives the probability of $x = a$, $x = b$, $x = c$, and $x = d$ regardless of the value y of Y, and it is obtained by summing the corresponding columns of the joint probability matrix. The corresponding marginal distribution of Y is $(\frac{1}{4}, \frac{1}{4}, \frac{1}{4}, \frac{1}{4})$.

The conditional entropy is defined as:

$$H(X|Y) = \sum_{1}^{4} p(Y = y) \times H(X|Y = y).$$

The actual value of $H(X|Y)$ is:

$$H(X|Y) = \frac{1}{4}H(\frac{1}{2}, \frac{1}{4}, \frac{1}{8}, \frac{1}{8}) + \frac{1}{4}H(\frac{1}{4}, \frac{1}{2}, \frac{1}{8}, \frac{1}{8}) + \frac{1}{4}H(\frac{1}{4}, \frac{1}{4}, \frac{1}{4}, \frac{1}{4}) + \frac{1}{4}H(1, 0, 0, 0).$$

or

$$H(X|Y) = \frac{1}{4} \times \frac{7}{4} + \frac{1}{4} \times \frac{7}{4} + \frac{1}{4} \times 2 + \frac{1}{4} \times 0 = \frac{11}{8} \; bits.$$

Theorem. The joint entropy of two random variables X and Y, H(X,Y), the entropy of X and Y, H(X) and H(Y), and the conditional entropy, H(X|Y) and H(Y|X), are related:

$$H(X, Y) = H(X) + H(Y|X) = H(Y) + H(Y|X).$$

The proof of this theorem is left as an exercise for the reader.

The reduction in uncertainty of a random variable X due to another random variable Y is called the mutual information.

Definition. The *mutual information of two random variables* X and Y is:

$$I(X; Y) = H(X) - H(X|Y) = \sum p(x, y) \times log\frac{p(x, y)}{p(x) \times p(y)}.$$

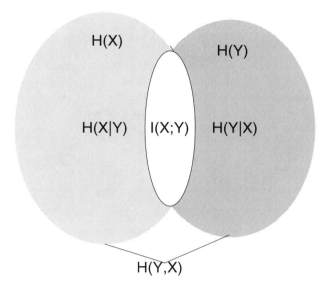

Fig. 2.4 The relations between entropy, conditional entropy, joint entropy, and mutual information.

The mutual information $I(X, Y)$ is a measure of the dependence between the two random variables; it is symmetric in X and Y and always non-negative.

Example. If in the previous example the four outcomes of X are equally likely then:

$$H(X) = -4 \times \frac{1}{4} \times log_2 \frac{1}{4} = log_2 4 = 2 \; bits.$$

and

$$I(X;Y) \;=\; H(X) \;-\; H(X|Y) = 2 - \frac{11}{8} = \frac{5}{8} \; bits.$$

The relations between entropy, conditional entropy, joint entropy, and mutual information is illustrated in Figure 2.4. As we can see:

$$\begin{aligned} H(X) &= H(X|Y) + I(X;Y). \\ H(Y) &= H(Y|X) + I(X;Y). \\ H(X,Y) &= H(X) + H(Y) - I(X;Y). \end{aligned}$$

2.2.3 Binary Symmetric Channels

The input X and the output Y of a communication channel are random variables that take values over the channel alphabet. A communication channel is characterized by a probability transition matrix that determines the conditional distribution of the output given the input. If the input symbols are independent, then the information per symbol at the input of a channel is $H(X)$ and the information for n symbols is $n \times H(X)$.

The question we address now is how much of this information goes through the channel. To answer this question we examine first very simple channel models.

A *binary channel* is one where $X = \{0, 1\}$ and $Y = \{0, 1\}$. A unidirectional binary communication channel is one where the information propagates in one direction only, from the source to the destination.

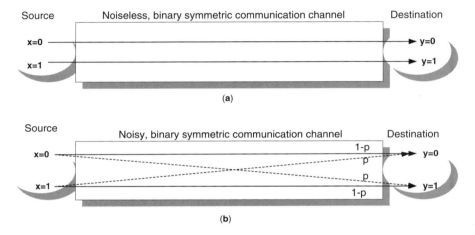

Fig. 2.5 (a) A noiseless binary symmetric channel maps a 0 at the input into a 0 at the output and a 1 into a 1. (b) A noisy symmetric channel maps a 0 into a 1, and a 1 into a 0 with probability p. An input symbol is mapped into itself with probability $1 - p$.

A *noiseless binary channel* transmits each symbol in the input alphabet without errors, as shown in Figure 2.5(a). The noiseless channel model is suitable in some cases for performance analysis but it is not useful for reliability analysis when transmission errors have to be accounted for.

In the case of a *noisy binary symmetric channel*, let $p > 0$ be the probability that one input symbol is received in error, a 1 at the input becomes a 0 at the output and a 0 at the input becomes a 1 at the output, as shown in Figure 2.5(b).

Assume that the two input symbols occur with probabilities q and $1 - q$ In this case:

$$H(Y|X) = -\sum_{x \in X} p(X = x) \times H(Y|X = x)$$

$$H(Y|X) = q \times (p \times log_2 p + (1 - p) \times log_2(1 - p))$$
$$+ (1 - q)(p \times log_2 p + (1 - p) \times log_2(1 - p))$$

$$H(Y|X) = p \times log_2 p + (1 - p) \times log_2(1 - p).$$

Then the mutual information is:

$$I(X;Y) = H(Y) + p \times log_2 p + (1 - p) \times log_2(1 - p).$$

We can minimize $I(X;Y)$ over q to get the channel capacity per symbol in the input alphabet as:

$$C_s = 1 + p \times log_2 p + (1 - p) \times log_2(1 - p).$$

When $p = \frac{1}{2}$ this capacity is 0 because the output is independent of the input. When $p = 0$ or $p = 1$, the capacity is 1, and we have in fact a noiseless channel.

2.2.4 Information Encoding

The problem of transforming, repackaging, or encoding information is a major concern in modern communication. Encoding is used to:

(i) make transmission resilient to errors,

(ii) reduce the amount of data transmitted through a channel, and

(iii) ensure information confidentiality.

A first reason for information encoding is error control. The error control mechanisms transform a noisy channel into a noiseless one; they are built into communication protocols to eliminate the effect of transmission errors.

An error occurs when an input symbol is distorted during transmission and interpreted by the destination as another symbol from the alphabet. *Coding theory* is concerned with this aspect of information theory. Error control is discussed in Section 2.2.6.

Another reason for encoding is the desire to reduce the amount of data transferred through communication channels and to eliminate redundant or less important information. The discipline covering this type of encoding is called *data compression*; encoding and decoding are called *compression* and *decompression*, respectively. Data compression is discussed in Chapter 5.

Last, but not least, we want to ensure information confidentiality, to restrict access to information to only those who have the proper authorization. The discipline covering this facet of encoding is called *cryptography* and the processes of encoding/decoding are called *encryption/decryption*. Data encryption is discussed in Section 2.8.

In all these cases there is a mapping from an original message to a transformed one done at the source and an inverse mapping done at the destination. The first process is called *encoding* and the second one *decoding*.

Source Encoding and Channel Encoding. Information may be subject to multiple stages of encoding as shown in Figure 2.6 for the error control case on a binary channel. In Figure 2.6(a) the source uses a four-letter alphabet and the source encoder maps these four symbols into two-bit strings. The source decoder performs the inverse

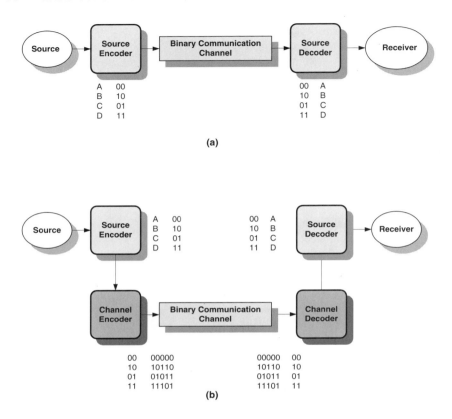

Fig. 2.6 Encoding. (a) The source alphabet consists of four symbols, A,B,C, and D. The *source encoder* maps each input symbol into a two-bit code, A is mapped to 00, B to 10, C to 01, and D to 11. The *source decoder* performs an inverse mapping and delivers a string consisting of the four input alphabet symbols. If a one-bit error occurs when the sender generates the symbol *D*, the source decoder may get 01 or 10 instead of 11 and decode it as either C or B instead of D. (b) The *channel encoder* maps a two-bit string into a five-bit string. If a one-bit or a two-bit error occur, the *channel decoder* receives a string that does not map to any of the valid five-bit strings and detects an error. For example, when 10110 is transmitted and errors in the second and third bit positions occur, the channel decoder detects the error because 11010 is not a valid code word.

mapping. In Figure 2.6(b) the channel encoder increases the redundancy of each symbol encoded by the source encoder by mapping each two-bit string into a five-bit string. This mapping allows the channel decoder to detect a single bit error in the transmission of a symbol from the source alphabet.

In general, the *source encoding* is the process of transforming the information produced by the source into messages. The source may produce a continuous stream of symbols from the source alphabet and the source encoder cuts this stream into blocks of fixed size. The channel encoder accepts as input a set of messages of fixed length and maps the source alphabet into a channel alphabet, then adds a set of redundancy symbols, and finally sends the message through the channel. The channel decoder first determines if the message is in error and takes corrective actions. Then it removes the redundancy symbols, maps back the channel alphabet into the source alphabet, and hands each message to the source decoder who in turn processes the message and passes it to the receiver.

2.2.5 Channel Capacity: Shannon's Theorems

So far we have discussed two properties of a communication channel, the bandwidth and latency. Now we address a more subtle question: How much information may be transmitted through a communication channel?

Definition. Given a communication channel with input X and output Y, the *channel capacity* is defined as the highest rate the information can be transmitted through the channel:

$$C \; = \; max \; I(X;Y).$$

We are interested in two fundamental questions regarding communication over noisy channels: (i) Is it possible to encode the information transmitted over a noisy channel to minimize the probability of errors? (ii) How does the noise affect the capacity of a channel?

The intuition behind the answer to the first question is illustrated by the following analogy. If we want to send a delicate piece of china using a parcel delivery service, we have to package it properly. The more packaging material we add, the more likely it is that the delicate item will arrive at the destination in its original condition, but, at the same time, we increase the weight of the parcel and add to the cost of shipping.

As far as the second question is concerned, we know that whenever the level of noise in a room or on a phone line is high, we have to repeat words and sentences several times before the other party understands what we are saying. Thus, the actual rate we are able to transmit information through a communication channel is lowered by the presence of the noise.

Rigorous answers to both questions, consistent with our intuition, are provided by two theorems due to Claude Shannon, [35, 36, 37], who founded the information theory in the 1950s. Shannon uses the simple models of a communication channel presented earlier to establish the first fundamental result, the so-called Shannon's *coding theorem*: Given a noisy channel with capacity C, for any $0 < \epsilon < 1$ there is a coding scheme that allows us to transmit information through the channel at a rate arbitrarily close to channel capacity, C, and with a probability of error less than ϵ.

This result constitutes what mathematicians call a theorem of existence; it only states that a solution for transforming a noisy communication channel into a noiseless one exists, without giving a hint of how to achieve this result. In real life various sources of noise distort transmission and lower the channel capacity. This effect is expressed by Shannon's *channel capacity theorem for noisy channels*:

$$C = B \times log_2(1 + \frac{Signal}{Noise})$$

where B is the bandwidth, $Signal$ is the average power of the signal, and $Noise$ is the average noise power. Achieving Shannon's limit is a challenging task for any modulation scheme.

The signal-to-noise ratio is usually expressed in decibels (dB) given by the formula: $10 \times log_{10}(\frac{Signal}{Noise})$. A signal-to -noise ratio of 10^3 corresponds to 30 dB, and one of 10^6 corresponds to 60 dB.

Example: Consider a phone line that allows transmission of frequencies in the range 500 Hz to 4000 Hz and has a signal-to-noise ratio of 30 dB. The maximum data rate through the phone line is

$$C = (4000 - 500) \times log_2(1 + 1000) = 3500 \times log_2(1001) = 35Kbps.$$

If the signal-to-noise ratio improves to 60 dB, the maximum data rate doubles, to about 70 Kbps. However, improving the signal-to-noise ratio of a phone line by three orders of magnitude, from 10^3 to 10^6, is extremely difficult or even unfeasible from a technical stand point.

2.2.6   Error Detecting and Error Correcting Codes

Coding is a discipline of information theory building on Shannon's results. The approach taken in coding is to add additional information to increase the redundancy of a message. The intuition behind error detection and error correction is to artificially increase the distance between code words so that the transmission errors cannot possibly transform one valid code word into another valid code word.

Suppose we want to transmit a text written in an alphabet with 32 letters. Assuming the channel alphabet is binary, we can assign five bits to each letter of the source alphabet and we can rewrite the entire text in the binary alphabet accepted by the channel. Using this encoding strategy, we cannot correct errors during transmission. However, if we use more than five bits to represent each letter of the original alphabet, we have a chance to correct a small number of errors.

Error detection is the process of determining if a received message is in error. Accepting a message in error has severe implications on the correct functioning of a system and most communication protocols rely on error control mechanisms to detect when a message is in error. Data link and transport protocols, discussed in Chapter 4, use the automatic repeat request (ARQ) strategy to request the re-transmission of a message in error.

Example. A simple example of an error detection scheme is the addition of a parity check bit to a block of bits, or word, of a given length. This simple scheme is very powerful; it allows us to detect any number of odd errors but fails if an even number of errors occurs. For example, consider a system that enforces even parity for each eight-bit word. Given the string (10111011), we add one more bit to ensure that the total number of 1's is even, in this case a 0 and we transmit the nine-bit string (101110110). The error detection procedure is to count the number of 1's; we decide that the string is in error if this number is odd.

This example also hints to the limitations of error detection mechanisms. A code is designed with certain error detection capabilities and fails to detect error patterns not covered in the original design of the code.

Error correction is the process of restoring a message in error to its original content [40]. The ARQ strategy is unsuitable for real-time applications and serious consideration is given nowadays to the use of error correcting codes for critical applications with real-time delivery constraints.

Retransmission of a message in error is not an option because of the timing constraints. Different types of real-time applications address the problem of communication errors differently: multimedia applications discussed in Chapter 5 are typically less sensitive to errors and could either ignore a message in error or attempt to reconstruct the missing information by interpolation; other applications such as telesurgery or remote control of scientific instruments are more likely to use error correcting codes.

2.2.6.1 Block Codes. Now we provide a number of definitions necessary for understanding the basic concepts of coding theory.

Let A be an *alphabet* of q symbols. For example, $A = \{0, 1\}$ is the *binary alphabet*. The set of symbols that could be transmitted through a communication channel constitute the *channel alphabet*. Throughout this section we use the terms *vector* and *word* interchangeably for n-tuple, an ordered set of n symbols from the channel alphabet.

Definition. A *block code* of length n over the alphabet A is a set of M, n-tuples where each n-tuple takes its components from A and is called a *code word*. We call the block code an $[n, M]$-code over A.

2.2.6.2 Encoding for Block Codes. Figure 2.7 illustrates the encoding process for a block code. The source encoder maps messages, information that the source wants to transmit, into groups of k symbols from the channel alphabet. For example, assume that the channel alphabet consists of q symbols, the integers, 0 to $q - 1$, prefixed by the # sign and we want to transmit a text consisting of $s < q$ sentences. The channel encoder maps each sentence to one of the symbols, and then creates tuples of k such symbols. Next, the channel encoder maps each tuple of k symbols into one of $n = k + r$ symbols. The channel encoder transmits the code words, but the n-tuples received by the channel decoder may be affected by transmission errors, thus, they may or may not be code words.

The quantity $r = n - k > 0$ is called the *redundancy* of the code. The channel encoder adds redundancy, and this leads to the expansion of a message. While the added redundancy is desirable from the point of view of error control, it decreases the efficiency of the communication channel by reducing its effective capacity. The ratio $\frac{k}{n}$ measures the efficiency of a code.

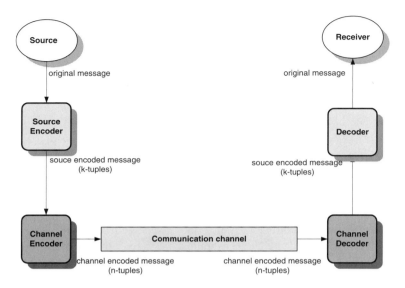

Fig. 2.7   Coding using block codes. The source encoder maps messages into blocks on k symbols from the code alphabet, the channel encoder adds r symbols and transmits n-tuples, with $n = k + r$. At the destination the channel decoder maps n-tuples into k-tuples, and the decoder reconstructs messages.

Definition. The *rate* of an $[n, M]$-code that encodes k-tuples into n-tuples is

$$R = \frac{k}{n}.$$

2.2.6.3   Hamming Distance.   We now introduce a metric necessary to establish the error detecting and error correcting properties of a code.

Definition. The *Hamming distance* $d(\mathbf{x}, \mathbf{y})$ between two code words $\mathbf{x}$ and $\mathbf{y}$ is the number of coordinate positions in which they differ.

Example. Given two binary code words $\mathbf{x} = (010110)$ and $\mathbf{y} = (011011)$. Their Hamming distance is $d(\mathbf{x}, \mathbf{y}) = 3$. Indeed if we number the bit position in each code word from left to right as 1 to 6, the two code words differ in bit positions 3, 4, and 6.

Theorem. The Hamming distance is a metric. For all n-tuples $\mathbf{x}, \mathbf{y}$ and $\mathbf{z}$ over an alphabet A:

1. $d(\mathbf{x}, \mathbf{y}) \geq 0$, with equality if and only if $\mathbf{x} = \mathbf{y}$.

2. $d(\mathbf{x}, \mathbf{y}) = d(\mathbf{y}, \mathbf{x})$.

3. $d(\mathbf{x}, \mathbf{y}) + d(\mathbf{y}, \mathbf{z}) \geq d(\mathbf{x}, \mathbf{z})$ (triangle inequality).

We leave the proof of this theorem as an exercise for the reader.

Definition. Let C be an $[n, M]$-code. The *Hamming distance d of code* C is

$$d = \min\{d(\mathbf{x}, \mathbf{y}) : \quad \mathbf{x}, \mathbf{y} \in C, \mathbf{x} \neq \mathbf{y}\}.$$

The Hamming distance of a code is the minimum distance between any pairs of code words.

Example. Consider $C = \{\mathbf{c}_0, \mathbf{c}_1, \mathbf{c}_2, \mathbf{c}_3\}$ where $\mathbf{c}_0 = (000000)$, $\mathbf{c}_1 = (101101)$, $\mathbf{c}_2 = (010110)$, $\mathbf{c}_3 = (111011)$. This code has distance $d = 3$. Indeed $d(\mathbf{c}_0, \mathbf{c}_1) = 4$, $d(\mathbf{c}_0, \mathbf{c}_2) = 3$, $d(\mathbf{c}_0, \mathbf{c}_3) = 5$, $d(\mathbf{c}_1, \mathbf{c}_2) = 5$, $d(\mathbf{c}_1, \mathbf{c}_3) = 3$, $d(\mathbf{c}_2, \mathbf{c}_3) = 4$.

To compute the Hamming distance for an $[n, M]$-code C, it is necessary to compute the distance between the $\binom{M}{2}$ pairs of code words and then to find the pair with the minimum distance.

2.2.6.4 Channel Decoding Policy.

We now define a policy for the channel decoder for $[n, M]$-code C with distance d. This policy tells the channel decoder what actions to take when it receives an n-tuple $\mathbf{r}$ and consists of two phases:

(1) The recognition phase, when the received code word, $\mathbf{r}$ is compared with all the code words in the code until a match is found or we decide that $\mathbf{r}$ is not a code word.

(2) The error correction phase, when the received tuple $\mathbf{r}$ is mapped into a code word.

The actions taken by the channel decoder are:

(i) If $\mathbf{r}$ is a code word, conclude that no errors have occurred and accept that the code word sent was $\mathbf{c} = \mathbf{r}$.

(ii) If $\mathbf{r}$ is not a code word, conclude that errors have occurred and either correct $\mathbf{r}$ to a code word $\mathbf{c}$ or declare that correction is not possible.

Before continuing our discussion we should observe that this strategy fails when $\mathbf{c}$, the code word sent, was affected by errors and transformed into another valid code word, $\mathbf{r}$. This is a fundamental problem with error detecting and error correcting code and we return to it later. Once we accept the possibility that the channel decoder may fail to decode properly in some cases, our goal is to take the course of action with the greatest probability of being correct.

The decoding strategy called *nearest neighbor decoding*, requires that a received vector is decoded to the code word "closest" to it, with respect to Hamming distance: If an n-tuple $\mathbf{r}$ is received, and there is a unique codeword $\mathbf{c} \in C$ such that $d(\mathbf{r}, \mathbf{c})$ is a minimum, then correct $\mathbf{r}$ to the $\mathbf{c}$. If no such $\mathbf{c}$ exists, report that errors have been detected, but no correction is possible. If multiple code words are at the same minimum distance from the received code word we select at random one of them.

For the following analysis we make the assumption that errors are introduced by the channel at random, and that the probability of an error in one coordinate is independent of errors in adjacent coordinates. Consider a code over an alphabet of q symbols and let the probability that an error occurs on symbol transmission be p. The probability that a symbol is correctly transmitted over the channel is then $1 - p$. We assume that if an error occurs, each of the $q - 1$ symbols aside from the correct one is equally likely, its probability to be received is $p/(q - 1)$. This hypothetical channel is called the *q-ary symmetric channel*.

To justify the nearest-neighbor decoding policy we discuss a strategy known as *maximum likelihood decoding*. Under this strategy, of all possible code words, $\mathbf{r}$ is decoded to that code word $\mathbf{c}$ which maximizes the probability $P(\mathbf{r}, \mathbf{c})$ that $\mathbf{r}$ is received, given that $\mathbf{c}$ is sent. If $d(\mathbf{r}, \mathbf{c}) = d$, then

$$P(\mathbf{r}, \mathbf{c}) = (1 - p)^{n-d} \left(\frac{p}{q - 1} \right)^d .$$

Indeed, $n - d$ coordinate positions in $\mathbf{c}$ are not altered by the channel; the probability of this event is $(1 - p)^{n-d}$. In each of the remaining d coordinate positions, the symbol in $\mathbf{c}$ is altered and transformed into the corresponding symbol in $\mathbf{r}$; the probability of this is $(p/(q - 1))^d$.

Suppose now that $\mathbf{c}_1$ and $\mathbf{c}_2$ are two code words. Assume that we receive $\mathbf{r}$ such that:

$$d(\mathbf{r}, \mathbf{c}_1) = d_1, \quad d(\mathbf{r}, \mathbf{c}_2) = d_2.$$

Without loss of generality we assume that $d_1 \leq d_2$ and that:

$$P(\mathbf{r}, \mathbf{c}_1) > P(\mathbf{r}, \mathbf{c}_2).$$

It follows that

$$(1 - p)^{n-d_1} \left(\frac{p}{q - 1} \right)^{d_1} > (1 - p)^{n-d_2} \left(\frac{p}{q - 1} \right)^{d_2}$$

$$(1 - p)^{d_2 - d_1} > \left(\frac{p}{q - 1} \right)^{d_2 - d_1}$$

and

$$\left(\frac{p}{(1 - p)(q - 1)} \right)^{d_2 - d_1} < 1.$$

If $d_1 = d_2$, this is false, and in fact, $P(\mathbf{r}, \mathbf{c}_1) = P(\mathbf{r}, \mathbf{c}_2)$. Otherwise, $d_2 - d_1 \geq 1$ and the inequality is true if and only if

$$\frac{p}{(1 - p)(q - 1)} < 1, \text{ i.e., } p < \frac{(q - 1)}{q}.$$

In conclusion, when the probability of error $p < (q - 1)/q$ and we receive n-tuple $\mathbf{r}$, we decide that code word c at the minimum distance from $\mathbf{r}$ is the one sent by the source.

Example. Consider the binary code $\mathcal{C} = \{(000000), (101100), (010111), (111011)\}$ and assume that $p = 0.15$. If $\mathbf{r} = (111111)$ is received, $\mathbf{r}$ is decoded to (111011) because the probability $P(\mathbf{r}, (111011))$ is the largest. Indeed:

$$P(\mathbf{r}, (000000)) = (0.15)^6 = 0.000011$$
$$P(\mathbf{r}, (101100)) = (0.15)^3 \times (0.85)^3 = 0.002076$$
$$P(\mathbf{r}, (010011)) = (0.15)^3 \times (0.85)^3 = 0.002076$$
$$P(\mathbf{r}, (111011)) = (0.15)^1 \times (0.85)^5 = 0.066555$$

A code is capable of *correcting e errors* if the channel decoder is capable of correcting any pattern of e or fewer errors, using the algorithm above.

2.2.6.5 Error Correcting and Detecting Capabilities of a Code.
The ability of a code to detect and/or correct errors is a function of its distance, d, previously defined as the minimum Hamming distance between any pair of code words.

Definition. Let c_i, $1 \leq i \leq M$ be the codewords of $\mathcal{C}$, an $[n, M]$-code. Let S be the set of all n-tuples over the alphabet of $\mathcal{C}$ and define

$$S_{\mathbf{c}_i} = \{\mathbf{x} \in S : \ d(\mathbf{x}, \mathbf{c}_i) \leq e\}$$

$S_{\mathbf{c}_i}$ is called the *sphere of radius e* around the code word $\mathbf{c}_i$. It consists of all n-tuples within distance e of the code word $\mathbf{c}_i$, which is at the *center* of the sphere.

Example. The sphere of radius 1 around the code word (000000) consists of the center and all binary six-tuples, that differ from (000000) in exactly one bit position:

$$\{(000000), (100000), (010000), (001000), (000100), (000010), (000001)\}.$$

Theorem. Let $\mathcal{C}$ be an $[n, M]$-code with an odd distance, $d = 2e + 1$. Then $\mathcal{C}$ can correct e errors and can detect $2e$ errors.

Proof. We first show that for $\mathbf{c}_i \neq \mathbf{c}_j$ we must have $S_{\mathbf{c}_i} \cap S_{\mathbf{c}_j} = \emptyset$. Assume by contradiction that $\mathbf{x} \in S_{\mathbf{c}_i} \cap S_{\mathbf{c}_j}$. Then $d(\mathbf{x}, \mathbf{c}_i) \leq e$ and $d(\mathbf{x}, \mathbf{c}_j) \leq e$. The triangle inequality:

$$d(\mathbf{c}_i, \mathbf{x}) + d(\mathbf{x}, \mathbf{c}_j) \geq d(\mathbf{c}_i, \mathbf{c}_j)$$

and hence

$$d(\mathbf{c}_i, \mathbf{c}_j) \leq 2e.$$

But every pair of distinct code words has a distance of at least $2e + 1$. Thus we conclude that

$$S_{\mathbf{c}_i} \cap S_{\mathbf{c}_j} = \emptyset.$$

Hence if code word $\mathbf{c}_i$ is transmitted and $t \leq e$ errors are introduced, the received word $\mathbf{r}$ is an n-tuple in the sphere $S_{\mathbf{c}_i}$, and thus $\mathbf{c}_i$ is the unique code word closest to $\mathbf{r}$. The decoder can always correct any error pattern of this type. If we use the code for error detection, then at least $2e + 1$ errors must occur in the code word to carry it

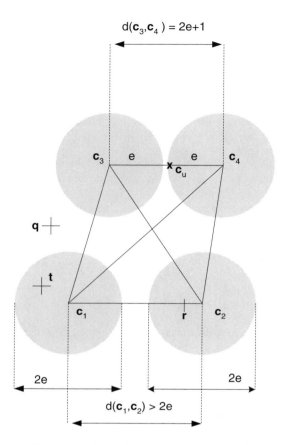

Fig. 2.8 A geometric illustration of error detection and error correction capabilities of a code. A code $\mathcal{C} = \{c_1, c_2, c_3, c_4, ..\}$ with minimum distance $d = 2e + 1$ is used simultaneously for error correction and for error detection. According to the channel decoding rules any n-tuple $\mathbf{t}$, in the sphere of radius e about code word c_1, is decoded as the center of the sphere, c_1. If at most $2e$ errors occur when c_1 is transmitted, the received n-tuple, $\mathbf{r}$ cannot be masquerading as a valid code word, c_2 since the distance between c_1 and c_2 is at least $2e + 1$. Some n-tuples, such as $\mathbf{q}$, are not located within any sphere; thus, they cannot be corrected to any valid code word. Patterns of $e + 1$ errors escape detection and are decoded incorrectly if the code is used simultaneously for error correction and for error detection. This is the case of c_u obtained from c_3 when $e + 1$ errors occur.

into another code word. If at least 1 and at most $2e$ errors are introduced, the received word will never be a code word and error detection is always possible.

Figure 2.8 provides a geometric interpretation for the previous theorem. The code $\mathcal{C} = \{c_1, c_2, c_3, c_4, ..\}$ with distance $d = 2e + 1$ is used simultaneously for error correction and for error detection.

The spheres of radius e around all code words do not intersect because the minimum distance between any pair of code words is $2e + 1$. According to the channel decoding rules, any n-tuple t in the sphere of radius e around code word c_1 is decoded as the center of the sphere c_1.

If at most $2e$ errors occur when the code word a is transmitted, the received n-tuple, r cannot be masquerading as a valid code word c_2 since the distance between c_1 and c_2 is at least $2e + 1$.

The distance of a code may be even or odd. The case for even distance is proved in a similar manner. Let $\lfloor a \rfloor$ denote the largest integer smaller than or equal to a.

Theorem. Let C be an $[n, M]$-code with distance d. Then C can correct $\lfloor \frac{(d-1)}{2} \rfloor$ errors and can detect $d - 1$ errors.

From Figure 2.8 we see that there are n-tuples that are not contained in any of the spheres around the code words of a code C. If an n-tuple q is received and the decoder cannot place it in any of the spheres, then the decoder knows that at least $e + 1$ errors have occurred and no correction is possible.

If a code C with distance $2e + 1$ is used *simultaneously* for error detection and error correction some patterns of less than $2e$ errors could escape detection. For example, patterns of $e + 1$ errors that transform a code word c_3 into a received n-tuple, c_u in sphere S_{c_4}, and force the decoder to correct the received n-tuple to c_4. In this case the $(e + 1)$-error pattern is undetected and a false correction is performed.

In conclusion, when $d = 2e + 1$, the code C can correct e errors in general, but is unable to simultaneously detect additional errors. If the distance of the code is even, the situation changes slightly.

Theorem. Let C be an $[n, M]$-code having distance $d = 2k$. Then C can correct $k - 1$ errors and simultaneously detect k errors.

Proof. By a previous theorem C can correct up to

$$\lfloor \frac{d - 1}{2} \rfloor = \lfloor \frac{2k - 1}{2} \rfloor = \lfloor k - \frac{1}{2} \rfloor = k - 1$$

errors. Since the spheres around code words have radius $k - 1$, any pattern of k errors cannot take a code word into a word contained in some sphere around another code word. Otherwise, the code words at the centers of these two spheres would have distance at most $k + k - 1 = 2k - 1$, which is impossible since $d = 2k$. Hence, a received word obtained from a code word by introducing k errors cannot lie in any code word sphere and the decoder can detect the occurrence of errors. The decoder cannot detect $k + 1$ errors in general, since a vector at distance $k + 1$ from a given code word may be in the sphere of another code word, and the decoder would erroneously correct such a vector to the code word at the center of the second sphere.

Example. Consider the code $C = \{c_1, c_2, c_3, c_4\}$ where

$$c_1 = (000000) \quad c_2 = (101100) \quad c_3 = (010111) \quad c_4 = (111011)$$

C has distance $d = 3$, and hence can correct 1 error. The set S of all possible words over the alphabet $\{0,1\}$ consists of all possible binary 6-tuples, hence, $|S| = 64$. Let us now construct the four spheres of radius 1 about each code word:

$$S_{c_i} = \{(000000), (100000), (010000), (001000), (000100), (000010), (000001)\}$$

$$S_{c_2} = \{(101100), (001100), (111100), (100100), (101000), (101110), (101101)\}$$

$$S_{c_3} = \{(010111), (110111), (000111), (011111), (010011), (010101), (010110)\}$$

$$S_{c_4} = \{(111011), (011011), (101011), (110011), (111111), (111001), (111010)\}$$

These spheres cover 28 of the 64 6-tuples in S. Let S^* be the set of 6-tuples not in any sphere and $|S^*| = 64 - 28 = 36$.

Suppose the decoder receives $\mathbf{r} = (000111)$. The distance to each code word is computed.

$$d(c_1, \mathbf{r}) = 3, \quad d(\mathbf{c}_2, \mathbf{r}) = 4, \quad d(\mathbf{c}_3, \mathbf{r}) = 1, \quad d(\mathbf{c}_4, \mathbf{r}) = 4.$$

Since there is a unique minimum distance, $\mathbf{r}$ is decoded to $\mathbf{c}_3$. Notice that $\mathbf{r}$ lies in the sphere $S_{\mathbf{c}_3}$.

To evaluate the reliability of the nearest neighbor decoding strategy we have to compute the probability that a code word $\mathbf{c}$ sent over the channel is decoded correctly. Let us consider an $[n, M]$-code $\mathcal{C}$ with distance d over an alphabet A with q symbols, $|A| = q$. Assume a probability of error p, such that $0 \le p \le (q - 1)/q$.

When code word c is sent, the received n-tuple will be decoded correctly if it is inside the sphere of radius $e = \lfloor (d - 1)/2 \rfloor$ about $\mathbf{c}$, $S_{\mathbf{c}}$ of radius e. The probability of this event is

$$\sum_{\mathbf{r} \in S_c} P(\mathbf{r}, \mathbf{c}) = \sum_{i=0}^{e} \binom{n}{i} p^i (1 - p)^{n-i}.$$

Indeed, the probability of receiving an n-tuple with i positions in error is $\binom{n}{i} p^i (1 - p)^{n-i}$ and i takes values in the range from 0, no errors, to a maximum of e errors. This expression gives a lower bound on the probability that a transmitted code word is correctly decoded.

2.2.6.6 Hamming Bound.
In the previous section we established that the ability of a code to detect and correct errors is determined by the distance of the code. To construct a binary code with k information bits and r redundancy bits we have to select a subset of n-tuples with $n = k + r$ so that the minimum distance between any pair of code words is d.

Now we examine the question of the minimum number of redundancy bits necessary to construct a code able to correct any single error, the so-called Hamming bound.

To establish this bound we make several observations:

(i) To construct an $[n, M]$ block code means to select $M = 2^k$ n-tuples as code words out of 2^n n-tuples.

(ii) To correct all 1-bit errors, all spheres of radius one around the M code words must not intersect each other.

(iii) A sphere of radius one around an n-tuple consists of $(n+1)$ n-tuples. In addition to the center of the sphere, there are n n-tuples at distance one from the center, one for each bit position, see also the first example in Section 2.2.6.5.

Then:

$$M \times (n+1) \leq 2^n.$$

This relation says that the total number of n-tuples in the M spheres of radius one cannot exceed the total number on n-tuples. This can be written as:

$$2^k \times (k+r+1) \leq 2^{(k+r)}.$$

or

$$2^r - r \geq k+1.$$

For example, if $k = 15$, the minimum value of r is 5.

2.2.7   Final Remarks on Communication Channel Models

The communication channel models discussed in this section are useful to understand how to handle communication errors, one of the main concerns in the design of a distributed system.

A communication channel is characterized by its bandwidth B, or by its capacity C related to the bandwidth by Shannon's channel capacity theorem for noisy channels. Sometimes, instead of channel capacity, we talk about the maximum rate R of a channel.

Information theory allows us to define primitive concepts such as entropy, mutual information, and the capacity of a communication channel using statistical arguments. Shannon's coding theorem establishes that communication with an arbitrary low probability of undetected errors is possible and provides the foundations for coding theory.

In practice a code should be designed according to the expected error rate. A code constructed to detect x-errors may fail if a larger number of errors occurs.

Some communication protocols have error control mechanisms based on error detection and retransmission of messages in error. New real-time applications are opening the door for error correcting codes simply because the timing constraints do not allow retransmission of messages in error.

2.3   PROCESS MODELS

2.3.1   Processes and Events

The model presented in this section is based on the assumption that a channel is a unidirectional bit pipe of infinite bandwidth and zero latency, but unreliable. Messages

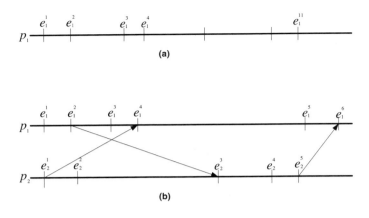

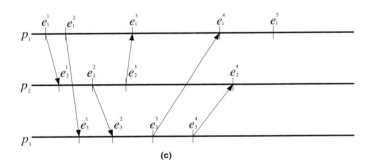

Fig. 2.9 Space-time diagrams. (a) All events in case of a single process are local. Multiple processes interact by means of communication events, (b) and (c).

sent through a channel may be lost, distorted, or the channel may fail. We also assume that the time a process needs to traverse a set of states is of no concern and processes may fail.

The activity of any process is modeled as a sequence of *events*. There are two types of events, local and communication events. An event causes the change of the process state. The *state of a process* consists of all the information necessary to restart a process once it has been stopped. The *local history of a process* is a sequence of events, possibly an infinite one, and can be presented graphically as a *space-time diagram* where events are ordered by their time of occurrence. For example, in Figure 2.9(a) the history of process p_1 consists of 11 events, $e^1, e^2, ..., e^{11}$. The process is in state σ_1 immediately after the occurrence of event e^1 and remains in that state until the occurrence of event e^2.

Distributed systems consist of multiple processes active at any one time and communicating with each other. *Communication events* involve more than one process and occur when the algorithm implemented by a process requires sending or receiving a message to another process. Without loss of generality we assume that communication among processes is done only by means of *send(m)* and *receive(m)* communication events where m is a message. Completion of every step of the algorithm is a *local event* if it does not involve communication with other processes. The space-time diagram in Figure 2.9(b) shows two processes, p_1 and p_2 with local histories $h_1 = (e_1^1, e_1^2, e_1^3, e_1^4, e_1^5)$ and $h_2 = (e_2^1, e_2^2, e_2^3, e_2^4)$.

A *protocol* is a finite set of messages exchanged among processes to help them coordinate their actions. Figure 2.9(c) illustrates the case when communication events are dominant in the local history of processes, p_1, p_2 and p_3. In this case only e_1^5 is a local event; all others are communication events. The protocol requires each process to send messages to all other processes in response to the a message from the coordinator, process p_1.

2.3.2 Local and Global States

The informal definition of the state of a single process can be extended to collections of communicating processes. The global state of a distributed system consisting of several processes and communication channels is the union of the states of the individual processes and channels [2].

Call h_i^j the history of process p_i up to and including its j-th event, e_i^j and σ_i^j the local state of process p_i following event e_i^j. Consider a system consisting of n processes, $p_1, p_2, ..., p_n$, its global state is an n-tuple of local states:

$$\Sigma = (\sigma_1, \sigma_2, ..., \sigma_n).$$

The state of the channels does not appear explicitly in this definition of the global state because the state of the channels is encoded as part of the local state of the processes communicating through the channels.

The global states of a distributed computation with n processes form an n-dimensional lattice. The elements of this lattice are global states $\Sigma^{j1,j2,....jn}(\sigma_1^{j1}, \sigma_2^{j2}, ..., \sigma_n^{jn})$.

Figure 2.10(a) shows the lattice of global states of the distributed computation in Figure 2.9(b). This is a two-dimensional lattice because we have two processes, p_1 and p_2. The lattice of global states for the distributed computation in Figure 2.9(c) is a three-dimensional lattice, the computation consists of three concurrent processes, p_1, p_2, and p_3.

The initial state of the system in Figure 2.9(b) is the one before the occurrence of any event and is denoted by $\Sigma^{0,0}$. The only global states reachable from $\Sigma^{0,0}$ are $\Sigma^{1,0}$ and $\Sigma^{0,1}$. The communication events limit the global states the system may reach. In this example the system cannot reach the state $\Sigma^{4,0}$ because process p_1 enters state σ_4 only after process p_2 has entered the state σ_1.

Figure 2.10(b) shows the six possible sequences of events to reach the global state $\Sigma^{2,2}$: $(e_1^1, e_1^2, e_2^1, e_2^2)$, $(e_1^1, e_2^1, e_1^2, e_2^2)$, $(e_1^1, e_2^1, e_2^2, e_1^2)$, $(e_2^1, e_2^2, e_1^1, e_1^2)$, $(e_2^1, e_1^1, e_1^2, e_2^2)$, $(e_2^1, e_1^1, e_2^2, e_1^2)$.

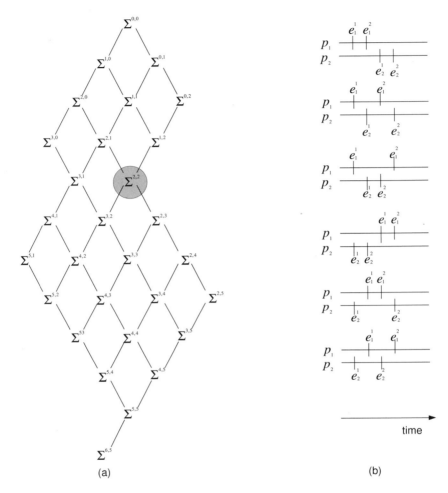

Fig. 2.10 (a) The lattice of the global states of the distributed computation in Figure 2.9(b). (b) Sequences of events leading to the state $\Sigma^{2,2}$.

2.3.3 Process Coordination

A major concern in any distributed system is *process coordination in the presence of channel failures*. There are multiple modes for a channel to fail and some lead to messages being lost. In the most general case, it is impossible to guarantee that two processes will reach an agreement in case of channel failures.

Many problems in network computing systems are instances of the *global predicate evaluation problem (GPE)* where the goal is to evaluate a Boolean expression whose elements are a function of the global state of the system. In many instances we need to perform an action when the state of the system satisfies a particular condition.

The coordination problem can be solved sometimes by constructing fairly complex communication protocols. In other cases even though no theoretical solution exists, in practice one may use channels with very low error rates and may tolerate extremely low probabilities of failure.

Let us now prove the assertion that no finite exchange of messages allows two processes to reach consensus when messages may be lost.

Statement. Given two processes p_1 and p_2 connected by a communication channel that can lose a message with probability $\varepsilon > 0$. No protocol capable of guaranteeing that two processes will reach agreement exists, regardless how small ε is.

Proof. The proof is by contradiction. Assume that such a protocol exists and it consists of n messages. Since we assumed that any message might be lost with probability ε it follows that the protocol should be able to function when only $n - 1$ messages reach their destination, one being lost. Induction on the number of messages proves that indeed no such protocol exists, see Figure 2.11.

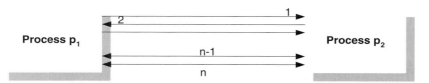

Fig. 2.11 Process coordination in the presence of errors. Each message may be lost with probability p. If a protocol consisting of n messages exists, then the protocol would have to function properly with $n - 1$ messages reaching their destination, one of them being lost.

2.3.4   Time, Time Intervals, and Global Time

Virtually all human activities and all man-made systems depend on the notion of time. We need to measure *time intervals*, the time elapsed between two events and we also need a *global concept of time* shared by all entities that cooperate with one another. For example, a computer chip has an *internal clock* and a predefined set of actions occurs at each clock tick. In addition, the chip has an *interval timer* that helps enhance the system's fault tolerance. If the effects of an action are not sensed after a predefined interval, the action is repeated.

When the entities collaborating with each other are networked computers the precision of clock synchronization is critical [25]. The event rates are very high, each system goes through state changes at a very fast pace. That explains why we need to measure time very accurately. Atomic clocks have an accuracy of about 10^{-6} seconds per year.

The communication between computers is unreliable. Without additional restrictions regarding message delays and errors there are no means to ensure a perfect synchronization of local clocks and there are no obvious methods to ensure a global ordering of events occurring in different processes.

An isolated system can be characterized by its *history* expressed as a sequence of events, each event corresponding to a change of the state of the system. Local timers provide relative time measurements. A more accurate description adds to the system's history the time of occurrence of each event as measured by the local timer.

The mechanisms described above are insufficient once we approach the problem of cooperating entities. To coordinate their actions two entities need a common perception of time. Timers are not enough, clocks provide the only way to measure distributed duration, that is, actions that start in one process and terminate in another. *Global agreement on time* is necessary to *trigger actions* that should occur concurrently, e.g., in a real-time control system of a power plant several circuits must be switched on at the same time. Agreement on *the time when events occur* is necessary for distributed recording of events, for example, to determine a precedence relation through a temporal ordering of events. To ensure that a system functions correctly we need to determine that the event causing a change of state occurred before the state change, e.g., that the sensor triggering an alarm has indeed changed its value before the emergency procedure to handle the event was activated. Another example of the need for agreement on the time of occurrence of events is in replicated actions. In this case several replica of a process must log the time of an event in a consistent manner.

Timestamps are often used for event ordering using a global time-base constructed on local virtual clocks [29]. Δ-protocols [16] achieve total temporal order using a global time base. Assume that local virtual clock readings do not differ by more than π, called *precision* of the global time base. Call g the granularity of physical clocks. First, observe that the granularity should not be smaller than the precision. Given two events a and b occurring in different processes if $t_b - t_a \leq \pi + g$ we cannot tell which of a or b occurred first [41]. Based on these observations it follows that the order discrimination of clock-driven protocols cannot be better than twice the clock granularity.

2.3.5 Cause-Effect Relationship, Concurrent Events

System specification, design, and analysis require a clear understanding of cause-effect relationships. During the system specification phase we view the system as a state machine and define the actions that cause transitions from one state to another. During the system analysis phase we need to determine the cause that brought the system to a certain state.

The activity of any process is modeled as a sequence of *events*; hence, the binary relation cause-effect should be expressed in terms of events and should express our intuition that the cause must precede the effects. Again, we need to distinguish between local events and communication events. The latter affect more than one process and are essential for constructing a global history of an ensemble of processes. Let h_i denote the local history of process p_i and let e_i^k denote the k-th event in this history. The binary cause-effect relationship between two events has the following properties:

1. Causality of local events can be derived from the process history. If $e_i^k, e_i^l \in h_i$ and $k < l$ then $e_i^k \rightarrow e_i^l$.

2. Causality of communication events. If $e_i^k = send(m)$ and $e_j^l = receive(m)$ then $e_i^k \rightarrow e_j^l$.

3. Transitivity of the causal relationship. If $e_i^k \rightarrow e_j^l$ and $e_j^l \rightarrow e_m^n$ then $e_i^k \rightarrow e_m^n$.

Two events in the global history may be unrelated, neither is the cause of the other; such events are said to be *concurrent*.

2.3.6 Logical Clocks

A logical clock is an abstraction necessary to ensure the clock condition in absence of a global clock. Each process p_i maps events to positive integers. Call $LC(e)$ the local variable associated with event e. Each process time-stamps each message m sent with the value of the logical clock at the time of sending, $TS(m) = LC(send(m))$. The rules to update the logical clock are:

$LC(e) := LC + 1$ if e is a local event or a $send(m)$ event.

$LC(e) := max(LC, TS(m) + 1)$ if $e = receive(m)$.

Figure 2.12 uses a modified *space-time diagram* to illustrate the concept of logical clocks. In the modified space-time diagram the events are labeled with the logical clock value. Messages exchanged between processes are shown as lines from the sender to the receiver and marked as communication events.

Logical clocks do not allow a global ordering of events. For example, in Figure 2.12 there is no way to establish the ordering of events e_1^1, e_2^1 and e_3^1. The communication events help different processes coordinate their logical clocks. Process p_2 labels event e_2^3 as 6 because of message m_2, which carries information about the logical clock value at the time it was sent as 5. Recall that e_i^j is the j-th event in process p_i.

Logical clocks lack an important property, *gap detection*. Given two events e and e' and their logical clock values, $LC(e)$ and $LC(e')$, it is impossible to establish if an

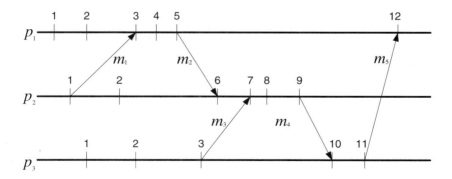

Fig. 2.12 Three processes and their logical clocks. The usual labeling of events as $e_1^1, e_1^2, e_1^3, \ldots$ is omitted to avoid overloading the figure; only the logical clock values for local or communication events are indicated. The correspondence between the events and the logical clock values is obvious: $e_1^1, e_2^1, e_3^1 \rightarrow 1$, $e_1^5 \rightarrow 5$, $e_2^4 \rightarrow 7$, $e_3^4 \rightarrow 10$, $e_1^6 \rightarrow 12$, and so on. Process p_2 labels event e_2^3 as 6 because of message m_2, which carries information about the logical clock value at the time it was sent as 5. Global ordering of events is not possible; there is no way to establish the ordering of events e_1^1, e_2^1 and e_3^1.

event e'' exists such that $LC(e) < LC(e'') < LC(e')$. For example, in Figure 2.12, there is an event, e_1^4 between the events e_1^3 and e_1^5. Indeed $LC(e_1^3) = 3$, $LC(e_1^5) = 5$, $LC(e_1^4) = 4$, and $LC(e_1^3) < LC(e_1^4) < LC(e_1^5)$. However, for process p_3, events e_3^3 and e_3^4 are consecutive though, $LC(e_3^3) = 3$ and $LC(e_3^4) = 10$.

2.3.7 Message Delivery to Processes

The communication channel abstraction makes no assumptions about the order of messages; a real-life network might reorder messages. This fact has profound implications for a distributed application. Consider for example a robot getting instructions to navigate from a monitoring facility with two messages, "turn left" and "turn right", being delivered out of order.

To be more precise we have to comment on the concepts of messages and packets. A message is a structured unit of information, it makes sense only in a semantic context. A packet is a networking artifact resulting from cutting up a message into pieces. Packets are transported separately and reassembled at the destination into a message to be delivered to the receiving process. Some local area networks (LANs) use a shared communication media and only one packet may be transmitted at a time, thus packets are delivered in the order they are sent. In wide area networks (WANs) packets might take different routes from any source to any destination and they may be delivered out of order. To model real networks the channel abstraction must be augmented with additional rules.

A *delivery rule* is an additional assumption about the channel-process interface. This rule establishes when a message received is actually delivered to the destination process. The receiving of a message m and its delivery are two distinct events in a causal relation with one another, a message can only be delivered after being received, see Figure 2.13:

$$receive(m) \rightarrow deliver(m).$$

First in first out *(FIFO) delivery* implies that messages are delivered in the same order they are sent. For each pair of source-destination processes (p_i, p_j) FIFO delivery requires that the following relation be satisfied:

$$send_i(m) \rightarrow send_i(m') \Rightarrow deliver_j(m) \rightarrow deliver_j(m').$$

Even if the communication channel does not guarantee FIFO delivery, FIFO delivery can be enforced by attaching a sequence number to each message sent. The sequence numbers are also used to reassemble messages out of individual packets.

Causal delivery is an extension of the FIFO delivery to the case when a process receives messages from different sources. Assume a group of three processes, (p_i, p_j, p_k) and two messages m and m'. Causal delivery requires that:

$$send_i(m) \rightarrow send_j(m') \Rightarrow deliver_k(m) \rightarrow deliver_k(m').$$

Message delivery may be FIFO, but not causal when more than two processes are involved in a message exchange. Figure 2.14 illustrates this case. Message m_1 is delivered to process p_2 after message m_3, though message m_1 was sent before m_3.

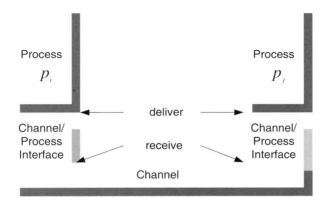

Fig. 2.13 Message receiving and message delivery are two distinct operations. The channel-process interface implements the delivery rules, e.g., FIFO delivery.

Indeed, message m_3 was sent by process p_1 after receiving m_2, which in turn was sent by process p_1 after sending m_1.

Call $TS(m)$ the time stamp carried by message m. A message received by process p_i is *stable* if no future messages with a time stamp smaller than $TS(m)$ can be received by process p_i.

When using logical clocks, a process p_i can construct consistent observations of the system if it implements the following delivery rule: *deliver all stable messages in increasing time stamp order.*

Let us now examine the problem of consistent message delivery under several sets of assumptions. First, assume that processes cooperating with each other in a distributed environment have access to a global real-time clock and that message

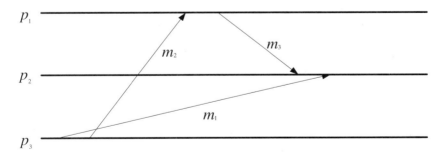

Fig. 2.14 Violation of causal delivery. Message delivery may be FIFO but not causal when more than two processes are involved in a message exchange. From the local history of process p_2 we see that $deliver(m_3) \rightarrow deliver(m_1)$. But: (i) $send(m_3) \rightarrow deliver(m_3)$; (ii) from the local history of process p_1, $deliver(m_2) \rightarrow send(m_3)$; (iii) $send(m_2) \rightarrow deliver(m_2)$; (iv) from the local history of process p_3, $send(m_1) \rightarrow send(m_2)$. The transitivity property and (i), (ii), (iii) and (iv) imply that $send(m_1) \rightarrow deliver(m_3)$.

delays are bounded by δ and that there is no clock drift. Call $RC(e)$ the time of occurrence of event e. Each process includes in every message the time stamp $RC(e)$ where e is the send message event. The delivery rule in this case is: *at time t deliver all received messages with time stamps up to t $-$ δ in increasing time stamp order.* Indeed, this delivery rule guarantees that under the bounded delay assumption the message delivery is consistent. All messages delivered at time t are in order and no future message with a time stamp lower than any of the messages delivered may arrive.

For any two events e and e', occurring in different processes, the so called *clock condition* is satisfied if:

$$e \rightarrow e' \Rightarrow RC(e) < RC(e').$$

Oftentimes, we are interested in determining the set of events that caused an event knowing the time stamps associated with all events, in other words, to deduce the causal precedence relation between events from their time stamps. To do so we need to define the so-called strong clock condition. The *strong clock condition* requires an equivalence between the causal precedence and the ordering of time stamps:

$$\forall e, e' \quad e \rightarrow e' \equiv TC(e) < TC(e').$$

Causal delivery is very important because it allows processes to reason about the entire system using only local information. This is only true in a closed system where all communication channels are known. Sometimes the system has *hidden channels* and reasoning based on causal analysis may lead to incorrect conclusions.

2.3.8 Process Algebra

There are many definitions of a process and process modeling is extremely difficult. Many properties may or may not be attributed to processes [3]. Hoare realized that a language based on execution traces is insufficient to abstract the behavior of communicating processes and developed *communicating sequential processes (CSP)* [20]. More recently, Milner initiated an axiomatic theory called the *Calculus of Communicating System (CCS)* [30].

Process algebra is the study of concurrent communicating processes within an algebraic framework. The process behavior is modeled as a set of equational axioms and a set of operators. This approach has its own limitations, the real-time behavior of processes, the true concurrency still escapes this axiomatization. Here we only outline the theory called *Basic Process Algebra (BPA)* , the kernel of *Process Algebra*.

Definition. An *algebra* **A** consists of a set A of elements and a set of operators, f. A is called the domain of the algebra **A** and consists of a set of constants and variables. The operators map A^n to A, the domain of an algebra is closed with respect to the operators in f.

Example. In Boolean algebra **B** $= (B, xor, and, not)$ with $B = \{0, 1\}$.

Definition. *BPA* is an algebra, **BPA** $= (\Sigma_{BPA}, E_{BPA})$. Here Σ_{BPA} consists of two binary operators, $+$ and $\times$, as well as a number of constants, $a, b, c, ...$

and variables, $x, y, \dots$. The first operator, $\times$ is called the *product* or the *sequential composition* and it is generally omitted, $x \times y$ is equivalent to xy and means a process that first executes x and then y. $+$ is called the *sum* or the *alternative composition*, $x + y$ is a process that either executes x or y but not both. E_{BPA} consists of five axioms:

$$
\begin{aligned}
x + y &= y + x & (A1) &- \text{Commutativity of sum} \\
(x + y) + z &= x + (y + z) & (A2) &- \text{Associativity of sum} \\
x + x &= x & (A3) &- \text{Idempotency of sum} \\
(x + y)z &= xz + yz & (A4) &- \text{Right Distributivity of product} \\
(xy)z &= x(yz) & (A5) &- \text{Associativity of product}
\end{aligned}
$$

Nondeterministic choices and branching structure. The alternative composition, $x + y$ implies a nondeterministic choice between x and y and can be represented as two branches in a state transition diagram.

The fourth axiom $(x + y)z = xz + yz$ says that a choice between x and y followed by z is the same as a choice between xz, and yz and then either x followed by z or y followed by z.

Note that the following axiom is missing from the definition of BPA:

$$
x(y + z) = xy + xz.
$$

The reason for this omission is that in $x(y + z)$ the component x is executed first and then a choice between y and z is made while in $(xy + xz)$ a choice is made first and only then either x followed by y or x followed by z are executed.

Processes are thus characterized by their branching structure and indeed the two processes $x(y + z)$ and $(xy + xz)$ have different *branching structures*. The first process has two subprocesses and a branching in the second subprocess, whereas the second one has two branches at the beginning.

2.3.9 Final Remarks on Process Models

The original process model presented in this section is based on a set of idealistic assumptions, e.g., the time it takes a process to traverse a set of states is of no concern. We introduced the concepts of states and events and showed that in addition to the local state of a process, for groups of communicating processes we can define the concept of global state.

We also discussed the Global Coordination Problem and showed that a process group may not be able to reach consensus if any message has a non-zero probability of being lost. Once we introduce the concept of time we can define a causality relationship. We also introduced the notion of virtual time and looked more closely at the message delivery to processes.

2.4   SYNCHRONOUS AND ASYNCHRONOUS MESSAGE PASSING SYSTEM MODELS

2.4.1   Time and the Process Channel Model

Given a group of n processes, $G = (p_1, p_2, ..., p_n)$, communicating by means of messages, each process must be able to decide if the lack of a response from another process is due to: (i) the failure of the remote process, (ii) the failure of the communication channel, or (iii) there is no failure, but either the remote process or the communication channel are slow, and the response will eventually be delivered.

For example, consider a monitoring process that collects data from a number of sensors to control a critical system. If the monitor decides that some of the sensors, or the communication channels connecting them have failed, then the system could enter a recovery procedure to predict the missing data and, at the same time, initiate the repair of faulty elements. The recovery procedure may use a fair amount of resources and be unnecessary if the missing data is eventually delivered. This trivial example reveals a fundamental problem in the design of distributed systems and the need to augment the basic models with some notion of time.

Once we take into account the processing and communication time in our assumptions about processes and channels, we distinguish two types of systems, asynchronous and synchronous ones. Informally, synchronous processes are those where processing and communication times are bounded and the process has an accurate perception of time. Synchronous systems allow detection of failures and implementation of approximately synchronized clocks. If any of these assumptions are violated, we talk about asynchronous processes.

2.4.2   Synchronous Systems

Let us examine more closely the relation between the real time and the time available to a process. If process p_i has a clock and if $C_{p_i}(t)$ is the reading of this clock at real time t, we define *the rate drift of a clock* as

$$\rho = \frac{C_{p_i}(t) - C_{p_i}(t')}{t - t'}.$$

Formally, a process p_i is *synchronous* if:

(a) There is an upper bound δ on message delay for all messages sent or received by p_i and this bound is known.

(b) There is an upper bound on the time required by process p_i to execute a given task, and

(c) The rate of drift of the local clock of all processes p_i is communicating with is bounded for all $t > t'$.

We now present several examples of synchronous processes and algorithms exploiting the bounded communication delay in a synchronous system. The first example

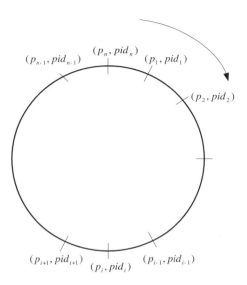

Fig. 2.15 A unidirectional ring of n synchronous processes. Process p_i receives messages from process p_{i-1} and sends them to process p_{i+1}. Each process p_i has a unique identifier.

presents an algorithm for electing a leader in a token passing ring or bus. Token passing systems provide contention-free or scheduled access to a shared communication channel. The second and third examples cover collision-based methods for multiple access communication channels.

In a ring topology any node is connected to two neighbors, one upstream and one downstream, see Figure 2.15. In a token passing bus there is a logical ringlike relationship between nodes, each node has an upstream and a downstream neighbor.

A node is only allowed to transmit when it receives a token from its upstream neighbor and once it has finished transmission it passes the token to its downstream neighbor. Yet tokens can be lost and real-life local area networks based on a ring topology have to address the problem of regenerating the token. For obvious reasons we wish to have a distributed algorithm to elect a node that will then be responsible to regenerate the missing token.

A *multiple access communication channel* is one shared by several processes, see Figure 2.16(a). Only one member of the process group $G = (p_1, p_2, ..., p_n)$ may transmit successfully at any one time, and all processes receive every single message sent by any other member of the group; this is a *broadcast* channel. A common modeling assumption for a multiple access system is that time is slotted and in every slot every member of the group receives *feedback* from the channel. The feedback is ternary, the slot may be:

(i) *an idle slot* when no process transmits, or

(ii) *a successful slot* when exactly one process transmits, or

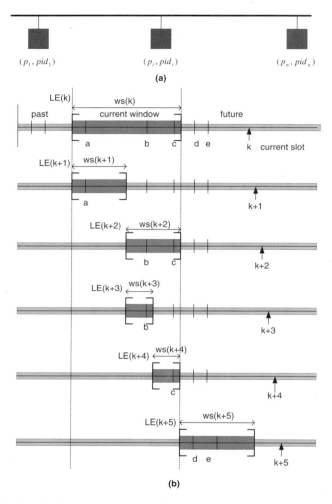

Fig. 2.16 (a) A multiple access communication channel. n processes $p_1, p_2, \ldots p_n$ access a shared communication channel and we assume that the time is slotted. This is a synchronous system and at the end of each slot all processes get the feedback from the channel and know which one of the following three possible events occurred during that slot: *successful transmission* of a packet when only one of the processes attempted to transmit; *collision*, when more than one process transmitted; or *idle slot* when none of the processes transmitted. (b) The FCFS splitting algorithm. In each slot k all processes know the position and size of a window, LE(k) and ws(k) as well the state $s(k)$. Only processes with packets within the window are allowed to transmit. All processes also know the rules for updating $LE(k), ws(k)$ and $s(k)$ based on the feedback from the communication channel. The window is split recursively until there is only one process with a packet within the window.

(iii) *a collision slot*, when two or more processes in the group attempt to transmit.

The communication delay is bounded, and after a time $\tau = 2\frac{D}{V}$, with D the length of the physical channel and V the propagation velocity, a node attempting to transmit in a slot will know if it has been successful or not.

Coordination algorithms for multiple access communication channels are also called *splitting algorithms* for reasons that will become apparent later. We present two such algorithms, the First Come First Served (FCFS) algorithm of Gallagher and the stack algorithm.

Example. Consider a unidirectional ring of n synchronous processes, see Figure 2.15, each identified by a *unique process identifier*, *pid*. The process identifier can be selected from any totally ordered space of identifiers such as the set of positive integers, N^+, the set of reals, and so on. The only requirement is that the identifiers be unique. If all processes in the group have the same identifier, then it is impossible to elect a leader. We are looking for an algorithm to elect the leader of the ring, when exactly one process will output the decision that it is the leader by modifying one of its state variables.

The following algorithm was proposed by Le Lann, Chang and Roberts [27] : Each process sends its process identifier around the ring. When a process receives an incoming identifier, it compares that identifier with its own. If the incoming identifier is greater than its own it passes it to its neighbor; if it is less it discards the incoming identifier; if it is equal to its own, the process declares itself to be the leader.

Assuming that the sum of the processing time and the communication time in each node are bounded by τ, then the leader will be elected after at most $n \times \tau$ units of time. If the number n of processes and τ are known to every process in the group then each process will know precisely when they could proceed to execute a task requiring a leader.

Example. The FCFS, splitting algorithm allows member processes to transmit over a multiple access communication channel precisely in the order when they generate messages, without the need to synchronize their clocks [7].

The FCFS algorithm illustrated in Figure 2.16(b) is described informally now. The basic idea is to divide the time axis into three regions, the past, present and future and attempt to transmit messages with the arrival time in the current window. Based on the feedback from the channel each process can determine how to adjust the position and the size of the window and establish if a successful transmission took place. The feedback from the channel can be: successful transmission, *success*, collision of multiple packets, *collision*, or an idle slot, *idle*.

For example, in slot k we see two packets in the past, three packets (a, b, c) within the window, and two more packets (d, e) in the future. The left edge of the current window in slot k is $LE(k)$ and the size of the window is $w(k)$.

All processes with packets with a time stamp within the window are allowed to transmit, thus in slot k we have a collision among the three packets in the window. In slot $k + 1$ the window is split into two and its left side becomes the current window. All processes adjust their windows by computing $LE(k + 1)$ and $ws(k + 1)$. It turns out that there is only one message with a time stamp within the new window, thus, in slot $k + 1$ we have a successful transmission. The algorithm allows successful transmission of message c in slot $k + 4$, and the window advances.

For the formal description of the algorithm we introduce a state variable $s(k)$ that can have two values, L (left) or R (right), to describe the position of the window in that slot. By default the algorithm starts with $s(0) = L$. The following actions must be taken in slot k by each process in the group:

if *feedback = empty* then:

$$\begin{aligned} LE(k) &= LE(k-1) \\ ws(k) &= \frac{ws(k-1)}{2} \\ s(k) &= L \end{aligned}$$

if *feedback = success* and $s(k-1) = L$, then:

$$\begin{aligned} LE(k) &= LE(k-1) + ws(k-1) \\ ws(k) &= ws(k-1) \\ s(k) &= R \end{aligned}$$

if *feedback = empty slot* and $s(k-1) = L$, then:

$$\begin{aligned} LE(k) &= LE(k-1) + ws(k-1) \\ ws(k) &= \frac{ws(k-1)}{2} \\ s(k) &= L \end{aligned}$$

if *feedback = empty slot* and $s(k-1) = R$, then:

$$\begin{aligned} LE(k) &= LE(k-1) + ws(k-1) \\ ws(k) &= min[ws_0, (k - LE(k))] \\ s(k) &= R \end{aligned}$$

Here ws_0 is a parameter of the algorithm and defines an optimal window size after a window has been exhausted. The condition $ws(k) = min[ws_0, (k - LE(k))]$ simply states that the window cannot extend beyond the current slot.

The FCFS algorithm belongs to a broader class of algorithms called *splitting algorithms* when processes contending for the shared channel perform a recursive splitting of the group allowed to transmit, until the group reaches a size of one. This splitting is based on some *unique* characteristic of either the process or the message. In case of the FCFS algorithm this unique characteristic is the arrival time of a message. Clearly if two messages have the same arrival time, then the splitting is not possible.

The FCFS splitting algorithm is *blocking*, new arrivals have to wait until the collision between the messages in the current window are resolved. This implies that a

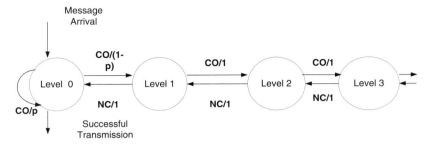

CO/1   - transition takes place in case of collsion with probability 1
CO/p   - transition takes place in case of collsion with probability p
CO/(1-p) - transition takes place in case of collsion with probability 1-p
NC/1   - transition takes place in case of acollsion-free slot with probability 1

Fig. 2.17   The stack algorithm for multiple access.

new station may not join the system because all nodes have to maintain the history to know when a collision resolution interval has terminated.

Example. We sketch now an elegant algorithm distributed in time and space that allows processes to share a multiple access channel without the need to maintain state or know the past history. The so-called *stack* algorithm, illustrated in Figure 2.17, requires each process to maintain a local stack and follow these rules:

- When a process gets a new message it positions itself at stack level zero. All processes at stack level zero are allowed to transmit.

- When a collision occurs all processes at stack level $i > 0$ move up to stack level $i + 1$ with probability $q = 1$. Processes at stack level 0 toss a fair coin and with probability $q < 1$ remain at stack level zero, or move to stack level one with probability $1 - q$.

- When processes observe a successful transmission, or an idle slot, they migrate downward in the stack, those at level i migrate with probability $q = 1$ to level $i - 1$.

The stack-splitting algorithm is nonblocking, processes with new messages enter the competition to transmit immediately. In summary, synchronous systems support elegant and efficient distributed algorithms like the ones presented in this section.

2.4.3 Asynchronous Systems

An asynchronous system is one where there is no upper bound imposed on the process-ing and communication latency and the drift of the local clock [10]. Asynchronous system models are very attractive because they make no timing assumptions and have simple semantics. If no such bounds exist, it is impossible to guarantee the successful completion of a distributed algorithm that requires the participation of all processes in a process group, in a message-passing system. Asynchronous algorithms for mutual exclusion, resource allocation, and consensus problems targeted to shared-memory systems are described in Lynch [27].

Any distributed algorithm designed for an asynchronous system can be used for a synchronous one. Once the assumption that processing and communication latency and clock drifts are bounded is valid, we are guaranteed that a more efficient distributed algorithm to solve the same problem for a synchronous system exists. From a practical viewpoint there is no real advantage to model a system as a synchronous one if there are large discrepancies between the latency of its processing and communication components.

In practice, we can accommodate asynchronous systems using *time-outs* and be prepared to take a different course of action when a time-out occurs. Sometimes time-outs can be determined statically, more often communication channels are shared and there is a variable queuing delay associated with transmissions of packets at the intermediate nodes of a store and forward network and using the largest upper bound on the delays to determine the time-outs would lead to very inefficient protocols.

Example. Often, we need to build into our asynchronous system *adaptive behavior*, to cope with the large potential discrepancies between communication delays. For example, the Transport Control Protocol (TCP) of the Internet suite guarantees the reliable delivery of data; it retransmits each segment if an acknowledgment is not received within a certain amount of time. The finite state machine of the TCP sched-ules a retransmission of the segment when a time-out event occurs. This time-out is a function of the round trip time (RTT) between the sender and the receiver.

The Internet is a collection of networks with different characteristics and the net-work traffic has a large variability. Thus, the sample value of RTT may have large variations depending on the location of the sender and receiver pair and may vary be-tween the same pair, depending on the network load and the time of day. Moreover, an acknowledgment only certifies that data has been received, thus may be the ac-knowledgment for the segment retransmission and not for the original segment. The actual algorithm to determine the TCP time-out, proposed by Jacobson and Karels [21] consists of the following steps:

1. Each node maintains an $estimatedRTT$ and has a weighting factor $0 \leq \delta \leq 1$. The coefficients μ and ϕ are typically set to 1 and 0, respectively. A node measures a $sampleRTT$ for each communication act with a given partner provided that the segment was not retransmitted.

2. The node calculates

difference $=$ *sampleRTT* $-$ *estimatedRTT*

estimatedRTT $=$ *estimatedRTT* $+$ ($\delta \times$ *difference*)

deviation $=$ *deviation* $+$ $\delta \times$ (|*difference*| $-$ *deviation*)

timeout $=$ $\mu \times$ *estimatedRTT* $+$ $\phi \times$ *deviation*

This algorithm is used for TCP congestion control, see Section 4.3.7.

2.4.4 Final Remarks on Synchronous and Asynchronous Systems

The models discussed in this section tie together the two aspects of a distributed system: computing and communication. Synchronous systems have a bounded communication delay, there is an upper limit of the time it takes a process to carry out its task and clock drifts are bounded.

Several algorithms exploiting the characteristics of synchronous systems are presented, including the election of a leader in a token passing ring and two slitting algorithms for multiple access communication.

In a wide-area distributed system communication delays vary widely and communication protocols rely on time-outs determined dynamically to implement mechanisms such as error control or congestion control.

2.5 MONITORING MODELS

Knowledge of the state of several, possibly all, processes in a distributed system is often needed. For example, a supervisory process must be able to detect when a subset of processes is deadlocked. A process might migrate from one location to another or be replicated only after an agreement with others. In all these examples a process needs to evaluate a predicate function of the global state of the system.

Let us call the process responsible for constructing the global state of the system, the *monitor*. The monitor will send inquiry messages requesting information about the local state of every process and it will gather the replies to construct the global state. Intuitively, the construction of the global state is equivalent to taking snapshots of individual processes and then combining these snapshots into a global view. Yet, combining snapshots is straightforward if and only if all processes have access to a global clock and the snapshots are taken at the same time; hence, they are consistent with one another.

To illustrate why inconsistencies could occur when attempting to construct a global state of a process consider an analogy. An individual is on one of the observation platforms at the top of the Eiffel Tower and wishes to take a panoramic view of Paris, using a photographic camera with a limited viewing angle. To get a panoramic view she needs to take a sequence of regular snapshots and then cut and paste them together. Between snapshots she has to adjust the camera or load a new film. Later, when pasting together the individual snapshots to obtain a panoramic view, she discovers

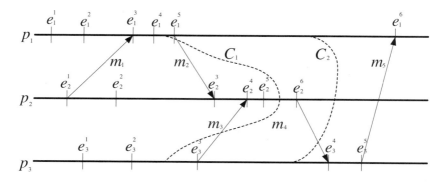

Fig. 2.18 Inconsistent and consistent cuts. The cut $C_1 = (4, 5, 2)$ is inconsistent because it includes e_2^4, the event triggered by the arrival of message m_3 at process p_2 but does not include e_3^3, the event triggered by process p_3 sending m_3. Thus C_1 violates causality. On the other hand $C_2 = (5, 6, 3)$ is a consistent cut.

that the same bus appears in two different locations, say in Place Trocadero and on the Mirabeau bridge. The explanation is that the bus has changed its position in the interval between the two snapshots. This trivial example shows some of the subtleties of global state.

2.5.1 Runs

A total ordering R of all the events in the global history of a distributed computation consistent with the local history of each participant process is called a *run*. A run

$$R = (e_1^{j1}, e_2^{j2}, ..., e_n^{jn})$$

implies a sequence of events as well as a sequence of global states.

Example. Consider the three processes in Figure 2.18. The run $R_1 = (e_1^1, e_2^1, e_3^1, e_1^2)$ is consistent with both the local history of each process and the global one. The system has traversed the global states $\Sigma^{000}, \Sigma^{100}, \Sigma^{110}, \Sigma^{111}, \Sigma^{211}$. $R_2 = (e_1^1, e_1^2, e_3^1, e_1^3, e_3^2)$ is an invalid run because it is inconsistent with the global history. The system cannot ever reach the state Σ^{301}; message m_1 must be sent before it is received, so event e_2^1 must occur in any run before event e_1^3.

2.5.2 Cuts; the Frontier of a Cut

A *cut* is a subset of the local history of all processes. If h_i^j denotes the history of process p_i up to and including its j-th event, e_i^j, then a cut C is an n-tuple:

$$C = \{h_i^j\} \text{ with } i \in \{1, n\} \text{ and } j \in \{1, n_i\}$$

The frontier of the cut is an n-tuple consisting of the last event of every process included in the cut. Figure 2.18 illustrates a space-time diagram for a group of three processes, p_1, p_2, p_3 and it shows two cuts, C_1 and C_2. C_1 has the frontier $(4, 5, 2)$, frozen after the fourth event of process p_1, the fifth event of process p_2 and the second event of process p_3, and C_2 has the frontier $(5, 6, 3)$.

Cuts provide the necessary intuition to generate global states based on an exchange of messages between a monitor and a group of processes. The cut represents the instance when requests to report individual state are received by the members of the group. Clearly not all cuts are meaningful. For example, the cut C_1 with the frontier $(4, 5, 2)$ in Figure 2.18 violates our intuition regarding causality; it includes e_2^4, the event triggered by the arrival of message m_3 at process p_2 but does not include e_3^3, the event triggered by process p_3 sending m_3. In this snapshot p_3 was frozen after its second event, e_3^2, before it had the chance to send message m_3. Causality is violated and the a real system cannot ever reach such a state.

2.5.3 Consistent Cuts and Runs

A cut closed under the causal precedence relationship is called a *consistent cut*. C is a consistent cut iff for all events e, e', $(e \in C) \wedge (e' \rightarrow e) \Rightarrow e' \in C$.

A consistent cut establishes an "instance" for a distributed computation. Given a consistent cut we can determine if an event e occurred before the cut.

A run R is said to be consistent if the total ordering of events imposed by the run is consistent with the partial order imposed by the causal relation, for all events $e \rightarrow e'$ implies that e appears before e' in R.

2.5.4 Causal History

Consider a distributed computation consisting of a group of communicating processes $G = \{p_1, p_2, ..., p_n\}$. The *causal history of event e* is the smallest consistent cut of G including event e:

$$\theta(e) = \{e' \in G \mid e' \rightarrow e\} \cup \{e\}.$$

The causal history of event e_2^5 in Figure 2.19 is:

$$\theta(e_2^5) = \{e_1^1, e_1^2, e_1^3, e_1^4, e_1^5, e_2^1, e_2^2, e_2^3, e_2^4, e_2^5, e_3^1, e_3^2, e_3^3\}.$$

This is the smallest consistent cut including e_2^5. Indeed, if we omit e_3^3, then the cut $(5, 5, 2)$ would be inconsistent, it would include e_2^4, the communication event for receiving m_3 but not e_3^3, the sending of m_3. If we omit e_1^5 the cut $(4, 5, 3)$ would also be inconsistent, it would include e_2^3 but not e_1^5.

Causal histories can be used as clock values and satisfy the strong clock condition provided that we equate clock comparison with set inclusion. Indeed $e \rightarrow e' \equiv \theta(e) \subset \theta(e')$.

The following algorithm can be used to construct causal histories. Each $p_i \in G$ starts with $\theta = \emptyset$. Every time p_i receives a message m from p_j it constructs $\theta(e_i) = \theta(e_j) \cup \theta(e_k)$ with e_i the *receive* event, e_j the previous local event of p_i, e_k the *send* event of process p_j.

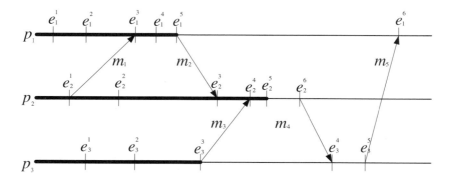

Fig. 2.19   The causal history of event e_2^5 is the smallest consistent cut including e_2^5.

Unfortunately, this concatenation of histories is impractical because the causal histories grow very fast.

2.5.5   Consistent Global States and Distributed Snapshots

Now we present a protocol to construct consistent global states based on the monitoring concepts discusses previously. We assume a strongly connected network.

Definition. Given two processes p_i and p_j the state of the channel, $\xi_{i,j}$, from p_i to p_j consists of messages sent by p_i but not yet received by p_j.

The snapshot protocol of Chandy and Lamport. The protocol consists of three steps [11]:

1. Process p_0 sends to itself a "take snapshot" message.

2. Let p_f be the process from which p_i receives the "take snapshot" message for the first time. Upon receiving the message, p_i records its local state, σ_i, and relays the "take snapshot" along all its outgoing channels without executing any events on behalf of its underlying computation. Channel state $\xi_{f,i}$ is set to empty and process p_i starts recording messages received over each of its incoming channels.

3. Let p_s be the process from which p_i receives the "take snapshot" message beyond the first time. Process p_i stops recording messages along the incoming channel from p_s and declares channel state $\xi_{s,i}$ as those messages that have been recorded.

Each "take snapshot" message crosses each channel exactly once and every process p_i has made its contribution to the global state when it has received the "take snapshot" message on all its input channels. Thus, in a strongly connected network with n processes the protocol requires $n \times (n-1)$ messages. Each of the n nodes is connected with all the other $n - 1$ nodes. Recall that a process records its state the first time it receives a "take snapshot" message and then stops executing the underlying computation for some time.

Example. Consider a set of six processes, each pair of processes being connected by two unidirectional channels as shown in Figure 2.20. Assume that all channels are empty, $\xi_{i,j} = 0$, $i \in 0, 5$, $j \in 0, 5$ at the time p_0 issues the "take snapshot" message. The actual flow of messages is:

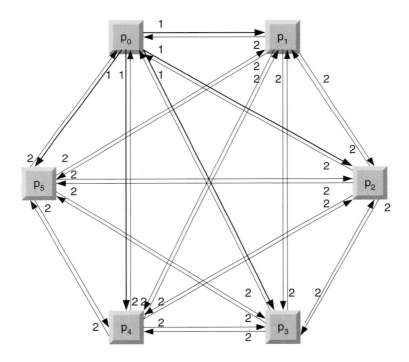

Fig. 2.20 Six processes executing the snapshot protocol.

- In step 0, p_0 sends to itself the "take snapshot" message.

- In step 1, process p_0 sends five "take snapshot" messages labeled (1) in Figure 2.20.

- In step 2, each of the five processes, p_1, p_2, p_3, p_4, and p_5 sends a "take snapshot" message labeled (2).

A "take snapshot" message crosses each channel from process p_i to p_j exactly once and $6 \times 5 = 30$ messages are exchanged.

2.5.6 Monitoring and Intrusion

Monitoring a system with a large number of components is a very difficult, even an impossible, exercise. If the rate of events experienced by each component is very high, a remote monitor may be unable to know precisely the state of the system. At the same time the monitoring overhead may affect adversely the performance of the system. This phenomenon is analogous to the uncertainty principle formulated in 1930s by the German physicist Werner Heisenberg for quantum systems.

The Heisenberg uncertainty principle states that any measurement intrudes on the quantum system being observed and modifies its properties. We cannot determine as accurately as we wish both the coordinates $\bar{x}$, and the momentum $\bar{p}$ of a particle:

$$\Delta\bar{x} \times \Delta\bar{p} \geq \frac{h}{4\pi}$$

where $h = 6.625 \times 10^{-34}$ *joule* $\times$ *second* is the Plank constant, $\bar{x} = (x, y, z)$ is a vector with x, y, z the coordinates of the particle, and $\bar{p} = (p(x), p(y), p(z))$ are the projections of the momentum along the three axes of coordinates.

The uncertainty principle states that the exact values of the coordinates of a particle correspond to complete indeterminacy in the values of the projections of its momentum. According to Bohm [8], "The Heisenberg principle is by no means a statement indicating fundamental limitations to our knowledge of the microcosm. It only reflects the limited applicability of the classical physics concepts to the region of microcosmos. The process of making measurements in the microcosm is inevitably connected with the substantial influence of the measuring instrument on the course of the phenomenon being measured."

The intuition behind this phenomenon is that in order to determine very accurately the position of a particle we have to send a beam of light with a very short wavelength. Yet, the shorter the wavelength of the light, the higher the energy of the photons and thus the larger is the amount of energy transferred by elastic scattering to the particle whose position we want to determine.

2.5.7 Quantum Computing, Entangled States, and Decoherence

In 1982 Richard Feynman [18] speculated that in many instances computation can be done more efficiently using quantum effects. His ideas were inspired by previous work of Bennett [4, 5] and Benioff [6].

Starting from basic principles of thermodynamics and quantum mechanics, Feynman suggested that problems for which polynomial time algorithms do not exist can be solved; computations for which polynomial algorithms exist can be speeded up considerably and made reversible; and zero entropy loss reversible computers would use little, if any, energy.

The argument in favor of quantum computing is that in quantum systems the amount of parallelism increases exponentially with the size of the system; in other words, an exponential increase in parallelism requires only a linear increase in the amount of space needed. The major difficulty lies in the fact that access to the results of a quantum computation is restrictive, access to the results disturbs the quantum state. The process of disturbing the quantum state due to the interaction with the environment is called *decoherence*.

Let us call a *qubit* a unit vector in a two-dimensional complex vector space where a basis has been chosen. Consider a system consisting of n particles whose individual states are described by a vector in a two-dimensional vector space. In classical mechanics the individual states of particles combine through the cartesian product; the possible states of the system of n particles form a vector space of $2 \times n$ dimensions; given n bits, we can construct 2^n n-tuples and describe a system with 2^n states.

Individual state spaces of n particles combine quantically through the tensor product. Recall that if X and Y are vectors, then the vector product $X \times Y$ has dimension $dim(X) + dim(Y)$; the tensor product $X \otimes Y$ has dimension $dim(X) \times dim(Y)$.

In a quantum system, given n qubits the state space has 2^n dimensions. The extra states that have no classical analog are called *entangled states*.

The catch is that even though a quantum bit can be in infinitely many superposition states, when the qubit is measured, the measurement changes the state of the particle to one of the two basis states; from one qubit we can only extract a single classical bit of information.

To illustrate the effects presented above consider the use of polarized light to transmit information. A photon's polarization state ψ can be modeled by a unit vector and expressed as a linear combination of two basis vectors denoted as $| \uparrow >$ and $| \rightarrow >$:

$$|\psi > \ = \ a| \uparrow > + b| \uparrow > \qquad |a|^2 + |b|^2 = 1.$$

The state of the photon is measured as $| \uparrow >$ with probability $|a|^2$ and as $| \rightarrow >$ with probability $|b|^2$. Clearly, there is an infinite number of possible orientations of the unit vector $|\psi >$, as shown in Figure 2.21(a). This justifies the observation that a qubit can be in infinitely many superposition states.

An interesting experiment that sheds light (pardon the pun) on the phenomena discussed in this section is presented in [32]. Consider that we have a source S capable of generating randomly polarized light and a screen E where we measure the intensity of the light. We also have three polarized filters: A, polarized vertically, $\uparrow$; B polarized horizontally, $\rightarrow$; and C polarized at 45 degrees, $\nearrow$.

Measuring the polarization is equivalent with projecting the random vector $|\psi >$ onto one of the two bases. Note that filter C measures the quantum state with respect to a different basis than filters A and B; the new basis is given by:

$$\{\frac{1}{\sqrt{2}}(| \uparrow > + | \uparrow >), \ \frac{1}{\sqrt{2}}(| \uparrow > - | \uparrow >)\}.$$

Using this experimental setup we make the following observations:

(i) Without any filter the intensity of the light measured at E is I, see Figure 2.21(b).

(ii) If we interpose filter A between S and E, the intensity of the light measured at E is $I' = I/2$, see Figure 2.21(c).

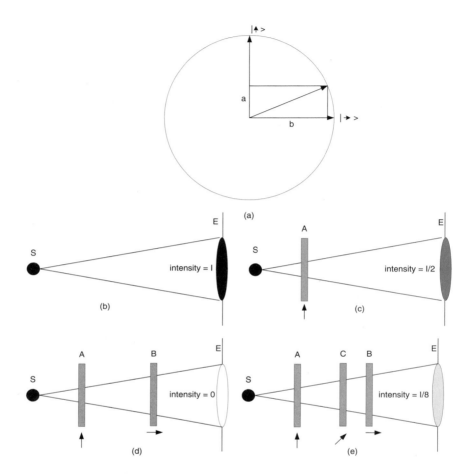

Fig. 2.21 (a) The polarization of a photon is described by a unit vector $|\psi >$ with projections $a| \uparrow>$ and $b| \to>$ on a two-dimensional space with basis $| \uparrow>$ and $| \to>$. Measuring the polarization is equivalent to projecting the random vector $|\psi >$ onto one of the two basis. (b) Source S sends randomly polarized light to the screen; the measured intensity is I. (c) Filter A measures the photon polarization with respect to basis $| \uparrow>$ and lets pass only those photons that are vertically polarized. About 50% of the photons are vertically polarized and filter A lets them pass; thus the intensity of the light measured at E is about $I/2$. (d) Filter B inserted between A and E measures the photon polarization with respect to basis $| \to>$ and lets pass only those photons that are horizontally polarized; but all incoming photons to B have a vertical polarization due to A, thus the intensity of the light measured at E is 0. (e) Filter C inserted between A and B measures the photon polarization with respect to basis $| \nearrow>$. The photons will be measured by C as having polarization $\nearrow$, will be only 50% of those coming from A, and those measured by B as $\to$ will only be 50% of those measured by C; thus the intensity of the light measured at E is $(\frac{1}{2})^3 = \frac{1}{8}$.

(iii) If between A and E in the previous setup we interpose filter B, then the intensity of the light measured at E is $I'' = 0$, see Figure 2.21(d).

(iv) If between filters A and B in the previous setup we interpose filter C, the intensity of the light measured at E is $I''' = I/8$, see Figure 2.21(e).

The explanation of these experimental observations is based on the fact that photons carry the light and that the photons have random orientations as seen in Figure 2.21(a).

Filter A measures the photon polarization with respect to basis $|\uparrow>$ and lets pass only those photons that are vertically polarized. About 50% of the photons will be measured by A as being vertically polarized and let to pass, as seen in Figure 2.21(c); recall that measuring polarization is equivalent to projecting a vector with random orientation onto the basis vectors.

Filter B will measure the photon polarization with respect to basis $|\rightarrow>$ and let pass only those photons that are horizontally polarized; but all incoming photons have a vertical polarization induced by filter A, see Figure 2.21(d), thus the intensity of the light reaching the screen will be zero.

Filter C measures the photon polarization with respect to basis $|\nearrow>$. The photons measured by C as having polarization $\nearrow$ will be only 50% of those coming from A, and those measured by B as $\rightarrow$ will only be 50% of those measured by C; thus the intensity of the light on the screen is $\frac{1}{8}$, see Figure 2.21(e).

These facts are intellectually pleasing but two questions come immediately to mind:

1. Can such a quantum computer be built?

2. Are there algorithms capable of exploiting the unique possibilities opened by quantum computing?

The answer to the first question is that only three-bit quantum computers have been built so far; several proposals to build quantum computers using nuclear magnetic resonance, optical and solid state techniques, and ion traps have been studied.

The answer to the second question is that problems in integer arithmetic, cryptography, or search problems have surprisingly efficient solutions in quantum computing. In 1994 Peter Shor [38] found a polynomial time algorithm for factoring n-bit numbers on quantum computers and generated a wave of enthusiasm for quantum computing. Like most factoring algorithms, Shor's algorithm reduces the factoring problem to the problem of finding the period of a function, but uses quantum parallelism to find a superposition of all values of the function in one step. Then the algorithm calculates the quantum Fourier transform of the function, which sets the amplitudes into multiples of the fundamental frequency, the reciprocal of the period. To factor an integer then the Shor algorithm measures the period of the function.

Problem 16 at the end of this chapter discusses another niche application of quantum computing: public key distribution in cryptography.

2.5.8   Examples of Monitoring Systems

Now we discuss two examples of monitoring in a distributed system. The first example addresses the very practical problem encountered by the Real-Time Protocol (RTP), used to deliver data with timing constraints over the Internet. The second is related to scheduling on a computational grid.

First, consider a radio station broadcasting over the Internet. In Chapter 5 we discussed multimedia communications; here, we only note that the audio information is carried by individual packets and each packet may cross the Internet on a different path and experience a different delay; even the delay on the same path is affected by the other traffic on the network and differs from packet to packet.

The difference in the time it takes consecutive packets to cross the network is called *jitter*. However, the receiver has to play back the packets subject to timing constraints. The actual protocols for multimedia communication requests that individual receivers provide periodic feedback regarding the quality of the reception, in particular, they report the magnitude of the jitter.

If the rate of the feedback reports is not correlated with the actual number of stations providing the reports, then the total amount of feedback traffic will hinder the audio broadcast. Indeed, due to congestion created in part by the feedback reports, the packets sent by the broadcaster will arrive late at the receivers or will be dropped by the routers. To avoid this phenomenon, the rate of the transmission quality reports should decrease when the number of receivers increases. For example, when the number of stations increases by one order of magnitude, a station should increase the time between reports by an order of magnitude; if it sent a report every second, then after the increase it should send a report every 10 seconds.

Consider now a grid with thousands of nodes and with a very high rate of events at each node. Two types of monitoring are of special interest in this environment:

1. Application-oriented: monitoring done by a supervisory process controlling a computation distributed over a subset of nodes of a grid.

2. System-oriented: monitoring done by a "super-scheduler" controlling the allocation of resources on a subgrid.

Novel monitoring models are used in a wide-area distributed system. For example, *subscription-based monitoring*, permits a monitoring process to subscribe to various types of events generated by a set of processes. The contractual obligation of a process in the set is to send a message to the monitor as soon as the corresponding event occurs. Clearly if the interval between two consecutive internal events of interest, $\delta t_i^{j,j+1} = t_{e_i^{j+1}} - t_{e_i^j}$ is shorter than the propagation time $t_{prop}^{i,0}$ between process p_i and the monitor, process p_0, the monitor will believe that p_i is in state σ_i^j, while the process has already reached state σ_i^{j+1}.

The intrusion due to the monitoring process has several manifestations:

(i) The amount of traffic in the network increases. For example, assuming that a super-scheduler wants to determine the global state of a subgrid with n nodes every τ seconds and a monitoring message has length $\bar{l}$ then the data rate for monitoring is:

$$\frac{n \times (n-1) \times \bar{l}}{\tau}$$

(ii) Each process being monitored is slowed down. For example, in the snapshot protocol let t_{stop} denote the time spent by process p_i from the instance it got the first "take snapshot" message until it got the same message on all input channels. If process p_i receives a "take snapshot" message in state σ_i^j, the residence time in this state will increase from $\delta t_i^{j,j+1}$ to $\delta t_i^{j,j+1} + t_{stop}$.

2.5.9   Final Remarks on Monitoring

Determining the global state of a system consisting of set of concurrent processes is a challenging task. First of all, there is the peril of inconsistent global states where the causal relationships are violated. This problem is solved by snapshot protocols. Second, we have to be aware of the conceptual limitations of monitoring and the intrusion of the monitor on the processes being monitored.

In practice a monitoring process can never be informed of every change of state of every process because of: (i) the finite time it takes a message to cross the network from the process being monitored to the monitor, (ii) practical limitations on the volume of monitoring traffic, and (iii) the monitoring overhead imposed on the process being monitored.

As a result of these challenges, the resource management and process coordination on a wide-area system is a nontrivial task and often we need to make decisions with incomplete or inaccurate information.

2.6   RELIABILITY AND FAULT TOLERANCE MODELS. RELIABLE COLLECTIVE COMMUNICATION

In any networked system processes and communication links are subject to failures. A failure occurring at time t is an undesirable event characterized by its:

- manifestation - the timing of events, the values of state variables, or both could be incorrect.

- consistency - the system may fail in a consistent or inconsistent mode.

- effects - the failure may be benign or malign.

- occurrence mode - we may have singular or repeated failures.

The cause of a failure is called a *fault*. In turn, a fault is characterized by its (a) character, it could be intentional or a chance occurrence; (b) reason, it can be due to design problems, physical failure of components, software failures, and possibly other causes; (c) scope, internal or external; and (d) persistence, it could be temporary or permanent.

2.6.1   Failure Modes

Our model of a distributed system is based on two abstractions, processes and communication channels, thus, we are concerned with the failures of both. The desired behavior of a process is prescribed by the algorithm implemented by the process. If the actual behavior of a process deviates from the desired one, the process is *faulty*. A communication channel is expected to transport messages from the source to the destination; a faulty channel does not exhibit the prescribed behavior.

Communicating processes and communication channels may fail in several modes summarized in Table 2.2. In this table we see that a variety of modes processes and

Table 2.2   Failure modes of processes and channels listed in the order of severity from less severe to more severe.

Failure Mode	Faulty Process	Faulty Channel
Crash	Does nothing. The correct behavior of the process stops suddenly.	Stops suddenly transporting the messages.
Fail-Stop	Halts and this undesirable behavior is detectable by other processes.	
Send Omissions	Intermittently does not send messages or stops prematurely sending messages.	
Receive Omissions	Intermittently does not receive messages or stops prematurely receiving messages.	
General Omissions	Intermittently does not send and/or receive messages or stops prematurely sending and/or receiving.	Intermittently fails to transport messages.
Byzantine	Can exhibit any behavior.	Any behavior is possible.
Arbitrary with message authentication	May claim to have received a message even if it never did.	
Timing	The timing of events change in an unpredictable manner. May happen only in synchronous systems.	

channels may fail. For example, a process may halt abruptly and other processes may be able to infer that the process is faulty because it will not respond to messages from any other process. The fact that a process or a communication channel has crashed may not be detectable by other processes. Unless the system is synchronous it is not possible to distinguish between a slow process and one that has stopped or between a slow communication channel and one that has crashed. Byzantine failures are the most difficult to handle, a process may send misleading messages, a channel may generate spurious messages.

Failures have different levels of *severity*. An algorithm may tolerate a low severity failure but not a high severity one. The failure modes are listed in Table 2.2 in the order of their severity. The crash is the least severe, followed by send and receive omissions, then the general omissions followed by the arbitrary failures with message authentication, and finally the arbitrary failures. Timing failures are only possible in synchronous systems.

2.6.2 Redundancy

Adding components able to detect errors and prevent them from affecting the functionality of a system and to protect the important information manipulated by the system enhances the dependability of a system. Three modes of redundancy are encountered in practice:

1. *Physical resource redundancy* is the process of replicating physical resources of a system to mask the failure of some of the components. For example, some ring networks consist of two rings with information propagating in opposite directions. When one of the rings fails, the other one is activated.

2. *Time redundancy* is the replication of an action in the time domain. For example, several copies of a critical process may run concurrently on different processors. If one of the processors fails, then one of the backup copies will take over.

3. *Information redundancy* is the process of packaging information during storage and communication in containers able to sustain a prescribed level of damage, as discussed earlier.

Passive and *active redundancy* are the two models used to exploit redundant organization of systems. In the passive model, redundant resources are only activated after a system failure, while in the active model all resources are activated at the same time.

Several types of passively redundant systems are known. *Fail-silent* systems either deliver a correct result or they do not deliver any result at all. A *fail-stop* system is a fail-silent system with the additional property that the standby resources are informed when the primary resources have failed.

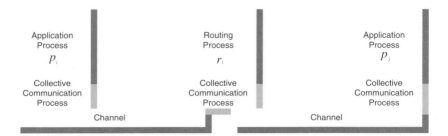

Fig. 2.22   Collective communication model. The collective communication processes at an application site and at a routing site implement the broadcast/multicast algorithm.

2.6.3   Broadcast and Multicast

Sending the same information to all or to a subset of processes are called *broadcast* and *multicast*, respectively. These forms of collective communication are used to achieve consensus among processes in a distributed system. One-to-many and many-to-one collective communications require that reliable broadcast/multicast protocols exist and that they are capable of sending messages repeatedly on outgoing channels and receiving repeatedly on incoming channels [9].

Collective communication has important practical applications. For example, message routing in ad hoc mobile networks is based on broadcasting. At the same time, multicasting of audio and video streams is a particularly challenging problem in the Internet. Broadcasting and multicasting are also critical components of parallel algorithms when partial results have to be made known to multiple threads of control.

Figure 2.22 illustrates the model for collective communication. At the sending site the application process delivers the message to the collective communication process and the collective communication process, in turn, sends repeatedly the message on its outgoing channels. If the network is fully connected, all destinations can be reached directly from any source, otherwise the collective communication process at intermediate sites has to deliver the message to the local application process and at the same time send it on its outgoing channels.

If the collective communication process at an intermediate site uses a routing algorithm called *flooding* to send a broadcast message on all its outgoing channels, there is a chance that a collective communication process will receive duplicate copies of the same message. To prevent repeated delivery of the same message to the application process, each message is uniquely identified by its sender and by a sequence number. Sometimes a strategy called *source routing* is used. In this case the collective communication process at the sending site calculates all delivery routes using, for example, a minimum spanning tree routed at the source node.

2.6.4   Properties of a Broadcast Algorithm

Since multiple components are involved in collective communication, see Figure 2.22 and each component may fail independently, a broadcast or a multicast message may reach only a subset of its intended distribution or successive messages may be delivered out of order.

Table 2.3 Desirable properties of a broadcast algorithm.

Property	Comments
Validity	If a correct collective communication process broadcasts a message m, then all correct collective communication processes eventually deliver m.
Agreement	If a correct collective communication process delivers message m, then all correct processes eventually deliver m.
Integrity	For any message m, every correct collective communication process delivers m at most once, and only if m was previously broadcast by a collective communication process.
FIFO Order	If a collective communication process broadcasts a message m before m', then no correct collective communication process delivers m' unless it has previously delivered m.
Causal Order	If the broadcast of a message m causally precedes the broadcast of a message m', then no correct process delivers m' unless it has previously delivered m.
Total Order	If two correct collective communication processes p and q both deliver messages m and m', then p delivers m before m' if and only if q delivers m before m'.

The desirable properties of a broadcast algorithm are listed in Table 2.3. The first three properties are critical to ensure that all processes in the broadcast group receive precisely once every message broadcasted by a member of the group.

2.6.5 Broadcast Primitives

A *reliable broadcast* is one that satisfies the first three properties, namely, validity, agreement, and integrity. Validity guarantees that if a correct collective communication process broadcasts a message m, then all correct collective communication processes eventually deliver m. Agreement ensures that all collective communication processes agree on the messages they deliver and no spurious messages are delivered. Integrity guarantees that for any message m, every correct collective communication process delivers m at most once, and only if m was previously broadcast by a collective communication process. An *atomic broadcast* is a reliable broadcast augmented with total ordering of messages.

Table 2.4   Broadcast primitives and their properties.

Type	Validity	Agreement	Integrity	FIFO Order	Causal Order	Total Order
Reliable	Yes	Yes	Yes			
FIFO	Yes	Yes	Yes	Yes		
Causal	Yes	Yes	Yes	Yes	Yes	
Atomic	Yes	Yes	Yes			Yes
FIFO Atomic	Yes	Yes	Yes	Yes		Yes
Causal Atomic	Yes	Yes	Yes	Yes	Yes	Yes

There are several other flavors of broadcast primitives. A *FIFO broadcast* is a reliable broadcast augmented with FIFO order, a *causal broadcast* is a reliable broadcast augmented with FIFO and causal order. A reliable broadcast augmented with total order is called an atomic broadcast, one augmented with total and FIFO order is called FIFO atomic and a FIFO atomic broadcast with causal order is causal atomic broadcast. Table 2.4 summarizes the broadcast primitives and their properties and Figure 2.23 follows Hadzilakos and Toueng [19] to show the relationships among these primitives.

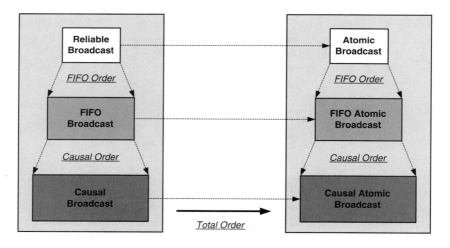

Fig. 2.23   The broadcast primitives and their relationships. The three types of nonatomic broadcast are transformed into the corresponding atomic broadcast primitives by imposing the *total order* constraint. In each group of broadcast modes the *FIFO order* and the *causal order* constraints lead to FIFO and Causal broadcast primitives, respectively

Note that a causal atomic broadcast enables multiple processes to make decisions based on the same message history. For example, in a real-time control system all replicated processes must operate on the same sequence of messages broadcast by the sensors.

2.6.6 Terminating Reliable Broadcast and Consensus

So far we have assumed that *all* processes in the process group, $\forall p \in \mathcal{P}$, p may broadcast a message, $m \in \mathcal{M}$; moreover, processes have no a priori knowledge of the time when a broadcast message may be sent, or the identity of the sender. There are instances in practice when these assumptions are invalid. Consider, for example, a sensor that reports periodically the temperature and pressure to a number of monitoring processes in a power plant; in this case, the time of the broadcast and the identity of the sender are known.

We now consider the case when a single process is supposed to broadcast a message at known times m and all correct processes must agree on that message. A *terminating reliable broadcast (TRB)* is a reliable broadcast with the additional *termination* property; in this case that correct processes always deliver messages. Note that the message delivered in this case could be that the *sender is faulty (SF)*. In this case the set of messages is $\mathcal{M} \cup SF$.

Let us now examine a situation related to TRB when all correct processes first propose a value $v \in \mathcal{V}$ using a primitive $propose(v)$ and then have to agree on the proposed values using another primitive, $decide(v)$. There are two situations: We have consensus when all processes propose the same value v, or there is no consensus and then the message sent is No Consensus (NC). The *consensus problem* requires that:

(i) Every correct process eventually decides on some value $v \in \mathcal{V} \cup NC$ (termination).

(ii) If all correct processes execute $propose(v)$, then all correct processes eventually execute $decide(v)$ (validity).

(iii) If a correct process executes $propose(v)$, then all correct processes eventually execute $decide(v)$ (agreement).

(iv) Every correct process decides at most one value, and if it decides $v \neq NC$ then some process must have proposed v.

2.7 RESOURCE SHARING, SCHEDULING, AND PERFORMANCE MODELS

Resource sharing is a reality common to many aspects of our lives. It is mandated by the fact that resources are finite, by space limitations, by cost, and sometimes by functionality requirements. We all share the natural resources of our planet that are finite.

The members of a community share roads, parks, libraries, airports, shopping centers, and other costly elements of urban infrastructure. The employees of an organization share the communication and computing infrastructure of that organization.

So we should not be surprised that resource sharing is a pervasive problem in all areas of computer science and engineering. The bandwidth available for packet radio networks or for satellite communication is finite, thus, a large number of subscribers of cellular phone or satellite communication services have to share the airwaves. The very high bandwidth fiber optic channel connecting two backbone Internet routers is shared by packets coming from many sources and going to many different destinations. The CPU of a personal computer is shared among a set of processes, some of them invoked directly by the user, others acting on behalf of the operating system running on the PC. A network file system is shared among the users of an organization. A Web server is a shared resource expected to provide replays to requests generated by a large number of clients.

Sharing resources requires: (i) scheduling strategies and policies to determine the order in which individual customers gain access to the resource(s) and for how long they are allowed to utilize it, and (ii) quantitative methods to measure, on one hand, how satisfied the customers are and, on the other hand, how well the resource is utilized.

Queuing models support a quantitative analysis of resource sharing. A queuing system consists of customers, one or more servers, and one or more queues where customers wait their turn to access the servers, see Figure 2.24(a).

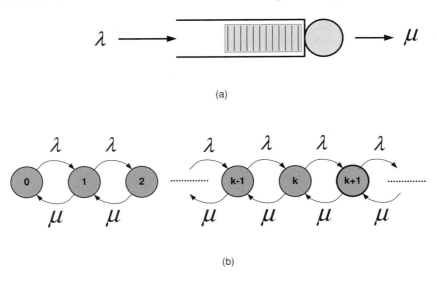

Fig. 2.24   (a) A queue associated with server S. The arrival rate is λ, the service rate is μ. (b) The state diagram of the discrete-parameter birth-death process.

Customers arrive in the system, join the queue(s), and wait until their turn comes, then enter the service and, on completion of the service, leave the system. The scheduling policy decides the order the customers are served; for example, in a FIFO system, the position of a customer in the queue is determined by the order of arrival. In this section we provide only an informal introduction to queuing models. We consider only systems with a single server and discuss two simple models, the M/M/1 and the M/G/1 systems. Several excellent references [14, 22, 39] cover in depth queuing models.

2.7.1   Process Scheduling in a Distributed System

Scheduling is concerned with optimal allocation of resources to processes over time. Each process needs computational, communication, and data resources to proceed. The goal of a *scheduling algorithm* is to create a schedule that specifies when a process is to be executed and which resources it will have access to at that time, subject to certain constraints, including the need to optimize some *objective function*. Many scheduling problems are NP-hard and polynomial time algorithms for them do not exist. When *scheduling algorithms,exact* which give an optimal solution do not exist, we seek *scheduling algorithms,approximate*. A *scheduability test* is an algorithm to determine if a schedule exists.

Given a process group we classify the scheduling problems based on six criteria:

1. if there are deadlines for processes in the process group,

2. if the scheduling decisions are made at run time or a schedule is computed prior to execution of the process group,

3. if once an activity is started it can be preempted or not,

4. if schedules are computed in a centralized or distributed fashion,

5. if resources needed by the competing processes are controlled by a central authority or by autonomous agents,

6. if a process needs one or more resources at the same time, or equivalently if the members of a process group need to be scheduled at the same time because they need to communicate with one another.

We now discuss each of the six classification criteria listed above:

1. We recognize three scheduling situations: (a) no deadlines for completion of tasks carried out by processes exist; (b) there are *soft deadlines*, when the violation of a timing constraint is not critical; and (c) there are *hard real-time* constraints, when the deadlines of all critical processes must be guaranteed under all possible scenarios.

The properties of a schedule can be analyzed by analytical methods or by simulation. In turn, analytical methods can be based on an average case analysis, a technique used for case (a) and sometimes for case (b) above, or worst case analysis, suitable for case (c).

Scheduling for hard real-time systems cannot be based on stochastic simulations because we have to guarantee timeliness under all anticipated scenarios. We have to know in advance the resource needs of every process and all possible interactions among processes.

2. The schedules can be produced offline or online, during the process execution.

A *static scheduler* takes into account information about all processes in the process group, e.g., the maximum execution times, deadlines, precedence constraints, mutual exclusion conditions, etc. and generates a dispatching table before the actual execution takes place. Then at run time a *dispatcher* decides what process to run and what resources to assign to it based on the dispatching table. The overhead of the dispatcher is relatively small.

A *dynamic scheduler* makes its scheduling decisions at run time knowing the current state of the system and bases its decisions on the actual level of resource consumption, not on maximal levels. A dynamic scheduler may have full knowledge of the past but it cannot anticipate the future requests, thus, we need to revise our definition of optimality for a dynamic scheduler.

Definition. We say that a dynamic scheduler is optimal if it can find a schedule whenever a *clairvoyant scheduler* with full knowledge of the past and of the future could find one.

A dynamic scheduler is itself a process that needs to monitor system resources and process execution, thus, its overhead can be substantial. Moreover the communication delays between the scheduler and individual processes and resource agents prevent the dynamic scheduler from determining accurately the current state of the system, as we discussed in Section 2.5.

3. Some scheduling algorithms are *non-preemptive*, once a process is launched into execution it cannot be interrupted. Other scheduling strategies are *preemptive*, they allow a process to be preempted, its execution stopped for a period of time and then continued, provided that safety constraints are observed.

Sometimes the very nature of the process makes it non-preemptive. For example, packet transmission at the physical level is a non-preemptive process, we cannot stop in the middle of a packet transmission because each packet has to carry some control information, such as the source and destination addresses, type, window size. We cannot simply send a fragment of a packet without such information.

The transmission time of a packet of length L over a channel with the maximum transmission rate R is $\tau_{packet} = \frac{L}{R}$. Communication with real-time constraints requires an agile packet scheduler and, in turn, this requirement limits the maximum transmission time of a packet and its maximum size. For example, the *asynchronous transmission mode ATM*, limits the size of packets, called *cells* in ATM speak, to 53 bytes. In Chapter 5 we discussed the advantages of this approach in terms of the ability to satisfy timing constraints, but we also pointed out that a small packet size decreases the useful data rate, because each packet must carry the control information, and the maximum data rate through a router, because a router incurs a fixed overhead per packet.

Fragmentation and reassembly may occur in the Internet but it is a time-consuming proposition and it is done by the network protocol, in the case of the Internet by the Internet Protocol, IPv4. A newer version of the protocol, IPv6, does not support packet fragmentation.

The same situation occurs for CPU scheduling when the *time slice* allocated to a process is comparable to the time required for context switching.

4. The schedules can be computed in a centralized manner, one *central scheduler* controls all resources and determines the schedules of all processes in the group. This approach does not scale very well and has a single point of failure, thus, it is not highly recommended.

Distributed scheduling algorithms are of considerably more interest because they address the shortcomings of centralized algorithms, scalability, and fault tolerance, but are inherently more complex.

Hierarchical distributed scheduling algorithms are very appealing, they minimize the communication overhead, and, at the same time, have the potential to simplify decision making, because tightly coupled processes and resources related with one another are controlled by the same agent.

5. An important question is whether the scheduler, in addition to making scheduling decisions, is able to enforce them, in other words if the scheduler controls resource allocation. While this is true in single systems or systems with a central authority, this may or may not be true in distributed systems.

Resources in a distributed system are typically under the control of autonomous agents, see Figure 2.25. In such cases a resource is guarded by a local agent that interacts with schedulers and enforces some resource access policy. The agent may attempt to optimize resource utilization or another cost function and it may or may not accept reservations.

As a general rule, reservations are the only mechanism to provide quality of service guarantees, regardless of the load placed on a system. Only if we reserve the exclusive use of a supercomputer from say 6 a.m. till 8 a.m. can we have some guarantees that the results of a computation that takes 100 minutes will be available for a meeting starting at 8 : 30 a.m. the same day. If the system is lightly loaded, then we may be able to carry out the computation before the deadline, but there are no guarantees.

This simple example outlines some of the more intricate aspects of resource reservation schemes. We need to have good estimates of the execution time, a very challenging task in itself. To minimize the risk of being unable to complete a task by its deadline we tend to overestimate its resource needs, but this approach leads to lower resource utilization. There are other drawbacks of resource reservation schemes: There is an additional overhead for maintaining the reservations, the system is less able to deal with unexpected situations.

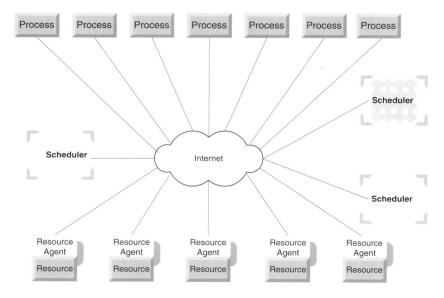

Fig. 2.25 Schedulers and resource guarding agents in a distributed environment.

Dynamic distributed scheduling in an environment where resources are managed by autonomous agents is even more difficult when the agents do not accept reservations. Market-oriented algorithms have been suggested, where consumer agents and resource agents place bids and broker agents act as a clearinghouse and match requests with offerings. Once a resource management agent makes a commitment it has to abide by it. Several systems based on market-oriented algorithms have been proposed [12].

6. Oftentimes a process needs several types of resources at the same time. For example, a process must first be loaded into the main memory of a computer before being able to execute machine instructions. An operating system relies on a long-term scheduler to decide what processes should be loaded in the main memory and a short-term scheduler allocates the CPU to processes. The long-term scheduler is a component of the memory management subsystem and the short-term scheduler is part of the process management subsystem.

Most operating systems support virtual memory, thus a process may be given control of the CPU only to experience a "page-fault" that will force it to suspend itself and relinquish its control of the CPU. This approach may lead to a phenomenon called *thrashing* when processes with large working sets, sets of pages needed for execution, are activated by the short-term scheduler, only to experience a page-fault, because the memory management system has removed some of the pages in the process working set from the physical memory. This simple example illustrates the problems occurring when multiple resources needed by a process are controlled by independent agents.

An equivalent problem occurs in a distributed system when all members of a process group $G = \{p_1, p_2, \ldots, p_n\}$ need to be scheduled concurrently because the algorithm requires them to communicate with one another during execution.

This process is called *co-scheduling* and it is very challenging in a distributed system consisting of autonomous nodes, e.g., clusters of workstations. Clusters of workstations are used these days as a cost-effective alternative to supercomputers. In this case the nodes have to reach an agreement when to schedule the process group [1].

However, when the system has a unique scheduler controlling all resources, then all processes in the process group can be scheduled at the same time. This is the case of tightly coupled parallel machines where a process group of size n will only be scheduled for execution when a set of n processors becomes available.

2.7.2 Objective Functions and Scheduling Policies

A scheduling algorithm optimizes resource allocation subject to a set of constraints. Consider a process group $G = (p_1, p_2, \ldots p_n)$ and set of resources available to it $R = (r_1, r_2, \ldots, r_q)$. Let $c^j_{i,k}$ be the cost of allocating resource r_i to process p_j and of p_j using this resource for completion of its task under schedule s_k. If s_k does not require process p_j to use r_i, then $c^j_{i,k} = 0$. The schedule s_k in the set $S = (s_1, s_2, \ldots s_k, \ldots s_p)$ is optimal if its cost is minimal:

$$C = \min_{(k)} C(s_k) = \min_{(k)} \sum_{j=1}^{n} \sum_{i=1}^{q} c^j_{i,k}$$

The optimality criteria above takes into account not only the cost of using resources but also the scheduling overhead. This situation is consistent with the observation that in a dynamic scheduling environment the scheduler itself is a process and requires resources of its own to complete its task.

In a real-time system all schedules in the set $S = (s_1, s_2, \ldots s_k, \ldots s_p)$ must guarantee that all critical processes in the process group meet their deadlines.

In a soft real-time system or in a system with no deadlines we can define the *makespan* t_k *of a schedule* s_k as the maximum completion time of any process in the process group G, under s_k. If t^i_k denotes the completion time of process p_i under schedule s_k then:

$$t_k = \max_{(i)} (t^i_k)$$

An optimality criteria may be to minimize the makespan, t_k, to complete all processes in the group as early as possible. An alternative optimality criteria is to consider the average completion time under the schedules in the set S and attempt to minimize it.

When the scheduler and the resource management agent are integrated into one entity the objective may be to maximize the resource utilization or the throughput.

A number of *scheduling policies* have been proposed and are implemented by various systems.

(i) *Round Robin with a time slice* is a widely used policy when processes that need to use a resource join a single queue and are allocated the resource for a time slice, Δ, and after that time they release the resource and rejoin the queue until they complete their execution.

(ii) *Priority scheduling* is based on a multiqueue approach where each process is assigned a priority and joins one of the q queues. In each scheduling cycle, each queue gets a share of the resource according to a prearranged scheme. For example, the highest priority queue gets 50% of the cycle, and each of the $q - 1$ remaining queues gets a fraction of the residual 50%, time, function of the priority of the corresponding queue.

(iii) *First Come First Serve (FCFS)*, also called first in first out (FIFO) is a non-preemptive strategy that assigns a resource to customers in the order they arrive.

(iv) *Last Come First Serve (LCFS)*, also called last in first out (LIFO) is a non-preemptive strategy when customers are served in the reverse order of their arrival.

(v) *Shortest Laxity First (SLF)* is a common scheduling policy for real-time system.

Definition. The *laxity* of process p_j is defined as $l_j = d_j - e_j$.

In this strategy the customer with the minimum difference between its deadline and its execution time is served first.

2.7.3   Real-Time Process Scheduling

Consider now a real-time system and a process group $G = \{p_1, p_2, ...p_n\}$. The members of this process group have deadlines $(d_1, d_2, ...d_n)$ and execution times $(e_1, e_2, ..., e_n)$.

In a real-time system we recognize periodic and aperiodic or sporadic processes. If we know the initial request time of a periodic task and the period, we can compute all future request times of the process. Assuming that all processes $p_j \in G$ are periodic with period τ_j and we have a system with N processors, then a necessary schedulabity test is that the system is stable, the utilization of each N processors is at most one, or:

$$\mu = \sum_i^N \mu_i = \sum_i^N e_i/\tau_i \leq N.$$

2.7.4   Queuing Models: Basic Concepts

A stochastic process is a collection of random variables with the common distribution function.

Definition. Consider a discrete-state, discrete-time process and let X_n denote the discrete value of the random process at its nth step. If

$$P[X_n = j | X_{n-1} = i_{n-1}, \ldots X_1 = i_1] = P[X_n = j | X_{n-1} = i_{n-1}.$$

then we say that X is a discrete-state, discrete-time Markov process.

A Markov process is a memoryless process, the present state summarizes its past history.

A queuing system is characterized by the arrival process and the service process. The arrival process describes the rate at which customers enter the system and the distribution of the interarrival times. Common arrival processes are: deterministic, uniform, normal, exponential, batch, and general. The service process describes the service rate, and the distribution of the service time. Uniform, normal, and exponential, are commonly used distributions of the service time.

A queuing model is characterized by the arrival process, the service process, the number of servers, and the maximum queue capacity or buffer size. For example, an $M/M/1$ model means that the arrival process is Markov (M), the service process is Markov (M), there is only one server (1), and the buffer size is not bounded. An M/G/1 model has a general (G) service process. An $M/M/1/m$ is an $M/M/1$ model with finite buffer capacity equal to m.

Definition. We denote by λ the *arrival rate*, by μ the *service rate*, and by ρ the *server utilization* defined as:

$$\rho = \frac{\lambda}{\mu}.$$

The *interarrival time* is $\frac{1}{\lambda}$ and the *service time* is $\frac{1}{\mu}$.

Example. Consider a process characterized by an arrival rate of $\lambda = 10$ customers/hour and a service rate of $\mu = 12$ customers/hour. In this case the interarrival time is 6 minutes and the service time is 5 minutes. In a deterministic system precisely six customers enter the system every hour and they arrive on a prescribed pattern, say, the first 1 minute after the hour, the second 10 minutes after the hour, and so on. If the interarrival time has an exponential distribution, then once a customer has arrived we should expect the next one after an exponentially distributed interval with expected value $\frac{1}{\lambda}$. The expected number of customers is six every hour, though there may be hour-long intervals with no customers and other intervals with 10 customers, but such events are rare. If the distribution of the interarrival times is uniform, then the customers arrive every 6 minutes with high probability. In a system with batch arrivals, groups of customers arrive at the same time.

A necessary condition for a system to be *stable* is that the length of the queue is bounded. This implies that the server utilization cannot be larger than one:

$$\rho \leq 1.$$

If the arrival rate in the previous example increases from $\lambda = 10$ to $\lambda = 15$, then a customer enters the system every 4 minutes on average, and, as before, one customer leaves the system every 5 minutes on average, thus, the number of customers in the systems grows continually.

Important figures of merit for a queuing model are: the average number in the system, $\bar{N}$, the average time in system, T, the average waiting time, W, the number in the queue, N_q, and the average service time $\frac{1}{\mu}$.

2.7.4.1   Little's Law.   The number in system, the time in system, and the arrival rate are related as follows:

$$\bar{N} = \lambda T.$$

The intuitive justification of this relationship is that when a "typical" customer leaves the system after a "typical" time in system, T, it sees a "typical" number of customers, N, that have arrived during T at a rate λ customers per unit of time.

From Little's law it follows immediately that:

$$\bar{N}_q = \lambda W$$

In a G/G/m system, one with a general arrival and service process and with m servers, we have:

$$\bar{N}_q = \bar{N} - m \times \rho.$$

We are only concerned with single-server, *work-preserving systems*, when the server is not allowed to be idle while customers wait in the queue. Thus:

$$\bar{N} = \bar{N}_q + 1$$

and

$$T = W + \frac{1}{\mu}.$$

2.7.5   The M/M/1 Queuing Model

Let us turn our attention to a system with one server, Markov arrival and service processes, and an infinite buffer. First of all, the Markovian assumption means that the probability of two of more arrivals at the same time is very close to zero.

Such a system can be modeled as a discrete-state system. The system is in state k if the number of customers in the system is k. Moreover, from state k there are only two transitions possible, to state $k + 1$ if a new customer arrives in the system, or to state $k - 1$ if a customer finishes its service and leaves the system. The corresponding transition rates are λ and μ. The number of states of the system is unbounded. Such a process is also called a *birth and death* process and its state transition diagram is presented in Figure 2.24(b).

Let us denote by p_k the probability of the system being in state k. Clearly:

$$\sum_{k=0}^{k=\infty} p_k = 1.$$

We are only interested in the steady-state behavior of the system. In this case, the transitions from state $(k-1)$ to state (k) is $p_{k-1} \times \lambda$ and equals the transitions from state k to state $(k-1)$, namely $p_k \times \mu$. Applying recursively this relationship we obtain:

$$p_k = (1 - \rho) \times \rho^k.$$

Then the average number in system, the average time in system, and the average waiting time are:

$$\bar{N} = \frac{\rho}{1 - \rho}$$

$$T = \frac{\frac{1}{\mu}}{1 - \rho}$$

$$W = \frac{\frac{\rho}{\mu}}{1 - \rho}.$$

The variance of the number in system is:

$$\sigma_N^2 = \frac{\rho}{(1 - \rho)^2}.$$

Figure 2.26(a) illustrates the dependence of the time in system on the server utilization. When the server utilization increases, the time in system increases; when ρ is getting very close to 1 then the time in system is unbounded.

The quantity of the service provided by the server is measured by the throughput, the number of customers leaving the system per unit of time, while the quality of the service is measured by the time spent in the system by a customer. A fundamental dilemma in the design of systems with shared resources is to achieve an optimal trade-off between the quantity and the quality of service.

2.7.6 The M/G/1 System: The Server with Vacation

We discussed briefly contention-free or scheduled multiple-access. In this scheme a station transmits when it gets a token then waits for the next visit of the token. For this reason, the model capturing the behavior of such a system is called *server with vacation*.

Once a station acquires the right to transmit, several *service strategies* are possible. The name of the strategy and the packets transmitted in each case are:

(i) Exhaustive – all packets in the queue.

(ii) k-limited – at most k-packets; a particular case is one-limited, only one packet is transmitted.

(iii) Gated - all packets in the queue at the time the token arrived, but not the ones that arrived after the token. If there were q packets in the queue at the time when the station got the token and if q' packets arrived since, then the station will transmit q, leaving q' in the queue.

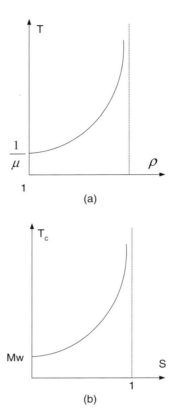

Fig. 2.26   (a) The expected time in system, function of the server utilization for an M/M/1 system. (b) The cycle time in a token passing ring with exhaustive service, function of the ring throughput.

(iv) Semigated – as many packets as necessary to reduce the number of packets in the queue by one. If there were q packets in the queue at the time when the station got the token and if q' packets arrived since, then the station will transmit $q' + 1$, leaving $q - 1$ behind.

Let us now outline a very simple derivation of the cycle time for the exhaustive service strategy in this model. For this analysis we need to define several parameters of the system:

M – the number of stations in the ring.

w – the walk time, the time it takes the token to move from station i to station $i + 1$.

λ – the packet arrival rate at a node.

R – the channel rate

l – the packet size (a random variable),

$\bar{l}$ – the mean packet size.

m – mean number of packets stored at a station.

S – the throughput, $S = M \times \frac{\lambda \times \bar{l}}{R}$.

T_c – the cycle time (a random variable).

$\bar{T}_c$ – the mean cycle time

During one cycle the token visits each of the M stations, at each station, it has to transmit in average $m \times \bar{l}$ bits and the time to do so is $\frac{m \times \bar{l}}{R}$. Then it walks to the next station. Thus

$$T_c = M \times \left(\frac{m \times \bar{l}}{R} + w \right)$$

When the system reaches a steady-state all the m packets queued at a station when the token arrives have accumulated during one cycle time.

$$m = \lambda \times \bar{T}_c.$$

Thus:

$$T_c = M \times \left(\frac{\lambda \times T_c \times \bar{l}}{R} + w \right).$$

Finally:

$$T_c = \frac{M \times w}{1 - S}$$

Figure 2.26(b) illustrates the dependence of the cycle time on the throughput in a token passing ring with exhaustive service. Again, when the throughput S, defined as the data rate transmitted divided by the channel rate, is getting very close to one the cycle time becomes unbounded, the same phenomenon we observed earlier for the M/M/1 system, see Figure 2.26(a).

2.7.7 Network Congestion Example

In this example we focus on a router in the Internet with two connections passing through it, see Figure 2.27(a). An internal router is part of the Internet core, it is connected with other routers, while an edge router connects local area networks and hosts with the rest of the Internet.

In a store and forward packet-switched network, a router forwards incoming packets on its input communication channels, or links, to output channels. There is a queue of packets associated with each input and output link. Packets in an input link queue wait to be handled by the switching fabric and packets in an output link queue wait to be transmitted.

When the rate at which packets accumulate in a queue is larger than the rate at which they can be processed, we witness a phenomenon called *congestion*. Real life routers have finite resources, including buffer space, and in case of congestion they start dropping packets.

In our example in Figure 2.27(a) there are two connections passing through router d, one originating in router b and the other in router c. Both connections go to router e via d. All communication channels have capacity C. We assume that the two connections are symmetric and the traffic on both is similar. We make an idealistic assumption, namely, that the output queue associated with the communication channel connecting d with e has an infinite buffer space allocated to it.

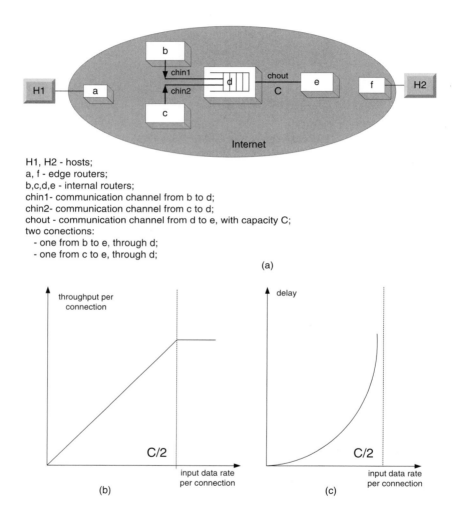

H1, H2 - hosts;
a, f - edge routers;
b,c,d,e - internal routers;
chin1- communication channel from b to d;
chin2- communication channel from c to d;
chout - communication channel from d to e, with capacity C;
two conections:
   - one from b to e, through d;
   - one from c to e, through d;

(a)

(b)

(c)

Fig. 2.27   (a) Four Internet core routers, b, c, d, e, connected by channels with capacity C. Two connections pass through router d, they are symmetric and the traffic on both is similar. The output queue associated with the communication channel connecting d with e has an infinite capacity. (b) The throughput of each connection is limited to $C/2$. (c) The delays experienced by the packets are very large when the packet arrival rate is close to the capacity of the communication channel

In this example the maximum input packet rate for the router cannot exceed $C/2$ on each of the two connections simply because the capacity of the output channel is equal to C, see Figure 2.27(b). But the time in queue of a packet grows as indicated in Figure 2.27(c). We see again a manifestation of the same phenomenon, the delays experienced by the packets are very large when the packet arrival rate is close to the capacity of the communication channel.

2.7.8   Final Remarks Regarding Resource Sharing and Performance Models

Resource sharing is a pervasive problem in the design of complex systems. Physical limitations, cost, and functional constraints mandate resource sharing among customers: the bandwidth of communication channels among flows; hardware resources of a computer such as the CPU, the main memory, and the secondary storage devices among processes; Internet servers among clients.

Scheduling covers resource access policies and mechanisms for shared resources and answers the question when a resource is made available to each customer waiting to access it. Scheduling and enforcement of scheduling decisions in a system consisting of autonomous systems is an enormously difficult task.

Performance models provide abstractions to determine critical system parameters such as resource utilization, the time a customer spends in systems, the conditions for stability. A very important conclusion drawn from performance analysis is the relationship between the quality of service expressed by the time required to get the service, or by the time between successive visits of a server with vacation and the quantity of service expressed by the throughput or the resource utilization.

2.8   SECURITY MODELS

Networked computer systems are built to support information and resource sharing and system security is a critical concern in the design of such systems. Information integrity and confidentiality can be compromised during transmission over insecure communication channels or while being stored on sites that allow multiple agents to modify it.

Malicious agents may pose as valid partners of a transaction or prevent access to system resources. System security ensures confidentiality and integrity of the information stored and processed by a system as well as authentication, verification of the identity of the agents manipulating the information, and it allows controlled access to system resources.

There are a number of misconceptions and fallacies regarding system security. A common misconception is that security can be treated as an afterthought in the design of a complex system. Another misconception is that adding cryptography to a system will make it secure. Several fallacies, e.g., a good security model is a sufficient condition for a secure system and the security of each component of a system guarantees the security of the entire system are often encountered.

Before discussing in depth these fallacies we examine the standard features of a secure system and introduce the basic terms and concepts, then we present a security model.

2.8.1 Basic Terms and Concepts

Confidentiality is a property of a system that guarantees that only agents with proper credentials have access to information. The common method to support confidentiality is based on *encryption*. Data or *plaintext* in cryptographic terms is mathematically transformed into *ciphertext* and only agents with the proper key are able to decrypt the ciphertext and transform it into plaintext.

The algorithms used to transform plaintext into ciphertext and back form a *cipher*cipher. A *symmetric cipher* uses the same key for encryption and decryption. *Asymmetric or public key ciphers* involve a *public key* that can be freely distributed and a secret *private key*. Data is encrypted using the public key and it is decrypted using the private key. There are *hybrid systems* that combine symmetric and asymmetric ciphers.

Data integrity ensures that information is not modified without the knowledge on the parties involved in a transaction. Downloading a malicious program designed to exploit the inadequacy of the local operating system may lead to the loss of locally stored data and programs, the alteration of the input data will always lead to incorrect results of a computation and so on. A *message digest* is a special number calculated from the input data. The encrypted message digest is called a *signature* and it is used to ensure the integrity of the data. The message digest is computed at the sending site, encrypted, and sent together with the data. At the receiving site the message digest is decrypted and compared with a locally computed message digest, this process is called the *verification of the signature*. If the confidentiality is compromised there are no means to ensure integrity. A *message authorization code (MAC)* is a message digest with an associated key.

The process of proving identity is called *authentication* [17]. Often, the agents involved in a transaction use an asymmetric cipher for authentication and then after a session has been established they continue their exchange of information using a symmetric cipher. For example, consider the operation of a hybrid client-server system. Both parties use initially an asymmetric cipher to agree on a private or session key then continue their session using a symmetric cipher.

Authorization is the process of controlling access to system resources. An access control model defines the set of resources each principal has access to and possibly the mode the principal may interact with each resource as a two dimensional matrix.

Figure 2.28 illustrates the secret and public key cryptography.

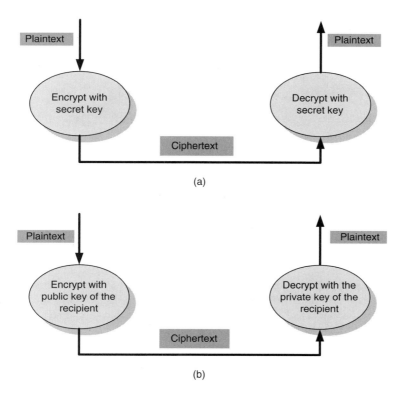

Fig. 2.28 (a) Secret key cryptography. (b) Public key cryptography.

2.8.2 An Access Control Model

The access control model presented in Figure 2.29 is due to Lampson [26]. In this model principals generate requests to perform operation on resources or objects protected by monitors. The requests are delivered to the monitors through channels. The monitor is responsible for authenticating a request and for enforcing the access control rules.

This model helps us to understand why security is a much harder task in a distributed system than in a centralized one. In a centralized system the operating system implements all channels and manages all processes and resources.

In a distributed system the monitor must authenticate the communication channel as well. The path from the principal to the monitor might crosses multiple systems with different levels of trust and multiple channels. Each system may implement a different security scheme. Moreover, some of the components of this path may fail and all these conditions make authentication more difficult. The authorization is

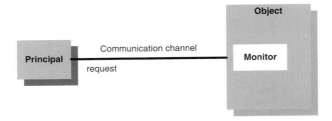

Fig. 2.29 The access control model. The monitor should be aware of the source of the request and the access rules. *Authentication* means to determine the principal responsible for the request. *Access control* or *authorization* requires interpretation the access rules.

also complicated by the fact that a distributed system may have different sources of authority.

A secure distributed environment typically relies on a *trusted computing base (TCB)* the subset of the software and hardware that the entire system security depends on. The system components outside TCB can fail in a fail-secure mode, i.e., if such a nontrusted component fails, the system may deny access that should be granted but it will not grant access that should have been denied.

2.9   CHALLENGES IN DISTRIBUTED SYSTEMS

Distributed systems research is focused on two enduring problems: concurrency and mobility of data and computations. Figure 2.30 summarizes distributed systems concurrency and mobility attributes and models. Now we discuss briefly these two critical aspects of distributed system design.

2.9.1   Concurrency

Concurrency is concerned with systems of multiple, simultaneously computing active agents interacting with one another and covers both tightly coupled, synchronous parallel systems as well as asynchronous and loosely coupled asynchronous systems.

Concurrent programs, as opposed to sequential ones, consist of multiple threads of control, thus, the interactions between the computing agents are more subtle and phenomena such as race conditions, deadlock, and interference, unknown to sequential programs, may occur. Very often concurrent programs are *reactive* – they do not terminate but interact continuously with their environment. For reactive programs the traditional concept of coreteness to relate inputs to the outputs on termination is no longer applicable.

Concurrency models are based on the assumption that systems perform atomic actions. These models are classified along three dimensions: observability, the type of concurrency, and description.

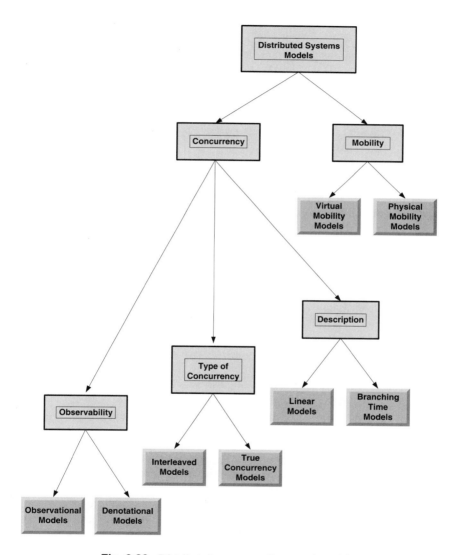

Fig. 2.30 Distributed system attributes and models.

(i) Observational versus denotational models. *Observational models* view the system in terms of states and transitions among states. Examples of observational models are Petri nets, various process algebra models, e.g. the *Communicating Sequential Processes (CSP)* of Hoare [20] and the *Calculus of Communicating Systems (CCS)*, of Milner [30]. *Denotational models* are based on a set of observations of the system and the concept of a *trace*, a sequence of atomic actions executed by the system.

(ii) Interleaving versus true concurrency models. *Interleaving* models consider that at any one time only one of the several threads of control is active and the others are suspended and reactivated based on the logic of the concurrent algorithm. *True concurrency* models are based on the assumption that multiple threads of control may be active at any one time.

(iii) Linear versus branching time models. *Linear models* describe the system in terms of sets of their possible partial runs. They are useful for describing the past execution history. *Branching time models* describe the system in terms of the points where computations diverge from one another. Such models are useful for modeling the future behavior of the system.

2.9.2 Mobility of Data and Computations

Mobility of data and computations constitute a second fundamental challenge in designing distributed systems. Communication is unreliable, messages may be lost, affected by errors, duplicated, and, in the most general case, there is no bound on communication delays. For distributed systems with unreliable communication channels the problem of reaching consensus does not have a general solution. Performance problems due to latency and bandwidth limitations are of major concern. Moreover, in the general case we are unable to distinguish between performance problems and failures.

There are two primary forms of mobility that in practice may interact with one another:

(i) Mobile computations/virtual mobility - a running program may move from one host to another. *Virtual mobility* is consistent with the idea of network-centric computing when hardware as well as software resources are distributed and accessible over the Internet. This paradigm is viewed primarily as a software issue and it is appealing for two reasons. First, it simplifies the problem of software distribution, instead of buying and installing a program on one of the systems in the domain of an organization, we may simply "rent" an executable one for a limited time and bring it to one of our systems. Second, it may improve the quality of the solution, by: (a) improving performance as seen by the user as well as by reducing the network traffic and (b) providing a more secure environment. Instead of moving a large volume of data to a remote site where data security cannot be guaranteed, we bring in the code to our domain and run it in a controlled environment.

(ii) Mobile computing/physical mobility - a host may be reconnected at different physical locations. *Physical mobility* is a reality we have to face at the time of very rapid advances in wireless communication and nomadic computing, and it is viewed primarily as a hardware issue. We want uninterrupted connectivity and we wish to trigger and monitor complex activities performed by some systems in the Internet, from a simple device with limited local resources, connected to the Internet via a low-bandwidth wireless channel.

Mobility allows novel solutions to existing problems but it also creates new and potentially difficult problems. Mobility allows us to overcome latency problems by moving computations around and making remote procedure calls local. At the same time we can eliminate bandwidth fluctuations and address the problem of reliability in a novel way by moving away from nodes when we anticipate a failure. Mobility forces us to address the problem of trust management because mobile computations may cross administrative domains to access local resources on a new system.

2.10 FURTHER READING

The book edited by Mullender [31] contains a selection of articles written by leading researchers in the field of distributed systems. The articles in this collection cover a wide range of topics ranging from system specification to interprocess communication, scheduling, atomic transactions, and security.

A comprehensive discussion of distributed algorithms can be found in a book by Lynch [27]. A good reference for information theory is the textbook by Cover and Thomas [15]. Vanstone and VanOorschot [40] is a readable introduction to error correcting and error detecting codes. Splitting algorithms are presented by Bertsekas and Gallagher [7].

Several papers by Shannon [35, 36, 37] present the mathematical foundations of the theory of communication. The paper by Lamport [24] addresses the problem of synchronization in distributed systems while the one due to Chandy and Lamport [11] introduce an algorithm for distributed snapshots.

Concurrency theory is discussed in the *Communicating Sequential Processes, CSP*, of Hoare [20], and the *Calculus of Communicating Systems, CCS*, of Milner [30]. A good reference for Process Algebra is a book by Baeten and Weijland [3].

There is a vast body of literature on scheduling, among the numerous publications we note [1, 13, 23, 34].

2.11 EXERCISES AND PROBLEMS

Problem 1. Let $X_1, X_2, \ldots X_n$ be random variables with the joint probability density function, $p(x_1, x_2, \ldots x_n)$.

(i) Show that the joint entropy of $X_1, X_2, \ldots X_n$ is the sum of the conditional entropies:

$$H(X_1, X_2, \ldots X_n) = \sum_{i=1}^{n} H(X_i | X_{i-1}, X_{i-2}, \ldots X_1).$$

(ii) If Y is another random variable show the following relationship for mutual information between $X_1, X_2, \ldots X_n$ and Y:

$$I(X_1, X_2, \ldots X_n; Y) = \sum_{i=1}^{n} H(X_i; Y | X_{i-1}, X_{i-2}, \ldots X_1).$$

Problem 2. Intuitively, given a random variable X, the knowledge of another random variable Y reduces the uncertainty in X. To prove this formally, we need to show that conditioning reduces entropy:

$$H(X) \geq H(X|Y).$$

with equality iff X and Y are independent.

Hint: Prove first that $I(X; Y) \geq 0$ using Jensen's inequality:

$$E[f(X)] \geq f(E[X]).$$

where f is a convex function. Recall that a function $f(x)$ is said to be convex over an interval (a, b) if for every $x_1, x_2 \in (a, b)$ and $0 \leq \lambda \leq 1$ we have:

$$f(\lambda x_1 + (1 - \lambda)x_2) \leq \lambda f(x_1) + (1 - \lambda)f(x_2).$$

Using Taylor series expansion one can prove that if the second derivative of $f(x)$ is non-negative, $f''(x) \geq 0, \quad \forall x \in (a, b)$ the function is convex in that interval.

Problem 3. Given a discrete random variable X and a function of X, $f(X)$ show that:

$$H(X) \geq H(f(X)).$$

Hint: Prove first that:

$$H(X, f(X)) = H(X) + H(f(X)|X) = H(f(X)) + H(X|f(X)).$$

Then show that:

$$H(f(X)|X) = H(X|f(X)) = 0.$$

Problem 4. Prove that $d(x, y)$, the *Hamming distance* between two n tuples over an alphabet A, defined in Section 2.2.6.1 is indeed a metric.

Problem 5. $w(x)$, the Hamming weight of an n-tuple x over an alphabet A, is defined as the number of nonzero elements of x; the parity of x is the parity of $w(x)$. Show that:

(i) $w(x + y)$ is even iff x and y have the same parity.

(ii) $w(x + y) = d(x, y)$.

(iii) $w(x + y) = w(x) + w(y) - 2p$ where p is the number of positions in which both x and y are 1.

Problem 6. Extend the Hamming bound presented in Section 2.2.6.6 for codes capable of correcting q errors. *Hints:* Recall that the Hamming bound provides a lower bound on the number of parity check symbols needed for a $[n, k]$ block code.

Problem 7. Consider a code that adds two parity check bits, one over all odd-numbered bits and one over all even-numbered bits. What is the Hamming distance of this code?

Problem 8. Consider the FCFS splitting algorithm presented in Section 2.4.2.

(i) Explain why when $s(k) = L$ and the feedback indicates an empty slot the following rules apply:
$$LE(k) = LE(k - 1) + ws(k - 1)$$
$$ws(k) = \frac{ws(k)}{2}$$
$$s(k) = L.$$

(ii) We assume that the arrival process is Poisson with rate λ. Compute the expected number of packets G_i in an interval that has been split i times.

(iii) If instead of Poisson arrival we assume bulk arrivals would the FCFS algorithm still work? What property of the Poisson process is critical for the FCFS algorithm.

(iv) Draw the state transition diagram of the Markov chain for the FCFS algorithm. Identify a state by a pair consisting of the level of splitting of the original interval and the position of the current subinterval, L or R. Consider that the original state is $(0, R)$.

(v) Call $P_{i,L,R}$ the probability of a transition from state (i, L) to the state (i, R); such a transition occurs in case of a successful transmission in state (i, L). Show that:
$$P_{i,L,R} = \frac{G_i \times e^{-G_i}(1 - e^{-G_i})}{1 - (1 + G_{i-1}) \times e^{-G_{i-1}}}.$$

(vi) Call $P_{i,R,0}$ the probability of a transition from state (i, R) to the state $(0, R)$; such a transition occurs in case of a successful transmission in state (i, R). Show that:
$$P_{i,L,R} = \frac{G_i \times e^{-G_i}}{1 - e^{-G_i}}.$$

Problem 9. Construct the lattice of global states for the system in Figure 2.18 and the runs leading to the global state $\Sigma_{(5,6,3)}$.

Problem 10. Consider the system in Figure 2.18. Construct the snapshot protocol initiated in each of the following states: $\Sigma_{(4,6,3)}$, $\Sigma_{(5,5,3)}$, $\Sigma_{(5,6,2)}$, and $\Sigma_{(5,6,3)}$.

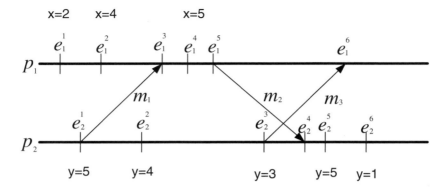

Fig. 2.31   A system with two processes. Messages m_1 and m_3 communicate the value of y computed by process p_2, to p_1 while m_2 transmits to p_2 the value of x computed by p_1.

Problem 11. Consider the system consisting of two processes shown in Figure 2.31. Identify the states when the predicate $x = y$ is satisfied. Is this predicate stable?

Problem 12. Let us call $\preceq$ the *reduction* relationship. Given two problems, $\mathcal{A}$ and $\mathcal{B}$ we say that $\mathcal{B} \preceq \mathcal{A}$ if there is a transformation $\mathcal{R}_\mathcal{A} \to \mathcal{B}$ that may be applied to any algorithm for $\mathcal{A}$ and transform it into an algorithm for $\mathcal{B}$. Two problems $\mathcal{A}$ and $\mathcal{B}$ are equivalent if each is reducible to the other, $(\mathcal{B} \preceq \mathcal{A}) \wedge (\mathcal{A} \preceq \mathcal{B})$.

   (i) To show a reduction of Causal Broadcast to FIFO Broadcast, design an algorithm that transforms any FIFO Broadcast into a Causal Broadcast.

   (ii) Using reduction show that there are no deterministic Atomic Broadcast algorithms for asynchronous systems.

Problem 13. Prove that in synchronous systems *Consensus* is equivalent to TRB while in asynchronous systems they are not equivalent.

Problem 14. Let X be a random variable with an exponential distribution. Its probability density function $f(x)$ and cumulative density functions $F(x)$ are:

$$
\begin{aligned}
f(x) &= \lambda e^{-\lambda x} \quad \text{if } x > 0 \text{ and } 0 \text{ otherwise.} \\
F(x) &= 1 - e^{-\lambda x} \quad \text{if } 0 \leq x < \infty \text{ and } 0 \text{ otherwise.}
\end{aligned}
$$

Prove the *memoryless* or *Markov* property of the exponential distribution. If X models the number of customers in a system with one server and if the interarrival time is exponentially distributed, then this number does not depend on the past history. If X models the time a component of a computer system has been functioning, the distribution of the remaining lifetime of the component does not depend on how long the component has been operating, [39].

Hint. Define a new random variable $Y = X - t$. Call $G_t(y)$ the conditional probability that $Y \leq y$ given that $X > t$. Show that $G_t(y)$ is independent of t:

$$G_t(y) = 1 - e^{-\lambda y}.$$

Problem 15. Consider a queuing system with arrival rate λ and with m servers each with service rate μ. If the interarrival times are exponentially distributed with the expected interarrival time $\frac{1}{\lambda}$ and the service time is also exponentially distributed with expected value $\frac{1}{\mu}$, then we have an $M/M/m$ queue.

(i) Draw the state transition diagram of the system.

(ii) Show that the expected number of customers, N, in the system is:

$$E[N] = m \times \rho + \rho \times \frac{(m \times \rho)^m}{m!} \times \frac{p_0}{(1 - \rho)^2}.$$

where $\rho = \frac{\lambda}{m \times \mu}$ and

$$p_0 = [\sum_{i=0}^{m-1} \frac{(i \times \rho)^i}{i!} + \frac{(m \times \rho)^m}{m!} \times \frac{1}{(1 - \rho)}]^{-1}.$$

(iii) Show that the expected number of busy servers is:

$$E[M] = \frac{\lambda}{\mu}.$$

(iv) Show that the probability of congestion is:

$$P_{queuing} = \frac{(m \times \rho)^m}{m!} \times \frac{p_0}{(1 - \rho)}.$$

Problem 16. Quantum key distribution is a very elegant solution to the key distribution problem. Assume that in addition to an ordinary bidirectional open channel, Alice uses a quantum channel to send individual particles, e.g., photons and Bob can measure the quantum state of the particles.

The quantum key distribution consists of the following steps:

(a) Alice uses two bases, b_1 and b_2, for encoding each bit into the state of a photon. She randomly selects one of the two bases for encoding each bit in the sequence of Q bits sent over the quantum channel.

(b) Bob knows the two bases and measures the state of each photon by randomly picking up one of the two bases.

(c) After the bits have been transmitted over the quantum channel, Alice sends Bob over the open channel the basis used for encoding the Q bits and Bob uses the same open channel for sending Alice the basis for decoding each bit in the sequence.

(d) Both Alice and Bob identify the bits for which the base used by Alice to encode and the basis used by Bob to decode the sequence on Q bits are the same. These bits will then be used as the secret key.

(i) What is the average number of bits sent over the quantum channel to have a key of length 1024 bits.

(ii) Eve is eavesdropping on both the open and quantum channel. Can Alice and Bob detect Eve's presence? What prevents Eve from determining the key?

REFERENCES

1. M. J. Atallah, C. Lock Black, D. C. Marinescu, H. J. Siegel, and T. L. Casavant. Models and Algorithms for Co-scheduling Compute-Intensive Tasks on a Network of Workstations. *Journal of Parallel and Distrbuted Computing*, 16:319–327, 1992.

2. Ö Babaoğlu and K. Marzullo. Consistent Global States. In Sape Mullender, editor, *Distributed Systems*, pages 55–96. Addison Wesley, Reading, Mass., 1993.

3. J. C. M. Baeten and W. P. Weijland. *Process Algebra*. Cambridge University Press, Cambridge, 1990.

4. C. H. Bennett. Logical Reversibility of Computation. *IBM Journal of Research and Development*, 17:525–535, 1973.

5. C. H. Bennett Thermodinamics of Computation – A Review. *International Journal of Theoretical Physics*, 21:905–928, 1982.

6. P. Benioff. Quantum Mechanical Models of Turing Machines that Dissipate no Energy. *Physical Review Letters*, 48:1581–1584, 1982.

7. D. Bertsekas and R. Gallager. *Data Networks*, second edition. Prentice-Hall, Saddle River, New Jersey, 1992.

8. A. Bohm. *Quantum Mechanics : Foundations and Applications*. Springer – Verlag, Heidelberg, 1993.

9. T. D. Chandra and S. Toueg. Time and Message Efficient Reliable Broadcasts. In Jan van Leeuwen and Nicola Santoro, editors, *Distributed Algorithms, 4th Int. Workshop, Lecture Notes in Computer Science*, volume 486, pages 289–303. Springer – Verlag, Heidelberg, 1991.

10. T.D. Chandra and S. Toueg. Unreliable Failure Detectors for Asynchronous Systems. In *PODC91 Proc. 10th Annual ACM Symp. on Principles of Distributed Computing*, pages 325–340, ACM Press, New York, 1992.

11. K. M. Chandy and L. Lamport. Distributed Snapshots: Determining Global States of Distributed Systems. *ACM Transactions on Computer Systems*, 3(1):63–75, 1985.

12. A. Chavez, A. Moukas, and P. Maes. Challenger: A Multi-Agent System for Distributed Resource Allocation. In *Proc. 5th Int. Conf. on Autonomous Agents*, pages 323–331. ACM Press, New York, 1997.

13. S. Cheng, J. A. Stankovic, and K. Ramamritham. Scheduling Algorithms for Hard Real-Time Systems–A Brief Survey. In J. A. Stankovic and K. Ramamritham, editors, *Tutorial on Hard Real-Time Systems*, pages 150–173. IEEE Computer Society Press, Los Alamitos, California, 1988.

14. R. Cooper. *Queuing Systems*. North Holland, Amsterdam, 1981.

15. T. M. Cover and J. A. Thomas. *Elements of Information Theory*. Wiley Series in Telecommunications. John Wiley & Sons, New York, 1991.

16. F. Cristian, H. Aghili, R. Strong, and D. Dolev. Atomic Broadcast From Simple Message Diffusion to Byzantine Agreement. In *15th Int. Conf. on Fault Tolerant Computing* pages 200–206. IEEE Press, Piscataway, New Jersey, 1985.

17. D. Dolev and H. R. Strong. Authenticated Algorithms for Byzantine Agreement. Technical Report RJ3416, IBM Research Laboratory, San Jose, March 1982.

18. R.P. Feynman *Lecture Notes on Computation* Addison Wesley, Reading, Mass., 1996.

19. V. Hadzilacos and S. Toueg. Fault-Tolerant Broadcasts and Related Problems. In S. Mullender, editor, *Distributed Systems*, pages 97–145. Addison Wesley, Reading, Mass., 1993.

20. C. A. R. Hoare. Communicating Sequential Processes. *Comm. of the ACM*, 21(8):666–677, 1978.

21. V. Jacobson. Congestion Avoidance and Control. *ACM Computer Communication Review; Proc. Sigcomm '88 Symp., 1988*, 18(4:)314–329, 1988.

22. L. Kleinrock. *Queuing Systems*. John Wiley & Sons, New York, 1975.

23. H. Kopetz. Scheduling in Distributed Real-Time Systems. In *Advanced Seminar on R/T LANs*, INRIA, Bandol, France, 1986.

24. L. Lamport. Time, Clocks, and the Ordering of Events in a Distributed System. *Comm. of the ACM*, 21(7):558–565, 1978.

25. L. Lamport and P. M. Melliar-Smith. Synchronizing Clocks in the Presence of Faults. *Journal of the ACM*, 32(1):52–78, 1985.

26. B. Lampson, M. Abadi, M. Burrows, and E. Wobber. Authentication in Distributed Systems: Theory and Practice. *ACM Trans. on Computer Systems*, 10(4):265–310, 1992.

27. N. A. Lynch. *Distributed Algorithms*. Morgan Kaufmann, San Francisco, 1996.

28. D. C. Marinescu, J. E. Lumpp, Jr., T. L. Casavant, and H.J. Siegel. Models for Monitoring and Debugging Tools for Parallel and Distributed Software. *Journal of Parallel and Distributed Computing*, 9(2):171–184, 1990.

29. F. Mattern. Virtual Time and Global States of Distributed Systems. In M. Cosnard et. al., editor, *Parallel and Distributed Algorithms: Proc. Int. Workshop on Parallel & Distributed Algorithms*, pages 215–226. Elsevier Science Publishers, New York, 1989.

30. R. Milner. *Lectures on a Calculus for Communicating Systems. Lecture Notes in Computer Science*, volume 197. Springer – Verlag, Heidelberg, 1984.

31. S. Mullender, editor. *Distributed Systems*, second edition. Addison Wesley, Reading, Mass., 1993.

32. E. Rieffel and W. Polak. *An Introduction to Quantum Computing for Non-Physicists, ACM Computing Surveys*, 32(3):300-335, 2000.

33. F. B. Schneider. What Good Are Models and What Models Are Good? In Sape Mullender, editor, *Distributed Systems*, pages 17–26. Addison Wesley, Reading, Mass., 1993.

34. L. Sha, R. Rajkumar, and J. P. Lehoczky. Priority Inheritance Protocols: An Approach to Real-Time Synchronization. *IEEE Trans. on Computers*, 39(9):1175–1185, 1990.

35. C. E. Shannon. Communication in the Presence of Noise. *Proceedings of the IRE*, 37:10–21, 1949.

36. C. E. Shannon. Certain Results in Coding Theory for Noisy Channels. *Information and Control*, 1(1):6–25, 1957.

37. C. E. Shannon and W. Weaver. *The Mathematical Theory of Communication*. University of Illinois Press, Urbana, 1963.

38. P. Shor *Algorithms for Quantum Computation: Discrete Log and Factoring. Proc. 35 Annual Symp. on Foundatiuons of Computer Science*, pages 124–134, IEEE Press, Piscataway, New Jersey, 1994.

39. K. Trivedi. *Probability and Statistics with Reliability, Queuing, and Computer Science Applications*. Prentice Hall, Saddle River, New Jersey, 1981.

40. S. A. Vanstone and P. C. VanOorschot. *An Introduction to Error Correcting Codes with Applications*. Kluwer Academic Publishers, Norwell, Mass., 1989.

41. P. Veríssimo and L. Rodrigues. A Posteriori Agreement for Fault-Tolerant Clock Synchronization on Broadcast Networks. In Dhiraj K. Pradhan, editor, *Proc. 22nd Annual Int. Symp. on Fault-Tolerant Computing (FTCS '92)*, pages 527-536. IEEE Computer Society Press, Los Alamitos, California, 1992.

3

Net Models of Distributed Systems and Workflows

3.1 INFORMAL INTRODUCTION TO PETRI NETS

In 1962 Carl Adam Petri introduced a family of graphs, called Place-Transition (P/T), nets, to model dynamic systems [25]. P/T nets are bipartite graphs populated with tokens that flow through the graph. A *bipartite graph* is one with two classes of nodes; arcs always connect a node in one class with one or more nodes in the other class. In the case of P/T nets the two classes of nodes are *places* and *transitions*; arcs connect one place with one or more transitions or a transition with one or more places.

To model the dynamic behavior of systems, the places of a P/T net contain tokens; firing of transitions removes tokens from some places, called input places, and adds them to other places, called output places. The distribution of tokens in the places of a P/T net at a given time is called the *marking* of the net and reflects the state of the system being modeled.

P/T nets are very powerful abstractions and can express both concurrency and choice. P/T nets are used to model various activities in a distributed system; a transition may model the occurrence of an event, the execution of a computational task, the transmission of a packet, a logic statement, and so on. The *input places* of a transition model the preconditions of an event, the input data for the computational task, the presence of data in an input buffer, the preconditions of a logic statement. The *output places* of a transition model the postconditions associated with an event, the results of the computational task, the presence of data in an output buffer, or the conclusions of a logic statement.

P/T nets, or Petri nets (PNs), as they are commonly called, provide a very useful abstraction for system analysis and for system specification, as shown in Figure 3.1. To analyze a system we first construct a PN model, then the properties of the net are analyzed using one of the methods discussed in this chapter, and, finally, the results of this analysis are mapped back to the original system, see Figure 3.1(a).

Another important application of the net theory is the specification of concurrent systems, using the Petri net language, see Figure 3.1(b). In this case a concurrent system is described as a net, then the properties of the net are investigated using PN tools, and, when satisfied that the net has a set of desirable properties, the Petri net description is translated into an imperative computer language, that, in turn, is used to generate executable code.

P/T nets are routinely used to model distributed systems, concurrent programs, communication protocols, workflows, and other complex software, or hardware or systems. Once a system is modeled as a P/T net, we can perform static and dynamic analysis of the net. The *structural analysis* of the net is based on the topology of the graph and allows us to draw conclusions about the static properties of the system modeled by the net, while the analysis based on the markings of the net allow us to study its dynamic properties.

High-Level Petri nets, HLPNs, introduced independently by Jensen [13], and Genrich and Lautenbach [8] in 1981, provide a more concise, or folded, graphical representation for complex systems consisting of similar or identical components. In case of HLPNs, tokens of different colors flow through the same subnet to model the dynamic behavior of identical subsystems. An HLPN can be unfolded into an ordinary P/T net.

To use PNs for performance analysis of systems we need to modify ordinary P/T nets, where transitions fire instantaneously, and to augment them with the concept of either deterministic or random time intervals. Murata [20], Ramamoorthy [27], Sifakis [28], and Zuberek [30] have made significant contributions in the area of timed Petri nets and their application to performance analysis. The so called Stochastic Petri nets (SPNs), introduced independently by Molloy [19] and Florin and Natkin [7] in 1982 associate a random interval of time with an exponential distribution to every transition in the net. Once a transition is ready to fire, a random interval elapses before the actual transport of tokens triggered by the firing of the transition takes places. An SPN is isomorphic with a finite Markov chain. Marsan and his co-workers [18] extended SPNs by introducing two types of transitions, timed and immediate.

Applications of stochastic Petri nets to performance analysis of complex systems is generally limited by the explosion of the state space of the models. In 1988 Lin and Marinescu [16] introduced Stochastic High-Level Petri nets (SHLPNs) and showed that SHLPNs allow easy identification of classes of equivalent markings even when the corresponding aggregation of states in the Markov domain is not obvious. This

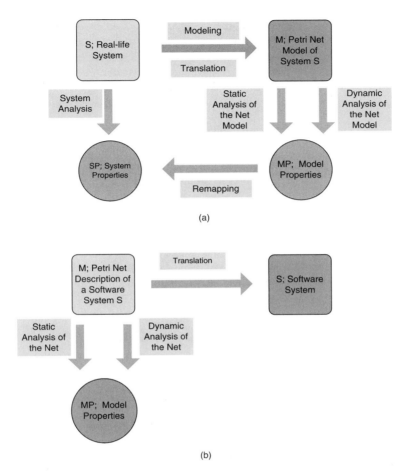

Fig. 3.1 Applications of Petri nets. (a) PNs are often used to model complex systems that are difficult or impossible to analyze by other means. In such cases one may construct a PN model of the system, M, then carry out a static and/or dynamic analysis of the net model and from this analysis infer the properties of the original system S. If S is a software system one may attempt to translate it directly into a PN rather than build a model of the system. (b) A software system could be specified using the PN language. The net description of the system can be analyzed and, if the results of the analysis are satisfactory, then the system can be built from the PN description.

aggregation could reduce the size of the state space by one or more orders of magnitude depending on the system being modeled.

This chapter is organized as follows: we first define the basic concepts in net theory, then we discuss modeling with Petri nets and cover conflict, choice, synchronization, priorities, and exclusion. We discuss briefly state machines and marked graphs, outline marking independent, as well as marking dependent properties, and survey Petri net languages. We conclude the discussion of Petri net methodologies with an introduction to state equations and other methods for net analysis. We then review applications of Petri nets to performance analysis and modeling of logic programs. Finally, we discuss the application of Petri nets to workflow modeling and enactment, and discuss several concepts and models introduced by van der Aalst and Basten [1, 2] for the study of dynamic workflow inheritance.

3.2   BASIC DEFINITIONS AND NOTATIONS

In this section we provide a formal introduction to P/T nets and illustrate the concepts with the graphs in Figures 3.2 (a)-(j). Throughout this chapter the abbreviation *iff* stands for *if and only if*.

Definition – Bag. A *bag* $\mathcal{B}(\mathcal{A})$ is a multiset of symbols from an alphabet, $\mathcal{A}$; it is a function from $\mathcal{A}$ to the set of natural numbers.

Example. $[x^3, y^4, z^5, w^6 \mid P(x, y, z, w)]$ is a bag consisting of three elements x, four elements y, five elements z, and six elements w such that the $P(x, y, z, w)$ holds. P is a predicate on symbols from the alphabet. x is an element of a bag A denoted as $x \in A$ if $x \in \mathcal{A}$ and if $A(x) > 0$.

The sum and the difference of two bags A and B are defined as:

$$A + B = [x^n \mid x \in \mathcal{A} \ \wedge \ n = A(x) + B(x)]$$
$$A - B = [x^n \mid x \in \mathcal{A} \ \wedge \ n = max(0, (A(x) + B(x)))]$$

The empty bag is denoted as **0**.

Bag A is a *subbag* of B, $A \leq B$ iff $\forall x \in \mathcal{A} \ \ A(x) \leq B(x)$.

Definition – Labeled P/T net. Let U be a universe of identifiers and L a set of labels. An L-labeled P/T Net is a tuple $N = (p, t, f, l)$ such that:

1. $p \subseteq U$ is a finite set of *places*.
2. $t \subseteq U$ is a finite set of *transitions*.
3. $f \subseteq (p \times t) \cup (t \times p)$ is a set of directed arcs, called *flow relations*.
4. $l : t \rightarrow L$ is a labeling or a weight function.

The weight function describes the number of tokens necessary to enable a transition. Labeled P/T nets as defined above describe a static structure. Places may contain *tokens* and the distribution of tokens over places defines the state of the P/T net and is called *the marking of the net*. We use the term marking and state interchangeably throughout this chapter. The dynamic behavior of a P/T net is described by the structure together with the markings of the net.

Definition – Marked P/T net. A marked, L-labeled P/T net is a pair (N, s) where $N = (p, t, f, l)$ is an L-labeled P/T net and s is a bag over p denoting the markings of the net.

The set of all marked P/T nets is denoted by $\mathcal{N}$.

Definition – Preset and Postset of Transitions and Places. The *preset* of transition t_i denoted as $\bullet t_i$ is the set of input places of t_i and the *postset* denoted by $t_i \bullet$ is the

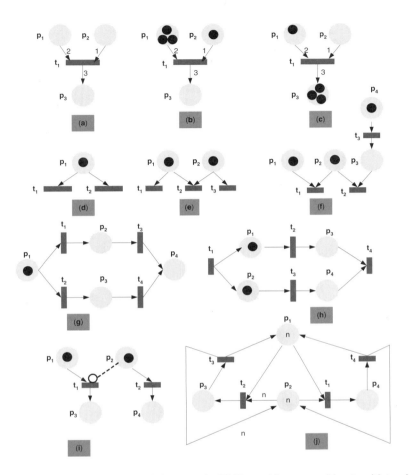

Fig. 3.2 Place Transition Nets. (a) An unmarked P/T net with one transition t_1 with two input places, p_1 and p_2 and one output place, p_3. (b)-(c) The net in (a) as a Marked P/T net before and after firing of transition t_1. (d) Modeling choice with P/T nets. Only one of transitions t_1, or t_2 may fire. (e) Symmetric confusion; transitions t_1 and t_3 are concurrent and, at the same time, they are in conflict with t_2. If t_2 fires, then t_1 and t_3 are disabled.y (f) Asymmetric confusion; transition t_1 is concurrent with t_3 and it is in conflict with t_2 if t_3 fires before t_1. (g) A state machine; there is the choice of firing t_1, or t_2; only one transition fires at any given time, concurrency is not possible. (h) A marked graph allows us to model concurrency but not choice; transitions t_2 and t_3 are concurrent, there is no causal relationship between them. (i) An extended P/T net used to model priorities. The arc from p_2 to t_1 is an inhibitor arc. The task modeled by transition t_1 is activated only after the task modeled by transition t_2 is activated. (j) Modeling exclusion: the net models n concurrent processes in a shared memory environment. At any given time only one process may write but all n may read. Transitions t_1 and t_2 model writing and respectively reading.

set of the output places of t_i. The *preset* of place p_j denoted as $\bullet p_j$ is the set of input transitions of p_j and the *postset* denoted by $p_j \bullet$ is the set of the output transitions of p_j

Figure 3.2(a) shows a P/T net with three places, p_1, p_2, and p_3, and one transition, t_1. The weights of the arcs from p_1 and p_2 to t_1 are two and one, respectively; the weight of the arc from t_1 to p_3 is three.

The preset of transition t_1 in Figure 3.2(a, b, c) consists of two places, $\bullet t_1 = \{p_1, p_2\}$ and its postset consist of only one place, $t_1 \bullet = \{p_3\}$. The preset of place p_4 in Figure 3.2(g) consists of transitions t_3 and t_4, $\bullet p_4 = \{t_3, t_4\}$ and the postset of p_1 is $p_1 \bullet = \{t_1, t_2\}$.

Definition – Source and Sink Transitions; Self-loops. A transition without any input place is called a *source transition* and one without any output place is called a *sink transition*. A pair consisting of a place p_i and a transition t_j is called a *self-loop* if p_i is both the input and output of t_j.

Transition t_1 in Figure 3.2(h) is a source transition, while t_4 is a sink transition.

Definition – Pure Net. A net is *pure* if there are no self loops.

Definition – Ordinary Net. A net is *ordinary* if the weights of all arcs are 1.

The nets in Figures 3.2(c, d, e, f, g, h) are ordinary nets, the weights of all arcs are 1.

Definition – Start and Final Places. A place without any input transitions is called a *start place* and one without any output transition is called a *final place*; p_s is a start place iff $\bullet p_s = \emptyset$ and p_f is a final place iff $p_f \bullet = \emptyset$.

Definition – Short-Circuit Net. Given a P/T net $N = (p, t, f, l)$ with one start place, p_s and one final place p_f the network $\tilde{N}$ obtained by connecting p_f to p_s with an additional transition $\tilde{t_k}$ labeled τ is called the short-circuit net associated with N.

$$\tilde{N} = (p, t \cup \{\tilde{t_k}\}, f \cup \{(p_f, \tilde{t_k}), (\tilde{t_k}, p_s)\}, l \cup \{(\tilde{t_k}, \tau)\})$$

Definition – Enabled Transition. A transition $t_i \in t$ of the ordinary net (N, s) *is enabled* iff each of its input places contain a token, $(N, s)[t_i > \Leftrightarrow \bullet t_i \in s$. Here s is the initial marking of the net. The fact that t_i is enabled is denoted as, $(N, s)[t_i >$.

The marking of a P/T net changes as a result of transition firing. A transition must be enabled in order to fire. The following firing rule governs the firing of a transition.

Definition – Firing Rule. *Firing of the transition t_i of the ordinary net (N, s) means that a token is removed from each of its input places and one token is added to each of its output places. Firing of transition t_i changes a marked net (N, s) into another marked net $(N, s - \bullet t_i + t_i \bullet)$.

Definition – Finite and Infinite Capacity Nets. The *capacity of a place* is the maximum number of tokens the place may hold. A net with places that can accommodate an infinite number of tokens is called an *infinite capacity net*. In a *finite capacity net* we denote by $K(p)$ the capacity of place p.

There are two types of firing rules for finite capacity nets, strict and weak, depending on the enforcement of the capacity constraint rule.

Definition – Strict and Weak Firing Rules. The *strict firing rule* allows an enabled transition t_i to fire iff after firing the transition t_i, the number of tokens in each place of its postset $p_j \in \bullet t_i$, does not exceed the capacity of that place $K(p_j)$. The *weak firing rule* does not require the firing to obey capacity constraints.

Figure 3.2(b) shows the same net as the one in Figure 3.2(a) with three token in place p_1 and one in p_2. Transition t_1 is enabled in the marked net in Figure 3.2(b); Figure 3.2(c) shows the same net after firing of transition t_1. The net in Figure 3.2(b) models synchronization; transition t_1 can only fire if the condition associated with the presence of two tokens in p_1 and one token in p_2 are satisfied.

In addition to regular arcs, a P/T net may have *inhibitor arcs* that prevent transitions to be enabled.

Definition – Extended P/T Nets. P/T nets with inhibitor arcs are called *extended P/T nets*.

Definition – Modified Transition Enabling Rule for Extended P/T Nets. A transition is not enabled if one of the places in its preset is connected with the transition with an inhibitor arc and if the place holds a token.

For example, transition t_1 in the net in Figure 3.2(i) is not enabled while place p_2 holds a token.

3.3 MODELING WITH PLACE/TRANSITION NETS

3.3.1 Conflict/Choice, Synchronization, Priorities, and Exclusion

P/T nets can be used to model concurrent activities. For example, the net in Figure 3.2(d) models *conflict* or *choice*; only one of the transitions t_1 and t_2 may fire but not both. Transition t_4 and its input places p_3 and p_4 in Figure 3.2(h) model synchronization; t_4 can only fire if the conditions associated with p_3 and p_4 are satisfied.

Two transitions are said to be *concurrent* if they are causally independent, as discussed in Chapter 2. Concurrent transitions may fire before, after, or in parallel with each other, as is the case of transitions t_2 and t_3 in Figure 3.2(h). The net in this figure models concurrent execution of two tasks, each one associated with one of the concurrent transitions and transition t_4 models synchronization of the two tasks.

When choice and concurrency are mixed, we end up with a situation called *confusion*. *Symmetric confusion* means that two or more transitions are concurrent and, at the same time, they are in conflict with another one. For example, in Figure 3.2 (e) transitions t_1 and t_3 are concurrent and in the same time they are in conflict with t_2. If t_2 fires either one or both of them will be disabled. *Asymmetric confusion* occurs when a transition t_1 is concurrent with another transition t_3 and will be in conflict with t_2 if t_3 fires before t_1 as shown in Figure 3.2 (f).

Place Transition Nets, can be used to model *priorities*. The net in Figure 3.2(i) models a system with two tasks, $task_1$ and $task_2$; $task_2$ has higher priority than $task_1$. Indeed, if both tasks are ready to run, both places p_1 and p_2 hold tokens. When both tasks are ready, transition t_2 will fire first, modeling the activation of

$task_2$. Only after t_2 is activated transition t_1, modeling of activation of $task_1$, will fire.

P/T nets are able to model *exclusion*. For example, the net in Figure 3.2(j), models a group of n concurrent tasks executing in a shared-memory environment. All tasks can read at the same time, but only one may write. Place p_3 models the tasks allowed to write, p_4 the ones allowed to read, p_2 the ones ready to access the shared memory and p_1 the running tasks. Transition t_2 models the initialization/selection of tasks allowed to write and t_1 of those allowed to read, whereas t_3 models the completion of a write and t_4 the completion of a read.

Indeed p_3 may have at most one token while p_4 may have at most n. If all n tasks are ready to access the shared memory all n tokens in p_2 are consumed when transition t_1 fires. However, place p_4 may contain n tokens obtained by successive firings of transition t_2.

3.3.2 State Machines and Marked Graphs

Structural properties allow us to partition the set of nets into several subclasses: (a) state machines, (b) marked graphs, (c) free-choice nets, (d) extended free-choice nets, and (e) asymmetric choice nets. This partitioning is based on the number of input and output flow relations from/to a transition or a place and by the manner in which transitions share input places as indicated in Figure 3.3.

Finite state machines can be modeled by a subclass of L-labeled P/T nets called *state machines* with the property that *each transition has exactly one incoming and one outgoing arc or flow relation*. This topological constraint limits the expressiveness

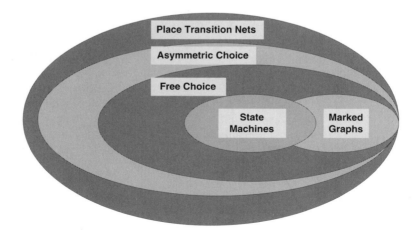

Fig. 3.3 Subclasses of Place Transition nets. State Machines do not model concurrency and synchronization; Marked Graphs do not model choice and conflict; Free Choice nets do not model confusion; Asymmetric-Choice Nets allow asymmetric confusion but not symmetric one.

of a state machine, no concurrency is possible. In the followings we consider marked state machines (N, s) where marking $s_0 \in s$ corresponds to the initial state.

For example, in the net from Figure 3.2(g) transitions t_1, t_2, t_3, and t_4 have only one input and output arc, the cardinality of their presets and postsets is one. No concurrency is possible; once a choice was made by firing either t_1, or t_2 the evolution of the system is entirely determined.

Recall that a marking/state reflects the disposition of tokens in the places of the net. For the net in Figure 3.2 (g) with four places, the marking is a 4-tuple (p_1, p_2, p_3, p_4). The markings of this net are $(1, 0, 0, 0), (0, 1, 0, 0), (0, 0, 1, 0), (0, 0, 0, 1)$.

Definition – State Machine. Given a marked P/T net, (N, s_0) with $N = (p, t, f, l)$ we say that N is a *state machine* iff $\forall t_i \in t \; (\mid \bullet t_i \mid = 1 \wedge \mid t_i \bullet \mid = 1)$.

State machines allow us to model choice or decision, because each place may have multiple output transitions, but does not allow modeling of synchronization or concurrent activities. Concurrent activities require that several transitions be enabled concurrently. The subclass of L-labeled P/T nets called *marked graphs* allow us to model concurrency.

Definition – Marked Graph. Given a marked P/T net, (N, s_0) with $N = (p, t, f, l)$ we say that N is a *marked graph* iff $\forall p_i \in p \mid \bullet p_i \mid = 1 \wedge \mid p_i \bullet \mid = 1$.

In a marked graph each place has only one incoming and one outgoing flow relation; thus, marked graphs do not allow modeling of choice.

3.3.3 Marking Independent Properties of P/T Nets

Dependence on the initial marking partitions the set of properties of a net into two groups: structural properties, those independent of the initial marking, and behavioral or marking-dependent properties. Strong connectedness and free-choice are examples of structural properties, whereas liveness, reachability, boundeness, persistance, coverability, fairness, and synchronic distance are behavioral properties.

Definition – Strongly Connected P/T Net. A P/T net $N = (p, t, f, l)$ is *strongly connnected* iff $\forall x, y \in p \cup t \quad x f^* y$.

Informally, strong connectedness means that there is a directed path from one element $x \in p \cup t$ to any other element $y \in p \cup t$. Strong connectedness is a static property of a net.

Definition – Free Choice, Extended Free Choice, and Asymmetric Choice P/T Nets. Given a marked P/T net, (N, s_0) with $N = (p, t, f, l)$ we say that N is a *free-choice net* iff

$$(\bullet t_i) \cap (\bullet t_j) = \emptyset \Rightarrow \mid \bullet t_i \mid = \mid \bullet t_j \mid.$$

when $\forall t_{i,j} \in t$.

N is an *extended free-choice net* if $\forall t_i, t_j \in t$ then $(\bullet t_i) \cap (\bullet t_j) = \emptyset \Rightarrow \bullet t_i = \bullet t_j$.
N is an *asymmetric choice net* iff $(\bullet t_i) \cap (\bullet t_j) \neq \emptyset \Rightarrow (\bullet t_i \subseteq \bullet t_j)$ or $(\bullet t_i \supseteq \bullet t_j)$.

In an extended free-choice net if two transition share an input place they must share all places in their presets. In an asymmetric choice net two transitions may share only a subset of their input places.

3.3.4 Marking Dependent Properties of P/T Nets

Definition – Firing Sequence. Given a marked P/T net, (N, s_0) with N = (p,t,f,l), a nonempty sequence of transitions $\sigma \in t^*$ is called a *firing sequence* iff there exist markings $s_1, s_2, ...s_n \in \mathcal{B}(p)$ and transitions $t_1, t_2, ...t_n \in t$ such that $\sigma = t_1 t_2 ....t_n$ and for $i \in (0, n)$, $(N, s_i)t_{i+1} >$ and $s_{i+1} = s_i - \bullet t_i + t_i \bullet$. All firing sequences that can be initiated from marking s_0 are denoted as $\sigma(s_0)$.

Firing of a transition changes the state or marking of a P/T net, the disposition of tokens into places is modified.

Reachability is the problem of finding if marking s_n is reachable from the initial marking s_0, $s_n \in \sigma(s_0)$. Reachability is a fundamental concern for dynamic systems. The reachability problem is decidable, but reachability algorithms require exponential time and space.

Definition – Liveness. A marked P/T net (N, s_0) is said to be *live* if it is possible to fire any transition starting from the initial marking, s_0. We recognize several levels of liveness of a P/T net. A transition t is

- *L0-live, dead* if it cannot be fired in any firing sequence in $\sigma(s_0)$,

- *L1-live, potentially firable* if it can be fired at least once in $\sigma(s_0)$,

- *L2-live* if given an integer k it can be fired at least k times in some firing sequence in $\sigma(s_0)$,

- *L3-live* if it appears infinitely often in some firing sequence in $\sigma(s_0)$.

The net in Figure 3.4(a) is live; in Figure 3.4(b) transition t_3 is L0-live, transition t_2 is L1-live, and transition t_1 is L3-live.

Corollary. The absence of deadlock in a system is guaranteed by the liveness of its net model.

Definition – Syphons and Traps. Given a P/T net N, a nonempty subset of places Q is called a *siphon/deadlock* if $(\bullet Q) \subseteq (Q \bullet)$ and it is called a *trap* if $(Q \bullet) \subseteq (\bullet Q)$.

In Figure 3.4(c) the subnet Q is a siphon; in Figure 3.4(d), the subnet R is a trap.

Definition – Boundedness. A marked P/T net (N, s_0) is said to be *k-bounded* if the number of tokens in each place does not exceed the finite number k for any reachable marking from s_0.

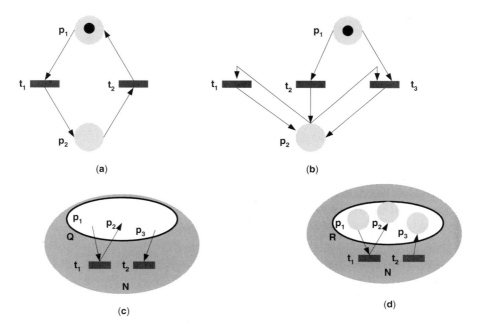

Fig. 3.4 Behavioral properties of P/T nets. The net in (a) is bounded, live, and reversible. In (b) transition t_3 is L0-live, transition t_2 is L1-live, and transition t_1 is L3-live. In (c) the subnet Q is a siphon. In (d) the subnet R is a trap.

Definition – Safety. A marked P/T net (N, s_0) is said to be *safe* if it is 1-bounded, for any reachable marking $s' \in [N, s_0 >$ and any place $p' \in p, s'(p) \le 1$.

Definition – Reversibility. A marked P/T net (N, s_0) is *reversible* if for any marking $s_n \in \sigma(s_0)$, the original marking s_0 is reachable from s_n. More generally a marking s' is a *home state* if for every marking $s \in \sigma(s_0)$, s' is reachable from s.

Reversibility of physical systems is desirable; we often require a system to return to some special state. For example, an interrupt vector defines a set of distinguished states of a computer system we want to return to, when an interrupt occurs. Reversibility is a property of a net necessary to model reversible physical systems; it guarantees that a net can go back to its initial marking.

Definition – Persistence. A marked P/T net (N, s_0) is *persistent* if for any pair of two transitions (t_i, t_j), firing of one does not disable the other.

Persistency is a property of conflict-free nets, e.g., all marked graphs are persistent because they do not allow conflicts and choice. Moreover, a safe persistent net can be transformed into a marked graph by duplicating some places and transitions.

Definition – Synchronic Distance. Given a marked P/T net (N, s_0), the *synchronic distance* between two transitions t_i and t_j is $d_{i,j} = max|\bar{\sigma}(t_i) - \bar{\sigma}(t_j)|$, with σ a firing sequence and $\bar{\sigma}(t_i)$ the number of times transition t_i fires in σ.

The synchronic distance gives a measure of dependency between two transitions. For example, in Figure 3.2(j) $d(t_2, t_3) = 1$, and $d(t_1, t_2) = \infty$. Indeed, once a task is allowed to write, it will always complete the writing, while reading and writing are independent.

Definition – Fairness. Given a marked P/T net (N, s_0), two transitions t_i and t_j, are in a *bounded-fair, B-fair,* relation if the maximum number one of them is allowed to fire while the other one not firing is bounded. If all pairs of transitions are in a B-fair relation then the P/T net is a *B-fair net*. A firing sequence σ is *unconditionally fair* if every transition in σ appears infinitely often.

Definition – Coverability. A marking s of a marked P/T net (N, s_0), is *coverable* if there exist another marking s' such that for every place p, $s'(p) \geq s(p)$, with $s(p)$ denoting the number of tokens in p under marking s.

Coverability is related to L1-liveness.

3.3.5   Petri Net Languages

Consider a finite alphabet $\mathcal{A} = a, b, c, d, ...w$ with w the null symbol. Given a marked P/T net, $N = (p, t, f, l)$ with a start place p_s and a final place p_f, $p_s, p_f \in p$, let us label every transition $t_i \in t$ with one symbol from $\mathcal{A}$. Multiple transitions may have the same label.

Definition – Petri net Language. The set of strings generated by every possible firing sequence of the net N with initial marking $M_0 = (1, 0, 0, ...0)$, when only the start place holds a token, and terminates when all transitions are disabled, defines a language $L(M_0)$.

Example. The set of strings generated by all possible firing sequences of the net in Figure 3.5 with the initial marking M_0, defines the Petri net language

$$L(M_0) = \{(ef)^m (a)^n (b)^p (c)^q \ \ m \geq 0, 0 \leq n < 2, p \geq 0, q \geq 0, \}.$$

Every state machine can be modeled by a Petri net, thus every regular language is a Petri net language. Moreover it has been proved that all Petri net languages are context sensitive [24].

3.4   STATE EQUATIONS

Definition – Incidence Matrix. Given a P/T net with n transitions and m places, the *incidence matrix* $F = [f_{i,j}]$ is an integer matrix with $f_{i,j} = w(i, j) - w(j, i)$. Here $w(i, j)$ is the weight of the flow relation (arc) from transition t_i to its output place p_j, and $w(j, i)$ is the weight of the arc from the input place p_j to transition t_i. In this expression $w(i, j)$ represents the number of tokens added to the output place p_j and $w(j, i)$ the ones removed from the input place p_j when transition t_i fires. F^T is the transpose of the incidence matrix.

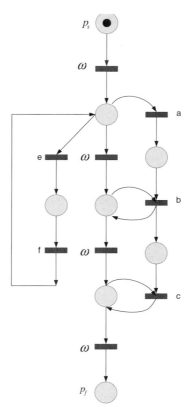

Fig. 3.5 A Petri net language $\{(ef)^m(a)^n(b)^p(c)^q \; m \geq 0, 0 \leq n < 2, p \geq 0, q \geq 0\}$.

A marking s_k can be written as a $m \times 1$ column vector and its j-th entry denotes the number of tokens in place j after some transition firing.

The necessary and sufficient condition for transition t_i to be enabled at a marking s is that $w(j, i) \leq s(j) \; \forall s_j \in \bullet t_i$, the weight of the arc from every input place of the transition, must be smaller or equal to the number of tokens in the corresponding input place.

Consider a firing sequence σ and let the k-th transition in this sequence be t_i. In other words, the k-th firing in σ will be that of transition t_i. Call s_{k-1} and s_k the states/markings before and after the k-th firing and u_k the firing vector, an integer $n \times 1$ row vector with a 1 for the k-th component and 0's elsewhere.

The dynamic behavior of the P/T net N is characterized by the state equation relating consecutive states/markings in a firing sequence:

$$s_k = s_{k-1} + F^T u_k.$$

Reachability can be expressed using the incidence matrix. Indeed, consider a firing sequence of length d, $\sigma = u_1 u_2, ... u_d$ from the initial marking s_0 to the current marking s_q. Then:

$$s_q = s_0 + F^T \sum_{k=1}^{d} u_k$$

or

$$F^T x = \Delta s$$

with $x = \sum_{k=1}^{d} u_k$ called a *firing count vector*, an $n \times 1$ column vector of non-negative integers whose i-th component indicates how many times transition t_i must fire to transform the marking s_0 into s_q with $\Delta s = s_q - s_0$.

Definition – T and S invariant. An integer solution of the equation $F^T x = 0$ is called a T invariant. An integer solution of the equation $Fy = 0$ is called an S invariant.

Intuitively, place invariants of a net with all flow relations (arcs) of weight 1 are sets of places that do not change their token count during firing of transitions; transition invariants indicate how often, starting from some marking, each transition has to fire to reproduce that marking.

3.5   PROPERTIES OF PLACE/TRANSITION NETS

The liveness, safeness and boundedess are orthogonal properties of a P/T net, a net may posses one of them independently of the others. For example, the net in Figure 3.4(a) is live, bounded, safe, and reversible. Transitions t_1 and t_2 are L3-live, the number of tokens in p_1 and p_2 is limited to one and marking $(1, 0)$ can be reached from $(0, 1)$. The net in Figure 3.4(b) is not live, it is bounded, safe, and not reversible.

A number of transformations, e.g., fusion of Series/Parallel Places/Transitions preserve the liveness, safeness, and boundedss of a net as seen in Figure 3.6

We now present several well-known results in net theory. The proof of the following theorems is beyond the scope of this book and can be found elsewhere.

Theorem – Live and Safe Marked P/T Nets. If a marked P/T net (N, s_0) is live and safe then N is strongly connected. The reciprocal is not true, there are strongly connected nets that are not live and safe. The net in Figure 3.4(d) is an example of a strongly connected network that is not live.

State machines enjoy special properties revealed by the following theorem.

Theorem – Live and Safe State Machines. A state machine (N, s_0) is live and safe iff N is strongly connected and if marking s_0 has exactly one token.

A marked graph can be represented by a directed graph with nodes corresponding to the transitions and arcs corresponding to places of the marked graph. The presence of tokens in a place is shown as a token on the corresponding arc. Firing of a transition corresponds to removing a token from each of the input arcs of a node of the directed graph and placing them on the output arcs of that node. A directed circuit in the

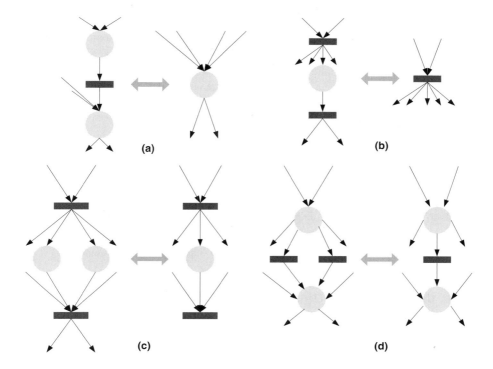

Fig. 3.6 Transformations preserving liveness, safeness, and boundedess of a net. (a) Fusion of Series Places. (b) Fusion of Series Transitions. (c) Fusion of Parallel Places. (d) Fusion of Parallel Transitions.

directed graph consists of a path starting and terminating in the same node. In this representation a marked graph consists of a number of connected directed circuits.

Theorem – Live Marked Graph. A marked graph (N, s_0) is live iff marking s_0 places at least one token on each directed circuit in N.

Indeed, the number of tokens in a directed circuit is invariant under any firing. If a directed circuit contains no tokens at the initial marking, then no tokens can be injected into it at a later point in time, thus, no transitions in that directed circuit can be enabled.

Theorem – Safe Marked Graph. A live marked graph (N, s_0) is safe iff every place belongs to a directed circuit and the total count of tokens in that directed circuit in the initial marking s_0 is equal to one.

Theorem – Live Free-Choice Net. A free-choice net (N, s_0) is live iff every syphon in N contains a marked trap.

We now present two theorems that show that a live and safe free-choice net can be seen as the interconnection of live and safe state-machines, or, equivalently, the interconnection of live and safe marked graphs.

A state machine component of a net N is a subnet constructed from places and transitions in N such that each transition has at most one incoming and one outgoing arc and the subnet includes all the input and output places of these transitions and the connecting arcs. A marked graph component of a net N is a subnet constructed from places and transitions in N such that each place has at most one incoming and one outgoing arc and the subnet includes all the input and output places of these transitions and the connecting arcs.

Theorem – Safe Free-Choice Nets and State Machines. A live free-choice net (N, s_0) is safe iff N is covered by strongly connected state machine components and each component state machine has exactly one token in s_0.

Theorem – Safe Free-Choice Nets and Marked Graphs. A live and safe free-choice net (N, s_0) is covered by strongly connected marked graph components.

3.6   COVERABILITY ANALYSIS

Given a net (N, s_0) we can identify all transitions enabled in the initial marking s_0 and fire them individually to reach new markings; then in each of the markings reached in the previous stage we can fire, one by one, the transitions enabled and continue ad infinitum.

In this manner we can construct a tree of all markings reachable from the initial one; if the net is unbounded, this tree will grow continually. To prevent this undesirable effect we use the concept of a coverable marking introduced earlier.

Recall that a marking s of a marked P/T net (N, s_0) with $|P|$ places is a vector, $(s(p_1), s(p_2), s(p_3), \dots s(p_i), \dots s(p_{|P|}))$; component $s(p_i)$ gives the number of tokens in place p_i. Marking s is said to be coverable if there exists another marking s' such that for every place, the number of tokens in p_i under marking s' is larger, or at least equal to the one under marking s, $s'(p_i) \geq s(p_i)$, $1 \leq i \leq |P|$.

For example, in Figure 3.7(a) the initial marking is $(1, 0, 0)$, one token in place p_1 and zero tokens in p_2 and p_3. In this marking two transitions are enabled, t_1 and t_5. When t_1 fires we reach the marking $(1, 0, 1)$ and when t_5 fires we stay in the same marking, $(1, 0, 0)$. Marking $(1, 0, 1)$ covers $(1, 0, 0)$.

We discuss now the formal procedure to construct the finite tree representation of the markings. First, we introduce a symbol ω with the following properties: given any integer n, $\omega > n$, $\omega \pm n = \omega$, and $\omega \geq \omega$. Each node will be labeled with the corresponding marking and tagged with the symbol *new* when it is visited for the first time, *old* when it is revisited, or *dead end* if no transitions are enabled in the marking the node is labeled with. The algorithm to construct the coverability tree is:

- Label the root of the tree with the initial marking s_0 and tag it as *new*.

- While nodes tagged as *new* exist do:

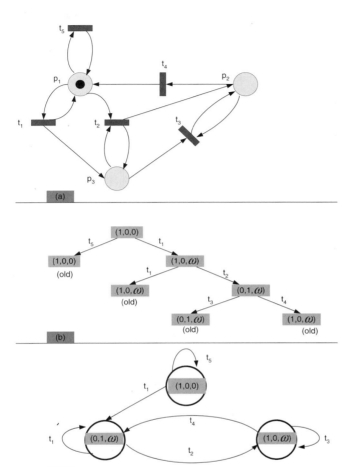

Fig. 3.7 (a) A Petri net. (b) The coverability tree of the net in (a). (c) The coverability graph of the net in (a).

- Select a node tagged as *new* labeled with marking s.
- If there is another node in the tree on the path from the root to the current node with the same label s, then tag the current node as *old* and go to the first step.
- If no transitions are enabled in marking s then tag the node as *dead end* and go to the first step.
- For all transitions t_j enabled in marking s:
  * fire t_j and determine the new marking s',
  * add a new node to the graph,

* connect the new node to the parent node by an arc labeled t_j,
* tag the new node as *new*, and
* determine the label of this node as follows: if on the path from the root to the parent node exists a node labeled $s'' \neq s'$ such that s' is coverable by s'' then identify all places p_i such that $s'(p_i) > s''(p_i)$ and replace $s'(p_i) = \omega$; else label the new node s'.

Figure 3.7(b) illustrates the construction of the coverabilty graph for the net in Figure 3.7(a). As pointed out earlier, marking $(1, 0, 1)$ covers $(1, 0, 0)$ thus the node in the graph resulting after firing transition t_1 in marking $(1, 0, 0)$ is labeled $(1, 0, \omega)$.

From the coverability tree T we can immediately construct the coverability graph G of the net, as shown in Figure 3.7(c). G is the state transition graph of the system modeled by the Petri net.

In our example, the net can only be in one of three states, $(1, 0, 0), (1, 0, \omega), (0, 1, \omega)$; transition t_5 leads to a self-loop in marking $(1, 0, 0)$, transition t_1 to a self-loop in state $(1, 0, \omega)$, and transition t_3 to a self-loop in marking $(0, 1, \omega)$. Transition t_2 takes the net from the marking $(1, 0, \omega)$ to $(0, 1, \omega)$ and transition t_4 does the opposite. Firing transition $t2$ in marking $(1, 0, \omega)$ leads to the marking $(0, 1, \omega)$, and so on.

The coverability tree, T, is very useful to study the properties of a net, (N, s_0). We can also identify all the markings s' reachable from a given marking s. If a transition does not appear in the coverabilty tree, it means that it will never be enabled; it is a dead transition. If the symbol ω does not appear in any of the node labels of T, then the net is bounded. If the labels of all nodes contain only 0's and 1's then the net is safe.

3.7   APPLICATIONS OF STOCHASTIC PETRI NETS TO PERFORMANCE ANALYSIS

In this section we introduce SPNs, and SHLPNs. Then we present an application.

3.7.1   Stochastic Petri Nets

SPNs are obtained by associating with each transition in a Petri net a possibly marking dependent transition rate for the exponentially distributed firing time.

Definition. An SPN is a quintuple:

$$SPN = (p, t, f, s, \lambda)$$

1. p is the set of places.
2. t is the set of transitions.
3. $p \cap t = \emptyset, p \cup t \neq \emptyset$.
4. f is the set of input and output arcs; $f \subseteq (p \times t) \cup (t \times p)$.
5. s is the initial marking.
6. λ is the set of transition rates.

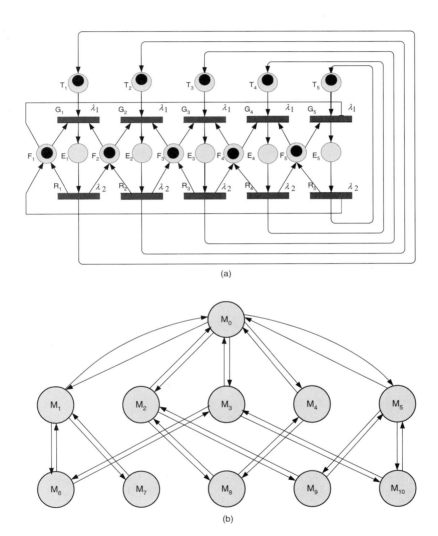

(a)

(b)

Fig. 3.8   (a) The SPN model of the philosopher system. (b) The state transition diagram of the system.

The SPNs are isomorphic to continuous time Markov chains due to the memoryless property of the exponential distribution of firing times. The SPN markings correspond to the states of the corresponding Markov chain so that the SPN model allows the calculation of the steady-state and transient system behavior.

In SPN analysis, as in Markov analysis, ergodic (irreducible) systems are of special interest. For ergodic SPN systems, the steady-state probability of the system being in any state always exists and is independent of the initial state. If the firing rates do not depend on time, a stationary (homogeneous) Markov chain is obtained. In particular, k-bounded SPNs are isomorphic to finite Markov chains. We consider only ergodic, stationary, and k-bounded SPNs (or SHLPNs) and Markov chains.

Example of SPN modeling. Consider a group of five philosophers who spend some time thinking between copious meals. There are only five forks on a circular table and there is a fork between two philosophers. Each philosopher needs the two adjacent forks. When they become free, the philosopher hesitates for a random time, exponentially distributed with average $1/\lambda_1$, and then moves from the thinking phase to the eating phase where he spends an exponentially distributed time with average $1/\lambda_2$. This system is described by the SPN in Figure 3.8(a). The model has 15 places and 10 transitions, all indexed on variable i; $i \in [1, 5]$ in the following description.

T_i is the "thinking" place. If T_i holds a token, the ith philosopher is pretending to think while waiting for forks.

E_i is the "eating" place. If E_i holds a token, the ith philosopher is eating.

F_i is the "free fork" place. If F_i holds a token, the ith fork is free.

G_i is the "getting forks" transition. This transition is enabled when the hungry philosopher can get the two adjacent forks. The transition firing time is associated with $1/\lambda_1$ and it is related to the time the philosopher hesitates before taking the two forks and starting to eat.

R_i is the "releasing forks" transition. A philosopher releases the forks and returns to the thinking stage after the eating time exponentially distributed with average $1/\lambda_2$.

The SPN model of the philosopher system has a state space size of 11 and its states (markings) are presented in Table 3.1. The state transition diagram of the corresponding Markov chain is shown in Figure 3.8(b). The steady-state probabilities that the system is in state i, p_i, can be obtained:

$$
p_i = \begin{cases}
\dfrac{\lambda_2^2}{5\lambda_1(\lambda_1 + \lambda_2) + \lambda_2^2} & i = 0 \\[3ex]
\dfrac{\lambda_1\lambda_2}{5\lambda_1(\lambda_1 + \lambda_2) + \lambda_2^2} & i = 1, 2, 3, 4, 5 \\[3ex]
\dfrac{\lambda_1^2}{5\lambda_1(\lambda_1 + \lambda_2) + \lambda_2^2} & i = 6, 7, 8, 9, 10.
\end{cases}
$$

Table 3.1 The markings of the philosopher system in the SPN modeling example.

	T_1	T_2	T_3	T_4	T_5	E_1	E_2	E_3	E_4	E_5	F_1	F_2	F_3	F_4	F_5
M_0	1	1	1	1	1						1	1	1	1	1
M_1		1	1	1	1	1							1	1	1
M_2	1		1	1	1		1				1			1	1
M_3	1	1		1	1			1			1	1			1
M_4	1	1	1		1				1		1	1	1		
M_5	1	1	1	1						1		1	1	1	
M_6		1		1	1	1		1							1
M_7		1	1		1	1			1				1		
M_8	1		1		1		1		1		1				
M_9	1		1	1			1			1				1	
M_{10}	1	1		1				1		1		1			

3.7.2 Informal Introduction to SHLPNs

Our objective is to model the same system using a representation that leads to a model with a smaller number of states. The following notation is used throughout this section: $a \oplus b \pmod{p}$ stands for addition modulo p. $|\{\}|$ denotes the cardinality of a set. The relations between the element and the set, $\in$ and $\notin$, are often used in the predicates.

The SHLPNs will be introduced by means of an example that illustrates the fact than an SHLPN model is a scaled down version of an SPN model, it has a smaller number of places, transitions, and states than the original SPN model. Figure 3.9(a) presents the SHLPN model of the same philosopher system described in Figure 3.8 using an SPN. In the SHLPN model, each place and each transition stands for a set of places or transitions in the SPN model. The number of places is reduced from 15 to 3, the place T stands for the set $\{T_i\}$, E stands for $\{E_i\}$, and F stands for $\{F_i\}$, for $i \in [1, 5]$. The number of transitions is reduced from ten to two; the transition G stands for the set $\{G_i\}$ and R stands for the set $\{R_i\}$ with $i \in [1, 5]$.

The three places contain two types of tokens, the first type is associated with the philosophers and the second is associated with forks, see Figure 3.9(a). The arcs are labeled by the token variables. A token has a number of attributes, the first attribute is the type and the second attribute the *identity*, *id*.

The tokens residing in the place E, the eating place, have four attributes; the last two attributes are the *ids* of the forks currently used by the philosopher. The transition G is associated with the predicate which specifies the correct relation between a philosopher and the two forks used by him. The predicate inscribed on transition G, see Figure 3.9(a), as $i = j$ is a concise form of expressing that the second attribute of a (p, i) token should be equal to the second attribute of the two tokens representing the forks. This means that a philosopher can eat only when two adjacent forks are free;

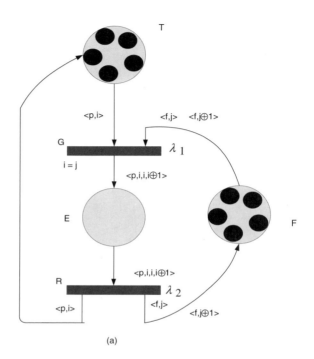

(a)

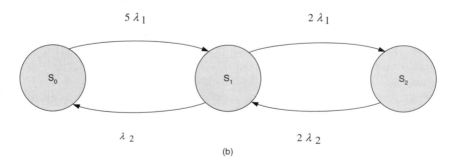

(b)

Fig. 3.9 (a) The SHLPN model of the philosopher system. (b) The state transition diagram of the philosopher system with compound markings.

for example, the forks $(f, 3)$ and $(f, 4)$ must be free in order to allow the philosopher $(p, 3)$ to move to the eating place.

A predicate expresses an imperative condition that must be met in order for a transition to fire. A predicate should not be used to express the results associated with the firing of a transition. There is no predicate associated with transition R in Figure 3.9(a), although there is a well-defined relationship between the attributes of the tokens released when R fires.

In an SHLPN model, the transition rate associated with every transition is related to the markings that enable that particular transition. To simplify the design of the model, only the transition rate of the individual markings is shown in the graph, instead of the transition rate of the corresponding compound markings. For example, in Figure 3.9(a), the transition rates are written as λ_1 for the transition G and λ_2 for the transition R.

As shown in Figure 3.9(b) the system has three states, S_i with $i \in [0,1,2]$ representing the number of philosophers in the eating place. The actual transition rates corresponding to the case when the transition G fires are $5 \times \lambda_1$ and $2 \times \lambda_1$ depending on the state of the system when the transition G fires. If the system is in state S_0, then there are five different philosophers who can go to the eating place; hence, the actual transition rate is $5 \times \lambda_1$.

The problem of determining the compound markings and the transition rates among them is discussed in the following. The markings (states) of the philosopher system based on HLPN are given in Table 3.2. The initial population of different places is five tokens in T, five tokens in F, and no token in E. When one or more philosophers are eating, E contains one or more tokens.

In many systems, a number of different processes have a similar structure and behavior. To simplify the system model, it is desirable to treat similar processes in a uniform and succinct way. In the HLPN models, a token type may be associated with the process type and the number of tokens with the same type attribute may be associated with the number of identical processes. A process description, a subnet, can specify the behavior of a type of process and defines variables unique to each process of that type. Each process is a particular and independent instance of an execution of a process description (subnet).

The tokens present in SHLPNs have several attributes: type, identity, environment, etc. In order to introduce compound markings, such attributes are represented by variables with a domain covering the set of values of the attribute.

In the philosopher system, we can use a variable i to replace the *identity* attribute of the philosopher and the *environment variable* attribute representing fork tokens to each philosopher process. The domain set of the variable i is [1,5], i.e., the (p, i) represents anyone among $(p, 1)$, $(p, 2)$, $(p, 3)$, $(p, 4)$, $(p, 5)$, and the (f, i), represents anyone among $(f, 1)$, $(f, 2)$, $(f, 3)$, $(f, 4)$, $(f, 5)$. The compound marking (state) table of the philosopher system is shown in Table 3.3. The size of the state space is reduced compared to the previous case. Our compound marking concept is convenient for computing the reachability set and for understanding the behavior of the system modeled.

Table 3.2 The states of the philosopher system with individual markings. Each state is described by the disposition of all tokens in every place.

State	Place		
	T	E	F
0	$< p, 1 >, < p, 2 >, < p, 3 >,$ $< p, 4 >, < p, 5 >$	0	$< f, 1 >, < f, 2 >, < f, 3 >$ $< f, 4 >, < f, 5 >$
1	$< p, 2 >, < p, 3 >, < p, 4 >,$ $< p, 5 >$	$< p, 1, 1, 2 >$	$< f, 3 >, < f, 4 >, < f, 5 >$
2	$< p, 1 >, < p, 3 >, < p, 4 >,$ $< p, 5 >$	$< p, 2, 2, 3 >$	$< f, 1 >, < f, 4 >, < f, 5 >$
3	$< p, 1 >, < p, 2 >, < p, 4 >,$ $< p, 5 >$	$< p, 3, 3, 4 >$	$< f, 1 >, < f, 2 >, < f, 5 >$
4	$< p, 1 >, < p, 2 >, < p, 3 >,$ $< p, 5 >$	$< p, 4, 4, 5 >$	$< f, 1 >, < f, 2 >, < f, 3 >$
5	$< p, 1 >, < p, 2 >, < p, 3 >,$ $< p, 4 >$	$< p, 5, 5, 1 >$	$< f, 2 >, < f, 3 >, < f, 4 >$
6	$< p, 2 >, < p, 4 >, < p, 5 >$	$< p, 1, 1, 2 >,$ $< p, 3, 3, 4 >$	$< f, 5 >$
7	$< p, 2 >, < p, 3 >, < p, 5 >$	$< p, 1, 1, 2 >,$ $< p, 4, 4, 5 >$	$< f, 3 >$
8	$< p, 1 >, < p, 3 >, < p, 5 >$	$< p, 2, 2, 3 >,$ $< p, 4, 4, 5 >$	$< f, 1 >$
9	$< p, 1 >, < p, 3 >, < p, 4 >$	$< p, 2, 2, 3 >,$ $< p, 5, 5, 1 >$	$< f, 4>$
10	$< p, 1 >, < p, 2 >, < p, 4 >,$	$< p, 3, 3, 4 >,$ $< p, 5, 5, 1 >$	$< f, 2>$

The markings of Table 3.3 correspond to the Markov chain states shown in Figure 3.9(b) and are obtained by grouping the states from Figure 3.8(a). The transition rates between the grouped states (compound markings) can be obtained after determining the number of possible transitions from one individual marking in each compound marking to any individual marking in another compound marking. In our case, there

Table 3.3 The states of the philosopher system with compound markings

State	Place		
	T	E	F
0	$<p,i>,<p,i\oplus1>,$ $<p,i\oplus2>,$ $<p,i\oplus3>$ $<p,i\oplus4>$	0	$<f,i>,<f,i\oplus1>,$ $<f,i\oplus2>,$ $<f,i\oplus3>$ $<f,i\oplus4>$
1	$<p,i\oplus1>,$ $<p,i\oplus2>,$ $<p,i\oplus3>,$ $<p,i\oplus4>$	$<p,i,i\oplus1>$	$<f,i\oplus2>,$ $<f,i\oplus3>$ $<f,i\oplus4>$
2	$<p,i\oplus1>,$ $<p,i\oplus3>,$ $<p,i\oplus4>$	$<p,i,i\oplus1>,$ $<p,i\oplus2,i\oplus2,i\oplus3>$	$<f,i\oplus4>$

is one possible transition from only one individual marking of the compound marking S_0 to each individual marking of the compound marking S_1 with the same rate. So, the transition rate from S_0 to S_1 is $5\lambda_1$. Using a similar argument, we can obtain the transition rate from S_1 to S_2 as $2\lambda_2$, and from S_1 to S_0 as λ_2. The steady-state probabilities of each compound marking (grouped Markov state) can be obtained as

$$p_0 = \frac{\lambda_2^2}{5\lambda_1(\lambda_1+\lambda_2)+\lambda_2^2},$$

$$p_1 = \frac{5\lambda_1\lambda_2}{5\lambda_1(\lambda_1+\lambda_2)+\lambda_2^2},$$

$$p_2 = \frac{5\lambda_1^2}{5\lambda_1(\lambda_1+\lambda_2)+\lambda_2^2}.$$

The probability of every individual marking of a compound marking is the same and can be easily obtained since the number of individual markings in each compound marking is known.

The previous example has presented the advantage of using high-level Petri nets augmented with exponentially distributed firing times.

3.7.3   Formal Definition of SHLPNs

Definition A high-level Petri net, HLPN consists of the following elements.

1. A directed graph (p, t, f) where

   p is the set of places

   t is the set of transitions

   f is the set of arcs; $f \subseteq (p \times t) \cup (t \times p)$

2. A structure of Σ consisting of some types of individual tokens (u_i) together with some operations (op_i) and relations (r_i), i.e. $\Sigma = (u_i, ..., u_n; op_1, ..., op_m; r_1, ..., r_k)$.

3. A labeling of arcs with a formal sum of n attributes of token variables (including the zero attributes indicating a no-argument token).

4. An inscription on some transitions being a logical formula constructed from the operation and relations of the structure Σ and variables occurring at the surrounding arcs.

5. A marking of places in p with n attributes of individual tokens.

6. A natural number k that assigns to the places an upper bound for the number of copies of the same token.

7. *Firing rule*: Each element of t represents a class of possible changes of markings. Such a change, also called *transition firing*, consists of removing tokens from a subset of places and adding them to other subsets according to the expressions labeling the arcs. A transition is enabled whenever, given an assignment of individual tokens to the variables which satisfies the predicate associated with the transition, all input places carry enough copies of proper tokens, and the capacity K of all output places will not be exceeded by adding the respective copies of tokens. The *state space of the system* consists of the set of all markings connected to the initial marking through such occurrences of firing.

Definition A continuous time stochastic high-level Petri net is an HLPN extended with the set of markings related, transition rates, $\lambda = \{\lambda_1, \lambda_2, ..., \lambda_R\}$. The value of R is determined by the cardinality of the reachability set of the net.

To have an equivalence between a timed Petri net and the stochastic model of the system represented by the net, the following two elements need to be specified:

(i) the rules for choosing from the set of enabled transitions the one that fires, and

(ii) the conditioning based on the past history.

The sojourn time in any state is given by the minimum among the exponential random variables associated with the transitions enabled by that particular state. The

SHLPNs do not have immediate transitions. The predicate associated with a transition performs the selection function using the attributes of the tokens in the input places of the transition. A one-to-one correspondence between each marking of a stochastic high-level Petri net and a state of a Markov chain representing the same system can be established.

Theorem. Any finite place, finite transition, stochastic high-level Petri net is isomorphic to a one-dimensional, continuous-time, finite Markov chain.

As in the case of SPNs, this isomorphism is based on the marking sequence and not on the transition sequence. Any number of transitions between the same two markings is indistinguishable.

3.7.4 Compound Marking of an SHLPN

The compound marking concept is based on the fact that a number of entities processed by the system exhibit an identical behavior and they have a single subnet in the SHLPN model. The only distinction between such entities is the *identity* attribute of the token carried by the entity. If, in addition, the system consists of identical processing elements distinguished only by the identity attribute of the corresponding tokens, it is possible to lump together a number of markings in order to obtain a more compact SHLPN model of the system. Clearly, the model can be used to determine the global system performance in case of homogeneous systems when individual elements are indistinguishable.

Definition. A compound marking of an SHLPN is the result of partitioning an individual SHLPN marking into a number of disjoint sets such that:

(i) the individual markings in a given compound marking have the same distribution of tokens in places, except for the identity attribute of tokens of the same type,

(ii) all individual markings in the same compound marking have the same transition rates to all other compound markings.

Let us now consider a few properties of the compound marking.

(i) A compound marking enables all transitions enabled by all individual markings lumped into it.

(ii) If the individual reachability set of an SHLPN is finite, its compound reachability set is finite.

(iii) If the initial individual marking is reachable with a nonzero probability from any individual marking in the individual reachability set, the SHLPN initial compound marking is reachable with a nonzero probability from any compound marking in the compound reachability set.

We denote by p_{ij} the probability of a transition from the compound marking i to the compound marking j and by $p_{i_n j_k}$ the probability of a transition from the individual marking i_n to the individual marking j_k, where $i_n \in i$ and $j_k \in j$. The relation between the transition probability of individual markings is

$$p_{ij} = \sum_k p_{i_n j_k}.$$

The relation between the transition rate of compound markings and the transition rate of individual markings is

$$q_j(t) = \frac{d\left(\sum_i p_{ij}\right)}{dt} = \frac{\sum_i d\left(\sum_k p_{i_n j_k}\right)}{dt}.$$

$$q_{ij}(t) = \frac{dp_{ij}}{dt} = \frac{\sum_k d(p_{i_n j_k})}{dt}.$$

If the system is ergodic, then the sojourn time in each compound marking is an exponentially distributed random variable with average

$$\left[\sum_{i \in h} (q_{jk})_i\right]^{-1}.$$

where h is the set of transitions that are enabled by the compound marking and q_{jk} is the transition rate associated with the transition i firing on the current compound marking j.

Since there is an isomorphism between stochastic high-level Petri nets and Markov chains, any compound markings of an SHLPN correspond to grouping or lumping of states in the Markov domain.

In order to be useful, a compound marking must induce a correct grouping in the Markov domain corresponding to the original SHLPN. Otherwise, the methodology known from Markov analysis, used to establish whether the system is stable and to determine the steady-state probabilities of each compound marking, cannot be applied. The compound marking of an SHLPN induces a partition of the Markov state space that satisfies the conditions for grouping.

3.7.5   Modeling and Performance Analysis of a Multiprocessor System Using SHLPNs

We concentrate our attention on *homogeneous systems*. Informally, we define a homogeneous system as one consisting of identical processing elements that carry out identical tasks. When modeled using SHLPNs, these systems have subsets of *equivalent* states. Such states can be grouped together in such a way that the SHLPN model of the system with compound markings contains only one *compound state* for each

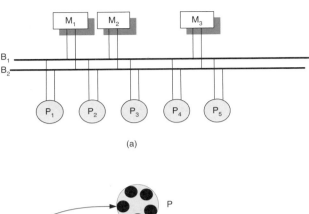

(a)

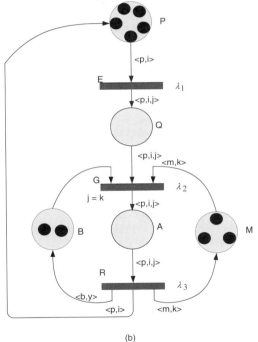

(b)

Fig. 3.10   (a) The configuration of the multiprocessor system used in SHLPN modeling. (b) The SHLPN model of the multiprocessor system.

group of *individual states* in the original SPN model. In this case, an *equivalence relationship* exists among the SHLPN model with compound markings and the original SPN model.

To assess the modeling power of SHLPNs, we consider now a multiprocessor system as shown in Figure 3.10 (a). Clearly, the performance of a multiprocessor system depends on the level of contention for the interconnection network and for the common memory modules.

There are two basic paradigms for interprocessor communication determined by the architecture of the system, namely, message passing and communication through shared memory. The analysis carried out in this section is designed for shared memory communication, but it can be extended to accommodate message passing systems. To model the system, we assume that each processor executes in a number of domains and that the execution speed of a given processor is a function of the execution domain. The model assumes that a random time is needed for the transition from one domain to another.

First, we describe the basic architecture of a multiprocessor system and the assumptions necessary for system modeling, then we present the SHLPN model of the system. The methodology to construct a model with a minimal state space is presented and the equilibrium equations of the system are solved using Markov chain techniques. Performance analysis is based on the steady-state probabilities associated with system states.

3.7.5.1 *System Description and Modeling Assumptions.* As shown in
Figure 3.10(a), a multiprocessor system consists of a set of n processors $P = \{P_1, P_2, \cdots, P_n\}$ interconnected by means of an interconnection network to a set of q common memory modules $M = \{M_1, M_2, \cdots, M_q\}$. The simplest topology of the interconnection network is a set of r buses $B = \{B_1, B_2, \cdots, B_r\}$. Each processor is also connected to a private memory module through a private bus.

As a general rule, the time to perform a given operation depends on whether the operands are in local memory or in the common one. When more than one processor is active in common memory, the time for a common memory reference increases due to contention for buses. The load factor ρ, is defined as the ratio between the time spent in an execution region located in the common domain and the time spent in an execution region located in the private domain.

A common measure of the multiprocessor system performance is the processing power of a system with n identical processors expressed as a fraction of the maximum processing power (n times the processing power of a single processor executing in its private memory). Consider an application decomposed into n identical processes; in this case the actual processing power of the system depends on the ratio between local memory references and common memory ones.

The purpose of our study is to determine the resource utilization when the load factor increases. The basic assumptions of our model are:

(i) All processor exhibit identical behavior for the class of applications considered. It is assumed that the computations performed by all processors are similar and they have the same pattern of memory references. More precisely, it is assumed that each processor spends an exponentially distributed random time with mean $1/\lambda_1$, while executing in its private domain and then an exponentially distributed random time with mean $1/\lambda_3$ while executing in a common domain. We assume that after finishing an execution sequence in private memory, each processor draws a random number k, uniformly distributed into the set $[1, q]$, which determines the module where its next common memory reference will be. This assumption reflects the fact that common memory references are evenly spread into the set of available common memory modules.

(ii) The access time to common memory modules has the same distribution for all modules and there is no difference in access time when different buses are used.

(iii) When a processor acquires a bus it starts its execution sequence in the common memory and it releases the bus only after completing its execution sequence in the common domain.

The first assumption is justified since common mapping algorithms tend to decompose a given parallel problem into a number of identical processes, one for every processor available in the system. The second and the third assumptions are clearly realistic due to hardware considerations.

3.7.5.2 Model Description.

Figure 3.10(b) presents an SHLPN model of a multiprocessor system. Although the graph representing the model is invariant to the system size, the state space of the SHLPN model clearly depends on the actual number of processors n, common memory modules q, and buses r. For our example, $n = 5$, $q = 3$ and $r = 2$.

The graph consists of five places and three transitions. Each place contains tokens whose type may be different. A token has a number of attributes; the first attribute is the type of the token. We recognize three different types: p–processor, m–common memory, b–bus. The second attribute of a token is its *identity*, id, a positive integer with values depending on the number of objects of a given type. In our example, when type = p, the id attribute takes values in the set [1,5]. The tokens residing in place Q have a third attribute: the id of the common memory module they are going to refer next.

The meaning of different places and the tokens they contain are presented in Figure 3.10 b). The notation used should be interpreted in the following way: the place P contains the set of tokens of type processors with two attributes (p, i), with $i \in [1,5]$. The maximum capacity of place P is equal to the number of processors.

The transition E corresponds to an end of execution in the private domain and it occurs with a transition rate exponentially distributed with mean λ_1. As a result of this transition, the token moves into place Q where it selects the next common memory reference. A token in place Q has three attributes (p, i, j) with the first two as before and the third attribute describing the common memory module $j \in [1,3]$ to be accessed by processor i. The processor could wait to access the common memory module when either no bus is available or the memory module is busy.

Transition G occurs when a processor switches to execution in common domain, and when the predicate $j = k$ is satisfied, see Figure 3.10 (b). This is a concise representation of the condition that the memory module referenced by the processor i is free. Another way of expressing this condition is: the third attribute of token (p, i, j) is equal to the second attribute of token (m, k). The place B contains tokens representing free buses and the place M contains tokens representing free memory modules. The maximum capacities of these places are equal to the number of buses and memory modules. The rate of transition G is λ_2 and it is related to the exponentially distributed communication delay involved in a common memory access. The place A contains tokens representing processes executing in the common domain.

The maximum capacity of the places in our graph are:

$$
\begin{aligned}
\text{Capacity } (P) &= n \\
\text{Capacity } (Q) &= n \\
\text{Capacity } (M) &= q \\
\text{Capacity } (B) &= r \\
\text{Capacity } (A) &= \min(n, q, r).
\end{aligned}
$$

The compound markings of the system are presented in Table 3.4. To simplify this table, the following convention is used: Whenever the attributes of the tokens do not have any effect on the compound marking, only the number of the tokens present in a given place is shown. When an attribute of a token is present in a predicate, only that attribute is shown in the corresponding place if no confusion about the token type is possible.

For example, the marking corresponding to state 2 has four tokens in place P (the token type is p according to the model description), two tokens in place B (type $= b$), zero tokens in place A. Only the third attribute i of the token present in place Q (the id of the memory module of the next reference) is indicated. Also shown are the ids of the tokens present in place M, namely i, j, and k.

As a general rule, it is necessary to specify in the marking, the attributes of the tokens referred to by any predicate that may be present in the SHLPN. In our case, we have to specify the third attribute of the tokens in Q and the second attribute of the tokens in M, since they appear in the predicate associated with transition G.

Table 3.4 shows the state transition table of the system. For example, state 2 can be reached from the following states, state 1 with the rate $15 \times \lambda_1$, state 18 with the rate λ_3, and state 19 with the transition rate equal to λ_3. From state 2, the system goes to state 3 with a transition rate equal to $8 \times \lambda_1$, to state 4 with rate $4 \times \lambda_1$, or to state 17 with rate λ_2.

State 2 corresponds to the situation when any four processors execute in the private domain and the fifth has selected the memory module of its next common domain reference to be module i. It should be pointed out that state 2 is a *macrostate* obtained due to the use of the compound marking concept and it corresponds to 15 atomic states. These states are distinguished only by the identity attributes of the tokens in two places, P and Q, as shown in Table 3.5. The transition rate from the compound marking, denoted as state 1 in Table 3.4, to the one denoted by state 2 is $15 \times \lambda_1$, since there are 15 individual transitions from one individual marking of state 1 to the 15 individual markings in the compound marking corresponding to state 2.

3.7.6 Performance Analysis

To determine the average utilization of different system resources, it is necessary to solve the equilibrium equations and then to identify the states when each resource is idle and the occupancy of that state, and the number of units of that resource that are idle. The following notation is used: Size $[B]_i$ is the occupancy of place B when the system is in state i, and p_i is the probability of the system being in state i. Then the

Table 3.4 The states of the multiprocessor system model.

Marking (State)	Place Index				
	P	Q	M	B	A
1	5	0	i,j,k	2	0
2	4	i	i,j,k	2	0
3	3	i,j	i,j,k	2	0
4	3	i,i	i,j,k	2	0
5	2	i,j,k	i,j,k	2	0
6	2	i,i,j	i,j,k	2	0
7	2	i,i,i	i,j,k	2	0
8	1	i,i,j,k	i,j,k	2	0
9	1	i,i,i,j	i,j,k	2	0
10	1	i,i,j,j	i,j,k	2	0
11	1	i,i,i,i	i,j,k	2	0
12	0	i,i,i,j,k	i,j,k	2	0
13	0	i,i,j,j,k	i,j,k	2	0
14	0	i,i,i,i,j	i,j,k	2	0
15	0	i,i,i,j,j	i,j,k	2	0
16	0	i,i,i,i,i	i,j,k	2	0
17	4	0	j,k	1	i
18	3	j	j,k	1	i
19	3	i	j,k	1	i
20	2	j,k	j,k	1	i
21	2	i,j	j,k	1	i
22	2	i,i	i,k	1	j
23	2	i,i	j,k	1	i
24	1	i,j,k	j,k	1	i
25	1	i,i,j	i,k	1	j
26	1	i,i,j	j,k	1	i
27	1	i,i,i	i,k	1	j
28	1	i,i,i	j,k	1	i
29	0	i,i,j,k	j,k	1	i
30	0	i,i,i,k	i,k	1	j
31	0	i,i,j,j	i,j	1	k
32	0	i,j,j,k	j,k	1	i
33	0	i,i,i,i	i,k	1	j
34	0	i,i,i,j	j,k	1	i
35	0	i,i,j,j	j,k	1	i
36	0	i,i,i,j	i,k	1	j
37	0	i,i,i,i	j,k	1	i
38	3	0	k	0	i,j
39	2	k	k	0	i,j
40	2	i	k	0	i,j
41	1	i,i,k	i,k	1	j
42	1	i,k	k	0	i,j
43	1	i,j	k	0	i,j
44	1	i,i	k	0	i,j
45	0	i,i,k	k	0	i,j
46	0	i,i,i	i	0	j,k
47	0	i,j,j	j	0	i,k
48	0	i,j,k	k	0	i,j
49	0	i,i,i	k	0	i,j
50	0	i,i,j	k	0	i,j
51	1	k,k	k	0	i,j

Table 3.5 The 15 individual markings (states) for places P and Q, corresponding to the compound marking defined as macrostate 2 in Table 3.4.

P				Q
$< p, 2 >$	$< p, 3 >$	$< p, 4 >$	$< p, 5 >$	$< p, 1, 1 >$
				$< p, 1, 2 >$
				$< p, 1, 3 >$
$< p, 1 >$	$< p, 3 >$	$< p, 4 >$	$< p, 5 >$	$< p, 2, 1 >$
				$< p, 2, 2 >$
				$< p, 2, 3 >$
$< p, 1 >$	$< p, 2 >$	$< p, 4 >$	$< p, 5 >$	$< p, 3, 1 >$
				$< p, 3, 2 >$
				$< p, 3, 3 >$
$< p, 1 >$	$< p, 2 >$	$< p, 3 >$	$< p, 5 >$	$< p, 4, 1 >$
				$< p, 4, 2 >$
				$< p, 4, 3 >$
$< p, 1 >$	$< p, 2 >$	$< p, 3 >$	$< p, 4 >$	$< p, 5, 1 >$
				$< p, 5, 2 >$
				$< p, 5, 3 >$

average utilization of a processor η_p, a common memory module η_m, and a bus η_b are defined as

$$\eta_p = 1 - \sum_{i \in S} \frac{p_1 \times \text{ size } [Q]_i}{n}.$$

$$\eta_m = 1 - \sum_{i \in S} \frac{p_1 \times \text{ size } [M]_i}{q}.$$

$$\eta_b = 1 - \sum_{i \in S} \frac{p_1 \times \text{ size } [B]_i}{l}.$$

The load for common resources is defined as

$$\rho = \frac{\lambda_1}{\lambda_2}.$$

The number of original states is very high, larger than 500, and we have reduced the model to only 51 states. As mentioned earlier, the same conceptual model can be used to model a message passing system. In such a case, λ_2 will be related to the time necessary to pass a message from one processor to another, including the processor communication overhead at the sending and at the receiving site, as well as the transmission time dependent upon the message size and the communication delay. In case of a synchronization message passing system, λ_3 will be related to the average blocking time in order to generate a reply.

3.8 MODELING HORN CLAUSES WITH PETRI NETS

The material in this section covers applications of the net theory to modeling of logic systems and follows closely Lin et al. [15]. A Horn clause of propositional logic has the form

$$B \leftarrow A_1 \wedge A_2, \ldots, \wedge A_n.$$

This notation means that holding of all conditions A_1 to A_n implies the conclusion B. Logical connectiveness is expressed using the $\leftarrow$ (implication) and $\wedge$ (conjunction) symbols. A Horn clause is a clause in which the conjunction of zero or more conditions implies at most one conclusion.

There are four different forms of Horn clauses. The Petri net representations of Horn clauses are:

1. The Horn clause with non-empty condition(s) and conclusion

$$B \leftarrow A_1 \wedge A_2, \ldots, \wedge A_n \text{ with } n \geq 1.$$

For example, the clause $C \leftarrow A \wedge B$ is represented by the Petri net in Figure 3.11(a). When the conditions A and B are true, the corresponding places A and B hold tokens, transition t fires, and a token is deposited in place C, i.e., the conclusion C is true.

2. The Horn clause with empty condition(s)

$$B \leftarrow .$$

This type of Horn clause is interpreted as an assertion of a fact. A fact B can be represented in a Petri net model as a transition system with a *source* transition, as shown in Figure 3.11(b). The source transition t is always enabled and this means that the formula B is always true.

3. The Horn clause with empty conclusion

$$\leftarrow A_1 \wedge A_2, \ldots, A_n \text{ with } n \geq 1.$$

This type of Horn clause is interpreted as the goal statement, which is in the negation form of what is to be proven. In a Petri net model a condition such as 'A and B' is represented as a goal transition system with a *sink transition*, as shown in Figure 3.11(c).

4. The null clause, which is interpreted as a contradiction. There is no representation of such clause, the *empty net* is not defined in the net theory.

Given a set of Horn clauses consisting of n clauses and m distinct symbols, the $n \times m$ incidence matrix $F = [F_{ij}]$ of a Petri net corresponding to the set of clauses can be obtained by the following procedure given by Murata and Zhang [22].

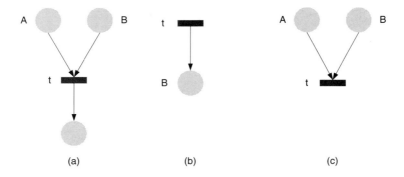

Fig. 3.11 Modeling Horn clauses with Petri nets. (a) A Horn clause with two conditions and a conclusion. (b) A Horn clause with no condition. (c) A Horn clause with empty conclusion.

Step 1: Denote the n *clauses* by $t_1, \ldots, t_n$. The clause t_i represents the ith row of F.

Step 2: Denote the m *predicate symbols* by $p_1, \ldots, p_m$. The symbol p_j represents the jth column of F.

Step 3: The $(i, j)^{th}$ entry of F, F_{ij}, is the sum of the arguments in the ith clause and the jth symbol. The sum is taken over all the jth symbols appearing in the ith clause. All the arguments to the left side of the $\leftarrow$ operator are taken as positive, and all the arguments to the right side of it are taken as negative. Thus the elements F_{ij} can be either '0', or '1' or '-1'.

The following example shows the translation procedure.

Example: (based on Peterka and Murata [23]).
Consider the following set of Horn clauses represented in the conventional way

1) A	2) B
3) $A \wedge B \rightarrow C$	4) $C \wedge B \rightarrow D$
5) $D \rightarrow A$	6) $D \rightarrow C$

To prove that $D \wedge C$ is true, one can apply the satisfiability principle. Let S be a set of first order formulae and G be a first order formula. G is a *logic consequence* of S iff $S \cup (\neg G)$ is unsatisfiable. The following result is obtained by adding the negation of $D \wedge C$ to the set of clauses

1) A	2) B
3) $C \vee \neg A \vee \neg B$	4) $D \vee \neg B \vee \neg C$
5) $A \vee \neg D$	6) $C \vee \neg D$
7) $\neg D \vee \neg C$	

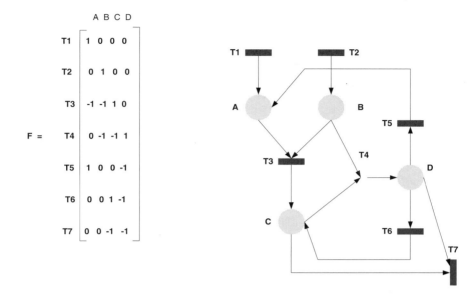

$$F = \begin{array}{c} \\ T1 \\ \\ T2 \\ \\ T3 \\ \\ T4 \\ \\ T5 \\ \\ T6 \\ \\ T7 \end{array} \begin{array}{cccc} A & B & C & D \\ 1 & 0 & 0 & 0 \\ 0 & 1 & 0 & 0 \\ -1 & -1 & 1 & 0 \\ 0 & -1 & -1 & 1 \\ 1 & 0 & 0 & -1 \\ 0 & 0 & 1 & -1 \\ 0 & 0 & -1 & -1 \end{array}$$

Fig. 3.12 The incidence matrix and the Petri net for the set of Horn clauses in the example from Section 3.8.

The Petri net representation of this set of Horn clauses and its incidence matrix are shown in Figure 3.12.

Sinachopoulos [29], Lautenbach [14], and Murata [23] have investigated the necessary and sufficient conditions for a set of Horn clauses to contain a contradiction based on analysis of the Petri net model of such clauses. These conditions are:

Theorem. A necessary net theoretical condition for a set of clauses J, to be unsatisfiable is that the net representation of J has a non-negative T-invariant.

Theorem. A sufficient net theoretical condition for a set of Horn clauses J, to be unsatisfiable is that J contains at least one source transition, at least one sink transition, and has a nonzero T-invariant.

Theorem. Let N be a Petri net representation of a set of Horn clauses. Let t_g be a goal transition in t. There exists a firing transition sequence that reproduces the empty marking $(M = 0)$ and fires the goal transition t_g in N iff N has a T-invariant X such that $X \geq 0$ and $X(t_g) \neq 0$. X is a vector and the value of its t_g^{th} element is given by $X(t_g)$.

3.9 WORKFLOW MODELING WITH PETRI NETS

The idea of using Petri nets for modeling and enactment of workflows can be traced back to a paper published in 1993 by Ellis and Nutt [6]. It was soon discovered that Petri nets support modeling of dynamic changes within workflow systems [4] and the net-based workflow modeling was included in a book published in 1996 on modeling, architecture, and implementation of workflow management systems [9]. The WorkFlow nets and the concept of workflow inheritance were introduced in 1999 by van der Aalst and Basten [1].

Recall from Chapter 1 that in workflow management we handle *cases*, individual activations of a workflow, and for each case we execute *tasks* or *activities* in a certain order. Each task has *preconditions* that must be satisfied before the task can be executed; after the execution of a task its *postconditions* must hold.

3.9.1 Basic Models

The basic Petri net workflow modeling paradigm is to *associate tasks with transitions, conditions with places, and cases with tokens*. A workflow is modeled by a net with a start place, p_s, corresponding to the state when the case is accepted for processing and a final place, p_f, corresponding to the state when the processing of the case has completed successfully. We also require that every condition and activity contributed to the processing of the case. This requirement means that every node, be it a place or a transition, be located on a path from p_s to p_f. These informal requirements translate into the following definition

Definition – Workflow Net. The P/T net $N = (p, t, f, l)$ is a Workflow net iff: (a) N has one start and one finish place, p_s and p_f and (b) $\tilde{N}$, its short-circuit counterpart is strongly connected.

The *initial marking*, s_{init}, of a workflow net corresponds to the state when there is only one token in the start place, p_s, and the *final marking* s_{final} corresponds to the state when there is only one token in the finish place, p_f.

We are interested in Workflow nets that have a set of desirable structural and behavioral properties. First, we require a net to be safe; this means that in all markings every place has at most one token. Indeed, places in the net correspond to conditions that can either be true and the place contains one token, or false and the place contains no tokens. Second, we require that it should be always possible to reach the final marking, s_{final} from the initial marking s_{init}. This requirement simply implies that we can always complete a case successfully. Third, we require that there are no dead transitions; for each activity of the workflow there is an execution when the activity is carried out. This set of minimal requirements leads to the so-called soundness of the Workflow net.

Definition – Sound Workflow Net. The workflow net $[N, s_{init}]$ is sound iff: (i) it is safe, (ii) for any reachable marking $s \in [N, s_{init}]$ $s_{final} \in [N, s]$, and (iii) there are no dead transitions.

A workflow net $[N, s_{init}]$ is sound iff its associated short-circuit net, $[\tilde{N}, s_{init}]$, is live and safe [1]. Workflow definition languages used in practice lead to free-choice Worflow nets and for such nets the soundness can be decided in polynomial time.

3.9.2   Branching Bisimilarity

We often partition the set of objects we have to manipulate, in equivalence classes such that all objects with a set of defining properties belong to the same class. This approach allows us to structure our knowledge, to accommodate the diversity of the environment, and to formulate consistent specifications for systems with similar or identical functionality.

The basic idea of branching bisimilarity is to define classes of equivalent systems based on the states the systems traverse in their evolution and the actions causing transitions from one state to another. When defining this equivalence relationship we can insist on a stronger or weaker similarity, thus, we can define two different types of relationships.

Informally, if two systems are capable of replicating every action of each other and traversing similar states they are strongly equivalent for the corresponding set of consecutive actions. Consider two chess players; every time one makes a move, the other one is able to mirror the move. We bend the traditional chess rules and after each pair of moves of the two players, either player may move first. Clearly, this mirroring process can only be carried out for a relatively small number of moves. At some point in time one of the players will stop replicating the other's move because of either conflicts due to the rules of the game or because it will lead to a losing position.

To define a weaker notion of equivalence we introduce the concept of *silent* or internal actions, actions that cannot be noticed by an external observer. For example, a casual listener of an audio news broadcast may not distinguish between a digital reception over the Internet, played back by a Real Networks player running on a laptop, and an analog broadcast played by a traditional radio receiver.

The two systems have some characteristics in common: both receive an input information stream, process this stream to generate an analog audio signal, and finally feed this signal into the loudspeakers. Yet, internally, the two systems work very differently. One is connected to the Internet and receives a digital input stream using a transport protocol, unpacks individual voice samples in the same packet, interpolates to re-construct missing samples as discussed in Chapter 5, then converts the digital samples into an analog signal. The other has an antenna and receives a high-frequency radio signal, amplifies the signal, extracts the analog audio signal from the high-frequency carrier using analog audio circuitry.

Clearly, the equivalence relationship is an ad hoc one; it only reflects the point of view of a particular observer. A more astute observer would notice differences in the quality of the sound produced by the two systems. When modeling the two processes described in this example, all actions of the digital Internet audio player that are different from those performed by the analog receiver, and vice versa, are defined as silent actions.

We now first define the concept of strong and weak bisimulation and then we introduce branching bisimilarity of Petri nets.

Definition – Strong Bisimulation. A binary relation R over the states s_i of a labeled transition system with actions $a \in Actions$ is a strong bisimulation iff:

$$\forall (s_1, s_2) \in R, \ \ \forall (a) \in Actions$$

$$(s_1 \xrightarrow{a} s_1' \ \Rightarrow \ \exists \, s_2 \xrightarrow{a} s_2', \ s_1' R s_2') \wedge (s_2 \xrightarrow{a} s_2' \ \Rightarrow \ \exists \, s_1 \xrightarrow{a} s_1', \ s_1' R s_2')$$

In this equation $s_1 \xrightarrow{a} s_1'$ means that the system originally in state s_1 moves to state s_1' as a result of action a. Two states s_1 and s_2 are strongly bisimilar iff there is a strong bisimulation R such that $s_1 R s_2$. This definition can be extended to two different systems by setting them next to each other and considering them as a single system. The largest strong bisimulation, the one with the highest number of actions, is an equivalence relation called *strong bisimulation equivalence*.

If processes contain internal actions, labeled τ denote:

$$\overset{a}{\Rightarrow} \ := \ ((\xrightarrow{\tau})^* \xrightarrow{a} (\xrightarrow{\tau})^*), \ \ a \in Actions$$

and

$$\overset{\tilde{a}}{\Rightarrow} \ := \ \left\{ \begin{array}{ll} \overset{a}{\Rightarrow} & if \ a \neq \tau \\ (\xrightarrow{\tau})^* & if \ a = \tau \end{array} \right\}$$

Definition – Weak Bisimulation. A binary relation R over the states s_i of a labeled transition system with actions $a \in Actions$ is a weak bisimulation if:

$$\forall (s_1, s_2) \in R, \ \ \forall (a) \in Actions$$

$$(s_1 \xrightarrow{a} s_1' \ \Rightarrow \ \exists \, s_2 \overset{\tilde{a}}{\Rightarrow} s_2', \ s_1' R s_2') \wedge (s_2 \xrightarrow{a} s_2' \ \Rightarrow \ \exists \, s_1 \overset{\tilde{a}}{\Rightarrow} s_1', \ s_1' R s_2')$$

Two states s_1 and s_2 are weakly bisimilar iff there is a weak bisimulation R such that $s_1 R s_2$. This definition can be extended to two different systems by setting them next to each other and considering them as a single system. The largest weak bisimulation, the one with the highest number of actions, is an equivalence relation called *weak bisimulation equivalence*.

Note that in this case instead of an observable action a we require that when one of the systems reaches state s_j' as a result of the action a in state s_j, then the other system in state s_i reaches state s_i' after zero or more internal or silent actions followed by a, possibly followed by zero or more silent actions: $s_1 \xrightarrow{\tilde{a}} s_1'$ and $s_2 \xrightarrow{\tilde{a}} s_2'$ respectively.

Strong bisimilarity between a Petri net and a finite-state system is decidable [10] while the weak bisimilarity between a Petri net and a finite-state system is undecidable [11].

The weak bisimulation relation is used to construct classes of equivalent Petri nets. We define an equivalence relation among marked labeled P/T nets by introducing silent actions modeled as transitions with a special label τ. Such transitions correspond to internal actions that are not observable. Two marked labeled P/T nets are branching bisimilar if one of them is able to simulate any transition α of the other one after performing a sequence of zero or more silent actions. The two must satisfy an additional requirement: both must either deadlock or terminate successfully.

Definition – Behavioral Equivalence of Workflow Nets. Two workflow nets, $[N, s_{init}]$ and $[Q, q_{init}]$ are behaviorally equivalent iff a branching bisimilarity R relation between them exists.

$$[N, s_{init}] \cong [Q, q_{init}] \iff ([N, s_{init}]R[Q, q_{init}]$$

3.9.3 Dynamic Workflow Inheritance

The theoretical foundation for the concept of dynamic workflow inheritance discussed now is based on work done by van Aalst and Basten [1] for workflow modeling and analysis on the equivalence relation among labeled P/T, nets, called branching bisimilarity. This equivalence relation is related to the concept of observable behavior. We distinguish two types of actions, those that are observable and the silent ones, actions we cannot observe. In this context an action is the firing of a transition. Two P/T nets that have the same observable behavior are said to be equivalent. A labeled P/T net can evolve into another one through a sequence of silent actions and a predicate expressing the fact that a net can terminate successfully after executing one or more silent actions.

The intuition behind inheritance is straightforward, given two workflows v and w, we say that w is a subclass of v or extends v iff w inherits "some" properties of v. Conversely, we say that v is a superclass of w. The subclass may redefine some of the properties of its superclass.

The components of workflows are actions; hence a necessary condition for workflow w to be a subclass of v is to contain all the actions of v and some additional ones. But the action subset relation between an extension and its superclass is not sufficient, we need to relate the outcomes of the two workflows, to make them indistinguishable from one another under some conditions imposed by actions in w but not in v. Two such conditions are possible: (a) block the additional actions, and (b) consider them as unobservable, or silent.

Two basic types of dynamic inheritance, have been defined [1]. (1) *Protocol inheritance:* if by blocking the actions in w that are not present in v it is not possible to distinguish between the behavior of the two workflows we say that w inherits the protocol of v. (2) *Projection inheritance:* w inherits the projection of v if by making the activities in w that are not in v unobservable, or silent it is not possible to distinguish between the behavior of the two workflows.

Figure 3.13 inspired from van der Aalst and Basten [1] illustrates these concepts. Each workflow is mapped into a P/T net. The P/T net transitions correspond to workflow actions. The workflows in (b), (c), (d), and (e) are subclasses of the workflow in (a) obtained by adding a new action D. The workflow in (b) is a subclass with respect to projection and protocol inheritance. When either blocking or hiding action D, (b) is identical to (a). The workflow in (c) is a subclass with respect to protocol inheritance

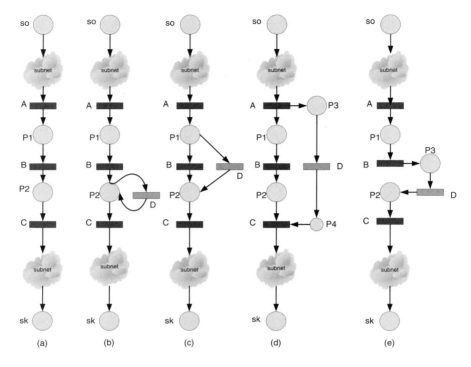

Fig. 3.13 Dynamic workflow inheritance. The workflows in (b), (c), and (d) are subclasses of the workflow in (a) obtained by adding a new action D. The workflow in (b) is a subclass with respect to projection and protocol inheritance. When either blocking or hiding action D, (b) is identical to (a). The workflow in (c) is a subclass with respect to protocol inheritance but not under projection inheritance. When blocking activity D, (c) is identical to (a) but it is possible to skip activity B by executing action D. The workflow in (c) is not a subclass with respect to projection inheritance. The workflow in (d) is a subclass of the one in (a) with respect to projection inheritance. The workflow in (e) is not a subclass with respect to either projection or protocol inheritance.

but not under projection inheritance. When blocking activity D, (c) is identical to (a) but it is possible to skip activity B by executing action D. The workflow in (c) is not a subclass with respect to projection inheritance. The workflow in (e) is not a subclass with respect to either projection or protocol inheritance.

3.10 FURTHER READING

A Web site maintained by the Computer Sciences Department at University of Aarhus in Denmark, http://www.daimi.au.dk/PetriNets/bibl, provides extensive information related to Petri nets, including: groups working on different aspects on net theory and applications; standards; education; mailing lists; meeting announcements; and the Petri nets newsletter.

A comprehensive bibliography with more than 2500 entries is available from http://www.daimi.au.dk/PetriNets/bibl/aboutpnbibl.html.

A fair number of Petri net software tools have been developed over the years. A database containing information about more than fifty Petri net tools can be found at http://www.daimi.au.dk/PetriNets/tools/db.html.

The vast literature on Petri nets includes the original paper of Carl Adam Petri [25] and his 1986 review of the field [26]. The book by Peterson [24] is an early introduction to system modeling using Petri nets; the tutorial by Murata [21] provides an excellent introduction to the subject.

The proceedings of the conferences on Petri nets and applications, held annually since early 1980, have been published by Springer-Verlag in the Lecture Notes on Computer Science series, e.g., LNCS volumes 52, 254, 255, and so on. Conferences on Petri nets and performance models have taken place every two years since 1985 and the papers published in the proceedings of these conferences cover a wide range of topics from from methodology to tools and to algorithms for analysis [17].

The book edited by Jensen and Rozenberg [12] provides a collection of papers on the theory and application of high-level nets. Timed Petri nets (TPNs) are discussed by Zuberek [30]. Stochastic Petri nets are presented by Molloy [19], Florin and Natkin [7], Marsan and his co-workers [18], Lin and Marinescu [16].

Applications to performance evaluation are discussed by Sifakis [28], Ramamoorthy [27], and Murata [20]. Applications to modeling logic systems are presented by Murata et al. [22, 23], Marinescu et al. [3, 15], and others [14, 29]. Applications of Petri nets to workflow modeling and analysis are the subject of papers by Ellis et al. [4, 6, 5], van der Aalst and Basten [1, 2], and others [9]. Work on branching bisimulation and Petri nets is reported in [10, 11].

3.11 EXERCISES AND PROBLEMS

Problem 1. A toll booth accepts one and five dollar bills, one dollar, half dollar, and quarter coins. Passenger cars pay $1.75 or $3.25, depending on the distance traveled, while trucks and buses pay $3.50 and $ 6.50. The machine requires exact change.

Design a Petri net representing the state transition diagram of the toll booth.

Problem 2. Translate the formal description of the home loan application process of Problem 2 in Chapter 1 into a Petri net; determine if the resulting net is a free-choice net.

Problem 3. Translate the formal description of the automatic Web benchmarking process of Problem 3 in Chapter 1 into a Petri net; determine if the resulting net is a free-choice net.

Problem 4. Translate the formal description of the grant request reviewing process of Problem 5 in Chapter 1 into a Petri net; determine if the resulting net is a free-choice net.

Problem 5. Construct the coverability graphs of the net in Figure 3.2(j) and of the nets you have constructed for Problems 1,2, 3, and 4 above.

Problem 6. Show that iff the token count on the subset of places $P' \subset P$ never changes under arbitrary transition firings, the condition $F \times y = 0$, where y is an vector of integers with $|P|$ components and has nonzero components corresponding to all places in P'.

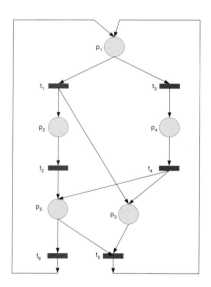

Fig. 3.14   Petri net for Problem 7.

Problem 7. Compute the S-invariants of:

(i) the net in Figure 3.14;

(ii) the four nets you have constructed for Problems 1,2, 3, and 4 above.

Problem 8. Compute the T-invariants of the four nets you have constructed for Problems 1,2, 3, and 4 above.

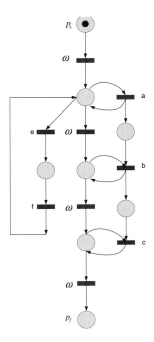

Fig. 3.15 A net similar to the one in Figure 3.5.

Problem 9. Provide a definition for the Petri net language described by the net in Figure 3.15.

Problem 10. Prove that a live free-choice Petri net(N, s_0) is safe iff it is covered by strongly connected state machines and each state machine has exactly one token in s_0.

REFERENCES

1. W.M.P. van der Aalst and T. Basten. Inheritance of Workflows: An approach to tackling problems related to change. Computing Science Reports 99/06, Eindhoven University of Technology, Eindhoven, 1999.

2. T. Basten and W.M.P. van der Aalst. A Process-Algebraic Approach to Life-Cycle Inheritance: Inheritance = Encapsulation + Abstraction. Computing Science Reports 96/05, Eindhoven University of Technology, Eindhoven, 1996.

3. A. Chaudhury, D. C. Marinescu, and A. Whinston. Net-Based Computational Models of Knowledge-Processing Systems. *IEEE Expert*, 8(2):79–86, 1993.

4. C. A. Ellis, K. Keddara, and G. Rozenberg. Dynamic Changes with Workflow Systems. In N. Comstock, C. A. Ellis, R. Kling, J. Mylopoulos, and S. Kaplan, editors, *Conference on Organizational Computing*, pages 10–21. ACM Press, New York, 1995.

5. C. A. Ellis, K. Keddara, and J. Wainer. Modeling Workflow Dynamic Changes Using Timed Hybrid Flow Nets. In W.M.P. van der Aalst, G. De Michelis, and C. A. Ellis, editors, *Workflow Management: Net-based Concepts, Models, Techniques and Tools (WFM'98), Computing Science Reports*, volume 98/7, pages 109–128. Eindhoven University of Technology, Eindhoven, 1998.

6. C. A. Ellis and G.J. Nutt. Modeling and Enactment of Workflow Systems. In M. Ajmone Marsan, editor, *Applications and Theory of Petri Nets 1993, Lecture Notes in Computer Science*, volume 691, pages 1–16. Springer-Verlag, Heidelberg, 1993.

7. G. Florin and S. Natkin. Evaluation Based upon Stochastic Petri Nets of the Maximum Throughput of a Full Duplex Protocol. In C. Girault and W. Reisig, editors, *Application and Theory of Petri Nets: Selected Papers from the First and the Second European Workshop, Informatik Fachberichte*, volume 52, pages 280–288, Springer-Verlag, Heidelberg, 1982.

8. H. J. Genrich and K. Lautenbach. System Modelling with High-Level Petri Nets. *Theoretical Computer Science*, 13(1):109–136, 1981.

9. S. Jablonski and C. Busser. *Workflow Management: Modeling Concepts, Architecture, and Implementation*. International Thompson Computer Press, London, 1995.

10. P. Jančar. Decidability Questions for Bisimilarity of Petri Nets and Some Related Problems. *Lecture Notes in Computer Science*, volume 775, pages 581–592. Springer–Verlag, Heidelberg, 1994.

11. P. Jančar. Undecidability of Bisimilarity for Petri Nets and some Related Problems. *Theoretical Computer Science*, 148(2):281–301, 1995.

12. K. Jensen and G. Rozenberg. *High Level Petri Nets*. Springer–Verlag, Heidelberg, 1995.

13. K. Jensen. A Method to Compare the Descriptive Power of Different Types of Petri Nets. In P. Dembinski, editor, *Mathematical Foundations of Computer Science 1980, Proc. 9th Symp., Lecture Notes in Computer Science*, volume 88, pages 348–361. Springer–Verlag, Heidelberg, 1980.

14. K. Lautenbach. On Logical and Linear Dependencies. GMD Report 147, GMD, St. Augustin, Germany, 1985.

15. C. Lin, A. Chaudhury, A. Whinston, and D. C. Marinescu. Logical Inference of Horn Clauses in Petri Net Models. *IEEE Transactions on Knowledge and Data Engineering*, 5(3):416–425, 1993.

16. C. Lin and D. C. Marinescu. Stochastic High Level Petri Nets and Applications. *IEEE Transactions on Computers*, C-37, 7:815–825, 1988.

17. D. C. Marinescu, M. Beaven, and R. Stansifer. A Parallel Algorithm for Computing Invariants of Petri Net Models. In *Proc. 4th Int. Workshop on Petri Nets and Performance Models (PNPM'91)*, pages 136–143. IEEE Press, Piscataway, New Jersey, 1991.

18. M. Ajmone Marsan, G. Balbo, and G. Conte. A Class of Generalised Stochastic Petri Nets for the Performance Evaluation of Multiprocessor Systems. *ACM Transactions on Computer Systems*, 2(2):93–122, 1984.

19. M. Molloy. Performance Analysis Using Stochastic Petri Nets. *IEEE Transactions on Computers*, C31(9):913–917, 1982.

20. T. Murata. Petri Nets, Marked Graphs, and Circuit-System Theory – A Recent CAS Application. *Circuits and Systems*, 11(3):2–12, 1977.

21. T. Murata. Petri Nets: Properties, Analysis, and Applications. *Proceedings of the IEEE*, 77(4):541–580, 1989.

22. T Murata and D. Zhang. A Predicate-Transition Net Model for Parallel Interpretation of Logic Programs. *IEEE Transactions on Software Engineering*, 14(4):481–497, 1988.

23. G. Peterka and T. Murata. Proof Procedure and Answer Extraction in Petri Net Model of Logic Programs. *IEEE Trans. on Software Engineering*, 15(2):209–217, 1989.

24. J. L. Peterson. *Petri Net Theory and the Modeling of Systems*. Prentice Hall, Englewood Cliffs, 1981.

25. C. A. Petri. *Kommunikation mit Automaten*. Schriften des Institutes fur Instrumentelle Mathematik, Bonn, 1962.

26. C. A. Petri. Concurrency theory. In W. Brauer, W. Reisig, and G. Rozenberg, editors, *Advances in Petri Nets 1986, Part I, Petri Nets: Central Models and Their Properties, Lecture Notes in Computer Science*, volume 254, pages 4–24. Springer–Verlag, Heidelberg, 1987.

27. C. V. Ramamoorthy and G. S. Ho. Performance Evaluation of Asynchronous Concurrent Systems Using Petri Nets. *IEEE Transactions on Software Engineering*, 6(5):440–449, 1980.

28. J. Sifakis. Use of Petri Nets for Performance Evaluation. *Acta Cybernetica*, 4(2):185–202, 1978.

29. A. Sinachopoulos. Derivation of a Contradiction by Resolution Using Petri Nets. *Petri Net Newsletter*, 26:16–29, 1987.

30. W. M. Zuberek. Timed Petri Nets and Preliminary Performance Evaluation. In *Proceedings of the 7th annual Symposium on Computer Architecture, Quarterly Publication of ACM Special Interest Group on Computer Architecture*, 8(3):62–82, 1980.

4

Internet Quality of Service

The Internet is a worldwide ensemble of computer networks that allow computers connected to any network to communicate with one other (see Figure 4.1). The computers connected to the Internet range from supercomputers, to mainframes, servers, workstations, desktops, laptops, palmtops, and an amazing range of wireless devices.

In the future we expect a new breed of nontraditional devices such as: sensors, "smart appliances", personal digital assistants (PDAs), new hybrid devices, and a mix of portable phones with palm top computers and cameras. Mobile devices will be connected to the Internet using wireless networks.

The milestones in the brief history of the Internet are outlined here. In December 1969, a network with four nodes connected by 56 Kbps communication channels became operational [16]. The network was funded by the Advanced Research Project Agency and it was called the ARPANET.

In 1985 the National Science Foundation, initiated the development of the NSFNET. The NSFNET had a tree-tiered architecture connecting campuses and research organizations to regional centers that were connected with each other via backbone links. In 1987 the backbone channels were upgraded to T1 lines with a maximum speed of 1.544 Mbps, and in 1991 they were again upgraded to T3 lines with a maximum

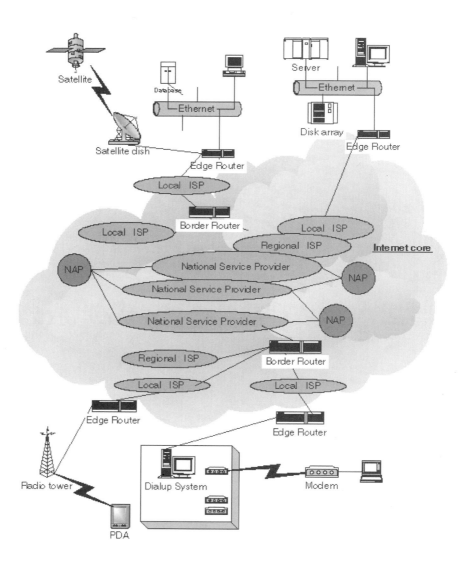

Fig. 4.1 The Internet is a network of networks. The Internet core consists of routers and communication lines administered by autonomous national, regional, and local service providers. National service providers are interconnected to each other at network access points (NAPs). Terrestrial lines, satellite, and packet-radio networks are used to transport data. At the edge of the network, computers belonging to autonomous organizations are connected with each other via edge routers.

speed of 45 Mbps. The very high-speed backbone network service (vBNS), based on 155-Mbps transit networks was launched in 1995.

The NSFNET was decommissioned in 1995 and the modern Internet was born. Commercial companies are now the Internet service providers, the regional networks were replaced by providers such as MCInet, ANSnet, Sprintlink, CICnet, and CERFnet.

Over the past two decades, the Internet has experienced an exponential, or nearly exponential, growth in the number of networks, computers, and users, as seen in Figure 4.2. We have witnessed a 12-fold increase in the number of computers connected to the Internet over a period of 5 years, from 5 million in 1995 to close to 60 million in 2000. At the same time, the speed of the networks has increased dramatically.

The Internet is the infrastructure that someday will allow individuals and organizations to combine individual services offered by independent service providers into super-services. The end-to-end quality of service in this vast semantic Web depends

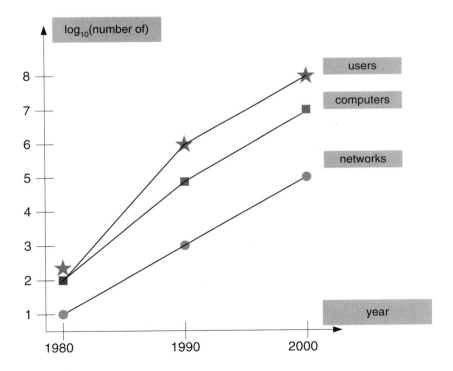

Fig. 4.2 The exponential increase of the networks, computers, and users of the Internet. On the vertical axis we show the logarithm of the the number of networks, computers, and users in million units.

on the quality of service of each component, including communication services. This justifies our interest in the quality of communication service provided by the Internet.

The Internet was designed based on the "best effort" service model. In this model there are no quality of service (QoS) guarantees. It is impossible to guarantee the bandwidth allocated to a stream, or to enforce an upper limit on the time it takes a packet to cross the Internet, to guarantee that the jitter of an audio stream will be bounded, or that a video stream will get the necessary bandwidth.

Now, faced with multimedia applications, where audio and video streams must be delivered subject to bandwidth and timing constraints, we need to consider other service models that do provide QoS guarantees [12]. But QoS guarantees require a different approach to resource management in the network. Only a network architecture supporting resource reservations is capable of guaranteeing that bandwidth and timing constraints are satisfied, regardless of the load placed on the network.

However, from queuing models we know that the queuing delay at various routers along the path of a packet could be kept low if network resources, such as channel capacity, router speed, and memory, are abundant for a given network load. Hence, the idea of overprovisioning, or providing resources well beyond those actually needed. The overprovisioning is clearly a stopgap measure as discussed in Chapter 5.

The "best - effort" service model played a very significant role in the explosive development of the Internet, a more restrictive model would have limited the number of autonomous organizations willing to participate. Migrating now to a different service model is a nontrivial proposition because of the scale of the system and the technical questions related to the prolonged transition period, when both models coexist and have to be supported.

The natural path for all areas of science and engineering is to develop systems based on the current level of knowledge, and, as the experience with existing systems accumulates and the science advances, to transfer the newly acquired knowledge and understanding into better engineering designs. Indeed, the fact that turbulence phenomena in fluid dynamics is not completely understood does not prevent us from flying airplanes or building propellers for ships. Our incomplete knowledge of the human genes does not preclude the continuing effort to identify genetic diseases and develop drugs to cure them.

Yet, once a technology is adopted, only changes that do not affect the basic assumptions of the model supporting the technology are feasible. The future of the Internet is a subject of considerable interest, but it is impossible to anticipate all the technical solutions that will enable this vast system to evolve gracefully into the next generation Internet.

In this chapter we present the Internet as it is today with emphasis on quality of service. First, we introduce basic networking terminology and concepts. We discuss applications and programming abstractions for networking, the layered network architecture and the communication protocols, the basic networking techniques, local area, wide-area, and residential access networks, routing in store-and-forward networks, networking hardware, and the mechanisms implemented by communication protocols.

Then, we survey addressing in the Internet. We present Internet address encoding, subnetting, classless addressing, address mapping, dynamic address assignment, packet forwarding, tunneling, and wireless communication and mobile IP.

We discuss routing in the Internet, we start with hierarchical routing and autonomous systems, interdomain routing, and then present several protocols in the Internet stack: the Internet protocol (IP), the Internet control message protocol (ICMP), the transport control protocol (TCP), the user datagram protocol (UDP), the routing information protocol (RIP), and the open shortest path first protocol (OSPF).

Finally, we address the problem of QoS guarantees. We present several service models, introduce flows, and discuss resource allocation in the Internet. Then, we cover traffic control, present packet scheduling, and review constrained routing and the resource reservation protocol (RSVP). We conclude with a survey of Internet integrated and differentiated services.

4.1 BRIEF INTRODUCTION TO NETWORKING

A computer network consists of nodes connected with communication lines. An ideal computer network is a fully connected graph; the processing elements in each node have an infinite speed and unlimited memory; the communication channels have an infinite bandwidth, zero delay, and no losses. Network models based on such assumptions are useful to reason about some aspects of network design but cannot possibly capture important aspects related to the functionality and performance of real networks.

The degree of connectivity of the computer networks in the real world is limited by cost and physical constraints; the information sent by one node has to cross several nodes before reaching its destination. The information is stored in each node and then forwarded to the next node along the paths, thus the name *store-and-forward network* given to such networks.

Some of the nodes of a store-and-forward network generate and consume information, they are called *hosts*, other nodes called *switches* act as go between. The hosts are located at the *network edge*; some of the switches, the routers, and the links between them form the so-called *network core*. *Routing*, deciding how a message from one host can reach another host, is a major concern in a store-and-forward network.

The propagation of physical signals through communication channels is affected by noise therefore the information sent through a network is distorted. Thus we need *error control* mechanisms to detect errors and take appropriate measures to recover the information.

The propagation delay on a physical channel is finite, the laws of physics, as well as cost, limit the processing speed and the memory available on the switches. When the network is congested the switches start dropping packets. This leads to nonzero end-to-end communication delay and to information loss. In turn, these limitations imply that a physical network has a finite capacity to transmit information. Thus we

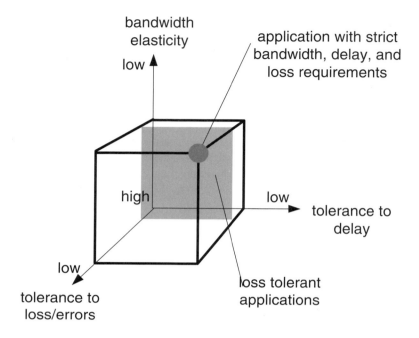

Fig. 4.3 Bandwidth, delay, and loss are three of the four dimensions of application QoS requirements; the fourth is the jitter. Some applications are bandwidth elastic and can adapt to the amount of bandwidth, some are delay insensitive, some are loss tolerant, some are jitter intolerrant. Other applications have strict bandwidth, delay, loss, and jitter requirements, or a combination of them.

need *congestion control* mechanisms to limit the amount of information sent through a network.

Moreover, the physical computers communicating with one another have finite and possibly different speeds and amounts of physical memory; thus, we need some form of feedback to allow a slow receiver to throttle down a fast sender, a mechanism called *flow control*. To hide losses, mask the end-to-end delays, control the bandwidth allocation, and support congestion control and flow control, we have to design complex networking software.

The network is just a carrier of information, the actual producers and consumers of information are the applications. The network applications discussed in depth in the next chapter depend on the bandwidth, the end-to-end delay, and the losses of a computer network. This three-dimensional space, see Figure 4.3, is populated with various types of applications with different bandwidth, end-to-end delay, and loss requirements. Some applications are bandwidth elastic, some are delay insensitive, some are loss tolerant. Other applications have strict bandwidth, delay, or loss requirements or a combination of them.

4.1.1   Layered Network Architecture and Communication Protocols

Application processes expect a virtual communication channel that:

(i) Guarantees message delivery.

(ii) Delivers messages in the same order they are sent.

(iii) Delivers at most one copy of each message.

(iv) Supports arbitrarily large messages.

(v) Supports synchronization between sender and receiver.

(vi) Allows the receiver to apply flow control to the sender.

(vii) Supports multiple application processes on each host.

The complex task of accommodating the communication needs of individual applications is decomposed into a set of subtasks with clear interfaces among themselves and with a well-defined set of functions assigned to every subtask. Such a decomposition is called a *network architecture*. Several network architectures have been proposed over the years; the Internet architecture discussed has been so far the most successful one. Figure 4.4 illustrates the gap filled in by the communication protocols for a given networking architecture.

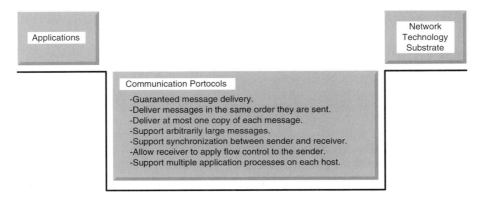

Fig. 4.4   Communication protocols bridge the gap between the expectations of applications and what the underlying technology provides.

A network architecture provides a set of abstractions that help hide the complexity of a computer network. The common abstractions encountered in networking are processes, communication channels, sessions, messages, peers, and communication protocols. The active entities in a computer network are processes running on hosts interconnected by communication channels and exchanging information packaged into messages.

Sometimes communicating processes establish a longer term relationship called a *session* and exchange a set of messages; in other instances a *connectionless* exchange takes place. Two entities running on different nodes are called *peers* if they share some common knowledge about the state of their relationship, for example, the identity of each other, the amount of data transferred, and so on.

The communication discipline is encapsulated into communication protocols. Communication protocols fill in the gap between what applications expect and what the underlying technology provides.

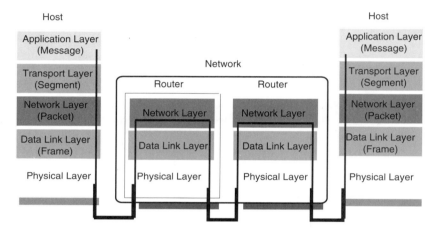

Fig. 4.5 Layered network architecture and the corresponding protocol stack. The information unit at each layer is indicated in parenthesis. A layered architecture is based on peer-to-peer communication. A layer communicates directly with the adjacent layers on the same node and it is logically related to its peer on the destination node. Thick lines represent communication lines, thinner vertical lines indicate the flow of information through the layers on a host or router.

Abstraction naturally leads to layering. Layering encourages a modular design, by decomposing the problem of building a computer network into manageable components. Figure 4.5 illustrates a network architecture with several layers:

The physical layer is responsible for signal propagation. It is implemented entirely by the communication hardware.

The data link layer is responsible for communication between two nodes directly connected by a line. The data link layer is partially implemented in hardware and partially in software. The hardware performs functions related to medium access control, decides when to send, and when information has been received successfully. Data link protocols transform a communication channel with errors into an errorless bit pipe. In addition to error control, data link protocols support flow control. Data link protocols are implemented by the system communication software running on hosts, bridges, and routers, see Section 4.16.

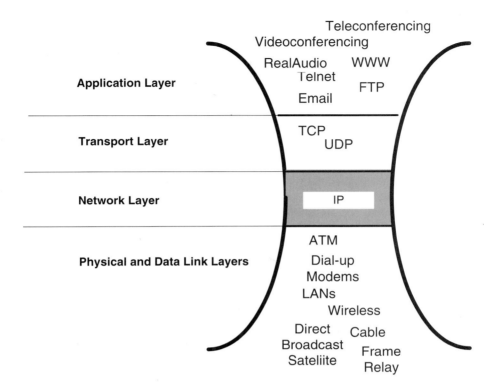

Fig. 4.6 The hourglass architecture of the Internet: wide at the top to support a variety of applications and transport protocols; wide at the bottom to support a variety of network technologies; narrow in the middle. All entities involved need only to understand the IP protocol.

The network layer is responsible for routing. The peers are network layer processes running on hosts and some switches called routers. Routing protocols are used to disseminate routing information and routing algorithms are used to compute optimal routes.

The transport layer is responsible for end-to-end message delivery. The peers are system processes running on the hosts involved in the exchange. A network architecture typically supports several transport protocols by implementing different error control and flow control mechanisms.

The application layer is responsible for sending and receiving the information through the network. The peers are the application processes running on the hosts communicating with one another. Each class of application requires its own application protocol.

A network architecture like the one in Figure 4.5 is implemented as a *protocol stack*; the stack defines the protocols supported at each layer. Except at the hardware level when peers communicate directly over communication lines, each protocol communicates with its peer by passing messages to a lower level protocol that in turn delivers messages to the next layer. We may have alternative abstractions at each layer; for example, we may have multiple data link, network, and transport protocols.

The Internet is based on an hourglass shaped architecture [6], see Figure 4.6, that reflects the basic requirements discussed earlier:

(i) Wide at the top to support a variety of applications and transport protocols.

(ii) Wide at the bottom to support a variety of network technologies such as: Ethernet, fiber distributed data interface (FDDI), asynchronous transmission mode (ATM) networks, and wireless netwoks.

(iii) Narrow in the middle. IP is the focal point of the architecture, it defines a common method for exchanging packets among a wide collection of networks [5]. The only requirement for an organization to join the Internet is to support the IP. This flexibility is responsible for the explosive growth of the Internet.

4.1.2 Internet Applications and Programming Abstractions

The ultimate source and destination of a message are applications running on hosts connected to the network. Programming languages for network applications have to support a communication abstraction allowing them to establish, open, and close a connection, and to send and receive data. These functions are similar with the ones supported by a file system: mount a file, open and close a file, read from a file, and write into a file.

It is not surprising that the networking abstraction, called a *socket*, allowing processes to communicate with each other, is similar to a file. A socket is explicitly created by the programmer, and, at creation time, one must specify the transport protocol used by the the socket. A socket is an end point of a logical communication channel; it consists of two queues of messages, one to send and one to receive messages, see Figure 4.7.

Each socket is completely specified by a pair of integers, the port number, and the transport protocol number. There is a one-to-one mapping from the protocol name to a protocol number. A *port* is a logical address used to reach a process on a host. A process may create several sockets and may use more than one transport protocol. Thus, a process may be able to communicate using several ports.

To communicate with a process one needs to know the host were the process runs as well as the port number and the protocol used by the process. Some of the most common applications available on virtually every system connected to the Internet run at *known ports*. Table 4.1 provides a summary of widely used applications, the transport protocol used, and their port number(s).

Several applications and the corresponding application protocols in the Table 4.1 are discussed in this chapter; the dynamic host reconfiguration protocol (DHCP) is

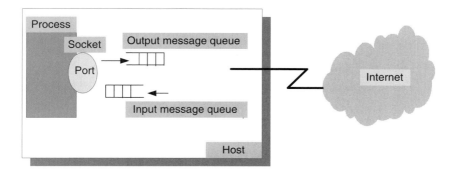

Fig. 4.7 A socket is an end point of a logical communication channel; it allows a process to send and receive messages.

presented in Section 4.2.5, other applications such as domain name services, the electronic mail, and the World Wide Web are discussed in depth in Chapter 5.

The same network has to support families of applications with very different requirements, a daunting endeavor that can only be accomplished by a combination of hardware and software solutions.

4.1.3 Messages and Packets

So far, we have been rather vague about the format of the information transmitted over the network. Now we take a closer look at the practical aspects of information exchange and we start by introducing various information units flowing through a computer network.

Table 4.1 The transport protocol and the port number of commonly used applications.

Application	Application Protocol	Transport Protocol	Port Number
Remote Login	Telnet	TCP	23
Electronic Mail	SMTP	TCP	25
Domain Name Service	DNS	TCP & UDP	53
Dynamic Host Configuration	DHCP	UDP	67
World Wide Web	HTTP	TCP	80
Internet Mail Access	POP	TCP & UDP	109,110
Internet Mail Access	IMAP	TCP & UDP	143,220
Lotus Notes	Lotus Notes	TCP & UDP	352
Directory Access Service	LDAP	TCP & UDP	389
Network File System	NFS	TCP & UDP	2049
X Windows	X Windows	TCP	6000-6003

Application processes communicate with each other by exchanging messages. *A message* is a logical unit of information exchanged by two communicating entities. A request sent by a client and the response generated by a server, an image, or an Email are examples of messages. The actual size of a message may vary widely, from a few bytes in an acknowledgment to hundreds of bytes for an Email message, few Mbytes for an image, Gbytes for a complex query, or possibly Tbytes for the results of an experiment.

A semantic action is triggered only after the entire message is received. A server cannot react unless it receives the entire request, a program used to display an image cannot proceed if it gets only some regions of an image, an Email cannot be understood if only fragments reach the recipient.

There are several reasons why arbitrarily long messages have to be fragmented into units of limited size during transmission through the network. Fairness is one of the reasons; while we transmit a continuous stream of several Gbytes of data, the communication channel, a shared resource, cannot be used by other processes. Moreover, the switches along the message path may not have enough storage capacity for an arbitrarily long message. Last, but not least, in case of an error we would have to retransmit the entire message.

The unit of information carried by a protocol layer is called a *protocol data unit* (PDU). The application, transport, network, and data link layer PDUs are called messages, segments, packets, and frames, respectively, see Figure 4.5.

The size of a PDU differs from layer to layer, from one network architecture to another, and from one implementation to the next. The *transport data unit* (TDU), is called a *segment*. TCP is one of the Internet transport protocols and the *maximum segment size* (MSS), depends on the TCP implementation. In practice, typical values for MSS range from 512 to 1500 bytes.

A *packet* is a network layer PDU. The theoretical maximum size of an IP packet in the Internet is 65,536 bytes. A *frame* is a data link layer PDU. The maximum size of a frame is dictated by the network used to send the frame. For example, the Ethernet allows a maximum frame size of 1500 bytes.

The process of splitting a unit of information into pieces is called *fragmentation* and the process of putting the fragments together is called *reassembly*. The packets crossing from one network to another may suffer fragmentation and then the fragments have to be reassembled.

4.1.4   Encapsulation and Multiplexing

When a message is sent down the protocol stack, each protocol adds to the message a *header* understood only by its peer. In the case of application and transport protocols the peer is running on the destination host; for network and data link protocols the peer may be running on a switch or on a host, see Figure 4.5.

A header contains control information, e.g., sequence number, session id. The process of adding a header to a payload is called *encapsulation*. In Figure 4.8 we see that on the sending side the payload at level i consists of the header and the payload at level $(i - 1)$.

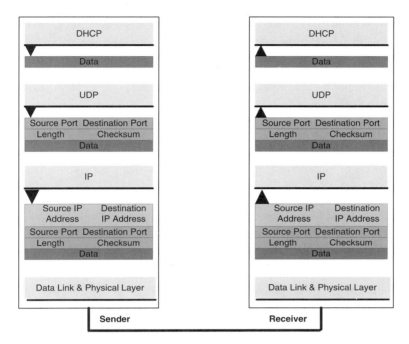

Fig. 4.8 Encapsulation and decapsulation in the case of communication between a client and a DHCP server using an application protocol called DHCP. On the sending site each protocol in the stack adds a header with information for its peer. On the receiving site the peer removes the header and uses the information to perform its functions.

The peer at the receiving site removes the header, takes actions based on the information in the header, and passes up the protocol stack only the data. This process is called *decapsulation*.

Example. Figure 4.8 shows the encapsulation and decapsulation for the case of the dynamic host reconfiguration service. This service allows a host to acquire dynamically an IP address, see Section 4.2.5. A client process running on the host sends a request to the DHCP server and gets back a response.

The communication between the client and the server is implemented by the DHCP. The DHCP protocol uses the transport services provided by UDP. In turn, UDP uses the network services provided by IP.

On the sending side the application generates the data and the DHCP creates a message and passes it to the transport protocol. UDP adds a header containing the source and the destination port, the length of the TDU and the checksum. The checksum allows the recipient to detect transmission errors as discussed in Chapter 2. Then IP adds the source and destination IP address to identify the hosts and passes the packet to the data link layer that constructs a frame and transmits it.

On the receiving site the data link layer extracts the IP packet from the frame. The IP protocol identifies the transport protocol and passes the transport data unit to UDP. Then UDP extracts the destination port and hands over the data to the application protocol, DHCP. In turn, DHCP parses the message and delivers its contents to the application, either the client side running on a host or the server side running on a dedicated system.

A protocol may be used by multiple protocols from an adjacent layer. In Figure 4.37 we see that several application layer protocols use TCP and UDP; in turn, both TCP and UDP use services provided by IP.

The process of combining multiple data streams into one stream is called *multiplexing*; the reverse process, splitting a stream into multiple ones is called *demultiplexing*. Figure 4.9 illustrates the case when the streams generated by three protocols, P1, P2, and P3 are multiplexed into one stream at the sending side and demultiplexed at the receiving side of a connection. In this example, one process running the P4 protocol cooperates with three processes, one running the P1 protocol, one running P2, and one running P3. On the sending side the three PDUs created by P1, P2 and P3 are encapsulated and the header of each PDU produced by P4 identifies the source protocol. The PDUs produced by P4 on the sending side is used by its peer, the process implementing the P4 protocol on the receiving side, to distribute the PDUs to P1, P2, and P3.

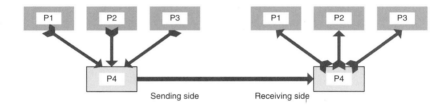

Fig. 4.9 The data streams generated by protocols P1, P2, and P3 are multiplexed into one stream at the sending side and the stream received by P4 is demultiplexed into three streams at the receiving side of a connection.

4.1.5   Circuit and Packet Switching. Virtual Circuits and Datagrams

There are two practical switching methods: circuit switching and packet switching, see Figure 4.10. Circuit switching is favored by analog networks, when information is carried by continuous-time continuous-amplitude signals, whereas packet switching is favored by digital networks. Digital networks sometimes resort to circuit switching as well.

In a circuit-switched network a physical connection between the input line and the desired output line of every switch along the path from the producer of information to the consumer is established for the entire duration of a session. After a connection is

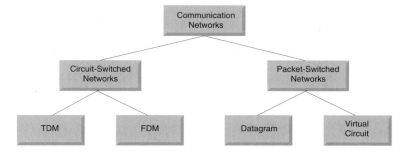

Fig. 4.10 Network taxonomy. Circuit switching is favored by networks where information is carried by analog signals. Packet switching is the method of choice for digital networks.

established, the signals carrying the information follow this path and travel through a "continuous" communication channel linking the source with the destination. At the end of the session the circuit is torn down.

There are two types of circuit-switched networks, see Figure 4.11, one based on time division multiplexing (TDM), and one based on frequency division multiplexing (FDM). TDM allocates individual time slots to each connection. FDM splits the bandwidth of a channel into several sub-channels and allocates one subchannel for each connection.

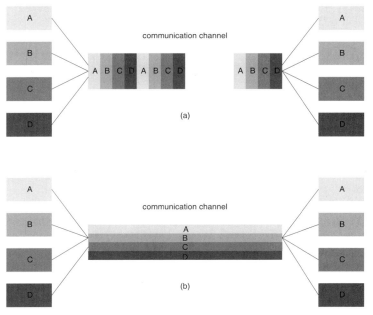

Fig. 4.11 (a) Time Division Multiplexing. The time is slotted and each connection is assigned one slot per period. (b) Frequency Division Multiplexing. The channel bandwidth split into four channels, one for each connection.

Circuit switching has the overhead to establish a circuit, but once the circuit is established the information is guaranteed to reach its destination with no additional overhead. This technique is efficient for relatively long-lived sessions and it was used for many years in telephony. A phone conversation between humans consists of an exchange of several messages as well as silence periods, thus the duration of the session is quite long compared with computer-to-computer communication. All the resources along the path are allocated for the entire session, and are wasted during the silence periods.

Computer-to-computer communication is very bursty, a large file may require a few seconds to be transferred and then no activity will occur for the next few hours. Circuit switching is rather ineffective in this case.

Packet switching is used in store-and-forward computer networks. Packets arrive at a switch where they are first stored, then the information about their final destination is extracted, and finally the packets are forwarded on one of the output lines of a switch. A switch performs two functions: *routing*, the process of constructing the knowledge base, in fact, a table, to make a forwarding decision; *forwarding*, the handoff of one packet from an input to an output line.

In a packet, switched network we have two options to route the packets from one source to one destination: (i) route each packet individually, or (ii) establish a path and route all packets along the same path. In the first case, no connection is established between the two parties involved, while in the second case a connection is necessary. The first approach based on *connectionless communication* is called *datagram* and the second, based on *connection-oriented communication* based upon a *virtual circuit*.

Datagram services incur less overhead, but do not provide guaranteed delivery or assurance that the packets arrive in the same order as they are sent, whereas virtual circuits are closer to an ideal lossless communication channel. However, a virtual circuit implies a contract involving a number of autonomous entities, including switches and communication channels in multiple networks, and demands dedicated resources throughout the duration of the contract.

Both paradigms have correspondents in real life: the U.S. Postal Service and the Western Union provide connectionless services, whereas the phone system supports connection-oriented services. All services provided by these institutions are necessary and this indicates to us that ultimately a computer network has to support both datagram and virtual circuit services.

When we discuss connectionless versus connection-oriented communication in a computer network we have to examine both the network and the transport layers. The network layer may provide a datagram or a virtual circuit service. In turn, the transport layer may implement both datagram and virtual circuit services regardless of the service offered by the network layer, see Figure 4.12. A connection-oriented, reliable, transport protocol can be built on top of an unreliable datagram network service.

The designer of a network may decide against virtual circuit support at the network layer because the establishment of a virtual circuit requires all routers on all networks along the path of a connection to allocate resources to the virtual circuit. This proposition is more difficult to implement and possibly more costly than to support only a datagram network service.

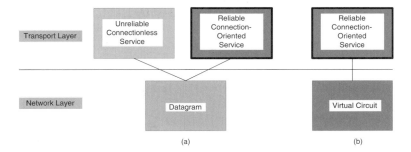

Fig. 4.12 The network layer may provide a datagram or a virtual circuit service; the transport layer may support an unreliable connectionless service and/or a reliable connection-oriented service. (a) The network layer provides a datagram service and the transport layer supports a reliable connection-oriented service and an unreliable datagram service. (b) The network layer provides a virtual circuit service and the transport layer supports a reliable connection-oriented service.

The Internet network architecture is based on IP, a datagram network protocol but provides connection-oriented as well as connectionless transport protocols, TCP and UDP, respectively.

4.1.6 Networking Hardware

In this section we survey basic components of the networking hardware. We discuss communication channels, network interfaces, modems, hubs, bridges, and routers.

4.1.6.1 Communication Channels. Communication channels, or lines, are physical media supporting propagation of signals.

Twisted pairs, coaxial cables, wireless channels, satellite links, and the optic fiber used by modern cable TV systems are all communication channels with different bandwidth, latency, and error rates. The bandwidth of a communication channel varies from few Kbps to hundreds of Gbps.

Latency depends on the length of the line and propagation velocity of the signal in the channel media. The propagation velocity of electromagnetic waves in ether or in fiber optic cables is equal to the speed of light, $c = 3 \times 10^{10}$ cm/second. The propagation velocity of electromagnetic waves in copper is about $2/3 \times c$. The error rates depend on the sensitivity of the media to electromagentic interference.

Twisted-pairs are used almost exclusively by phone companies to connect the handset to the end office. Such a pair consists of two copper wires, about 1 mm thick, twisted together to reduce the electrical inference, and enclosed in a protective shield. They are used to provide residential Internet access via dial-up, integrated service data network (ISDN), and asymmetric data service line (ADSL) networks. The data rates supported range from 56 Kbps for dial-up, to 128 Kbps for ISDN, and 10 Mbps for ADSL.

Unshielded twisted-pairs (UTPs) are typically used for LANs. Category 3 UTPs are used for data rates up to 10 Mbps, while category 5 UTPs can handle data rates of up to 100 Mbps.

Baseband coaxial cable or 50-ohm cable, is used in LANs for 10 Mbps Ethernets. It consists of two concentric copper conductors and allows transmission of digital signals without shifting the frequency.

Broadband coaxial cable or 75-ohm cable, is used in LANs and cable TV systems. The digital signal is shifted to a specific frequency band and the resulting analog signal is transmitted through the cable.

Fiber optics is a medium that conducts pulses of light, supports data rates of up to thousands of Gbps, has very low signal attenuation, and is immune to electromagnetic interference [22].

Terrestrial and satellite radio channels carry electromagnetic signals. Mobile services allow data rates of tens of Kbps, wireless LANs support data rates of up to tens of Mbps, and satellite links allow data rates of hundreds of Gbps [10]. Communication using geostationary satellites is subject to large delays of about 250 milliseconds.

Radio and satellite communication is subject to atmospheric perturbation and the error rates are considerably larger than those experienced by terrestrial lines. The maximum distance between a sender and receiver depends on the the frequency band used, the power of the transmitter, and the atmospheric conditions.

The great appeal of wireless networks is that no physical wire needs to be installed, a critical advantage for mobile communication devices.

4.1.6.2 Network Adaptors and Physical Addresses.
Any network device, be it a host, a switch, a printer, or a smart appliance is connected to a network by means of one or more network adaptors. A host, is generally connected to one LAN; a switch may be connected to multiple networks. LANs, are discussed in Section 4.1.8

From the point of view of a host, the LAN is yet another I/O device connected to the I/O bus. The block diagram of a network adaptor, see Figure 4.13, shows two components, the bus interface and the link interface that work asynchronously and have different speeds; the speed of the host I/O bus is generally higher than the speed of the communication line. The asyncronicity mandates that the two components be interconnected using two queues: frames sent by the host are buffered in an Out queue and sent to the network when the medium access protocol determines that a slot is available; frames received from the LAN are buffered in an In queue until the I/O bus can transfer the payload of the frame to the main memory.

The host interface of a network adaptor implements the hardware protocol for the I/O bus. The link interface implements the medium access control protocol for a LAN technology such as carrier sense multiple access with collision detection (CSMA/CD), FDDI, token ring, or ATM.

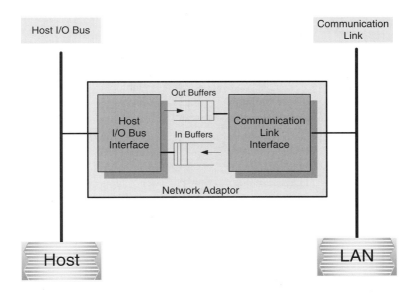

Fig. 4.13 A network adaptor connects a host to a LAN. The host interface implements the hardware protocol of the I/O bus. The communication line interface implements the medium access control protocol for a particular type of LAN technology such as 10 Mbps Ethernet, 100 Mbps Ethernet, ATM, or FDDI.

A network adaptor has a unique physical address hardwired by the manufacturer. A network adaptor for a broadcast channel is expected to identify the destination address field in a data link frame, compare that address with its own physical address, and transfer the frame to a buffer in the memory of the computer in case of a match. The network adaptor also recognizes broadcast and multicast addresses.

Figure 4.14 shows the format of an Ethernet frame. The network adaptor uses the preamble to recognize the beginning of a frame and then determines the source and destination addresses. If the destination address matches its own physical address

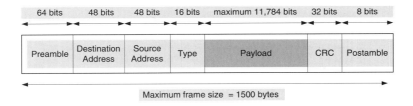

Fig. 4.14 The format of an Ethernet frame.

then the network adaptor identifies the type of the frame and the payload, then it performs a parity check, and finally delivers the payload.

Physical addresses form a flat addressing space. The size of the physical address space for different medium access control schemes is rather large. The size of the address space for Ethernet and token rings is 2^{48}. Large blocks of physical addresses are assigned to individual manufacturers of network hardware by the IEEE and the manufacturers select individual addresses from that block for each network adaptor they build.

4.1.6.3 Modems.

The information is transported through a communication channel by a *carrier*. A carrier is a periodic signal, a physical perturbation of the electromagnetic, optical, or accoustics field traveling through the transmission media. Common carriers are electric signals in metallic conductors such as twisted pairs or coaxial cable; electromagnetic waves in the ether; optical signals in an optical cable; and audio signals through ether or water. The process of inscribing the information on a carrier is called *modulation*; the process of extracting the information from the carrier is called *demodulation* [15].

A periodic signal is characterized by three parameters: amplitude, frequency, and phase. The information can be inscribed on a carrier by modifying either one of these three parameters; thus, we have amplitude, frequency, and phase modulation. For example, a straightforward way to transmit a binary sequence is to map a 1 to an electrical pulse of some amplitude, say, $+1$ Volt and a 0 to a pulse of a different amplitude, say, -1 Volt.

More sophisticated amplitude modulation schemes are used in practice. In the Manchester encoding scheme, described in standard communication and computer networking texts such as Kurose and Ross [14], a binary 1 is mapped into a positive pulse followed by a negative pulse, and a binary 0 is mapped into a negative pulse followed by a positive one. Figure 4.15 illustrates the encoding of the binary string 11011000 into a train of binary pulses using Manchester encoding.

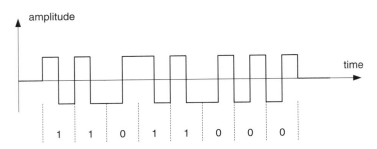

Fig. 4.15 In the Manchester encoding scheme a binary 1 is mapped into a positive pulse followed by a negative pulse, and a binary 0 is mapped into a negative pulse followed by a positive one.

The maximum data rate through a channel is determined by the duration of each pulse, the shorter the duration, the higher the rate. The data rate could be increased without shortening the duration of a pulse by increasing the number of signal levels. For example, with four signals levels we can encode combination of two bits. In this case, the data rate is twice the *baud rate*, the rate the amplitude of the signal changes.

A *modem* is a physical device performing modulation and demodulation. Digital computers can only send and receive digital signals and a modem is used to map digital into analog signals and back before transmission and after reception through an analog communication channel.

A typical modem allows transmission rates of up to 56 Kbps using standard phone lines. Often the line connecting a home with the end office consists of twisted pairs and the actual rate is much lower than this maximum. ADSL allows much higher data rates up to 10 Mbps. ADSL modems use more sophisticated frequency modulation schemes.

4.1.6.4 **Switches: Hubs, Bridges, and Routers.**   Until 1950s the circuit switched network called the telephone system depended on switchboards and human operators to physically connect subscribers with one another. Modern computer networks need a considerably faster and more reliable solution for switching.

A *switch* is a device with multiple inputs and outputs capable of connecting any input with any output. A switch in a computer network has multiple network adaptors, one for each input and output line; its main function is *packet forwarding*.

Switching in a packet-switched network means that a packet from an input line is transmitted on one of the output lines connected to the switch. In a circuit-switched network, a physical connection is established between the input and the output lines. Switching in a computer network can be done by an ordinary computer or by specialized devices described in this section called hubs, bridges, and routers.

There are some differences as well as similarities between switching in a LAN and switching in a WAN. A LAN consists of LAN segments interconnected by hubs and bridges and connected to the rest of the world via routers. A WAN consists of one or more networks interconnected by routers. The subject of routing in the Internet is discussed in depth in Section 4.2.6; here, we only present the routers.

LANs are often organized hierarchically; hosts are connected to LAN segments; in turn, LAN segments are connected among themselves via hubs, multiple hubs may be connected using a bridge, and multiple bridges may be connected to a router. Other LAN topologies are possible, for example, a LAN may have a backbone connecting individual hubs, or the hubs may be connected via bridges. In Figure 4.16 we see host A in LAN 1 connected to a hub, multiple hubs connected to a bridge, and several bridges connected to a router.

Two packet-switch architectures are used: (i) store-and-forward and (ii) cut-through. In a *store-and-forward switch* the entire packet must arrive before the switch can start its transmission, even when the queue associated with the output line is empty. In a *cut-through* switch once the header of the packet containing the destination address has arrived, the packet transmission may be initiated.

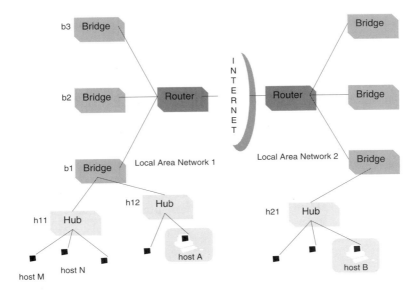

Fig. 4.16 Hubs, bridges, and routers. Host A in LAN 1 is connected to a hub, several hubs are connected to a bridge, and several bridges are connected to a router. All LAN segments connected to a hub share the same collision domain. Bridges isolate collision domains from one another.

Packets must be buffered inside a switch for a variety of reasons: multiple incoming packets on different input lines may need to travel on the same output line; the switching fabric may be busy; the output line may not be available. If the capacity of a buffer is exceeded, then the switch starts dropping packets.

Switching can be done at the physical, data link, or network layer. Hubs are physical layer switches, bridges are data link layer switches, and routers are network layer switches. A physical layer switch does not need any information to route the frames, it simply broadcasts an incoming frame on all the lines connected to it. A data link switch uses the information in the data link header to route a frame. The most complex switch is a router, a network layer switch, that uses information provided by the network layer header to forward each incoming packet.

Hubs are physical layer switches; they broadcast every incoming bit on all output lines. Hubs can be organized in a hierarchy with two or more levels; in a two-level topology, backbone hubs connect several hubs to the backbone of the LAN, other hubs connect LAN segments to the backbone hub.

In case of a collision-based multiple access LAN, such as Ethernet, all LAN segments connected to a hub share the same *collision domain*, only a single host from all segments may transmit at any given time. This effect limits the cumulative throughput of all segments connected to a hub to the maximum throughput of a single segment. For example, let us assume that the three LAN segments, in LAN 1, connected to the hub on the left side of Figure 4.16, are 10 Mbps Ethernets; then the total throughput of the subnet connected to the hub is 10 Mbps.

Each LAN technology defines a maximum distance between any pair of nodes and the medium access control protocol requires that all hosts are physically connected to the shared communication media, see Section 4.1.8. When the network cable is severed the LAN segment is no longer functional. Hubs extend the maximum distance between nodes and help isolate network faults.

Bridges are data link layer switches. Bridges can be used to connect LANs based on different technologies, e.g., 10-Mbps and 100-Mbps Ethernets.

In addition to forwarding, a bridge performs *filtering*, it forwards frames selectively. The bridge uses a forwarding table to determine if a frame should be forwarded as well as the address of the network adaptor it should be sent to.

For example, the bridge b1 in LAN 1, in Figure 4.16 isolates the traffic in the two subnets, one connected to the hub h11 and the other connected to the hub h12, from one another. A frame sent by host M connected to the hub h11 for host N in one of the segments connected to the same hub is also received by the bridge b1 but it is not forwarded to the hub h12, see Figure 4.16. However, if the destination address of the frame is host A, then the bridge b1 forwards the frame to the hub h12.

The forwarding table of a bridge is built automatically without the intervention of network administrators. If the destination address of a frame received by the bridge is not already in the forwarding table, then a new entry is added and the frame is broadcasted on all network adapters. If the destination address is already in the table, the frame is sent only to the network adapter for that destination.

An entry in the forwarding table of a bridge consists of the physical address of the source, the physical address of the network adaptor the frame arrived from, and a time stamp when the entry was created. An entry is deleted if no other frames from the same source arrive during a certain a period of time.

Routers are the most sophisticated type of switches. In addition to packet forwarding, they have to construct and update the forwarding tables that control routing. The routing algorithms for a WAN are rather complex and the number of entries in a forwarding table could be very large. Moreover, routers are expected to have a high throughput, some of them connect multiple very high-speed lines, each capable of delivering millions of packets per second [19].

A router consists of input ports connected to output ports via a switching fabric and a routing processor, see Figure 4.17. The routing processor constructs and updates the forwarding table. Input ports are independent processing elements capable of runing the data link protocol, examine each incoming packet, identify its destination address, perform a lookup in the forwarding table to determine the output port, and finally buffer the packet until the switching fabric is able to deliver it to the right output port. In turn, output ports are independent processing elements capable of buffering the packets for the output line, run the data link layer protocol for that particular line, and finally transmit the packet.

The load placed on a router depends on the placement of the router and the network topology. Based on their function and implicitly on the traffic, the routers can be classified as:

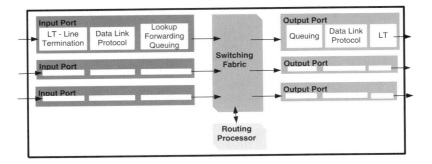

Fig. 4.17 The architecture of a router. The input ports are connected to output ports via a switching fabric. The routing processor constructs and updates the forwarding table.

(i) *Edge routers*, which connect a LAN or a set of LANs to the the the Internet. They forward only packets to/from the LAN(s) thus the intensity of the traffic handled by edge routers is generally lower than for other types of routers. Edge routers may perform additional functions related to network security and/or traffic control; they may act as firewalls and/or implement packet admission policies for congestion control.

(ii) *Internal routers*, which connect high-speed lines within a single administrative domain with one another. The intensity of the traffic could be very high.

(iii) *Border routers*, which connect administrative domains with one another.

Switching could be a time consuming function that limits the maximum throughput of a network. The switching overhead is virtually nonexistent for the physical layer switches, larger for data link layer switches, and even larger for network layer switches. For every incoming packet a router has to perform a table lookup and it may have to copy the packet from one buffer area to another. Figure 4.18 illustrates the layers crossed by a message from host A in LAN 1 to host B in LAN 2 in Figure 4.16.

4.1.7 Routing Algorithms and Wide Area Networks

Packet forwarding requires each router to have some knowledge of how to reach each node of the network. Each router builds the forwarding tables and determines the route for the packets using a *routing algorithm*.

Graph theory provided the foundation for studying routing algorithms. Consider the graph $\mathcal{G} = (\mathcal{N}, \mathcal{V})$ where $\mathcal{N}$ is the set of network nodes, the places where routing decisions are made, and $\mathcal{V}$ is the set of communication links. Each link v_i has a cost c_i associated with it. A *path* is an ordered sequence of links from source to the destination. An *optimal path* is a path of least-cost; the least cost path from a source to a destination has several properties:

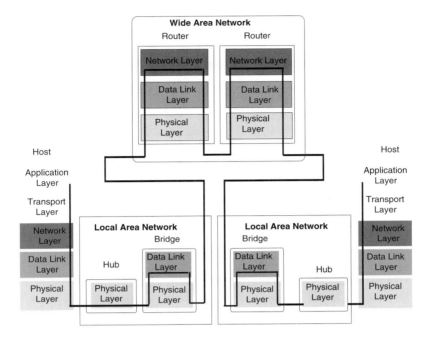

Fig. 4.18 The protocol layers crossed by a message on hosts and various types of switches for communication between host A in LAN 1 and host B in LAN 2 in Figure 4.16. A hub is a physical layer switch, a bridge is a data link layer switch, a router is a network layer switch.

(i) the first link in the path is connected to the source;

(ii) the last link in the path is connected to the destination;

(iii) $\forall (v_i, v_{i-1}) \in \mathcal{V}$ in the path they are connected to the same node $n_j \in \mathcal{N}$;

(iv) the sum of the costs of the links on the path is minimal for the least-cost path.

When all costs are the same, the least-cost path is identical with the shortest path. The problem of defining the cost of a link in a computer network is nontrivial, it is discussed at length in the literature and treated in depth by many networking texts, [7, 14, 20].

Computing optimal routes in a network is a much harder problem than the theoretical graph problem of finding the least-cost path from a source to a destination for two reasons:

(i) the network topology changes in time;

(ii) the costs associated with different links change due to network traffic.

There are two broad classes of routing algorithms: centralized and decentralized. *Centralized routing algorithms* use global knowledge; they need complete state information, the topology of the network, as well as the cost of all links. In the decentralized case no node has complete information about the costs of all network links or the topology of the network.

Another classification distinguishes between static and dynamic algorithms. *Static routing algorithms* can be used when the routes change slowly over time often as a result of human intervention. *Dynamic routing algorithms* are capable of accommodating changes of the routing patterns based on topological information when links and routers go up and come down and network load, based on congestion information. Dynamic routing algorithms can cause instability and oscillating behavior.

We examine two commonly used algorithms, the link state (LS) algorithm due to Djikstra, and the distance vector (DV) algorithm also known as Bellman-Ford.

4.1.7.1 *The Link State Routing Algorithm.*   The LS algorithm computes the path from a given source, node a, to all destinations. The algorithms consists of an initialization phase and a main computational loop.

Call $n(a)$ the set of immediate neighbors of node a and denote by $d(v)$ the distance between the node a and node v; then the two phases of the algorithm are:

$/ *$ *Initialization of the LS algorithm* $*/$
$\mathcal{B} = \{a\}$
$\forall v \in \mathcal{V}$
   $if \in n(a)$
      $then\ d(v)\ =\ cost(a,v)$
   $else\ d(v)\ =\ \infty$
$/ *$ *Iterations of the LS algorithm* $*/$
do
   $find\ w \notin \mathcal{B}\ such\ that\ d(w)\ is\ a\ minimum$
   $add\ w\ to\ \mathcal{B}$
   $(\forall v \notin \mathcal{B}) \bigwedge (v \in n(w))$
      $d(v) = min(d(v), d(w) + cost(w,v))$
      $until\ all\ nodes\ are\ in\ \mathcal{B}$
$enddo$

When the algorithm terminates, for each node, we have its predecessor along the least-cost path from the source node. For each predecessor we have also its predecessor. The complexity of the algorithm is $\mathcal{O}(N^2)$ where N is the number of nodes of the network and the communication complexity is $\mathcal{O}(N \times V)$ messages, with V the number of links in the network.

4.1.7.2 *The Distance Vector (DV) Algorithm.*   Each node maintains a distance table. This table gives the distance to every destination via each of the immediate neighbors of the node. To find the distance to a node: search all the neighbors and determine the distance to each one of them; add the distance to each neighbor to the distance the neighbor reports; and select the minimum among all neighbors.

The DV algorithm has a number of distinctive features; it is:

(i) *Distributed:* each node receives some information from its directly connected neighbors, performs a calculation, and then distributes it again to its immediate neighbors.

(ii) *Iterative:* continues until no more information is exchanged between neighbors.

(iii) *Asynchronous:* nodes do not work in lock step.

Call:

$n(a)$ the set of immediate neighbors of node a,

$\mathcal{Y}$ the set of all possible destinations,

e_1 the event that cost of the link from a to neighbor v changes by δ,

e_2 the event that node a receives an update from neighbor $v \in n(a)$ regarding destination $y \in \mathcal{Y}$. Call this update μ.

$D^a(y, v)$ is the distance from node a to node y via neighbor v of a.

$Cost(a, v)$ is the cost associated with the link connecting node a with its immediate neighbor v.

With these notations the algorithm can be described as follows:

$/ *$ *Initialization of the DV algorithm at node a* $ * /$
$\forall v \in n(a)$
$\quad D^a(x, v) = \infty \ if \ x \in \mathcal{V};$
$\quad D^a(v, v) = Cost(a, v);$
$\quad \forall y \in \mathcal{Y} \ send \ to \ v \ min_v[d(y, v)];$
$/ *$ *The DV algorithm at node a* $ * /$
do
$\quad wait \ for \ (e_1 \bigvee e_2)$
$\quad if(e_1)$
$\quad\quad then \ \forall \ y \in \mathcal{Y} \ \ D^a(y, v) = Cost(y, v) + \delta;$
$\quad if(e_2)$
$\quad\quad then \ for \ y \in \mathcal{Y} \ \ D^a(y, v) = Cost(a, v) + \mu;$
$forever$

In case of the first event, e_1, the cost of a link to neighbor v changes, node a changes the costs to all destination by the amount of the change, δ. When a receives an update from neighbor v regarding destination y, event e_2, then it updates its own distance to that destination.

The number of messages required by the DV algorithm is smaller than those for the LS routing algorithm. Message are exchanged only between directly connected

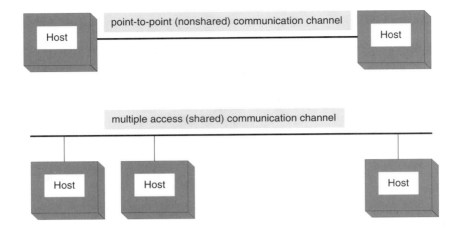

Fig. 4.19 Point-to-point and multiple-access communication channels. In case of multiple access channels a medium access control protocol is necessary to coordinate the sharing of the channel.

neighbors at each iteration; only changes that affect the costs of the least-cost path for the nodes attached to that link are transmitted. But the DV algorithm can converge slowly and can have routing loops; it can advertise incorrect least paths to all destinations.

4.1.8 Local Area Networks

A LAN, connects a relatively small number of computers, belonging to the same organization, administered by the same authority, and located within a geographic area of a few hundred meters or less.

Computers can be connected by point-to point channels or by broadcast channels, see Figure 4.19. Broadcast channels, also called multiple-access channels, are very popular for LANs.

The native communication mode for a broadcast channel is one-to-many, a frame sent by one node is received by all nodes connected to the channel. One-to-one communication for a broadcast channel is implemented as a particular case of the one-to-many mode; though all nodes receive all frames, only the one recognizing its address in the destination field of a frame, picks it up and processes it.

Broadcast or shared channels are more attractive for LANs than point-to-point channels because wiring is expensive. However, a single channel limits the communication bandwidth available to every single system sharing it. Broadcast communication presents security risks; networks using one wire also have the disadvantages of a single point of failure.

Broadcast channels have a wide spectrum of applications; in addition to LANs, they are used for satellite communication and for wireless communication based on packet radio networks. A problem that is nonexistent for full-duplex, point-to-point channels, but critical for broadcast channels is scheduling the transmission of a frame. This problem was discussed in Section 2.4, here, we only summarize the important concepts related to multiple-access channels used in LANs.

For simplicity in this discussion we consider a time-slotted channel with frames of fixed size and equal to the duration of a slot. In any given slot only one node may transmit successfully; if more than one node transmits, then we have a *collision* and all the parties involved have to reschedule the transmission. Channel sharing in a multiple access channel is defined by a media access control (MAC) layer, included in the data link layer.

There are two basic methods for channel sharing:

1. *collision-free multiple access* methods based on scheduled access. Token passing rings and busses schedule transmissions such that only one of the n nodes connected to a shared channel transmits in any given slot.

2. *collision-based multiple access* or *random multiple access* (RMA) methods, where collisions are allowed, and then *collision resolution algorithms* (CRA), or other methods are used to determine the order in which nodes transmit.

RMA algorithms were first used in practice in the Alohanet, a packet-switched network designed by Abramson at the University of Hawaii in late 1960s [1]. The Aloha algorithm allows a node with a new frame to transmit immediately and a *backlogged* node, one involved in a collision, is required to wait a random amount of time before retransmitting the frame. The efficiency of an Aloha system can be computed with relative ease but this derivation is beyond the scope of this book and can be found in most standard texts such as [2]. The efficiency of the Aloha algorithm is 0.18%:

$$\eta_{aloha} = \frac{1}{2e}.$$

An improved version of the algorithm, the *slotted Aloha*, requires the nodes to transmit only at the beginning of a slot and has an efficiency of 0.36%:

$$\eta_{saloha} = \frac{1}{e}.$$

These figures are impressive considering the simplicity of the algorithms involved. Aloha algorithms inspired the invention of the Ethernet, a very popular technology for LANs [17].

In this section we discuss only the multiple access method used by the Ethernet technology. *CSMA/CD* is an algorithm that requires each node to monitor or sense the channel before sending a frame and to refrain from sending the frame if the channel is busy.

Carrier sensing does not prevent collisions because two or more nodes may sense that the channel is idle and transmit at the same time. If the maximum distance between any pair of nodes is L and propagation velocity is v, then a node knows that it has managed to transmit successfully only if the channel feedback indicates no interference with its transmission after an interval equal to $\tau = 2 \times t_p$ where $t_p = \frac{L}{v}$ is the propagation time between the pair of the farthest two nodes.

When a collision occurs, the nodes involved in the collision use a binary exponential backoff algorithm to resolve the collision. Conceptually, the *binary exponential backoff algorithm* requires that the nodes involved in a collision flip a coin and retransmit with probability $1/q$ in one of the following q slots, with q initially set to 2 and doubling after each subsequent collision. It is likely that only two nodes were involved in the initial collision and flipping the coin will allow each of the two nodes to transmit alone in one of the next two slots based on a random drawing. If a subsequent collision occurs it is possible that more than two nodes were involved in the initial collision and each of them is likely to draw a different slot in the pool consisting of the next four slots. The process continues until the collision is resolved. A collision resolution interval lasts an integer number of slots of length τ.

The original Ethernet invented in 1973 by Boggs and Metcalfe at Xerox Park Research Center, ran at 2.94 Mbps and linked some 256 hosts within a mile from each other. The 10-Mbps Ethernet became immensely popular in the early 1980s and continues to be widely used as a LAN even today. Faster Ethernet networks, 100-Mbps and even 1-Gbps, are available nowadays.

Collisions limit the actual throughput of an Ethernet network to a value lower than the maximum throughput [3]. The *channel efficiency*, defined as the useful time spent transmitting data versus the total time, decreases as the speed of an Ethernet network increases, see Figure 4.20. Consider three networks with the same topology and number of nodes, but with different speeds: 10 Mpbs, 100 Mbps, and 1 Gbps, respectively. The collision resolution interval contains the same number of slots of duration τ, for a given packet arrival pattern at the nodes.

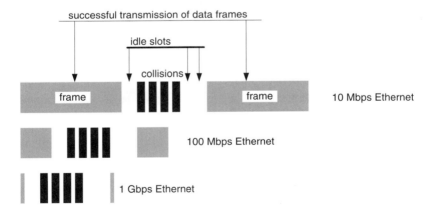

Fig. 4.20 Channel efficiency decreases as the speed of an Ethernet network increases. The time spent transmitting the data is getting shorter and shorter as we move from 10 Mbps to 100 Mbps and to 10 Gbps while the time for collision resolution stays the same if the number of nodes and network topology are the same. τ, the length of a slot, does not change when the transmission speed increases.

But τ depends only on the maximum distance between any pair of two nodes and the propagation velocity v, and it is invariant to the transmission speed. Thus, the useful time spent transmitting a frame shrinks when transmission speed increases, while the scheduling overhead for each frame stays the same. This conclusion is valid for all collision-based schemes for multiple access.

If we denote by t_f the time to transmit a frame, the Ethernet efficiency can be approximated by the following expression [2]:

$$\eta_{ethernet} = \frac{1}{1 + 5 \times \frac{t_p}{t_f}}.$$

4.1.9 Residential Access Networks

In the previous sections we saw that institutions use LANs connected to an edge router to access the Internet. The use of LANs is possible because the computers are located within the same geographic area, belong to the same organization, and are administered by the same authority. This solution cannot be used for residential Internet access because these assumptions are violated.

Installing new lines to every home is an expensive proposition and residential access networks take advantage of the existing lines laid down by the telephone and cable companies. Satellite channels provide a very attractive alternative, but, at the time of this writing, they account for a very small percentage of homes connected to the Internet.

We discuss first three residential access networks based on the telephone system, dial-up, ADSL, and ISDN. The dial-up does not impose any special requirements, whereas ISDN and ADSL require that special equipment be installed by the local carrier. Here, the term "local carrier" refers to the company providing local telephone services. Then we present HFC, a residential access network using the cable system.

The solution available to anyone with a phone line into the home is dial-up, see Figure 4.21. A home computer is connected to the phone line via a modem. The Internet service provider (ISP) has a modem farm and each incoming call is routed through one of the modems to a dial-up system.

Modems are communication devices converting digital to analog signals and back. The maximum speed allowed by modern modems is 56 Kbps, but the quality of the line connecting a home with the end office limits this speed to lower values.

The ADSL is a newer service provided by phone companies [9]. ADSL uses more sophisticated encoding techniques to achieve much higher data rates. ADSL is based on frequency division multiplexing and provides three channels: a high-speed downstream channel; a medium-speed upstream channel; and an ordinary phone channel.

The word "asymmetric" in ADSL reflects the uneven data rates for transmission to/from the home computer; the high-speed downstream channel, providing data to the home computer supports up to 8 Mbps and the upstream channel, from the home computer to the ISP, supports only about 1 Mbps. The built-in asymmetry comes from the realization that a home computer consumes more data than it produces. Indeed, a significant fraction of the traffic is related to Web activity.

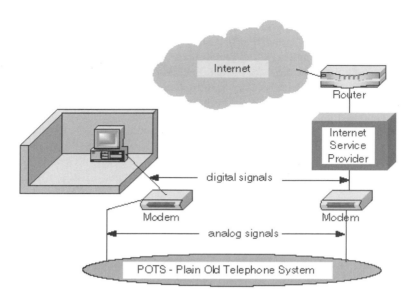

Fig. 4.21 Dial-up access network. Modems convert digital signals generated by computers to analog signals to be transmitted through the phone system and convert analog signals received at the other end into digital signals.

ISDN is another alternative to connect a home computer with the Internet, but requires the telephone company's switches to support digital connections. A digital signal, instead of an analog signal, is transmitted across the line, see Figure 4.22.

This scheme permits a much higher data transfer rate than analog lines, up to 128 Kbps. ISDN has other advantages too; while a modem typically takes 30-60 seconds to establish a connection, this interval is reduced to less than 2 seconds for an ISDN call. Multiple devices may operate concurrently because ISDN supports multiple digital channels through the regular phone wiring used for analog lines.

Last, but not least, cable companies now offer the hybrid fiber coaxial cable (HFC), services. HFC requires cable modems connected to a home computer via Ethernet. The downstream channel could provide up to 10 Mbps while the upstream channel rates are limited to, say, 1 Mbps. The actual rates depend on the service provider. Moreover the HFC network has a tree topology (see Figure 4.23) and the amount of bandwidth available to individual customers depends on the actual traffic in the network.

4.1.10   Forwarding in Packet-Switched Network

To fully understand the advantages and the challenges posed by each type of packet-switched network, we now discuss the problem of packet forwarding in datagram and virtual circuit networks.

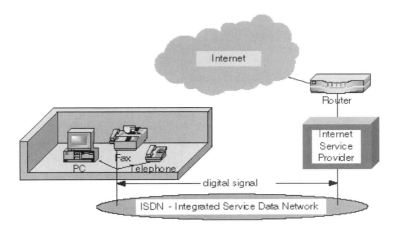

Fig. 4.22 ISDN network access. Multiple devices share a digital communication channel.

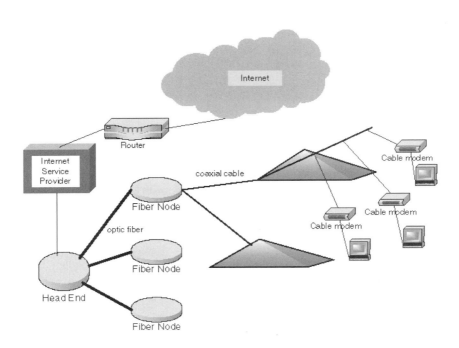

Fig. 4.23 A hybrid cable access network has a tree topology. The Head End is connected to Fiber Nodes using fiber optics and coaxial cable connects individual homes to a Fiber Node.

Packet forwarding is done by devices called switches, see Section 4.18. A switch is similar to a post office sorting center where incoming letters are sorted based on their destination address; those with the destination addresses within the same region are put into one bag and sent to a regional distribution center. A switch has several input and output lines, each line is identified locally by a port number. Each incoming packet is forwarded on one of the output lines.

A necessary condition for packet forwarding is to identify each possible network destination by an address. An in-depth discussion of addressing in Internet is presented in Section 4.2, for now we only assume that each host and router has one or more unique addresses. In addition to the ability to identify the destination address of each packet a switch has to maintain a knowledge base, or a *forwarding table*, on how to reach each possible network destination.

In datagram-based networks the network header of each packet carries its final destination address and the forwarding table maps each possible destination into a port connected to an output line. The task of the switch is to: (a) identify the destination address of a packet, (b) look up in the forwarding table the entry corresponding to the destination address, and (c) send the packet to the output port.

This process is slightly more complicated in case of a virtual circuit network. First, we have to establish a virtual circuit (VC) between the sender and the receiver. Once the VC is established all packets follow the same route.

Now, each entry in the forwarding table of a switch consists of a four tuple: the input port number, the input VC number, the output port number, and the output VC number, $inPort, inVC, outPort, outVC$.

To establish a full-duplex connection, two VCs are created on each line between the two end points of the circuit.

The VC numbers for each line are assigned by the network layer of the host generating the request or by the switch receiving a request to establish a VC. The host or the switch searches its database and assigns a VC number not used on the outgoing line. Thus, the VC numbers for the same VC inevitably change from line to line.

Figure 4.24 illustrates the establishment of a VC. Initially, a process on host a requests the establishment of a full-duplex connection with a peer on host b.

Host a examines its database and determines that:

(i) The VC should go through switch A

(ii) It is directly connected to switch A. The connection runs from port 1 of a to port 2 of A.

(iii) A full-duplex circuit is desired. The two VC numbers available on the line to A are 12 and 13.

Host a updates its forwarding table accordingly and sends the request to switch A.

Switch A examines its database and determines that:

(i) The request should be forwarded to switch B.

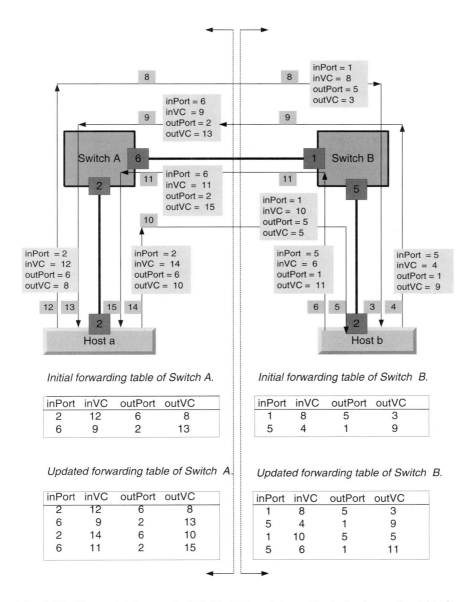

Fig. 4.24 The establishment of a VC. The VCs and the entries in the forwarding table for: switch A on the left side and for switch B on the right side. Initially, we have a full-duplex VC between a process on host a and one on host b. Then another process on host a initiates the establishment of a second full-duplex VC between a and b. The VCs on each line are: 12, 13, 14, 15 between a and A; 8, 9, 10, 11 between A and B; 3, 4, 5, 6, between B and b. The first two entries in each list correspond to the the initial full-duplex connection and the last two to the second one. On each virtual circuit we show the entries corresponding to each of the two switches. The ports of A, B, a, b are $(2, 6)$, $(1, 5)$, (2), and (2), respectively.

(ii) It is directly connected to switch B. The connection runs from port 6 of A to port 1 of B.

(iii) A full-duplex VC is requested.

(iv) The VC numbers on the line to a are 12 and 13, as determined by host a.

(v) The first two available VC numbers on the line to B are 8 and 9.

Switch A adds two new entries to its forwarding table: $2, 12, 6, 8$ for the circuit from a to b and $6, 9, 2, 13$ for the one from b to a and then forwards the request to switch B.

In turn, switch B examines its own database and determines that:

(i) The request should be forwarded to host b.

(ii) It is directly connected with host b. The connection runs from port 5 of B to port 2 on b.

(iii) A full-duplex VC is requested.

(iv) The VC numbers on the line to A are 8 and 9, as determined by switch A.

(v) The first two available VC numbers on the line to b are 3 and 4.

Switch B adds two new entries to its forwarding table: $1, 8, 5, 3$ for the circuit from a to b and $5, 4, 1, 9$ for the one from b to a and then forwards the request to host b.

Finally, host b gets the request and determines that:

(i) It is the terminal point for the VC.

(ii) It is directly connected to switch B. The connection runs from port 5 of B to port 2 of b.

(iii) A full-duplex circuit is desired. The two VC numbers available on the line to B are 3 and 4, as assigned by B.

Host b updates its forwarding table and sends an acknowledgment to a.

As pointed out earlier, the full-duplex VC consists of two VC, one from a to b and one from b to a. Each of the two circuits consists of three segments and has a different VC number on each segment $12, 8, 3$ for the first and $4, 9, 13$ for the second.

Assume now that another process on host a requests another VC to b. Figure 4.24 illustrates the updated segment of the forwarding tables for the two switches assuming that no other VCs connecting the two switches have been established from the moment of the previous request.

Once the VC was established, for every incoming packet a switch goes through the following procedure: (a) get the packet from an input port, (b) extract the VC number from the header of the packet, (c) perform a look-up to determine the output port and VC number, knowing the input port and VC number, (d) construct a new header with the new circuit number, and (e) forward the packet to the output port.

4.1.11   Protocol Control Mechanisms

Earlier we pointed out that communication protocols have to bridge the gap between applications and networking technology. The list of the features expected by applications, see Section 4.1.1, can be condensed into several mechanisms that communication protocols have to support:

(i)   error control - mechanisms for error detection and error handling,

(ii)   flow control - mechanisms to coordinate sending and receiving of PDUs, and

(iii)   congestion control - mechanisms to prevent overloading the network.

Error control and flow control are built into the protocols at several layers of a communication architecture. Data link protocols must implement error and flow control. It makes no sense for a router to transmit further a packet in error, thus the need for error control at the data link layer. A slow router connected to a fast one via a fast communication channel would run out of buffer space and be forced to drop the packets, thus the need for flow control at the data link layer.

Yet, error control and flow control at the data link layer are insufficient to guarantee end-to-end error control and flow control in a datagram network. A router along the path may fail after getting the packets from the incoming line, but before being able to send them on the output line. The per-hop flow control does not guarantee that the slow router will have enough buffer space to forward the packets coming from a fast router and a fast line to a slow router connected via a slow line. Therefore, the need to build error control and flow control into the transport layer protocols.

Application layer protocols may choose to implement error control and flow control. This solution is wasteful; it leads to a duplication of effort and it is seldom used. Instead, applications rely on transport protocols to support these functions.

From this brief discussion we conclude that a protocol stack should contain several transport protocols supporting various degrees of end-to-end error control and a flow control mechanism. An application protocol would then be able to choose the transport mechanism best suited for the application.

Let us now address the issue of congestion control. A computer network can be regarded as a storage system containing the packets in transit at any given time. This storage system has a finite capacity; when the system is close to its capacity, the network becomes congested and the routers start dropping packets. The role of a congestion control mechanism is to prevent network congestion.

Congestion control is a global network problem, it can only be enforced if all participants to the traffic cooperate. In a datagram-based network, congestion control cannot be addressed at the network layer because each packet is treated by the network individually; the only solution is to provide transport layer congestion control. But, connectionless transport protocols cannot support any form of congestion control; connection-oriented transport protocols only support congestion control for the processes at the end points of a connection.

As we already know, the Internet is a datagram network based on the Internet protocol and there are two transport protocols: UDP, a connectionless datagram protocol and TCP, a connection-oriented protocol. TCP is the only transport protocol supporting congestion control.

We now cover the first two control mechanisms presented above, error control and flow control and defer an in-depth discussion of congestion control for Section 4.3.7. In the following presentation we talk about PDUs, instead of frames or segments because error control and flow control mechanisms are implemented both at the data link and at the transport layer.

4.1.11.1   *Error Control.*   We encounter two potential problems, PDUs in error and lost PDUs. First, we address the problem of transmission errors. In Chapter 2 we discussed error detecting/correcting codes and we know that a message must be encoded prior to transmission to enable any type of error control.

Recall that a code is designed with well-defined error detection/correction capabilities and is unable to detect/correct error patterns outside its scope. This means that there is always a chance, we hope a very small one, that a particular error pattern may go undetected/uncorrected.

Communication protocols use almost exclusively error detecting codes. Error correcting codes were seldom used in the past, but this may be changing for applications with timing constraints when retransmission is not an option.

Traditionally, communication protocols use a procedure called automatic repeat request (ARQ): once an error is detected the receiver requests the retransmission of the PDU. To support ARQ we need to:

(i) request the receiver to provide feedback to the sender regarding individual PDUs. This feedback is in the form of *acknowledgments*.

(ii) address the problem of lost PDUs and/or acknowledgments.

To support (i) we have to stamp each PDU and each acknowledgment with a unique *sequence number* and *acknowledgment number*, respectively. This information is included into the corresponding protocol header.

To support (ii) we have to associate a timer and *timeout* with each individual PDU and request the sender to obey the following set of rules:

1. Set a timer immediately after transmitting a PDU;

2. Wait for an acknowledgment for that particular PDU. When the acknowledgment arrives reset the timer and transmit the next PDU.

3. If a timeout occurs before receiving the acknowledgment, re-transmit the PDU associated with that timer. In this scheme the receiver only acknowledges frames without errors.

To illustrate the intricacies of error control mechanisms we discuss the "alternating bit protocol." This simple stop-and-wait protocol uses only one bit for the sequence number and one for the acknowledgment number. The sender sends one PDU and waits for the acknowledgment before sending the next PDU.

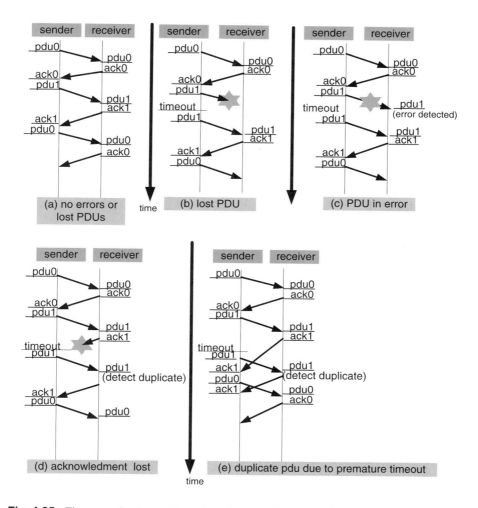

Fig. 4.25 Five scenarios for an alternating-bit protocol: (a) normal operation of the protocol when no errors or PDU losses occur; (b) a timeout and a retransmission of a lost PDU; (c) a PDU in error is received; (d) a timeout occurs when an acknowledgment is lost; and (e) a premature timeout causes a duplicate PDU to be sent. Scenarios (a), (b), (d), and (e) are similar with the ones described in [14].

Figure 4.25 depicts five scenarios for an alternating-bit protocol:

(a) an exchange without errors or lost PDUs;

(b) a PDU is lost and this causes a timeout and a retransmission;

(c) a PDU in error is detected;

(d) an acknowledgment is lost; and

(e) a duplicate PDU is sent due to a premature timeout.

The role of the sequence numbers is illustrated by the last two examples; the receiver could not detect a duplicated PDU without a sequence number, even though only one PDU is transmitted at a time.

The functioning of a communication protocol is best described as a state machine. The state machine of a protocol is characterized by: (1) the set of states; (2) the set of transitions among states; (3) the set of events (each transition is caused by an event); and (4) the set of actions (any event may trigger an action).

Let us now consider the efficiency of a stop-and-wait protocol. We first introduce a measure of the communication delay called the round trip time (RTT). RTT measures the time it takes a PDU to travel from one end of a communication channel to the other and back. The efficiency of a stop-and-wait protocol is:

$$\eta_{stopAndWait} = \frac{t_{PDU}}{t_{PDU} + RTT}$$

where $t_{PDU} = L/B$ is the transmission time of a PDU of length L over a channel with maximum speed B, see Figure 2.2 in Chapter 2.

Example. Given an optical cable 450 Km long the RTT is:

$$RTT = 2 \times \frac{4.5 \times 10^7 cm}{3 \times 10^{10} cm/sec} = 3 \times 10^{-3} seconds.$$

The transmission time of a 1000 bit PDU over a 1 Gbps channel is:

$$t_{PDU} = \frac{10^3 bits}{10^9 bits/sec} = 10^{-6} seconds.$$

Thus:
$$\eta_{stopAndWait} = \frac{10^{-6}}{3 \times 10^{-3} + 10^{-6}} = 3.4\%.$$

While this is an extreme example, it should be clear that the stop-and-wait protocol has a low efficiency; the shorter the PDU, the higher the channel speed, and the larger the RTT, the less efficient this protocol is.

4.1.11.2 *Flow Control.*

It is important to remember that data link protocols perform hop-to-hop flow control, while transport protocols perform end-to-end flow control. End-to-end flow control can only be provided by connection-oriented transport protocols.

The brief description of the stop-and-wait algorithm indicates that acknowledgments are important not only for error control but also for flow control. A receiver is able to throttle down the sender by withholding acknowledgments.

An obvious and at the same time significant improvement over the stop-and-wait algorithm is to support *pipelining*, to allow the sender to transmit a range of N PDUs without the need to wait for an acknowledgment. The sequence numbers of the PDUs a process is allowed to send at any given time are said to be in the *sender's window*; this window advances in time, as the sender receives acknowledgments for PDUs; thus, the name *sliding-window* protocols.

Sliding-window communication protocols achieve a better efficiency than stop-and-wait protocols at the expense of a more complex protocol state machine and additional buffer space to accommodate all the PDUs in the sender's window. The efficiency of this protocol family is further increased by *cumulative acknowledgments*. By convention, when the sender receives an acknowledgment for the PDU with sequence number seq_i, this means that the entire range of PDUs, up to seq_i has been received successfully.

The condition to keep the pipeline full, assuming that the round trip time is RTT and all PDUs are of the same size and have the same transmission time, t_{PDU}, is:

$$N > \frac{RTT}{t_{PDU}}.$$

This brings us to the issue of sequence numbers. If in the protocol header we allocate n bits for the sequence number and an equal number of bits for the acknowledgment number, the sequence numbers wrap around modulo 2^n PDUs. But the PDUs within the window must have distinct sequence numbers so we need at least $log_2(N)$ bits for a pipelined protocol with the window size equal to N. It turns out that n has to be twice this limit, see Problem 3 at the end of this chapter.

So far we have concentrated only on the sending side of a connection. Let us now turn our attention to the receiving side. First, we note that on the receiving side of a sliding-window protocol with a window size N, the peer must also maintain a window of size N. Indeed, the N PDUs the peer on the sender side is allowed to transmit without an acknowledgment may arrive at the peer on the receiver side before the consumer of the PDUs may be able to accept any of them. The peer would have to buffer them for some time and delay sending the acknowledgment until all or some of the PDUs have been disposed of. The consumer of PDUs for the transport layer is the application; for the data link layer the consumer is the network layer protocol, see Figure 4.5.

The next question is whether the PDUs accepted by the receiver must be in order. There are two types of window-based communication protocols and each answers this question differently; in the *Go-Back-N* algorithm the receiver maintains an $expected\_seqn$ and only accepts PDUs in order; the *Selective Repeat* is more flexible and allows out-of-order PDUs.

In Figure 4.26 we see a snapshot of the sender's window. The sender maintains three pointers, $window\_base$ to the lower side of the window, $window\_base+(N-1)$ to the upper side of the window, and $next\_seqn$ to the next available sequence number. PDUs already sent and acknowledged have sequence numbers lower than the lower side of the window. Some of the PDUs, the ones with sequence numbers in the range $window\_base \leq seqn < next\_seqn$ have already been sent and the acknowledgments for them have not been received yet. The peer on the sender's side can only accept from its upper layer PDUs with sequence numbers in the range

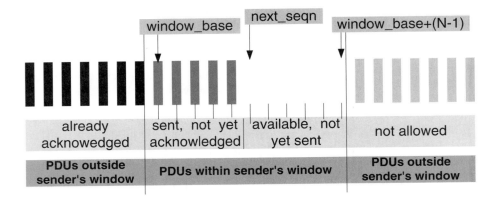

Fig. 4.26 The sender's window for a Go-Back-N protocol. The sender maintains three pointers, $window\_base$ to the lower side of the window, $window\_base + (N - 1)$ to the upper side of the window, and $next\_seqn$ to the next available sequence number. The PDUs with sequence numbers in the range $window\_base \leq seqn < next\_seqn$ have already been sent and the acknowledgments for them have not been received yet. The protocol can only accept from its upper layer PDUs with sequence numbers in the range $next\_seqn \leq seqn < window\_base + (N - 1)$ and is able to send them immediately.

$next\_seqn \leq seqn < window\_base + (N - 1)$ and is able to send them immediately. The $window\_base$ is updated every time an acknowledgment for a PDU with sequence number larger than its current value is received. When a timeout for a PDU, $seqn_{timeout}$ occurs, the sender must retransmit all PDUs in the range $window\_base \leq seqn \leq seqn_{timeout}$.

The receiver only accepts a PDU if its sequence number is equal to $expected\_seqn$, otherwise it drops it. This strategy does not allow cumulative acknowledgments and limits the efficiency of the Go-Back-N algorithm.

The limitations of the Go-Back-N algorithm are overcome by the selective repeat (SR) algorithm. In SR the receiver accepts out-of-order PDUs. The sender's window advances when acknowledgments for its left margin are received. PDUs already sent and acknowledged may appear in the window. Figure 4.27 shows a snapshot of sender's window for a selective repeat algorithm.

4.2 INTERNET ADDRESSING

In this section we present Internet addressing and then discuss routing in an internetwork. A communication system must identify the end points of a logical communication channel to deliver any type of information. The end points of all logical communication channels form an *address space*. Examples of address spaces are the set of all telephone numbers in North America and the set of all postal addresses in the United States.

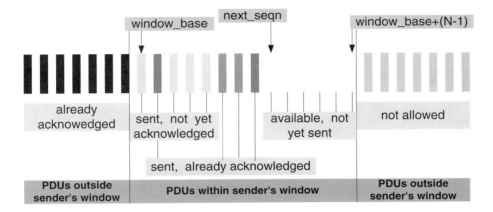

Fig. 4.27 A snapshot of sender's window for a selective repeat protocol. The window advances when acknowledgments for its left margin are received.

The organization of an address space is known as an *addressing scheme*. Communication systems may use a hierarchical, or a flat addressing scheme. In *hierarchical addressing*, the address space is structured, it forms a tree. At each level i of the tree we have a set disjoint *domains*, in turn each domain at level i, consists of a set of disjoint subdomains, at level $i + 1$. To deliver the information we need to traverse the tree from the sender to the receiver. The telephone system uses a hierarchical addressing scheme.

In a hierarchical addressing scheme the actual address of a destination entity is different for different senders, depending on the relative position in the tree of the two entities. To call a phone number in Paris from another country we need to dial first the country code, then the city code, and finally the phone number in Paris. In this example, the three components of the phone number are concatenated, the country prefix, the city prefix, and the phone number in Paris form a unique phone number to be used when calling from outside France. To call the same number from within France we concatenate the city prefix and the phone number in Paris.

When the entire address space consists of a single domain, we have a *flat addressing* scheme. In this case, an address is assigned by a central authority and it does not provide any information about the location of the entity. For example, the Social Security numbers (SSNs) form a flat addressing space; the SSNs are assigned by the Social Security Administration and the SSN of an individual does not reveal where the individual lives.

Sometimes we need a multiple addressing scheme to combine the need to have an invariant name for an object with the desire to introduce some structure in the address space and/or to have mnemonic names. For example, an automobile has a serial number and a license plate. The serial number is stamped for the lifetime of the automobile, while the license plate depends on the residence of the owner and may change in time. The correspondence between the two is established by the registration papers.

Communication can be *one-to-one* or may involve groups of entities, a paradigm known as *collective communication*. Collective communication is pervasive in our daily life: announcers at an airport address particular groups of travelers; a presidential address is broadcast by radio and TV stations for everybody.

We now present a classification of Internet addressing modes based on the relationship between the end points of the communication channel(s). The first addressing mode supports one-to-one communication while the last three support collective communication:

(i) *Unicast*: the address identifies a unique entity; the information is delivered to this entity.

(ii) *Multicast*: the address identifies a group of entities; the information is delivered to all of them.

(iii) *Anycast*: the address identifies a group of entities; the information is delivered to only one of them selected according to some criteria.

(iv) *Broadcast*: the address identifies all entities in the address space; the information is delivered to all of them.

Internet uses multiple addressing schemes to identify a host. A network adaptor has a physical address, a logical address, and a name. Physical addresses are hard-wired into network adaptors and cannot be changed, while logical or IP addresses are assigned based on the location of the computer and may change. In Section 4.2.4 we discuss a mechanism to relate the physical and IP addresses and we defer the discussion of the correspondence between IP addresses and Internet names for Chapter 5.

4.2.1 Internet Address Encoding

An *Internet address*, also called an *IP address*, uniquely identifies a network adaptor connecting a host or a router to the Internet. An IP address consists of the pair $(NetworkId, HostId)$, the network id or network number and the host id. Recall that the port number is not part of the IP address, it is an additional component of the address of a process within a host, identified in the header of a transport protocol.

A host may have multiple connections to the Internet and may have multiple IP addresses, one for each connection, as seen in Figure 4.36. However, a router always has multiple connections to the Internet. Thus, a router has multiple IP addresses.

We now turn to the more complex problem of logical addressing in the Internet. Two versions of the addressing scheme and consequently two version of the network protocol are supported, IPv4 and IPv6. The first is based upon 32-bit IP addresses and the second on 128-bit IP addresses. Unless stated otherwise our discussion throughout this chapter covers 32-bit IP addressing. IPv6 is presented in Section 4.3.3.

An IPv4 address is encoded as a 32-bit number. The leftmost 4 bits encode an address class, the next group of bits encode the $NetworkId$ and the rightmost bits encode the $HostId$. An IPv4 address is typically presented as a sequence of four integers, one for each byte of the address. For example, 135.10.74.3

The IP addresses are grouped together in several classes. There are four classes of IP addresses in use today A,B,C, and D. Class D is used for IP multicasting, class E is reserved for future use. The actual number of bits encoding the $NetworkId$ and the $HostId$ differs for classes A,B, and C. This scheme illustrated in Figure 4.28 is called *classful addressing*.

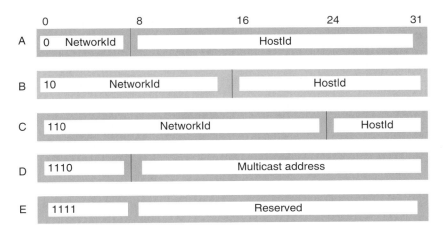

Fig. 4.28 IPv4 address format.

The encoding scheme described above for IPv4 has some limitations:

(i) The size of the address space is limited to 2^{32}. This means that the maximum number of network hosts is about 4×10^9. This seems an impressive number, but the structure imposed on the address space by the classful addressing scheme discussed in this section generates a large number of unusable IP addresses. Only a relatively small fraction of this address space is usable.

(ii) Class C addresses are not in demand. Many networks have more 255 hosts and cannot use Class C addresses.

(iii) Class B addresses are in high demand. But a network with $n < 65,535$ hosts uses only a fraction $\frac{n}{65,535}$ of these addresses.

Scalability is a serious concern in the Internet. In Section 4.2.6 we discuss this problem in depth; here, we only note that routing in the Internet requires each router to have a *forwarding table* telling it how to reach different networks. The more networks in the Internet, the larger is the size of the forwarding tables and the larger is the overhead to locate an entry. Keeping the size of the forwarding tables relatively small is an enduring objective of Internet designers.

University campuses or large corporations typically having a large number of networks are administered independently. Assigning distinct network numbers to networks belonging to the same organization not only leads to the depletion of the address space, but it also increases the size of the forwarding tables.

In Sections 4.2.2 and 4.2.3 we discuss two techniques designed to address the concerns related to classful Internet addressing: subnetting and classless addressing.

4.2.2 Subnetting

Subnetting is one of the solutions to the problems discussed in the previous section. The basic idea of subnetting is to allocate a single network number to a collection of networks. To this end we introduce another level of hierarchy in the addressing scheme and split the $HostId$ component of a Class B address into a $SubnetId$ and a $HostId$, as shown in Figure 4.29.

A subnet is now characterized by a *subnet number* and a *subnet mask*. The bitwise AND of the IP address and the subnet mask is the same for all hosts and routers in a subnet and it is equal to the subnet number.

The forwarding table of a router now contains one entry for every subnet. Each entry consists of the tuple $(SubnetNumber, SubnetMask, NextHop)$. To compute the $SubnetNumber$ a router performs a bitwise AND between the destination address of a packet and the $SubnetMask$ of all entries and forwards the packet to the $NextHop$ given by the entry where a match if found.

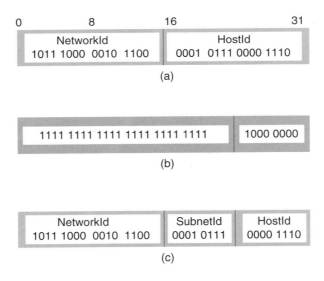

Fig. 4.29 Subnet address format.   (a) An example of Class B address format: 184.44.23.14 (b) A subnet mask: 255.255.255.128.   (c) The subnet address consists $(NetworkId, SubnetId, HostId)$.

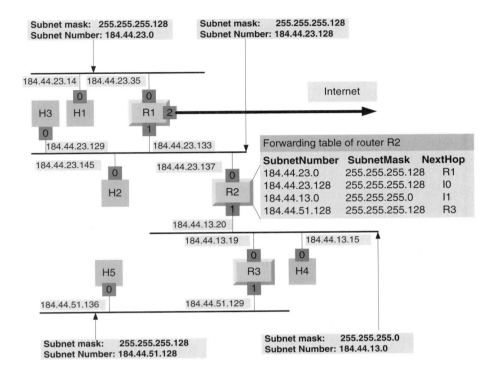

Fig. 4.30 Internet subnetting. The four subnets share a single class B address, $184.44.xx.yy$ and are interconnected via routers $R1$, $R2$, and $R3$. The forwarding table of router $R2$ contains one entry for every subnet. Each entry consists of a tuple $(SubnetNumber, SubnetMask, NextHop)$.

Let us turn to an example to illustrate the advantages, the problems, and the inner workings of subnetting. In Figure 4.30 we show four subnets that share a single class B address, $184.44.xx.yy$ and are interconnected via routers $R1$, $R2$, and $R3$. The four subnets are connected to the Internet via router $R1$.

The network adaptor of hosts and routers in a subnet have the same subnet number obtained by a bitwise AND of the IP address and the subnet mask.

Network adaptor 0 of H1: $(184.44.23.14)AND(255.255.255.128) = 184.44.23.0$

Network adaptor 0 of R1: $(184.44.23.35)AND(255.255.255.128) = 184.44.23.0$

Network adaptor 0 of H2: $(184.44.23.145)AND(255.255.255.128) = 184.44.23.128$

Network adaptor 0 of H3: $(184.44.23.129)AND(255.255.255.128) = 184.44.23.128$

Network adaptor 1 of R1: $(184.44.23.133)AND(255.255.255.128) = 184.44.23.128$

Network adaptor 0 of R2: $(184.44.23.137)AND(255.255.255.128) = 184.44.23.128$

A packet for $H5$ is forwarded by router $R2$ as follows:

$(184.44.51.136)$ AND $(255.255.255.128)$ = 184.44.51.128, no match to 184.44.23.0.

$(184.44.51.136)$ AND $(255.255.255.128)$ = 184.44.51.128, no match to 184.44.23.128.

$(184.44.51.136)$ AND $(255.255.255.0)$ = 184.44.51.128, no match to 184.44.13.0.

$(184.44.51.136)$ AND $(255.255.255.128)$ = 184.44.51.128, match to 184.44.51.128.

Thus, the packet is sent directly to router $R3$.

Let us now see how packets with other destination IP addresses are forwarded by router $R2$:

A packet for $H1$ is sent to router $R1$. Indeed, the destination IP address 184.44.23.14 matches the first entry in the forwarding table of router $R2$:
$(184.44.23.14)$ AND $(255.255.255.128)$ = 184.44.23.0.

A packet for $H2$ is sent to network adaptor 0. Indeed, the destination IP address 184.44.23.145 matches the second entry in the forwarding table of router $R2$:
$(184.44.23.145)$ AND $(255.255.255.128)$ = 184.44.23.128.

A packet for $H4$ is sent to network adaptor 1. Indeed, the destination IP address 184.44.13.15 matches the third entry in the forwarding table of router $R2$:
$(184.44.13.15)$ AND $(255.255.255.0)$ = 184.44.13.0.

All networks in this example have fewer than 255 hosts so in this case four class C addresses would have been sufficient. Now all distant networks need only to know one network number, 184.44 for the four networks.

This example also illustrates the limitations of subnetting. The subnets sharing the same class B address need to be in the proximity of each other because distant routers will select a single route to all the subnets. All packets from the outside world for the network with the network number 184.44 are sent to router R1.

4.2.3 Classless IP Addressing

Another solution to the problem of depletion of the IP address space and large forwarding tables in backbone routers is supernetting, or aggregation of several networks into one. This technique known as *classless interdomain routing* (CIDR) allocates a variable rather than a fixed number of bits to the $networkID$ component of an IP address.

In CIDR a block of class C addresses are aggregated and have a common prefix. For example consider the block of 32 class C addresses starting with

$$195.2.32.XX \quad \rightarrow \quad 11000101\ 00000010\ 00100000\ xxxxxxxx$$

and ending with

$$195.2.63.XX \quad \rightarrow \quad 11000101\ 00000010\ 00011111\ yyyyyyyy.$$

All addresses in this block have a common prefix of length 18, 11000101 00000010 00. In this bloc we have $2^{14} = 16,384$ distinct IP addresses. If the following two conditions are satisfied:

1. all potential $16,384$ hosts with IP addresses in this block are in LANs connected to the same router, and

2. all routers in the Internet understand that they have to use the leftmost 18 bits in the IP address of a packet during the lookup phase of packet forwarding.

   Then we have succeeded in:

   (a) reducing the number of entries in the routing tables of backbone routers; instead of $2^6 = 64$ entries, we now have only one entry.

   (b) avoiding wasting class B addresses, which are in high demand. At the same time, we avoided wasting the $65,536$ class B addresses for only $16,384$ hosts.

The problem raised by CIDR is that the lookup phase of the packet forwarding must be changed. Given an IP address a router now has to determine the longest match of the IP address with entries in its forwarding table. Let us assume that a router has two entries in its forwarding table, and one is the prefix of the other. For example, 195.2 for a 16-bit prefix, and the other 195.2.36 for a 24-bit prefix. A packet with the destination IP address 195.2.36.214 matches both, but should be forwarded according to the longest match.

4.2.4 Address Mapping, the Address Resolution Protocol

In this section we discuss the automatic mapping of IP addresses to hardware addresses in a LAN. From our previous discussion we know that:

(i) Once a packet reaches a router connecting the network specified in the destination IP address, the router extracts the network component from the IP address and forwards the packet to a switch connecting the LAN where the host is located to the network. In Figure 4.31 all packets for hosts in the LAN are first delivered to the switch connecting the LAN to the Internet.

(ii) In turn, the switch creates a data link frame to deliver the packet to the destination host.

(iii) The data link protocol requires the physical addresses of the destination host. The switch in Figure 4.31 needs to know the physical address of the host with a given IP address.

Thus, we need a mechanism to translate the $hostId$, the host component of the destination IP address, to the physical address of the host. To minimize network maintenance, the mappings between the IP and physical addresses of a network interface must be done automatically.

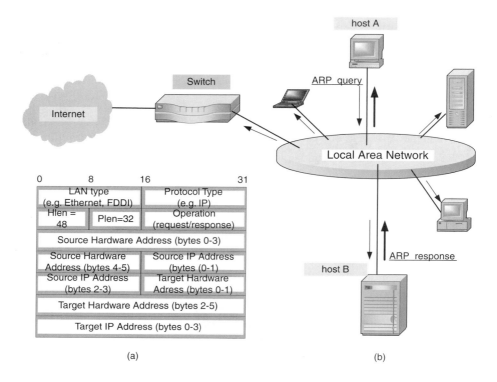

0	8	16	31
LAN type (e.g. Ethernet, FDDI)		Protocol Type (e.g. IP)	
Hlen = 48	Plen=32	Operation (request/response)	
Source Hardware Address (bytes 0-3)			
Source Hardware Address (bytes 4-5)		Source IP Address (bytes (0-1)	
Source IP Address (bytes 2-3)		Target Hardware Adress (bytes 0-1)	
Target Hardware Address (bytes 2-5)			
Target IP Address (bytes 0-3)			

(a)   (b)

Fig. 4.31 The address resolution protocol. To deliver a packet to a host the switch connecting a LAN to the Internet needs to map the IP address of each host in the LAN to its the physical. (a) The ARP packet format. (b) The ARP operation. Host A broadcasts an ARP query containing the IP address of host B as well as its own physical and IP addresses. All nodes receive the query. Only B, whose IP address matches the address in the query, responds directly to A.

The *address resolution protocol* (ARP) is used to create a mapping table relating the IP and physical addresses for the local hosts. Each node connected to a LAN must cash a copy of this table and perform a lookup for every packet sent. In practice, instead of creating an additional mapping table, the results of the ARP protocol are stored as an extra column in the forwarding table.

Once the host recognizes that the destination IP address is in the same network, it creates a frame with the corresponding physical address and sends it directly to the destination. If the destination is in another network, the frame is sent to a switch or to a host with multiple network interfaces, capable of reaching the destination network.

The process illustrated in Figure 4.31 exploits the fact that virtually all LANs are broadcast networks. In this example, host A knows the IP address of host B and realizes that it is in the same LAN, yet it cannot communicate with B because it does not know its physical address.

Host A broadcasts an *ARP query* containing the IP address of host B as well as its own physical and IP addresses. All nodes receive the query and update the entry for A in their own table if it was obsolete. Only B, whose IP address matches the address in the query, responds directly to A with a unicast packet.

4.2.5 Static and Dynamic IP Address Assignment

We now discuss the question of how IP addresses are assigned. Assigning network addresses is done by a central authority for class A and B addresses and by the network administrator within an organization for class C addresses.

The network administrator has the authority to assign IP addresses within an administrative domain. This solution, practicable when few computers were connected to the Internet, places a heavy burden on system maintenance nowadays, when every organization has thousands of systems. Scaling of the network management is a serious concern at this stage in the evolution of the Internet.

Moreover, in the age of laptops and other mobile computing devices, static IP address assignment raises many questions. For example, should an IP address be assigned permanently to a line even though no computer may be connected to it for long periods of time? How should a mobile device with a wireless connection moving from one network to another be treated?

The automatic or dynamic IP address assignment is an example of a function delegated to a network service. This service allows network managers to configure a range of IP addresses per network rather than one IP address per host.

A DHCP server is named after the communication protocol used to access its services, *dynamic host configuration protocol (DHCP)*. A pool of IP addresses is allocated to a DHCP server. Whenever a computer is connected to the network it sends a request to the server, the server gets the request and assigns *temporarily* one of the addresses in its pool to the client.

There is a subtle aspect of the dynamic address assignment; the server has a finite pool of addresses, and, without a mechanism to reuse addresses, the sever could run out of IP addresses. To circumvent this problem a DHCP server *leases* an IP address to a client and reclaims the address when the lease expires. This clever mechanism places the burden on the client to renew its lease periodically for as long it needs the IP address. Once the client is disconnected, the address automatically returns to the pool.

A DHCP server is shared among a number of LANs; installing one in every LAN would be wasteful and would complicate the network management. However, a newly connected host can only send frames to systems in the same LAN; it cannot send IP packets and cannot communicate directly with a DHCP server located outside the LAN.

The solution to this problem is to have in every LAN a *DHCP relay* that knows the address of a DHCP server, which could be located in another network, see Figure 4.32. The DHCP relay acts as a go-between for a client in the same LAN and a remote DHCP server.

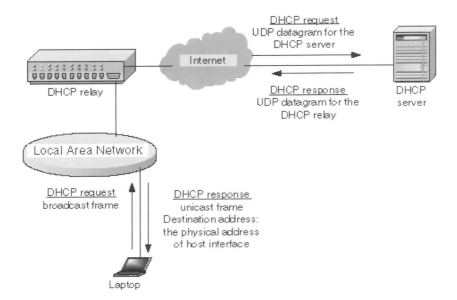

Fig. 4.32 The operation of a DHCP server. A DHCP relay knows the address of a remote DHCP server and acts as an intermediary. It receives a DHCP request broadcasted by a newly connected host, encapsulates the request into an UDP datagram and sends it to the DHCP server. The server sends the response to the relay in a UDP datagram; the relay decapsulates the UDP datagram, extracts the response, and forwards a frame containing the response to the client.

A newly connected client broadcasts a DHCP request containing its own physical address. The broadcast is picked up by the DHCP relay and it is forwarded to the DHCP server. In turn, the DHCP response, which contains the newly assigned IP address, is sent to the relay. Finally, the relay forwards the response to the client, using its physical address.

DHCP uses the UDP transport protocol, as shown in Figure 4.8 in Section 4.1.4.

4.2.6   Packet Forwarding in the Internet

It is now time to take a closer look at packet forwarding in the Internet. We already know that the Internet is a datagram network and packets are routed individually; a router or a host examines the destination address in the IP header and then performs a lookup in its forwarding table and delivers the packet to one of the network interfaces connecting it with other routers.

In Figure 4.33 we see one router and several hosts in four separate LANs. We also see the forwarding tables of the router and of one of the hosts. Let us first observe that the four LANs have class C IP addresses, which means that the IP addresses of the hosts in the same LAN have the third byte either 1, 2, 3, or 4. The router has five

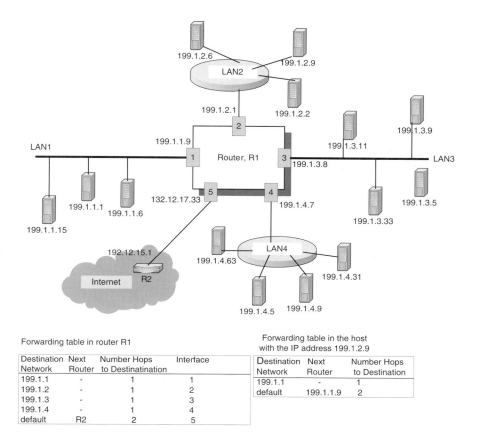

Fig. 4.33 A router and its forwarding table. The router connects four LANs to the Internet and has five network interfaces.

entries in its forwarding table, one for each LAN and one for the interface connecting it with an edge router in the Internet.

Consider a packet with the destination IP address 199.1.2.9 arriving on interface 5 of router $R1$. The router finds a match with the second entry of its forwarding table and learns that:

(i) the packet should be delivered to interface 2 and

(ii) the destination host is one hop away, which means that $R2$ is directly connected to the destination host via some LAN. Then the router looks up the physical address of the destination host and sends the frame using the appropriate data link protocol.

Let us now consider three destinations for a packet sent by the host with IP address 199.1.2.9, in LAN2, to another host with the IP address:

(1) 199.1.2.6 in the same LAN. The sender learns that the destination host is in the the same LAN. Indeed, the IP address of the destination matches the first entry in its forwarding table. The sender accesses its ARP cache to find the physical address of the destination and then uses the data link protocol to send a frame on LAN2.

(2) 199.1.3.11 in LAN3. The sender cannot find a match for the destination IP address and uses the default; it sends the packet to router $R1$ after determining the physical address of interface 2 in LAN2. The packet reaches $R1$ who finds a match between the destination IP address and the third entry in its forwarding table. Then $R2$ determines the physical address corresponding to the IP address 199.1.3.11 and sends the frame on interface 3 connected to LAN3.

(3) 132.23.53.17 in another network reachable via $R2$. The sender cannot find a match for the destination IP address and uses the default; it sends the packet to router $R1$. The router $R1$ fails to find a match, uses its default entry, and sends the packet via interface 5 to router $R2$.

4.2.7 Tunneling

Several Internet applications require a virtual point-to-point channel between two nodes separated by an arbitrary number of networks. For example, a large corporation may have several campuses at different geographic locations and wants to establish an Intranet connecting these campuses together.

The solution is to establish a *tunnel* between two routers, one at each end of the tunnel. When the router at the entrance of the tunnel wants to send a packet through the tunnel, it encapsulates the packet in an IP datagram addressed to the router at the tunnel's exit. The router at the exit of the tunnel finds out that the datagram has its own address as the destination, removes the IP header and looks inside the packet. There it finds another IP packet with its own source and destination IP addresses and forwards this new packet as it would any other IP packet. For a full-duplex operation each router is both an entry and an exit point in a tunnel.

Figure 4.34 shows an Intranet of an organization with two campuses interconnected by a tunnel. Router $R1$ connects one LAN, with a class C address 192.10.5, to a network with a class B address 129.5; and router $R2$ connects another LAN, with a class C address 195.4.50, to a network with a class B address 135.12. A host with the IP address 192.10.5.14 in the first LAN sends a packet for a host with the IP address 195.3.50.3.

Router $R1$ determines that the network 195.4.50 is reachable via a virtual interface and encapsulates the original IP packet into one with a source IP address the same as its own address and a destination IP address the same as the address of $R2$.

4.2.8 Wireless Communication and Host Mobility in Internet

Wireless networks play an increasingly more important role in the Internet. More and more producers and consumers of data are connected to the Internet and are mobile.

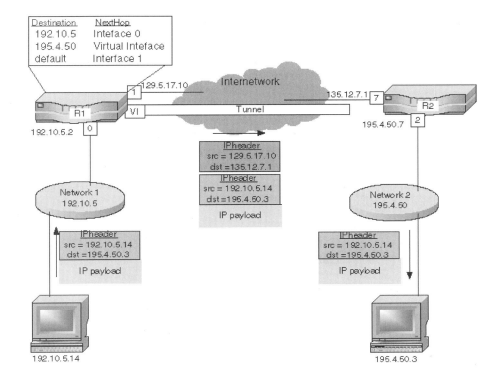

Fig. 4.34 An IP tunnel. The router at the entrance of the tunnel encapsulates an IP datagram into a new one. This source and the destination IP addresses of the new datagram correspond to the IP addresses of the two routers at the entrance and exit of the tunnel, respectively. The router at the exit of the tunnel decapsulates the IP datagram, extracts the original datagram, determines the IP address of the actual destination, and sends the original datagram to its actual destination. The forwarding table of the routers at both ends of the tunnel have a separate entry for a virtual interface.

The producers of data are often sensors installed on objects that are changing their position, e.g., cars, trucks, and ships. The consumers of data are individuals with hand-held devices who are on the move themselves. Some production processes, e.g., airplane assembly, require the use of wearable computing devices. In such cases there is no alternative to support mobility other than wireless networks.

Wireless networks based on packet-radio communication systems have a number of appealing features. In addition of being able to accommodate physical mobility they have lower start up costs, there is no need to install and maintain expensive communication lines. However, they have several problems:

(i) The technology is still under development.

(ii) The bandwidth capacity is limited.

(iii) Error rates are much larger than in traditional networks.

(iv) The communication range is limited and decreases as transmission speed increases. The power of the signals decreases as $1/d^2$, with d the distance between the sender and the receiver.

(v) There is radio interference between transmitting stations.

(vi) Transmissions are prone to eavesdropping.

In case of wireless communication there is a fixed infrastructure to forward packets. When crossing from one geographic area to another, the mobile device is handed off from one station to another. There are also *ad hoc networks* where this infrastructure is missing, the mobile nodes are themselves involved in packet forwarding.

To support mobility in the Internet we need a mobile version of the IP protocol. The *mobile IP* should allow a host to move subject to two constraints :

1. The movement should be transparent to applications. A network application running on the mobile host should continue sending and receiving data without any disturbance of transport services.

2. The solution should not affect existing networking software running on non-mobile hosts.

DHCP does not provide an adequate solution to continuous-time mobility. It does not support a seamless transition while a host moves from one network to another; all network activities are interrupted until the host gets a new IP address in a foreign network. Figure 4.35 illustrates a solution compatible with the two requirements stated above.

The network architecture for host mobility is based on several key ideas: a mobile host has a *home network* and a *home IP address*; there is a *home agent* located in the home network providing a forwarding service; there is a *a foreign agent* in a foreign network providing a mailbox service.

The mobile host learns the IP address of the home agent before leaving its home network. Once it moves to a foreign network, the mobile host learns the address of the foreign agent and registers with it. This registration request sent by the mobile host includes (1) its own physical address and IP address and (2) the IP address of the home agent. A tunnel is established between the foreign agent and the home agent.

A packet for the mobile host, sent by a third party, is intercepted by the home agent; then the home agent forwards it to the foreign agent, and finally the foreign agent delivers it to the mobile host. This solution requires answers to a few questions: How does a mobile host learn the IP addresses of the home and foreign agents? How does the home agent know when the mobile host has moved? How does the home agent intercept the packets for the mobile host? How does the foreign agent communicate with the mobile host.

The answer to the first question is that both agents periodically advertise their services; moreover, the foreign agent can be a process running on the mobile host as

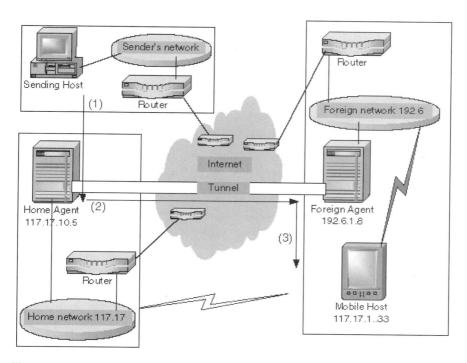

Fig. 4.35 Internet support for host mobility. The mobile host has a *home network* and a *home IP address*. Before leaving its home network, the mobile host has to know the IP address of a *home agent*. Once it moves to a foreign network, the mobile host registers with a *foreign agent* and provides the address of the home agent. A tunnel is established between the foreign agent and the home agent. A packet for the mobile host sent by a third party: (1) is intercepted by the home agent, (2) the home agent forwards it to the foreign agent, and (3) the foreign agent delivers it to the mobile host.

discussed below. Once it receives a registration request, the foreign agent informs the home agent that the mobile host has moved, provides the IP addresses of the mobile host, and establishes a tunnel with the home agent. At that moment, the home agent issues an unsolicited or *gratuitous ARP* response, informing all hosts in the home network that all frames for the mobile host should be sent to him; the ARP response associates the IP address of the mobile host with the physical address of the home agent. The foreign agent uses the physical address to communicate with the mobile host as long as they are in the same network.

Let us now consider the case when the foreign agent is a process running on the mobile host. Immediately after joining the foreign network, it requests a new IP address from a DHCP server connected to the foreign network. After getting the new IP address, it sends a gratuitous ARP response informing all nodes in the foreign network about its physical and IP address. Then it establishes a virtual tunnel with the home agent.

An important point is that the area covered by ground stations in packet-radio networks overlap. As a mobile host moves farther from one ground station and approaches another one, the carrier from the first station becomes weaker and the one from the second becomes stronger. When it starts picking up the signal from the second station and realizes that the gradient of the signal is positive, the foreign agent process on the host initiates the DHCP request.

4.2.9 Message Delivery to Processes

Message delivery in the Internet resembles the delivery of traditional mail. A letter for someone in Paris, first reaches France, then a distribution center in Paris, then a distribution center in one of the boroughs (arondissement) in Paris, and finally it is delivered to the mail box of its intended recipient at her home address.

The Internet is a collection of networks. The entities exchanging messages are processes, processes run on hosts, hosts are connected to networks, as seen in Figure 4.36.

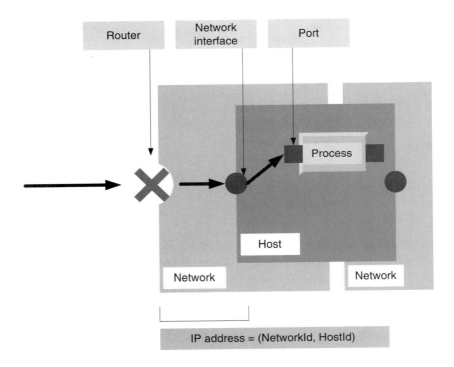

Fig. 4.36 Network-host-process chain for PDU delivery in the Internet. The PDU is first delivered to a router connected to the destination network then the router delivers it to the host via a network interface. Finally, the PDU is delivered to a process at a port specified by the transport protocol. The pair $(NetworkId, HostId)$ identifies an IP address, see Section 4.2. Each network interface has a unique IP address.

This hierarchy suggests a procedure used to deliver a packet to its destination:

(i) Deliver the packet to a router connected to the destination network. The packet may cross multiple networks on its way to its destination.

(ii) Deliver the packet to the network interface of that host. A switch connected to the destination network is able to identify the destination host, find its physical address, and use a data link protocol to deliver the frame.

(iii) Once a packet is delivered to a host, the networking software uses information provided by the transport protocol to deliver the segment to a process at a given *port*, as shown in Figure 4.36.

4.3 INTERNET ROUTING AND THE PROTOCOL STACK

There are more than 60 million hosts, several million routers, and close to $100,000$ networks in the Internet today. These numbers are expected to grow in the future; thus, scalability is a serious concern for such a system. The architecture, the algorithms, the mechanisms and policies employed in the Internet today should continue to work well when the Internet will grow beyond today's expectations [11].

Routing is a critical dimension of the effort to ensure the scalability of the Internet; if the forwarding tables continue to grow, then the number of computing cycles needed to forward each packet increase and the throughput of a router is not able to keep up with the fast optical links of the future.

In this section we discuss first a hierarchical organization that supports scalability and is consistent with an internetwork linking together a large number of autonomous networks. Then we present the Internet protocol stack.

The protocols in the Internet protocol stack, shown in Figure 4.37, are: IP at the network layer; TCP and UDP for the transport layer; ICMP, a network layer control protocol; RIP, OSPF, protocols used to transport routing information; RSVP, a protocol used for QoS support.

Application protocols such as hypertext transfer protocol (HTTP), file transfer protocol (FTP), and Telnet are based on TCP; other application protocols such as network file system RPC (NFS-RPC), domain name services (DNS), and simple mail transfer protocol (SMTP) are based on UDP.

4.3.1 Autonomous Systems. Hierarchical Routing

We have stated repeatedly that the Internet is a collection of autonomous networks administered by separate organizations. Each organization in turn can group its routers into regions or *autonomous systems* (AS). Routers in the same AS run the same routing protocols. One can, in fact, take advantage of this hierarchical organization to ensure scalabilty of the system.

Figure 4.38 shows such an AS and indicates that there are two types of routers: those concerned with routing within the AS, the so-called *intra-AS routers* and one

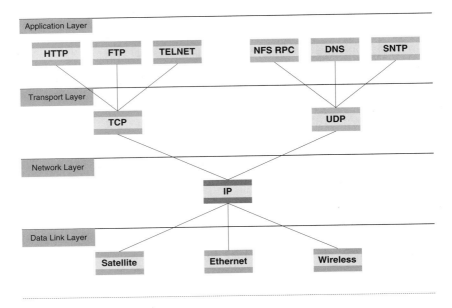

Fig. 4.37 The protocols in the Internet stack.

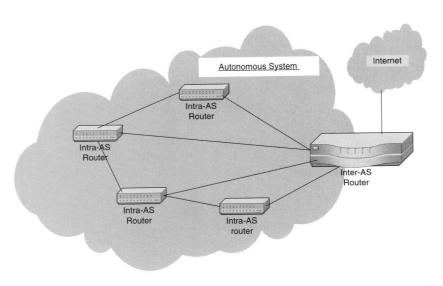

Fig. 4.38 Intra-AS and Inter-AS routing. An Intra-AS router needs only information about the AS and should be able to recognize when the destination address is outside the AS. Inter-AS routers need only to know how to reach each AS, without knowing how to reach individual hosts in each AS.

or more routers connecting an AS to other ASs, the so-called *inter-AS routers*. The forwarding tables of intra-AS routers need only have information about the AS and be able to recognize when the destination address is outside the AS. In this case one of the inter-AS routers would be able to deliver the packet to another AS.

An autonomous system may be organized hierarchically into several *areas* with *border routers* used to connect one area with the rest of the world and *internal routers* responsible for routing within each area. *Boundary routers* are then used to interconnect areas among themselves and with *backbone routers*, as shown in Figure 4.39.

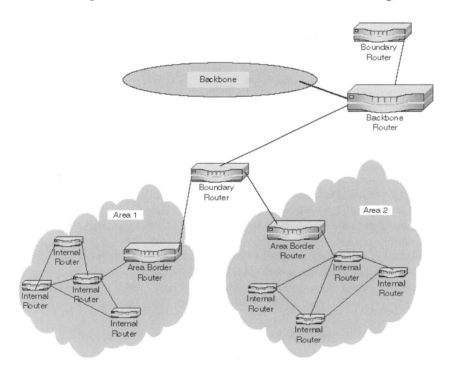

Fig. 4.39 Hierarchical routing. Each AS is split into several areas. Area border routers connect individual areas with one another through area boundary routers. A border router connects several areas to a backbone router.

4.3.2   Firewalls and Network Security

Network security is a serious concern in the Internet [18]. The scale of the system and domain autonomy make it very difficult to prevent attacks and to detect the source of the attack after the fact.

Threats to data integrity and denial-of-service attacks are among the top concerns in today's Internet. The media often report on sensitive data such as credit card information, product information, new designs being stolen, and on widely used services being interrupted for relatively long periods of time.

Denial-of-service attacks occur when an intruder penetrates several sites and installs code capable of sending a high rate of requests to targeted servers. Oftentimes, the code used to attack the target sites does not use the domain name server; instead they have the IP address of the target hardwired. They also masquerade the sender's IP address. With these precautions taken by the attacker, locating the source of the attack becomes a very difficult task.

A firewall is a router that filters packets based on the source, the destination address, or both. Recall that a service is identified by a four tuple: (source IP address, source port, destination IP address, destination port).

The router is given a set of access patterns it should inhibit. Wild cards are often used; for example, (*,*,128.6.6.5, 80) blocks all access to a Web server running on a host with IP address 128.6.6.5 from outside the network of an organization. In this case, all service requests from outside have to pass through the firewall and the firewall rejects them. Attackers from outside an organization cannot either access internal data or orchestrate a denial-of-service attack. Of course, the firewall cannot prevent insider attacks.

There are also new problems created by firewalls. There are applications that do not run at known ports or that select dynamically the ports used for data transfer once a connection to a server running at a known port is established. Such is the case of the FTP, which requires establishing of a new TCP connection for each file transfer; in this case the ports are assigned dynamically and applications such as FTP require the firewall to support dynamic filters.

A *proxy-based firewall* is a process that imitates both a client and a server; it acts as a server for the client and as a client for the server.

The limitations of the proxy-based firewall are that:

(i) it does not isolate internal users from each other,

(ii) it cannot keep mobile code out,

(iii) it is not effective in a wireless environment.

The proxy-based firewall does not need to understand the specific application protocol. For example, a cluster of Web servers can be protected by a front end that gets the HTTP request and then forwards it to a specific back-end system, as discussed in Section 5.5.7.

4.3.3   IP, the Internet Protocol

The Internet is a collection of networks, or an internetwork, where all networks use the IP addressing conventions and support the IP network protocol. The IP is the focal point of the hourglass-shaped Internet architecture, see Figure 4.6.

IP is a connectionless network layer protocol that has evolved in time. The original version, IPv4, is based on 32-bit IP addresses, whereas the newer version, IPv6, uses 128-bit IP addresses.

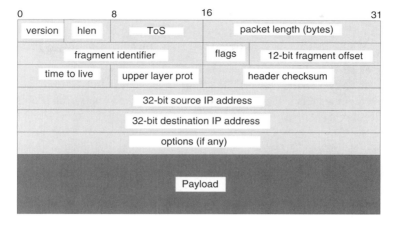

Fig. 4.40   The format of an IPv4 datagram. The header has a variable format; it is at least 20 bytes long. The payload has a variable length too.

Figure 4.40 shows the header of an IPv4 datagram. The minimum header length is 20 bytes but when options are present the header can be longer. The fields of the header and the number of bits for each are:

Version (4) - currently version 4.

Header Length, hlen (4) - the number of 32-bit words in the header.

Type of service, ToS (4) - not widely used in the past.

Length (16) - number of bytes in the datagram.

Identity (16) - used for the fragmentation mechanism to identify a packet several fragments belong to.

Flags (4) - used for the fragmentation mechanism.

Offset (12) - used for the fragmentation mechanism to identify the position of a fragment in a packet.

Time to live (TTL) (8) - number of hops the datagram has traveled.

Protocol (8) - key indicating the transport protocol the datagram should be delivered to at the receiving site, e.g., TCP=6, UDP=17.

Header checksum (8) - IP treats every two bytes of the header and sums them using 1's complement arithmetic. Routers discard datagrams when an error is detected.

Source IP address (32) - the IP address of the source.

Destination IP address (32) - the IP address of the destination.

Options - field of variable length.

Fragmentation of IP packets is due to the fact that some data link protocols in a network limit the *maximum transport unit* (MTU). If the MTU on an outgoing link of a router is smaller than the size of the datagram, then the datagram is fragmented.

Example of IP fragmentation. Assume that a datagram of 4400 bytes arrives at a router and the MTU on the network the datagram must be delivered to is 1500 bytes. Then the router cuts this datagram into three fragments and sends each fragment as a separate datagram:

- the first fragment has a payload of 1480 bytes and a 20-byte IP header. The segmentation-related fields in the header will be:

$$fragment_{id} = 7775, \quad fragment_{offset} = 0.$$

Data should be inserted at the beginning of the reassembled datagram, $flags = 1$, more fragments are coming.

- the second fragment has a payload of 1480 bytes and a 20-byte IP header. The segmentation-related fields in the header will be:

$$fragment_{id} = 7775, \quad fragment_{offset} = 1480.$$

Data should be inserted with an offset of 1480 bytes in the reassembled datagram, $flags = 1$, more fragments are coming.

- the third fragment has a payload of 1440 bytes and a 20-byte IP header. The segmentation-related fields in the header will be:

$$fragment_{id} = 7775, \quad fragment_{offset} = 2960.$$

Data should be inserted with an offset of 2960 bytes in the reassembled datagram, $flags = 0$, this is the last fragment.

The fact that the IPv4 header has a variable length increases the packet-forwarding overhead in a router. Packet fragmentation is another factor limiting the packet rate through a router. To minimize the fragmentation overhead, a source should send packets smaller than the smallest MTU of all networks traversed by a packet.

The smallest MTU size for all networks connected to the Internet is $MTU = 576$. This implies that if a transport protocol sends a payload of at most 536 bytes, no fragmentation will occur. Last but not least, computing the checksum of the header requires additional CPU cycles in every router the datagram crosses on its path from source to the destination.

These problems, as well as the limitations of the address space supported by IPv4, are addressed in IPv6 [13]:

(i) Supports 128-bit IP addresses.

(ii) Supports anycast addressing; a packet may be delivered to any one of a group of hosts. This feature, discussed in Section 4.2, allows load balancing among a set of servers providing the same service.

(iii) Supports flow labeling and priorities as discussed in Section 4.4.

(iv) Does not support packet fragmentation.

(v) IPv6 header has a fixed format, it is 40 bytes long.

Figure 4.41 shows the format of the IPv6 header. The *priority* field is equivalent to the *ToS* field in IPv4; the *flow label* identifies the flow the segment belongs to, flows are introduced in Section 4.4.2; the *next header* field points to the header of the transport protocol the paylod is delivered to at the destination; the hop count is decremented by each router and the datagram is discharged when this field reaches zero.

IPv6 addresses are written as a sequence of 8 hexadecimal numbers separated by semicolons, e.g., $4B2A; CCCC; 1526; BF22; 1FFF; EEEE; 7DC1; ABCD$.

Today only a subset of hosts and routers support IPv6 and the two protocols coexist in today's Internet. IPv6-enabled nodes have two protocol stacks one running IPv4 and the other IPv6. This *dual-stack* approach allows two nodes, one running IPv4 and the other IPv6-enabled, to communicate based on their common denominator, IPv4. Two IPv6 enabled nodes communicate among themselves through a tunnel.

An intriguing question is why in the present Internet only a subset of nodes support IPv6. The answer is that a system like the Internet has a very significant inertia and it is very difficult or impossible to enforce a change.

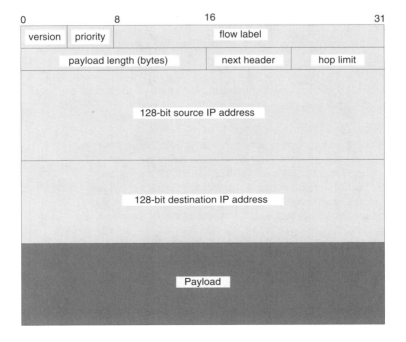

Fig. 4.41 The format of an IPv6 datagram. The header is 40 bytes long.

Table 4.2   The ICMP codes.

Type	Code	Description
0	0	echo reply (to ping)
3	0	destination network unreachable
3	1	destination host unreachable
3	2	destination protocol unreachable
3	3	destination port unreachable
3	6	destination network unknown
3	7	destination host unknown
4	0	source quench (congestion control)
9	0	router advertisement
10	0	router discovery
11	0	TTL expired
12	0	bad IP header

4.3.4   ICMP, the Internet Control Message Protocol

The *ICMP* is used by hosts and routers to exchange network layer information; its main function is error reporting. ICMP resides just above the IP layer.

An ICMP message consists of the type and code fields as well as the first eight bytes of the original datagram. Table 4.2 summarizes the error codes used by ICMP.

The `traceroute` network utility uses ICMP to report the path to a node and the time it takes a datagram to reach it. This utility sends a series of datagrams with $TTL = 1, 2, 3, \ldots$ and starts timers after sending each datagram. A router n hops away from the source discards a datagram with $TTL = n$ and sends a warning message, ICMP type 11, code 0, including the name of the router and its IP address.

A typical output of the `traceroute` utility follows:

```
cisco5 (128.10.2.250) 2 ms 2 ms 2 ms
cisco-tel-242.tcom.purdue.edu (128.210.242.22) 1 ms 3 ms
abilene.tcom.purdue.edu (192.5.40.10) 9ms 8 ms 7 ms
kscy-ipls.abilene.ucaid.edu (198.32.8.5) 19 ms 17 ms
hstn-kscy.abilene.ucaid.edu (198.32.8.61) 32 ms 32 ms
losa-hstn.abilene.ucaid.edu (198.32.8.21) 64 ms 64 ms
USC--abilene.ATM.calren2.net (198.32.248.85) 65 ms 65 ms
ISI--USC.POS.calren2.net (198.32.248.26) 64 ms 68 ms
UCLA--ISI.POS.calren2.net (198.32.248.30) 69 ms 65 ms
JPL--UCLA.POS.calren2.net (198.32.248.2) 67 ms 66 ms
CIT--JPL.POS.calren2.net (198.32.248.6) 73 ms 67 ms
BoothBorder-Calren.caltech.edu (192.41.208.50) 66 ms 67 ms
Thomas-RSM.ilan.caltech.edu (131.215.254.101) 68 ms 67 ms
ajax.ecf.caltech.edu (131.215.127.75) 70 ms * 70 ms
```

From this output we see a message from `arthur.cs.purdue.edu`, 128.10.9.1, that reached `ajax.caltech.edu`, 131.215.127.75 after 14 hops, and 70 milliseconds.

The datagram first reached the router 128.10.2.250 connecting the CS Department with Purdue backbone, it was then forwarded to the router 128.210.242.22 connecting Purdue with the `abilene` network, traveled through seven routers in the `abilene network`, and finally reached a router connecting Caltech with `abilene` 192.41.208.50. Once at Caltech, the datagram was sent to a router connecting `ecf` facilities with the backbone.

4.3.5 UDP, the User Datagram Protocol

UDP is a connectionless transport protocol; it only provides a best-effort service and a straightforward checksum to detect transmission errors. The question that comes to mind immediately is why a datagram transport protocol, why not use IP directly?

The only additional function supported by UDP is demultiplexing. The communicating entities at the transport layer are processes; while IP transports a datagram to a host we need to deliver the datagram to a particular process running on that host.

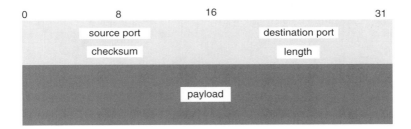

Fig. 4.42   The format of a UDP datagram. The UDP header includes the *source port*, the *destination port*, a *checksum*, and the length of the datagram.

Figure 4.42 shows that indeed the UDP header identifies the two end points of the communication channel, the sender and the receiver port. The *checksum* is similar to the IP checksum and covers the UDP header, the UDP payload, and the so-called *pseudoheader* consisting of three fields from the IP header: the source IP address, the destination IP address, and the protocol number.

UDP is the simplest possible transport protocol, thus, it is very efficient. On the sending side, UDP gets a message from the application process, attaches to it the source and destination port number, the length of the datagram, computes the checsum and adds it to the datagram, and then passes the datagram to the network layer. On the receiving side UDP verifies the checksum and passes the payload to the application process at the destination port.

4.3.6 TCP, the Transport Control Protocol

TCP is a full-duplex, byte-stream, connection-oriented transport protocol providing reliable end-to-end delivery, end-to-end flow control, and congestion control in the

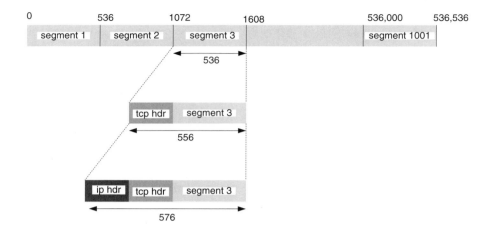

Fig. 4.43 Segmentation of an input stream of 536,536 bytes. The MTU is 576 bytes and each of the TCP and IP headers is 20 bytes; thus, MSS is set to 536 and 1001 segments are sent.

Internet. Full-duplex means that each of the two processes linked by a TCP connection act as senders and receivers.

4.3.6.1 TCP Segments and the TCP Header.
A byte-stream transport protocol accepts a sequence of bytes from a sender process, breaks them into segments, and sends them via IP; on the other side, the receiving process reads a number of bytes from its input stream up to the *maximum segment size* (MSS), see Figure 4.43.

During the connection establishment phase the sender and the receiver negotiate an acceptable value for the MSS. The default value for MSS is 512 bytes but most TCP implementations propose an MSS that is 40 bytes less than the MTU of the data link protocol. For example, a host connected via an Ethernet interface proposes $1500 - 40 = 1460$ bytes. To avoid IP fragmentation, knowing that all networks support an MTU of at least 576 bytes, TCP implementations often use an MSS = 536, see Figure 4.43

An important question is when should a TCP segment be transmitted; as soon as the application process delivers data to TCP, or should we wait until the application process has delivered enough data to fill a segment of size equal to MSS. The first solution minimizes the sending delay but the processing overhead increases and the channel efficiency decreases; for the same amount of data we transmit a larger number of segments and each segment carries a fixed-size header. The second solution minimizes the overhead but increases the delay until segments are transmitted. A better alternative is provided by Nagel's algorithm: send a segment if either the amount of data available is close to MSS or all segments sent have already been acknowledged.

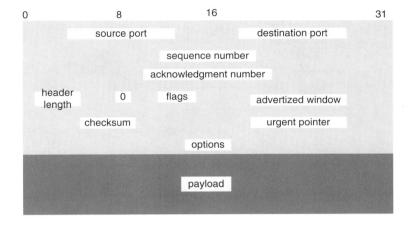

Fig. 4.44   The format of a TCP segment. The TCP header includes a variable length option field that may or may not be present. The minimum header size is 20 bytes. A TCP connection is identified by a four tuple: *(source port, source IP address, destination port, destination IP address)*. The *advertised window*, the *sequence number*, and the *acknowledgement number* are used for error, flow, and congestion control.

Figure 4.44 shows the format of a TCP segment. The fields in the TCP header are described below; the length of each field in bits follows the name of the field:

- *source port, (16)* and *destination port, (16)*: used to identify the two communicating processes. A TCP connection is identified by a four tuple: *(source port, source IP address, destination port, destination IP address)*.

- *sequence number, (32)*: the byte stream number of the first byte of the segment.

- *acknowledgment number, (32)*: the segment number of the next byte the receiver expects.

- *header length, (4)*: the length of the TCP header in 32- bit words.

- *flags, (6)*: $ACK, SYN, RST, FIN, PUSH, URG$.
  When set:
  ACK - the value carried in the acknowledgment field is valid.
  SYN, RST, FIN - used for connection establishment and tear-down.
  $PUSH$ - the data should be passed to the upper layer immediately.
  URG- there is "urgent" information in the data.

- *advertised window, (16)*: the flow control and congestion control window.

- *checksum, (16)*: covers the TCP header and the payload.

- *urgent pointer, (16):* pointer to one byte of urgent data, typically used for out-of-band signaling. Out-of-band signaling provides mechanisms for requesting immediate actions.

- *options (variable length):* used to negotiate (1) the MSS, (2) the window-scaling factor for high-speed networks.

4.3.6.2 The TCP State Machine.   TCP is a sophisticated communication protocol and its complexity is reflected in its state machine shown in Figure 4.45. Every

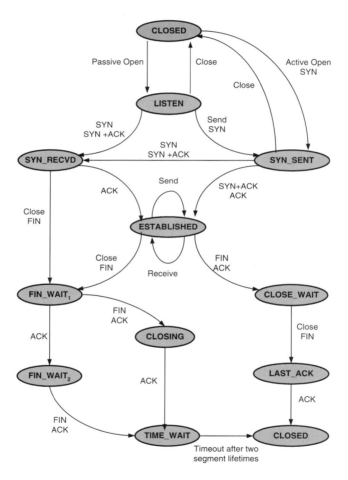

Fig. 4.45   TCP state machine. The establishment of a connection is an asymmetric process, the server performs a passive open, while clients perform an active open, they connect to an existing port the server listens to. Once a connection is established, then both parties can send and receive data. The connection tear-down is a symmetric process, either party may initiate it.

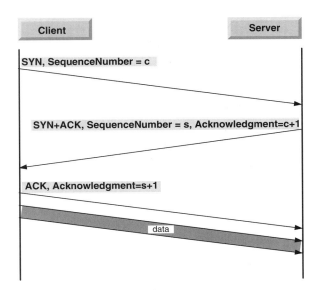

Fig. 4.46 TCP three-way handshake. The client sets the SYN flag on in the TCP header and proposes a start-up sequence number c; the server responds with a segment with SYN and ACK flags on, proposes its own initial sequence number s, and requests next byte from the client $c + 1$; then the client sends a segment with the ACK flag on and requests the next byte from the server $s + 1$.

transition in this diagram is labeled by the action taken and the flags set in the header. Two types of events trigger a transition in the TCP state diagram:

(1) a segment arrives from the peer, and

(2) the local application process invokes an operation on TCP.

TCP favors client-server communication. The establishment of a TCP connection is an asymmetric activity: a server does a *passive open* while a client does an *active open*, see Figure 4.45. Connection termination is symmetric; each side has to close the connection independently; one side can issue a close, meaning that it can no longer send data, but the other side may keep the other half of the connection open and continue sending data.

After a passive open, the server moves to a *listen* state and is prepared to accept connections initiated by a client. Figure 4.46 shows the actual message exchanges for the establishment of a TCP connection, a process known as the *three-way handshake*. The two parties have to agree on the starting numbers for their respective byte streams.

The client sets the SYN flag on in the TCP header and proposes a startup sequence number c; the server responds with a segment with SYN and ACK flags on, proposes its own initial sequence number s, and requests next byte from the client $c + 1$; then the client sends a segment with the ACK flag on and requests the next byte from the server $s + 1$. Now the connection is established and the client can send its first request

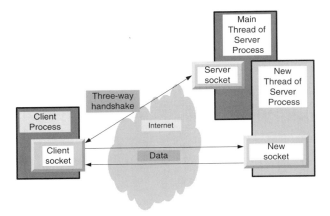

Fig. 4.47 Client-server communication with TCP. The main thread of control of the server receives connection requests from a client and goes through the three-way handshake process. Once the connection is established, the server starts a new thread of control and opens a new socket. The client now communicates directly with the newly started thread while the main thread is able to establish new TCP connections and start additional threads in response to clients requests.

in a data-carrying segment. Both the client and the server side of the connection are in the $ESTABLISHED$ state.

Let us now take a closer look at the actual communication between a server and several client processes. A server is a shared resource; it may receive multiple requests simultaneously. A single-threaded server is unable to process a new request until it has completed the processing of the current one.

In the case of a multithreaded server, the request from a client to establish a TCP connection is processed by the server's main thread of control, see Figure 4.47. Once the connection is established, the server starts a new thread and creates a new socket for each client. Then the client communicates directly to the thread assigned to it.

The mechanism described above ensures parallel communication channels between a multithreaded server and the each of its clients. The main thread of control of the server acts as a dispatcher the actual responses are produced by the individual threads, one associated with each client.

A TCP connection can be closed by the client, the server, or both. The three ways to close a connection and the corresponding states traversed by the the two parties are:

(i) This side closes first:

$$ESTABLISHED \rightarrow FIN\_WAIT\_1 \rightarrow FIN\_WAIT_2 \rightarrow TIME\_WAIT \rightarrow CLOSED$$

(ii) The other side closes first:

$$ESTABLISHED \rightarrow CLOSE\_WAIT \rightarrow LAST\_ACK \rightarrow CLOSED$$

(iii) Both sides close at the same time:

$$ESTABLISHED \rightarrow FIN\_WAIT_1 \rightarrow CLOSING \rightarrow TIME\_WAIT \rightarrow CLOSING$$

4.3.6.3 Wraparound.
Using TCP a byte with a sequence number *seq* may be sent at one time and then on the same connection a byte with the same sequence number may be sent again. This phenomenon called *wraparound* is a consequence of the fact that the TCP header has two 32-bit fields to identify the sequence number of a segment and the sequence number of an acknowledgment.

However, the maximum lifetime of an IP datagram in the Internet is 120 seconds, thus we need to have a wraparound time at least as long. In other words, we need to guarantee that in the worst case two datagrams with the same sequence number will not be present on any TCP connection.

For slow links there is no danger of wraparound. Indeed, as we can see from Table 4.3 the wraparond time for a 10-Mbps network is around 687 seconds; if we transmit at full speed through a 10-Mbps network the sequence numbers will repeat after 687 seconds. In this case, the datagram is dropped by the IP protocol after 120 seconds and this undesirable phenomena is avoided.

Yet column three of Table 4.3 shows that for high-speed networks such as fiber optic networks we should be concerned with this phenomena. For example, when the sender is allowed to transmit continually on an STS-12 link with a bandwidth of 622 Mbps the sequence numbers will experience the wraparound phenomenon after 110 seconds, while for an STS-24 link with a bandwidth of 1244 Mbps this time is only 55 seconds.

Table 4.3 The time until wraparound, WT, and the window size, $WS = RTT \times B$, necessary to keep the pipe full for a given bandwidth, B, and a $RTT = 50$ milliseconds.

Network	Bandwidth (Mbps)	WT (seconds)	WS (Kbytes)
Ethernet	10	6871	62.5
Ethernet	100	687.1	625
STS-12	622	110.5	3887.5
STS-24	1244	55.25	7775.0

4.3.6.4 The Window Size to Keep the Pipeline Full.
We may look at a network as a storage system. The total amount of data in transit through a communication channel, WS, is the product of the channel bandwidth, B, and the propagation delay reflected in the round trip time (RTT):

$$WS = RTT \times B.$$

To keep the pipe full we need a window size at least equal to WS. As we may recall, the window size is encoded in the TCP segment header, as a field of 16 bits, thus the largest integer that can be expressed is $65,535$. This is quite sufficient for 10 Mbps networks but not for faster networks, as we can see in the last column of Table 4.3. For fast optical networks, the amount of data that can possibly be in transit is several orders of magnitude higher than a 16-bit window could accommodate to keep the pipeline full. The solution is to express the window in multiples of m bytes, e.g., in units of, say, $m = 2^8$ bytes.

4.3.7 Congestion Control in TCP

Congestion control is a mechanism to inform senders of packets that the network is congested and they have to exercise restraint and reduce the rate at which they inject packets into the network. Congestion control can be built into transport protocols or can be enforced by edge routers controlling the admission of packets into a network supporting multiple classes of traffic.

Internet hosts communicating using TCP are subject to congestion control. Congestion control in TCP is an example of host-centric, feedback-based resource allocation policy in a network. This mechanism requires the two hosts, the end points of a TCP connection, to maintain, in addition to the flow control window, a congestion control window and to observe the lowest limit placed by either of the two windows.

The flow control window is manipulated by the receiving side that uses acknowledgments to enforce the rate it is able to process the incoming segments. The congestion control window is affected by the timing of the acknowledgments; a late or missing acknowledgment signals that the network is congested.

Let us now take a closer look at actual implementation of congestion control in TCP. Each side of a TCP connection has a receive buffer and a send buffer and maintains several state variables, see Figure 4.48. The advertised window is:

$$advertisedWindow = min(flowControlWindow, congestionControlWindow).$$

The amount of unacknowledged data a sender may have in transit cannot be larger than the advertised window:

$$lastByteSent - lastByteAcknowledged \leq advertisedWindow.$$

4.3.7.1 The TCP Acknowledgment Policy. A TCP receiver sends an acknowledgment whenever it receives a segment, whether it is in order or out of order. If the receiver gets an out-of-order segment, it sends a duplicate acknowledgment for the last in-order segment it has received.

TCP uses a *fast retransmit* policy: after the third acknowledgment for the same segment the sender does not wait for the timer to expire, it sends immediately the segment following the one acknowledged.

There are several similarities between the TCP flow control and the selective repeat (SR) policy discussed earlier, in Section 4.1.11:

(i) the receiver accepts segments out of order and buffers them;

(ii) the sender sets a timeout for each segment.

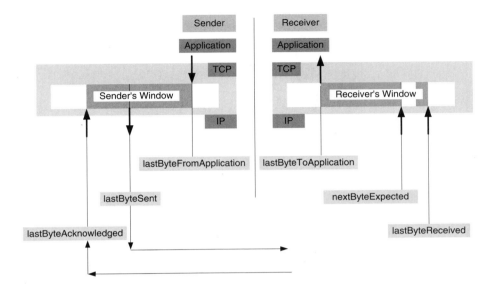

Fig. 4.48 The sender and receiver windows in TCP. The sender's window left margin is determined by the last byte acknowledged by the receiver and its upper margin by the last byte the application pushed into TCP. The receiver's window left margin is determined by the last byte the application pulled from TCP and its upper margin by the last byte the receiver got from the sender. TCP accepts segments out of order; thus, the receiver's window may have gaps corresponding to missing segments.

There are also some differences between TCP and SR motivated by the need to optimize TCP, reduce the network traffic, as well as the time a sender waits to retransmit a segment. These differences are:

(i) TCP uses cumulative acknowledgments to reduce traffic; SR does not.

(ii) The acknowledgment for a segment is delayed for up to 500 milliseconds in TCP.

If another in-order segment arrives, then a cumulative acknowledgment is sent.

(iii) Three duplicate acknowledgments trigger a fast retransmit in TCP.

A communication protocol must be safe and live; it should never reach an undesirable state and progress must be guaranteed. To guarantee liveness TCP allows the sender to probe the receiver with a 1-byte segment even if its advertised window is zero. This is done to avoid the danger of reaching a state when the sender has already received acknowledgments for all segments sent and, at the same time, the receiver's window is full thus the advertised window is zero and no progress is possible.

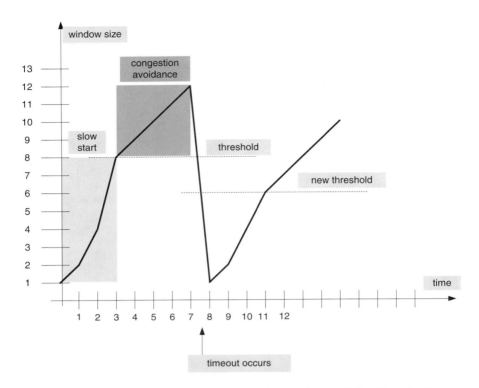

Fig. 4.49 The slow start phase, the congestion avoidance phase, and the effect of a timeout on the size of the congestion window in the *AIMD* algorithm used for TCP congestion control.

4.3.7.2 The Additive Increase Multiplicative Decrease (AIMD) Congestion Control Algorithm.
TCP uses the AIMD algorithm, for congestion control, see Figure 4.49. The algorithm maintains two state variables: `congestionControlWindow` and `threshold`.

Initially, the size of the congestion window is one segment. If the current segment is acknowledged before its timeout expires, then we send two MSS segments and continue doubling the number of segments as long as the following two conditions are met:

1. The acknowledgments arrive before the timeouts for the corresponding segments.

2. The `threshold` is not exceeded.

This *slow start* continues as long as the window size is smaller than the `threshold`. After the `threshold` is reached, we move to another phase called *congestion avoidance* when the exponential growth is replaced by a linear growth, as long as the acknowledgments arrive in time.

When a timeout occurs:

(i) The `threshold` is set to half of the current congestion window size.

(ii) The congestion window size is set to 1.

The TCP congestion control mechanism described in this section is dependent on the ability of the two sides of a TCP connection to estimate the RTT. An algorithm for estimating the RTT was described earlier in Section 2.4.3.

The congestion control limits the actual throughput of a TCP connection. Call W the maximum size of the congestion window and assume that W and RTT are essentially constant during the lifetime of a connection. Then:

$$maximumTransmissionRate = (W \times MSS)/RTT.$$
$$minimumTransmissionRate = (W \times MSS)/2 \times RTT.$$
$$averageTransmissionRate = 0.75 \times (W \times MSS)/RTT.$$

4.3.8   Routing Protocols and Internet Traffic

In this section we overview two commonly used routing protocols used to disseminate routing information in the Internet, one used for intra-AS routing, the other for inter-AS routing. Then we report on results regarding the Internet traffic.

4.3.8.1   *Routing Information Protocol (RIP).*   This routing protocol is used for intra-AS routing. it is an application layer protocol, it sends/receives information using UDP packets at port 520. RIP was included in the original BSD Unix in 1982. In Unix there is an application process called *routed daemon* that implements the RIP protocol.

RIP is based on a distance vector (DV) routing algorithm. It uses the hop count as a cost metric and limits the number of hops to 15. The routing tables are exchanged between neighbors every 30 seconds; a message contains at most 25 destination routes. If a router does not hear from its neighbor once every 180 seconds, that host is considered to be out of reach.

4.3.8.2   *Open Shortest Path First Protocol (OSPF).*   OSPF is a protocol used for intra-AS routing. The OSPF protocol is based on a link state (LS) routing algorithm. OSPF uses flooding to disseminate link state information and assigns different costs for the same link depending on the `type of service` (TOS).

Periodically, a router sends the distance between itself and all its immediate neighbors, to all other routers in the autonomous system. Messages are authenticated; only trusted routers participate. Each router constructs a complete topological map of the autonomous system.

OSPF supports unicast and multicast routing; it also supports hierarchical routing in a single domain among several areas. There are four types of OSPF routers, see Figure 4.39: (i) internal area router; (ii) border area router; (iii) boundary area router; and (iv) backbone router.

4.3.8.3 The Internet Traffic.

Several studies of Internet traffic were conducted in recent years. The results reported in the literature show that 90% to 95% of the total amount of data is carried by TCP and 5% to %10% by UDP.

The Web accounts for 65% to 75% of the TCP traffic and the balance of the TCP traffic is covered by News, 10%, Email, 5%, FTP, 5%, and Napster, 1%.

The UDP traffic is split between DNS, Realaudio, and games.

4.4 QUALITY OF SERVICE

Many insiders believe that the great success of the Internet is due to its best-effort service model and to the relative autonomy of the service providers. Recall from the previous section that the autonomous systems in the Internet may use their own routing protocols and may, or may not support connection-oriented network protocols.

The success of the Internet has invited new applications, such as multimedia services, and, in this process, has revealed the limitations of the best-effort model, a service model incapable of accommodating bandwidth, delay, delay jitter, reliability, and cost guarantees of Internet applications. The jitter reflects the variability of end-to-end communication delays.

Multimedia services, as well as other real-time applications, require quality of service (QoS), guarantees from the network. A substantial effort was invested in recent years to support QoS guarantees in the Internet.

Significant changes in the Internet architecture and protocols are considerably more difficult at this stage. In recent years we have witnessed the slow transition from IPv4 to IPv6, from HTTP 1.0 to HTTP 1.1, though the newer protocols have significant advantages over the older versions. Recall from the previous section that IPv6 does not support segment fragmentation and provides a considerably larger IP address space, features that increase the speed of the packet forwarding process in routers and accommodate in a straightforward manner the increasing number of hosts connected to the Internet. In Chapter 5, we show that HTTP 1.1 eliminates the cost of multiple TCP connections and overcomes the bandwidth limitations due to the initial slow-start phase of each TCP connection in HTTP 1.0.

The inherent inertia of a complex system leads us to believe that we are a long way before the QoS guarantees expected by existing and future real-time applications will be fully integrated into the Internet. In absence of magical solutions, the philosophy of the Internet designers to support QoS guarantees with the current architecture, is *overprovisioning*, building networks with a capacity far greater than the level warranted by the current traffic. For example, if the peak traffic through a network segment is 1 Gbps, use a 100 Gbps channel.

This philosophy is justified by the fact that in a lightly loaded network sufficient bandwidth can be allocated to individual application, the routers have enough buffer space and only rarely do they drop packets. The end-to-end delay can be predicted and controlled in a lightly loaded network.

The variability of the end-to-end delay is due to queuing in the routers and to packets being dropped due to insufficient buffer space in the routers. For example, experience shows that when the network load is kept at a level of 10% of its capacity the audio quality is quite good.

Overprovisioning can only be accepted as a stop-gap measure for at least two important reasons:

(1) the traffic will continue to increase and fill out the available capacity; and

(2) We need end-to-end service guarantees for critical applications. For example, some applications of telemedicine such as remote surgery are inconceivable without firm end-to-end delay and bandwidth guarantees.

Overprovisioning may work for the network backbone with relatively few high-performance routers interconnected by high-capacity fiber optic channels, but the complexity of the network is at the edge and overprovisioning at the network edge is prohibitively expensive.

In this section we first introduce service models, flows, and address the problem of resource allocation in the Internet. Then we discuss mechanisms to support QoS guarantees. Finally, we introduce integrated and differentiated services.

4.4.1 Service Guarantees and Service Models

At the beginning of this chapter we classified network applications based on their bandwidth, delay, and loss requirements. A closer evaluation of Internet applications indicates that we need to address several kinds of guarantees:

- Bandwidth; for audio and video streaming applications.

- Delay; for remote instrumentation, games, audio and video streaming.

- Jitter; for audio applications.

- Reliability; for loss-intolerant applications

- Cost; for virtually all applications.

Consider first bandwidth guarantees. We can guarantee a maximum bandwidth, a minimum bandwidth, or provide no guarantee at all. In the first case, a flow cannot send more than its maximum reserved bandwidth; in the second case, we guarantee a minimum bandwidth and allow the flow to use more bandwidth, if available; the third case corresponds to the best-effort service. As far as the delay is concerned, a network may provide a maximum guaranteed delay and implicitly a jitter delay guarantee, or no delay guarantees.

Table 4.4 Service models and their attributes.

Model	Bit Rate Guarantees	Bandwidth Guarantees	Packet Timing Guarantees	Network Congestion	In Order Delivery	Packet Losses
CBR	yes	yes	yes	no	yes	no
VBR	yes	yes	yes	no	yes	no
ABR	minimum rate	minimum rate	no	feedback provided	no	yes
UBR	no	no	no	yes	yes	yes
BEF	no	no	no	yes	no	yes

Table 4.4 summarizes the attributes of several service models defined for ATM networks: the constant bit rate (CBR); the variable bit rate (VBR); the available bit rate (ABR); the unspecified bit rate (UBR). We also list the corresponding attributes of the best effort (BEF) model. CBR is the most appealing model for real-time applications; it guarantees a constant rate and bandwidth, the packets are in order, no packet is lost, the packet timing is maintained, and there is no congestion in the network. VBR is very similar, but the source rate is allowed to vary within some limits. ABR guarantees a minimum transmission rate and bandwidth and provides feedback regarding network congestion. At the bottom of the scale, UBR is slightly better than BEF, it guarantees in-order delivery of packets.

In turn, the Internet Engineering Task Force (IETF) defined two more service models, the *controlled load* and the *guaranteed service*. These models are discussed in Section 4.4.11.

The controlled load is based on overprovisioning philosophy discussed earlier and translates into maintaining the network load at a level well below network capacity to ensure predictable and bounded end-to-end delay, but no guarantees are provided for the jitter or the delay. The guaranteed service is a stronger model where upper bounds of the end-to-end delay are guaranteed.

4.4.2 Flows

Once we have the additional service models described in Table 4.4 we have to address the question of how to implement them in a packet-switched network where IP provides a connectionless datagram service. As discussed in the previous section, the TCP and UDP transport protocols implement two end-to-end abstractions: a reliable virtual bit pipe and a connectionless, unreliable channel. Both abstractions are implemented based only on resources at the edge of the network, without any support from the network protocol IP.

The QoS support is certainly related to the allocation of resources, the bandwidth of communication links, CPU cycles, and memory in the routers. To understand the issue of resource allocation in the Internet and the means to provide QoS guarantees we need to focus on the consumers of these resources.

A *flow* is a sequence of packets with one common characteristic based on any field of the packets. A *layer-N flow* is a sequence of packets where the common characteristic is a layer-N attribute. For example, a layer-4 or transport layer flow consists of all the packets exchanged between two processes at a given pair of ports. A layer-3 flow, or a network flow, is characterized by a source-destination IP address pair.

Transport layer flows can be defines for TCP and UDP. Recall that a TCP connection is characterized by a four-tuple, including the source and destination IP addresses as well as the source and destination port. A sequence of UDP datagrams exchanged by two processes is also characterized by source-destination IP and port pairs.

In a connectionless network a flow is *implicit*, whereas in a connection-oriented network the flow is *explicit*. In the first case, a router may identify a flow by examining the source and the destination of packets traveling between the same points. In this case the router does not maintain any state information about the flow.

However, a virtual circuit in a connection-oriented network is explicitly established by *setup* packets. The routers along the path of the flow maintain *hard state information*. The attribute "hard" is related to the fact that this type of state information can only be removed by packets signaling the closing of the connection.

We are now in a position to understand that flows are the consumer of network resources. To provide QoS guarantees means to allocate enough resources to each flow so that the bandwidth and timing requirements specific to the flow are met. Thus, we need to take a closer look at the problem of resource allocation in the Internet.

4.4.3 Resource Allocation in the Internet

There are three basic questions related to resource allocation in the Internet:

1. who makes the decision to allocate resources;

2. what is the basis for the decision; and

3. how are these decisions enforced.

Decisions can originate from two sources: the hosts at the edge of the network or the routers at the network core. In case of *host-centric* decision making, the hosts monitor the traffic, then regulate the packet injection into the network based on their observations, the routers simply drop packets whenever their capacity is exceeded. In case of *router-centric* decision making, each router decides what packets should be dropped and it may inform the hosts how many packets they are allowed to send.

The basis for the decisions regarding resource allocation may be the need of each flow or the actual state of the network. In the first case, the hosts make *reservations* at the time a flow is established. Each router then allocates resources necessary for the flow if they are available, or the reservation is denied in case of insufficient resources along the path of the flow. In the second case, there are no reservations and hosts adjust their traffic dynamically based on the *feedback* from the network.

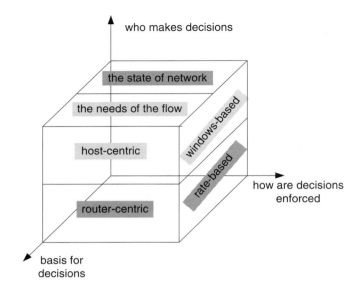

Fig. 4.50 Resource allocation dimensions: decisions can be host- or router-centric; the bases for decisions are the needs of a flow or the state of the network; the mechanisms for enforcing the decisions are window-based or rate-based

There are two mechanisms to enforce the allocation of resources, *window-based* and *rate-based*. We have already discussed window-based flow control and congestion control mechanisms for TCP and know that the sender can only transmit packets within a window. Once a sender has exhausted its window, it must refrain from sending. In the case of rate-based enforcement, the host is allowed to send packets up to a maximum rate.

Not all the possible combinations of these three dimensions of resource allocation policies are possible, see Figure 4.50. For example, a reservation-based system is only possible in the context of router-centric decision making. Note also that reservation schemes are potentially wasteful and in absence of a pricing structure, individual flows may attempt to reserve resources in excess of what they actually need. Resource reservations also require a more disciplined network, one where once a router has accepted a reservation, it has signed a contract and has to abide by it.

Last but not least, reservation schemes require routers to maintain state for all flows passing through a router and this has a negative impact on scalability. To support reservations we need a *reservation table* with one entry per flow.

The number of flows crossing a high-throughput router connected to high-speed links, could be of the order of few millions over a period of a few hours. For example, assume that a router connects three incoming and three outgoing OC-12 links and that each carries GSM-encoded audio streams. The number of flows could be as large as:

$$3 \times \frac{622.080 Mbps}{13 Kbps} = 143,556$$

A router has to maintain an entry for every flow passing through it. Clearly, the space required to maintain this information, as well as the CPU cycles necessary to retrieve the information when forwarding packets are prohibitive. Recall that we encountered a similar problem when discussing routing in a virtual circuit network in Section 4.1.10; at that time we observed that a router has to maintain an entry for every virtual circuit passing through it.

The next question is how to differentiate between flows: Should we look at flows individually, or should we split them in a few classes and then deal uniformly with the flows in each class? To answer these questions, Internet supports two categories of services, integrated and differentiated. *Integrated services* support fine-grain QoS, applied to individual flows, see Section 4.4.11; *differentiated services* support course grain QoS, applied to large classes of aggregated traffic, see Section 4.4.12.

Before discussing in some detail these two categories of services, we take a closer look at other important mechanisms for packet queuing and dropping strategies.

4.4.4 Best-Effort Service Networks

Now we discuss bandwidth allocation for several service models. We start with the best-effort service based on the assumption that all IP packets are indistinguishable and want to get the same service. Then, we consider two other service models where instead of packets we consider flows; guarantees are given to individual flows. A maximum guaranteed bandwidth service allows a flow to transmit only up to a maximum rate. When a minimum rate is guaranteed, then the flow has priority as long its current rate does not exceed the guaranteed value, but it may exceed that limit if other traffic permits.

Best-effort service networks cannot provide any QoS guarantees, but should at least allocate resources fairly. A *fair bandwidth allocation policy* is based on a *max-min* algorithm that attempts to maximize the bandwidth allocation for flows receiving the smallest allocation. To increase the bandwidth allocation of one flow, the system has to decrease the allocation of another flow.

Consider for simplicity a network with multiple unidirectional flows and routers with infinite buffer space. In such a network the link capacity is the only limiting factor in bandwidth allocation for individual flows. The following algorithm [7] guarantees a *min-max fair bandwidth allocation* among all flows:

- Start with an allocation of zero Mbps for each flow.

- Increment equally the allocation for each flow until one of the links of the network becomes saturated. Now all the flows passing through the saturated link get an equal fraction of the link capacity.

- Increment equally the allocation for each flow that does not pass through the first saturated link until a second link becomes saturated. Now all the flows passing through the saturated link get an equal fraction of the link capacity.

- Continue by incrementing equally the allocations of all flows that do not use a saturated link until all flows use at least one saturated link.

The fairness of bandwidth allocation is a slightly more complex phenomenon than the previous algorithm tends to suggests, it is strongly affected by:

(i) The routers; when the network becomes congested the routers drop packets.

(ii) The end systems; when the network becomes congested end systems use congestion control to limit the traffic of each level-4 flow. Congestion control is a mechanism to inform senders of packets that the network is congested and they have to exercise restraint and reduce the rate at which they inject packets into the network. Congestion control can be built into transport protocols or can be enforced by edge routers controlling the admission of packets into a network supporting multiple classes of traffic.

4.4.5 Buffer Acceptance Algorithms

To better understand congestion control in the Internet, we take a closer look at the strategies used by a router to determine: (a) when to drop a packet; and (b) which packets should be dropped.

Buffer acceptance algorithms control the number of packets in the buffers of a router, attempt to optimize the utilization of the output links, and enforce some degree of fairness among the flows crossing the router. We discuss two buffer acceptance algorithms, the tail drop and the random early detection; one provides a passive, the other one an active queue management solution.

4.4.5.1 *The Tail Drop Algorithm.* A packet arriving at a queue with maximum capacity maxThr will be dropped with probability 1 if the number of packets in the queue is $n = maxThr$. The algorithm is very simple and easy to implement and works well for large buffers.

However, the tail drop algorithm makes no distinction between several flows. It is not an optimal solution for TCP traffic and could have a devastating effect on an audio or video stream. Such flows are bursty and there is a large probability that consecutive packets from the same stream will be dropped when the network becomes congested and the forward error correction schemes discussed in Chapter 5 could not be used to provide an acceptable audio or video reception.

4.4.5.2 *RED, the Random Early Detection Algorithm.* The RED buffer acceptance algorithm is a more sophisticated strategy used by routers to manage their packet queues. Rather than waiting for a queue to fill up and then drop all incoming packets with probability $p = 1$, the algorithm uses a variable probability to drop a packet. The router maintains several state variables:

$minThr, maxThr$ - thresholds for queue length.

$sampleQueueLength$ - the instantaneous value of queue length.

$averageQueueLength$ - average value of the queue length.

$dropProb$ - probability of dropping a packet.

$maxDropProb$ - value of $dropProb$ when $averageQueueLength = maxThr$

w - a weighting factor $0 \leq w \leq 1$.

$count$ - keeps track of how many arriving packets have been queued while

$$minThr < averageQueLen < maxThr$$

The algorithm works as follows:

1. If $(averageQueueLength \leq minThr)$ - queue the packet.

2. If $(minThr < averageQueueLength < maxThr)$

   - calculate $dropProb$
   - drop the arriving packet with probability $dropProb$.

3. If $(averageQueueLength \geq maxThr)$ - drop the packet.

The parameters of the algorithm are computed as follows:

$averageQueueLength =$

$$(1 - w) \times averageQueueLength + w \times sampleQueueLength.$$

$$tempDropProb = \frac{maxDropProb \times averageQueueLength - minThr}{maxThr - minThr}$$

$$dropProb = \frac{tempDropProb}{1 - count \times tempDropProb}$$

We now provide the intuition behind these expressions. There are three regimes of operations for the router: low, intermediate, and high load. The router identifies the current operating regime by comparing the average queue length with minimum and maximum thresholds. At low load the router does not drop any packets, at high load it drops all, and in the intermediate regime the drop probability increases linearly with the average queue length.

The average queue length is a weighted average, the computation gives more weight to the past history reflected by the $averageQueueLength$ value, than to the instantaneous value, $sampleQueueLength$, typically $w < 0.2$. We know that flows often have bursty spurts and we want to prevent packets from the same stream to be dropped. We increase slowly the drop probability based on the number of packets received since the last drop increase, $dropProb$ increases as $count$ increases.

Figure 4.51 illustrates the application of RED strategy for enforcing the admission control policy at the edge router of a network supporting two classes of traffic, *premium*, or *in*, and *regular*, or *out*. This algorithm is called *random early detection with in and out classes (RIO)* .

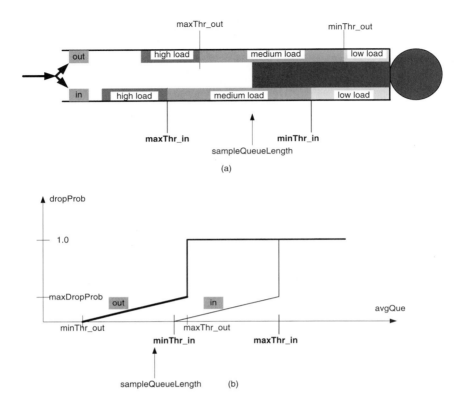

Fig. 4.51 RIO, Random early detection with in and out packet drop strategy. (a) Two classes of services are supported: "in" corresponds to premium service and "out" to regular service. The three regimes of operations for the router, low, intermediate, and high load are different for the two classes. At low load the router does not drop any packets, at high load it drops all, and in the intermediate regime the drop probability increases linearly with the average queue length. (b) An edge router has two different drop probabilities, $dropProb_{in} < dropProb_{out}$ and adjusts both of them dynamically based on the sample queue length, $sampleQueueLength$, and the average queue length, $averageQueueLength$.

The drop probability of the two classes of traffic are different. The transition from low to intermediate regime occurs earlier for the regular packets than for the premium ones, $minThr_{out} < minThr_{in}$; the transition from intermediate to high occurs later for premium packets, $maxThr_{in} > maxThr_{out}$; during the intermediate regime the drop probability of premium packets is lower than the one for regular packets.

This preferential treatment of the premium class justifies the *in* and *out* subscripts in the description of the RIO. The same idea can be applied to multiple classes of traffic and the corresponding strategy is called *weighted random early detection* (WRED).

The empirical evidence shows that RED lowers the queuing delay and increases the utilization of resources. Yet, the algorithm is difficult to tune, the procedures to determine optimal values for the parameters of the algorithm are tedious. At the same time, using suboptimal values may lead to worse performance than the much simpler tail drop algorithm.

4.4.6 Explicit Congestion Notification (ECN) in TCP

The TCP congestion control mechanism discussed earlier has a major flow; it detects congestion after the routers have already started dropping packets. Network resources are wasted because packets are dropped at some point along their path, after using link bandwidth as well as router buffers and CPU cycles up to the point where they are discharged.

The question that comes to mind is: Could routers prevent congestion by informing the source of the packets when they become lightly congested, but before they start dropping packets? This strategy is called *source quench*.

There are two possible approaches for the routers to support source quench:

1. Send explicit notifications to the source, e.g., use the ICMP. Yet, sending more packets in a network that shows signs of congestion may not be the best idea.

2. Modify a *congestion notification* flag in the IP header to inform the destination; then have the destination inform the source by setting a flag in the TCP header of segments carrying acknowledgments.

There are several issues related to the deployment of ECN [8]. First, the TCP must be modified to support the new flag. Second, routers must be modified to distinguish between ECN-capable flows and those who do not support ECN. Third, IP must be modified to support the congestion notification flag. Fourth, TCP should allow the sender to confirm the congestion notification to the receiver, because acknowledgments could be lost.

4.4.7 Maximum and Minimum Bandwidth Guarantees

When we wish to enforce a maximum or a minimum flow rate we have to consider two main tasks:

1. Classify individual packets; identify the flow a packet belongs to.

2. Measure the rate of a flow and enforce the flow limit.

4.4.7.1 Packet Classification. Packet classification can be done at several layers. At the network layer, layer-3 flows can be defined in several ways. For example, we can define a flow between a source and a destination with known IP addresses; alternatively, a flow can be defined as the IP traffic that goes to the same border router.

Packet classification at each router is prohibitively expensive. A practical solution is to require an edge router to classify the packets entering the Internet and force all other routers to rely on that classification. This proposition requires that a field in the IP header be used for packet marking, or the addition of an extra header for marking.

An easy to implement solution, in line with the first approach, is the use of the 5-bit type-of-service (TOS) field in the IP header for packet marking.

An alternative solution is to add an extra header in front of the IP header. The *multiprotocol label switch (MPLS)* approach changes the forwarding procedure in a router. Now a router decides the output port and the output label of a packet based on the incoming port and the MPLS label of the incoming packet.

We have already discussed transport, or layer-4 flows, and we only mention briefly application layer flows. First of all, identifying applications is a difficult or sometimes an impossible exercise because not all applications are known; some that are known do not always use the same ports. Moreover, the use of encrypted tunnels hide the TCP and UDP headers. Even if we are able to identify the application layer, classification of packets is extremely expensive.

4.4.7.2 Flow Measurements.

Let us turn our attention to the second problem, measuring the rate of a flow. The easiest solution is to count the number of bytes in a given interval and produce an average rate. This is not necessarily the best approach because the result is heavily influenced by the choice of the measurement interval. A small measurement interval makes it difficult to accommodate bursty traffic where we have to limit not only the average rate but also the amount of traffic during a given period of time.

An alternative solution is to use a token bucket, see Figure 4.52. The basic idea is that a flow can only consume as much bandwidth as the token bucket associated with the flow allows. The token bucket has a maximum capacity of B tokens and accumulates tokens at a rate of one token every $1/r$ seconds, where r is the average flow rate. Thus, if a flow starts with a full bucket, then in any given period of T seconds the maximum number of bytes it may transmit is: $B + T \times r$. If a packet of length L arrives when there are C tokens in the bucket, then:

```
if ( L <= C ) {
    accept the packet;
    C = C - L;
}
else
    drop the packet;
```

4.4.7.3 Traffic Shaping.

The token bucket could be modified to shape the traffic by adding a buffer, see Figure 4.53. The shaping buffer delays the packets that do not conform to the traffic shape rather than dropping them. Then, the handling of a packet of length L is slightly modified:

```
if ( L <= C ) {
    accept the packet;
    C = C - L;
```

```
}
else {
    /* the packet arrived early, delay it */
    while ( C < L ) {
      wait;
    }
    transmit the packet;
    C = C - L;
}
```

A flow may be characterized by several (r, B) pairs and a pair may describe several flows. The closer the characterization is to the actual average and burst rate of the

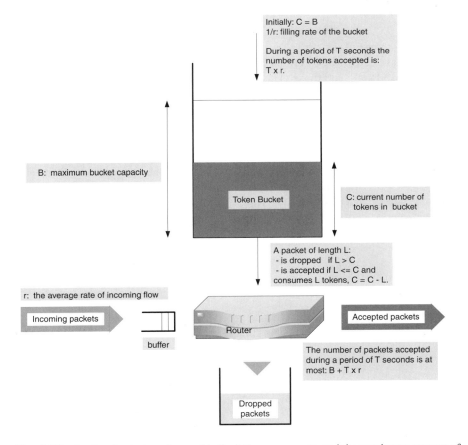

Fig. 4.52 A token bucket can be used to limit the average rate and the maximum amount of traffic a flow is allowed to transport during any period of time. Tokens accumulate in the bucket at a constant rate; tokens are consumed by the flow to transmit the packets. A simple token bucket does not have a buffer. A modified token bucket uses the buffer to shape the traffic.

flow, the more accurate the reservations will reflect the actual needs of the flow. For example, a flow may transport data for 9 seconds at a rate of 1 Mbps followed by 1 second at 20 Mbps. This flow can be described by a (2.9 Mbps, 20 MB) bucket but the same bucket could describe a flow with a constant rate of 2.9 Mbps.

The idea of the token bucket filter is that the probability that several flows crossing a router reach their burst rate at the same time is reduced because of the constraints imposed by the average rate. Flows accumulate tokens at the average rate and, at the same time, they have to consume tokens to sustain the average rate.

For the sake of argument, consider a mischievous flow that monitors the traffic through a router and decides to throw in its burst rate when all the other flows are at, or near, their burst rate. To do so the mischievous flow has to accumulate tokens and wait for the right moment to spend them. Though it may be successful at times, to sustain the average rate it has declared, the flow cannot hold the accumulated tokens for an indefinite amount of time.

4.4.7.4 *Packet Marking.*

To guarantee that a flow receives a minimum bandwidth we have to measure the rate of a flow and then mark the packets within the minimum bandwidth and those exceeding the minimum bandwidth. The marking of packets can be done in a deterministic or nondeterministic fashion.

Deterministic marking can be based on extensions to the token bucket algorithm. Following [4] the packets belonging to one flow could be classified in three categories with the scheme in Figure 4.53.

Here *cir* is the *committed information rate*, the rate we guarantee that packets will be accepted at; *cbr* is the *committed burst rate*, packets falling into this category will be given priority; and *ebr* is the *excess burst rate*, packets in this category are guaranteed to be accepted but given lower priority.

The extended bucket filling algorithm is:

```
Initially:
  C = cbr;
  CE = ebr;
Every 1/cir do {
    if ( C < cbr)  C = C + 1;
    else
        if (CE < ebr) CE = CE + 1;
        else do nothing;
}
```

The classification algorithm for a packet of length L is:

```
if ( L <= C ) {
   C = C - L;
   mark packet as red;
}
else if ( L <= CE ) {
       CE = CE - L;
```

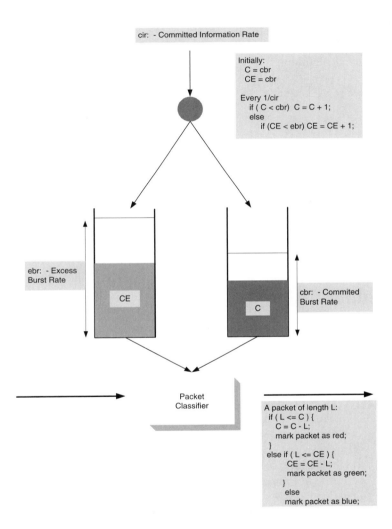

Fig. 4.53 An extended token bucket is used to classify packets in three categories.

```
      mark packet as green;
}
  else
  mark packet as blue;
```

In case of probabilistic marking a packet in a flow whose average rate exceeds the the minimum guaranteed rate are marked with probability p function of the excess rate. The actual algorithm is:

```
if ( averageFlowRate <= guaranteedMinimumRate) {
   mark packet as red;
}
else {
   p = (averageFlowRate - guaranteedMinimumRate)
                            / averageFlowRate;
   mark packet as blue with probability p;
   mark packet as red with probability (1-p);
   }
```

Once packets are marked then we can use one of the buffer acceptance algorithms discussed earlier to discard packets selectively. If we have only two classes of packets, we can use RIO and give priority to one class of packets, e.g., the red packets; if we have several classes of packets we can use the WRED buffer acceptance algorithm and give the highest priority to red, the next priority to green, and the lowest priority to blue packets.

4.4.8 Delay Guarantees and Packet Scheduling Strategies

The question we address in this section is how to modify the functions of a router for a multiservice network to support both best-effort traffic and traffic with delay guarantees. Inherently, a router multiplexes several classes of traffic, for example, best-effort and traffic with delay guarantees and we want to make sure that the traffic with delay guarantees has priority over the best-effort traffic.

It should be clear by now that packet classification, traffic shaping, and buffer acceptance are critical components of traffic control. But they are not sufficient when we have to deal with delay guarantees; we need a packet scheduling mechanism to actually allow packets to be transmitted based on their priority, packets with delay guarantees first and best efforts packets with a lower priority.

Figure 4.54 shows the architecture of a QoS-capable router and introduces several new components of the system. A *classifier* identifies the flow an incoming packet belongs to; then adds an internal flow ID to each packet; finally, it sends the packet to the next component, the policer, when the flow follows the rules, or to the shaper, when it does not.

The *policer* uses the internal flow ID and the current rate and assigns a priority to each packet:

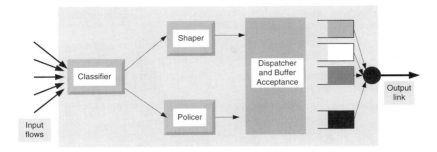

Fig. 4.54   The processing of several flows at the output link of a QoS capable router in a multiservice network.

(i) low priority is given to best-effort packets and to excess packets from minimal bandwidth guaranteed flows;

(ii) high priority is assigned to maximum bandwidth packets and to nonexcess packets from minimum guaranteed bandwidth flows.

The *shaper* delays flows that do not follow the rules. Here we show the shaping of output router traffic; one could also shape the input traffic by placing a shaper in front of the queue associated with each input link.

Finally, the packets reach a *dispatcher* that assigns packets to queues based on their priority and also rejects packets selectively, using an RED strategy. Figure 4.54 shows that instead of a single FIFO queue now we have several queues and packets from the same flow are placed in the same queue when the flow obeys its contract.

4.4.8.1 *Packet Size and Packet Scheduling.*   Before discussing the scheduling algorithms used for packet scheduling we review several concepts introduced in Chapter 2. There are two classes of scheduling algorithms: those that do not allow a server to be idle while there is work to be done are called *work-conserving*; *nonwork-conserving* scheduling algorithms may defer the transmission of a packet even though there are packets waiting and the output link is available. Such scheduling algorithms can provide delay jitter guarantees.

Scheduling strategies can be *preemptive* or *non-preemptive*. In case of a preemptive strategy the server may interrupt its work to schedule a higher priority request. All packet scheduling policies are non-preemptive, once the first bit of a packet is transmitted, there is no way to interrupt the transmission and reschedule a higher priority packet. In turn, the transmission time of a packet depends on the length of the packet and the speed of the communication channel:

$$\mu(seconds) \ = \ packetLength(bits)/channelBandwidth(bps)$$

Example. The transmission time for a 2-Kbyte packet over a 100-Mbps channel is: $2048 \times 8 \ \times 1/100 \times 10^6 \ = \ 163.8 \times 10^{-6}$ seconds; the transmission time for the same 2-Kbyte packet over a 2.5-Gbps, OC 48 channel is 25 times shorter, 6.5×10^{-6} seconds.

The transmission time of an ATM cell over the 100-Mbps channel is $53 \times 8 \times 1/100 \times 10^6 = 4.24 \times 10^{-6}$ seconds; the transmission time for the same ATM cell over the OC 48 channel is as expected, 25 times shorter, or about 0.17×10^{-6} seconds.

The incoming packet rate for a router connected to an OC 48 link is:

- 152, 587 packets/second for the 2-Kbyte packets.
- 5, 896, 226 packets/second for the 53-byte ATM cells.

The number of CPU cycles used by a router for packet forwarding is independent of packet size; to support the same traffic rate for small and large packets alike a router must be much faster than one handling only large packets.

This simple example outlines a basic dilemma encountered in the design of a network: the shorter the maximum packet size, the more able the network is to deal with real-time constraints, and guarantee a lower jitter, but the higher are the packet rates a router must handle when connected to high-speed links.

Let us now examine several packet scheduling strategies for QoS-capable routers.

4.4.8.2 Processor Sharing (PS) and Generalized Processor Sharing (GPS).

If the capacity of the output channel is C and the number of nonempty queues at time t is $N_{nonempty}(t)$, then the rates $R_i^{PS}(t)$ and $R_i^{GPS}(t)$ at which the PS and the GPS strategies, respectively, serve the queue Q_i with weight w_i are:

$$R_i^{PS}(t) = C \times \frac{1}{N_{nonempty}(t)}.$$
$$R_i^{GPS}(t) = C \times \frac{w_i}{\sum_{j \in N_{nonempty}(t)} w_j}.$$

PS and GPS are work-conserving packet-scheduling strategies, an elegant theoretical solution but not implementable in practice. No packets are discharged in either case; the service is min-max fair in case of PS.

GPS does not allow starvation of low priority flows. A GPS scheduler guarantees an upper bound for the delay equal to R/B for token-bucket (R, B)-constrained flows.

4.4.8.3 Round Robin (RR), Weighted Round Robin (WRR), and Deficit Round Robin (DRR).

The queues are served one after another. In WRR, if active, the flow with weight w_i gets the corresponding fraction of the total bandwidth.

In Figure 4.55, we see four flows with the same arrival rate λ and the same packet length and service rate μ, and with weights, $12, 6, 4, and 3$, respectively. A scheduling cycle consists of up to 25 slots, the server visits q_1 for up to 12 slots, then q_2 for up to 6 slots, then q_3 for up to 4 slots, and finally q_4 for up to 3 slots. As a result of this scheduling policy, we expect the average queue length of q_4 to be twice that of q_3, three times that of q_2, and four times that of q_1. This scheduling algorithm is work-conserving; thus, the "up to" qualifications in the algorithm description above.

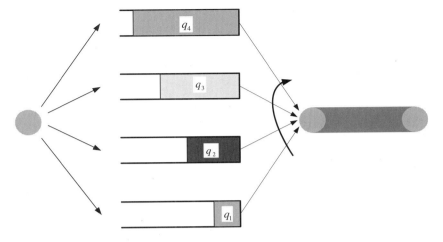

Fig. 4.55 Weighted queuing.

A slight modification allows the RR strategy to be fair even when variable length packets are transmitted. DRR associates a counter $c(i)$ with a queue, $q(i)$ for flow i; if the length of the first packet in a queue is larger than the counter, the queue is skipped. The algorithm used by DRR increases the counter every time the queue, $q(i)$ is visited: $c(i) = c(i) + \delta$. If L is the length of the packet at the head of queue $q(i)$ then:

```
if ( L > c(i) {
    do not transmit the packet;
    }
else {
    transmit the packet;
    c(i) = c(i) - L;
    }
```

RR and DRR strategies are fair for fixed-length packets and can be easily implemented in hardware. If the server finishes processing the requests in any queue earlier than the maximum allotted number of slots, then it moves to the next queue.

4.4.8.4 Priority Scheduling. The queues are served in order of their priority. All the packets in a high-priority queue are transmitted before any packet in the next priority queue. Once all packets in some queue are transmitted, the scheduler starts transmitting packets from the highest priority nonempty queue. This may lead to the starvation of low-priority flows.

4.4.8.5 Weighted Fair Queuing, WFQ. WFQ is a practical version of GPS, it is a weighted scheduling algorithm; it calculates the finishing time of transmission for each packet and transmits the packets in the order of their finishing time.

4.4.9 Constrained Routing

In the previous sections we discussed mechanisms to support QoS at the router level in a datagram network. To provide end-to-end guarantees for bandwidth, delay, jitter, cost, or loss rate, we have first to find a path satisfying constraints involving the characteristics of individual links.

Recall from Section 4.2.6 that we have two basic classes of routing algorithms: link state (LS) and distance vector (DV) algorithms. Internet routers distribute information about network load using the OSPF protocol discussed in Section 4.3.8 and based on an LS algorithm. The algorithm requires each router to know the topology of the net. Internet routers use RIP to distribute routing tables. The RIP protocol is a DV algorithm and it is not really suitable to provide information needed for constrained routing.

As we already know from Chapter 2, the state of a wide-area system cannot be distributed instantaneously to all nodes. Routers have to make decisions based on incomplete and/or outdated information. While topological changes occur relatively seldom, the variation of the load could be significant, even over short periods of time.

A critical issue is how often should the information needed for constrained routing be exchanged; if it is exchanged too often, then a significant fraction of the network capacity is used for network control and even more important, oscillations are likely to occur. However, if the information is distributed too seldom, then the routing decisions are made with obsolete knowledge and may no longer be suboptimal but could be plain wrong.

Indeed, assume that two cities are linked by two parallel routes. Consider the behavior of the traffic on a busy day; assume that a radio traffic report delivers the news that one route is congested in both directions while the traffic on the other is fluid. If there are frequent crossover points from one route to the other, then many drivers will cross from the congested route to the one with fluid traffic when hearing the news. This route will immediately become congested and the next traffic report will disseminate this information, causing many drivers to change routes again. Some drivers will end up crossing from one route to another and make little progress toward their destinations. However, if no traffic reports are available one of the routes may be congested while the traffic on the other is very light.

If the path has n links and d_i, B_i, and e_i are the delay, bandwidth, and loss rate on link i respectively, routing may be subject to several types of constraints.

Our first example is to find a path where all links have a bandwidth larger than B; in this case we impose a *concave constraint*:

$$min(B_i)_{i=1,n} > B.$$

This can be done easily; we construct a modified network graph with all the links that do not satisfy the constraint removed. Then, we run the LS algorithm on the modified network.

If we wish to find a path such that the total delay is lower than d, we have an *additive constraint*:

$$\sum_{i=1}^{n} d_i < d.$$

However, if we wish to find a path such that the loss rate is smaller than e, we impose a *multiplicative constraint*:

$$\prod_{i=1}^{n} e_i < e.$$

Satisfying a single additive or multiplicative constraint is straightforward for LS algorithms; we add a node to the path if it minimizes the desired constraint. The problem becomes NP hard when we have two or more constraints.

In practice, constrained routing is only considered for intradomain routing. A proposal favored by the IETF is to extend OSPF and add to each link four new parameters: maximum bandwidth, maximum reservable bandwidth, unreserved bandwidth, and resource class.

Let us now consider the practical aspects of establishing and controlling constrained network paths for individual flows. There are two basic approaches: (1) define a separate protocol to establish, release, and deal with changes in the flow requirements or with changes in the environment; (2) use special packets in the flow for the establishment and release of resources. For obvious reasons the two methods are called *out-of-band* and *in-band flow management*.

The out-of-band method is well suited for networks based on virtual circuits but not very popular for datagram networks. Individual routers have to maintain the state of each flow and the routes are fixed. ISDN, see Section 4.1.9, uses this method of flow management.

4.4.10 Resource Reservation Protocol (RSVP)

RSVP is used to establish a path for a flow and then to reserve resources along this path [23]. RSVP messages are exchanged as IP datagrams as seen in Figure 4.56.

There are two ways to establish the path of a flow, the hop-by-hop approach and the source-controlled approach. In the first case, each router decides the next hop, in the second one, the source computes explicit paths.

Before describing the RSVP protocol we need to stipulate several requirements for a network architecture that supports reservations.

First, we need to accommodate faults, due either to routers that crash or to links that fail. Since reservation requires maintaining state information about each flow in every router the flow crosses, we need to provide a mechanism to provide end-to-end connectivity in the presence of faults.

The solution is to maintain a *soft state* in the routers, i.e., to allocate resources, in this case entries in the reservation tables, on a temporary basis. The initiator of a reservation request is only allowed to *lease* entries in the reservation tables for a limited amount of time. To keep the entries the initiator of the reservation request has to renew the lease periodically.

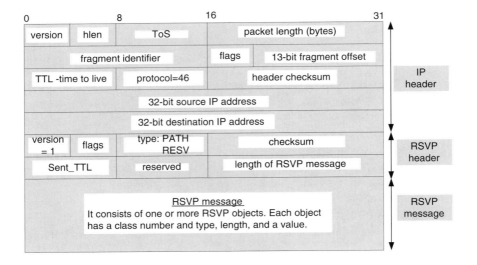

Fig. 4.56 The RSVP message is encapsulated into an IP datagram with protocol number equal to 46. In addition to the 20-byte IP header, the message is prefixed by an 8-byte RSVP header.

Under these conditions, once a router fails or a link goes down, the end-to-end connection abstraction will detect the breakdown of the virtual circuit and will eventually reestablish a new one without the need to contact all routers along the path and delete the entries corresponding to the now defunct connection. These entries are deleted automatically when their leases expire.

Second, we need to support not only unicast but also multicast connections. In case of a multicast topology, e.g., one employed by an Internet radio or video broadcast service, different receivers have different requirements. These requirements are based on: the capabilities of the end station; the speed of the connection links; the specific needs of the application; the cost of subscribing to the service; and possibly other factors. Thus RSVP is based on a *receiver-oriented* reservation scheme, the receiver is responsible to make the reservation request.

The basic operation of RSVP is depicted in Figure 4.57. In response to a connection request the sender inserts its flow specifications, the so-called TSpec, into a PATH RSVP message and forwards this message to the receiver. Each router along the path, adds to this RSVP message its own ID and identifies the upstream router. After the path is established reservations coming from downstream will be sent to the upstream router. The specification of services requested by the client are described by a so-called RSpec.

Once the PATH message reaches its destination, the receiver creates an RESV message containing the characteristics of the flow, as described by the sender, and adds its own characteristics, the so-called, RSpec, see Section 4.4.11. The RESV message travels upstream and, if all routers accept the reservation, a new entry is added to the

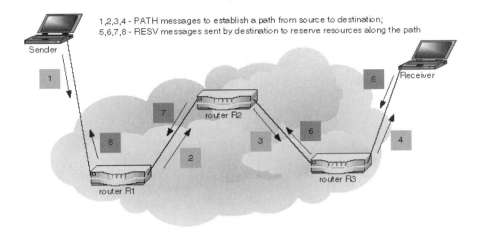

1,2,3,4 - PATH messages to establish a path from source to destination;
5,6,7,8 - RESV messages sent by destination to reserve resources along the path

Fig. 4.57 Connection establishment and resource reservation with RSVP. 1,2,3, and 4 are PATH messages used to establish a path from sender to receiver; 5,6,7, and 8 are RESV messages used to reserve resources in each router along the established path. A router forwards the RESV only if it is able to allocate the resources. The individual messages are: (1) the sender identifies flow requirements; (2) router R1 decides to route the flow through router R2; (3) router R2 decides to route the flow via router R3; (4) router R3 reaches destination; (5) destination requests R3 to reserve resources; (6) R3 reserves resources and forwards the request to R2; (7) R2 reserves resources and forwards the request to R1; (8) R1 reserves resources and sends to the source a confirmation that the necessary resources along the path have been reserved.

reservation table of each of the routers along the path. The new entry is added after the sender gets the RESV message and responds to it with a new PATH message.

The receiver sends the same RESV message every 30 seconds or so for the entire duration of the period it intends to keep its reservation. These messages are interpreted by each router as requests to renew the lease of the flow. In turn, the sender issues PATH messages every 30 seconds or so.

A router unable to make the reservation does not forward the RESV packet upstream. In time, all the routers downstream will drop their reservations. Indeed, in absence of a RESV message, the sender does not send a new PATH message. Missing the PATH message, the receiver assumes that the reservation has failed and does not send the required RESV message to renew the lease.

In case of router or link failure, the routing protocols create a new path from the sender to the receiver and update the forwarding tables of the routers along the path. Each router discovers changes in its forwarding table. All routers along the original path send PATH messages every 30 seconds or so. The first such message after the new path is stable will carry the information about the new path to the receiver that will respond to it with an RESV message that will travel along the new path.

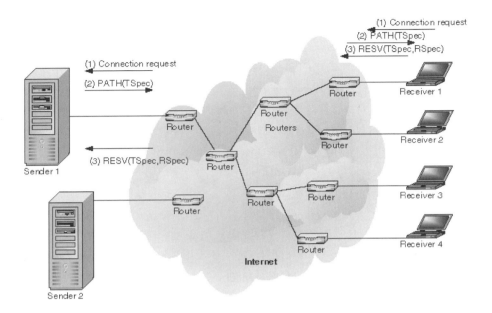

Fig. 4.58 RSVP multicast. (1) A receiver requests a connection to a multicast sender. (2) After receiving the connection request, the sender issues a PATH message containing the flow specifications; the message propagates downstream on the multicast tree to the receiver. (3) The receiver sends up the tree a RESV message to reserve resources along the path. Routers create entries in their reservation tables; if the the reservation is accepted by all the routers along the path, then the sender receives the RESV message. As long as the receiver wants to keep the reservation it sends the same RESV message every 30 seconds or so to renew its lease.

The resources along a path can be released by explicit tear-down requests. The PATHtear allows a sender to end a flow and the RESVtear allows a reciver to end the flow.

The basic operation of RSVP in case of multicast operations is depicted in Figure 4.58. In response to a connection request the sender inserts its TSpec in a PATH message and forwards this message to the receiver. Once the PATH message reaches its destination, the receiver creates a RESV message containing the TSpec of the sender along with its own RSpec.

Reservations are aggregated by the routers on the multicast tree whenever possible. In case of receivers with different service requirements, the RESV messages are merged and the maximum of the downstream reservations are sent upstream. For example, once a router has accepted a reservation guaranteeing a maximum delay of d milliseconds, all reservations for $d_h \geq d$ will be automatically satisfied and no new reservations are necessary. To upgrade the reservation for a flow to a new value, $d_l < d$, each router along the path sends the new reservation upstream and, if accepted by all routers along the path, the new reservation is installed.

If multiple senders are involved, for example, in case of video conferences, each destination may use a filter to specify the sources that can benefit from the reservation.

In conclusion, RSVP provides the means to establish flows with guaranteed reservations in a datagram network and supports both unicast and multicast operations. RSVP uses a soft state approach to resource reservations and it is able to accommodate link and router failures as well as the failure of the sender or the receiver.

4.4.11 Integrated Services

Integrated services support fine grain QoS for individual flows and provide delay and bandwidth guarantees for unicast and multicast communication, without the need to alter the routing protocols [21]. Integrated services coexist with best-effort service models.

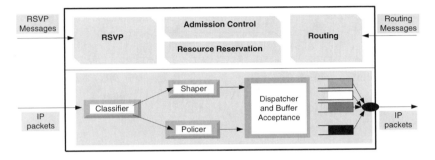

Fig. 4.59 The IP packet and the control information flow through an integrated service router.

Figure 4.59 illustrates the flow of IP packets and of control information through an integrated services enabled router. In addition to routing and packet forwarding, the router supports resource reservations. The forwarding function is more complex, individual IP packets are classified and handled differently for best-effort and QoS guaranteed services.

A closer examination shows that for fine-grain QoS we need four types of mechanisms, one for each of the following problems: (1) *specification of flow requirements*; (2) *admission decisions*; (3) *resource reservation and policing*; and (4) *policy enforcement*.

The four mechanisms supporting integrated services in the Internet are: Flowspecs, admission control, resource reservation and policing, and packet scheduling. We have already examined resource reservation, packet scheduling and policy enforcement, now we discuss only flow specification and admission control.

4.4.11.1 *Specification of flow requirements, Flowspecs.* Flow specification, abbreviated *Flowspecs* supports two mechanisms: one called TSpec to specify the traffic characteristics; and one called RSpec to describe the services required from the network.

Recall that IETF supports two service models, controlled load and guaranteed service. RSpec for controlled load does not require any parameters just the information that the flow is content with the controlled load model. RSpec for guaranteed service requires the flow to specify the acceptable delay or another parameter of the flow that can be used to derive the delay. TSpec is used by the admission control policy to decide if a flow is admitted or not.

Description of traffic characteristics is a more delicate issue. Many streaming applications generate a bursty traffic, with silence periods with little or no traffic and periods with very heavy traffic. In many cases, the *burst rate* is considerably higher than the *average rate*.

The naive approach based on average rate requirements has obvious drawbacks. The decision to admit a flow based on the average rate is obviously flawed because it does not take into account temporal properties of a flow. The sum of the actual rate requirements of all flows passing through a router at time t may exceed the capacity of that router, though the sum of the average rate requirements is well below the capacity of the router. An alternative is to require each flow to declare its burst rate. The admission control policy based on the burst rate of each flow is wasteful.

A better solution, though still an imperfect one, is to use the *token bucket* abstraction that takes into account both the burst rate and the average rate of a flow. A so-called r, B *token bucket,filter* is described by two parameters, r the average rate and B the depth, see Section 4.4.7.

4.4.11.2 *Admission Control.*

Admission control is a binary decision whether there are enough resources to match the TSpec and RSpec of a flow. Each router knows the fraction of its capacity already committed and if it uses a weighted fair scheduling it can decide easily if it can accommodate the flow. Thus, for guaranteed service the decision is "yes" if all routers along the path can accommodate the new flow and "no" if at least one router along the path cannot accommodate it. In case of controlled load, one could use some heuristics, e.g., use past information about the interaction of similar flows with a load similar to the existing one, or simply make a decision based on the heaviest load reported by any router along the path.

There is also the question of how to handle flows that exceed their allotted quota. We need a policing mechanism to make decisions on a per-packet basis and we need a policy to handle the offending packets. The simplest such policy is to drop packets once a flow exceeds its allotted quota. An alternative policy is to allow the packets from the offending flows in, but mark them low priority and, in case of congestion, empower the routers to drop such packets first.

The integrated service, or *Intserv* architecture defines two basic classes of services: *guaranteed services* (GS), and *controlled load* (CL).

The first, GS, supports a service model approximating the one provided by a direct physical link between the source and the destination or the destinations. Conforming packets are guaranteed a maximum end-to-end delay but not an average delay; there are no jitter guarantees either. Packet losses may occur due to bit errors, remember that routers drop packets when the checksum fails, but buffers are reserved in all routers along the path and packet loss due to buffer overflow is prevented. Nonconforming packets are treated as best effort.

Packet conformity in GS is based on token buckets defined in terms of the peak, or the average traffic rate. If L_{max}, and L are the maximum and the average packet size, respectively, and r_{peak} and r the peak and the average traffic rate in bytes/sec rate, respectively, then the maximum amount of traffic due to the flow during an interval of T seconds is bounded for a peak rate token bucket, (L_{max}, r_{peak}) and for an average rate token bucket (L, r). Packets with a size larger than L_{max} are treated as best effort. One can carry out an exact analysis of the GS service model and obtain bounds for the delay.

The second, CL, approximates the performance of a best-effort model in a lightly loaded network, it provides no guarantees for end-to-end delay, jitter, or losses. In practice, the CL policy requires a router to detect nonconforming packets and then use multiple queues for scheduling their transmission: (i) one could have only two queues, a CL queue for all flows and one best-effort queue; or (ii) individual CL queues for each flow and one or more best-effort queues.

There are obvious problems with integrated services. Some applications are unable to specify with any accuracy their communication requirements. To accommodate critical applications unable to specify their requirements the network supports a "better" best-effort service, the so-called *null* service. This class of service allows applications to specify only their MTU

Moreover, as we can see from Figure 4.59, packet forwarding is a considerably more involved process. The QoS guarantees, bandwidth/delay guarantees for the GS model and bandwidth guarantees for the CL model, require routers to reserve resources along the path of each flow. This requirement limits the scalability of the integrated service architecture: each flow has to send one PATH/RESV message per refresh period; each router has to maintain state information for each flow; for each packet a router has to identify the state of the flow and check the traffic contract and the reservations.

4.4.12 Differentiated Services

The overhead of handling individual flows and managing multiple queues could be too much for the high-speed routers that have to forward millions of packets per second in the Internet. Thus a second alternative that supports only two classes of traffic, *regular* and *premium* is considered by the IETF.

In case of *differentiated services*, a router gives preferential treatment to a packet from a premium flow. At this point it should be clear that no end-to-end guarantees are possible, because there is no mechanism to ensure a consensus among all the routers along the path of a flow from its source to its destination, as in the case of RSVP. For this reason we can only talk about "per-hop behaviors" abbreviated as PHBs.

There are two obvious question: Who decides if the packets of a flow should be marked as premium? What precisely does preferential treatment mean? The answer to the first question is straightforward: the edge router accepting a flow makes this decision based on the pricing structure of the Internet service provider. If a customer pays more, it is entitled to a better service.

The second question translates into what kinds of preferences can be given to a packet, or the types of PHBs to be supported. The answer is that we can forward the packet with minimal delay and loss, the so-called *expedited forwarding* (EF), or use a packet dropping policy to minimize the probability that a premium packet is dropped, the so-called *assured forwarding* (AF).

To implement the EF policy we need weighted fair queuing with two classes. The weight of the premium class should be high enough to allow such packets to be forwarded with minimal delay but leave enough bandwidth for the regular traffic and for the control traffic supporting network management. We also need to limit the level of premium traffic entering the domain through some form of admission policy.

The AF policy requires that we assign different drop probabilities to the two classes, a lower probability for the premium packets and a higher probability for the regular packets. In Section 4.4.7 we presented the advantages of the RED scheme, when the drop probability is adjusted dynamically, and of its versions for multiple service classes, RED with "In" and "Out" classes (RIO) and weighted RED (WRED).

4.4.13 Final Remarks on Internet QoS

We discussed at length the problems of Internet QoS because the quality of the communication services affects the end-to-end quality of external network services offered by autonomous providers connected at the periphery of the Internet. Moreover, some of the service models, as well as the techniques used to support QoS guarantees in the Internet can be extended for end-to-end QoS guarantees. Supporting multiple classes of services, multiple queues, rejection of service requests when the load placed on a server reaches a predetermined threshold, shaping of the requests, all are ideas that can be extended to external network services.

The fact that the Internet is based on a network layer datagram service makes it more difficult to support QoS guarantees. At the same time, the scale of the Internet makes any global changes very difficult or even impossible.

It would be unwise to predict how the Internet will evolve. It is plausible that it may end up as a superposition of different internetworks, some supporting QoS gurantees, others without any QoS provisions. Two networks in the first class may be connected with one another via a tunnel crossing only networks in the same class and be capable of guaranteeing end-to-end bandwidth, delay, and jitter, or if such a path does not exist, may not be able to provide the guarantees.

4.5 FURTHER READING

The Web site: `ftp://ftp.internic.net/rfc` is the repository for *requests for comments (RFCs)*. The first request for comments, RFC 001, "Host Software" is by S. Crocker.

In August 1980 J Postel defined UDP (RFC 768) followed in September 1981 by IPv4 and ICMP (RFC 792), and TCP (RFC 793).

The UDP checksum is described by R. Braden, D. Borman, and C. Partridge (RFC 1071); the extensions to TCP are defined by V. Jacobson, S. Braden, and D. Borman (RFC 1323). IPv6 is defined by S. Bradner and A. Mankin (RFC 1752). The addressing architecture in IPv6 is introduced by R. Hinden and S. Deering (RFC 2373).

ARP was defined in November 1982 by D.C. Plummer (RFC 826).

In August 1985 J. Mogul and J. Postel defined standard Internet subnetting (RFC 950). Classeless interdomain routing (CIDR) was introduced in September 1993 by V. Fuller, T. Li, J. Yu, and K. Varadhan (RFC 1519).

RIP was defined by C. L. Hendrick (RFC 1058) and G. Malkin (RFC 1723). The guaranteed service specification is defined by S. Shenker, C. Partridge, and R. Guerin (RFC 2212).

The Tspec and Rspec are defined in RFCs 2210 and 2215.

Several textbooks cover in depth different aspects of networking; [2, 7, 14, 20] are among them. A very good presentation of digital communication can be found in a textbook by Lee and Messerschmidt [15]. Optical networks are treated in [22] and internetwork routing in [11].

4.6 EXERCISES AND PROBLEMS

Problem 1. Perform a `traceroute` between your system and another location and measure the delays. Use two locations, one in North America and another one on a different continent, and perform statistical data analysis of the delay for both sites.

  (i) Repeat the measurements 10 times within a 60 minutes period to collect the data necessary to compute the average value and the variance of the delay.

 (ii) Pick three different times of the day, say, morning, midday, and evening and repeat the measurements for at least seven days.

(iii) Compute a 95% confidence interval for the mean.

Problem 2. Compare two entities (algorithms, protocols, mechanisms, features). In each case you are expected to: (i) describe *briefly* the function of the two entities and their most relevant properties; (ii) list a number of criteria used to compare the two entities and explain why each criteria you propose to use in your comparison is important; (iii) present the advantages and disadvantages of each of the two entities based on each of the criteria you defined in (ii).

  a. Connection-oriented versus connectionless communication.

  b. Persistent versus nonpersistent HTTP connections.

  c. IP v4 versus IP v6

    d. Short versus long packet size, fixed length versus variable length packets.

    e. Interdomain versus intradomain routing.

    f. Error correction versus error detection.

    g. Collision-based versus collision-free multiple access.

    h. Flow control versus congestion control.

    i. Link state versus distance vector routing algorithms.

    j. Static versus dynamic IP address assignment.

Problem 3. A fiber optic cable is 100 miles long and runs at a T3 rate.

    (i) How many bits fit into the cable?

    (ii) What is the efficiency of a stop-and-wait protocol for 53-, 200-, and 2000-bit frames?

Problem 4. The encapsulation and multiplexing mechanisms described in Section 4.1.4 allow a protocol to identify the consumer of the PDUs it receives. Can the IP protocol running on a router apply the same procedure to identify the application each packet crossing the router belongs to?

Problem 5. Identify the states, the transitions, the events, and the actions for the alternating-bit protocol described in Section 4.1.11. Draw the state transition diagram.

Problem 6. If in the protocol header we allocate n bits for the sequence number and an equal number of bits for the acknowledgment number, the sequence numbers wrap around modulo 2^n.

The PDUs within a window must have distinct sequence numbers so we need at least $log_2(N)$ bits for a pipelined protocol with the window size equal to N. Show that n has to be twice this limit.

Problem 7. Consider a slotted Aloha system with m nodes with no buffering space. Assume that: (1) at time t there are n backlogged nodes, nodes with packets that have previously collided and have to be retransmitted, and $m - n$ active, nodes; (2) the arrival process of new packets has an exponential distribution with rate $\frac{\lambda}{m}$; (3) each backlogged node retransmits with a fixed probability, p_r, until a successful retransmission occurs.

    (i) Show that p_a the probability that an active node transmits a packet in a given slot is $p_a = 1 - e^{-\frac{\lambda}{m}}$.

    (ii) Compute $T^a_{(i,n)}$ the probability that i active nodes transmit in a given slot.

    (iii) Compute $T^b_{(i,n)}$ the probability that i backlogged nodes transmit in a given slot.

(iv) Describe the behavior of the system as a discrete-time Markov chain such that in state n there are n backlogged nodes. Draw the state transition diagram of the system.

(v) Express $P_{(n,n+i)}$ the probability of a transition from state n to state $n + i$ in terms of $T_{(i,n)}^a$, $T_{(i,n)}^b$ for the following cases:

$i < -1$ more than one of the backlogged nodes are successful in a given slot.

$i = -1$ exactly one backlogged node is successful in a given slot.

$i = 0$ one active node transmits while none of the backlogged nodes transmit; or no active node transmits and more than one of the already backlogged nodes transmit.

$i = 1$ one active and one or more of the backlogged nodes transmit.

$2 \leq i \leq m - n$ more than one active nodes transmit.

Problem 8. Consider a 100-Mbps Ethernet. Assume a frame length of 100 bytes and no repeaters.

(i) What is the maximum distance between a node and a hub to have an efficiency of 25%, 50%, and 70%.

(ii) Repeat the same calculations for a 1-Gbps Ethernet.

Problem 9. You have a router with five incoming and five outgoing OC-24 links carrying GSM-encoded audio streams (13 Kbps).

(i) Define the concept of a "flow".

(ii) Explain how flows are used to ensure QoS.

(iii) Compute the number of flows passing through the router.

(iv) Assuming that you need 100 bytes for an entry, what would be the size of the flow management table for that router?

(v) What are explicit and implicit flows.

(vi) What resource management problems are associated with explicit flows.

(vii) What is "resource leasing"? Would it solve the problem you encounter in (vi)? Give an example when resource leasing is useful.

Problem 10. Consider a path of length n connecting hosts H_1 and H_2. Assume that each router along the path drops a packet with probability p independently of the other routers. What are the mean numbers of:

(i) Hops traveled by a packet before being discarded.

(ii) Retransmissions of a packet.

Problem 11. Show that if L_{max}, and L are the maximum and the average packet size, respectively, and r_{peak} and $\bar{r}$ the peak and the average traffic rate, respectively, in bytes/sec, then for guaranteed service the maximum amount of traffic due to the flow during an interval of T seconds is:

$$L_{max} + min[(r_{peak} \times T), (L \times T + \bar{r} - L_{max})].$$

Problem 12. Consider the *additive-increase, multiplicative decrease* (AIMD) algorithm for congestion control in TCP. Plot the congestion window (in segments) function of the number of transmissions assuming that:

(i) transmissions occur at discrete times t=0,1,2,...,15;

(ii) the original threshold for the slow start is $w = 8$;

(iii) the first and only loss occurs at $t = 7$.

Explain how you computed the size of the congestion window and the moments when transition from one mode to another occur.

Problem 13. Estimate the effect of a congestion control mechanism with a static window size, $wSize$ on the transmission time of a file. Assume that no transmission errors occur. You know: $fileSize$, the size of the file; R, the maximum transmission rate; RTT, the round trip time; MSS, the maximum segment size. Call $sTime = \frac{MSS}{R}$, the transmission time for one segment.

(i) Examine first the case when there is no stalling, the acknowledgment for the first segment in the window arrives before the window is exhausted:

$$wSize \times sTime > RTT + sTime.$$

Draw a timing diagram and show that in this case:

$$transTime_{noStall} = 2 \times RTT + \frac{fileSize}{R}.$$

(ii) Then examine the case when the transmission stalls when the window is exhausted before the acknowledgment for the first segment in the window arrives:

$$wSize \times sTime < RTT + sTime.$$

Draw a timing diagram and show that now:

$$tranTime_{stall} = transTime_{noStall} + (q - 1)$$

$$\times (sTime + RTT - wSize \times sTime).$$

Here $q = fileSize/(wSize \times MSS)$, rounded up to the next integer.

Problem 14. Determine the effect of the AIMD congestion control mechanism on the transmission time of a file. Assume that no transmission errors occur. You know: $fileSize$, the size of the file; R, the maximum transmission rate; RTT, the round trip time; MSS, the maximum segment size.

(i) Show that $nWindows$ the number of windows that cover the file is:

$$nWindows = \lceil log_2(\frac{fileSize}{MSS} + 1) \rceil.$$

Hint: AIMD allows first a window size of one segment, then two segments, and so on.

(ii) The sender may stall after transmitting the i-th window, waiting for an acknowledgement. Compute the stall time after the transmission of the i-th window, $stallTime_i$ as:

$$stallTime_i = timeFirstAck_i - timeTransmitWindow_i.$$

where $timeFirstAck_i$ is the time when the sender receives the acknowledgment for the first segment in the window and $timeTransmitWindow_i$ is the time to transmit the i-th window of size: $2^{(i-1)} \times sTime$.

(iii) Compute the total stall time:

$$totalStallTime = max[0, \sum_{i=1}^{nWindows} stallTime_i].$$

(iv) Show that the transmission latency when AIMD is in place is:

$$transTime_{AIMD} = transTime_{noStall} + totalStallTime$$

where $transTime_{noStall} = 2 \times RTT + \frac{fileSize}{R}$.

Problem 15. In Section 4.4.7 we presented an extended token bucket used to classify the packets of a flow into three categories. Imagine a scheme when an edge router uses a similar scheme to classify the packets into four categories and then uses weighted fair queuing to forward these packets on an output link. Compute the expected time between successive visits of the server to the highest priority queue.

REFERENCES

1. N. Abramson. Development of the Alohanet. *IEEE Trans. on Information Theory*, IT-31:119–123, 1985.

2. D. Bertsekas. *Linear Network Optimization. Algorithms and Codes.* MIT Press, Cambridge, Mass., 1991.

3. D. Boggs, J. Mogul, and C. Kent. Measured Capacity of an Ethernet: Myth and Reality. In *Proc. ACM SIGCOMM'88, ACM Computer Communication Review* volume 18(4):222–234, 1988.

4. O. Bonaventure. Traffic Control and Quality of Service, QoS, in IP Networks. URL http://www.infonet.fundp.ac.be., 2000.

5. V. Cerf. A Protocol for Packet Networks Interconnections. *IEEE Trans. on Comm. Technology*, COMM-22:627–641, 1974.

6. D.D. Clark. The Design Philosophy of the DARPA Internet Protocols. In *Proc. ACM SIGCOMM'88, ACM Computer Communication Review* volume 18(4):106–114, 1988.

7. D. Comer. *Interconnecting with TCP/IP. Vol 1: Principles, Protocols, and Architecture*, fourth edition. Prentice Hall, Englewood Cliffs, New Jersey, 2000.

8. S. Floyd. TCP and Explicit Congestion Notification. *ACM Computer Communication Review*, 24:10–23, 1994.

9. ADSL Forum. ADSL Tutorial. URL http://www.adsl.com., 1998.

10. Wireless Data Forum. CDPD System Specification, Release 1.1. URL http://www.2wirelessdata.org., 1998.

11. B. Halabi. *Internet Routing Architectures*. CISCO Press, Indianapolis, Indiana, 1997.

12. F. Halsall. *Multimedia Communications: Applications, Networks, Protocols, and Standards*. Addison Wesley, Reading, Mass., 2001.

13. C. Huitema. *IPv6: The New Internet Protocol*, second edition, Prentice Hall, Englewood Cliffs, N.J., 1992.

14. J. Kurose and K. W. Ross. *Computer Networks*. Addison Wesley, Reading, Mass., 2000.

15. E. A. Lee and D.G. Messerschmidt. *Digital Communication*. Kluwer Academic Publishers, Norwell, Mass., 1988.

16. B. Leiner, V. Cerf, D. Clark, R. Kahn, L. Kleinrorock, D. Lynch, J. Postel, L. Roberts, and S. Woolf. A Brief History of the Internet. URL http://www.isoc.org./internet history brief.html, 1999.

17. R. M. Metcalfe and D. R. Boggs. Ethernet: Distributed Packet Switching for Local Computer Networks. *Comm. of the ACM*, 19(7):395–404, 1976.

18. R. Molva. Internet Security Architecture. *Computer Networks and ISDN Systems*, 31(8):787–804, 1999.

19. C. Partridge. A Fifty Gigabit per Second IP Router. *IEEE/ACM Trans. on Networking*, 6(3):237–248, 1998.

20. L. L. Peterson and B. S. Davie. *Computer Networks: A Systems Approach*, second edition, Morgan Kaufmann, San Francisco, California, 2000.

21. R. Rajan, D. Varma, S. Kamat, E. Felsteine, and S. Herzog. A Policy Framework for Integrated and Differentiated Services in the Interenet. *IEEE Network Magazine*, Sept.-Oct.:36–41, 1999.

22. R. Ramaswami and K. Sivarajan. *Optical Networks: A Practical Perspective*. Morgan Kaufmann, San Francisco, California, 1998.

23. L. Zhang, S. Deering, D. Estrin, S. Shenker, and D. Zappala. RSVP: A New Resource Reservation Protocol. *IEEE Network Magazine* , 7(9):8–18, 1993.

5

From Ubiquitous Internet Services to Open Systems

5.1 INTRODUCTION

It is now time to turn our attention from the network core to the periphery of the Internet. We start the chapter with an overview of ubiquitous Internet services that have experienced an explosive growth over the past years and we end the chapter with a discussion of open systems.

In the previous chapters we argued that concurrency and distribution of computations and data pose enduring challenges for designers and users of a distributed system. In spite of these challenges a number of distributed services such as electronic mail and file transfer have been widely used for more than two decades.

Another Internet service, the World Wide Web, introduced in the early 1990s, has been immensely successful. At the same time, the Web has exposed the limitations of the current Internet technology and has left many individuals wondering if ad hoc solutions to delicate problems in the area of network architecture, computer security, network management, and so on, will withstand the test of time. Another sensitive question is how a solution to a technical problem once adopted and used at the scale of the Internet could be replaced by a better one, and what will be the costs of such changes.

The success of the World Wide Web has intrigued and motivated many entrepreneurs to think about new Internet services. The question whether the Internet could support the development of a new economy, as well as new approaches to education, health care, entertainment, and so on, is an open one. The progress in the last years in many areas including distance learning, telemedicine, and business-to-business applications is very encouraging and it is already beginning to affect all aspects of our lives.

There is a complex relationship between the core and the periphery of the Internet. The explosive growth at the periphery of the Internet has generated new requirements for the network core and, in turn, technological changes at the core have affected the quality and the quantity of services provided at the periphery of the Internet.

It is impossible to develop new types of services without some understanding of the Internet core. At the same time, it is unwise to argue about changes at the Internet core without understanding the services the network is expected to support in the future.

The human aspect of widespread use of *information technology (IT)* including the Internet, is another factor that increases the inertial component of the technology. Once a large group of individuals become familiar with a set of products, it becomes very difficult to replace them with better products with a different user interface. Thus, the agonizing question of when to release an IT product for widespread use: as soon as possible, to exploit the commercial advantages of being the first to the market, or to hold it back until you have a deeper understanding of all the technical problems involved.

This chapter is organized as follows: First, we discuss briefly the client-server paradigm and examine the Internet directory service. Then, we discuss the electronic mail and the World Wide Web. We present multimedia applications and conclude the chapter with a discussion of open systems.

5.2 THE CLIENT-SERVER PARADIGM

Relatively early in the development of applications and of operating systems it was recognized the need to construct modular rather than monolithic systems and to allow a clear separation between the modules requesting a function and the ones providing the function was recognized. Once the interface of the module providing a function was well defined, then multiple modules could use the same function to support a more complex functionality without the need to duplicate the code.

Operating Systems (OS) are complex control programs that run on every computer. Examples of widely used operating systems are Unix and its various flavors, Linux, and different flavors of Windows. The primary functions of an OS are to manage local resources and to provide convenient access to local and remote resources. The term *resources* refers here to: (i) hardware resources such as CPU cycles, main memory, secondary storage, and interfaces for various input/output devices including network interfaces; (ii) software resources, programs that are continuously running, or are started on demand. Among the components of an OS are the CPU scheduler, responsible for sharing the CPU cycles among the active processes; the real and virtual memory management system responsible for long-term scheduling decisions and allocation of memory; the file system that supports functions needed to store and retrieve files from the secondary storage system.

The modular design of OSs and the producer-consumer relationship evolved gradually into the so-called *client-server paradigm*. The consistent application of this paradigm in practice led to systems that are easier to build, maintain, extend, and analyze.

The most impressive advantage of the client-server paradigm became apparent after the operating systems incorporated network-access functions and it became possible to support *remote services* as if they were available locally. Suddenly, the environment presented by the OS to the user became considerably richer; the user gained access to hardware and software resources well beyond those available locally. One of the very first applications of the client-server paradigm was the development of network file systems that supported transparent access to files stored on several computers as if they were available on the local machine.

The typical exchange between a client and a server is usually described as *request-response* communication, the client initiates the contact by sending a request and the server responds. The client-server paradigm requires well-defined communication protocols. Remote procedure call (RPC), protocols allow clients to invoke services provided by remotely located servers.

In the RPC execution model, a client generates a request, the information is packaged into a message and sent to the server while the client blocks waiting for the response. At the other end, the server decodes the message carrying the request and the information associated with it, performs the actions as requested by the client, packages the response into a message and sends it back to the client. On the receipt of the response, the client unpacks the response and continues as shown in Figure 5.1. The RPC communication model supports the mobility of the flow of control from the client to the server and back and is a natural extension of the traditional local procedure call.

Asynchronous RPCs operate differently: the client continues execution after sending the request and may only block if the response is not available at the time when it is needed.

The RPC execution model empowers us to look at servers as shared resources. One server is used by many clients; thus, this model has the potential advantages and disadvantages known in resource sharing: lower costs to provide the service, easier maintenance, but at the same time, quality of service dependent on the load, single point of failure, and so on.

A server is brought to service and then repeats a sequence of operations: wait for a request to come, serve the incoming request, send back the response. This execution model is called *reactive execution*, because the server reacts to incoming requests only.

There are two types of servers:

1. Stateless - no state information is maintained between successive interactions between a client and the server.

2. Statefull - state information is maintained.

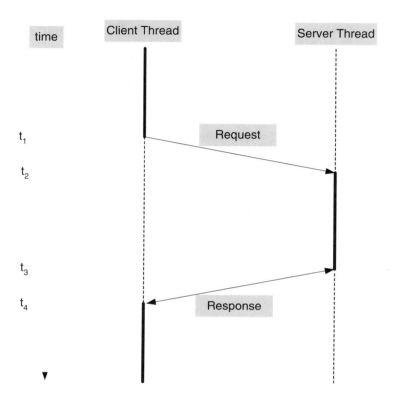

Fig. 5.1   A synchronous RPC supports the migration of the flow of control from a client thread to a server thread. At time t_1 the client sends a request and blocks; at time t_2 the server receives the request, wakes up, and starts the service; at time t_3 the server generates the response; at time t_4 the response reaches the client and the client thread continues its execution.

The advantages of a stateless server are simplicity, performance, scalability, fault tolerance, and ease of use. Once a server is required to maintain state information, it cannot scale beyond a certain limit determined by the amount of resources available to it. Here scalability refers to the size of the population of potential clients. The number of clients that can be served simultaneously is also limited by the amount of resources available.

At the same time, the performance of a state-based server may be limited because it needs to maintain and search a large database of state information. As far as fault tolerance is concerned, a stateless server may fail and then come back up without affecting the clients that did not request services during the period the server was unavailable. However, a server maintaining state information may be able to provide a better quality service because it knows more about the client. An interesting alternative is to maintain state information at the client's site. Web servers use cookies to this end. This solution is not without its own pitfalls, related primarily to client privacy.

One final observation regarding communication between a client and a server: we distinguish two types of services, connection-oriented and connectionless services. In the first case, a client needs to establish a connection first and only then may it request services. After the service is provided the connection is closed. As pointed out in the previous chapter, the connection-oriented communication in the Internet is supported by the TCP that guarantees reliable and in-order delivery of packets, as well as flow control and congestion control. Indeed, Internet services such as file transfer or Web services, need a reliable communication channel between the client and the server.

The connectionless communication is supported in the Internet by the UDP that does not guarantee reliable delivery or in-order delivery, and does not support either flow control or congestion control. These attributes, in particular the absence of error control and congestion control, makes UDP ideal for multimedia applications that are less sensitive to errors but sensitive to timing delays potentially caused by the retransmission mechanism used by TCP for error control. Congestion control also has a potentially devastating effect on on-time delivery of multimedia streams.

RPCs were the first widely used mechanism for structuring distributed systems [12]. SunRPC is probably the most popular and its latest version is a proposed standard for the Internet. Other distributed systems have defined their own RPC protocols, e.g., Sprite [55] and Amoeba [47]. The V system was built around the versatile message transaction protocol (VMTP) claimed to be extremely efficient.

5.3   INTERNET DIRECTORY SERVICE

Humans remember computers by name, while computers prefer numeric values to identify other computers. Therefore, Internet hosts are identified by names as well as IP addresses and there is a need for services capable of mapping host names to IP addresses.

The Internet directory service is an internal service mapping host names into IP addresses. We call it an internal service because it is rarely invoked by users directly; typically other network services use the directory service. Applications such as electronic mail, file transfer, or the World Wide Web allow users to specify a host by name and rely on a *name server* to map the name to an IP address.

A host is allowed to have multiple names or aliases and name servers map all aliases to a *canonical host name*. When parsed from right to left a *full host name* first identifies the Internet domain name (valid domain names in the US are *com, org, gov, mil, edu*), then the domain where the host is located, and finally the name of the computer in that domain. Here the term *domain* identifies the LAN where the host is located. For example, the IP address of the host *arthur.cs.purdue.edu* is *128.10.2.1*, the Internet domain is edu, the domain is cs.purdue, and the host name in that domain is arthur.

The Domain Name System (DNS), specified in RFC 1034 and 1035, is a distributed database consisting of a hierarchy of *name servers*. Each organization has one or more *local name servers*. When the local name server cannot satisfy a query it behaves as

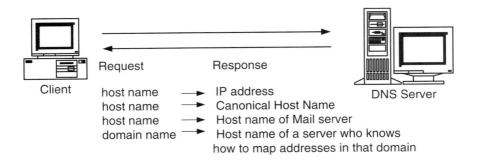

Fig. 5.2   The request-response communication between a client and a DNS server. Four types of request-response pairs are shown. These responses correspond to the four types of DNS records: ANAME, CNAME, MX, and NS.

a DNS client and queries a *root name server*. In turn, a root name server unable to answer a query generates a request and sends it to an *authoritative name server*. Each host in the Internet is registered with an authoritative name server.

A DNS database is a collection of DNS records. A DNS record is a tuple consisting of four fields *Name, Value, Type, TimeToLive*. There are four types of DNS records: *ANAME* and *CNAME* map a host name to an IP address and a canonical host name, respectively; *MX* maps a host name to the mail server name; *NS* maps a domain name to the host name of a server who knows how to map addresses in that domain. The request-response communication between a client and a DNS server is illustrated in Figure 5.2.

Figure 5.3 illustrates a plausible sequence of service requests and responses generated by a user access to a Web page. In this example, a user provides a *uniform resource locator (URL)*, to access a resource, a Web page. The browser contacts a name server that resolves the host name portion of the URL into an IP address and only then the browser establishes a TCP connection with the host identified by the IP address. Once the TCP connection is established, the client sends the HTTP request to the Web server on that host. An in-depth discussion of URLs, browsers, and HTTP is provided in Section 5.5; here, we are only concerned with the implicit invocation of DNS during a Web access.

To avoid the long chain of requests illustrated by Figure 5.3, name servers cache DNS records for a period specified by the `time to live` entry of the record. If the local name server in this example had cached a record for the Web server, it would have been able to respond immediately.

DNS uses an application layer protocol to query and, more recently, to update DNS databases. The DNS protocol runs over UDP and the DNS server is available at port 53.

In addition to mapping host names to IP addresses, DNS supports *load balancing*. If a service is provided by a group of servers then the DNS can distribute the incoming requests to the servers in the group.

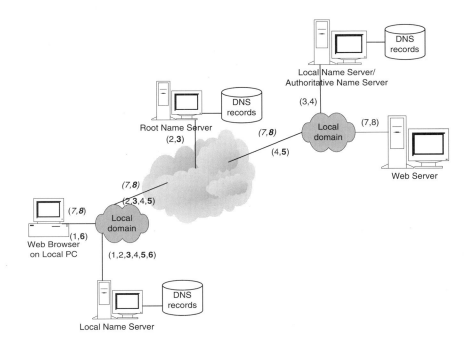

Fig. 5.3 DNS access from a Web browser in response to a user request to access a page from *etrade.com*, a Web server. The following requests and responses flow over the network: (1) request from the Web browser to the local name server; (2) request from the local name server to the root name server; (**3**) response from the root name server providing the address of an authoritative name server; (4) request from the local name server to the authoritative name server; (**5**) response from the authoritative name server to the local name server providing the IP address of the web server; (**6**) response of the local name server to browser; (7) HTTP request sent by the browser to the Web server; (**8**) the Web page provided by the Web server. On each communication link we indicate the request-response pair transmitted over that link. For example, on the link connecting the local PC to the local domain we show two pairs: (1,6) consists of the request generated by the Web browser and the response provided by DNS; (7,8) the request to the Web server with the IP address provided by the DNS server and the response from the Web server. Responses are in bold.

For example, if multiple mirror images of a Web server are available, the authoritative name server will permute the list of IP addresses and hint to clients to use different servers. Assume that a company has a Web site http://www.hector.com with thirty Web servers. Each server has an IP addresses in the range 128.9.7.35 – 128.9.7.65. The authoritative name server will respond to a DNS request with the first address in the list, say 128.9.7.35, then it will permute the list. The response to a second DNS request could be 128.9.7.36, a third request will be answered 128.9.7.37, and so on.

5.4 ELECTRONIC MAIL

5.4.1 Overview

Electronic mail is one of the oldest applications of the client-server paradigm, designed to support *asynchronous communication* between the sender and the recipient of a message. Since the user's PC may be connected to the Internet only intermittently, the electronic mail in transit is typically stored by a mail server permanently connected to the Internet. The mail is then retrieved asynchronously by its intended recipient from her mail server at her convenience. Mail servers are shared resources, typically maintained either by the organization a user belongs to or by an Internet service provider (ISP).

Originally, a user could only send and receive electronic mail by logging on the mail server and starting a mail reader program such as *mail* or *elm*. Nowadays, Web browsers incorporate sophisticated mail programs such as *Messenger* from Netscape or *Outlook Express* from Microsoft.

Figure 5.4 presents the Email communication model. Both sender and receiver are connected to mail servers. The sender "pushes" the message into an "outbox" on the mail server. Then the mail server on the sender's site "pushes" the message into the "inbox" of the recipient located on some mail server. Finally, the recipient "pulls" the message from the "inbox" on its own mail server. SMTP is used in the first two phases POP3 or IMAP access protocols are used in the third phase.

Electronic mail has evolved over time; originally a message was limited to ASCII text, nowadays it supports transmission of multimedia. In addition to text encoded in different formats, an Email message may contain audio or video attachments. We will witness an increase in audio and video messages once multimedia devices such as video cameras and microphones, and the necessary software, drivers for these devices, as well as audio and video players, become a common fixture of PCs, laptops, and palm PCs.

5.4.2 Simple Mail Transfer Protocol

The simple mail transfer protocol (SMTP) is an application layer protocol developed in the early 1980s to transport Internet electronic mail. SMTP uses TCP as a transport protocol. Recall from Chapter 4 that TCP is the reliable stream-oriented transport protocol in the Internet protocol suite.

In SMTP a mail client initiates a persistent TCP connection with the mail server. Once a persistent TCP connection is established the client sends requests and the server responds to each request with a code.

Each SMTP command such as: HELO, TO, FROM, MAIL FROM, RCPT TO, DATA, QUIT is sent as the header of a separate message terminated by a marker (a carriage return, CR, and a line feed, LF). Multiple messages may be sent using the same connection, but a predefined sequence of commands starting with HELO must be repeated before the actual Email message is included.

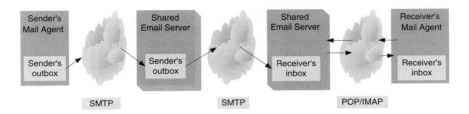

Fig. 5.4   The asynchronous Email communication model. The sender and the receiver of Email are each identified by a pair (`userid, domain name`). Four agents are involved in the process of sending and receiving Email: two mail agents, one acting on behalf of the sender and the other one on behalf of receiver; two mail servers, one for the sender and one for the receiver. The sequence of events to send and receive Email is: (1) the mail agent of the sender uses SMTP to "push" the message into the "outbox" of the sender located on its Email server; (2) the Email server of the sender locates the Email server of the receiver using the DNS services and uses SMTP to "push" the message into the receiver's "inbox" on that server; (3) the mail agent of the receiver uses either the POP or IMAP protocols to "pull" the message from the receiver's Email server.

An Email message consists of a series of mail header lines including `From:`, `To:`, `Subject:` and possibly other headers, followed by a blank line and then by the body of the Email message. The receiver adds a *Received:* header line indicating the host the message originated from, the mail server, and a timestamp.

The connection is terminated when the mail server receives a *QUIT* command.

5.4.3   Multipurpose Internet Mail Extensions

The body of the a message sent using the SMTP protocol may contain text, still images, audio, or video clips. Text messages contain only ASCII characters and can be sent without any transformation. The ASCII character set uses only a subset of all possible 8-bit combinations to represent the characters of the English alphabet.

An image or an audio clip may contain any possible combination of bits and transmission of such *binary data* requires encoding. Recall from the previous chapter that data link communication protocols use specific bit combinations as *control characters* to delimit the beginning of the text body or to synchronize transmission. A binary stream generated during multimedia transmission may contain combinations of bits identical to those used as control characters; thus, the need to encode a binary stream as ASCII characters.

Multipurpose Internet mail extensions (MIME), use several techniques to transform binary data into ASCII text; one of these techniques is `Base64` encoding. The `Base64` encoding algorithm consists of the following steps:

- Take a 24-bit sequence from the source. If fewer than 24 bits are available use the "=" character for padding.

- Separate the sequence into four 6-bit characters.

- View each character as the lower 6 bits of an 8-bit character by padding it to the left with 00. With 6 bits one could encode $2^6 = 64$ characters.

- Use each 8-bit character constructed in the previous step as an index into the Base64 alphabet: "ABCDEFGHIJKLMNOPQRSTUVWXYZabcdefghijklmno pqrstuvwxyz0123456789+/="

To send a multimedia message, in addition to the headers presented earlier new headers must be included. The *Content-Transfer-Encoding* header is used to specify the encoding method and the *Content-Type* header to describe the contents of the message and to guide the receiver in how to interpret the data.

Several top-level media types supported by SMTP are: *text, image, audio, video, application*. For each data type there are several subtypes:

- text

    - `text/plain; charset=us-ascii,`

    - `text/plain; charset="ISO-8859-1",`

    - `text/html.`

- still images

    - `image/jpeg,`

    - `image/gif.`

- video

    - `video/mpeg,`

    - `video/quicktime.`

More information about the media formats is provided in Section 5.6.5.

The mail agent at the receiver's site decodes the data using the information provided by the *Content-Transfer-Encoding* header and then invokes the program registered for the data type given by the *Content-Type* header. For example, a web browser is invoked for `html` data type, an Adobe Acrobat Reader for `pdf` data type, a ghostview reader for `ps`.

Example. In this example we illustrate the operation of SMTP and the SMTP interactions with a mail server. First, we establish a TCP connection with the mail server listening at port 25 on host *arthur.cs.purdue.edu* and then we emulate the behavior of the sender agent to send a gif-encoded image.

We connect to the server by typing "telnet arthur.cs.purdue.edu 25". The sender is *joe@merlin.cs.purdue.ed* and the receiver is *jim@arthur.cs.purdue.edu*. Server responses are prefixed with a code. A transcript of an SMTP session follows.

```
220 arthur.cs.purdue.edu
HELO merlin.cs.purdue.edu
250 hello merlin.cs.purdue.edu, please to meet you
MAIL FROM joe@merlin.cs.purdue.edu
250 joe@merlin.cs.purdue.edu ... Sender OK
RCPT TO: jim@arthur.cs.purdue.edu
250 jim@merlin.cs.purdue.edu ...Recipient OK
DATA
From: joe@merlin.cs.purdue.edu
To: jim@arthur.cs.purdue.edu
Subject: JPEG image
MIME-Version: 1.0
Content-Transfer-Encoding: base64
Content-Type: image/gif
.
base64 encoded data
.
250 Message accepted for delivery
QUIT
221 arthur.cs.purdue.edu closing connection
```

5.4.4 Mail Access Protocols

The mail agent running on the user's machine uses the electronic mail access protocol to download electronic messages from the mail server to the local system. Two mail access protocols, both based on TCP are in use today: POP3, the post office protocol version 3; and IMAP, the Internet mail access protocol.

The POP3 protocol consists of three stages: authorization, transactions, and update. In the first phase, the agent provides the user name and the password to authenticate the user. Messages are retrieved during the second phase, and, in the last phase, the server deletes the messages downloaded by the agent if so requested.

IMAP is a more complex mail access protocol than POP3. It allows a user to manipulate mailboxes on the mail server as if they were local, to create and maintain multiple folders on the remote mail server, and to obtain components of a message. The last feature is useful to retrieve only the header of a message, or to selectively retrieve components of a long message if connected to the server via a low bandwidth channel.

SMTP is defined by RFC 821, MIME by RFC 822, the format of extra headers by RFCs 2045 and 2046, POP3 by RFC 1939, IMAP by RFC 1730. The Internet media types supported by MIME are registered with Internet Assigned Numbers Authority (IANA) and are described by RFC 1590.

5.5 THE WORLD WIDE WEB

The World Wide Web, or simply the Web, was first introduced by T. Berners-Lee and his coworkers [9, 10], as an environment allowing groups involved in high-energy physics experiments at the European Center for Nuclear Research, CERN, in Geneva, Switzerland, to collaborate and share their results.

The Web is the "killer application" that has made the Internet enormously popular and triggered its exponential growth. Introduced in the 1990s, the web is widely regarded as a revolution in communication technology with social and economic impacts similar to the ones caused by the introduction of the telephone in the 1870s and of the broadcast radio and television of the 1920s and 1930s. In 1998 more than 75% of the Internet traffic was Web-related.

The Web is based on a global naming scheme for distributed objects. A *uniform resource locator (URL)* is used to locate an object, or *resource* in Web terminology. For example, all the information available for students taking the undergraduate networking class offered by the Computer Sciences Department at Purdue University is available from `http://webct.cc.purdue.edu/SCRIPT/CS422/scripts`.

URLs are pairs consisting of: (i) an Internet host name and (ii) a path to a file on that host. In this example the host name is `webct.cc.purdue.edu` and the path is: `SCRIPT/CS422/scripts`.

An object called a *Web page* is a multimedia file containing text, images, video, or audio clips. The *hypertext markup language (HTML)* is used to describe the format of a Web page, using a set of tags and *hyperlinks*, the URLs of various objects referenced by the page. The information in each page is encoded using a standard format, e.g., the graphics interchange format (GIG) or JPEG for images, MPEG for video clips, and so on.

The *hypertext transfer protocol (HTTP)* is the application protocol used by browsers to communicate with an Web server.

5.5.1 HTTP Communication Model

The Web is an application of the client-server paradigm: Someone collects information and stores it on a server and clients "pull" it from the server. A stateless *Web server*, also called an *HTTP server* houses a collection of Web pages. A client, called a *Web browser*, allows users to request individual Web pages or resources. The server and the clients communicate using an application layer protocol called HTTP.

An HTTP server, listens to a well-known port, typically port 80, for HTTP requests from clients, see Figure 5.5. Once a request arrives, the server logs the request and then provides a response. Most HTTP servers log the IP address, the domain name, the browser used by the client, and the machine being used.

Each request identifies a *method* the client invokes on the HTTP server. Once a request arrives at the server, a new thread of control to handle the request is started. The request is parsed and the target page is located in the local cache or brought in from the secondary storage. An error code is generated when the page cannot be

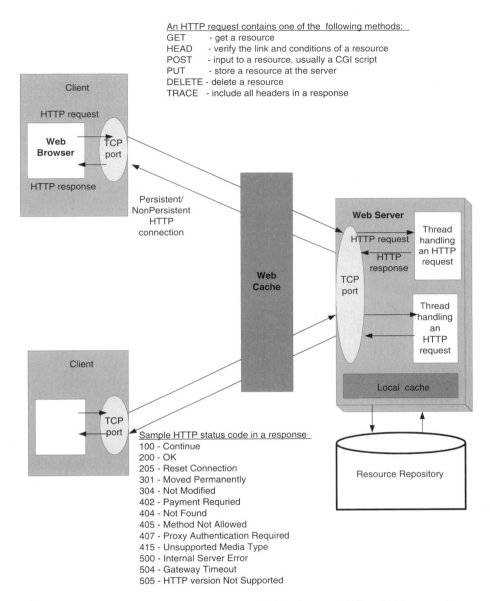

Fig. 5.5 The HTTP communication model. An HTTP client establishes a TCP connectiopn with an HTTP server. An HTTP request sent by a client identifies the method or the function requested. An HTTP response provided by the server contains a status code. The server may be multithreaded, each request may be handled by a separate thread. The resource requested from the server may be available from the local cache of the server or may be retrieved from the secondary storage. The Web cache may or may not be present. The TCP connections may be persistent or nonpersistent.

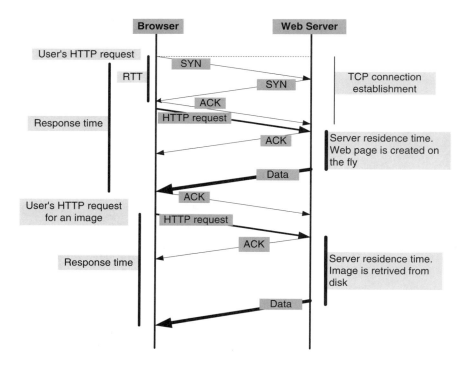

Fig. 5.6   Message exchanges for a persistent HTTP connection and various components of the *response time*, the time elapsed from the instance an HTTP request is sent and the time the response arrives. RTT stands for round-trip time. The *server residence time* is the interval elapsed from the instance the HTTP request arrives at the server and the time the response is sent by the server. The residence time differs for a page created on the fly, one available in the local cache of the server, and one that has to be retrieved from the disk.

found, the client is not authorized to access the page, or the format of the request is invalid. Sometimes, pages are generated on the fly, for example a page could be assembled by the server to match the profile or preferences of an individual user.

HTTP uses TCP because it needs a reliable transport mechanism between a client and a server. The establishment of the TCP connection is triggered by an HTTP request and involves the three-way handshake procedure illustrated in Figure 5.6.

The actual HTTP request could be piggybacked onto the TCP acknowledgment sent by the client in the third phase of the three-way handshake, or sent separately immediately after the acknowledgment. The HTTP server responds by providing the Web page or by delivering an error message.

The data rate supported by a TCP connection changes in time to adapt to the network traffic. In Chapter 4 we discussed in some depth the congestion control mechanism built into TCP. Initially, the connection only allows a low data rate, the so-called *slow start phenomena*, and in time, attempts to determine the maximum rate the network is able accommodate by a process of trial and error.

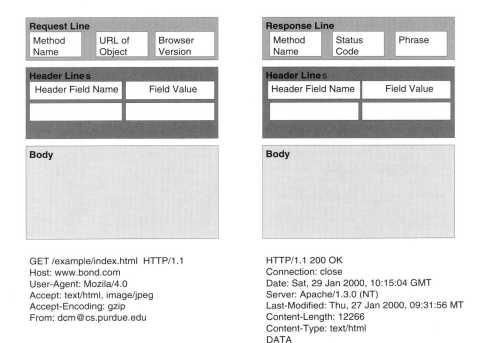

GET /example/index.html HTTP/1.1
Host: www.bond.com
User-Agent: Mozila/4.0
Accept: text/html, image/jpeg
Accept-Encoding: gzip
From: dcm@cs.purdue.edu

HTTP/1.1 200 OK
Connection: close
Date: Sat, 29 Jan 2000, 10:15:04 GMT
Server: Apache/1.3.0 (NT)
Last-Modified: Thu, 27 Jan 2000, 09:31:56 MT
Content-Length: 12266
Content-Type: text/html
DATA

Fig. 5.7   The format of an HTTP request and response.

5.5.2   Hypertext Transfer Protocol (HTTP)

HTTP is a request-response protocol. Each message is composed of several lines of human-readable text. An HTTP request consists of a *request line* that identifies: (i) the HTTP method, (ii) the URL of the target object, (iii) the type and the version of the browser, and (iv) several header lines.

Each header line provides additional information, e.g., the type of data the browser is willing to accept.

An HTTP response consists of a *status line* that describes: (i) the protocol version, (ii) the status of the request, and (iii) several header lines.

Figure 5.7 shows the actual format of an HTTP request and response together with an example. We now describe the HTTP methods and various headers in HTTP requests and responses.

Methods supported by the HTTP standard are:

GET - request the body of the resource. Check for the modification of the resource.

HEAD - verify the link.

POST - submit data to a resource on the server. The POST method is used by a browser to submit a *form*, a Web page containing input fields.

PUT - store resources at the server's site. *PUT* supports Web-based editing. The difference between *POST* and *PUT* is that in the first case the resource, the form is passed for processing at the server's site, while in second case the resource is actually stored there. The HTTP standard does not specify what happens after a server accepts a body via a *POST*.

DELETE - remove resources from the server. *PUT* and *DELETE* provide a functionality similar with the one supported by the standard file transfer protocol.

OPTIONS - query the server about its capabilities.

TRACE - force the server to respond with a message containing all the headers in the original request.

Request header fields specify some of the attributes or conditions for the delivery of the resource.

Accept - specify media types the client prefers,

Accept-Charset - request that a resource be delivered in a certain character set,

Accept-Encoding - the client accepts data encoding other than GZIP,

Accept-Language - natural languages acceptable for response,

Authorization - send the credentials of the client,

From - send the Email address of the user controlling the client,

User-Agent - provide a signature of the browser,

Host - differentiate between virtual hosts on the same machine,

Proxy Authorization - allow a client to validate itself,

Range - instead of the full resource the client requests only the byte range of the resource it does not have.

Entity headers describe the attributes of the body sent by either client or server:

Allow - informs the browser what methods are supported by the resource identified by a URL,

Content-Encoding - specifies the coding applied to the body before transmission,

Content-Language - the natural language of the resource being returned,

Contents-Length - the length of the resource,

Content-Type - the media type,

Content-Location - the location of the resource,

Content-MD5 - to provide a digital signature of the entire body of the resource,

Last-Modified - the time the server believes the resource was last modified.

General headers:

Connection - indicates the sender's desire to close the current connection once the response is sent,

Date - the time when the message (not the resource) was generated,

Upgrade - to negotiate a change in protocols,

Via - inserted by gateways and proxies to indicate the protocols and recipients that handled the data between the client and the server.

There are several types of conditional GET requests. *If-Modified-Since* or *If-Unmodified-Since* together with a date/time stamp are used to determine if the local copy of a resource stored in the browser's cache is fresh or stale. We say that the copy is fresh if the original resource has not been modified since the time the resource was cached locally. The browser sends a conditional request to the server to determine the status of the local copy. The server compares the time stamp provided by the browser in its request with the one of the resource. As a result of a conditional request the server returns a response code 304, Not Modified or it resends the resource if modified. Conditional requests help reduce the network traffic as discussed in Section 5.5.6.

An HTTP response message consists of: (i) a status line, (ii) one or more header lines, and (iii) an optional entity body. The status line contains a status code. The header fields may include: (i) authentication challenges, (ii) server name and version, (iii) location, (iv) warnings.

HTTP status codes in the response provided by an HTTP server and brief explanations of the codes are provided below.

100 - Continue

200 - OK

205 - Reset Connection

301 - Moved Permanently

304 - Not Modified

402 - Payment Required

404 - Not Found

405 - Method Not Allowed

407 - Proxy Authentication Required

415 - Unsupported Media Type

500 - Internal Server Error

504 - Gateway Timeout

505 - HTTP version Not Supported

5.5.3   Web Server Response Time

The *response time of a Web server* is the time measured by a client from the instance an HTTP request is sent and the time the response arrives. The response time depends on such factors as: network load, server load, amount of data to be transferred, distance between the client and the server, quality of the communication links.

The *residence time of a Web server* is the time between the instance an HTTP request is received and the time the response is handed over to the transport protocol on the server side of the TCP connection to be delivered to the client. The server residence time is dominated by the time to retrieve the page from secondary storage, or from cache, or the time to retrieve the objects necessary to compose the page.

To evaluate the response time we have to take into account the time to establish the TCP connection, the time it takes the server to construct the response, and the transmission time and propagation delay of the response, see Figure 5.6. The first and second phases of the three-way handshake require roughly one round trip time (RTT). Thus, the total response time in absence of transmission errors has three components: the propagation times, in our case $2 \times RTT$, the server residence time, and the transmission time of the resource:

$$ResponseTime = PropagationTime + ServerResidenceTime$$
$$+ ResourceTransmissionTime$$

5.5.4   Web Caching

Caching is a technique used to improve the performance of a system when there is a mismatch between the bandwidth of different components. For example, a microprocessor is considerably faster than the memory; thus, one needs a faster memory, a cache, to store instructions and data on the microprocessor itself. The cache helps bridge the gap between instruction execution speed and the memory speed.

In our case, the Web browser is the consumer of data and the Web server is the producer of data. The client and the server are connected via a network that limits the data rate available to the client. Thus, the need for Web caches.

Figure 5.8 shows that there are several levels of Web caches. Web resources can be cached by: (i) the browser itself, (ii) a publicly shared cache, or (iii) the server.

If the resource is in the browser's local cache, the server needs only to inform the browser that the resource has not been modified since last downloaded. This feature of the HTTP protocol, supported by the conditional GET request discussed earlier, helps reduce the network traffic.

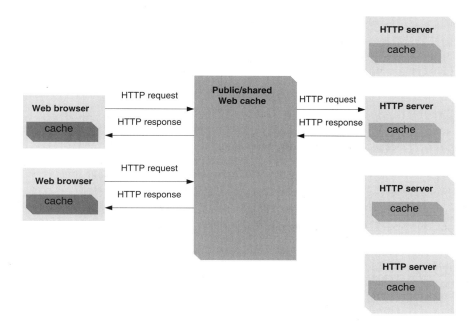

Fig. 5.8   There are several levels of Web caches. The Web browser caches pages locally. A shared Web cache is a proxy for several Web servers; it serves the page if it is available locally or forwards the request to the origin HTTP server. Each Web server has a local cache.

A publicly shared Web cache is a proxy that satisfies HTTP requests on behalf of a server. If the resource is in cache, the proxy sends it to the client immediately, else it forwards the request to the origin server. When the server responds, the proxy forwards the resource to the client and stores it locally, as shown in Figure 5.8. The Web cache has a local disk and acts as both client and server.

The goal of publicly shared Web caches is to reduce the network traffic and improve the response time as seen by a client. The origin Web server may run on a slow machine and may be connected to a slow network. If a client has a high-speed network connection to a fast proxy, then the response time for a resource cached by the proxy is considerably shorter because both data transmission and propagation times and the server residence times are shorter.

Last but not least, each server has its own local cache. If the Web resource is in cache, then the server residence time, discussed in the next section, is reduced. The access time to the secondary storage is considerably larger than the cache access time for the same resource.

The cache control is based on the idea of expiration time, a resource that has reached its expiration time is *stale*, otherwise it is *fresh*. The cache determines the age of a resource by taking into account the time spent in transit and the time spent as resident in cache. Once a cache has determined that a resource is fresh, the cache sends the resource to a client.

Responses to *POST, PUT, DELETE, OPTIONS, TRACE* as well as those including an authorization header are forbidden to be cached. But, as shown in Section 5.5.6, the bulk of all requests consist of *GET* and *HEAD* methods. The responses to *GET* and *HEAD* are allowed to be cached.

The following headers are used for cache control:

Age - the age of a response,

Expires - gives a date when the response should be considered stale,

Cache-Control - with several options, e.g., no-cache, no-store, max-age, max-stale, and so forth.

5.5.5 Nonpersistent and Persistent HTTP Connections

Any client-server application using TCP as a transport protocol has the choice to establish a connection for every request-response pair, or to allow multiple request-response pairs to be exchanged over the same connection. In case of HTTP, the first approach is called *nonpersistent HTTP connection* and it is supported by HTTP version 1.0 while the second one is called *persistent HTTP connection* and it is supported by HTTP version 1.1.

Let us examine first the nonpersistent case. A Web page may contain references to multiple objects. HTTP 1.0 allows a browser to request these objects one by one or in parallel. In the first case, there is only one TCP connection active at any time. In the second case, multiple TCP connections, one per object, are established between the client and the server, and the data are transferred in parallel on all these connections. The second alternative reduces the total time to gather all the objects at the client's side, but the price to be paid is the overhead for maintaining multiple TCP connections.

Establishing a TCP connection is time-consuming, each three-way handshake takes approximately $2 \times RTT$. In addition, each TCP connection requires the server to allocate buffers for the TCP socket. The slow start of the TCP protocol limits the data transmission rate on each connection compared with the case when a single TCP connection is used.

In the case of a persistent connection, the client may send multiple requests over the same connection. There are two possible alternatives, send a request and wait until the response arrives, or send multiple requests without waiting for responses, a strategy called *pipelining*. The default transmission mode supported by HTTP 1.1 is a persistent and pipelined connection.

Example. We have a base HTML page containing 15 JPEG images. The URL is www.hector.org/dog/bones.index.

The sequence of events for a nonpersistent HTTP connection is:

1. When you click on the link, the browser initiates a TCP connection to port 80 at server www.hector.org.

2. The browser sends the HTTP request to GET the object dog/bones.index. The HTTP methods, including GET, are discussed in Section 5.5.2.

3. The HTTP server creates an HTTP response and encapsulates the object into that response.

4. The server tells TCP to close the connection.

5. The browser receives the HTTP response and extracts the object.

6. The connection is closed at the instance the acknowledgment from the client reaches the server.

7. The same sequence is repeated for each of the 15 images.

If we ignore the server residence time and assume that the transmission time of all objects is the same, then the response time for the sequential and parallel nonpersistent connections can be approximated by:

$$ResponseTime_{Sequential}^{NonPersistent} = 16 \times (2 \times RTT) + 15 \times ObjectTransmissionTime$$

$$ResponseTime_{Parallel}^{NonPersistent} = 2 \times (2 \times RTT) + ObjectTransmissionTime$$

Using the same assumptions as above the corresponding response times for persistent nonpipelined and pipelined connections can be approximated by:

$$ResponseTime_{Nonpipelined}^{Persistent} = 2 \times RTT + 15 \times ObjectTransmissionTime$$

$$ResponseTime_{Pipelined}^{Persistent} = 2 \times RTT + ObjectTransmissionTime$$

The expressions above only approximate the response time. First, there is no guarantee that in the parallel nonpersistent or in the pipelined-persistent case all requests are sent at exactly the same time. Second, we cannot easily account for the effect of the congestion control window and compute the transmission time on a single TCP connection versus multiple connections.

5.5.6   Web Server Workload Characterization

A recent study of the workload placed on a Web server [3] provides useful hints for Web server and networks designers. The study reports results collected during the 1998 World Soccer Cup held in Paris.

The authors analyzed the logs of the Web servers for a period of two months starting prior to the first event of the World Soccer Cup. The data recorded for each access consists of: the IP address of the client; the remote login name of user; date and time of request; the HTTP request line; the HTTP response status code; and the length of the document transferred.

Table 5.1 Summary of results reported in the 1998 World Cup Web study [3].

Measured Parameter	Value
Total number of HTTP requests (requests)	1,352,804,107
Average number of requests (requests/minute)	10,756
Total amount of bytes transferred (Tbytes)	4.981
Total number of files transferred (files)	20,728
Total size of all files (MBytes)	307
Mean size of a file (KBytes)	15.524
Fraction of requests using HTTP 1.0 (%)	78.7
Fraction of requests using HTTP 1.1 (%)	21.3

The summary data in Table 5.1 gives us an idea of the request rates Web servers have to sustain, the total amount of traffic generated, the amount of data stored at the servers, the average size of files transferred, and shows that the number of browsers using HTTP 1.0 outnumbers those using HTTP 1.1 in a ratio of 4:1.

The design of shared Web caches and of the local caches of a Web server can only be based on an understanding of the *temporal locality of reference* of files requested by the clients. The detailed analysis of the data shows that a file referenced once is referenced again soon; though the total number of files stored by the Web server is fairly large, 20,728, after a file was referenced once, it was referenced again after an average of 106 references to other files. Moreover, the top 10% of the most popular files received 97% of all requests, generated almost 90% of all the network traffic to/from the Web servers, and occupied less than 7% of the storage space.

The measurements show a *heavy tail distribution of the file sizes* while most theoretical studies of Web workloads and the Web benchmarking environments assume a logonormal, normal after a logarithmic transformation, file distribution. Another argument for caching comes from the observation that the great majority of all requests were for static files, 88% for images and 10% for HTML files.

Almost 20% of all requests were conditional get requests that generated no additional traffic because the local copy of the browser had the same time stamp as the one on the server, indicating that the file had not been updated since it was referenced.

5.5.7 Scalable Web Server Architecture

The measurements reported in the previous section confirm what we have expected all along; namely, that Web servers could be subjected to very high "hit" rates of tens or even hundreds of requests per second. The amount of computing resources such as CPU cycles, memory, secondary storage, and network transfer rates, available on a single system are insufficient to provide a reasonable response time or even to guarantee responses to all requests. Thus, the need for a scalable Web Server architecture supporting clusters of servers.

In Section 5.3 we sketched such an architecture where access to a cluster of Web servers is controlled by the Authoritative Domain Name server that directs incoming requests to different servers in the cluster to ensure load balancing. Figure 5.9 presents two other configurations where requests are sent to a Front End system that dispatches them to different back-end servers. In Figure 5.9(a) the HTTP requests and responses are channeled through the front end, while in Figure 5.9(b), the HTTP responses are sent directly to the clients.

First let us consider several methods used by the front end to select which back-end server should process an HTTP request. These methods, called *dispatching strategies*, require the front end to examine an incoming request and make a decision. The more complex the dispatching strategy, the higher is the load placed on the front end, and the less scalable is the architecture.

The front end could perform only a *load-balancing* function, similar to the one discussed earlier. In this case, the front end does not need to maintain any information other than the identity of the server the last request has been sent to. A perfect load balancing is not feasible, the load placed on a server depends on the type of the request, the size of the resource, and other factors.

Another strategy is *customer class-based* dispatching. The system supports different classes of customers, e.g., has *premium* and *standard* service. The customers in the first class are dispatched to dedicated servers in the cluster whose load is kept at a low level to guarantee a very short server residence time. The front end examines the incoming HTTP request and dispatches it based on the IP address of the client.

Yet another strategy is *content-based* dispatching. Resources are spread on the cluster base and the front end need to examine the URL on the incoming request to decide which server is able to handle it. To do so, the front end must maintain a directory of all the objects on the site.

Let us now turn our attention to the path followed by the response. Clearly, the architecture in Figure 5.9(a) is less desirable because the front end becomes a bottleneck. Indeed, in the general case a response may contain a large object and handling these objects would stretch the capabilities of the front end. The architecture in Figure 5.9(b) is more promising, responses are delivered directly to the clients, avoiding the front end. But the price to pay is that we need a mechanism to "hand off" a TCP connection from the front end to a back-end. Recall from Chapter 4 that TCP is a state-oriented protocol and we need to pass this state from the front to the back-end system a nontrivial proposition.

5.5.8 Web Security

Oftentimes, an organization wishes to restrict access to an HTTP server to only a select group, for example, only to the employees of the organization. A widespread method to restrict access to computing resources is to hide them behind a firewall as shown in Figure 5.10(a); the firewall checks the source IP address of any incoming packet and drops those originating from sources whose access to the site is not explicitly permitted.

Figure 5.10(b) illustrates the use of a proxy server running on a system acting as a firewall. A proxy forwards HTTP requests originating from select IP addresses to the Web server and denies access to requests from other users.

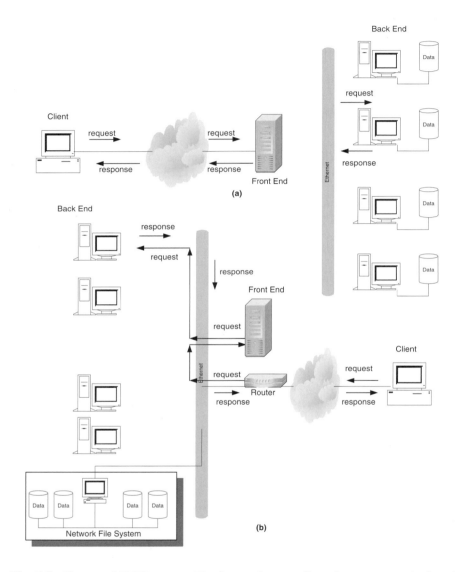

Fig. 5.9 Clusters of HTTP servers. The front end system dispatches requests to back-end Servers. In (a) the HTTP requests and responses are channeled through the front end which acts as a proxy. In (b) HTTP responses are sent directly to the clients.

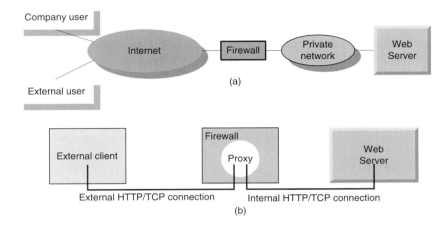

Fig. 5.10 (a) Firewall protection of a Web server. (b) A proxy forwards HTTP requests originating from select IP addresses to the Web server and denies access to requests from other users.

Before granting access to the documents they house, some Web servers require users to authenticate themselves by providing some credentials. The *basic authentication* supported by HTTP requires a user to provide a name and a password. This is a very weak authorization scheme, the credentials are not encrypted but encoded using the well-known `Base64` algorithm and sent over the network as plaintext to the server.

Digest authentication is a more sophisticated scheme, both client and server compute a digest value over a concatenation of a secret password and several other values using the `MD5` algorithm.

Cookies and log files allow servers to gather information about users and create the potential for security violations when confidential information is either disclosed to a third party or when the access to it is lax and intruders are able to penetrate the system. A *cookie* is a set of attribute-value pairs. Cookies provide a distributed mechanism for servers to gather information about users. Rather than maintain a database of all users, the servers store the information at the user's site in a cookie file. Cookies allow the server to remember user's preferences, to correlate various user actions, and to avoid the hassle of asking a user to provide credentials with every request when authentication is required. This solution reduces the load placed on the server and it is scalable.

The users of the Web are subject to various threats. Attacks against integrity, confidentiality, denial of service, and authentication are possible. On the client's side a first potential problem is the security of software distribution. An attacker can cause a user to download a modified browser and with a minimum level of sophistication cause severe damages, e.g., mail information about the browsing habits of the user to the attacker, modify the secure socket level (SSL), options to weaken security and compromise all interactions with secure servers, and so on.

Helper applications are often distributed from various sources and users download them for convenience. Assume for example that a user downloads a file of type *.ps*. Then the browser looks into one of its configuration files and determines that it needs a program called GSVIEW to present that format. If the program is not available locally the user is directed to download it from some Web site and we face again the problem of the security of software distribution. Helper applications open the user's site to serious attacks. For example, if a user configures its browser so that all files with the *.exe* extension be fed to the shell, then any file downloaded with this extension will be executed immediately. This is the procedure of choice for spreading computer viruses.

Local code is presumed to be trusted and no access control is applied to it. Such code inherits the privileges of the user running it. Mobile code, in particular unsigned applets, are a potential danger. Once downloaded, mobile code may request various system services, e.g., create and delete files, send messages, start new threads of control and so on. Often mobile code is confined to a *sandbox*, a restricted area, and it is not allowed access to anything outside it. One way to break the security rules is to make remote code look like local code.

5.5.9 Reflections on the Web

We looked more closely at the World Wide Web because it is a very popular application and illustrates very well the performance, security, and deployment problems in a large-scale open system.

First let us observe that the Web was made possible by the widespread acceptance of a rather large number of standards. An incomplete list of these standards is presented in Section 5.9.

Once in place, performance became of paramount concern and Web caching has been under scrutiny during the past years. Convenience of use is another major concern once the Web is used by a significant segment of the population. More and more functions are added to the Web: editing over the net and Email services are some of the new functions provided by Web browsers. Some question whether the Web browser should replace the traditional operating system running on a PC.

Last but not least, Web security is a major concern. There are legitimate questions as to whether Web technology is mature enough to support applications critical to the infrastructure of a nation, applications involving national security, banking, trading, health care, or other applications where confidentiality and privacy are critical.

5.6 MULTIMEDIA SERVICES

Historically, the telephone network was, and still is, the primary carrier for voice while the cable networks are the primary carriers for broadcast video and audio information. During the past decade, digital technologies have progressed to the point where audio and video information is routinely captured and stored in digital format. With the differences between data, voice, and video blurred, integrating different types of information into one stream seems a natural choice. Equally natural is to explore the use of the Internet to transport digital audio and video information along with data and to provide network multimedia services.

Emerging Internet multimedia services, e.g., voice over IP, radio services, video services, teleconferencing, videoconferencing, distance learning, telemedincine, interactive games, and so on, are the result of this line of thought. Yet the Internet is based on the best-effort model that does not match the needs of multimedia applications. Data transmission is loss sensitive, it does not tolerate bit errors or packet loss but there are no real-time requirements. However, transmission of audio and video, though they are to some extent loss tolerant, pose additional challenges in terms of the bandwidth and timing requirements.

5.6.1 Sampling and Quantization; Bandwidth Requirements for Digital Voice, Audio, and Video Streams

The Internet has the potential to provide a more economical and convenient solution to transport audio and video information along with data provided that this information is in a digital format. Audio and video information can be collected using analog devices or digital devices.

The process of transforming an analog signal into a digital one is called *sampling* and it is carried out by devices called *analog to digital converters*. The reverse process is called *digital to analog* conversion and it is necessary to reproduce digitally stored or transmitted audio or video information.

How often do we need to sample an analog signal? The answer to this question is provided by the *Nyquist theorem* that states that *if an analog signal is sampled at a rate that is at least twice the highest frequency in the spectrum of the signal, then one can reconstruct the original signal from the set of discrete samples.* An extended discussion of signal-processing concepts such as amplitude, frequency, phase, spectrum, bandwidth, modulation, demodulation can be found in [29].

The process of assigning an integer value to the amplitude of each sample is called *quantization*. The sampling and quantization necessary to transform a continuous-time signal into a set of digital values is called *pulse code modulation (PCM)*.

Quantization introduces *quantization errors*. The higher the quality of a digital recording, the larger is the number of quantization levels necessary to achieve the desired quality, for a particular type of data. The higher is the quality of digital multimedia the larger is the communication bandwidth necessary to transmit the stream, or the amount of secondary storage to keep it.

The number of bits per sample determine the number of quantization levels. For example, 8 bits and $2^8 = 256$ quantization levels are sufficient for voice, but we need 14 bits for CD-quality audio.

Digital audio or video require a considerably larger bandwidth than their analog counterpart and data compression is a critical component of data streaming.

Table 5.2 Standards and bandwidth requirements for uncompressed and compressed digitized voice, audio, and video streams.

Stream	Sampling Rate (Ksamples/sec)	Uncompressed Stream (Kbps)	Compressed Stream (Kbps)
Voice	8.0	PCM: 64	GSM: 13 G.729: 8 G.723.3: 6.4 and 5.3
CD Sound	44.1	705.6 (mono) 1,411 (stereo)	MP3 (MPEG 3): 128 or 112
Video	10,000.0	240,000	CD-ROM quality video (MPEG 1): 1500 High-quality DVD (MPEG 2): 3000-6000

Table 5.2 summarizes the sampling rates and the bandwidth requirements for uncompressed and compressed audio and video.

Instead of transmitting an analog signal carrying out voice over a communication channel, we can sample the voice at a rate of 8000 samples per second. If we use 8 bits per sample, then a digital voice channel requires a transmission rate of 64 Kbps.

To generate CD-quality sound we need 44,100 samples per second. Each sample consists of 16 bits because we need a much larger number of levels than in the case of voice to ensure the quality of the recording. We have two parity bits and 14 information bits so that we can distinguish between $2^{14} = 16,384$ levels of the signal. The data rate to transfer uncompressed CD-quality sound using PCM, is 705.6 Kbps for mono and 1.411 Mbps for stereo.

A 1024×1024 3-byte pixel still image requires 3 MB of storage space. At the time of this writing, high resolution digital cameras are able to collect 4 Mpixel still images. Most offer the option to store such images either uncompressed or with different levels of compression.

An analog video signal requires a sampling rate of about 10 Msamples/second. Assuming a 3-byte sample, we need a bandwidth of about $10 \times 10^6 samples/second \times 24 bits/sample = 240Mbps$. For color images the data rate is three times higher because we have to transmit three color carriers. Three bytes allow us to distinguish between $2^{24} = 16,777,216$ different colors for each pixel.

5.6.2   Delay and Jitter in Data Streaming

To playback multimedia data or to play out voice we need to transform the sequence of samples into a continuous signal. The data rate and the time when successive samples are available must be within well-defined limits. For example, for voice we need to get 8000 samples per second or one sample every 125 microseconds. Voice samples are buffered at the sender site and packets containing, say, 160 samples are

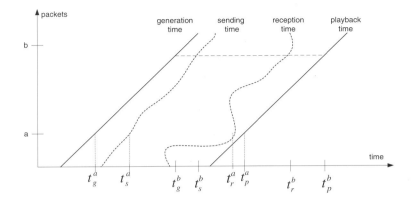

Fig. 5.11   The delay and jitter in data streaming.

sent every 20 milliseconds. Each packet carries along either a sequence number or a time stamp to guarantee the play-out order.

To illustrate the timing requirements for voice transmission, Figure 5.11 traces two packets, a and b, containing voice samples from the same talkspurt. Packet i is generated at time t_g^i, leaves the sender at time t_s^i, is received at the client at time t_r^i, and it is buffered until its playback time, t_p^i.

The overall delay between packet generation time and playback time includes a variable delay at the sender site, $\eta_{sender} = t_s^a - t_g^a$ and a variable delay for crossing the network, $\eta_{network} = t_r^a - t_s^a$. This first delay is due to contention for system resources at the sender, the second is due to transmission times, propagation delays, and queuing times at various routers along the path. In the general case $\eta_{sender} \ll \eta_{network}$ and depends on the load placed on the server.

Figure 5.12 shows a streaming server with multiple threads one for each data stream. The threads compete among themselves for CPU cycles and the real-time scheduler running at the server site guarantees each thread the fair share necessary to meet its deadlines.

To ensure that samples are available when needed, a buffer at the receiving site is provided, see Figure 5.12. This buffer is fed at a variable rate $x(t)$ from the network and drained by the player at a constant rate. The buffer allows the player to have a constant *play-out delay*. Yet this delay cannot be made arbitrarily large. A normal conversation can be carried out if the play-out delay, $t_p^a - t_g^a$, is lower than 400 milliseconds. A play-out delay lower than 100 milliseconds in not noticeable, while one larger than 400 milliseconds makes a conversation very difficult.

For interactive applications such as voice over IP, we are also concerned with the *jitter*, the variability in end-to-end delay for packets within the same stream. As a result of the jitter, the buffering time of the two packets $\eta_{buffer}^a = t_p^a - t_r^a$, and $\eta_{buffer}^a = t_p^b - t_r^b$ are different. A large jitter may cause packets to arrive after their scheduled play-out time. Such packets are discarded.

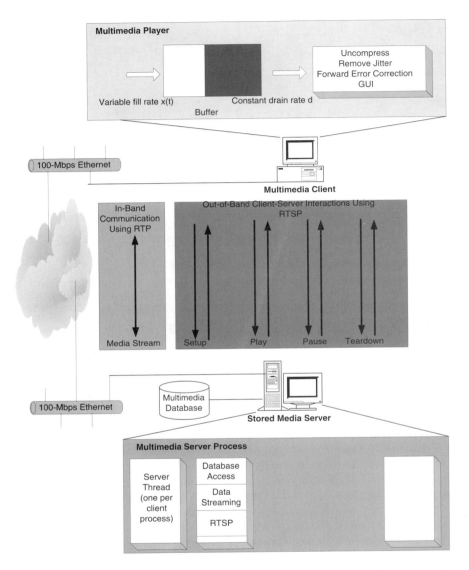

Fig. 5.12 Data streaming over the Internet. The client process has a buffer filled at a variable rate and drained by the player at a constant rate d. Two logical channels connect a multimedia server and a client: an *in-band* communication channel for data and an *out-of-band* channel for control information. The data stream is transmitted using RTP. The client and server processes interact using RTSP. The audio and video information is stored in a compressed format at the server site.

For voice over IP we can remove the jitter using either a fixed play-out delay or an adaptive one. The adaptive adjustment of the play-out delay takes advantage of the silent periods between talkspurts and compresses or dilates them.

To calculate the play-out time, we construct an estimate of the average packet delay, δ^i, and its variance, ν^i, after receiving the i-th packet as follows:

$$\delta^i = (1 - w) \times \delta^{i-1} + w \times (t_r^i - t_g^i)$$
$$\nu^i = (1 - w) \times \nu^{i-1} + w \times |t_r^i - t_g^i - \delta^i|$$

with $w = 0.01$ a factor that gives more weight to the more recent past. Recall that each packet carries its time stamp, t_g^i. If the i-th packet is the first in a talkspurt then its play-out time is:

$$t_p^i = t_g^i + \delta^i + K \times \nu^i$$

with K a constant. The larger the K, the more distant in the future is the play-out time and the lower the probability of packet loss.

5.6.3 Data Streaming

A *data stream* is a sequence of characters, or bytes, that flow out or into a process. For continuous media like audio or video, the data stream flows out of a *media server*, it is transported over the network and it is consumed by an application called a *media player*. In turn, a streaming client could generate a data stream and store it on the server.

The timing requirements of various streaming services are different:

(i) interactive services such as teleconferencing or voice over IP, are sensitive to communication delay and to the variation of this delay, but they are, to some extent, loss tolerant,

(ii) video streaming is rate sensitive and to some extent loss tolerant; an entire video frame must be available when it is scheduled to be displayed, at a rate of say 25 frames/second;

(iii) some applications in the general area of telemedicine and in remote instrument control are delay and loss sensitive;

(iv) stored media applications are less demanding.

Stored media applications could require a Web browser as an intermediary between the client and the server or may be based on direct interactions between them. In the first case, the multimedia files are stored as regular objects on a Web server and accessed via the HTTP protocol. At the client side, the contents-type header of the HTTP response indicates the specific audio or video encoding and activates the corresponding media player. Then, the data stream is passed from the browser to the player.

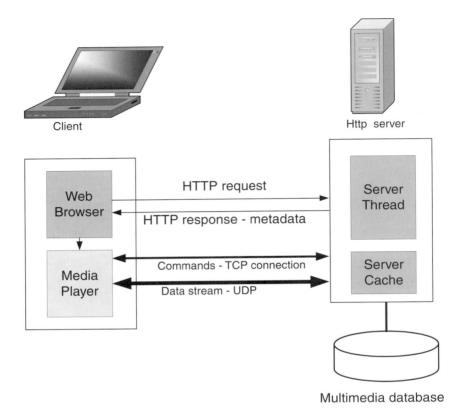

Fig. 5.13   A browser uses HTTP to download a *metafile* associated with the stream. The metafile provides information about the encoding of the contents and allows the browser to start up the corresponding player. The player sends commands to the server via a TCP connection. The UDP protocol is used for data streaming.

A Web browser is not well equipped to process long data streams, so in a second alternative there are two or even three logical communication channels between a client and the server. First, the browser uses HTTP, to download a *metafile* associated with the stream. The metafile provides information about the encoding of the contents and allows the browser to start up the corresponding player, then the player establishes a TCP connection, a UDP connection, or both with the server to download the audio or video stream. Figure 5.13 illustrates such a setup, where the player sends commands to the server via a TCP connection and the UDP protocol is used for data streaming.

Last, but not least, a player may communicate directly with the streaming server as illustrated in Figure 5.12. The audio and video information is stored in a compressed format at the server site. A server thread reads the data from the multimedia database and transmits the stream using RTP. The client process has a buffer filled at a variable rate and drained by the player at a constant rated d. To playback, the player performs several functions such as data decompression, jitter removal and forward error correction. The player provides a graphics user interface (GUI) to interact with the incoming stream. The client and server processes interact using the real-time streaming protocol (RTSP).

A media player allows the user to continuously play the audio or the video and to interact with the incoming data stream. For some applications, such as stored audio and video streaming, the user may request to pause, rewind, fast-forward, or index the data stream. Operations such as fast-forwarding are not possible for live audio or video applications.

A streaming server has access to a database of prerecorded audio and video information stored in a compressed format. Proprietary streaming servers and players are available from several companies including RealNetworks, a company who is currently the leader in audio and video streaming.

Once a player connects to a streaming server, the audio or video data is sent over the Internet using an application-level protocol built on top of one of the Internet transport protocols. The streaming player continuously processes the incoming stream, it uncompresses the data, removes the jitter, and handles packet losses. The removal of the jitter is done by buffering of incoming packets and delaying the play out, as discussed earlier.

Two recovery schemes deal with packet loss. The *forward error correction* scheme requires a sender to add redundant information enabling the receiver to reconstruct lost packets. For example, the sender may piggypack lower-quality information onto the original stream. In this scheme the payload of packet i consists of the original information plus a low-quality version of the multimedia information in packet $i-1$. If packet $i-1$ is lost, the low-quality version is available and will be used before processing packet i. *Interleaving* is a scheme where the original stream is scrambled before transmission. Packet i does not contain adjacent samples; thus, its loss of packet will not affect dramatically the quality of the reception. The receiver may interpolate the information it gets to compensate for the lost packets.

5.6.4 Real-Time Protocol and Real-Time Streaming Protocol

The streaming server and clients communicate with one another using an *in-band* protocol for the data stream and an *out-of-band* protocol for the commands, see Figure 5.12. Two protocols, RTP and RTSP, are now described briefly.

The real-time protocol is used to transport audio and video data streams. Applications insert and extract media chunks from RTP packets; thus, RTP can be viewed as an application-layer protocol. Earlier we indicated that audio streams are delay sensitive, and video streams are rate sensitive. For this reason, the transport protocol of choice for data streaming is UDP. The congestion control mechanism together with the error control mechanism built into TCP prevent rate and delay guarantees, thus TCP is seldom used to transport audio or video streams.

RTP is a connection-oriented protocol and it is used for both unicast and multicast communications. An application may use one or multiple parallel RTP sessions to transport the data stream between a client and a server, e.g., an audio and a video stream. The RTP multicast stream emanating from a single sender as in the case of an audio or video broadcast application, or from multiple senders in the case of audio or video conferencing generally belong to one RTP session.

RTP supports several audio formats including, PCM, GSM, G.722, and MPEG Audio and several video formats such as Motion JPEG, MPEG 1 and MPEG 2. Each RTP packet consists of a header and a payload. The header has several fields: the payload type, a magic number to identify the audio or video format; a sequence number of the packet; a time stamp; the synchronization source identifier, a random number associated with an RTP session.

RTP has its own control protocol called real-time control protocol (RTCP). There are two types of RTCP packets, sender and receiver reports. Senders generate periodically *RTCP source reports* containing the RTP session identifier, the application generating the stream, the address of the source, and so on. Periodical *RTCP receiver reports* carry feedback information such as the number of packets lost, the jitter, and the number of packets received. An application may use the data provided by RTCP reports for diagnostic purposes, to modify its transmission rates, or to synchronize several streams within an RTP session, e.g., the audio and video stream. In case of multicast applications, RTCP has a mechanism to limit the rate of receiver reports when the number of receivers increases. To maintain the control traffic to an acceptable level, the rates of sender and receiver RTCP report packets and the size of the packets are limited to some fraction, e.g., 5% of the total bandwidth allocated to the session.

Now we turn our attention to mechanisms to support interactive multimedia applications, where the client provides control information for the server. The playback of continuous media is controlled using an *out-of-band* protocol called real-time streaming protocol (RTSP), introduced by Schulzrinne and co-workers in 1997. This protocol consists of a set of methods indicating to the server what actions should be taken on the continuous media object stored locally and identified by a URL of the form `rtsp://continousMediaPathname`. RTSP also allows a client to store a continuous media stream on a server. Figure 5.12 shows a client setting up a connection, playing, pausing, and tearing down a connection using RTSP.

5.6.5   Audio and Video Compression

In Chapter 2 we mentioned that data encoding covers three generic methods to transform information: (i) error detection and error correction for transmission of information over noisy channels, (ii) data encryption to ensure the confidentiality of information during transmission, and (iii) data compression to reduce the bandwidth requirements. In all these cases the stream generated by the information source is encoded, then transmitted over the network, and it is decoded at the destination, prior to its use. The three encoding methods are used not only for data transmission but also for archiving, to guarantee the quality and the confidentiality of the data and to reduce the amount of storage.

Fig. 5.14   The information generated by a source is compressed prior to transmission to reduce the bandwidth requirements.

Compression reduces the redundancy and uncompression attempts to reconstruct the information transmitted by the source as accurately as possible, as shown in Figure 5.14. Compression and uncompression can be done by specialized software or hardware at the sender and receiver.

Table 5.2 in Section 5.6.1 summarizes the bandwidth requirements for uncompressed and compressed digitized speech, audio, and video streams and shows the dramatic bandwidth reduction and the corresponding reduction of the storage requirements due to data compression.

In this section we discuss basic principles and algorithms for compression of text, still images, and audio and video streams.

5.6.5.1 *Basic Concepts.*   There are two basic strategies for data compression. *Lossless compression* allows the receiver to reconstruct the information sent without any loss. Lossless compression is required by the transmission of text or data. *Lossy compression* tolerates some loss of information and is used for most multimedia applications. We now survey several lossless compression techniques

Differential encoding is a lossless compression technique based on the observation that sudden large variations in the amplitude of a signal generated by a sensor such as a microphone, scanner, or a video camera are relatively infrequent; thus, very often, after the analog to digital conversion, the numerical values of consecutive samples differ only slightly. Instead of transmitting the amplitude of a sample we only transmit the difference from the previous one because we need fewer bits to express the difference than the number of bits to express the value of the sample.

Entropy encoding is a lossless compression technique that attempts to remove the redundancy based on the entropy of the source of information. Two methods of entropy encoding are commonly used, run length and statistical encoding.

Run length encoding (RLE) is a technique based on the observation that the string of symbols generated by a source of information often consists of substrings repeating the same symbol. Instead of transmitting cnt copies of the symbol sy, we transmit the pair (cnt, sy). For example, instead of 11100001111101111000000 we transmit $3,1$ $4,0$ $5,1$ $1,0$ $4,1$ $6,0$.

Statistical encoding encodes different symbols based on their frequency of occurrence. Consider a source S that generates a string of length n of symbols from an alphabet $\mathcal{A}$. Let $p(c_i)$ the probability of occurrence of symbol c_i, $c_i \in \mathcal{A}$. As we recall from Chapter 2 the *entropy of source S* is:

$$H(S) = -\sum_{i=1}^{n} p(c_i) \times log_2 p(c_i).$$

Encoding could be done by associating a code word of variable length to every character or by cutting the string generated by source S into substrings and associating a code word w_j of length n_j with every substring s_j. If $p(s_j)$ is the probability of occurrence of substring s_j and m is the number of substrings, the average number of bits per code word is

$$\bar{B} = \sum_{j=1}^{m} n_j \times p(s_j).$$

The efficiency of a particular encoding scheme is the ratio of the entropy of the source to the average number of bits per code word.

Example 1: the alphabet used by S consists of 32 characters and they occur with equal probability. In this case,

$$H(S) = -\sum_{i=1}^{32} 1/32 \times log_2(1/32) = -log_2(1/32) = 5$$

Each character can be optimally encoded as a string of 5 bits.

Example 2: the string generated by S consists of 8 characters, A, B, C, D, E, F, G, H that occur with probabilities:

$$p_A = \frac{1}{2}, p_B = \frac{1}{4}, p_C = \frac{1}{8}, p_D = \frac{1}{16}, p_E = \frac{1}{64}, p_F = \frac{1}{64}, p_G = \frac{1}{64}, p_H = \frac{1}{64}$$

Since we have eight characters we would be tempted to use 3 bits to encode each character: $A \rightarrow 000$, $B \rightarrow 001$, ... $H \rightarrow 111$. But this encoding is not optimal. Indeed the entropy is:

$$H(S) = -\sum_{i=1}^{8} p(c_i) \times log_2 p(c_i) = -log_2(1/4) = 2$$

We show that an optimal encoding for this source is: $A \rightarrow 1$, $B \rightarrow 01$, $C \rightarrow 001$, $D \rightarrow 0001$, $E \rightarrow 000000$, $F \rightarrow 000001$, $G \rightarrow 000011$, and $H \rightarrow 000010$. For this optimal encoding the average length of a string is 2 bits and it is equal to the entropy.

Compression methods are specific to the media being transferred and we discuss separately compression of text, still images, audio, and video streams.

5.6.5.2 Text Compression.

Text compression is based on statistical encoding, it is lossless, and it is used to transmit unformatted, formatted, or hypertext documents. We can encode either individual characters or substrings.

There are two classes of methods for text compression, static and dynamic or adaptive. *Static encoding methods* require the sender and the receiver to agree before the transmission on the set of characters used during transmission and their frequency of occurrence. *Dynamic or adaptive encoding methods* allow the sender and the receiver to discover the characteristics of the text during the transmission.

Static Huffman Encoding. The algorithm assigns characters in the alphabet of the source variable length codewords based on their frequency of occurrence. The code generated by this algorithm is a *prefix code*, no code word is a prefix of another code word. The algorithm constructs an unbalanced binary tree called a *Huffman code tree* according to the following algorithm:

- Construct the list L_n of all n characters that appear in the text and their probability of occurrence.

- Repeat the following steps $n - 1$ times, for $i = n, n - 1, n - 2, \ldots 2$.
  - Regard L_i as a list of nodes of a binary tree and sort it in decreasing order of the probability of occurrence of each node, pr_w.
  - Assign to the bottom two entries in L_i the label of a branch, of a binary tree. One of the nodes, n_p, will be labeled 0 and the other, n_q, will be labeled 1.
  - Combine the two nodes and construct a new list, L_{i-1} where the two nodes, n_p and n_q are replaced by one node, n_r with a probability of occurrence $pr_r = pr_p + pr_q$.

- Put side to side the $n - 1$ lists starting with L_n at the left and ending with L_2 at the right.

- To determine the binary string encoding character x, identify the last list L_x where character x showed up as a node of the binary tree. Starting with L_2 trace back all the labels of the branches leading to character x. The binary string consisting of these labels is the code word for character x.

Let us now examine the Huffman encoding for the case in Example 2. Figure 5.15 shows the seven consecutive lists, the resulting Huffman tree and the binary strings used to encode the characters A, B, C, D, E, F, G, and H.

For the tree in Figure 5.15: (i) branches are labeled with two binary symbols 0 and 1; (ii) leaves are labeled as the pair (a character in the alphabet, its probability of occurrence); (iii) internal nodes are labeled by the cumulative probability of the subtree rooted at that node.

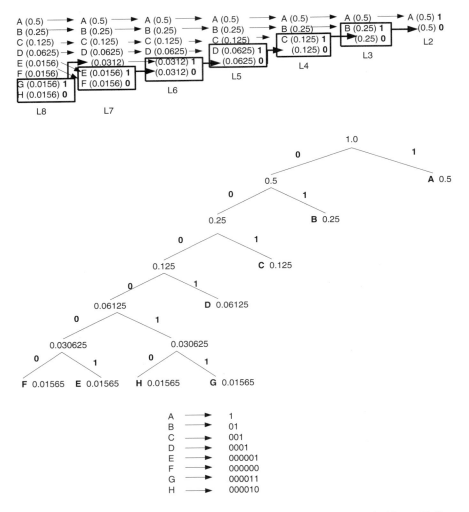

Fig. 5.15 Static Huffman compression. The seven lists used to construct the binary Huffman tree and the binary strings for encoding the characters in Example 2.

The code word for a character is the binary string consisting of the labels of branches encountered when traversing the tree from the root to the leaf labeled with that character. For example consider character G: it last appears in list $L8$ and its label is 1 and is connected to the fifth entry of $L7$ with no label, which in turn is connected to the fifth entry in $L6$ with label 1, which in turn is connected to the fifth entry in $L5$ with label 0, which is connected to the fourth entry in $L4$ with label 0, connected to the third entry in $L3$ with label 0, connected to the second entry in $L2$ with label 0. Thus the string of labels from G to the root is 110000, and its reverse, the string of labels from the root to G is 000011. By the same token, character A last appears in $L2$ and its label is 1 thus A is encoded as 1.

The decoding algorithm is based on the prefix property of the generated code: (i) starting from the root, traverse the tree guided by each input bit until you reach a leaf; (ii) the character labeling that leaf is the one corresponding to the traversal; (iii) once you identified a leaf, start a new traversal from the root. This is a static encoding algorithm and this means the receiver must have a copy of the tree before attempting to decode an input stream of characters.

Adaptive Huffman Encoding. The sender and the receiver build the tree dynamically. Each leaf node is labeled with a character and the count, the number of times that character has been encountered up to that point in time. In every tree there is a single leaf node called the *empty leaf* labeled Ef 0, with a 0 frequency of occurrence. An internal node is labeled only with the cumulative count of all the characters in the subtree rooted at that node. Each branch is labeled with a binary digit 0 or 1.

The sender and the receiver execute the following algorithm to build the binary tree: start with a tree with only the root node connected to Ef 0 node with a branch labeled 0; for every new character perform the following steps:

- If the character is already in the tree: the sender transmits the binary string encoding the character as the static Huffman encoder does; the receiver gets the binary string and decodes it as the static Huffman decoder does.

- If the character is encountered for the first time: the sender transmits the character without encoding it; the receiver gets the character and does not need to decode it.

- Update the tree. If the character is already in the tree, increment the count of the character. If the character is encountered for the first time, add the new character to the tree by replacing the empty leaf node with a new node labeled 1 and a subtree consisting of a left branch labeled 0 connected to a new Ef 0 and a right branch labeled 1 connected to the new character. Increment the labels of all internal nodes in the corresponding subtree (left or right) to reflect the addition of the new node.

- Construct a list of the nodes of the tree from left to right and from the bottom to the top, excluding the root. If this list contains nodes in the order imposed by their counts, starting with Ef 0, do nothing. Else, construct a modified list including all nodes sorted in increasing count order.

- Build a modified binary tree reflecting the modified list if necessary.

Figure 5.16 illustrates the first 5 steps to encode the string "alea jacta est", the famous sentence "the dice is cast" uttered on January 10-11, 49 b.c., by Julius Ceasar, on crossing the Rubicon, a small river separating Gaul from Italy. The crossing of the Rubicon marked the start of the Roman Civil War. Today this sentence means that an important decision has been made.

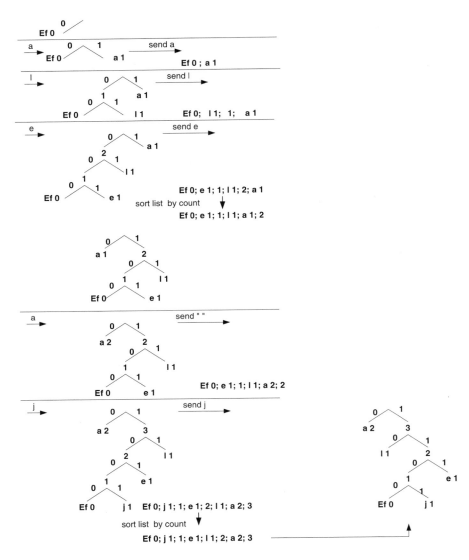

Fig. 5.16   Adaptive Huffman compression of the first five characters of string "alea jacta est."

Note that static and adaptive Huffman encoding produce optimal results only if the probabilities of occurrence of individual characters are integer powers of 2^{-1}.

Now we outline two methods to compress substrings, a static algorithm and a dynamic one.

Lempel-Ziv. The LZ algorithm is based on construction of a dictionary consisting of all the substrings found in the input stream. Instead of transmitting a substring we transmit the index of the substring in the dictionary. LZ is a static algorithm, the receiver is expected to have a copy of the dictionary and to use it to decode each substring.

Assume that: (i) the input string consists of N characters each represented as a code with n bits per character; (ii) the average length of a substring is L bits; (iii) the dictionary has $D = 2^d$ entries. The compression factor achieved by the LZ algorithm is:

$$LZ_{compression} = (N \times n)/(\frac{N}{L} \times d) = \frac{n \times L}{d}.$$

For example, assume that we transmit text with each character encoded as a 7-bit ASCII code, the dictionary has $2^{10} = 1024$ entries, and the average length of a string is 15 characters. Then $LZ_{compression} = 7 \times 15/10 = 10.5$

Lempel-Ziv-Welsh. The LZW algorithm is a dynamic algorithm, the dictionary is built simultaneously by the sender and the receiver during the transmission of the text. Both start with a dictionary consisting only of the character set used. For example the initial 128 entries of the dictionary may contain only the 128 binary codes for the ASCII characters. As the transmission of the text starts, for each character of the first word the corresponding binary representation is transmitted. Once we encounter the first separator, say a blank, after sending the character, both sender and receiver recognize that a word was transmitted and the word is entered in their local copy of the dictionary as the 129th entry. Next time the same word is encountered, its index in the dictionary is sent rather than the individual characters in the word.

5.6.5.3 *Still Image Compression.*

First let us recall a few basic properties of sources of light. A color source is characterized by two properties: *luminance* describing the brightness and *chrominance* describing the color. The luminance is determined by the *brightness*, the amount of energy that stimulates the eye. The brightness is independent of color. In turn, the *crominance* is concerned with the color and it is determined by two other basic properties of a source, the *hue*, the color of the source determined by the frequency associated with the corresponding light wave and the *saturation* given by the strength of that color, the intensity of the light wave. A color C can be produced on a screen by mixing the three primary colors, R (red), G (green), and, B (blue), in different proportions, e.g., $a \times R + b \times G + c \times B$. The luminance of the source, Y_s can be determined by summing the intensities of the three luminance signals, R_s, G_s, B_s:

$$Y_s = a \times R_s + b \times G_s + c \times B_s.$$

To transmit information about an image, we need to transmit either the coefficients a, b, c or the luminance of the source Y_s and two blue crominance, $C_b = B_s - Y_s$, and the red crominance, $C_r = R_s - Y_s$.

A still image consists of a two-dimensional array of pixels. In the case of a monochrome image each pixel is represented by an 8-bit gray value. For a color image each pixel is represented by an index into a table of $2^{24} = 16,777,216$ colors.

The 24-bit string identifies the color of that pixel; 8 bits are used to describe the contribution of each of the three primary colors, R, G, and B.

To store an uncompressed color $n \times m$ pixel image we need $3 \times n \times m$ bytes. For example several digital cameras available on the market capture 2048×1536 pixel images; we need 9 Mbytes to store this image.

We now overview several widely used still image compression schemes.

Graphics Interchange Format (GIF). This compression scheme reduces the number of colors present in the image from 2^{24} to 2^8 by choosing the 256 colors that best match the colors in the image and sending along with the compressed image the so-called *local color table* with 256 entries. GIF allows a compression factor of almost 3, instead of sending 24-bit pixels we send 8-bit pixels that are indexes in the local color table.

Using a strategy similar to the one of the LZW algorithm, we can extend the color table by adding to it additional entries corresponding to frequently used colors and compress the image even further. GIF also supports *interlaced* transmission allowing the receiver to build up the image progressively from low to high resolution as data arrives.

Joint Photographic Experts Group (JPEG). This is a lossy image compression method defined by the IS 10981 standard. JPEG is a transform encoding compression scheme where an image is first transformed using the discrete cosine transformation (DCT) and then encoded.

The basic idea of the algorithm is to decompose an image into blocks and then to transform individual blocks to the Fourier domain. In the Fourier domain we are able to identify high frequency components that correspond to rapid variations of the pixel intensity caused by details of the image. To each transform value we assign an integer in the dynamic range determined by the number of bits per sample, which, in turn, is determined by the maximum quantization error that can be tolerated. Finally, JPEG uses entropy encoding to transmit the sample values.

JPEG encoding consists of five stages, see Figure 5.17: image and block preparation, forward DCT, quantization, and entropy encoding.

Earlier we pointed out that for a color image we need three matrices, one for each of the R, G, and B quantized values or for the luminance values. Each pixel is represented as a triplet of integers in the range 0 to 255, the index into the corresponding color table. The pixel values are transformed to the range (-128) to $(+127)$, the 2D array of pixels is decomposed into blocks of 8×8 pixels, and the 2D DCT is performed:

$$F(i,j) = \frac{1}{4}C(i)C(j)\sum_{x=0}^{7}\sum_{y=0}^{7}P(x,y)cos\frac{(2x+1)i\pi}{16}cos\frac{(2y+1)i\pi}{16}$$

where $P(x,y)$ is the pixel value, $F(i,j)$ is the DCT, x, y, i, j are indices in the range 0 to 7, and $C(i), C(j) = \frac{1}{\sqrt{2}}$ for $i, j = 0$ and $C(i), C(j) = 1$ for $i, j \neq 0$.

The next step is the mapping of the floating point DCT coefficients to a range of integer values. The DCT quantization is the first stage of compression where losses

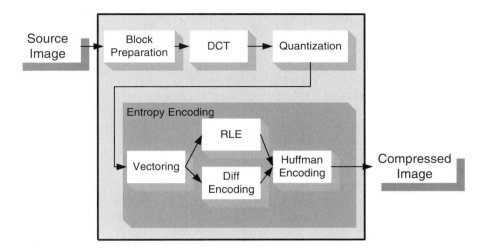

Fig. 5.17   Block diagram of JPEG encoding.

occur. The human eye responds to lower frequencies and to those components with intensities above a certain threshold. This threshold is component dependent.

A first step for quantization is to divide the DCT coefficients by an integer power of two. For example, dividing the coefficients by 32 saves 5 bits and eliminates the feeble components. Different components have different thresholds thus in practice the scaling of each component is controlled by a *quantization table*. As a result of DCT quantization typically we end up with a 2D matrix with mostly zero elements except a few nonzero coefficients in the upper left corner.

Entropy encoding requires a one dimensional structure. The *vectorization* process, see Figure 5.17, scans the 2D individual DCT blocks in a zig-zag pattern to create a one-dimensional array of integer values. Then, several entropy encoding methods are applied. Differential encoding reduces the dynamic range to express the DCT coefficients exploiting their slow variation pattern, run-length encoding takes advantage of large groups of zero coefficients, and the adaptive Huffman encoding attempts to create code words with an average length as close as possible to the entropy.

Typical compression ratios for JPEG are 10:1 to 20:1.

5.6.5.4 *Audio and Video Compression.* Uncompressed audio and video streams have very high bandwidth and storage requirements. Lossless compression of multimedia streams reduces these requirements slightly, but the real gain is provided by lossy audio and video compression that oftentimes results in compression ratios of 100:1 or more.

Is lossy compression of audio and video streams justified? The answer to this question is that the human hearing and vision systems are imperfect, they cannot process all the information provided by an "ideal" audio or video stream. Thus, we can reduce substantially the volume of data transferred, or stored, without affecting the quality of audio and video perceived by the human ear and eye. Understanding the human hearing and vision process helps us understand what information and under what conditions our sensory organs are able to process and thus design better audio and video compression algorithms.

For example, the retina of the human eye consists of approximately 6 million cones and 120 million rods that act as primary sensors of visual information. In turn, these cells are connected to so-called bipolar and then to ganglion cells, whose fibers form an optic nerve transmitting the information to the visual cortex. The optic nerve has about 1 million fibers. Thus, the network of bipolar and ganglion cells in the retina performs some sort of a lossy transformation of the incoming video signal, effectively "compressing" the results of 126 million sensors into just 1 million channels in the optic nerve connecting the sensors with the cortex.

Now we outline the compression of audio and video signals based on the methods proposed by the Motion Picture Expert Group (MPEG), charged by the International Standard Organization (ISO) with the formulation of standards for multimedia applications.

Other methods for compressing audio and video streams described in detail in Halsall[29] are: differential PCM, adaptive differential PCM, linear predictive coding, perceptual coding and Dolby for audio streams and H.261 and H263 for video streams.

Audio MPEG. The ISO Recommendation 11172-3 defines three layers of processing with the level of compression and perceptual quality increasing from layer 1 to 3; layer 1 provides Hi-fi quality at a rate of 192 Kbps/channel; layer 2 provides near CD-quality at a rate of 128 Kbps/channel; layer 3 provides CD-quality at 64 Kbps/channel. In practice, there are four types of audio: monophonic, dual monophonic, two-channel stereo, and single-channel stereo. For each layer, the dual monophonic and the two-channel stereo require twice the bandwidth listed above.

Let us discuss briefly some characteristics of the human hearing system. The human ear is sensitive to signals with frequency in the range 15 to 20,000 Hertz. The sensitivity depends on the frequency, the ear is most sensitive to the 2 to 5 KHz range. An intense signal at some frequency masks other signals, the so-called *frequency masking* effect, and a loud sound masks other sounds for a period of time, the so-called *temporal masking* effect.

The MPEG audio encoder and decoder structure is presented in Figure 5.18. The first step for audio MPEG encoding is the pulse code modulation consisting of sampling and quantization discussed in Section 5.6.1.

The PCM samples are then transformed using the discrete Fourier transform (DFT) analysis. Then the DFT values go through a quantization phase. In this phase the effects of frequency and temporal masking as well as the sensitivity of the ear to different frequencies in the audio spectrum are taken into account. Finally, the DFT coefficients are multiplexed into frames and the frames are transmitted over the network. At the receiving end the frames are demultiplexed, a DFT synthesis is performed, and the digital samples are then converted into an analog signal by the PCM decoder.

Video MPEG. There are two important standards: MPEG-1 for storing VHS quality audio and video with resolution up to 352×288 pixels on CD-ROM at bit rates up

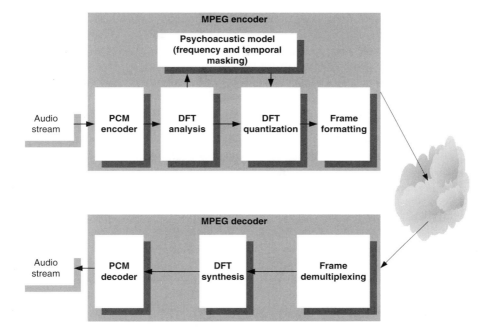

Fig. 5.18 Block diagram of audio MPEG encoder and decoder.

to 1.5 Mbps; MPEG-2 for storing and transmission of studio-quality audio and video with four possible resolutions, up to 1920×1152 pixels for wide-screen HDTV at bit rates of up to 80 Mbps.

A video stream is a sequence of digitized images or frames; thus, one could use JPEG independently in each frame. When discussing JPEG we pointed out the spatial redundancy in one frame. Additionally, there is a considerable correlation between successive frames of a video stream. Instead of sending individually composed frames we can transmit such frames from time to time and then predict the contents of the missing frames. In MPEG there are three types of frames: *intracoded* frames, or I-frames, and two types of predicted frames, *predictive*, or P-frames, and *bidirectional* or B-frames. I-frames are encoded without reference to other frames using the JPEG algorithm. They must be present in the output at regular intervals.

5.7 OPEN SYSTEMS

The next challenge is to design open systems and provide the infrastructure for assembling complex applications out of software components developed independently.

We restrict our attention to the *service overlay model* where services are introduced at the "edge" of the virtual infrastructure supported by the Internet. In this model service creation is relatively easy, but changing the infrastructure to support new services is a difficult proposition. For example, data streaming for multimedia applications requires QoS guarantees and resource reservation as discussed in Chapter 4.

Two other models have generated a considerable interest; one of the models attempts to modify the network core, the other to transform the data while crossing the network. The *active network model* is based on a programmable network infrastructure and allows users to modify the operational semantics of the network itself [61, 66]. There are serious concerns that a programmable network infrastructure is more vulnerable to attacks because some control mechanisms must be exposed and invite more complex attacks to the infrastructure.

The other model is based on *active media*; the media carries along the code necessary to transform the data. This model requires routers to execute mobile code and this increases their vulnerability. For example, the level of compression may be increased to reduce the bandwidth requirements of a video or of an audio stream on some branches of its multicast tree where congestion is experienced.

Figure 5.19 gives us a glimpse at the architecture of an open system based on the service overlay model. We recognize the familiar hourglass architecture of the Internet expanded with an additional layer of middleware services.

Originally, the client-server model implied a direct interaction between one client and a server. The implicit assumptions of the RPC protocols are that the client:

(a) knows the interface presented by the server,

(b) knows the exact location of the server, and

(c) blocks waiting for the response.

The servers are stateless, there are no provisions for reliability; if the sever goes down, the client will eventually discover the lack of a response and take proper actions.

These assumptions may no longer be valid in a large-scale open system. Indeed, a client may not be aware of the application program interface (API) to invoke the service, and may need to discover the exact location of a server. In a service-rich environment service providers may be grouped into classes and a client may be handed over to another service provider in the same class when the original one fails, its response time increases, the pricing structure becomes unfavorable, or for some other compelling reason. Some servers may be required to maintain state.

Security is a major concern in a global system and direct interactions between clients and servers may be discouraged to protect the integrity of the servers. Last but not least, a complex application may require the coordination of several, possibly many services.

5.7.1   Resource Management, Discovery and Virtualization, and Service Composition in an Open System

Let us first review the process of developing a computer application and outline the quantum leaps necessary to move outside the confines of a single administrative domain. To develop a traditional application for one computer, one needs familiarity

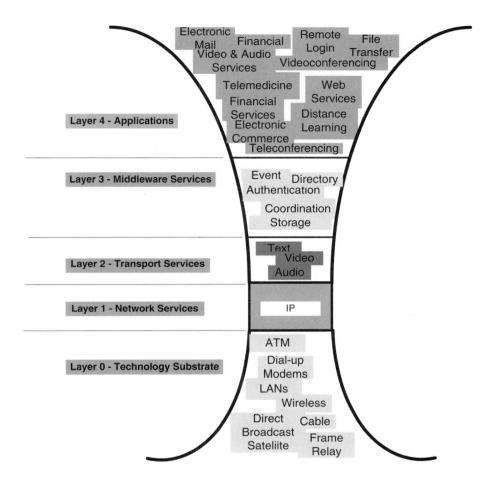

Fig. 5.19 The model of an open system extends the hourglass Internet model with middleware services.

with the local computing environment and a good understanding of the algorithms, the programming language, the run-time environment, as well as the domain specific libraries, e.g., mathematical, graphics, or system libraries like the X-window library, available locally.

Each operating system provides a set of low-level services to open, read, and write to a file, to open a socket in order to communicate over the network, to allocate and release storage, and so on. Each programming language supported by the system exposes APIs, for these services. The API specifies the exact syntax and the semantics of each service call in terms of the primitive data structures supported by the language. To use a library we first need to know if the library is installed and what modules are in the library, then we need to understand the syntax and the semantics of the call for each module.

In conclusion, the development of an application is a *process of composition* where user code is interlaced with calls to system services and to domain-specific libraries. Imperative languages used today require the precise knowledge of the APIs to system services and library modules.

Users do not have direct access to *system resources*, their access is mediated by the local operating system. The system administrator makes decisions on resource allocation policies and the operating system controls all hardware and software resources and enforces resource-sharing policies. For example, the system administrator establishes the disk quotas, the maximum amount of secondary storage for each user, assigns access rights to individual users, e.g., allows raw socket access only to super-users. The operating system returns an error code when user actions lead to a violation of established policies. At the same time, the operating system maintains the state of the system based on an exact knowledge of the state of each component.

Another important function of the operating system is *virtualization of resources*. It would be quite impractical to require individual users to know the actual amount of memory available on a system, the make of the disks connected to the system, or the type of the network interfaces and the speed of each communication link. Higher level abstractions like virtual memory, the concept of a file as a stream of bytes, a socket as an end point of a communication channel, and so on, provide some independence of the actual configuration of a system and make the development of applications easier.

Once we escape the confines of a single system the problems discussed above: (i)resource management(ii) resource discovery, (iii) virtualization of resources, and (iv) service composition, become considerably more difficult. The scale of the system, the open system requirements, the lack of a single administrative authority, and the need for even higher level abstractions for system resources are major concerns that need to be addressed in the design of wide-area, open distributed systems.

5.7.1.1 *Resource Management.*

In a wide-area system it is impossible for any single entity to be aware of all services available at any given time and to know the API of each service. Moreover, services, though long-lived, may dynamically join and leave the community.

In open distributed systems there is *no central authority to establish policies* on behalf of all service providers and all applications interested in these services and no system to enforce such policies. Services are provided by autonomous organizations and individual entities obtain the benefit of such services through mutual agreements with service providers.

Due to the scale of the system it is not feasible for any single entity to maintain the status of all resources. Nevertheless, a hierarchical decomposition of a system into domains may address the scalability issues. Entities may attempt to have some knowledge about other entities they interact with frequently but the state maintained by them may not be accurate at all times. For example a printing service may go down and at least for some time this fact will not be known to the entity providing a lookup service.

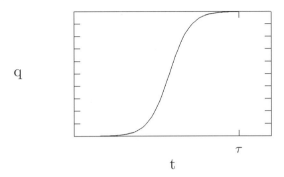

q

t

Fig. 5.20 The number of nodes known to a given entity, function of time. After time τ, each entity becomes aware of all the other nodes in the network

5.7.1.2 Resource Discovery. Resource discovery is an important function of the middleware. Mechanisms like *gossiping* based on *epidemic* algorithms [1, 31, 56], can be used effectively to spread information about the current state of resources in a wide-area system [6].

To model gossiping we use models similar to the ones for the spread of a contagious disease. An epidemic develops in a population of fixed size consisting of two groups, the infected individuals and the uninfected ones. The progress of the epidemic is determined by the interactions between these two groups.

We discuss here only a deterministic model. Given a group of n nodes this simple model is based on the assumption that the rate of change is proportional with the size of the group the entity is already aware of, y, and also with the size of the group the entity is unaware of, $n - y$. If k is a constant, we can express this relationship as follows:

$$y(t)' = k \times y(t) \times (n - y(t)).$$

The solution of this differential equation with the initial condition $y(0) = 0$ is:

$$y(t) = \frac{n}{1 + (n-1)e^{-knt}}$$

This function is plotted in Figure 5.20 and shows that after time τ an entity becomes aware of all the other nodes in the network. The parameter k as well as the value τ can be determined through simulation.

This deterministic model allows only a qualitative analysis. Rather than the smooth transition from 0 to n, we should expect a series of transitions, each one corresponding to a batch of newly discovered nodes.

We review briefly some of the algorithms presented in the literature, their basic assumptions, and the proposed performance measures to evaluate an algorithm. Virtually all algorithms model the distributed system as a directed graph in which each machine is a node and edges represent the relation "machine A knows about machine B." The network is assumed to be weakly connected and communication occurs in synchronous parallel rounds.

One performance measure is the *running time of the algorithm*, namely, the number of rounds required until every machine learns about every other machine. The amount of communication required by the algorithm is measured by: (a) the *pointer communication complexity* defined as the number of pointers exchanged during the course of the algorithm, and (b) the *connection communication complexity* defined by the total number of connections between pairs of entities.

The *flooding* algorithm assumes that each node v only communicates over edges connecting it with a set of initial neighbors, $\Gamma(v)$. In every round node v contacts all its initial neighbors and transmits to them updates, $\Gamma(v)^{updates}$ and then updates its own set of neighbors by merging $\Gamma(v)$ with the set $\{\Gamma(u)^{updates}\}$, with $u \in \Gamma(v)$. The number of rounds required by the flooding algorithm is equal to the diameter of the graph.

The *swamping* algorithm allows a machine to open connections with all its current neighbors not only with the set of initial neighbors. The graph of the network known to one machine converges to a complete graph on $O(log(n))$ steps but the communication complexity increases.

In the *random pointer jump* algorithm each node v connects a random neighbor, $u \in \Gamma(v)$ who sends $\Gamma(u)$ to v who in turn merges $\Gamma(v)$ with $\Gamma(u)$. A version of the algorithm called *the random pointer jump with back edge* requires u to send back to v a pointer to all its neighbors. There are even strongly connected graphs that require with high probability $\Omega(n)$ time to converge to a complete graph in the random pointer jump algorithm.

In the *name-dropper* algorithm during each round each machine v transmits $\Gamma(v)$ to one randomly chosen neighbor. A machine u that receives $\Gamma(v)$ merges $\Gamma(v)$ with $\Gamma(u)$. In this algorithm after $O(log^2 n)$ rounds the graph evolves into a complete graph with probability greater than $1 - 1/(n^{O(1)})$.

5.7.1.3 *Resource Virtualization.*

To support code mobility we need a common platform or a virtual machine. We also need higher level abstractions for clients to specify their needs in a "fuzzy" fashion. For example, once a laptop is connected to a new network it is desirable to specify that an application needs access to a high-speed color printer rather than know the name of the printer, its attributes, and its network address.

5.7.1.4 *Service Composition.*

Diversity is encouraged by the basic philosophy of an *open system*. Diversity implies the ability to develop new classes of applications and services, to develop a new service in a given class, or to create a new instance of an existing service. To develop a new class of services new standards must be developed. For example, the lightweight directory access protocol (LDAP) and its API define a new class of services.

To develop a new server for an existing class of services one needs to follow the standards for that class. For example, to develop a new Web server one needs to follow the specifications of the HTTP protocol [34]. To create a new instance of a given service one simply needs to use the generic API for that particular service.

Components developed independently must be able to interact with one another and *standards* supporting interoperability are a critical component of open systems. Yet, the scale of the system makes the development and deployment of standards difficult. New technologies, services, or policies require changes of existing standards and adoptions of new ones. But a sudden transition to a new standard is rarely feasible; one may need to support compatibility with older versions for many years.

In summary, the open distributed systems imply "globalization" of services and creation of a range of middleware services to mediate between a dynamic set of clients and a dynamic set of services that have agreed to obey a set of ever-changing standards.

5.7.2 Mobility

There are two notions of mobility, *virtual or code mobility* and *physical or hardware mobility*, see Figure 5.21. Cardelli [14] gives examples when the two interact and argues that intermittent connectivity can be caused by either network failures or by physical or virtual mobility.

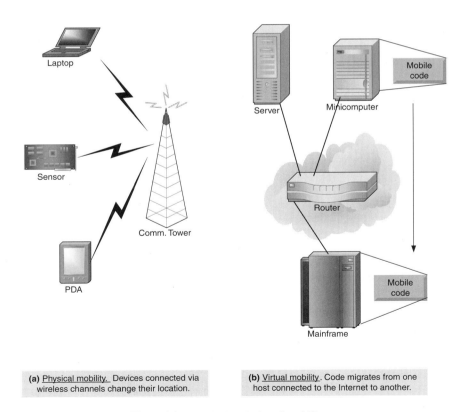

(a) Physical mobility. Devices connected via wireless channels change their location.

(b) Virtual mobility. Code migrates from one host connected to the Internet to another.

Fig. 5.21 Physical and virtual mobility.

Functionality and cost, performance, and security motivate the recent interest in mobile code. Recall that in an open system services are developed by independent service providers who are defining proprietary interfaces for each service. New devices, e.g., a camera, a scanner, a printer, or a mass storage system may be connected to the network and offer services.

The problem is further complicated because services and their interfaces evolve in time. In the absence of code mobility the software needed to access these services or devices would need to be installed and upgraded on every machine hosting a potential user of the service, the same way we install a new version of the operating system or a browser on our PCs. The alternative is to download on demand the code providing the human or programmable interface to these services. Java applets provide human interfaces to services while *plugins* or Jini proxies support programmable services. Code mobility has the potential to save significant administrative and software maintenance costs and provide convenient access to new services.

Another reason for code mobility is performance. Rather than moving large volumes of data to the site where the code runs, we can do the opposite. If we need repeated access to service, rather than traverse the network many times we can bring the service to the client's site and eliminate the problems caused by the fluctuations of the bandwidth in a wide area network. Last but not least, we may want to move together the client and the server because we do not trust the network but we do have the means to verify the mobile code.

We are primarily concerned with code mobility and discuss the problems it causes and the benefits it brings. According to the classification of Cugola et al. [19] there are three paradigms to build mobile code applications, see Figure 5.22:

(i) Code-on-Demand: A component running on a node of the network downloads code from a remote location and links it to a local task.

(ii) Remote Evaluation: A component running on a node of the network sends both the data and the code describing how to perform a service to a remote location.

(iii) Mobile Agents: A process migrates from one node of the network to another where it continues its execution from the state it was when migration was initiated.

There are two different contexts for mobility: systems confined to a local area network and those in a wide area network. In the first case, the distributed systems are built by linking together a set of possibly heterogeneous nodes by high-speed communication links and attempting to create stable and uniform environments simulating the ones available on main frames.

The main characteristics of LAN-based such distributed systems are *predictability* and a *single administrative domain*. Communication delays are bounded and response times of various servers can be estimated. The systems are generally well administered and protected from the outside attacks by firewalls. The network topology is hidden and the hosts are typically immobile.

In a LAN-based distributed system we distinguish three forms of mobility:

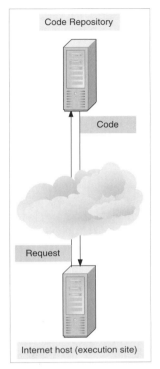

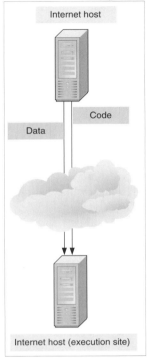

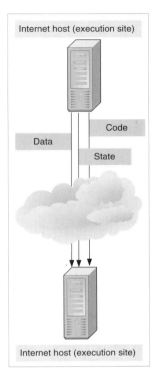

(a) <u>Code on Demand</u>. The Internet host loads the code from a repository and links it to an application.

(b) <u>Remote Evaluation</u>. An Internet host sends data and code to another host. The process starts execution at the new site.

(c) <u>Mobile Agents</u>. An Internet host sends the data, code, and state of a running process to another host. The process resumes execution at the new site.

Fig. 5.22   The three forms of virtual mobility. (a) Code on demand. (b) Remote evaluation. (c) Mobile agents.

1. Mobility of a thread of control and remote execution. Thread mobility is supported primarily by RPCs and entire computations can be delegated to a server.

2. Mobility of data and passive objects. Data is transported across machines.

3. Mobility of links/channels. The end points of a communication channel can be moved around.

Let us turn our attention to wide-area distributed systems. The Internet as a global information infrastructure has no reliable component or a single point of failure, and no centralized management/administrative authority. It is a dynamic collection of autonomous administrative domains, different from one another. The network topology is dynamic. Host mobility is pervasive, hosts may move from one network to another.

We need to introduce in this environment redundancy to archive reliability, replication for quality of service, and scalability. If we want to provide the same feeling in a wide-area distributed system as in a distributed system confined to a LAN we need to:

(i) Hide virtual and physical locations to ensure mobility.

(ii) Hide latency and bandwidth fluctuations.

Finally, note that a trust relationship must exist between a host and a mobile code, if a site does not trust the mobile code it will not allow it in; if the mobile code does not trust a site it will not visit it. Thus, code mobility poses technical and administrative, as well as political challenges; it requires a large segment of the user population to adhere to a set of new standards.

5.7.3 Network Objects

The object-oriented philosophy had a profound influence on software development for an extended period of time; it is only natural to expect that it plays an important role in open systems. In this section we discuss the single most important development in distributed object system, CORBA. First, we review the basic terminology of object-oriented programming.

Objects are instances of abstract data types called *classes*. An object consists of data, called *data members* or attributes, and functions that operate on the data, called methods or *member functions*. *Interfaces* describe the functions used to interact with an object. The classes of objects that respond to a particular interface are said to implement that interface.

An object is thus encapsulated, or hidden; we only expose the handles needed to interact with the object. This very simple idea had tremendous consequences in software engineering; the structure of an object may change but the rest of the world will not notice these changes as long as the methods used to manipulate the object are invariant.

The concept of *inheritance* is a cornerstone in the object-oriented philosophy; a new object may be built from an existing class by adding data members, and/or member functions. The *extended* class inherits the data members and the member functions of the original class.

Evolution and sharing are basic facts of life. Most man-made systems evolve over time, some of their components are modified while others remain unchanged. To reduce cost and development time and to improve reliability, most engineering disciplines attempt to reuse and share existing components as much as possible. Inheritance offers software systems the key to evolution and to component sharing.

The object-oriented approach allows the designers of a system to reuse solutions based on *recurring patterns* [22]. For example:

- The *observer* pattern allows the designer to define dependencies between objects so that when one object changes its state, all its dependents are notified and updated automatically.

- The *strategy* pattern encapsulates all the algorithms in a family of algorithms using a common interface; clients may change algorithms as needed.

- The *factory method* lets a class defer the instantiation to subclasses, each subclass being able to decide which class to instantiate.

- The *abstract class* pattern provides an interface for creating a family of related or dependent objects without specifying their concrete classes.

Serialization or flattening is the process of transforming an object that may contain pointers to other objects, into a unidimensional structure that can be stored on external storage or be transmitted over a communication channel. Serialization relies on protocols for packing/unpacking the data structure components of an object.

An object is *persistent* if it can be stored onto and retrieved from persistent storage. An *active object* has one or more threads of control. A *passive object* does not have a thread of control.

Objects need not be co-located, they may be distributed to hosts spread over a wide-area network and RPCs are used to invoke methods on remote objects. In turn, the leap to distributed object systems generates the need for higher level abstractions for handling remote objects.

When the objects are co-located, their interfaces, the language used for system development, the internal representation of data structures are known, and we have to deal with a single system image. Once objects are separated by a network, we have to address the typical problems encountered in a heterogeneous system with nodes with different architecture and system software. The need for higher level abstractions and middleware support for distributed object systems is motivated by several factors:

(i) The interfaces exposed by a remote object are language and system dependent.

(ii) Objects are passed around as arguments and as returned values and RPCs, which support a fairly limited number of primitive data types, are ill suited for distributed object applications. Some systems may support big-endian representation with the most significant byte first (MSB), others may be based on the least significant byte first (LSB), for little-endian representations.

(iii) An object may contain pointers to other objects and before being sent over the network a serial representation of the object must be constructed.

(iv) Socket-level programming in virtually all programming languages, including Java, is tedious; one must describe the type of socket connection desired, connect to services or alternatively listen for connections, accept them, and so on.

Two very different approaches for supporting distributed object systems are possible:

(1) accommodate the status quo, accept the heterogeneity of existing systems, and provide an operating system and programming language independent interface to all services and components;

(2) consider an ab initio solution and design a new platform for network objects. The term *platform* means an environment consisting of a new programming language, a virtual machine running under existing operating systems, or a new hardware.

The first solution was adopted by the designers of the CORBA system, the second by the designers of the Java platform.

5.7.3.1 The Common Object Request Broker Architecture (CORBA).

CORBA is a middleware project undertaken by more than 700 companies working together under the umbrella of a consortium, the Object Management Group (OMG) [52]. Microsoft is one of the few major software companies that did not join OMG and is developing its own competing distributed object system, DCOM, the distributed component object model [60].

A critical element of CORBA is the *interface definition language* (IDL), a purely declarative language used to specify the API and the error handling of methods used by CORBA components. IDL provides no implementation details and serves as the "glue" of the system.

The *object request broker* (ORB), is a software bus allowing remote objects to communicate transparently. The ORB hides the details of low-level communica-

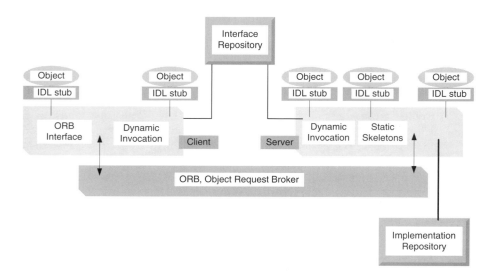

Fig. 5.23 A CORBA system. The ORB supports static and dynamic method invocation. IDL interface descriptions support interoperability in CORBA. The implementation language of client and server objects may be different.

tion and transport mechanisms, supports static and dynamic method invocation, and polymorphic messaging.

Static method invocation means that the method invocation is known at compile time; *dynamic method invocation* means that an object may discover at run time the interfaces exposed by a remote object and then use them. Every ORB supports an *interface repository*, a service describing the interfaces exposed by the objects in the ORB domain. Polymorphic messaging means that the same function has different effects depending on the target object.

The ORB has built-in security and transaction mechanisms and has high-level language bindings. The methods on remote objects can be invoked from any high language supported, regardless of the language the remote object is implemented in Figure 5.23 illustrates the basic architecture of a CORBA system. CORBA defines a set of services [53], each one providing one or more interfaces:

(i) *Life Cycle* - interfaces to create, delete, copy, move components.

(ii) *Naming* - interfaces to locate components.

(iii) *Event* - interfaces for components to register and unregister to receive events using the *event channel* abstraction.

(iv) *Persistence* - interfaces to store and retrieve components from databases or files.

(v) *Concurrency Control* - interfaces to a lock manager.

(vi) *Transactions* - interfaces to a two-phase commit protocol for flat and nested transactions.

(vii) *Query* - interfaces to SQL3 queries.

(viii) *Time* - interfaces for managing time-triggered events and for synchronization.

(xi) *Security* - interfaces for authentication, access control, and for managing credentials.

(x) *Yellow Pages* - interfaces for objects to advertise their services and bid for tasks.

(xi) *Externalization* - interfaces to get data in and out of components using a stream-like mechanism.

(xii) *Licensing* - interfaces for accounting and metering the use of components.

(xiii) *Properties* - interfaces to associate properties with components.

(xiv) *Relationship* - interfaces to create dynamic associations of components.

(xv) *Collection* - interfaces to manipulate collections.

(xvi) *Startup* - interfaces to automatically start up services.

CORBA favors three-tier client/server solutions as opposed tp the traditional two-tier architecture supported by RPCs, see Figure 5.24. Typically, light-weight objects reside on the client side; the middle tier consists of services like the ones listed above; the third tier consists of complex legacy applications.

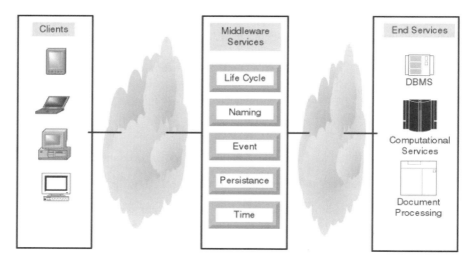

Fig. 5.24   Three-tier architecture. Light-weight objects reside on clients, middleware services facilitate access to end services provided by legacy applications.

5.7.3.2   Java.   Nowadays, Java is the object-oriented language of choice for building distributed applications [27]. Java is architecture-neural and supports socket-based communication [17]. The Java platform is based on the Java virtual machine (JVM) running under most operating systems [44]. JVM is embedded into Web browsers and maybe available in the future as specialized hardware.

5.7.4   Java Virtual Machine and Java Security

We now take a closer look at Java and Java-built distributed applications. As pointed out earlier, an application consists of user code interlaced with calls to system services and possibly to domain-specific libraries, and in the general case it is immobile. To support unrestricted code mobility it is necessary to:

   (i) develop a platform or a virtual machine and a programming language for it,

   (ii) implement and install the platform on virtually all hosts connected to the Internet, and

   (iii) require applications be developed in the language supported by the common platform.

At the time of this writing, Java virtual machine (JVM) is the common platform and Java is the programming language of choice for code mobility. Java bytecode produced on one machine can be transported over the network and the Java virtual machine embedded in the Web browser at the target site will execute it.

Figure 5.25 presents the Java environment consisting of the JVM and functions supporting t Java security. We discuss briefly the `classloader` and the `Java security manager`, objects that play a major role in enforcing security [17, 27, 44].

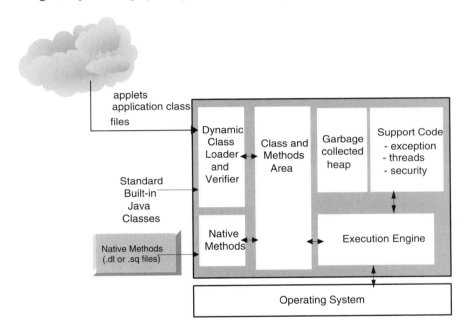

Fig. 5.25 Java environment.

Java objects or classes loaded from the network require a `classloader` to convert the bytecodes to the data structures representing Java classes and to verify that the remote code:

(i) does not violate access restrictions,

(ii) accesses objects by their correct type and methods with arguments of the correct type, and

(iii) does not allow the stack to overflow or forge any pointers.

Another important function of the `classloader` is to create a namespace for the downloaded code and make sure that a remote class does not overwrite local names, e.g., an applet does not overwrite the `classloader` itself.

The `Java security manager` allows only *safe* operations to be performed and throws a security exception when the policy does not allow the code to call a particular method. If an attacker is capable of defying the Java type system then she can circumvent all access control restrictions and run native code on a machine.

The Safe Internet Programming Group at Princeton [28] shows how to generate bytecodes and defeat the type system. Consider for example that C is a protected class and C' is a public class and two classes A and B refer to class C. A classloader could resolve A against C and B against C'. Assume now that an object of class C is allocated in class A and passed as an argument to a method of B. The method will treat the object as having class C'.

One may mail a page requesting a dangerous applet to a potential victim and the browser will automatically load the class file and run the applet. JVM limits the system calls the applet may execute. Most systems implement the *sandbox Java security model*, they only allow the applet to communicate with the host where it came from. But this policy was not properly enforced in earlier browser versions and a sophisticated attacker may be able to circumvent the policies enforced by the Java security manager or the classloader as pointed out earlier.

Denial of service prevents access to resources that would otherwise be available, for example, the attacker could modify the domain name system (DNS) and reroute all packets to/from a host. Most Web servers limit the number of accepted requests at any given time. An attacker may generate requests at a high rate, thus, denying access to legitimate users. Helper applications at the server's site pose similar threats as those at the client site and may allow an attacker to destroy or modify the information available at the server's site.

5.7.5 Remote Method Invocation

We need abstractions to hide the internals of a connection, data representation and network transport. The remote method invocation (RMI) in Java provides such abstractions.

RMI is a Java-specific implementation of a distributed object model. RMI allows objects in one JVM to invoke methods on remote objects residing within another JVM on the same host or located somewhere in the network.

Calls to remote objects differ from calls to local objects:

(i) An object passed as a parameter or returned from a method invoked on a remote object is passed by value not by reference. The object must be serializable or be an instance of a *Remote* object. Several methods with semantics based on object references have been modified for remote objects.

(ii) A remote object must implement one interface extending java.rmi.Remote interface. All interactions between a client and the remote object occur through these interfaces.

The RMI model is described in Figure 5.26. Here the *stub* is the client-side interface to the remote object. The stub initiates the call, marshals the arguments, passes them to a stream controlled by the *remote reference layer* and unmarshals the values returned. In turn, the *skeleton* unmarshals parameters from the marshal stream

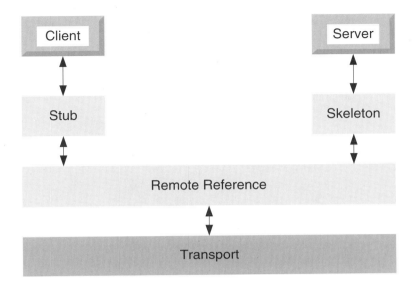

Fig. 5.26 The RMI model.

and marshals return values and exceptions for the client. The remote reference layer mediates between the stub and the skeleton and is responsible for lost connections; it maintains the persistence semantics for client-server connections. The transport substrate is provided by TCP.

5.7.6 Jini

Jini is a distributed computing environment. According to Sun Microsystems, the company that unveiled the Jini technology in early 1999, the goal is to provide "network plug and play," allowing devices to announce their presence and, once connected to the network, offer and request services and move freely throughout the network.

The devices supported by Jini range from computing and communication devices such as hand-held computers, portable phones, mass storage systems, printers, and scanners, to home appliances like toasters or heating and cooling systems. In this vision a heating and cooling system will be connected to the network and provide maintenance information to the company that installed it, report malfunctions to the manufacturer, contact a supplier to order new filters, the power company in case of a power failure, or the home owner in case of emergencies.

A Jini system consists of services, clients, and lookup services. A *Jini community* is a named collection of clients and services typically written in Java and communicating using Jini protocols. Jini addresses the scalability issue by allowing communities to be linked together into *Jini federations*.

When registering with a lookup service the server provides a copy of the code and Jini allows the actual code required to carry out the service to be downloaded to the client's side. Some of the devices may be too primitive to support the full Jini environment; they would only be able to run a wrapper able to gather data from a sensor and send it to a proxy located elsewhere. In this case, when registering with the lookup service, the sever will send a proxy rather than the service itself.

5.7.6.1 *Discovery.* Discovery is the process of finding and then joining Jini communities. The discovery protocols allow a Jini-aware entity to locate communities and discover the location of lookup services. The join protocol then allows it to publish services to the community.

There are several discovery protocols. Lookup services use a *multicast announcement protocol* to make public their presence when they become active. When a client or a service first becomes active it uses a *multicast request protocol* to locate active lookup services. The *unicast discovery protocol* is used by an entity that already knows the particular lookup service it want to connect to. As a result of discovery, the entity is provided with one or more references to the lookup services for the requested community.

5.7.6.2 *Lookup.* The lookup is a long-running service that keeps track of all services that have joined a Jini community. The lookup service maintains a set of objects called *service items*. In turn, a service item consists of a proxy object and a set of attributes describing the service. The proxy object serves as a "front end" for interacting with the service; it allows services and devices to carry with them the code necessary to use them.

A proxy provides an easy way to access a service, very much like a Java applet. The proxy is typically written by the developer of a service and downloaded by the users of that service. While applets are intended for humans, proxies can be used programmatically to compose services.

The server proxy is a serializable Java object stored by the lookup service and downloaded by a client. The interactions between the proxy and the service provider may be different; the proxy may:

(i) consist of an RMI stub used to access the service.

(ii) use a special protocol to talk to (a) the service implemented in a language other than Java, or (b) a primitive device unable to run JVM.

(iii) contain the code necessary to perform the service at the client's site.

It is expected that a set of common services for widely used network devices, e.g., cellular phones, printers, scanners, cameras, storage devices, etc. will be based on standardized interfaces. Clients will be able to search based on the type of the proxy and for nonstandard services they will use the attributes available in service items.

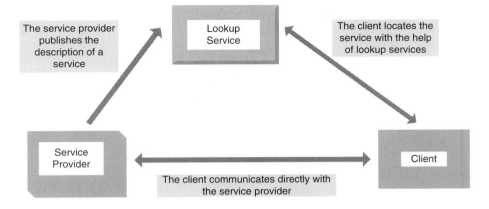

Fig. 5.27   Lookup services in Jini.

5.7.6.3 Leasing. Jini communities are expected to rely on long-running services, e.g., the lookup services, that can stay alive with little or no human intervention for months, possibly years. Traditional resource reservation mechanisms that grant access to resources for an unlimited amount of time are inadequate.

Instead, Jini resources can be leased and the lease must be periodically renewed. At any time the grantor of a lease may deny the request to renew it. The system also supports *third-party leasing*, an entity may delegate the process of lease renewal to a third party. This arrangement is convenient for cases when the service holding a lease is long-lived but rarely active; for example, a back-up service is activated nightly for a limited amount of time. Third-party leasing delegates the handling of events to another object, see Figure 5.28.

5.8 INFORMATION GRIDS

Electricity started to affect profoundly society only after interconnecting individual power stations into power grids. In the late 1990s the North American power grid had more than 10,000 generators, 100,000 transmission lines, 70,000 substations and 130 million customers. Today we cannot conceive life without electricity, black-outs are extremely rare events that remind us how dependent our society is on electric power. The failure of individual power stations goes unnoticed and we regard an entire power grid as a gigantic and very reliable power station. A power grid is a perfect example of a system where the value of the ensemble is higher than the sum of its parts.

There is an enormous diversity of home appliances, industrial installations, transportation systems, medical instruments, and other devices that cannot function without the energy produced by power grids. Yet, customers use electricity without any concern for where it was produced, the topology of the power grid, the type of generators

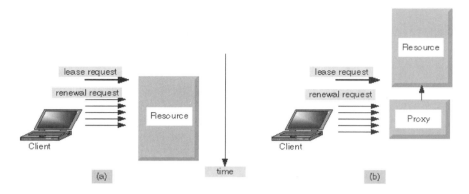

Fig. 5.28   Resource leasing. (a) Direct leasing; the client first sends a request to lease a resource, then sends lease renewal requests periodically. (b) Third-party leasing; a proxy receives the periodic lease renewal requests and updates the reservation table when the resource becomes available.

used, or the characteristics of the transmission lines. We carry along electric appliances from one country or continent to another, and expect them to function properly at a new location. Thus, it is only natural to ask ourselves if we could extend the positive lessons we learned from power distributions to other important areas of human endeavor.

Information, together with energy, are among the most important resources for a modern society. Access to information ensures competitiveness in business, allows industry to create technologically advanced products, creates a better learning environment for students at all levels, helps improve the quality of the health-care system, and supports a credible defense for a country. Information technology empowers scientists to look deeper into the microscopic universe and to understand the atomic structure of biological materials and uncover the structure of the matter, and to look further into the universe to understand how it all started billions of years ago.

Computers are man-made devices that provide the means to store and process information in ways that are qualitatively and quantitatively superior to those available to previous generations. It seems natural to think about creating information grids by linking computers together via high-speed communication channels.

Information grids are not unlike power grids; they are large collections of systems, in this case computers, owned and administered by autonomous organizations, interconnected with one another. Unlike power grids that are expected to deliver one product, electric power, with few, well-defined characteristics, e.g., voltage, intensity, and frequency, an information grid is expected to deliver a broad range of computing services. The set of services evolves in time, as new organizations join the grid while others disappear and the characteristics of services provided by each autonomous organization is subject to change. Thus, an information grid is a very dynamic system whereas a power grid is a static system.

Information grids enjoy favorable economics and allow access to a broad range of state-of-the art facilities to large communities of users. The rapid pace of technological development makes it very difficult for individuals and organizations to keep their own hardware and software state of the art. At the same time, the information grids facilitate collaborative efforts in research as well as industrial, commercial, and business applications.

The sustained effort to define a new computing infrastructure involves many researchers and practitioners. The Global Grid (GG) Forum is an organization whose goal is to study information grids and define standards for various aspects of grid computing. Several grid initiatives are under way: NEESgrid - the Network for Earthquake Engineering and Simulation, the DOE Science Grid, the EuroGrid, the Information Power Grid of NASA, the National Technology Grid, the European Data-Grid, GriPhyN - the Grid Physics Network, $DisCom^2$ - the Distance and Distributed Computing and Communication, Metasystems Thrust, and UNICORE [68]. The main thrust of the effort supported by the GG forum is towards the development of computational grids. Applications of grid computing in computational sciences and engineering are described in Foster and Kesselman [37].

Another notable effort to create a wide-area system to share computing resources, the *Peer-to-Peer (P2P)* working group, is supported by several vendors of computing equipment and software [70]. According to [69]: "Peer-to-peer computing is the sharing of computer resources and services by direct exchange between systems. These resources and services include the exchange of information, processing cycles, cache storage, and disk storage for files."

We distinguish several types of information grids: computational, service, and data grids. *Computational grids* treat computer systems connected at the edge of the Internet as large virtual machines and allow users to execute seamlessly complex computations on these machines when the resources needed are beyond those provided by any single system [24]. *Service grids* allow dynamic composition of services supported by independent service providers. *Data grids* allow controlled access to large volumes of data, spread over the network [59].

The boundaries between these concepts are fuzzy; the three types of grids emphasize: the autonomy of the resources placed at the edge of the Internet and the need for some form of temporal coordination of a subset of resources to obtain a coherent result.

5.8.1 Resource Sharing and Administrative Domains

The defining characteristic of information grids is resource sharing among a large user population in a network environment linking together autonomous systems.

In the context of an information grid the term *resource* is used in a wide sense; it means hardware and software resources, services, and content. *Content* generally means some form of static or dynamic data or knowledge. *Autonomy* implies that the resources are in different domains and resource sharing requires cooperation between the administrative authorities in each domain.

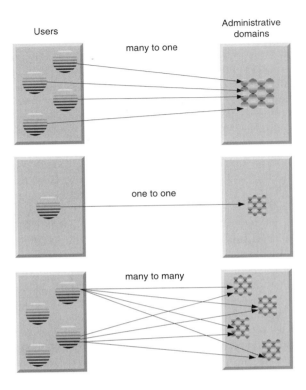

Fig. 5.29 The evolution of the mappings of users and administrative domains, from many-to-one, to one-to-one, and many-to-many. At the top there are multiuser systems, where a relatively small community of users share resources in a single administrative domain. In the middle we see personal computing with one user in one administrative domain. At the bottom a large user population shares resources available from multiple domains.

Sharing computer resources is driven by economics and has evolved over time, see Figure 5.29. In the early days, computer systems were relatively expensive, one system was usually shared among the members of the same organization, and sharing policies were established by a single administrative authority. With the introduction of commodity computing, a one-to-one mapping of users to systems became the norm and the more difficult problems posed by computing resource sharing were partially avoided by the massive introduction of personal computers.

Nowadays, we wish to combine the two paradigms and build an infrastructure allowing virtually an unlimited number of users to share a large numbers of autonomous systems in a transparent manner, subject to some level of quality of service guarantees.

Resource management is a critical aspect of grid design. We distinguish between several levels of resource management based on the granularity of resources. Fine-grain resource management on a grid is extremely challenging because of the scale of the system and the diversity and scope of user requests. To accomplish any task, an agent has to negotiate with the individual authorities controlling the resources needed by the task. The finer the granularity of the resources and the larger the number of entities controlling them, the more difficult the coordination problem becomes.

In addition to economics, there are other driving forces behind the effort to build information grids:

(i) Emerging applications with significant social and economic impact such as telemedicine, distance learning, and electronic commerce. Such applications require multiple services provided by several autonomous organizations.

(ii) Collaborative applications that require very large groups of individuals to co-ordinate their effort to solve a complex task, such as designing an airplane, conducting a high energy physics experiment, or business-to-business applications.

5.8.2   Services in Information Grids

An important feature of a grid is its dynamic and open-ended character. The grid evolves in time and new resources including services are constantly added to the grid, existing ones are modified, others are retired. Thus, a grid needs an infrastructure to mitigate access of the user community to the ever-changing service landscape.

In this section we take a closer look at the architecture of grid services and distinguish between several classes of services and a user-access layer. The service architecture of a grid is summarized in Figure 5.30.

Systemwide services supporting coordinated and transparent access to resources of an information grid are called *societal services*. Examples of societal services are: directory, event, service discovery, QoS support, and persistent storage services.

Specialized services accessed directly by end users are called *end services*. Content-provider services, legal, accounting, monitoring, and tracking are examples of end services. End services and societal services are expected to be offered by independent service providers.

A user-access layer provides uniform and transparent access to services. The most important function of this layer is to support dynamic service composition. Service composition and coordination is critical in a grid where a user is interested in a result that often requires an ad hoc assembly of end services as well as societal services and a mechanism to coordinate them.

There are qualitative and quantitative differences between different types of grids regarding the specific societal and end services provided to the user community.

A data grid allows a community of users to share content. A specialized data grid, supporting a relatively small user community is the one used to share data from high energy physics experiments.

The World Wide Web can be viewed as an example of a data grid. This grid is populated with HTTP, or Web servers, and audio and video streaming servers that provide the content. The user population accesses these servers via the Internet. Yet, in this particular grid societal services are limited and there are virtually no quality of service guarantees.

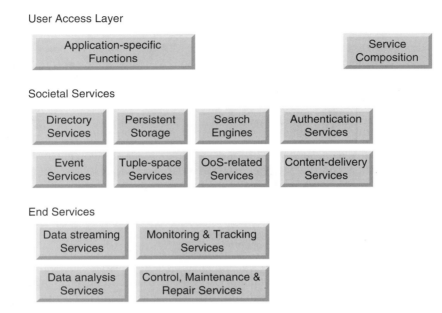

Fig. 5.30 A service-layered architecture model.

Societal services for the World Wide Web are provided by search engines, Web crawlers, and DNS, the Internet directory service. *Content-delivery* services such as those offered by Akamai are also societal services conceived to improve the quality of service without providing any QoS guarantees.

The content-delivery services replicate throughout the Internet some of the content of their client companies as shown in Figure 5.31. This replication removes the bottleneck due to single server access points and ensures the scalability of the Web. Indeed, no single server or cluster of servers could possibly have the communication bandwidth or the computing cycles to deal with the very bursty nature of Web demands where peak request rates can be orders of magnitude larger than the average request rates.

A content-delivery service such as Akamai places its servers at strategically located points in the Internet and replicates dynamically objects in high demand, at a point closer to their consumption.

Portals supports static service coordination in the Web. For example, after buying a book from Amazon.com one could request to have it delivered by FedEx and then access the tracking service provided by FedEx.

5.8.3 Service Coordination

A service grid is expected to support applications such as electronic commerce, telemedicine, distance learning, and business to business. Such applications require a wide spectrum of end services such as monitoring and tracking, remote control,

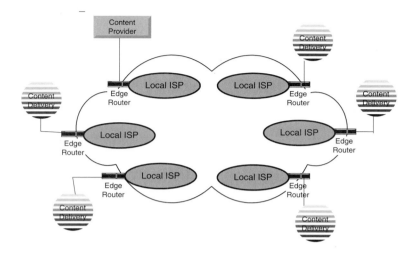

Fig. 5.31   Content-delivery services replicate throughout the Internet objects and audio and video streams from HTTP and data streaming servers, the so-called content providers.

maintenance and repair, online data analysis and business support, as well as services involving some form of human intervention such as legal, accounting, and financial services.

An application of a monitoring service in health care could be monitoring outpatients to ensure that they take the prescribed medication. Controlling the heating and cooling system in a home to minimize energy costs, periodically checking the critical parameters of the system, ordering parts such as air filters, and scheduling repairs is an example of control, maintenance, and repair service. Data analysis services could be used in conjecture with arrays of sensors to monitor traffic patterns or to document visitor's interest at an exhibition.

There are also qualitative differences between service and data grids. The content in a service grid is more dynamic; it is often the result of a cooperative effort of a number of service providers, involves a large number of sensors, and it is tailored to specific user needs. To create the dynamic content we need some form of dynamic service composition. Dynamic service composition has no counterpart in the current Web were portals supports static service coordination.

Consider the task of relocating a family as an example of dynamic service composition. Relocation is a complex activity involving buying and selling homes or renting apartments, registering and unregistering children to schools, closing and opening bank accounts, transferring medical records and locating new health-care providers, getting new license plates, and so on. The process is subject to a set of constraints and it is very different from one case to another. For example, instead of buying a new home one may temporarily rent an apartment and build a house. Some of the activities are themselves composite, for example, building a home may require real-estate, architectural, and financial, end services.

Societal services are also more demanding in a service grid. To avoid total chaos, a service provider should first establish a *contract* with a directory service. Such a contract provides a detailed description of the service in a universal service description language, it describes its preconditions and postconditions, provides a pricing model, the reward or payment model, the terms and conditions for providing the service, and possibly other clauses.

The QoS-oriented services are considerably more intricate in a service grid. For example, the content-delivery services may be difficult or impossible to replicate because of proprietary information. A service provider may have to establish a coalition with service provides in the same area, share with them proprietary information, and agree to back each other up, once the service request rate approaches the capacity of the original service provider.

5.8.4 Computational Grids

We turn our attention to an even more sophisticated type of grid. A *computational grid* is expected to provide transparent access to computing resources for applications requiring a substantial CPU cycle rate, very large memories, and secondary storage that cannot be provided by a single system.

`seti@home` is an example of a distributed application designed to take advantage of unused cycles of PCs and workstations. Once a system joins the project, this application is activated by mechanisms similar to the ones for screen savers. The goal of this project is to detect extraterrestrial intelligence. The participating systems form a primitive computational grid structure; once a system is willing to accept work it contacts a load distribution service, it is assigned a specific task and starts computing. When interrupted by a local user, this task is checkpointed and migrated to the load distribution service.

The requirements placed on the user access layer and societal services are even more stringent for a computational grid than for a service grid. The user access layer must support various programming models and the societal services of a computational grid must be able to handle low-level resource management.

In our view, the most significant difference between a data or service grid on one side and a computational grid on the other side regards the granularity of resource allocation and management, fine-grain for the latter and course-grain for the former.

A service bundles together all or most of the resources necessary for the completion of service. A server, e.g., a Web server, is fine-tuned to coordinate CPU scheduling with secondary storage and network bandwidth management. The internal resource allocation policies and mechanisms are completely invisible to the end user who simply posts a request and gets a reply.

However, an agent coordinating a computation on a computational grid must first dynamically acquire resources, then start up the computation, monitor the execution, check the results, and finally release the resources and shut down the computation. For example, a computational task may need at some point to use a linear system solver. To do so, it has to locate a site where it has execution privileges and where the necessary linear algebra library is available, determine the load on that site, and make sure that a new process can be started, that enough secondary storage to accommodate the input and the output are available on site, that sufficient communication bandwidth exists on the link connecting it to the site. The level of difficulties increases even further when the grid has to support computation steering and large volumes of data have to be transferred from the site where the computation takes place to the site were they are displayed.

Heterogeneity of the software and hardware is a serious concern in a computational grid. It does not really matter if a video server providing an MPEG stream is hosted by a system running Linux or Windows, or if the processor is Pentium or SPARC. Yet, the linear system solver in the previous example is more restrictive, the compilers for the language the linear system solver is written in, may produce slightly different object code for the four operating system/processor combinations discussed above. We may obtain slightly different results using these codes on the four systems.

There is an additional reason why large problems that require a high degree of coordination may be very difficult or even infeasible to solve on a grid. Even if we ignore for the moment the accounting and security issues, the overhead for coordination and control of an application amplifies the resources needed to solve the same problem on a grid.

Suppose that problem X, say a molecular dynamics computation, requires 10^{15} CPU cycles to produce a result. A substantial ratio of the cycles available on all systems connected to the Internet is wasted, one could argue that this particular problem could be solved in a matter of days using spare cycles.

Let us call this quantity the *raw cycle* requirement, r, and let o denote the overhead cycles needed by the system to provide the coordination infrastructure. Then the *adjusted cycle* requirement for this application becomes $a = r + o$.

We have to take into account the communication patterns of the application and the need to coordinate multiple threads of control. This coordination may require some processes to wait for the others at a synchronization point. Thus, the *true cycle* requirement t of a parallel application, running on a grid has an additional component w due to blocking, $t = r + o + w$.

Barrier synchronization is a communication pattern requiring all processes in a group to reach a certain point before any of them is allowed to continue. If we spawn say 1000 processes, each carrying the same computation on a subset of data and if the computation involves several phases, we probably need to synchronize at the end of each phase. If one process in the process group was preempted by the local scheduler, then all other processes in the group will waste a large number of cycles while waiting at the barrier. This leads to one of the more difficult problems in scheduling, the so-called *co-scheduling* or *gang scheduling* when all processes must be active at the same time.

In our example, one could envision a recovery service that would be alerted by the individual processes once they reach the barrier, and in turn this recovery service would either migrate the preempted process or negotiate with the local scheduler to reactivate it. In this case the w component can be reduced at the expense of the o component.

The *true cycle* requirement of a parallel application running on a grid could be orders of magnitude larger than the raw cycle requirements, $t >> r$. In the general case, t depends on the coordinating architecture, the more autonomy the individual nodes of the grid have, the larger the o and w components of t. The two additional components are dependent on the execution environment, e at time t: $o = o(e(t))$, and $w = w(e(t))$.

A qualitative analysis shows that when using N nodes the true cycle requirements per node, $t_N = t/N$ initially decreases because the o and w initially increase slowly when N increases. This translates into reduced execution time measured by the *speedup*.

The speedup of some application may be linear when the computation requires little coordination between the threads of control. In some cases we may even observe a super-linear speedup. Indeed, most systems support a memory hierarchy including cache, main memory, secondary, and ternary storage. Partitioning a large data set into increasingly smaller segments may allow a system to reduce the number of references to the elements of the storage hierarchy with higher latency and improve the cache hit ratios and to reduce the number of page faults or data-staging requests and this would actually contribute to a decrease of the r component.

As N increases the granularity of actual computation assigned to a single node measured by r/N decreases while the coordination and blocking component increase. Thus, we expect to speed up to reach a maximum and then decrease, a well-known fact in the parallel computing community. Alternatively, the curve showing the dependency of t_N on granularity of computation will show a minimum, see Figure 5.32.

Let us now examine the effect of the node autonomy on the true cycle requirement per node. Consider now a fixed number of nodes and several running environments starting with one where all the N nodes are under the control of a single scheduler, and continue with environments where an increasingly smaller number of nodes are under the control of a single scheduler. Clearly, the o and w components increase as the number of autonomous domains increases; we now have the additional overhead of coordination between the autonomous domains. The three curves, a, b, and c, in Figure 5.32 show this effect. Not only the optimal number of true cycle requirements per node increases but also the shape of the curve is likely to be altered, the performance degrades faster as we move away from the optimal functioning point.

5.9   FURTHER READING

The home pages of the World Wide Web Consortium, http://www.w3.org, and of the Apache software foundation, http://apache.org/, provide many useful references to activities related to the Web.

RPCs are defined in RFC 1831 and RFC 1832. DNS is specified in RFC 1034 and RFC 1035. A book by Albitz and Liu gives additional details regarding the domain name servers (DNS) [2].

SMTP, the simple mail transfer protocol, is defined in RFC 821, Multipurpose Internet Mail Extensions (MIME) in RFC 822, MIME formats in RFC 1521, the

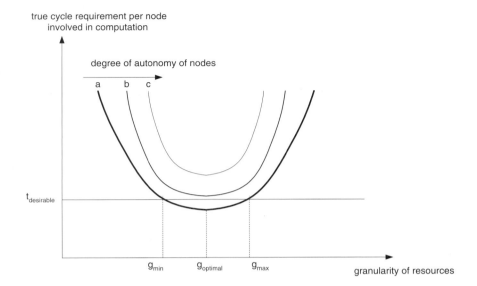

true cycle requirement per node
involved in computation

degree of autonomy of nodes

a   b   c

$t_{desirable}$

g_{min} $g_{optimal}$ g_{max}

granularity of resources

Fig. 5.32   The effect of resource allocation granularity and the degree of node autonomy on the true cycle requirement per node in a computational grid. The three curves correspond to different degrees of node autonomy, the autonomy increases from a to b and then to c.

format of extra headers in RFC 2045 and RFC 2046, POP3 in RFC 1939, IMAP in RFC 1730. The time format is defined in RFC 1123, GZIP in RFC 1952, the procedure to register a new media type with Internet Assigned Numbers Authority in RFC 1590,

There is a rather long list of RFCs pertinent to the Web. URLs are defined in RFC 1738 and RFC 1808. HTTP, the Hypertext Transfer Protocol, is defined by Fielding, Gettys, Mogul, Frystyk, and Berners-Lee in RFC 2068 and RFC 2069. HTML, the Hypertext Markup Language, is introduced by Berners-Lee and Connolly in RFC 1866. ICP, the Internet Caching Protocol is presented in RFC 2186. Other standards pertinent to the Web are US-ASCII coded character set defined by ANSI X3.4-1986, the Backus-Naur Form (BNF) used to define the syntax of HTTP presented in RFC 822, the Message Digest 5 (MD5) in RFC 1321, a protocol for secure software distribution in RFC 1805.

The web was first described by T. Berners-Lee and his co-workers in [9, 10]. The book by Hethmon gives an in-depth coverage of HTTP [34]. Web performance is the subject of several articles [8, 18, 46] and it is also covered in the book by Menasce and Almeida [43].

Web workload characterization is covered in [3, 4]. A good source for the Web security is [58]. Applications of the Web to real-time audio and video are presented in [16]. Information about *Jigsaw*, a Java-based web server is provided by [62].

Protocols for multimedia applications are the subject of several RFCs. RTP, the real-time transmission protocol is defined by Schulzrinne, Casner, Frederick, and

Jacobson in RFC 1889. RSVP, the resource reservation protocol is defined by Braden, Zhang, Berson, Herzog, and Jamin in RFC 2205. LDAP and its API are described by RFC 1777 and RFC 1823.

A good introduction to multimedia communication is provided in [67]. The book by Halsall [29] covers in depth multimedia applications and their requirements. The JPEG and MPEG standards are introduced in [64] and [38], respectively. Video streaming is discussed in [33, 41, 65]. QoS is discussed in [11].

Active networks are analyzed in [61, 66]. There is a wealth of literature on resource management in open systems, middleware for resource management, resource discovery [1, 6, 7, 30, 31, 32, 36, 40, 45, 49, 56]. Several papers present resource management in large scale systems [1, 15, 23, 25, 57].

Code mobility is discussed in [14, 19, 26, 39, 50, 63] and protocols supporting mobility in [42, 48].

There is vast literature on distributed object systems including [13, 22, 35, 52, 53, 54, 60]. Several books cover the Java language, Java threads, the Java virtual machine (JVM) networking and network programming, remote method invocation (RMI), and Jini [5, 17, 17, 20, 21, 27, 44, 51].

The *Global Grid forum* [68] provides up to date information about grid-related activities. The *P2P* site [69] points to various activities of the *Peer-to-Peer* organization. The book edited by I. Foster and C. Kesselman [37] contains a collection of papers devoted to various aspects of computing on a grid.

5.10 EXERCISES AND PROBLEMS

Problem 1. State the Nyquist theorem and then provide an intuitive justification for it. Define all the terms involved in your definition. Compute the amount of data on a CD containing 100 minutes of classical music (assume that the highest frequency in the spectrum is 24,000 Hz and that 256 levels are insufficient for discretization and more than 30,000 are not useful).

Problem 2. Facsimile transmission, commonly called FAX, uses the following procedure for sending text and images: the document is scanned, converted into a bit matrix, and the bit matrix is transmitted.

An 8×6 inch text has 12 characters/inch and 6 lines/inch. Assume that digitization uses a 100×100 dot matrix per square inch. Compare the bandwidth needed for facsimile transmission with the one needed when transmitting ASCII characters.

Problem 3. You want to provide access to a data streaming server from an Web browser.

(i) Describe the architecture of the system. Draw a diagram of the system.

(ii) List the six communication protocols involved and explain the function of each. Discuss the in-band and the out-band communication protocols in detail.

(iii) Describe the sequence of actions that take place starting with the instance you click on the URL of the data streaming server.

Problem 4. RTCP can be used in conjunction with multicasting of audio or video streams. In this case the bandwidth consumed by RTP is constant but the bandwidth consumed by RTCP grows linearly with the number of receivers.

(i) Imagine a scheme to keep the RTCP traffic limited to a fraction of the total bandwidth necessary for the multicast transmission.

(ii) Imagine your own scheme to compute the jitter and then compare it with the one in RFC

Problem 5. A scalable Web server architecture could be based on clusters of servers placed behind a front end, see Section 5.5.7. The front end may act as a proxy; alternatively, it may hand off the TCP connection to one of the nodes in the cluster, selected based on the contents of the request, the source of the request, the load of the individual nodes in the cluster, and so on.

(i) What is the advantage of the TCP connection hand off versus the proxy approach; discuss the case of persistent and nonpersistent HTTP connections.

(ii) Using the Web search engines, locate several papers describing systems based on this architecture.

(iii) The TCP protocol maintains state information at the server side. Identify the networking software in Linux that would be affected by the TCP connection hand off. What changes of the networking software in Linux would be necessary to support TCP connection hand off?

Problem 6. The Web page of an amateur photographer points to 10 still photos taken with a high-resolution digital camera. Each picture has 4.0 Mpixels and each pixel is 16 bits wide. A benchmarking program compares the response time for nonpersistent and persistent HTTP connections. Assume that $RTT = 10 msec$ and calculate the response time the benchmarking program is expected to determine in the two cases.

Problem 7. Write a Java server program `PicoServer.java` and client program, `PicoClient.java` communicating via a TCP connection.

(i) The client should read a local text file consisting of a set of lines and send it to the server. The server should search for the occurrence of a set of keywords in a thesaurus and send back to the client the lines of text containing any word in the thesaurus.

(ii) Modify the `PicoClient.java` program as follows: The client should first contact your Email server and retrieve an Email message using the POP3 protocol. Make sure that the Email message is not deleted from your Email server and that you do not hardcode the userid and the password into your code. Then, the client should send the text to your server, to determine if words in the thesaurus are found in the message. If a match is found, the client should use SMTP to send you the message with priority set to highest and with the word "Urgent" added to the Subject line and then to delete the original message. Use RFC 1939 to discover the syntax of the POP commands and RFC 821 for SMTP.

REFERENCES

1. D. Agrawal, A. Abbadi, and R. Steinke. Epidemic Algorithms in Replicated Databases. In *Proc. 16th ACM SIGACT-SIGMOD-SIGART Symp. on Principles of Database Systems*, pages 161–172, 1997.

2. P. Albitz and C. Liu. *DNS and BIND*. O'Reilly, Sebastopol, California, 1993.

3. M. Arlitt and T. Jin. A Workload Characterization Study of the 1998 World Cup Web Site. *IEEE Network*, May/June:30–37, 2000.

4. M. F. Arlitt and C. L. Williamson. Internet Web Servers: Workload Characterization and Performance Implications. *IEEE/ACM Transactions on Networking*, 5(5):631–645, 1997.

5. K. Arnold, A. Wollrath, B. O'Sullivan, R. Scheifler, and J. Waldo. *The Jini Specification*. Addison Wesley, Reading, Mass., 1999.

6. S. Assmann and D. Kleitman. The Number of Rounds Needed to Exchange Information within a Graph. *SIAM Discrete Applied Math*, (6):117–125, 1983.

7. A. Baggio and I. Piumarta. Mobile Host Tracking and Resource Discovery. In *Proc. 7th ACM SIGOPS European Workshop*, Connemara (Ireland), September 1996.

8. P. Barford and M. E. Crovella. Measuring Web Performance in the Wide Area. *Performance Evaluation Review*, 27(2):37-48, 1999.

9. T. Berners-Lee, R. Cailliau, J-F. Groff, and B. Pollermann. World-Wide Web: An Information Infrastructure for High-Energy Physics. *Proc. Workshop on Software Engineering, Artificial Intelligence and Expert Systems for High Energy and Nuclear Physics*, January 1992.

10. T. J. Berners-Lee, R. Cailliau, and J.-F. Groff. The World-Wide Web. *Computer Networks and ISDN Systems*, 25(4–5):454–459, 1992.

11. S. Bhatti and G. Knight. Enabling QoS Adaptation Decisions for Internet Applications. *Computer Networks*, 31(7):669–692, 1999.

12. A. Birell and B. Nelson. Implementing Remote Procedure Calls. *ACM TRans. on Computer Systems*, 2(1):39–59, 1984.

13. G. Booch. *Object–Oriented Analysis and Design with Applications.* Addison Wesley, Reading, Mass., 1994.

14. L. Cardelli. Abstractions for Mobile Computing. In *Secure Internet Programming: Security Issues for Mobile and Distributed Objects, Lecture Notes in Computer Science*, volume 1603, pages 51–94. Springer–Verlag, Heidelberg, 1999.

15. S. Chapin, D. Katramatos, J. Karpovich, and A. Grimshaw. Resource Management in Legion. In *Proc. 5th Workshop on Job Scheduling Strategies for Parallel Processing, at IPDPS 99, Lecture Notes in Computer Science*, volume 1659, pages 162–178. Springer–Verlag, Heidelberg, 1999.

16. Z. Chen, S. M. Tan, R. H. Campbell, and Y. Li. Real Time Video and Audio in the World Wide Web. *World Wide Web Journal*, 1, January 1996.

17. T. Courtois. *Java: Networking and Communication.* Prentice Hall, Englewood Cliffs, New Jersey, 1998.

18. M. Crovella and A. Bestavros. Self-Similarity in World Wide Web Traffic Evidence and Possible Causes. In *Proc. ACM SIGMETRICS 96, Performance Evaluation Review*, 24(1):160–169, 1996.

19. G. Cugola, C. Ghezzi, G.P. Picco, and G. Vigna. Analyzing Mobile Code Languages. In *Mobile Object Systems: Towards the Programmable Internet, Lecture Notes in Computer Science*, volume 1122. Springer–Verlag, Heidelberg, 1997.

20. T. B. Downing. *Java RMI.* IDG Books, 1998.

21. W. K. Edwards. *Core Jini.* Prentice Hall, Upper Saddle River, New Jersey, 1999.

22. E. Grama, R. Helm, R. Johnson, and J. Vlissides. *Design Patterns: Elements of Reusable Object-Oriented Software.* Addison Wesley, Reading, Mass., 1995.

23. S. Fitzgerald, I. Foster, C. Kesselman, G. Laszewski, W. Smith, and S. Tuecke. A Directory Service for Configuring High-Performance Distributed Computations. In *Proc. 6th IEEE Symp. on High-Performance Distributed Computing*, pages 365–375, 1997.

24. I. Foster, C. Kaasselman, and S. Tuecke. The Anatomy of the Grid: Enabling Scalable Virtual Organizations. Int. Journal of High Performance Computing Applications, 15(3):200-222, 2000.

25. I. Foster and C. Kesselman. Globus: A Metacomputing Infrastructure Toolkit. *Int. Journal of Supercomputer Applications and High Performance Computing*, 11(2):115–128, 1997.

26. A Fuggetta, G. P. Picco, and G. Vigna. Understanding Code Mobility. *IEEE Transactions on Software Engineering*, 24(5):342–361, 1998.

27. M. Grand. *Java Language.* O'Reilly, Sebastopol, California, 1997.

28. The Safe Internet Programming Group. URL http://www.cs.princeton. edu sip.

29. F. Halsall. *Multimedia Communications: Applications, Networks, Protocols, and Standards.* Addison-Wesley, Reading, Mass., 2001.

30. M. Harchol-Balter, T. Leighton, and D. Lewin. Resource Discovery in Distributed Networks. In *Proc. 18th Annual ACM Sym. on Principles of Distributed Computing, PODC'99*, pages 229–237. IEEE Press, Piscataway, New Jersey, 1999.

31. S. Hedetniemi, S. Hedetniemi, and A. Liestman. A Survey of Gossiping and Broadcasting in Communication Networks. *Networks*, (18):319–349, 1988.

32. W. R. Heinzelman, J. Kulik, and H. Balakrishnan. Adaptive Protocols for Information Dissemination in Wireless Sensor Networks. In *Proc. 5th Annual ACM/IEEE Int. Conf. on Mobile Computing and Networking (MobiCom-99)*, pages 174–185, ACM Press, New York, 1999.

33. M. Hemy, U. Hengartner, P. Steenkiste, and T. Gross. MPEG System Streams in Best-Effort Networks. In *Proc. Packet Video'99*, April 1999.

34. P.S. Hethmon. *Illustrated Guide to HTTP*. Manning, Greenwich, Conn., 1997.

35. S. Hirano, Y. Yasu, and H. Igarashi. Performance Evaluation of Popular Distributed Object Technologies for Java. *Concurrency: Practice and Experience*, 10(11–13):927–940, 1998.

36. J. Huang, R. Jha, W. Heimerdinger, M. Muhammad, S. Lauzac, and B. Kannikeswaran. RT-ARM: A Real-Time Adaptive Resource Management System for Distributed Mission-Critical Applications. In *Proc. IEEE Workshop on Middleware for Distributed Real-Time Systems and Services*, December 1997.

37. I. Foster and C. Kesselman, editor. *The Grid: Blueprint for a New Computer Infrastructure*, first edition. Morgan Kaufmann, San Francisco, 1999.

38. ISO. Coding of Moving Pictures and Associated Audio - for Digital Storage Media at up to about 1.5Mbits/sec. Technical Report, ISO, 1992.

39. D. Kotz and R. S. Gray. Mobile Code: The Future of the Internet. In *Proc. Workshop "Mobile Agents in the Context of Competition and Cooperation (MAC3)" at Autonomous Agents '99*, pages 6–12, 1999.

40. B. Li and K. Nahrstedt. A Control-Based Middleware Framework for Quality of Service Adaptations. *IEEE Journal of Selected Areas in Communications, Special Issue on Service Enabling Platforms*, 17(8):1632-1650, 1999.

41. X. Li, S. Paul, and M. Ammar. Layered Video Multicast with Retransmissions (LVMR): Evaluation of Hierarchical Rate Control. In *Proc. IEEE INFOCOM*

98, Proceedings IEEE, pages 1062–1073, IEEE Press, Piscataway, New Jersey, 1998.

42. D. Montgomery M. Ranganathan, M. Bednarek. A Reliable Message Delivery Protocol for Mobile Agents. In D. Kotz and F. Mattern, editors, *Agent Systems, Mobile Agents, and Applications, Lecture Notes on Computer Science*, volume 1882, pages 206–220. Springer–Verlag, Heidelberg, 2000.

43. D. A. Menascè and V. A. F. Almeida. *Capacity Planning for Web Performance: Metrics, Models, and Methods*. Prentice-Hall, Englewood Cliffs, New Jersey, 1998.

44. J. Meyer and T.B. Downing. *Java Virtual Machine*. O'Reilly, Sebastopol, California, 1997.

45. N. Minar, K. H. Kramer, and P. Maes. *Cooperating Mobile Agents for Dynamic Network Routing*, chapter 12. Springer–Verlag, Heidelberg, 1999.

46. D. Mosberger and T. Jin. httperf: A Tool for Measuring Web Server Performance. In *Proc. Internet Server Performance Workshop*, pages 59–67, 1998.

47. S. Mullender. Amoeba: A Distributed Operating System for the 1990s. *IEEE Computer*, 23(5):44–53, May 1990.

48. A. Murphy and G.P. Picco. A Reliable Communication for Highly Mobile Agents. In *Agent Systems and Architectures/Mobile Agents*, Lecture Notes on Computer Science, pages 141–150, Springer-Verlag, Heidelberg, 1999.

49. K. Nahrstedt, H. Chu, and S. Narayan. QoS-Aware Resource Management for Distributed Multimedia Applications. *Journal on High-Speed Networking, Special Issue on Multimedia Networking*, 2000.

50. B. Noble, M. Satyanarayanan, D. Narayanan, J. Tilton, J. Flinn, and K. Walker. Agile Application-aware Adaptation for Mobility. In *Proc. 16th ACM Symp. on Operating Systems and Principles, Operating Systems Review*, 31(5):276-287, 1997.

51. S. Oaks and H.Wong. *Java Threads*. O'Reilly, Sebastopol, California, 1997.

52. OMG. *The Common Object Request Broker : Architecture and Specification. Revision 2.3*. OMG Technical Committee Document 99-10-07, October 1999.

53. R. Orfali and D. Harkey. *Client/Server Programming with JAVA and CORBA*. John Wiley & Sons, New York, 1997.

54. R. Orfali, D. Harkey, and J. Edwards. *Instant CORBA*. John Wiley & Sons, New York, 1997.

55. J. K. Ousterhout, A.R. Cherenson, F. Douglis, M.N. Nelson, and B. B. Welch. The Sprite Network Operating System. *IEEE Computer*, 21(2):23–36, 1988.

56. A. Pelc. Fault-tolerant Broadcasting and Gossiping in Communication. *Networks*, (28):143–156, 1996.

57. R. Raman, M. Livny, and M. Solomon. Matchmaking: Distributed Resource Management for High Throughput Computing. In *Proc. 7th IEEE Int. Symp. on High Performance Distributed Computing*, pages 140–146, IEEE Press, Piscataway, New Jersey, 1998.

58. A. D. Rubin, D. Geer, and M. G. Ranum. *WEB Security Sourcebook*. John Wiley & Sons, New York, 1997.

59. I. Serafini, H. Stockinger, K. Stockinger, and F. Zini. Agent-based Querry Optimization in a Grid Environment. Technical Report, ITC - IRST, Povo(Trento), Italy, November 2000.

60. R. Sessions. *COM and DCOM: Microsoft's Vision for Distributed Objects*. John Wiley & Sons, New York, 1997.

61. J. Smith, K. Calvert, S. Murphy, H. Orman, and L. Peterson. Activating Networks: A Progress Report. *Computer*, 31(4):32-41, 1999.

62. W3C: The World Wide Web Consortium. Jigsaw: Java Web Server. URL `http://www.w3c.org`.

63. J. Waldo, G. Wyant, A. Wollrath, and S. Kendall. A Note on Distributed Computing. In *Mobile Object Systems: Towards the Programmable Internet, Lecture Notes in Computer Science*, volume 1997, pages 49–64. Springer–Verlag, Heidelberg, 1997.

64. G. K. Wallace. The JPEG Still Picture Compression Standard. *Communications of the ACM*, 34(4):30–44, 1991.

65. J. Walpole, R. Koster, S. Cen, C. Cowan, D. Maier, D. McNamee, C. Pu, D. Steere, and L. Yu. A Player for Adaptive MPEG Video Streaming over the Internet. In *Proc. 26th Applied Imagery Pattern Recognition Workshop AIPR-97, SPIE*, volume 3240, pages 270-281, 1998.

66. D. Wetherall, J. Guttag, and D. Tennenhouse. ANTS: A Toolkit for Building and Dynamically Deploying Network Protocols. *Proc. IEEE INFOCOM 98*, pages 117–129, IEEE Press, Piscataway, New Jersey, 1998.

67. L. Wolf, C. Gridwodz, and R. Steinmetz. Multimedia Communication. In *Proc. of the IEEE*, volume 85(12):1915–1933, 1997.

68. Global Grid Forum. URL `http://www.gridforum.org`., 2001.

69. Peer to Peer. URL `http://www.peertopeerwg.org`., 2001.

70. Will P2P Computing Survive or Evolve into Distributed Resource Management: a White Paper. URL `http://www.peertopeerwg.org`., 2001.

6

Coordination and Software Agents

Coordination is a very broad subject with applications to virtually all areas of science and engineering, management, social systems, defense systems, education, health care, and so on. Human life is an exercise in coordination, each individual has to coordinate his own activities with the activities of others, groups of individuals have to coordinate their efforts to achieve a meaningful result.

Coordination is critical for the design and engineering of new man-made systems and important for understanding the behavior of existing ones. Explicit coordination is at the heart of workflow management; the function of a workflow enactment engine is to ensure coordination of different component activities. For this reason we explore in this chapter coordination models, mechanisms, and technologies.

Coordination is an important dimension of computing. An algorithm describes the flow of control, the flow of data, or both; a program implementing the algorithm coordinates the software and the hardware components involved in a computation. The software components are library modules interspaced with user code executed by a single thread of control in case of sequential computations; in this case the hardware is controlled through system calls supported by the operating system running on the target hardware platform.

Coordination of distributed and/or concurrent computations is more complex, it involves software components based on higher level abstractions, such as objects, agents, and programs as well as multiple communication and computing systems. Throughout this chapter we are only concerned with coordination in an open system where individual components are course grain software systems running on computers interconnected via a wide area network. Each process description of an workflow provides an ad hoc linking of such systems.

Software agents provide an appealing technology for coordination. We discuss the autonomy, intelligence, and mobility and then we examine other defining attributes of an agent.

This chapter is organized as follows. In Section 6.1 we analyze the relationship between coordination and autonomy. In Sections 6.2 and 6.3 we present coordination models and techniques. We discuss the challenges of coordination in an open system interconnected by a wide area network and contrast endogeneous and exogeneous systems. In exogeneous systems the coordination is separated from the main functionality of the system. We overview coordination based on scripting languages, middle agents, and shared data spaces.

6.1 COORDINATION AND AUTONOMY

Coordination means managing the interactions and dependencies of the entities of a system. Interactions and dependencies are terms used in a broad sense, interactions cover any form of communication between system components, dependencies refer to spatial, temporal, causal relationships.

Virtually all man-made systems have a built-in coordination entity, the more complex the system, the more sophisticated this entity. The *control unit* (CU) of a microprocessor coordinates the execution of instructions. The CU does not produce any visible results, it only generates the control signals that trigger actions of other components that perform functions with visible side effects. For example, the *instruction fetch unit* brings in a new instruction from the main memory; the *instruction decoding unit* determines the operation to be performed and the operands; the *arithmetic and logic unit* (ALU) performs arithmetic and logic operations on integers; the *floating point unit* performs a similar function on floating point data.

The air traffic control system is an example of a complex coordination system that involves interactions between diverse entities such as humans, computer systems, mechanical systems, radar systems, communication systems, and weather systems. The interactions patterns among these systems are fairly complex and so are the resulting actions. Sensors display information about the parameters of the engines, the pilot declares an emergency condition, the air traffic controller grants permission to land, the pilot manipulates various levers, the engines produce less power, the control surfaces modify their geometry and orientation, the radar system reports the position of the airplane, and so on. The air traffic control system has to take into account an extraordinary number of dependencies: out of the few thousand airplanes in the air at any given time, no airplane can find itself within a safety box around any other airplane, no airplane can fly further than the amount of fuel in its tanks allows, an airplane cannot land before taking off, and so on.

In the general case, the components of a system are designed independently and expected to exhibit a certain degree of autonomy. *Autonomy* means that an entity may act independently, outside the spirit, or without the intervention of the coordinating entity(s). The pilot of an airplane, at his own initiative, may depart from his assigned flying path and take evasive actions to avoid another flying object. The airplanes must fly autonomously for prolonged periods of time when a power failure shuts down the air traffic control system.

The concept of autonomy of man-made systems deserves further scrutiny. The trait we described in the previous paragraph reflects *behavioral autonomy*. The *design autonomy* reflects the need to create components that are multifunctional. An airplane manufacturer uses the same basic design for passenger and cargo planes to defer large development costs. The *configuration autonomy* reflects the ability of individual organization to adjust a component to its own needs. For example, two different airlines may install different engines on the same airplane model, the number of passenger seats may be different.

The proper balance between autonomy and coordination is case-specific. Coordination in a microprocessor is very tight, a finite state machine describes precisely the states and the events causing transitions; the CU implements that state machine and reacts to each event causing a change of state. The coordination of an assembly line leaves little autonomy to the humans, or to the robots performing individual assembly tasks. At the opposite side of the spectrum, a student working on her doctoral dissertation, a climber attempting to reach the summit of K9, or a robot on a space probe, have a higher degree of autonomy.

The relationship between the autonomy of entities involved in a complex task and the coordination are very intricate. An intuitive analogy is to assimilate components with atoms, autonomy with repulsive forces attempting to keep them apart, and coordination with attraction forces binding them together, see Figure 6.1. At equilibrium the balance between the two types of forces determines the distance between atoms, or the proper balance between autonomy and coordination effects.

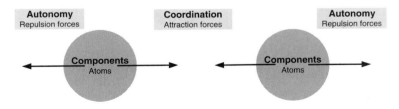

Fig. 6.1   A physical analogy of the interactions between autonomy and coordination.

We can examine the relationship between autonomy and coordination of a system with many components from the point of view of information theory. A larger degree of autonomy increases the entropy; given two system with identical components, the one consisting of components with additional degrees of freedom has a larger entropy. However, coordination tends to reduce the number of degrees of freedom of the system and decreases its entropy.

Coordination is an *invisible* activity, when properly conducted it leads to the successful completion of a complex task, with minimal overhead and best possible results. In the context of our previous example, if all airplanes land and depart precisely at the scheduled time, the air traffic control system has done a very good job.

While it is generally straightforward to assess the quality of service and the performance of individual components, it is harder to assess the quality and performance of coordination activities. We cannot possibly conclude that the air traffic system is faulty when the airplanes experience delays. Only a very intricate analysis may reveal that the endemic delays may be due to the airlines, the weather, the airports, the traffic control system, or to a combination of causes.

This uncertainty transcends man-made systems, it is encountered at various scales in social systems. For example, the administration of a University functioning very smoothly is transparent to both students and faculty and the only information available to the outside world is that the education and research missions of the university are accomplished flawlessly. However, an incompetent university administration may hide behind this uncertainty and blame the ills of a poorly functioning university on faculty and/or students.

We argued earlier, in Chapter 1, that coordination on a computational or service grid increases the overhead of carrying out a complex task. This is a general phenomenon, any form of coordination adds its own communication patterns and algorithms to assess the dependencies among components.

Can we define formal models of coordination that transcend the specifics of a particular application? Are there specific coordination abstractions? Can we separate the framework for expressing interactions from the interactions themselves? Can we talk about a coordination discipline?

The answers to some of these questions are not obvious to us. In most instances we can separate the coordination aspects of a complex activity from the tasks involved and encapsulate them into reusable software components. But, it is yet to be determined whether we can create a complete set of orthogonal coordination abstractions that can span the space, or, in other words, are suitable for all coordination schemes that may arise in practice.

An analysis of social experiments is not very helpful either. We can ask ourselves the question if the society can train successfully individuals whose role is to coordinate, regardless of the domain they are expected to work with. High-tech companies are examples of large organizations that require insightful coordination. If we analyze such companies, we see that some are led by individuals with sound technical background but no formal managerial training, others by individuals who have no formal technical training, but have an MBA degree. There are success stories as well as horror stories in each group.

Human-centric coordination has been the only form of coordination for some time. We are now in the process of delegating restricted subsets of coordination function to computers. This delegation can only be successful if we understand well the mechanisms and models used by humans.

6.2 COORDINATION MODELS

Let us now discuss coordination models. They provide the glue to tie together services and agents in globally distributed computing systems. We restrict our discussion to computer-centric coordination and to the communication media we have become familiar with, the Internet. Clearly, communication is a critical facet of coordination and this justifies our in-depth coverage of computer networks and distributed systems in previous chapters.

The great appeal of *stored program computers* is that they can be programmed to perform a very broad range of coordination functions, provided that they can be interfaced with sensors reporting the state of the system and with actuators allowing them to perform actions resulting in changes of the environment. Microprocessors are routinely used to coordinate various aspects of the interactions of a system with its environment; they are embedded into mechanical systems such as cars, airplanes, and into electromechanical systems, such as home appliances and medical devices, and into electronic systems, and so on.

Thus the entities involved in computer-centric coordination are processes. Yet, we are primarily interested in hybrid systems involving humans and computers. A subset of processes involved in coordination are connected to humans, sensors, actuators, communication systems, and other type of devices.

We want to further limit the scope of our discussion and Figure 6.2 illustrates a three-dimensional space for coordination models. The first dimension reflects the type of the network, an interconnection network of a parallel system, a local area network, or a wide area network; the second dimension describes the type of coordination, centralized, or distributed; the third dimension reflects the character of the system, closed, or open.

A computer network provides the communication substrate and its characteristics provide the first dimension of a coordination space. The individual entities can be co-located in space within a single system, they can be distributed over a LAN, or over a WAN. Our primary interest is in the WAN case, we are interested in Internet-wide coordination. In Chapter 4 we presented the defining attributes of a WAN and the effect of faults, communication delays, and limited bandwidth on applications running at the periphery of the network.

Coordination in a WAN is a more difficult problem than coordination confined to a LAN or to a single system; we have to deal with multiple administrative domains and in theory communication delays are unbounded. In a WAN it is more difficult to address performance, security, or quality of service issues.

There are two approaches to coordination, a centralized and a distributed one. Centralized coordination is suitable in some instances, for example, in case of *ad hoc service composition*. Suppose that one user needs a super service involving several services; in this case an agent acting on behalf of the user coordinates the composition.

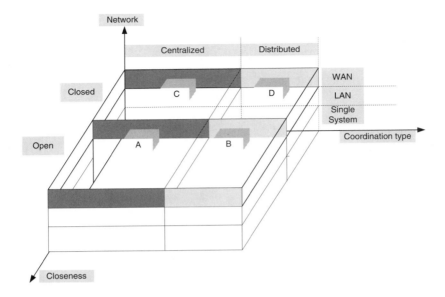

Fig. 6.2 A three-dimensional space for coordination models. The coordination can be centralized, or distributed; the components to be coordinated may be confined to a single system, to a LAN, or to a WAN; the system may be open, or closed. We are most interested in centralized and distributed coordination of open systems in WAN.

For now the term *agent* simply means a program capable of providing a user interface as well as interfaces with all the services involved.

In other cases, a distributed coordination approach has distinct benefits. Consider, for example, a complex weather service with a very large number of sensors, of the order of millions, gathering weather-related data. The system uses information from many databases; some contain weather data collected over the years, others archive weather models. The system generates short-, medium-, and long-range forecasts. Different functions of this service such as data acquisition, data analysis, data management, weather information services will most likely be coordinated in a distributed fashion. A hierarchy of coordination centers will be responsible for data collected from satellites, another group will coordinate terrestrial weather stations, and yet another set of centers will manage data collected by vessels and sensors from the oceans.

The last dimension of interest of the coordination space reflects whether the system is closed and all entities involved are known at the time when the coordination activity is initiated, or the system is open and allows new entities to join or leave at will. Coordination in an open system is more difficult than coordination in a closed system. Error recovery and fault tolerance become a major concern, a component suddenly fails or leaves the system without prior notice. The dynamics of coordination changes;

we cannot stick to a precomputed coordination plan, we may have to revise it. The state of the system must be reevaluated frequently to decide if a better solution involving components that have recently joined the system exits.

We concentrate on open systems because Internet resources, including services, are provided by autonomous organizations and such resources join and leave the system at will. We are primarily interested in coordination models of type A and B; type A refers to centralized coordination of open systems with the communication substrate provided by a WAN; type B refers to decentralized coordination of open systems with the communication substrate provided by a WAN.

To make our task even more challenging, we have to take into account component mobility. Some of the components may migrate from one location to another at runtime. Since communication among entities is a critical facet of coordination we reexamine the communication paradigms and accommodate entity mobility. For example, consider an agent communicating with a federation of agents using the TCP protocol. When the agent migrates to a new location we can either close the existing TCP connections and reopen them from the new site or hand off the connections to the new site. The first option is suitable when agent migration seldom occurs; the second option is technically more difficult.

Let us look now at coordination models from a constructive perspective and ask ourselves whether or not the coordination primitives must be embedded into individual components. Another question is how to support coordination mechanisms, see Figure 6.3.

The answer to the first question is that we may have *endogeneous* coordination systems and models where entities are responsible for receiving and delivering coor-

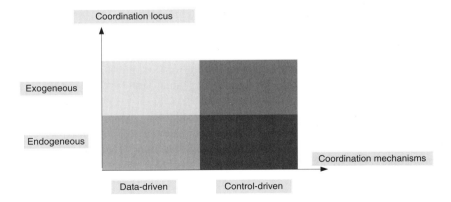

Fig. 6.3 A constructive classification of coordination systems and models: endogeneous versus exogeneous and data-driven versus control-driven. In endogeneous systems entities are responsible for receiving and delivering coordination information and, at the same time, for coordinating their actions with other components. In exogeneous systems, the entities are capable of reacting to coordination information, but the actual coordination is outside of their scope. In data-driven systems individual entities receive data items, interpret and react to them, whereas in control-driven systems the entities receive commands and react to them.

dination information and, at the same time, for coordinating their actions with other components. In *exogeneous* coordination systems and models the entities are capable of reacting to coordination information, but the actual coordination is outside of their scope, there are external coordinating entities whose only function is to support the coordination mechanisms. For example, in the case of workflow management the coordination functions are concentrated into the workflow enactment engine.

We believe that the exogeneous coordination models have distinct advantages; they exhibit a higher degree of:

   (i) design autonomy of individual components,

   (ii) behavioral autonomy; the coordination functions are concentrated in several entities that can adapt better to changing environments.

The answer to the second question is that we distinguish between data-driven or control-driven coordination models. In *data-driven* coordination models individual entities receive data items, interpret and react to them. In *control-driven* models the entities receive commands and react to them. The emphasis is on the control flow. The two models are dual; their duality mirrors the duality of message passing and remote method invocation.

Although these classifications are useful to structure the model space, sometimes the boundaries between different models are not clear. For example, the boundaries between data-driven and control-driven models may be quite fuzzy; if a resource requires periodic renewal of its lease, the very presence of a message indicates that the sender is alive and the lease is automatically renewed.

6.3 COORDINATION TECHNIQUES

We distinguish between low-level and high-level coordination issues. Low-level coordination issues are centered on the delivery of coordination information to the entities involved; high-level coordination covers the mechanisms and techniques leading to coordination decisions.

The more traditional distributed systems are based on *direct communication models* like the one supported by remote procedure call protocols to implement the client-server paradigm. A client connected to multiple servers is an example of a simple coordination configuration; the client may access services successively, or a service may in turn invoke additional services.

In this model there is a direct coupling between interacting entities in terms of name, place, and time. To access a service, a client needs to know the name of the service, the location of the service, and the interaction spans a certain time interval.

Mediated coordination models ease some of the restrictions of the direct model by allowing an intermediary, e.g., a directory service to locate a server, an event service to support asynchronous execution, an interface repository to discover the interface supported by the remote service, brokerage and matchmaking services to determine the best match between a client and a set of servers, and so on.

The software necessary to glue together various components of a distributed system is called middleware. The middleware allows a layperson to request services in human terms rather than become acquainted with the intricacies of complex systems that the experts themselves have troubles fully comprehending.

6.3.1 Coordination Based on Scripting Languages

Coordination is one application of a more general process called software composition where individual components are made to work together and create an ensemble exhibiting a new behavior, without introducing a new state at the level of individual components. A component is a black box exposing a number of interfaces allowing other components to interact with it.

The components or entities can be "glued" together with scripts. Scripting languages provide "late gluing" of existing components. Several scripting languages are very popular: `Tcl`, `Pearl`, `Python`, `JavaScript`, `ApleScript`, `Visual Basic`, languages supported by the `csh` or the `Bourne` Unix shells,

Scripting languages share several characteristics [60]:

(i) Support composition of existing applications; thus, the term "late gluing". For example, we may glue together a computer-aided design system (CAD), with a database for material properties (MPDB). The first component may be used to design different mechanical parts; then the second may be invoked to select for each part the materials with desirable mechanical, thermal, and electrical properties.

(ii) Rely on a virtual machine to execute bytecode. They are interpreted languages. `Pearl`, `Python`, and `Visual Basic` are based on a bytecode implementation, whereas `JavaScript`, `AppleScript`, and the `Bourne Shell` need an interpreter.

(iii) For rapid prototyping over performance. In the previous example, one is likely to get better performance in terms of response time by rewriting and integrating the two software systems, but this endeavor may require several men-years; writing a script to glue the two legacy applications together could be done in days.

(iv) Allow the extension of a model with new abstractions. For example, if one of the components is a CAD tool producing detailed drawings and specifications of the parts of an airplane engine, then the abstractions correspond to the airplane parts, e.g., wing, tail section, landing gear. Such high-level, domain-specific abstractions can be easily understood and manipulated by aeronautic and mechanical engineers with little or no computer science background.

(v) Generally, scripting languages are weakly typed, offer support for introspection and reflection, and for automatic memory management.

`Pearl`, `Python`, `JavaScript`, `AppleScript`, and `Visual Basic` are object-based scripting languages. All four of them are embedable, they can be included into existing applications. For example, code written in JPython, a Java version of Python, can be embedded into a data stream, sent over the network, and executed by an interpreter at the other site.

Pearl, Python, and JavaScript support introspection and reflection. Introspection and reflection allow a user to determine and modify the properties of an object at runtime.

Scripting languages are very popular and widely available. Tcl, Pearl, and Python are available on most platforms, JavaScript is supported by Netscape, the Bourne Shell is supported by Unix, and Visual Basic by Windows.

Script-based coordination has obvious limitations; it is most suitable for applications with one coordinator acting as an enactment engine, or in a hierarchical scheme when the legacy applications form the leaves of the tree and the intermediate nodes are scripts controlling the applications in a subtree. A script for a dynamic system, where the current state of the environment determines the course of action, becomes quickly very complex. Building some form of fault tolerance and handling exceptions could be very tedious.

In summary, script-based coordination is suitable for simple, static cases and has the advantage of rapid prototyping but could be very tedious and inefficient for more complex situations.

6.3.2 Coordination Based on Shared-Data Spaces

A shared-data space allows agents to coordinate their activities. We use the terminology *shared-data space* because of its widespread acceptance, though in practice the shared space may consist of data, knowledge, code, or a combination of them. The term *agent* means a party to a coordination effort.

In this coordination model all agents know the location of a shared data space and have access to communication primitives to deposit and to retrieve information from it. As in virtually all other coordination models, a prior agreement regarding the syntax and the semantics of communication must be in place, before meaningful exchanges of coordination information may take place.

The shared-data space coordination model allows *asynchronous communication between mobile agents in an open system*, as seen in Figure 6.4. The communicating components need not be coupled in time or space. The producer and the consumer of a coordination information item act according to their own timing; the producer agent may deposit a message at its own convenience and the consumer agent may attempt to retrieve it according to its own timing. The components need not be co-located; they may even be mobile. The only constraint is for each agent to be able to access the shared-data space from its current location. Agents may join and leave the system at will.

Another distinctive advantage of the shared-data space coordination model is its tolerance of heterogeneity. The implementation language of the communicating entities, the architecture, and the operating systems of the host where the agents are located play no role in this model. An agent implemented in Java, running in a Linux environment and on a SPARC-based platform, could interact with another one

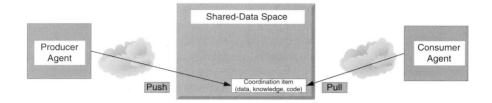

Fig. 6.4 A shared-data space coordination model. The producer of the coordination information pushes an item into the shared data space, a consumer pulls it out. Little, or no
state information needs to be maintained by the shared-data space. The model supports asynchronous communication between mobile agents. The agents may join and leave at will, the
model supports open systems.

implemented in C++, running under Windows on a Pentium platform, without any
special precautions.

Traditionally, a shared-data space is a *passive* entity, coordination information is
pushed into it by a source agent and *pulled* from it by the destination agent. The
amount of state information maintained by a shared-data space is minimal, it does not
need to know either the location or even the identity of the agents involved. Clearly,
there are applications where security concerns require controlled access to the shared
information, thus, some state information is necessary. These distinctive features
make this model scalable and extremely easy to use.

An alternative model is based on *active* shared-data spaces; here the shared-data
space plays an active role, it informs an intended destination agent when information
is available. This approach is more restrictive, it requires the shared-data space to
maintain information about the agents involved in the coordination effort. In turn,
this makes the system more cumbersome, less scalable, and less able to accommodate
mobility.

Several flavors of shared-data spaces exist. Blackboards were an early incarna-
tion of the shared-data space coordination model. Blackboards were widely used in
artificial intelligence in the 1980s.

Linda [16, 17] was the first system supporting associative access to a shared-data
space. *Associative access* raises the level of communication abstraction. Questions
such as who produced the information; when was it produced; who were the intended
consumers are no longer critical and applications that do not require such knowledge
to benefit from the additional flexibility of associative access.

Tuples are ordered collections of elements. In a shared-tuple space agents use
templates to retrieve tuples; this means that an agent specifies what kind of tuple to
retrieve, rather than what tuple.

Linda supports a set of primitives to manipulate the shared tuple space; out allows
an agent to deposit or write a tuple with multiple fields in the tuple space; in and rd
are used to read or retrieve a tuple when a matching has been found; inp and rdp are

nonblocking versions of in and rd; eval is a primitive to create an *active* tuple, one with fields that do not have a definite value but are evaluated using function calls.

Several types of systems extend some of the capabilities of Linda. Some, including T Spaces from IBM and JavaSpaces from Sun Microsystems, extend the set of coordination primitives, others affect the semantics of the language, yet another group modify the model. For example, T Spaces allows database indexing, event notification, supports queries expressed in the structured query language (SQL), and allows direct thread access when the parties run on the same Java Virtual Machine.

A survey of the state of the art in tuple-based technologies for coordination and a discussion of a fair number of systems developed in the last few years is presented in [58]. Several papers in reference [52] provide an in-depth discussion of tuple space coordination. More details on tuplespaces are provided in Chapter 8.

An interesting idea is to construct federations of shared tuple spaces. This architecture mirrors distributed databases and has the potential to lead to better performance and increased security for the hierarchical coordination model, by keeping communications local. Security is a major concern for tuplespace-based coordination in the Internet.

6.3.3 Coordination Based on Middle Agents

In our daily life middlemen facilitate transactions between parties, help coordinate complex activities, or simply allow one party to locate other parties. For example, a title company facilitates real estate transactions, wedding consultants and planners help organize a wedding, an auction agency helps sellers locate buyers and buyers find items they desire.

So it is not very surprising that a similar organization appears in complex software systems. The individual components of the system are called *entities* whenever we do not want to be specific about the function attributed to each component; they are called clients and servers when their function is well defined.

Coordination can be facilitated by agents that help locate the entities involved in coordination, and/or facilitate access to them. Brokers, matchmakers, and mediators are examples of middle agents used to support reliable mediation and guarantee some form of end-to-end quality of service (QoS). In addition to coordination functions, such agents support interoperability and facilitate the management of knowledge in an open system.

A *broker* is a middle agent serving as an intermediary between two entities involved in coordination. All communications between the entities are channeled through the broker. In Figure 6.5 we see the interactions between a client and a server through a broker. In this case, the broker examines the individual QoS requirements of a client and attempts to locate a server capable of satisfying them; moreover, if the server fails, the broker may attempt to locate another one, able to provide a similar service under similar conditions.

The broker does not actively collect information about the entities active in the environment, each entity has to make itself known by registering itself with the broker before it can be involved in mediated interactions. An entity uses an advertize

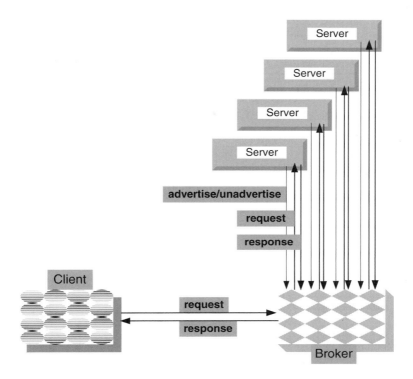

Fig. 6.5   A broker acts as an intermediary between a client and a set of servers. The sequence of events: (i) servers register with a broker; (ii) a client sends a request; (iii) the broker forwards the request to a server; (iv) the server provides the response to the broker; (v) the broker forwards the request to the client.

message, see Figure 6.5, to provide information about itself to the broker and an `unadvertize` to retract its availability.

The entities may provide additional information such as a description of services, or a description of the semantics of services. The broker may maintain a knowledge base with information about individual entities involved and may even translate the communication from one party into a format understood by the other parties involved.

A matchmaker is a middle agent whose only role is to pair together entities involved in coordination; once the pairing is done, the matchmaker is no longer involved in any transaction between the parties. For example, a matchmaker may help a client select a server as shown in Figure 6.6. Once the server is selected, the client communicates directly with the server bypassing the matchmaker.

The matchmaker has a more limited role; while the actual selection may be based on a QoS criterion, once made, the matchmaker cannot provide additional reliability support. If one of the parties fails, the other party must detect the failure and again contact the matchmaker. A matchmaker, like a broker, does not actively collect information about the entities active in the environment, each entity has to make itself known by registering itself with the matchmaker.

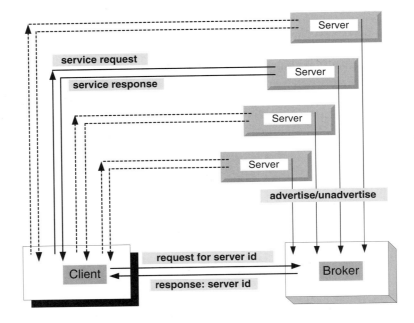

Fig. 6.6   A matchmaker helps a client select a server. Then the client communicates directly with the server selected by the matchmaker. The sequence of events: (i) servers register with the matchmaker; (ii) a client sends a request to a broker; (iii) the broker selects a server and provides its ID; (iv) the client sends a request to the server selected during the previous step; (v) the server provides the response to the client.

A mediator can be used in conjunction with a broker, or with a matchmaker to act as a front end to an entity, see Figure 6.7. In many instances it is impractical to mix the coordination primitives with the logic of a legacy application, e.g., a database management system. It is easier for an agent to use a uniform interface for an entire set of systems designed independently, than to learn the syntax and semantics of the interface exposed by each system. The solution is to create a wrapper for each system and translate an incoming request into a format understood by the specific system it is connected to; at the same time, responses from the system are translated into a format understood by the sender of the request.

6.4   SOFTWARE AGENTS

Until now we have used the term *agent* rather loosely, meaning a software component performing a well-defined function and communicating with other components in the process. Now we restrict our discussion to software agents.

Software agents, interface agents, and robotics are ubiquitous applications of artificial intelligence (AI). Interface agents are considered to be an evolutionary step in the development of visual interfaces. Robotics uses agents to model the behav-

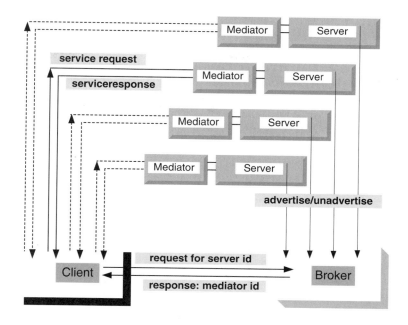

Fig. 6.7 A mediator acts as a front end or a wrapper to one or more servers; it translate requests and responses into a format understood by the intended recipient. A mediator may be used in conjunction with brokers or matchmakers.

ior of various types of devices capable of performing humanlike functions. Several references [5, 38, 39, 56, 57] address the theoretical foundations of agent research.

The software agents field witnesses the convergence of specialists from artificial Iintelligence and distributed object systems communities. The first group emphasizes the intelligence and autonomy facets of agent behavior. The second group sees agents as a natural extension of the object-oriented programming paradigm and is concerned with mobility; for this community *an agent is a mobile active object*. An *active object* is one with a running thread of control.

Various definitions of agency have been proposed. An agent is an entity perceiving its environment through sensors and acting on that environment through effectors and actuators [59]; a rational agent is expected to optimize its performance on the basis of its experience and built-in knowledge. Rational agents do not require a logical reasoning capability, the only assumption is that the agent is working towards its goal.

A *weak* notion of an agent is introduced in [72]: An agent is an entity that is (a) autonomous, (b) communicates, thus has some sort of social ability, (c) responds to perception - reactivity, and (d) is goal-directed, pro-activity.

The main difference between these definitions is that the one in [59] does not include the necessity of a separate goal or agenda, whereas the one in [72] includes the requirement of communication, not present in the other definitions.

Stronger notions relate agency to concepts normally applied to humans. For example, some use *mentalistic* notions such as knowledge, belief, intentions, and obligations to describe the behavior of agents. Others, consider *emotional agents* [5].

Although the separation between the strong and the weak notions of agency seems appropriate, we believe that using anthropomorphical terms is not particularly useful. Agent systems have to be evaluated individually to see if notions such as "knowledge" or "emotion" mean more than "database" or "state."

Figure 6.8 shows the interactions between an agent and the world. A reflex agent responds with reflex actions that do not require knowledge about the environment. A goal-based agent responds with goal-directed actions based on its model of the world. These goal-directed actions reflect an intelligent behavior based on inference, planning, and learning.

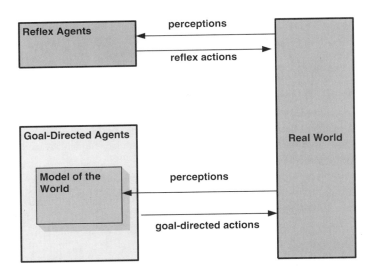

Fig. 6.8   Reflex agents react to the environment through reflex actions. Goal-directed agents respond with goal-directed actions.

6.4.1   Software Agents as Reactive Programs

A software agent is a reactive program. A *reactive* program is one designed to respond to a broad range of external and internal events. Functionally, the main thread of control of a reactive program consists of a loop to catch events; the reactive program may have one or more additional threads of control to process events. The lifetime of a reactive program is potentially unlimited once started, the program runs until either an error occurs, or it is shut down.

Ubiquitous examples of reactive programs are the kernel of an operating System (OS) or the program controlling the execution of a server. An OS kernel reacts to hardware and software events caused by hardware and software interrupts. Hardware events are due to timer interrupts, hardware exceptions, Input/Output (I/O) interrupts, and possibly other causes.

Hardware interrupts cause the activation of event handlers. For example, a timer interrupt caused by the expiration of the time slot allocated to a process may lead to the activation of the scheduler. The scheduler may suspend the current process and activate another one from the ready list. Software interrupts are caused by exceptional conditions such as overflow, underflow, invalid memory address, and invalid operations.

A server reacts to external events caused by requests from clients; the only internal events the server program reacts to are hardware or software exceptions triggered by an I/O operation, an error, or software interrupts.

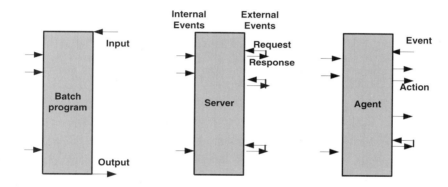

Fig. 6.9 Batch execution mode, and two types of reactive programs, servers and agents. Servers respond to requests, agents perform actions either as a reaction to an external event, or at their own initiative.

Other common types of programs are batch and interactive, see Figure 6.9. The main thread of control of a traditional *batch* program reads some input data, executes a specific algorithm, produces some results, and terminates. During its execution, the program may spawn multiple threads of control and may react to some external events; for example, it may receive messages, or may respond to specific requests to suspend or terminate execution. An *interactive* program is somehow similar to a batch program, it implements a specific algorithm, but instead of getting its input at once, it carries out a dialog with the user(s), responds to a predefined set of commands, and tailors its actions accordingly. In both cases the lifetime is determined by the algorithm implemented by the program.

A software agent is a special type of reactive program, some of the actions taken by the agent are in response to external events, other actions may be taken at the initiative of the agent. This special behavior of a software agent distinguishes it from other types of programs.

The defining attributes of a software agent are: autonomy, intelligence, and mobility [10], see Figure 6.10. *Autonomy*, or agency, is determined by the nature of

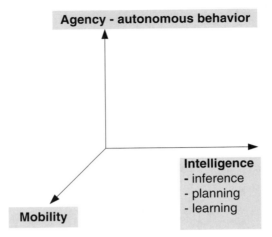

Fig. 6.10 The defining attributes of a software agent: autonomy, intelligence, and mobility. An agent may exhibit different degrees of autonomy, intelligence, and mobility.

the interactions between the agent and the environment and by the interactions with other agents and/or the entities they represent. *Intelligence* measures the degree of reasoning, planning, and learning the agent is capable of. *Mobility* reflects the ability of an agent to migrate from one host to another in a network.

An agent may exhibit different degrees of autonomy, intelligence, and mobility. For example, an agent may have inferential abilities, but little or no learning and/or planning abilities. An agent may exhibit strong or weak mobility; in the first case, the agent may be able to migrate to any site at any time; in the second case, the migration time and sites are restricted.

We now examine more closely the range of specific attributes we expect to find at some level in a software agent:

   (i) *Reactivity and temporal continuity.*

   (ii) *Persistence of identity and state.*

   (iii) *Autonomy.*

   (iv) *Inferential ability.*

   (v) *Mobility.*

   (vi) *Adaptability*

   (vii) *Knowledge-level communication ability.*

6.4.2   Reactivity and Temporal Continuity

Reactivity and temporal continuity provide an agent with the ability to sense and react over long periods of time. Reactivity is the property of agents to respond in a timely manner to external events. Reactivity implies an immediate action without planning or reasoning. Reactive behavior is a major issue for agents working in a real-time environment. In this case, the reaction time should be very short, in the microseconds to milliseconds range, so most reasoning models are much too slow.

Reactive behavior can be obtained using either a table lookup, or a neural network. Creating an explicit lookup table is difficult when the quantity of information in each item is very large as is the case with visual applications. In this case, segments of the table can be compressed by noting commonly occurring associations between inputs and outputs; such associations can be summarized in *condition-action rules*, or *situation-action rules* such as:

if *car-in-front-is-braking* **then** *initiate-braking*.

Agents exhibiting exclusively reactive behavior are called *simple reflex agents* [59]. Some agent systems follow biological systems where there is a division of labor between the conditional reactions controlled at the individual neurons or at the spine level and the planned behavior, which happens more at the cerebral cortex level, and dedicate a specific subsystem to reactive behavior.

6.4.3   Persistence of Identity and State

During its lifetime an agent maintains its identity, collects and keeps some perceptions as part of its *state*, and remembers the state.

The persistency models employed by agents depend on the implementation language. Prolog-based agents store their state in a knowledge-base as regular Prolog statements equivalent to clauses in a Horn logic. Lisp or Scheme-based agents also store the code and data in identical format. This strategy facilitates agent checkpointing and restarting.

It is more difficult to achieve persistency in compiled procedural or object-oriented languages such as C or C++, or partially compiled languages such as Java. A first step towards persistency is the ability to conveniently store internal data structures in an external format, a process called *serialization*.

Most object-oriented libraries, such as Microsoft Foundation Classes, Qt Libraries for C++, or the Java class libraries offer extensive support for serialization. Technically, serialization poses difficult questions, for example, the translation of object references from the persistent format to the internal format, the so-called *swizzling*; this can lead to a major performance bottleneck for complex data structures.

Serialization, however, is only one facet of persistency, the programmer must still identify the data structures to be serialized. *Orthogonal persistency*, the ability to store the current state of the entire computation to persistent storage, is a more advanced model of persistency.

A disadvantage of most persistency approaches is that they either require extensions to the languages, or they involve a postprocessing of the object code. For example, PJama, a persistent version of Java, uses a modified Java Virtual Machine, while the ObjectStore PSE of eXcelon corporation uses a postprocessing of the Java class files, adding persistency code after the Java compilation step. These approaches make the systems dependent on proprietary code without guaranteed support in the future, which is considered a disadvantage by many developers.

6.4.4 Autonomy

Autonomy gives an agent a proactive behavior and the ability to work toward a goal. Autonomy of agents can be perceived either in a weak sense, meaning "not under the immediate control of a human" to distinguish an agent from interactive programs, or in a strong sense meaning that "an agent is autonomous to the extent that its behavior is determined by its own experience."

Autonomy is closely related to *goal-directed behavior*. The agent needs a *goal* that describes desirable situations. The goal, together with the information about the current state of the world, determines the actions of agents.

Choosing actions that achieve the goal is the most difficult problem for a goal-directed agent. When a single action can achieve the goal, the problem can be addressed by a reactive agent. However, in many instances a number of actions should be taken to reach the goal and in such cases the agent should have planning abilities.

For the dynamic case, where the agent has to adapt its actions to a changing environment, more elaborate models are needed. The belief-desire-intention (BDI) model addresses this problem [56]. A BDI agent keeps its knowledge about the world in a set of logical statements called *beliefs*. The set of beliefs can be updated, or extended during the lifetime of the agent.

The goal of a BDI agent is captured in the set of statements called the *desires* of the agent. Desires are a high-level expression of the goal, and they can not be translated into immediately executable actions. Based on its desires and beliefs, the BDI agent generates a set of *intentions* that are immediately translatable into actions. The active component of the agent simply selects one from the current intentions, and executes it as an action.

6.4.5 Inferential Ability

Software agents act on abstract task specifications using prior knowledge of general goals and methods. The inferential ability of agents is reduced to the problem of knowledge manipulation; it is required that the agent has a knowledge of its goals, itself, the user, the world, including other agents.

The nature of the problem is greatly influenced by the choice made for *knowledge representation*. A fair number of choices are possible: knowledge representation based on logical statements; probabilistic and fuzzy logic; neural networks; and metaobjects.

6.4.6 Mobility, Adaptability, and Knowledge-Level Communication Ability

The relative merits of *agent mobility* is a controversial subject. An argument in favor of mobile agents is performance; it is more efficient to move a relatively small segment of code and state than a large data set. Moreover, a mobile agent can be customized to fit the local needs.

The Telescript system, developed in 1994 at General Magic, is the prototype for strong agent mobility. In this system the mobility is provided by an object-oriented programming language called Telescript, executed by a platform-independent *engine*. This engine supports persistent agents, every bit of information is stored in nonvolatile memory at every instruction boundary. This approach guarantees recovery from system crashes, and allows a Telescript program to be safely migrated at any time.

Adaptivity: ability to learn and improve with experience.

Knowledge-level communication ability: agents have the ability to communicate with persons and other agents using languages resembling humanlike "speech acts" rather than typical symbol-level program-to-program protocols.

6.5 INTERNET AGENTS

Applications of agents to the Internet and to information grids are topics of considerable interest [11, 42, 66]. Why are software agents considered the new frontier in distributed system development? What do we expect from them? The answer to these questions is that software agents have unique abilities to:

(i) Support intelligent resource management. Peer agents can negotiate access to resources and request services based upon user intentions rather than specific implementations.

(ii) Support intelligent user interfaces. We expect agents to be capable of composing basic actions into higher level ones, to be able of handling large search spaces, to schedule actions for future points in time, to support abstractions and delegations. Some of the limitations of direct manipulation interfaces, namely, difficulties in handling large search spaces, rigidity, and the lack of improvement of behavior, extend to most other facets of traditional approaches to interoperability.

(iii) Filter large amounts of information. Agents can be instructed at the level of goals and strategies to find solutions to unforeseen situations, and they can use learning algorithms to improve their behavior.

(iv) Adjust to the actual environment, they are network aware.

(v) Move to the site when they are needed and thus reduce communication costs and improve performance.

Once mobile agents are included in the system, new coordination models need to be developed. A simple-minded approach is to extend direct communication models of interagent interactions by tracking the movement of an agent. This is certainly expensive and does not scale very well. One may be able to interpose communication middleware but this approach is not scalable and does not provide the abstractions and metaphors required by more sophisticated interactions. In a *meeting-oriented* coordination model interactions are forced to occur in the context of special meeting points possibly implemented as agents, yet, the interacting agents need a priori knowledge of the identity of the special agents and their location.

Blackboard-based architectures allow agents to interact without knowing who the partners are and where they are located. This approach is better suited to support mobility, unpredictibility, and agent security. Since all transactions occur within the framework of a blackboard, it is easier to enforce security by monitoring the blackboard.

6.6   AGENT COMMUNICATION

To accomplish the complex coordinations tasks they are faced with, Internet agents are required to share knowledge. In turn, knowledge sharing requires the agents in a federation or groups of unrelated agents to communicate among themselves.

Knowledge sharing alone does not guarantee effective coordination abilities, it is only a necessary but not a sufficient condition for a federation of agents to coordinate their activities. Agents use inference, learning, and planning skills to take advantage of the knowledge they acquire while interacting with other agents.

The implementation languages and the domain assumptions of individual agents that need to coordinate their actions may be different. Yet, an agent needs to understand expressions provided by another agent in its own native language [23].

Agent communication involves sharing the meaning of propositions and of propositional attitudes. Sharing the meaning of propositions requires syntactic translation between languages and, at the same time, the assurance that a concept preserves its meaning across agents even if it is called differently. Ontologies provide taxonomies of terms, their definitions, and the axioms relating the terms used by different agents.

The propositional attitude aspect of agent communication implies that we are concerned with a more abstract form of communication between agents, above the level of bits, messages, or arguments of a remote method invocation. Agents communicate attitudes, they inform other agents, request to find agents who can assist them to monitor other entities in the environment, and so on.

6.6.1   Agent Communication Languages

Agent communication languages (ACLs) provide the practical mechanisms for knowledge sharing.

An agent communication language should have several attributes [43]. It should:

- be declarative, syntactically simple, and readable by humans,

- consist of a *communication language*, to express communicative acts, and a *contents language*, to express facts about the domain,

- have unambiguous semantics and be grounded in theory,

- lend itself to efficient implementation able to exploit modern networking facilities,

- support reliable and secure communications among agents.

The knowledge query and manipulation language (KQML), [21, 22] was the first ACL; more recently, the Foundation for Intelligent Physical Agents (FIPA) has proposed a new language, the FIPA ACL [24, 25]. Both are languages of propositional attitude.

Figure 6.11 illustrates the relationship between communication, representation, and the components related to inference, learning, and planning invoked by an agent coordinating its activity with other agents of a federation. The low-level communication between agents is based on a transport mechanism. ACLs communicate attitudes.

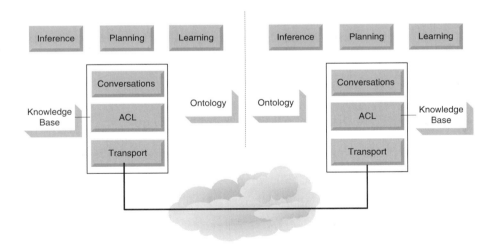

Fig. 6.11   An abstract model of agent coordination and the interactions between the agents in a federation. This model reflects communication, representation, and higher level agent activities. The low-level communication between agents uses some transport mechanism; ACLs communicate attitudes and require the agents to share ontologies to guarantee that a concept from one agent's knowledge base preserves its meaning across the entire federation of agents; inference, learning, and planning lead to the intelligent agent behavior required by complex coordination tasks.

The representation component consists of ontologies and knowledge bases. The agents share ontologies to guarantee that a concept from one agent's knowledge base preserves its meaning across the entire federation of agents. Inference, learning, and planning lead to the intelligent agent behavior required by complex coordination tasks.

An ACL defines the types of messages exchanged among agents and the meaning of them. But agents typically carry out *conversations* and exchange several messages.

6.6.2 Speech Acts and Agent Communication Language Primitives

Speech acts is an area of linguistics devoted to the analysis of human communication. Speech act theory categorizes human *utterances* into categories depending upon:

   (i) the intent of the speaker, the so-called illocutionary aspect,

   (ii) the effect on the listener, the so-called perlocutionary aspect, and

   (iii) the physical manifestations.

Since speech acts are human knowledge-level communication protocols, some argue that they are appropriate as programming language primitives [44], and in particular to construct agent communication protocols.

ACL primitives are selected from the roughly 4600 known speech acts grouped in several categories: representatives, directives, commissives, expressives, declarations, verdicatives. There is a division of labor between ACLs and the agent infrastructure to ensure that agents are ethical and trustworthy, and therefore the perlocutionary behavior of a speech act on the hearing agent is predictable.

6.6.3 Knowledge Query and Manipulation Language

The Knowledge Query and Manipulation Language (KQML) is perhaps the most widely used agent communication language [21, 22]. KQML is a product of the DARPA Knowledge Sharing Effort (KSE). This effort resulted also in a content language called Knowledge Interchange Format (KIF) [28]. KIF is based on the first-order logic and the set theory and an ontology specification language called Ontolingua [32].

KQML envisions a community of agents, each owning and managing a *virtual knowledge beliefs* database (VKB) that represents its model of the world. KQML does not impose any restrictions regarding the content language used to represent the model; the contents language could be KIF, RDF, SL or some other language.

The goal is to provide knowledge transportation protocol for information expressed in the content language using some ontology that the sending agent can point to and the receiving agent can access. Agents then query and manipulate the contents of each others VKBs, using KQML as the communication and transport language. KQML allows changes to an agent's VKB by another agent as part of its language primitives.

The KQML specification defines the syntax and the semantics for a collection of messages or performatives that collectively define the language in which agents communicate.

KQML is built around a number of performatives or instructions designed to achieve tasks at three conceptual layers: content, message, communication. There is a core set of reserved performatives. This set has been extended for different applications [4].

The performatives can be divided into several categories. The most important ones are:

(i) Queries - send questions for evaluation,

(ii) Responses - reply to queries and requests,

(iii) Informational - transfer information,

(iv) Generative - control and initiate message exchange,

(v) Capability - learn the capabilities of other agents and announce own capabilities to the community,

(vi) Networking - pass directives to underlying communication layers.

Agents can communicate directly with one another when they are aware of each other's presence or they may use an intermediary to locate an agent, to request to be informed about changes in the environment or about any type of event.

Figure 6.12(a) illustrates direct communication between agents X and Y. Agent X requests information from agent Y using the ask() performative; agent Y replays with the tell() performative.

Figure 6.12(b) shows the case when an intermediate agent dispatches events caused by a group of agents to one or more subscriber agents. Agent X monitors events caused by Y using the subscribe() performative; Y uses tell() to inform the mediator agent when an event occurs; finally, the mediator passes the information to X.

Figure 6.12(c) illustrates the recommendation process involving, a client, several potential servers, and a middle agent. Agent Y uses the advertise() performative to inform a middle agent about its existence and the functions it is capable of providing; agent X requests the middle agent to recommend one of the agents it is aware of; the middle agent uses the reply() performative to recommend X. Then X and Y communicate directly with one another.

Figure 6.12(d) illustrates the brokerage function; agent X uses the broker() performative to locate a partner Y.

6.6.4 FIPA Agent Communication Language

Like KQML, FIPA-ACL maintains orthogonality with the content language and is designed to work with any content language and any ontology. Beyond the commonalty

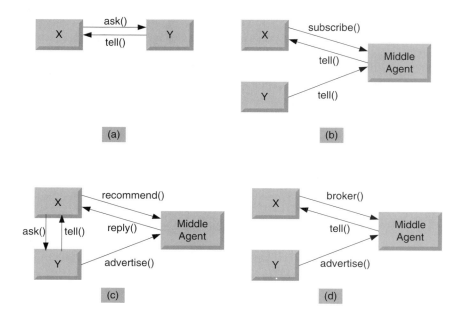

Fig. 6.12 KQML performatives are used for direct communication between two agents, or between agents and a mediator. (a) Agent X requests information from agent Y using the ask() performative; agent Y replays with the tell() performative. (b) Agent X monitors events cause by Y using the subscribe() performative; Y uses tell() to inform the mediator agent when an event occurs; finally, the mediator passes the information to X. (c) Agent Y uses the advertise() performative to inform a middle agent about its existence and the functions it is capable of providing; agent X requests the middle agent to recommend one of the agents it is aware of; the middle agent uses the reply() performative to recommend X. Then X and Y communicate directly with one another. (d) Agent X uses the broker() performative to locate a partner Y.

of goals and the syntax similarity, there are a number of significant differences between FIPA-ACL and KQML:

(i) In the FIPA-ACL semantic model, agents are not allowed to directly manipulate another agent's VKB. Therefore KQML performatives such as insert, uninsert, delete-one, delete-all, undelete are not meaningful.

(ii) FIPA-ACL limits itself to primitives that are used in communications between agent pairs. The FIPA architecture has an agent management system (AMS) specification that specifies services that manage agent communities. The AMS eliminates the need for register/unregister, recommend,recruit,broker and (un)advertise primitives in the ACL.

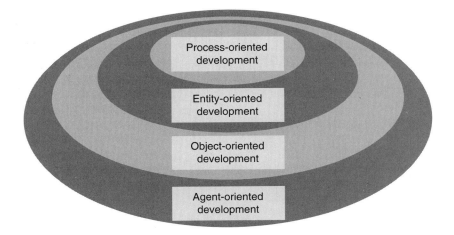

Fig. 6.13   Software development methods seen as a logical progression.

6.7   SOFTWARE ENGINEERING CHALLENGES FOR AGENTS

Imperative programming languages such as C are best suited for a process-oriented approach; descriptive languages such as SQL support entity-oriented style; object-oriented languages such as Smalltalk or C++ are designed for object-oriented programing. Languages such as Java seem best suited for agent-oriented programming [62], see Figure 6.13.

Different programming paradigms are associated with different levels of object granularity: low-level programming to binary data types, such as octal and hexadecimal; programming in high-level languages to basic data types such as floating point, integer, and character as well as structured data types such as sets, queues, lists, and trees; object-oriented programming with even more structured objects such as widgets and windows; agents with objects representing complex entities.

The methodology proposed in [74] sees an agent as a relatively coarse grain entity, roughly equivalent with a Unix process; it also assumes that the agents are heterogeneous, may be implemented in different programming languages. The methodology is designed for systems composed of a relatively small number of agents, less then 100, and it is not intended to design systems where there is a real conflict between the goals of the agents. The methodology considers an agent system as an artificial society or organization, and applies principles of organizational design. A key concept in this process is the idea of a *role*. As in a real organization, a role is not linked to an agent. Multiple agents can have the same role, e.g., salesperson, or an agent can have multiple roles.

The methodology divides the agent building process into analysis and design phases. During the analysis phase one prepares the organizational model of the agent system consisting of the *role model* and the *interaction model*. First, the key roles of the system must be identified, together with the associated permissions and responsabilities. Second, the interactions, dependencies, and relationships between different roles are determined. This step consists of a set of *protocol definitions*, one for each type of inter-role interaction.

The goal of the design step is to transform the analysis models into a sufficiently low level of abstraction, such that traditional design techniques such as object-oriented design can be used for implementation. The design process requires three models:

- The *agent model* identifies the *agent types* to be used in the system, and the *agent instances* to be instantiated.

- The *services model* identifies the main service types associated with each agent type.

- The *acquintance model* defines the communication links between agent types.

6.8 FURTHER READING

A recent collection of articles found in reference [52] attempts to provide a snapshot of the area of coordination models. Agent-based coordination is the subject of several papers including references [4, 15, 18, 19]. Tuple spaces are presented in [15, 16, 17, 34, 46, 67, 68].

There is a vast body of literature on software agents. Herbert Simon's thought provoking book [63], the modern text of Russell and Norvig [59], the excellent article of Bradshaw [10], and several other papers [26, 35, 40, 48, 53, 72] provide the reader with an overview of the field. The scalability of multi-agent systems is discussed in [55]. The AI perspective on agents is presented in [5, 31, 38, 39, 56, 57, 64].

Several agent communication languages have been proposed: KQML was introduced by Finnin and et al. [21, 22]; Elephant by John McCarthy [44]. Desiderata for agent communication languages are discussed by Mayfield et al. [43]. Agent-oriented programming is introduced by Shoham [62]. The Knowledge Interchange Format was defined by Genesreth and Fikes [28].

Attempts to define agent standards are due to FIPA [24, 25] and OMG [51].

Agent-oriented software engineering is the subject of many publications including [36, 50, 71, 73, 74],

A fair number of agent systems have been proposed and developed in a relatively short period of time: Telescript [69, 70], Aglets [41], Voyager [30], KAoS [11], NOMADS [65], ZEUS [47, 49], Grasshopper [6, 12], Hive [45], JavaSeal [13], Bond [8], JATLite [37], JACK [14], AgentBuilder [75].

Applications of software agents have been investigated in several areas such as manufacturing [2, 3, 61]; project management [54]; network management [20, 27]; air traffic control [33]; scientific and parallel computing [9, 29]; Web and news distribution [1, 7].

Applications of agents to grid computing are discussed in several papers presented at the First International Symposium on Cluster Computing and the Grid [42, 66].

6.9 EXERCISES AND PROBLEMS

Problem 1. Discuss the relative advantages and disadvantages of centralized versus decentralized coordination.

(i) Give examples of centralized and decentralized coordination in economical, social, military, and political systems.

(ii) Discuss the social, economical, and political coordination models used by the Roman Empire and compare them with the models used from about the eighth until the eighteenth century in today's Italy and Germany.

(iii) What is the effect of communication technology on the choice of centralized versus decentralized coordination models?

Problem 2. History books mention military geniuses such as: Caesar, Alexander the Great, William the Conqueror, Napoleon Bonaparte, Lord Nelson, Patton. Identify one famous battle won by each one of them and the strategy used in that battle.

Problem 3. Scripts are generally used to coordinate the execution of several programs running on the same system, they are very seldom used to coordinate execution across systems interconnected by a WAN.

(i) Give several sound reasons for the limitation of the use of scripts in a wide area system.

(ii) Scripts can be embedded into messages sent to a remote site and thus trigger the execution of a group of programs at the remote site. What are the limitations of this approach for ensuring global coordination?

Problem 4. Discuss the relative merits of endogeneous and exogeneous coordination models.

(i) Correlate the choice of an endogeneous or an exogeneous coordination model with the reaction time of the system. What type of model is suitable for an investment company, for traders on the floor of the stock exchange, for battlefield management, for disaster management, for a health care system, and for the air traffic control system.

(ii) Agent communication languages such as KQML allow the use of a contents language and of an ontology. Discuss the use of these options within the context of the choice between endogeneous and exogeneous coordination models.

Problem 5. Using the Web search engines, locate the agent Mobile Agent List and identify mobile agent systems that support strong and weak mobility.

(i) Provide several sound reasons why it is difficult for a run-time system to support strong mobility.

(ii) Several restrictions are imposed even on systems that support strong mobility. What are these restrictions?

(iii) Identify several applications that indeed require strong mobility.

Problem 6. Mobile agents are generally associated with heightened security risks. Discuss the:

(i) Risks posed to the mobile agents by the hosts they migrate to.

(ii) Risks posed to the hosts by mobile agents.

(iii) *Sandbox* security model adopted by Java and the limitations placed on the execution of applets.

Problem 7. The Web browser of a user limits the abilities of an applet to send messages to a third party. Imagine a scheme when the browser downloads an applet from a Web server and then distributes the local state information to a number of clients running on several systems.

Problem 8. Using the Web search engines identify a Java run-time environment that limits the amount of resources used by a thread of control and prevent the equivalent of denial of service attacks posed by mobile code.

(i) Discuss the mechanisms used to limit the CPU cycles and the rate of I/O requests used.

(ii) An agent may exhibit a bursty behavior, in other words, it may need to use a large number of CPU cycles and perform a large number of I/O operation over a short period of time while maintaining a relatively low average CPU and I/O rate. Imagine a mechanism based on a token bucketlike abstraction to support this type of scheduling.

Problem 9. Tuple spaces provide an extremely convenient way to accommodate communication in asynchronous systems.

(i) Identify a minimal set of primitives to be supported by tuple space servers.

(ii) What database management functions are very useful for a shared tuple space?

(iii) Discuss the security aspects of communication using shared tuple spaces.

(iv) What are the similarities and dissimilarities between IBM's T Spaces and Sun's Javaspaces?

Problem 10. Implement a secure persistent storage server based on IBM's T Spaces.

Problem 11. Discuss the application of tuple spaces for barrier synchronization. Using IBM's T Spaces, design a set of synchronization primitives allowing a group of n processes running on different hosts of a wide-area system to synchronize.

Problem 12. Active spaces extend the functionality of more traditional tuple spaces with the ability to send a notification when certain events occur.

(i) Using the Web search engines locate a system supporting active spaces.

(ii) CORBA lists event services as one of several services useful in a distributed object environment. Implement an event delivery service based on an active tuple space.

REFERENCES

1. L. Ardissono, C. Barbero, A. Goy, and G. Petrone. An Agent Architecture for Personalized Web Stores. In O. Etzioni, J. P. Müller, and J. M. Bradshaw, editors, *Proc. 3rd Annual Conf. on Autonomous Agents (AGENTS-99)*, pages 182–189. ACM Press, New York, 1999.

2. A. D. Baker. Metaphor or Reality: A Case Study Where Agents Bid with Actual Costs to Schedule a Factory. In Scott H. Clearwater, editor, *Market-Based Control*, pages 184–223. World Scientific Publishing, New Jersey, 1996.

3. S. Balasubramanian and D. H. Norrie. A Multi-Agent Intelligent Design System Integrating Manufacturing and Shop-Floor Control. In Victor Lesser, editor, *Proc. 1-st Int. Conf. on Multi–Agent Systems*, pages 3–9. MIT Press, Cambridge, Mass., 1995.

4. M. Barbuceanu and M. S. Fox. COOL: A Language for Describing Coordination in Multiagent Systems. In Victor Lesser, editor, *Proc. 1st Int. Conf. on Multi–Agent Systems*, pages 17–24. MIT Press, Cambridge, Mass., 1995.

5. J. Bates. The Role of Emotion in Believable Agents. *Communications of the ACM*, 37(7):122–125, 1994.

6. C. Bäumer, M. Breugst, S. Choy, and T. Magedanz. Grasshopper — A Universal Agent Platform Based on OMG MASIF and FIPA Standards. In A. Karmouch and R. Impley, editors, *1st Int. Workshop on Mobile Agents for Telecommunication Applications (MATA'99)*, pages 1–18. World Scientific Publishing, New Jersey, 1999.

7. D. Billsus and M. J. Pazzani. A Personal News Agent that Talks, Learns and Explains. In O. Etzioni, J. P. Müller, and J. M. Bradshaw, editors, *Proc. Third Annual Conf. on Autonomous Agents (AGENTS-99)*, pages 268–275. ACM Press, New York, 1999.

8. L. Bölöni, K. Jun, K. Palacz, R. Sion, and D. C. Marinescu. The Bond Agent System and Applications. In *Proc. 2nd Int. Symp. on Agent Systems and Applications and 4th Int. Symp. on Mobile Agents (ASA/MA 2000), Lecture Notes*

in Computer Science, volume 1882, pages 99–112. Springer–Verlag, Heidelberg, 2000.

9. L. Bölöni, D. C. Marinescu, P. Tsompanopoulou, J.R. Rice, and E.A. Vavalis. Agent-Based Networks for Scientific Simulation and Modeling. *Concurrency Practice and Experience*, 12(9):845–861, 2000.

10. J. M. Bradshaw. An Introduction to Software Agents. In *Software Agents*, pages 5–46. MIT Press, Cambridge, Mass., 1997.

11. J. M. Bradshaw, S. Dutfield, P. Benoit, and J.D. Woolley. KAoS: Toward an Industrial-Strength Open Agent Architecture. In *Software Agents*, pages 375–418. MIT Press, Cambridge, Mass., 1997.

12. M. Breugst, I. Busse, S. Covaci, and T. Magedanz. Grasshopper – A Mobile Agent Platform for IN Based Service Environments. In *Proc IEEE IN Workshop 1998*, pages 279–290. IEEE Press, Piscataway, New Jersey, 1998.

13. C. Bryce and J. Vitek. The JavaSeal Mobile Agent Kernel. In *Proc. 3rd Int. Symp. on Mobile Agents*, pages 103-116. IEEE Press, Piscataway, New Jersey, 1999.

14. P. Busetta, R. Rönnquist, A. Hodgson, and A. Lucas. JACK Intelligent Agents - Components for Intelligent Agents in Java. URL `http://agent-software.com.au/whitepaper/html/index.html`.

15. G. Cabri, L. Leonardi, and F. Zambonelli. Reactive Tuple Spaces for Mobile Agent Coordination. In K. Rothermel and F. Hohl, editors, *Proc. 2nd Int. Workshop on Mobile Agents*, *Lecture Notes in Computer Science*, volume 1477, pages 237–248. Springer–Verlag, Heidelberg, 1998.

16. N. Carriero and D. Gelernter. Linda in Context. *Communications of the ACM*, 32(4):444–458, 1989.

17. N. Carriero, D. Gelernter, and J. Leichter. Distributed Data Structures in Linda. Proc. 13th. Annual ACM Symp. on Principles of Programming Languages pages 236-242. ACM Press, New York, 1986.

18. P. Ciancarini, A. Knoche, D. Rossi, R. Tolksdorf, and F. Vitali. Coordinating Java Agents for Financial Applications on the WWW. In *Proc. 2nd Conf. on Practical Applications of Intelligent Agents and Multi Agent Technology (PAAM)*, pages 179–193. London, 1997.

19. P. Ciancarini, D. Rossi, and F. Vitali. A Case Study in Designing a Document-Centric Coordination Application over the Internet. In D. Clarke A. Dix, and F. Dix, editors, *Proc. Workshop on the Active Web*, pages 41–56. Staffordshire, UK, 1999.

20. S. Corley, M. Tesselaar, J. Cooley, and J. Meinkoehn. The Application of Intelligent and Mobile Agents to Network and Service Management. *Lecture Notes in*

Computer Science, volume 1430 pagesx 127–138. Springer–Verlag, Heidelberg, 1998.

21. T. Finin et al. Specification of the KQML Agent-Communication Language – Plus Example Agent Policies and Architectures, 1993.

22. T. Finin, R. Fritzon, D. McKay, and R. McEntire. KQML – A Language and Protocol for Knowledge and Information Exchange. In *Proc. 13th Int. Workshop on Distributed Artificial Intelligence*, pages 126–136. Seatle, Washington, 1994.

23. T. Finin, R. S. Cost, Y Labrou. Coordinating Agents using Agent Communication Languge Conversations. In A. Omicini, F. Zamborelli, M. Klush, and R. Tolksdorf, editors, *Coordination of Internet Agents: Models, Technologies and Applications*, pages 183–196. Springer–Verlag, Heidelberg, 2001.

24. Foundation for Intelligent Physical Agents. FIPA Specifications. URL http://www.fipa.org.

25. Foundation for Intelligent Physical Agents. FIPA 97 Specification Part 2: Agent Communication Language, October 1997.

26. S. Franklin and A. Graesser. Is it an Agent, or Just a Program? In *Proc. 3rd Int. Workshop on Agent Theories, Architectures and Languages, Lecture Notes in Computer Science*, volume 1193, pages 47-48. Springer–Verlag, Heidelberg, 1996.

27. C. Frei and B. Faltings. A Dynamic Hierarchy of Intelligent Agents for Network Management. *Lecture Notes in Computer Science*, volume 1437, pages 1–16. Springer–Verlag, Heidelberg, 1998.

28. M. R. Genesreth and R. E. Fikes. Knowledge Interchange Format, Version 3.0 Reference Manual. Technical Report Logic-92-1, Computer Science Department, Stanford University, 1992.

29. K. Ghanea-Hercock, J. C. Collis, and D. T. Ndumu. Co-operating Mobile Agents for Distributed Parallel Processing. In O. Etzioni, J. P. Müller, and J. M. Bradshaw, editors, *Proc. 3rd Annual Conference on Autonomous Agents*, pages 398–399, ACM Press, New York, 1999.

30. G. Glass. ObjectSpace Voyager — The Agent ORB for Java. *Lecture Notes in Computer Science*, volume 1368, pages 38–47. Springer–Verlag, Heidelberg, 1998.

31. M. Greaves, H. Holmback, and J. M. Bradshaw. What is a Conversation Policy? , Issues in Agent Communication, *Lecture Notes in Artificial Intelligence*, volume 1916, pages 118-131. Springer–Verlag, Heidelberg, 2000.

32. T. R. Gruber. Ontolingua: A Mechanism to Support Portable Ontologies, 1992.

33. H. Hexmoor and T. Heng. Air Traffic Control and Alert Agent. In C. Sierra, G. Maria, and J. S. Rosenschein, editors, *Proc. 4th Int. Conf. on Autonomous Agents (AGENTS-00)*, pages 237–238. ACM Press, New York, 2000.

34. IBM. TSpaces. URL http://www.almaden.ibm.com/cs/TSpaces.

35. C. Iglesias, M. Garrijo, and J. Gonzalez. A Survey of Agent-Oriented Methodologies. In J. Müller, M. P. Singh, and A. S. Rao, editors, *Proc. 5th Int. Workshop on Intelligent Agents: Agent Theories, Architectures, and Languages (ATAL-98), Lecture Notes in Artificial Inteligence*, volume 1555, pages 317–330. Springer–Verlag, Heidelberg, 1999.

36. N. Jennings and M. Wooldridge. Agent-Oriented Software Engineering. *Handbook of Agent Technology*, 2000.

37. H. Jeon, C. Petrie, and M. R. Cutkosky. JATLite: A Java Agent Infrastructure with Message Routing. *IEEE Internet Computing*, 4(2):87-96, 2000.

38. D. Kinny and M. Georgeff. Commitment and Effectiveness of Situated Agents. In *Proc. 12th Joint Conference on Artificial Intelligence*, pages 82–88, Sydney, Austalia, 1991.

39. D. Kinny, M. Georgeff, and A. . Rao. A Methodology and Modelling Technique for Systems of BDI Agents. In W. Van de Velde and J. W. Perram, editors, *Proc. 7th European Workshop on Modelling Autonomous Agents in a Multi-Agent World, Lecture Notes in Artificial Inteligence*, volume 1038, pages 56-62. Springer–Verlag, Heidelberg, 1996.

40. M. Knapik and J. Johnson. *Developing Intelligent Agents for Distributed Systems*. McGraw-Hill, New York, 1998.

41. D. B. Lange and M. Oshima. *Programming and Deploying Java Mobile Agents with Aglets*. Addison Wesley, Reading, Mass., 1998.

42. D.C. Marinescu. Reflections on Qualitative Attributes of Mobile Agents for Computational, Data, and Service Grids. In *Proc. of First IEEE/ACM Symp. on Cluster Computing and the Grid*, pages 442–449, May 2001.

43. J. Mayfield, Y. Labrou, and T. Finin. Desiderata for Agent Communication Languages. In *AAAI Spring Symposium on Information Gathering*, 1995.

44. J. McCarthy. Elephant 2000: A Programming Language Based on Speech Acts. 1992.

45. N. Minar, M. Gray, O. Roup, R. Krikorian, and P. Maes. Hive: Distributed Agents for Networking Things. In *Proc. 1st Int. Symp. on Agent Systems and Applications and 3rd. Int. Symp. on Mobile Agents, IEEE Concurrency* 8(2):24-33, 2000.

46. N. Minsky, Y. Minsky, and V. Ungureanu. Making Tuple Spaces Safe for Heterogeneous Distributed Systems. In *Proceedings of ACM SAC 2000: Special Track on Coordination Models, Languages and Applications*, pages 218–226, April 2000.

47. D. Ndumu, H. Nwana, L. Lee, and H. Haynes. Visualisation of Distributed Multi-Agent Systems. *Applied Artifical Intelligence Journal*, 13 (1):187–208, 1999.

48. H. Nwana and D. Ndumu. A Perspective on Software Agents Research. *The Knowledge Engineering Review*, 14(2):125-142, 1999.

49. H. Nwana, D. Ndumu, L. Lee, and J. Collis. ZEUS: A Tool-Kit for Building Distributed Multi-Agent Systems. *Applied Artifical Intelligence Journal*, 13 (1):129–186, 1999.

50. H. S. Nwana and M. J. Wooldridge. Software Agent Technologies. In *Software Agents and Soft Computing: Towards Enhancing Machine Intelligence, Lecture Notes in Artifical Intelligence*, pages 59–78. Springer–Verlag, Heidelberg, 1997.

51. OMG. MASIF - The CORBA Mobile Agent Specification. URL http://www.omg.org/cgi-bin/doc?orbos/98-03-09.

52. A. Omicini, F. Zamborelli, M. Klush, and R. Tolksdorf. *Coordination of Internet Agents: Models, Technologies and Applications*. Springer–Verlag, Heidelberg, 2001.

53. C. Petrie. Agent-Based Engineering, the Web, and Intelligence. *IEEE Expert*, 11(6):24–29, 1996.

54. C. Petrie, S. Goldmann, and A. Raquet. Agent-Based Project Management. In *Lecture Notes in Artificial Intelligence*, pages 339–362, volume 1600. Springer–Verlag, Heidelberg, 1999.

55. O. F. Rama and K. Stout. What is Scalability in Multi-Agent Systems. In *Autonomous Agents 2000*, pages 56–63. IEEE Press, Piscataway, New Jersey, 2000.

56. A. S. Rao and M. P. Georgeff. BDI Agents: From Theory to Practice. In Victor Lesser, editor, *Proc. 1st Int. Conf. on Multi–Agent Systems*, pages 312–319. MIT Press, Cambridge, Mass., 1995.

57. A. S. Rao and M. P. Georgeff. Modeling Rational Agents within a BDI-Architecture. In *Proc. of Knowledge Representation and Reasoning (KR&R-91)*, pages 473–484, 1999.

58. D. Rossi, G. Cabi, and E. Denti. Tuple-based Technologies for Coordination. In A. Omicini, F. Zamborelli, M. Klush, and R. Tolksdorf, editors, *Coordination of Internet Agents: Models, Technologies and Applications*, pages 83–109. Springer–Verlag, Heidelberg, 2001.

59. S. J. Russell and P. Norvig. *Artificial Intelligence. A Modern Approach*. Prentice-Hall, Englewood Cliffs, New Jersey, 1995.

60. J. G. Schneider, M. Lumpe, and O. Nierstrasz. Agent Coordination via Scripting Languages. In A. Omicini, F. Zamborelli, M. Klush, and R. Tolksdorf, editors, *Coordination of Internet Agents: Models, Technologies and Applications*, pages 153–175. Springer–Verlag, Heidelberg, 2001.

61. W. Shen, D. Xue, and D. H. Norrie. An Agent-Based Manufacturing Enterprise Infrastructure for Distributed Integrated Intelligent Manufacturing Systems. In H. S. Nwana and D. T. Ndumu, editors, *Proc. 3rd Int. Conf. on Practical Applications of Agents and Multi-Agent Systems (PAAM-98)*, pages 533–548. London, 1998.

62. Y. Shoham. Agent-Oriented Programming. *Artificial Intelligence*, 60:51–92, 1993.

63. H. A. Simon. *The Sciences of the Artificial*. MIT Press, Cambridge, Mass., 1969.

64. I.A. Smith, P.R. Cohen, J.M. Bradshaw, M. Greaves, and H. Holmback. Designing Conversation Policies Using Joint Intention Theory. In *Proc. Int. Conf. on Multi-Agent Systems (ICMAS-98)*, pages 269–276, 1998.

65. N. Suri, J. M. Bradshaw, M. R. Breedy, P.T. Groth, G.A. Hill, and R. Jeffers. Strong Mobility and Fine-Grained Resource Control in NOMADS. In D. Kotz and F. Mattern, editors, *Agent Systems, Mobile Agents, and Applications, Lecture Notes on Computer Science*, volume 1882, pages 2–15. Springer–Verlag, Heidelberg, 2000.

66. N. Suri, P.T. Groth, and J. M. Bradshaw. While You're Away: A System for Load-Balancing and Resource Sharing Based on Mobile Agents. In *Proc. First IEEE/ACM Symp. on Cluster Computing and the Grid*, pages 470–473. IEEE Press, Piscataway, New Jersey, 2001.

67. L. Tobin, M. Steve, and W. Peter. T Spaces: The Next Wave. *IBM System Journal*, 37(3):454–474, 1998.

68. J. Waldo. JavaSpace Specification - 1.0. Technical Report, Sun Microsystems, 1998.

69. P. Wayner. Agents Away. *Byte*, May 1994.

70. J. E. White. Telescript Technology: Mobile Agents. In Jeffrey Bradshaw, editor, *Software Agents*. AAAI Press/MIT Press, Cambride, Mass., 1996.

71. M. Wooldridge. Agent-Based Software Engineering. *IEEE Proceedings Software Engineering*, 144(1):26–37, 1997.

72. M. Wooldridge and N. R. Jennings. Intelligent agents: Theory and Practice. *The Knowledge Engineering Review*, 10(2):115–152, 1995.

73. M. Wooldridge and N. R. Jennings. Pitfalls of Agent-Oriented Development. In Katia P. Sycara and Michael Wooldridge, editors, *Proc. 2nd Int. Conf. on Autonomous Agents (AGENTS-98)*, pages 385–391. ACM Press, New York, 1998.

74. M. Wooldridge, N. R. Jennings, and D. Kinny. A Methodology for Agent-Oriented Analysis and Design. In O. Etzioni, J. P. Müller, and J. M. Bradshaw, editors, *Proc. 3rd Annual Conf. on Autonomous Agents (AGENTS-99)*, pages 69–76. ACM Press, New York, 1999.

75. Agentbuilder framework. URL `http://www.agentbuilder.com`.

7

Knowledge Representation, Inference, and Planning

7.1 INTRODUCTION

Can we effectively manage systems consisting of large collections of similar objects without the ability to reason about an object based on the generic properties of the class the object belongs to? Can we process the very large volume of information regarding the characteristics and the state of components of a complex system without structuring it into knowledge? Many believe that the answer to these questions is a resounding "no" and some think that software agents are capable of providing an answer to the complexity of future systems.

In the previous chapter we discussed agent-based workflow management and argued that software agents are computer programs that exhibit some degree of autonomy, intelligence, and mobility. In this chapter we concentrate on the autonomy and intelligence attributes of an agent. Intelligent behavior means that the agent:

(i) is capable of infering new facts given a set of rules and a set of facts;

(ii) has some planning ability: given its current state, a goal state, and a set of actions, it is able to construct a sequence of actions leading from the current state to the goal state; and

(iii) is able to learn and modify its behavior accordingly.

We address first the problem of knowledge representation and discuss two logic systems that support inference: propositional logic and first-order logic. Then we present concepts related to knowledge engineering and automatic reasoning systems. We conclude the chapter with a discussion of planning and introduce basic definitions and two planning algorithms.

7.2 SOFTWARE AGENTS AND KNOWLEDGE REPRESENTATION

7.2.1 Software Agents as Reasoning Systems

Software agents are programs that deal with abstractions of objects and relations among objects in the real world and explicitly represent and reason with knowledge [6]. Thus agents should be built as reasoning systems with a control structure isolated from knowledge and with the knowledge consisting of largely independent components.

The problem we address now is how to represent the knowledge about the world and allow agents to reason about complex objects and their relationships. A first question we ask ourselves is: If agents are programs, why can we not use existing data structures and why do we need special means to represent and process knowledge? The answer to this question is rather subtle and it is the subject of this section.

The ability to classify objects into categories and reason about an instance of an object based on the generic properties or attributes of the entire category is essential for intelligent behavior. We all know what a car is and though there are many models, each with its own characteristics, we still learn to drive a generic car.

Our knowledge about surrounding objects is structured; we are able to carry out primitive actions with very basic knowledge and learn gradually more facts about a certain domain and interact in an increasingly sophisticated manner with the environment.

Example. Consider the concept of a "router" and the operation of "packet forwarding." Recall from Chapter 4 that a router forwards packets based on their final destination address; it examines the header of every incoming packet and if it finds an entry in the routing table matching the destination address, then the packet is queued on the outgoing port corresponding to the entry. If no match is found, then the packet is queued on the output port corresponding to the default outgoing link. If the queue of an outgoing port is full then the packet is dropped.

A router is characterized by the number of incoming and outgoing ports; the volume of traffic it can handle in terms of number of packets per second; the software it runs; the switching fabric; the hardware resources, e.g., main memory and processor speed; the maker of the router, and so on.

When asked to determine why the rate of packets dropped by a particular router is excessive, an expert will probably follow the following steps. She will first identify the type, function, hardware, software, and other characteristics of the router. Then she will monitor the traffic and determine the rate of incoming and outgoing packets on all links connected to the router and will identify the output port were packets are dropped. Finally, she will determine the cause, e.g, that the amount of buffer memory of the output port is insufficient.

In principle we could write a C program capable of carrying out the same logic for monitoring and diagnostics. But the program would be extremely complex because:

(i) the decision leading to the diagnostics is rather complex;

(ii) we have to abstract and represent information about classes of objects. For example, all routers produced by company X run the same operating system, Q, but there are also some routers produced by company Y that run under Q;

(iii) we have to asses the range of values of various variables, e.g., packet rates. Moreover, some of the information changes dynamically, e.g., a new version of the operating system does memory management more effectively. Such rapid changes of the state of the world would require repeated changes of the monitoring and diagnostics program.

However, an agent would separate the control functions from the knowledge. It will set up queries to determine the model of the router, then look up its knowledge base to identify the proper monitoring procedure for a particular model; once traffic data is collected the agent will use a set of rules to identify the cause of the problem.

Yet, *the agent cannot operate on unstructured data, but on knowledge.* This means that the agent should be able to differentiate between the meaning of the term "rate" in the context of communication and processing; it should know that the channel rate is measured in bits per second, while the processing rate of the router is measured in packets per second. It should also be able to understand the relationship between different components of a router.

7.2.2   Knowledge Representation Languages

In programming languages we use a limited set of primitive data structures such as integers, floating-point, strings, as well as operations among them to implement an algorithm. A variable in a programming language such as C++ or Java, is an abstraction and has a number of attribute-value pairs, e.g., `name`, `address`, `value`, `lifetime`, `scope`, `type`, `size`.

For example, in Java the variable `int i`, means that the `name` attribute of the variable has value `i` and that the `type` attribute has value `int`. The type `int` is an abstract data type; thus, we can think about the qualities of an `int` and we are able to use or reason about them without the need to know how `int`'s are represented, nor how the operations among integers are implemented.

Abstract data types make it easier to develop, modify, and reuse code because both the types and the operations are designed in a single package that can be easily imported and one can replace one implementation of the modules with another one because importing programs cannot take advantage of hidden implementation.

Polymorphism means having many forms and polymorphic functions provide the same semantics for different data types. For example, we may define a generic operation, say, addition, that applies to vectors of floating point numbers, integers, and complex values though the implementation of the addition would be different for the three data types.

Object-oriented programming languages support abstract data types and generic and polymorphic functions, procedures, and modules based on parametrized types.

Modern procedural languages allow the design of programs that are more robust and secure. For example, the `class` construct of C++ or Java provides the means to declare a set of values and an associated set of operations or methods, while `struct` construct of C only allows the specification of a set of values.

A Java `interface` comprises a set of method declarations but does not supply implementations for the methods it declares. An interface identifies the set of operations provided by every class that implements the interface. An `abstract Java class` defines only part of an implementation and typically contains one or more abstract methods. A Java interface is used to define the set of values and the set of operations, the abstract data type. Then, various implementations of the interface can be made by defining abstract classes that contain shared implementation features and then by deriving concrete classes from the abstract base classes.

Even modern procedural programming languages such as Java do not support such features as:

(i) multiple inheritance;

(ii) dynamic attributes for an abstraction (for example, we cannot add to the data structure `int` a new attribute such as `last modified`);

(iii) multilevel hierarchies, e.g., allow construction of classes of classes;

(iv) specification of a range of values for an attribute of an abstract data type.

Yet, agents have to manipulate objects with properties inherited from multiple ancestors and changing in time. Agents should have some knowledge about the world and be able to reason about alternative courses of actions. An agent is expected to draw conclusions about objects, events, time, state of the world, and to take more complex actions than just react to changes in the environment. Thus, an agent needs a language to express the knowledge and the means to carry out reasoning in that language. Such a language is known as a *knowledge representation language*.

Knowledge representation languages map entities in the real world into beliefs of agents, as shown in Figure 7.1. Propositional logic maps facts; first-order logic and semantic networks map facts, objects, and relations; temporal logic maps all of the above and time into agent beliefs and assigns to each belief either the value true, false or unknown. Probability and fuzzy logic lead to degrees of belief. Ontologies have to do with the nature of realities and epistemologies with the states of the knowledge of an agent.

The *syntax* of a knowledge representation language describes the valid sentences and the *semantics* relates the sentences of the language with the facts of the real world.

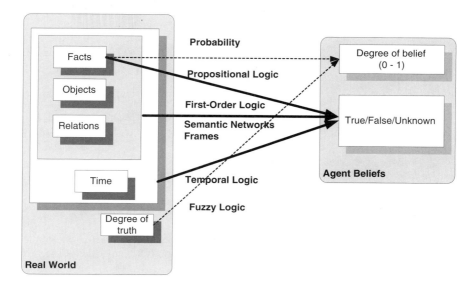

Fig. 7.1   Knowledge representation languages map entities in the real world into beliefs of agents.

Relations between sentences translate into relations between facts. For example, if s_1 and s_2 are sentences related semantically to facts f_1 and f_2, respectively, and if s_2 can be derived from s_1 then there is a causal relationship between facts f_1 and f_2, as shown in Figure 7.2. When the syntax and the semantics are precisely defined and we have *proof theory*, a set of rules to deduce the entailments, or consequences of a set of sentences, we speak about a formal system or a *logic*.

A *knowledge base* consists of a set of *sentences* in the knowledge representation language. The process of building a knowledge base is called *knowledge acquisition*. The process of reaching conclusions from existing premises is called *reasoning* or *inference*.

Knowledge representation languages are positioned somewhere in between programming languages and natural languages. Programming languages are designed to express algorithms and data structures, and are perfectly suited for describing *precisely* the state of a computation. Natural languages are considerably more expressive but less precise, they allow individuals to communicate, but often suffer from ambiguity because their representation power is limited.

From this brief discussion we conclude that knowledge representation languages should have several desirable properties. They should:

(i) be *expressive* - allow us to represent the knowledge we want to represent,

(ii) have a *well-defined syntax and semantics*; and

(iii) allow *new knowledge to be inferred* from a set of facts.

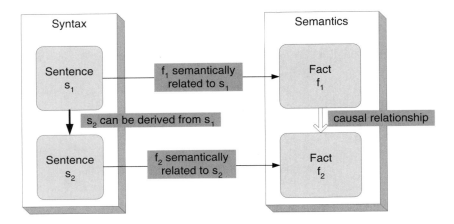

Fig. 7.2   Relations between sentences translate into relations between facts; s_1 and s_2 are sentences related semantically to facts f_1 and f_2, respectively. If s_2 can be derived from s_1, then there is a causal relationship between f_1 and f_2.

We discuss first two logic systems that support inference: propositional logic and first-order logic. In propositional logic symbols represent facts and they can be combined using Boolean connectives to form more complex sentences. In first-order logic we can represent objects as well as properties or relations among objects and we can use not only *connectives* but also *quantifiers* that allow us to express properties of entire collections of objects.

7.3   PROPOSITIONAL LOGIC

7.3.1   Syntax and Semantics of Propositional Logic

Definition. The Symbols of propositional logic are:

(i)   the logical constants `true` and `false`,

(ii)   symbols representing propositions,

(iii)   logical connectives:

$\vee$	`or`;
$\wedge$	`and`;
$\neg$	`not`;
$\Leftrightarrow$	`equivalence`;
$\Rightarrow$	`implies`;
$()$	`parenthesis`.

Table 7.1 The table of truth for logical connectives.

a	b	$\neg a$	$b \wedge a$	$a \vee b$	$a \Rightarrow b$	$a \Leftrightarrow b$
False	False	True	False	False	True	True
False	True	True	False	True	True	False
True	False	False	False	True	False	False
True	True	False	True	True	True	True

To resolve the ambiguity of complex sentences we impose the following order of precedence of connectives, from high to low: $\neg \wedge, \vee, \Rightarrow, \Leftrightarrow$.

Definition. Given two sentences P and Q, the following composite sentences are obtained using the logical connectives:

$P \wedge Q$	*conjunction,*
$P \vee Q$	*disjunction,*
$P \Leftrightarrow Q$	*equivalence.*
$P \Rightarrow Q$	*implication,*
$\neg P$	*negation.*

In an implication such as $P \Rightarrow Q$, P is called a *premise* or an *antecedent* and Q is a *conclusion* or *consequent*.

Definition. The BNF Syntax of the propositional logic is:

$Sentence \rightarrow AtomicSentence \mid ComplexSentence$
$AtomicSentence \rightarrow True \mid False \mid P \mid Q \mid R \mid \ .....$
$ComplexSentence \rightarrow$
$\qquad (Sentence) \mid Sentence\ Connective\ Sentence \mid \neg Sentence$
$Connective \rightarrow \vee \mid \wedge \mid \Leftrightarrow \mid \Rightarrow$

The semantics of propositional logic is defined by the interpretation of proposition symbols and by truth tables for the logical connectives. A proposition symbol may have any interpretation we choose. The sentence "In 1866 T.I. Singh measured the altitude of Lhasa and found it to be 3420 meters" may mean that "The Internet Telephony company Nighs will have a public offering at $18.66 a share on March 4, 2000 at the Ashla stock exchange."

The truth tables for the five logical connectives are given in Table 7.1. Given all possible combinations of truth values, True or False of boolean variables a and b we show the value of an expression giving several functions of a and b: negation of a, ¬a, and b ∧ a, or a ∨ b, implies a ⇒ b, and equivalence a ⇔ b.

Note that the implication connective does not require a causality relationship. For example, the sentence "After 1924 the Dalai Lama refused visas to anyone wanting to climb the mountain implies that K2 is higher than the Pioneer Peek" is true though there is no causality between the two sentences.

Table 7.2   Truth table showing that a $\Rightarrow$ b $\Leftrightarrow$ $\neg$a $\lor$ b

a	b	$\neg a$	$\neg a \lor b$	$a \Rightarrow b$
False	False	True	True	True
False	True	True	True	True
True	False	False	False	False
True	True	False	True	True

We are concerned with compositional languages where the meaning of a sentence is derived from the meaning of its parts by a process of decomposition and evaluation of its parts. Truth tables are used to test the validity of complex sentences.

Example. To evaluate an implication we construct a truth table for its premise and conclusions and decide that the implication is true if the conclusion follows from the premise for every possible combination of input sentences. Table 7.2 shows that a $\Rightarrow$ b $\Leftrightarrow$ $\neg$a $\lor$ b, a implies b is equivalent with $\neg$a or b, in other words, either the negation of a or b are true. The truth value for columns four and five of Table 7.2 are identical; the two expressions, $\neg$a $\lor$ b and a $\Rightarrow$ b have the same truth value regardless of the values of a and b .

Using the same method we can prove associativity and commutativity of conjunctions and disjunctions as well as the distributivity of $\land$ over $\lor$, of $\lor$ over $\land$, and de Morgan's laws:

$a \land (b \land c) \Leftrightarrow (a \land b) \land c$ (associativity of and)

$a \lor (b \lor c) \Leftrightarrow (a \lor b) \lor c$ (associativity of or)

$a \land b \Leftrightarrow b \land a$ (commutativity of and)

$a \lor b \Leftrightarrow b \lor a$ (commutativity of or)

$a \land (b \lor c) \Leftrightarrow (a \land b) \lor (a \land c)$ (distributivity of and)

$a \lor (b \land c) \Leftrightarrow (a \lor b) \land (a \lor c)$ (distributivity of or)

$\neg(a \land b) \Leftrightarrow \neg a \lor \neg b$ (de Morgan's laws)

$\neg(a \lor b) \Leftrightarrow \neg a \land \neg b$

7.3.2   Inference in Propositional Logic

Modeling is the process of abstracting the set of relevant properties of a system and identifying the relations between the components of the system as well as the relations of the system with the rest of the world. A reasoning system should be able to draw conclusions from premises regardless of the world the sentences refer to. In other words once we have modeled a system into a set of sentences, inference should be carried out without the need for additional information from the real world.

Given a knowledge base consisting of a set of statements and a set of inference rules, we can add new sentences to a knowledge base by inference.

Definition. A logic is *monotonic* if all the original sentences in the knowledge base are still entailed after adding to it new sentences obtained by inference.

Propositional logic is monotonic. Monotonicity is an important property, it allows us to determine the conclusion by examining only the sentences contained in the premise of the inference, rather than the entire knowledge base. Indeed, when the knowledge base is nonmonotonic, before deciding if the conclusion of an inference is entailed, one would need to check every sentence in the knowledge base.

Definition. An inference is *sound* if the conclusion is true when all premises are true. Note that the conclusion may also be true when some of the premises are false.

Now we discuss several patterns of inferences and show that they are sound. The notation

$$\frac{a}{b}$$

means that sentence b can be derived from a by inference.

Modus Ponens: infer a conclusion from an implication and one of the premises of the implication:

$$\frac{a \Rightarrow b, \; a}{b}$$

Sentence b is *true/false* if a implies b and if a is *true/false*.

Double Negation: infer a positive sentence, a, from a doubly negated one,

$$\frac{\neg \neg a \Rightarrow a}{a}$$

Unit Resolution: infer that one of the sentences of a disjunction is *true* if the other one is *false*,

$$\frac{a \vee b, \; \neg b}{a}$$

Transitivity of Implication:

$$\frac{a \Rightarrow b, \quad b \Rightarrow c}{a \Rightarrow c}$$

Table 7.3 proves that this inference is sound. Note that this rule can also be written as

$$\frac{a \vee b, \quad \neg b \vee c}{a \vee c}$$

Since b cannot be both *true* and *false* at the same time, one of the premises of the implications must be *true*, because each premise is a disjunction. Thus the conclusion, a disjunction itself must be *true*. Since $a \Rightarrow b \Leftrightarrow \neg a \vee b$ we can rewrite this as:

$$\frac{\neg a \Rightarrow b, \quad b \Rightarrow c}{\neg a \Rightarrow c}$$

Table 7.3 The transitivity property of an implication is sound. The four cases when both premises are **true** are in bold.

a	b	c	$a \Rightarrow b$	$b \Rightarrow c$	$a \Rightarrow c$
True	True	True	**True**	**True**	**True**
True	True	False	True	False	False
True	False	True	False	True	True
True	False	False	False	True	False
False	True	True	**True**	**True**	**True**
False	True	False	True	False	True
False	False	True	**True**	**True**	**True**
False	False	False	**True**	**True**	**True**

And Elimination: infer any conjunct of a conjunction:

$$\frac{a_1 \wedge a_2 \wedge \ ..... \ \wedge a_n}{a_i}$$

And Introduction: infer the conjunction of a number of sentences given individual sentences:

$$\frac{a_1, \ a_2, ... \ a_n}{a_1 \wedge a_2 \wedge \ ..... \ \wedge a_n}$$

Or Introduction: given a sentence, infer its disjunction with any other set of sentences:

$$\frac{a_i}{a_1, \ \vee \ a_2, ... \ \vee a_n}$$

The previous example and Table 7.3 show that the truth table method can be extended to all inference classes.

The complexity of the algorithms to determine the soundness of an inference is of concern for automatic reasoning systems like agents. If we have n proposition symbols, then the truth table will have 2^n rows, thus, the computation time to determine the soundness of inference is exponential.

Definition. A *Horn sentence* is one of the form: $p_1 \vee p_2 ... \vee p_n \Rightarrow q$, where p_i are non-negated atoms.

The inference procedure for Horn clauses is polynomial; indeed, we only need to check individual premises until we find one that is true.

Example. In this example an agent uses inference and propositional logic to identify the source of denial-of-service attacks on a Web server. The basic philosophy of the attacker is to generate TCP connection requests at a very high rate and send them to port 80 of the host where the Web server is located. This strategy prevents the server from responding to legitimate requests.

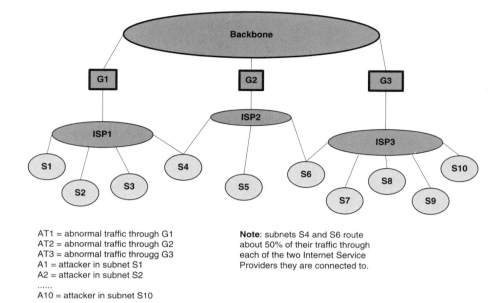

AT1 = abnormal traffic through G1
AT2 = abnormal traffic through G2
AT3 = abnormal traffic throug G3
A1 = attacker in subnet S1
A2 = attacker in subnet S2
......
A10 = attacker in subnet S10

Note: subnets S4 and S6 route
about 50% of their traffic through
each of the two Internet Service
Providers they are connected to.

Fig. 7.3   Network topology for the denial-of-service attack example.

The attacker takes several precautions to make tracking more difficult:

(i) it does not access the domain name server, instead the IP address of the Web
server is hardwired in the packets sent to establish the TCP connection, and

(ii) inserts a random sender IP address in each packet.

The three-way handshake required to establish the TCP connection cannot take
place because the IP address of the sender is incorrect and each connection request
times out, yet, the server wastes a large amount of resources.

The agent uses inference in propositional logic to identify the subnet most likely to
host the attacker. The search is narrowed down to three ISPs connected to the backbone
via gateways, G_1, G_2, G_3. There are ten suspected subnets, $S_1, S_2, ..., S_9, S_{10}$ as
shown in Figure 7.3.

The agent requests from each of the three gateways the information if an abnormal
traffic was observed. Gateway G_i, $i = 1, 3$ reports abnormal traffic if:

(i) the volume of the outgoing traffic is much larger than normal, and

(ii) a large number of outgoing TCP packets have the net address in the source IP
address different than the ones expected.

A fact is an assertion that some condition holds. For example, the fact AT_i means
that the traffic observed by gateway G_i is abnormal and $\neg AT_i$ means that the traffic

is normal and the attacker cannot be in one of the subnets connected to G_i. The fact $\neg A_j$ means that the attacker is not subnet S_j.

At some point in time the knowledge base contains three facts: $\neg AT_1$, $\neg AT_3$, AT_2, expressing the observations that abnormal traffic is only observed by G_2.

In addition to facts based on observations regarding the traffic, the agent has some knowledge of the environment expressed as rules. These rules reflect:

(i) the topology of the network, (rules 1 and 2) and

(ii) the routing strategy of subnets connected by two service providers (rule3).

The rules are:

Rule1 : $\neg AT_1 \;\Rightarrow\; \neg A_1 \;\wedge\; \neg A_2 \;\wedge\; \neg A_3 \;\wedge\; \neg A_4$. Subnets S_1, S_2, S_3, and S_4 are connected to gateway G_1, thus, the fact that G_1 does not report abnormal traffic means that the attacker is not in one of the subnets connected to it. In other words, none of the facts A_1, A_2, A_3, and A_4 are true.

Rule2 : $\neg AT_3 \;\Rightarrow\; \neg A_6 \;\wedge\; \neg A_7 \;\wedge\; \neg A_8 \;\wedge\; \neg A_9 \;\wedge\; \neg A_{10}$. Subnets A_6, A_7, A_8, A_9, and A_{10} are connected to gateway $G3$, thus, $G3$ will not report abnormal traffic if the attacker is not in one of the subnets connected to it.

Rule3 : $AT_2 \;\Rightarrow\; A_4 \;\vee\; A_5 \;\vee\; A_6$. If a subnet is connected to two ISPs, its outgoing traffic is split evenly on both ISPs.

We now follow the reasoning of the agent who applies successively the following inference rules:

(i) Modus Ponens to $rule1$ and obtains $\neg A_1 \wedge \neg A_2 \wedge \neg A_3 \wedge \neg A_4$. Then it applies End-Elimination to the previous result and gets: $\neg A_1$, $\neg A_2$, $\neg A_3$, $\neg A_4$. Thus the agent decides that the attacker is not subnets S_1, S_2, S_3 or S_4.

(ii) Modus Ponens to $rule2$ and obtains $\neg A_6 \wedge \neg A_7 \wedge \neg A_8 \wedge \neg A_9 \wedge \neg A_{10}$. Then it applies End-Elimination and gets: $\neg A_6$, $\neg A_7$, $\neg A_8$, $\neg A_9$, $\neg A_{10}$. Thus the agent decides that the attacker is not subnets S_6, S_7, S_8, S_9 or S_{10}.

(iii) Modus Ponens to $rule3$ and obtains $A_4 \;\vee\; A_5 \;\vee\; A_6$.

(iv) Unit Resolution to $A_4 \;\vee\; A_5 \;\vee\; A_6$, with a as $A_4 \;\vee\; A_5$ and b as A_6 and derives: $A_4 \;\vee\; A_5$.

(v) Unit Resolution to $A_4 \;\vee\; A_5$ with a as A_4 and b as A_5 and derives: A_5. Thus the attacker is in S_5.

Summary. From this example we see that an agent could use a model of the world to decide on its future actions. This model is a knowledge base consisting of sentences in a knowledge representation language, e.g., propositional logic. The agent uses inference to construct new sentences. The inference process must be sound, the new sentences must be true, whenever their premises are true.

7.4 FIRST-ORDER LOGIC

First-order logic is a representation language used in practically all fields of human activities to deal with objects and relations among them. While propositional logic assumes that the world consists of facts, first-order logic extends this perception to *objects* with individual *properties*, the *relations* and *functions* among these objects. First-order logic allows each domain to introduce its own representation of concepts necessary to express laws of nature or other rules like time, events, and categories.

Agents can use first-order logic to reason and maintain an internal model of the relevant aspects of the word and evaluate possible courses of action based on this knowledge.

7.4.1 Syntax and Semantics of First-Order Logic

A *term* represents an object and a *sentence* represents facts. Terms are built using constant symbols, variable symbols and function symbols while sentences consist of quantifiers and predicate symbols.

A *constant symbol* refers to only one object, a *variable symbol* can take a number of constant values.

A *predicate* refers to a particular relation in the model, e.g., the *teammate* predicate refers to members of a team. Some relations are *functional*, any object is related to only one other object by that function, e.g., the *routerProcessorOf( )* relation.

An atomic sentence is formed from a predicate symbol followed by a list of terms. For example, $ConnectedTo(ip_1, sf)$ states that input port ip_1 is connected to the switching fabric sf.

Logical connectives can be used to construct more complex sentences, e.g., the following sentence is true only if both input port ip_2 and output port op_3 are connected to the switching fabric: $ConnectedTo(ip_2, sf) \land ConnectedTo(op_3, sf)$.

The universal quantifier, $\forall$, allows us to express properties of entire collections of objects and the existential quantifier, $\exists$, properties of every object in a collection.

A term with no variables is called a *ground* term.

Definition. The BNF syntax of first-order logic is:

$$Sentence \;\rightarrow\; AtomicSentence \mid (Sentence)\; Connective\; (Sentence) \mid$$
$$\neg Sentence \mid Quantifier Variable, ... Sentence$$
$$AtomicSentence \;\rightarrow\; Predicate(Term, ...) \mid Term = Term$$
$$Term \;\rightarrow\; Function(Term, ...) \mid Constant \mid Variable$$
$$Connective \;\rightarrow\; \Rightarrow \mid \cup \mid \cap \mid \Leftrightarrow$$
$$Quantifier \;\rightarrow\; \forall \mid \exists$$
$$Constant \;\rightarrow\; sf \mid router_1 \mid server_i \; ...$$
$$Variable \;\rightarrow\; ?sf \mid ?router \mid ?server$$
$$Predicate \;\rightarrow\; Before \mid Faster \mid Router \mid \;....$$
$$Function \;\rightarrow\; Connected \mid ArrivalTime \mid \;....$$

7.4.2 Applications of First-Order Logic

To express knowledge about a domain using first-order logic we have to write a number of basic facts called *axioms* and then prove theorems about the domain. For example, in the domain of set theory, a discipline of mathematics, we want to represent elements of a set and individual sets, starting with an empty set, be able to decide if an element is a member of a set, construct the intersection and union of sets.

We only need:

(i) a constant called *empty set* and denoted by $\emptyset$,

(ii) three predicates, *Member*, *Set*, and *Subset*, denoted by $\in$, S, and $\subseteq$, respectively, and

(iii) three functions, *Add*, *Union*, and *Intersection* denoted by $\{\, element \mid set \,\}$, $\bigcup$, and $\bigcap$, respectively. The predicate $e \in s$ is true only if element e is a member of set s, $S(s)$ is true only if s is a set, $\{e \mid s\}$ denotes the set obtained by adding, element e to set s. A quantifier could be applied to more than one object, e.g., $\forall(e, s)$ or, equivalently, $\forall e, s$ means for all e and for all s.

The following eight independent axioms allow us to prove theorems in set theory:

A1. The empty set has no elements: $\quad \neg \exists(e, s) \; \{e \mid s\} \; = \; \emptyset$.

A2. A set s is either empty or one obtained by adding an element e to another set s_i: $\forall s \; S(s) \;\Leftrightarrow\; (s = \emptyset) \wedge \exists(e, s_i) \; S(s_i) \wedge s = \{e \mid s_i\}$

A3. Adding to a set s an element e already in the set has no effect:

$$\forall(e, s) \; e \in s \;\Leftrightarrow\; s = \{e \mid s\}$$

A4. A set s can be decomposed recursively into another set s_i and an element e_j added to it:

$$\forall(e, s) \, e \in s) \;\Leftrightarrow\; \exists(e_j, s_i) \; (s = \{e_j \mid s_i\} \wedge (e = e_j \vee (e \in s_i)))$$

A5. A set s_i is a subset of another set s_j if all members of s_i are also members of s_j

$$\forall(s_i, s_j) \; (s_i \subseteq s_j) \;\Leftrightarrow\; \forall e, (e \in s_i) \;\Rightarrow\; (e \in s_j)$$

A6. The intersection of two sets s_i and s_j consists of elements that are members of both sets:

$$\forall(e, s_i, s_j), \; (e \in s_i \cap s_j) \;\Leftrightarrow\; e \in s_i \wedge e \in s_j$$

A7. The union of two sets s_i and s_j consists of elements that are members of either set:

$$\forall(e, s_i, s_j), \; (e \in s_i \cup s_j) \;\Leftrightarrow\; e \in s_i \vee e \in s_j$$

A8. Two sets are equal if each one is a subset of the other:

$$\forall(s_i, s_j) \; (s_1 = s_2) \;\Leftrightarrow\; (s_i \subseteq s_j) \wedge (s_j \subseteq s_i)$$

Example. Using these axioms let us prove that the subset relation is transitive:

$$(s_i \subseteq s_j) \land (s_j \subseteq s_k) \Rightarrow s_i \subseteq s_k$$

Proof:

According to the axiom defining the subset relation:
$$(s_i \subseteq s_j) \Leftrightarrow \forall e, (e \in s_i) \Rightarrow (e \in s_j)$$
$$(s_j \subseteq s_k) \Leftrightarrow \forall e, (e \in s_j) \Rightarrow (e \in s_k)$$
Thus:
$\forall e, (e \in s_i) \Rightarrow (e \in s_k)$ and this is equivalent with $s_i \subseteq s_k$.

7.4.3 Changes, Actions, and Events

In the following we examine ensembles consisting of agents and their surrounding environments, the so-called *world*. An agent interacts with the world by perception and actions as shown in Figure 7.4. The world changes for a variety of reasons including the actions taken by the agent.

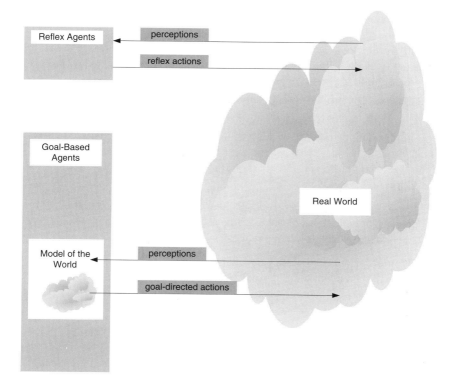

Fig. 7.4 The interactions between an agent and the world. Reflex agents classify their perceptions and act accordingly. Goal-directed agents maintain a model of the world and respond to changes with goal-directed actions.

An agent senses changes in the world and, in turn, performs actions that may change it. Based on their actions we recognize two types of agents, reflex agents and goal-directed agents. The first group simply classify their perceptions and respond through reflex actions. A traditional example of a reflex action is to step on the brakes when the traffic light is red. Another example of a reflex action is an agent monitoring the video stream at the site of a video client senses that the frame display rate is lower than the frame receive rate and starts dropping the frames before decoding them until the client catches up.

More sophisticated agents maintain a model of the world, where all relevant knowledge about the environment is kept. Such agents are goal-directed and their actions are subordinated to their goal. We are primarily concerned with agents that maintain a model of the world. The problem we address now is how to describe in the model the changes in the world.

Situation calculus is a method to express changes that is compatible with first-order logic. The idea is relatively simple; we take a snapshot of the world at discrete moments of time and link these snapshots/situations by the actions taken by the agent. The process described above is similar to recording the surroundings with a movie camera, each situation is equivalent with a frame. The properties of the situation taken after an action are indicated as in Figure 7.5, where $S(0)$, $S(1)$, ... , $S(n)$ are the situation constants.

The first-order logic axioms describing the effect of the actions are called *effect axioms*, the ones describing how the world stays the same are called *frame axioms* and those combining the two are called *successor state axioms*.

There are several problems in situation calculus:

(i) The *representational frame problem:* We need a very large number of frame axioms. This problem can be solved using successor state axioms. Such axioms say that a predicate will be true after an action, if the action made it true or if it was true before and the action did not affect it, and will stay true until an action reverses it.

(ii) The *inferential frame problem:* Whenever we have to reason about long sequences of actions we have to carry every property through all situations even when the property does not change.

(iii) Situation calculus cannot deal with continuous changes in time and it works best only when actions occur one at a time. Imagine a world where there are multiple agents each one performing independent actions. Clearly, situation calculus cannot handle continuous changes in time and we need to turn to a new approach called the *event calculus*.

The event calculus is a continuous version of the situation calculus. *An event* is a temporal and spatial "slice" of the environment, it may consist of many sub-events. *Intervals* are collections of subevents occurring in a given period of time. Examples of intervals are: the first week of October 2001, the time it took a packet from source to destination, etc. A packet that joins the queue of the input line of a router, beginning of the transmission of a packet are examples of events.

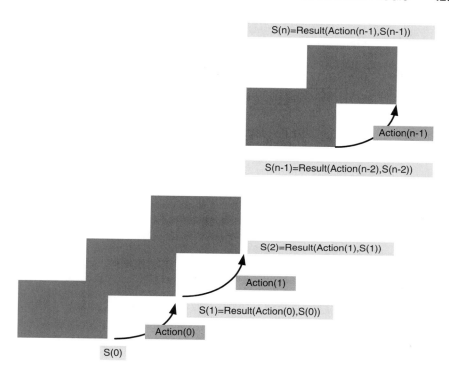

Fig. 7.5 Snapshots/situations linked by actions. A state, $S(i)$ is reached from a previous state, $S(i-1)$ as a result of an action, $A(i-1)$ or: $S(i) = Result(Action(i-1), S(i-1))$.

7.4.4   Inference in First-Order Logic

We introduce three new inference rules for first-order logic, that require substitution and then present a generalization of the Modus Ponens rule. In the general case, we define sentences in terms of variables, then substitute ground terms for these variables and infer new facts. The new rules are:

Universal Elimination.   Given a sentence a we can infer new facts by substituting the ground term g for variable v:

$$\frac{\forall v \; a}{Sub(\{v \mid g\}, \; a)}$$

For example, consider the predicate $SameDomain(x, y)$ that is true only if hosts x and y are in the same IP domain. We can use the substitution

$\{x/dragomirna.cs.purdue.edu, \; y/govora.cs.purdue.edu\}$ and infer

$SameDomain(dragomirna.cs.purdue.edu, \; govora.cs.purdue.edu)$

Existential Elimination. If there exists a variable v in sentence a, we can substitute a constant symbol k that does not appear in the knowledge base for v and infer a,

$$\frac{\exists v \; a}{Sub(\{v \mid k\}, \; a)}$$

For example, from $\exists x \; SameDomain(x, \; govora.cs.purdue.edu)$ we can infer $SameDomain(agapia.cs.purdue.edu, \; govora.cs.purdue.edu)$ as long as $agapia.cs.purdue.edu$ does not appear in the knowledge base.

Existential Induction. Given a sentence a, a variable v that does not occur in a, and a ground term g that does occur in a, we can substitute the ground term g by variable v:

$$\frac{a}{\exists v \; Sub(\{g \mid v\}, \; a)}$$

For example, from
$SameDomain(agapia.cs.purdue.edu, \; govora.cs.purdue.edu)$
we can infer $\exists \, x \; SameDomain(x, \; govora.cs.purdue.edu)$

Generalized Modus Ponens. This rule allows us to find a substitution for all variables in an implication sentence and the sentence to be matched:

$$\frac{p'_1, p'_2, ..., p'_n, \; (p_1 \wedge p_2 \wedge \; .... \; \wedge p_n \Rightarrow q)}{Sub(\theta, q)}$$

Example. To illustrate inference in first-order logic, consider the following facts: "If an individual reads an Email containing a virus and he clicks on the attachment the virus will damage his computer. There is a known virus called the LoveBug. The LoveBug virus comes with an Email message with the subject line 'I Love You' and with an attachment 'love.vcp'. John owns a computer and uses it to read his Email. John got an Email message with a subject line 'I Love You' and with an attachment 'love.vcp'. He clicked on the attachment."

Using these facts we want to prove that John's computer was damaged. To do so we first represent each fact in first-order logic:

"If an individual reads an Email containing a virus and he clicks on the attachment, the virus will damage his computer."
$$\forall x, y, z, w \; Person(w) \wedge Email(z) \wedge Computer(y) \wedge Virus(x) \wedge$$
$$ReadEmail(w, y, x, z) \wedge EmailCariesVirus(z, x) \wedge Click(z) \Rightarrow Damage(y) \quad (1)$$

"There is a known virus called the LoveBug."
$$Virus(LoveBug) \quad (2)$$

"The LoveBug virus comes with an Email message with the subject line 'I Love You' and with an attachment 'love.vcp'."

$\exists z \ Email(z) \wedge Subject(z, "ILoveYou") \wedge Attached(z, "love.vcp") \Rightarrow$
$EmailCariesVirus(z, LoveBug)$ (3)

"John owns a computer and uses it to read his Email."

$\exists y \ Person(John) \wedge Owns(John, y) \wedge Computer(y)$ (4)

"Using his computer John read an Email message with a subject line 'I Love You' and with an attachment 'love.vcp'. He clicked on the attachment."

$\exists x, y, z \ Email(z) \wedge ReadEmail(John, y, x, z) \wedge Subject(z, "ILoveYou") \wedge$
$Attached(z, "love.vcp") \wedge Click(z)$ (5)

From (4) and Existential Elimination we get:

$Person(John) \wedge Owns(John, C) \wedge Computer(C)$ (6)

From (5), (6) and Existential Elimination we get:

$\exists x \ Email(M) \wedge ReadEmail(John, C, x, M) \wedge Subject(M, "ILoveYou") \wedge$
$Attached(M, "love.vcp") \wedge Click(M)$ (7)

From (7) and And-Elimination we get:

$Email(M)$ (8.1)
$\exists x \ ReadEmail(John, C, x, M)$ (8.2)
$Subject(M, "ILoveYou")$ (8.3)
$Attached(M, "love.vcp")$ (8.4)

From (8.1), (8.3), (8.4) and And-Introduction we get:

$Email(M) \wedge Subject(M, "ILoveYou") \wedge Attached(M, "love.vcp") \Rightarrow$
$EmailCariesVirus, (M, LoveBug)$ (9)

If we apply to (1) Universal Elimination four times we get:

$Person(John) \wedge Email(M) \wedge Computer(C) \wedge Virus(LoveBug) \wedge$
$ReadEmail(John, C, LoveBug, M) \wedge EmailCariesVirus(M, LoveBug) \wedge$
$Click(M) \Rightarrow Damage(Y)$ (10)

From (6) and And-Elimination we get:

$Person(John)$ (11.1)
$Computer(C)$ (11.2)

From (11.1), (11.2), (2),(8.2), (8.5),(8.1), (9), (10) and Modus Ponens we get:

$Damage(C)$

7.4.5 Building a Reasoning Program

In this section we discuss the problem of building reasoning programs assuming that we use first-order logic as a knowledge representation language and apply to it the inference rules presented earlier. In the following, the substitution of a variable by another is called *renaming*, e.g., $ConnectedTo(x, switchingFabric)$ and $ConnectedTo(y, switchingFabric)$ are renaming of each other.

Canonical Forms. In the general case we have many inference rules and we have to decide the order in which to apply these rules. To simplify the inference process we restrict ourselves to a single inference rule, the Generalized Modus Ponens. This is possible when every sentence in the knowledge base is either an atomic sentence or a Horn sentence. Recall that a Horn sentence is an implication with a conjunction of atomic sentences on the left and a single atom on the right, and that Modus Ponens does not allow us to derive new implications, we can only derive atomic conclusions.

Definition. The process of transforming two atomic sentences p and q by some substitution so that they look the same is called *unification*.

θ, the unifier operator is defined formally as: $Unify(p, q) = \theta$ such that $Sub(\theta, p) = Sub(\theta, q)$.

Composition of substitutions. Often we need to apply several substitutions one after another: $Sub(Compose(\theta_1, \theta_2), p) = Sub(\theta_2, Sub(\theta_1, p))$

Forward-Chaining Algorithms. This is a data-driven procedure entirely capable of drawing irrelevant conclusions. As new facts come in, inferences that may or may not be helpful for solving the particular problem are drawn.

The basic idea of the algorithm is to generate all conclusions that can be derived after considering a new fact p. We have to consider all implications that have a premise matching p. If all remaining premises are already in the knowledge base, KB, then we can infer the conclusion.

Backward-Chaining Algorithms. The algorithm finds all answers to questions posed to KB. The idea is to examine the knowledge base to find out if the proof already exists. The algorithm then finds all implications whose conclusions unify with the query and attempts to establish the premises of these implications by backward chaining.

Figure 7.6 shows the proof that John's computer was damaged using backward chaining. For that we construct the proof tree and process it left to right, depth first.

Summary. First-order logic or, more precisely, first-order predicate calculus with equality, deals with *objects* and with relations or *predicates* among them and allows us to express facts about objects. Using first-order logic one can quantify over objects but not over relations and functions on those objects. Higher-order logic allows us to quantify over relations and functions as well as over objects.

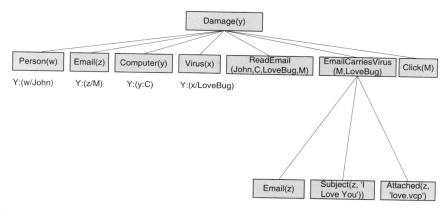

Fig. 7.6 The proof for the example in Section 7.4.4 based on the backward-chaining algorithm. We construct the proof tree and process it left to right, depth first.

7.5 KNOWLEDGE ENGINEERING

7.5.1 Knowledge Engineering and Programming

Knowledge engineering is the process of building a knowledge base and of writing some inference rules to derive new consequences, very much like programming is about writing and executing programs that may produce various outputs given some inputs. The steps taken for knowledge engineering mirror the ones taken when programming, see Figure 7.7:

(i) choose a logic/choose a programming language,

(ii) build a knowledge base/write the program,

(iii) implement the proof theory/select a compiler, and

(iv) infer new facts/execute the program.

Knowledge engineering is based on a declarative approach to system building, it provides methods to construct and use a knowledge base regardless of the domain. The task of a knowledge engineer is simpler than that of a programmer; she only needs to decide what objects to represent and what relations among objects hold. Once she specifies what is *true*, the inference procedures turn these facts into a solution. This task is simpler than writing a program when the algorithm must describe in detail the relations between the set of inputs and the outputs. Moreover, debugging a knowledge base is trivial, each sentence is either *true* or *false* by itself, while a decision about the correctness of a program is more involved.

So far we have seen two tools for knowledge representation and reasoning, predicate and first-order logic. Now we address the process of actually building knowledge

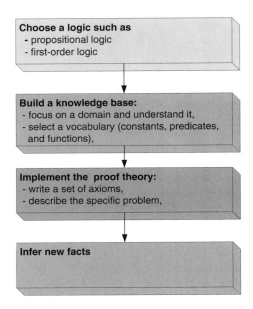

Fig. 7.7   Knowledge engineering.

bases, how to express facts in a given domain. A knowledge base is targeted toward humans and computers.

Several principles should be observed when building a knowledge base:

1. Automated inference procedures should allow us to obtain the same answers regardless of how the knowledge is encoded.

2. Facts entered into the knowledge base should be reused and as the system grows one should need fewer new facts and predicates.

3. Whenever we add a sentence to the knowledge base we should ask ourselves how general it is, can we express the facts that make it true instead, how does a new class relate to existing classes.

7.5.2   Ontologies

We can communicate effectively with one another if and only if there is agreement regarding the concepts used in the exchange. Confusion results when individuals or organizations working together do not share common definitions and the context of basic concepts. A former secretary of defense gives the following example [10]: "In managing DoD there are unexpected communication problems. For instance, when the Marines are ordered to *secure a building* they form a landing party and assault it. The same instruction will lead the Army to occupy the building with a troop of infantry. The Navy will characteristically respond by sending a yeoman to assure that the building lights are turned out. When the Air Force acts on these instructions, what results is a three year lease with option to purchase."

Humans, as well as programmed agents need a content theory of the domain to work coherently toward a common goal. Domain modeling is a critical research topic in areas as diverse as workflow management, databases, or software engineering. For example, workflow management systems have to agree on fundamental concepts such as process, resource, activity, to exchange information, or to support inter-organizational workflows. Regardless of the level of sophistication of a problem solver, whether it uses neural networks or fuzzy logic, it cannot work effectively without a content theory of the domain; thus, the continuing interest in ontologies. An ontology describes the structure of a domain at different levels of abstraction.

Researchers from different fields view ontologies differently; some, view ontologies as object models and are not concerned with the context. By contrast, the AI community views an ontology as a formal logic theory not only to define terms and relationships, but also the context where the relationships apply.

Ontologies can be classified based on formality, coverage, guiding principles, and point of view as follows:

(i) *upper ontologies* that cover concepts common across several domains;

(ii) *domain specific ontologies*;

(iii) *theory ontologies* that describe basic concepts such as space, time, causality; and

(iv) *problem-solving ontologies,* that describe strategies for solving domain problems.

Now, we overview several concepts of a general-purpose ontology and defer until later the discussion of a domain-specific ontology. A *general-purpose ontology* defines the broadest set of concepts, e.g., categories, composite objects, measures, time intervals, events and processes, physical objects, mental objects, and beliefs.

Categories. A category includes objects with common properties. The partition of objects into categories is important because we can reason at the level of categories and we can simplify knowledge bases through a process of *inheritance.*

Subclass relations based on taxonomies help us organize categories. For example, in Figure 7.8 we present a taxonomy of applications based on their timing constraints imposed on communication. Recall from Chapter 5 that real-time applications have timing constraints; thus, they are sensitive to communication delays and/or communication rates. Elastic applications are insensitive to communication delays and rates. Applications with real-time constraints are either tolerant or intolerant. Tolerant ones can be either adaptive or nonadaptive. Adaptive ones can be delay-adaptive or rate-adaptive. An example of delay-adaptive are video applications, whereas audio applications are rate-adaptive.

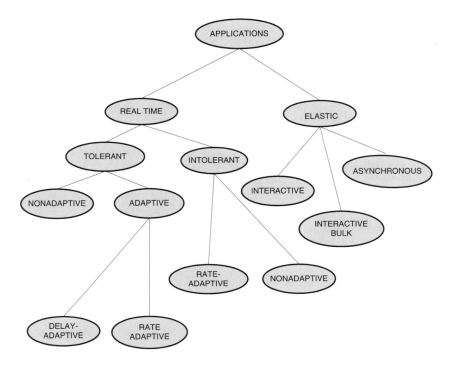

Fig. 7.8 Taxonomy of applications based on their timing constraints imposed on communication.

An object is a member of a category, a category is a subclass of another category, all members of a category have some properties in common, and a category has some properties. Two categories that have no members in common are said to be disjoint. For example, the *wirelessCommunicationChannel* category is disjoint from the category *fiberOpticsCommunicationChannel*.

An object may inherit from multiple categories. For example, the category describing a fiber optics channel, *fiberOpticsCommunicationChannel*, inherits from the communication channel category attributes such as bandwidth, latency, and attenuation; at the same time, it inherits from the fiber optics category attributes such as mode and wavelength.

In first-order logic categories are represented as unary predicates, e.g., *IPaddress(x), DHCPserver(x)* are predicates that are true for objects that are IP addresses and DHCP servers, respectively. *Reification* is the process of turning a predicate into an object in the language.

Composite Objects. Objects can be composed of other objects and first-order logic allows us to describe the *structure* of a composite object using the PartOf relation. The *PartOf* relation is transitive and reflexive.

Example. A router consists of input and output ports, switching fabric, and a routing processor, as shown in Figure 4.17. The structure of a router with n input and m output ports can be expressed using first-order logic:

$\forall r \ Router(r) \ \Rightarrow \ \exists ip_1, \ ip_2, \ ip_3, ..., \ ip_n, \ op_1, \ op_2, \ op_3, ..., \ op_m, \ sf, \ rp$

$InputPort(ip_1) \ \wedge \ InputPort(ip_2) ... \ \wedge \ InputPort(ip_n) \ \wedge$

$OutputPort(op_1) \ \wedge \ OutputPort(op_2) \ \wedge \ ... \ OutputPort(op_m) \ \wedge$

$SwitchingFabric(sf) \ \wedge \ RoutingProcessor(rp) \ \wedge \ ConnectedTo(rp, sf) \ \wedge$

$ConnectedTo(ip_1, sf) \wedge ConnectedTo(ip_2, sf) ... \wedge ConnectedTo(ip_n, sf) \wedge$

$ConnectedTo(op_1, sf) \ \wedge \ ConnectedTo(op_2, sf) ... \ \wedge \ ConnectedTo(op_m, sf)$

Here, a predicate like $SwitchingFabric(sf)$ means that sf is indeed a component of type $SwitchingFabric$ and $ConnectedTo(ip_1, sf)$ means that input port ip_1 is connected to the switching fabric, sf.

Since the *PartOf* relation is transitive and reflexive we have:

$PartOf \ (ip_1, \ router_k) \ \wedge \ PartOf \ (inputQueue_1, ip_1) \ \Rightarrow$
$PartOf \ (inputQueue_1, router_k).$

Time Intervals. The functions *Start* and *End* are used to identify the beginning and end of an interval, *Duration* the length of an interval, and *Time* the actual time during an interval.

$\forall Int \ Interval(Int) \ \Rightarrow$
$$Duration(Int) \ = \ (Time(End(Int)) \ - \ Time(Start(Int)))$$

Two intervals may be disjoint, one may be included in the other, they may overlap, or just be adjacent to one another. Several predicates define the following relations between two intervals: *Before, After, Meet, During, Overlap*, see also Figure 7.9:

$\forall Int_i, \ Int_j \ \ Before(Int_i, Int_j) \ \Leftrightarrow \ Time(End(Int_i)) \ < \ Time(Begin(Int_j))$

$\forall Int_i, \ Int_j \ \ After(Int_i, Int_j) \ \Leftrightarrow \ Time(Start(Int_i)) \ > \ Time(End(Int_j))$

$\forall Int_i, \ Int_j \ \ Meet(Int_i, Int_j) \ \Leftrightarrow \ Time(End(Int_i)) \ = \ Time(Start(Int_j))$

$\forall Int_i, \ Int_j \ During(Int_i, Int_j) \ \Leftrightarrow \ Time(Start(Int_i)) \ \geq \ Time(Start(Int_j)$
$\wedge \ Time(End(Int_i)) \ \leq \ Time(End(Int_j)$

$\forall Int_i, \ Int_j \ \ Overlap(Int_i, Int_j) \ \Leftrightarrow \ \exists t \ During(t, Int_i)) \ \wedge \ During(t, Int_j))$

Measures. Physical objects have properties such as mass, length, height, density, cost, and so on. A measure is a numerical value attached to such a property. The most important property of measures is that they can be *ordered*. For example, knowing that the bandwidth of channels A and B are 100 and 1000 Mbps, respectively, we conclude that channel B is faster:

$Bandwidth(channel_A) \ = \ Mbps(100) \ \wedge \ Bandwidth(channel_B) \ =$
$Mbps(1000) \ \Rightarrow \ Faster(channel_B, channel_A)$

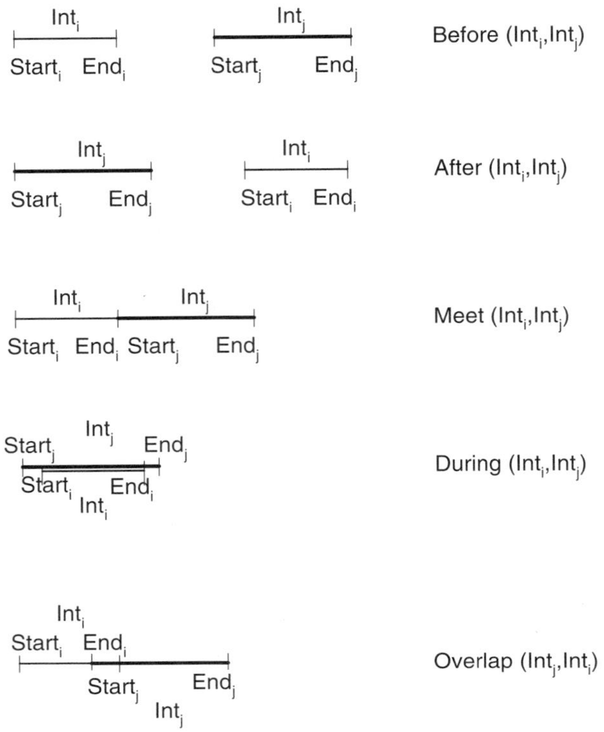

Fig. 7.9   A temporal logic predicate defines the relationship between two time intervals.

The measures can be expressed using different units. For example, the bandwidth of a communication channel can be expressed in Kilobits per second, Kbps, or in Megabits per second, Mbps/sec and the relationship between the two units is:

$$\forall b, \quad Kbps(b) = 1000 \times Mbps(b).$$

7.6   AUTOMATIC REASONING SYSTEMS

7.6.1   Overview

Automatic reasoning systems are capable of manipulating and reasoning with logic. Such systems can be broadly classified in several categories:

Logic programming languages such as Prolog. The implication is the primary representation in a logic programming language. Such languages typically (a) include nonlogical features such as input and output; (b) do not allow negation, disjunction, and equality; and (c) are based on backward-chaining.

Production systems are similar to logic programming languages but they interpret the consequent of each implicant as an action rather than a logical conclusion and use forward-chaining. The actions are insertions and deletions in the knowledge base and input and output. Expert systems such as Clips and Jess use the Rete pattern-matching algorithm, a forward-chaining algorithm [3].

Semantic networks represent objects as nodes of a graph with a taxonomic structure. The most important relations between concepts are the subclass relations between classes and subclasses, and instance relations between particular objects and their parent class. However, other relations are allowed.

The subclass and instance relations may be used to derive new information not explicitly represented. Semantic networks normally allow efficient inheritance-based inferences using special purpose algorithms. The drawbacks of semantic networks are: (1) they lack a well-defined semantics, e.g., a graph node with *router* written on it represents one router or all routers; (2) limited expressiveness, e.g., universal quantification is difficult to represent; and (3) ternary and higher order relations are cumbersome to represent. The links between nodes are binary relations.

Frame systems. The frame systems are similar to the semantic networks and we discuss in more depth an emerging standard called OKBC in Section 7.6.3.

Logic systems. Predicate logic is one of the most widely used knowledge representation languages. In predicate logic the meaning of a predicate is given by the set of all tuples to which the predicate applies. New meta-models that attempt to capture more of the domain semantics have been developed "on top" of predicate calculus (e.g, the *entity-relationship (ER)* model popular in the area of relational database systems) and *F-logic*.

Basic entities in ER modeling are conceptualized in conjunction with their properties and attributes, which are strictly distinguished from relations between entities. The *entity type* is defined by:

(i) a name,

(ii) a list of attributes with associated domains,

(iii) a list of attribute functions with associated signatures and implementations, and

(iv) a possibly empty set of *integrity constraints* (restrictions on admissible values of attributes).

A fundamental type of integrity constraint is a *key dependency*, that is a minimal set of attributes whose values identify an entity (it is a constraint, since it implies that their must be no pair of entities of the same type having the same values for their key attributes).

Relationships between entities can be either application domain specific or domain independent. There are two basic domain independent relationships: the *subclass* relationship and the *aggregation* relationship.

7.6.2 Forward- and Backward-Chaining Systems

Forward-Chaining Systems. The facts are represented in a continually updated working memory. The conditions are usually patterns that must match items in the working memory, while the actions usually involve adding or deleting items from the working memory. The interpreter controls the application of the rules based on a *recognize-act* cycle; first, it checks to find all the rules whose conditions hold, given the current state of working memory; then, selects one and performs the actions mandated by the rule.

Conflict resolution strategies are used to select the rules. The actions will result in a new working memory, and the cycle begins again. This cycle continues until either no rules fire, or some specified goal state is satisfied.

A number of conflict resolution strategies can be used to decide which rule to fire:

(i) Do not fire a rule twice on the same data.

(ii) Fire rules on more recent working memory elements before older ones. This allows the system to follow through a single chain of reasoning, rather than to keep on drawing new conclusions from old data.

(iii) Fire rules with more specific preconditions before ones with more general preconditions.

Backward-Chaining Systems. Given a goal state we wish to prove, a backward-chaining system will first check to see if the goal matches the initial facts given. If it does, then that goal succeeds. If it does not, the system will look for rules whose conclusions match the goal. One such rule will be chosen, and the system will then try to prove any facts in the preconditions of the rule using the same procedure, setting these as new goals to prove. Note that a backward-chaining system does not need to update a working memory. Instead, it needs to keep track of what goals it needs to prove at any given time given its main hypothesis.

7.6.3 Frames – The Open Knowledge Base Connectivity

Frames resemble closely objects and classes from object-oriented languages, but provide features such as multiple inheritance and meta-classes. The information relevant to a particular concept is stored in a single complex entity, called a *frame*. We examine briefly the *open knowledge base connectivity (OKBC)* [1], an emerging standard. Protege, a knowledge base creation and maintenance tool, is based on OKBC.

Definition. *The universe of discourse* is a set of entities we want to express knowledge about, as well as all constants of the basic types: true, false, integers, floating point numbers, strings, classes.

Definition. *Classes* are sets of entities, and all sets of entities are considered to be classes.

Definition. A *frame* is a primitive object that represents an entity. A frame that represents a class is called a *class frame*, and a frame that represents an individual is called an *individual frame*.

Definition. *Own slot.* A frame has associated with it a set of own slots, and each own slot of a frame has associated with it *slot values*.

Given a frame F, each value V of an own slot S of F represents the assertion (S F V) that the binary relation S holds for the entities represented by F and V. Since a relation can be an entity in the domain of discourse and hence representable by frames, a slot may be represented by a *slot frame* that describes the properties of the slot.

For example, the assertion that a communication channel is characterized by its bandwidth, latency, attenuation, and noise can be represented by a frame called communicationChannel. This frame has an own-slot called: communicationChannelProperties.

In turn, this own slot has four other frames as values:, communicationChannelBandwidth, communicationChannelLatency, communicationChannelAttenuation, and communicationChannelNoise.

Definition. *Own facet, facet value.* An own slot of a frame has associated with it a set of *own facets*, and each own facet of a slot of a frame has associated with it a set of entities called *facet values*.

Formally, a facet is a ternary relation, and each value OwnFacetValue of own facet OwnFacet of slot Slot of frame Frame represents the assertion that the relation OwnFacet holds for the relation Slot, the entity represented by Frame, and the entity represented by OwnFacetValue, i.e.,

(OwnFacet Slot Frame OwnFacetValue).

A facet may be represented by a *facet frame* that describes the properties of the facet since a relation can be an entity in the domain of discourse and hence representable by a frame. For example, the assertion that "voice over IP requires that the end-to-end delay be smaller than 150 milliseconds," can be represented by the facet :VALUE-TYPE of the DesirableProperties slot of the VoiceOverIP with the value Delay and the constraint smaller than 150 milliseconds.

Definition. *Class, instance, types, individuals, metaclasses.* A class is a set of entities. Each of the entities in a class is an instance of the class. An entity can be an instance of multiple classes, called its types. Entities that are not classes are referred to as individuals. Thus, the domain of discourse consists of individuals and classes. A class can be an instance of a class.

A class with instances that are themselves classes is called a meta-class, e.g., a particular router called CISCO Model XX is an instance of the Router class, which is itself an instance of an CommunicationHardware class.

Definition. A class frame has associated with it a collection of *template slots* that describe own slot values considered to hold for each instance of the class represented by the frame.

The values of template slots are said to be inherited to the subclasses and by the instances of a class. Formally, each value V of a template slot S of a class frame C represents the assertion that the relation template-slot-value holds for the relation S, the class represented by C, and the entity represented by V, i.e.,

(template-slot-value S C V).

That assertion, in turn, implies that the relation S holds between each instance I of class C and value V, i.e., (S I V). It also implies that the relation template-slot-value holds for the relation S, each subclass C_s of class C, and the entity represented by V, (template-slot-value (S C_s V)).

Thus, the values of a template slot are inherited by subclasses as values of the same template slot and to instances as values of the corresponding own slot. For example, the assertion that the gender of all female persons is female could be represented by template slot Gender of class frame Female-Person having the value Female. Then, an instance of Female-Person called Mary, Female is a value of the own slot Gender of Mary.

A template slot of a class frame has associated with it a collection of template facets that describe own facet values considered to hold for the corresponding own slot of each instance of the class represented by the class frame. As with the values of template slots, the values of template facets are said to inherit to the subclasses and instances of a class. Formally, each value V of a template facet F of a template slot S of a class frame C represents the assertion that the relation template-facet-value holds for the relations F and S, the class represented by C, and the entity represented by V, i.e., (template-facet-value F S C V). That assertion, in turn, implies that the relation F holds for relation S, each instance I of class C, and value V, i.e., (F S I V). It also implies that the relation template-facet-value holds for the relations S and F, each subclass C_s of class C, and the entity represented by V, i.e., $(template - facet - value F S C_s V)$. The values of a template facet are inherited to subclasses as values of the same template facet and to instances as values of the corresponding own facet.

Definition. *A knowledge base (KB)* is a collection of classes, individuals, frames, slots, slot values, facets, facet values, frame-slot associations, and frame-slot-facet associations. KBs are considered to be entities in the universe of discourse and are represented by frames. All frames reside in some KB.

Since frame systems are a variant of semantic nets, they retain most of their shortcomings.

Example. Protege is an integrated software tool to develop knowledge-based systems. This tool was created by a group at Stanford University [5].

The current version, *Protege-2000* is implemented in Java and it is based on the OKBC knowledge model [1].

The system consists of three basic components:

(i) A knowledge base server. In the default configuration an in-memory single user server is provided that supports a custom file format based on Clips syntax.

(ii) The control layer handles standard actions and connection between widgets and underlying knowledge base.

(iii) The widget layer provides user interface components that allow a small slice of the knowledge base to be viewed and edited.

We now present an example of use of Protege to construct a domain specific ontology. In Figure 7.10 we see that networking topic is mapped to a class. The top classes are: Internet, Layers, Protocols, Network Security, Network Management, Hardware, Software, and so on.

In turn, Internet consists of several classes: Network Core, Network Edge, Switching, Service Models, Topology, and so on. Each of these may have several subclasses; for example, the subclass Switching covers, Circuit, Packet and Message Switching, then Packet Switching consists of several subclasses, Store and Forward, Broadcast, and ATM. Note that ATM inherits from several classes; in addition to Switching it inherits from Hardware.

7.6.4 Metadata

Metadata is a generic term for standards used to describe the format of data. For example, the Hypertext Markup Language (HTML) provides a standard for describing documents accessible via a Web server. Without such a standard it would be impossible for clients, in this case Web browsers, to present the documents in meaningful format.

Metadata can be located either together with the data it describes or separately. In case of Web pages the metadata is stored together with the document itself. When the metadata is stored separately, multiple descriptions of the same data can appear in different locations and we need a distributed metadata representation model capable of:

(i) determining easily that two descriptions refer to the same data,

(ii) combining easily different descriptions referring to the same data, and

(iii) supporting descriptions of descriptions.

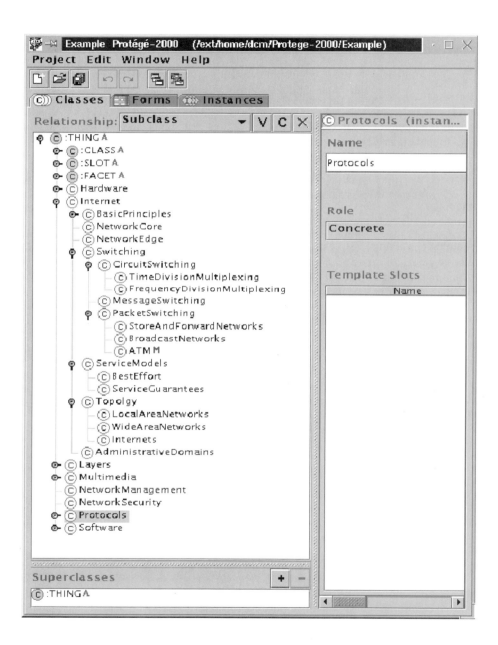

Fig. 7.10 A domain-specific ontology constructed using Protege-2000.

Extended Markup Language (XML). HTML and XML are derived from a powerful markup language called *Standard Generalized Markup Language (SGML).* HTML is a restriction of SGML, with a predefined vocabulary [7]. Whereas SGML does everything but is too complex, HTML is simple, but its parsing rules are loose, and its vocabulary does not provide a standard mechanism for extension. By comparison, XML is a streamlined version of SGML. It aims to meet the most important objectives of SGML without its complexity.

The major difference between HTML and XML markup languages is in semantics. While HTML tells *how to format a document*, XML describes the content of the document. XML clients can reorganize data in a way most useful to them, they are not restricted to the presentation format delivered by the server.

The XML format has been designed for the convenience of parsing, without sacrificing readability. XML imposes strong guarantees about the structure of documents: begin tags must have end tags, elements must nest properly, and all attributes must have values.

Java provides higher level tools to parse XML documents through the *Simple API for XML (SAX)* and the *document object model (DOM)* interfaces. The SAX and DOM parsers are de-facto standards implemented in several languages.

Resource Description Framework (RDF). RDF is a standard for metadata on the Internet proposed by the World Wide Web Consortium, [4, 8]. The syntax of RDF is defined in terms of XML and its data model is essentially that of semantic nets or frames.

An RDF description can be created about any resource that can be referred to using a *Uniform Resource Identifier (URI)* . Such a description is itself stored in a resource and can be referred to, using an URI, and thus be described by another RDF description.

An RDF description is a set of triples $(A\ u1\ u2)$, where A is the assertion identifier determining the property whose subject is described by URI $u1$ and whose value is described by URI $u2$. Unlike arbitrary XML documents such sets can be easily aggregated

The assertion identifier is a URI itself, which is considerably different from the approach in the ER model or the OKBC model.

In an ER model, typically every entity has an associated type; this type defines the attributes it can have, and therefore the assertions that are being made about it. Once a person is defined as having a name, address, and phone number, then the schema has to be altered or a new derived type of person must be introduced before one can make assertions about the race, sex, or age of a person.

The scope of the attribute name is the entity type, just as in object-oriented programming the scope of a method name is an object type or interface. By contrast, in the web, and thus in RDF, the hypertext link allows statements of new forms to be made about any object, even though this may lead to nonsense or paradox.

7.7 PLANNING

In Chapter 6 we argued that software agents are computer programs that exhibit some form of intelligent behaviour. Intelligent behavior has multiple facets, one of them is planning.

Planning is a deliberate activity that requires the knowledge of the current state of a system and of the set of all possible actions that the system may undertake to change its state. As a result of planning we generate a description of the set of steps leading to a desired state of the system.

In this section we first formulate the planning problem in terms of state spaces, then introduce the concept of partial and total order plans, and, finally, present planning algorithms.

7.7.1 Problem Solving and State Spaces

A system evolves over time by interacting with its environment through actions. As a result of these actions it traverses a set of states. Some of the states of a system may be more desirable than others and often we can identify goal states, states a system attempts to reach.

Physical systems are governed by laws of nature and they tend to reach an equilibrium. We can assimilate these states when the system is in equilibrium with goal states. For example, mechanical systems reach an equilibrium when the potential energy is minimal; a system with multiple components at different temperatures tend to reach a thermal equilibrium when all its components have the same temperature.

Man-made systems are designed to achieve an objective, e.g., the routers of a computer network attempt to deliver packets to their destination. Such systems have some feedback mechanism to detect the current state of the environment and adapt their behavior accordingly in order to reach their objectives.

Intelligent beings, e.g., humans, are often goal-driven, the motivation for their action is to achieve a goal. For example, the goal of the British expedition of 1924 led by George Mallory was to reach the peak of Mount Everest.

Problem-solving is the process of establishing a goal and finding sequences of actions to achieve that goal. More specifically, problem solving involves three phases:

1. goal formulation,

2. problem formulation, deciding on a set of actions and states, and

3. execution of the actions.

A problem is defined in an environment represented by a *state space*, and the system evolves from an *initial state*, the state the system finds itself in at the beginning of the process, toward a *goal state* following a *path* called a *solution*. Two functions are necessary for problem solving, a *goal test function* to determine when the system has reached its goal state and a *path cost function* to associate a cost with every path.

The goal test function is often easy to define and it is unambiguous; for example, the goal of reaching the summit of Mount Everest is unambiguous. However, the cost associated with a path may be more difficult to establish. For example, the cost associated with a link in a computer network should reflect the delay a packet experiences when traversing that link. Yet, finding practical means to estimate this delay is not a straightforward exercise. The cost may be associated with the length of the packet queue for the link; but the actual delay depends also on the link capacity, the length of the packets, and possibly other factors.

In general, finding an optimal path from the initial state to the goal state requires searching a possibly very large space of states. When several paths lead to the goal state, we are determined to find the *least cost path*. For example, the cost for transporting a packet from A to B in a computer network could be measured by the number of hops or by the total delay. For either measure we can compute the cost of every possible path and find optimal ones. Optimal network routing algorithms are known, e.g., the distance vector and the link state algorithms discussed in Chapter 4.

Often the *cost of finding a solution* is very important. In some cases there are stringent limitations; for example, the time to make a routing decision for a packet is very short, of the order of nanoseconds; the time to decide if the Everest expedition that has reached *Camp 7* could attack the summit in a given day is also limited, but on the order of minutes.

In the general case, problem solving requires the search of solution spaces with large branching factors and depth of the search tree. Techniques such as simulated annealing, or genetic algorithm are sometimes effective for solving large optimization problems.

Problem solving is made even more difficult because very often problems are ill formulated. Real life problems generally do not have an agreed upon formulation. Games such as the *8-queens problem, the tower of Hanoi, the missionaries and the cannibals, puzzels, tic-tac-toe* are cases when a toy problem is well defined and the goal is clearly specified.

For example, in the case of the *tic-tac-toe* game, the system can be in one of $3^9 = 19,683$ states. Once a player is assigned a symbol, there are 9 groups of winning combinations, or goal states. Indeed, there are 9 squares, each of them can be occupied by one of the two players. We use *marker* 1 for the player who starts first and 2 for the one who starts second and 0 for an empty square. We list the state as an 9-tuple starting from the upper left corner, continuing with the first row, then the second row from left to right, and finally the third row also from left to right. For example, $< 0,0,1,0,0,0,0,0,0 >$ corresponds with a 1 in the upper right corner and all other squares empty.

To win, a player needs to have his marker on all squares on the same:

(i) vertical line – 3 possibilities,

(ii) horizontal line – 3 possibilities, or

(iii) diagonal line – 2 possibilities.

The initial state is $< 0, 0, 0, 0, 0, 0, 0, 0, 0, 0 >$ and one group of goal states for the player that had the first move is $< 1, X, X, X, 1, X, X, X, 1 >$, where X stands for any of markers.

7.7.2   Problem Solving and Planning

Problem solving and planning are related, but there are several subtle differences between them. First, in problem solving we always consider a sequence of actions starting from the initial state. This restriction makes the problem very difficult, because for real-life problems the number of choices in the initial state is enormous.

In planning we can take a more reasonable approach; we may work on the part of the problem most likely to be solvable with the current knowledge first and hope that we can reach a state when the number of possible alternatives is small. For example, debugging a $100,000$-line program could be an extremely challenging task. Once we know that the program worked well before changing a 50-line procedure, the number of alternative plans for finding the problem is considerably reduced.

There is no connection between the order of planning and the order of execution. This property is exploited by several planning algorithms discussed later in this section.

Planning algorithms use a formal language, usually first-order logic, to describe states, goals, and actions. States and goals are represented by sentences; actions are represented by logical descriptions of their preconditions and effects.

Last but not least, in planning we can use a divide-and-conquer method to accomplish conjunctive goals. For example, the goal *reserve means of transportation* can be divided into independent goals, *reserve airline seats*, to reach a resort town, *reserve a car* to travel around the resort, and *reserve a boat ticket* for a day trip on a river from the resort town.

7.7.3   Partial-Order and Total-Order Plans

Definition. *A partial order* P on a set A is a binary relation with two properties: (i) it is not reflexive and (ii) it is transitive. Formally, this means:

- if $a \in A$ then $(a, a) \notin P$.

- if $(a, b) \in P$ and $(b, c) \in P$ then $(a, c) \in P$

A partial order can be depicted as a *graph with no cycles* where each node represents an element $a \in A$ and each element of P, a pair of elements of A, represents an edge. Consider the path from node a_i to node a_j in this graph and three consecutive nodes on this path a_{k-1}, a_k, a_{k+1}. Then the partial order relations among these elements are: $a_i \, P \, a_{k-1}, a_{k-1} \, P \, a_k, a_k \, P \, a_{k+1}$, and $a_{k+1} \, P \, a_j$. If nodes $b_n, n \in [1, q]$ belong to a subtree, b rooted at a_k, all the nodes of this subtree satisfy the same relationship their root, node a_k, satisfies; e.g., $a_{k-1} \, P \, b_n, n \in [1, q]$ and $b_n, n \in [1, q] \, P \, a_{k+1}$.

The graph representing a totally ordered set is a straight line; if $a_k \in A$ then there is at most one element $a_{k-1} \in A$ such that $a_{k-1} \, P \, a_k$ and at most one element $a_{k+1} \in A$ such that $a_k \, P \, a_{k+1}$.

Definition. *A plan* is an ordered set of elements called *steps*. There are two distinct elements of this set called *initial step* and *final step* and if P is the order relation among steps then:

$$(initial \; step) \; P \; (final \; step).$$

Definition. *A Partially Ordered Plan* Π is one when the precedence relation between steps is a partial-order relation.

Definition. *A Totally Ordered Plan* is one when the precedence relation between steps is a total-order relation.

A partial-order plan Π corresponds to a set of totally ordered plans and we call this set $Instances(\Pi)$. The cardinality of this set can be very large. If the number of steps in the plan is n then:

$$| \; Instances(\Pi) \; | \; = n! \; .$$

A total-order plan can be converted to a partial-order plan by removing constraints that do not affect its correctness. Results published in the literature show that given a total-order plan, the problem of finding the least-constrained version of it is NP-hard. There are heuristics to find suboptimal versions of total-order plans. For example, one can remove one by one the ordering constraints between the steps and verify if the plan is still correct and repeat this procedure until no more constraints can be removed. Yet, there is no guarantee that this leads to the least-constrained plan.

More formally a step is defined in conjection with a *planning operator*.

Definition. *A planning operator* α is an action that causes the system to move from one state to the next and it is characterized by:

(i) a name and a set of attributes

(ii) a set of preconditions, $Pre(\alpha)$

(iii) a set of postconditions, or effects, $Eff(\alpha)$

(iv) a cost

Consider a system and its state space S. The execution of a planning operator has side effects; it partitions the set of state variables into two disjoint subsets: those that are not affected by the operator and those that are affected.

Definition. Given a planning operator α, call $Del(\alpha)$ the set of state variables q negated by the operator:

$$\neg q \in Eff(\alpha).$$

Call T the set of state variables that are true after applying α, then:

$$T := (S - Del(\alpha)) \bigcup Eff(\alpha).$$

Definition. *A planning problem* is a triplet consisting of the initial state, the goal state, and the set of planning operators, $(init, goal, O)$.

Definition. *Causal Link:* given two planning operators, α and β, a causal link $cl = (\alpha \overset{p}{\mapsto} \beta)$ is a relation between α and β with three properties:

1. p is a postcondition or an effect of α,

2. p is a precondition of β, and

3. (α, β) is a partial-order relation.

Definition. *A partial-order plan;* Π is a four tuple:

$$\Pi = [\, Steps(\Pi),\ Order(\Pi),\ Binding(\Pi),\ CLink(\Pi) \,]$$

where:

$Steps(\Pi)$ is a set of steps,

$Order(\Pi)$ is a set of partially ordered constraints,

$Binding(\Pi)$ is a set of variable-binding constraints or choices,

$CLink(\Pi)$ is a set of causal links.

Definition. *Open Precondition:* a precondition p of a step α of a plan Π is an *open precondition* if there is no causal link $\gamma \overset{p}{\mapsto} \alpha$.

Definition. A *threat* to a causal link is a step that can nullify the link. Given three steps, α, β, γ, and a causal link, $cl = (\alpha \overset{p}{\mapsto} \beta)$, we say γ is a *negative threat* to the causal link cl iff:

(i) it is consistent to order γ between α and β, and

(ii) there is an effect of γ, $q = Eff(\gamma)$ that can delete p. The triple (cl, γ, q) is called a *conflict*.

Definition. *Positive Threat to a Causal Link:* the step γ is a positive threat if its inclusion between α and β would make step α useless.

There are three methods to remove a threat posed by step γ to a causal link p from step α to β :

1. *demotion*, order γ before α,

2. *promotion*, order γ after β, or

3. *separation*, making a choice by introducing a variable-binding constraint so that $\neg p$ and q will never be the same.

To actually carry out a plan it is necessary: to transform a partial-order plan into a total-order plan; make some choices by binding variables to constants; and last but not least, we need to show explicitly the *causal links* between steps.

Scheduling is related to planning and it deals with the problem of assigning resources to the tasks required by a plan. For example, scheduling on the factory floor means assigning machines to machine parts, scheduling on a computational grid means assigning computational tasks to computers on the grid. Scheduling can only be done once we have a plan, e.g., a dependency graph specifying a complex computational task.

The term PERT, project evaluation and review technique, describes a network consisting of activities constrained by a partial order.

Example. Consider the problem of planning a trip from the a town within the United States to France. To solve this problem one needs to:

(i) prepare for the trip and decide what cities to visit,

(ii) reserve airline seats for the round-trip to Paris,

(iii) reserve hotels in Paris and the other cities one plans to visit,

(iv) reserve a rental car, and

(v) confirm all reservations.

First, we have to define variables and constants for planning the trip.
Examples of variables:

```
?airline, ?hotelParis,
?arrivalDayParis, ?carRentalCompany,
?returnHomeDay, ?carRentalPrice,
?flightToParis,?uaFlightsToParis.
```
Examples of constants:
```
UnitedAirlines, AirFrance,
HotelPalaisBurbon, May15, June16.
```

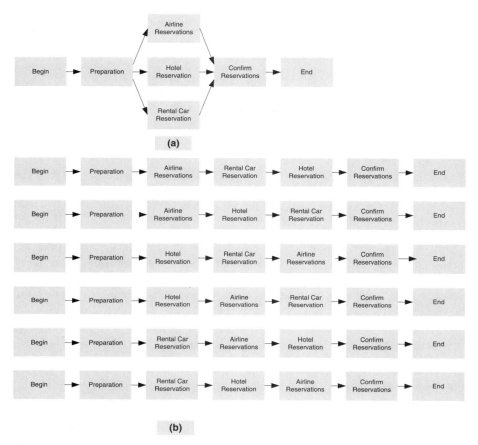

Fig. 7.11 Trip Planning. (a) A partial-order trip plan, (b) Six total-order trip plans

The actual steps of plan Π are depicted in Figure 7.11(a). To actually carry out the plan it is necessary to transform the partial-order plan into a total-order plan as shown in Figure 7.11(b).

Several total-order plans are presented, in each of these plans the order of the airline, hotel, and car reservation steps are different but consistent with the partial-order plan. The collection of all these total order plans forms $Instances(\Pi)$

In addition to ordering, planning requires making some choices. This process is known as *variable-binding constraints*. For example, ?hotelParis, a variable in the hotel reservation step, is bound to a particular constant in that step HotelPalaisBourbon, once a choice of hotels is made.

Particular types of binding constraints are *codesignation constraints* of the type $?x =?y$ that force the instantiations of $?x$ to be the same as the one for $?y$. For example, if one has frequent flyer miles with United Airlines and wishes to fly to Paris only with a UA flight, then the two variables are forced to take the same value: ?flightToParis=?uaFlightsToParis.

7.7.4 Planning Algorithms

A planning algorithm is a composition of planning operators and terminates either by finding a path from the initial state to the goal state or by failing. A planning algorithm is *sound* if every solution of it is correct, and it is *complete* if it will find a solution provided that a solution exists.

We discuss first systematic planning algorithms where actions are added incrementally and the space of plans is explored systematically. Systematic planning algorithms can be classified along two dimensions, the order and the direction of operator chaining. Thus we have partial- and total-order plans and forward- and backward-chaining plans.

Partial-Order Backward-Chaining Algorithm (POBC). The POBC algorithm starts with a set of planning operators O and an initial plan Π_{init} and terminates with a correct plan if a solution can be found. The initial plan consists of a begin step and an end step and the constraint that the begin step is before the end step.

The set of totally ordered plans, for the partial-order plan Π is $Instances(\Pi)$. The *correctness* of Π implies that $Instances(\Pi) \neq \emptyset$ and $\forall P \in Instances(\Pi)$, P is correct. But the size of $Instances(\Pi)$ could be very large and it may be impractical to check the correctness of every member of it.

The basic idea of the algorithm is to grow the plan backward, from the goal state. At each iteration we select a new goal, the precondition of the current step, identify the steps necessary to archive that precondition and add a new causal link to the plan. The process continues until we reach the initial state. Some of the operators may lead to conflict or may not be correct, may violate the partial ordering constraints.

In the description of the POBC algorithm we use several functions [9]:

Correct(Π) - a boolean function, which determines if a plan Π is correct,

Threats (T, Π) - a function that returns a list T of threats in plan Π,

ResolveThreat (t, Π) - a function that resolves threat t in plan Π,

EstablishPrecondition (s, Π) - a function that determines the precondition of step s in plan Π.

```
1   List = { Π_init }
2   repeat
3   Π = lowest cost plan in List
4     remove Π from List
5     if Correct (Π) =TRUE then    return (Π)
6     else
7      if Threats (T,Π) then
8        Let t be a threat. Successor:= ResolveThreat (t, Π)
```

```
 9     else
10        Successor := EstablishPrecondition (Π)
11     endif
12     Add all elements in Successor to LIST
13     endif
14  until LIST is empty
15  return (Fail)
```

The POBC algorithm for trip planning is illustrated in Figure 7.12. At each iteration we show only the steps that do not lead to conflicts. For example, at the second iteration the $HotelReservation$ step would lead to a conflict with $ConfirmReservations$.

Total-Order Forward-Chaining Algorithm. The basic idea of the algorithm is to start from an initial state description and move forwards by adding one step at a time. In this approach each node, N_{fc}, encodes all the information along the path traversed so far, $N_{fc} = <state,\ parent\ node,\ current\ step,\ cost>$.

In the description of the total-order forward-chaining algorithm we use two functions [9]:

$State - of(N_{fc})$ returns the state associated with node N_{fc}.

$Solution - Path(N_{fc})$ traces the steps from the current node to the root.

```
 1  List = { State_i, ∅, ∅, 0 }
 2  repeat
 3    N_fC = lowest cost node in List
 4    remove N_fC from List
 5    if State_q ⊆ State-of(N_fC) then return (Solution-Path(N_fC));
 6    else
 7      generate successor nodes of N_fC from applicable operators in O;
 8      for each successor node Succ do
 9        if State-of(Succ) is not previously expanded then
10          add Succ to List;
11        else
12          compare cost of Succ to previous path;
13          if Succ has lower cost then
14            add Succ to List;
15          endif
16        endif
17      endfor
18    endif
19  until List is empty;
20  return(fail);
```

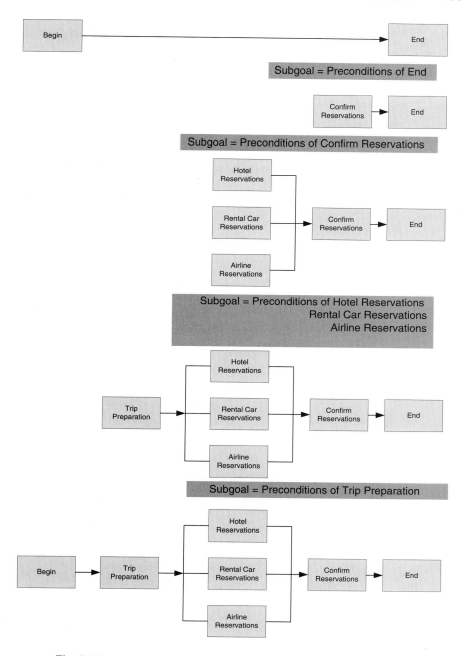

Fig. 7.12 The POBC algorithm applied to the Example in Section 7.7.4.

7.8 SUMMARY

Structuring the vast amount of information in an open system into knowledge represents a necessary condition to automate the process of coordination of various entities involved. Once this information is structured, software agents can use inference and planning to achieve their stated goals.

Problem solving is the process of establishing a goal and finding sequences of actions to achieve this goal. Often, problem solving requires the search of solution spaces with large branching factors and depth of the search tree. Techniques such as simulated annealing or genetic algorithm are sometimes effective for solving large optimization problems.

Software agents can be used for the management of a dynamic workflow; in this case planning sessions must be interleaved throughout the enactment of a process.

7.9 FURTHER READING

S. Russel and P. Norvig present the basic concepts in Artificial Intelligence from the perspective of intelligent agents in an authoritative text [6].

The monograph by Yang [9] provides a comprehensive presentation of planning.

The book by Giarratano and Riley covers expert systems and introduces Clips, a precursor of Jess, the Java expert system shell [2]. The World Wide Web Consortium provides several documents regarding the *resource description format (RDF)* [4, 8]. The *Protege 2000* systems [5] is described by several documents at Stanford University smi-web.stanford.edu/projects.

7.10 EXERCISES AND PROBLEMS

Problem 1. Define the following concepts: abstract data type, polymorphism, classes, introspection, reflections. Discuss each of these concepts in the context of several programming languages including C, C++, Java.

Problem 2. Justify the need for knowledge representation languages and discuss the limitation of traditional programming languages.

Problem 3. You have a video server capable of providing on demand video streams to clients whose resources including the: (i) display resolution; (ii) CPU power; (iii) disk space; and (iv) network connectivity are very different; a measurement of each one of these attributes reports an E, Excessive, A, Adequate, or I, Inadequate, value of the attribute. The server could deliver HQ, High Quality, GQ, Good Quality, and AQ, Acceptable Quality images by adjusting the compression level from low to high. Each data compression level requires a well-defined communication bandwidth; the higher the compression level, the lower the required communication bandwidth but the higher the CPU rate at the client site.

Once a client connects to the video server, a server and a client agent that will negotiate the quality of the transmission are created. The client agent evaluates the level of resources available at the client site, reserves the necessary resources, and performs measurements during transmission, e.g., the frame arrival rate, the display rate, the propagation delay. The server agent determines if the server is capable of supporting a new client and determines the quality of the video stream delivered by the server.

(i) Construct the set of rules used by the server and client agents. Identify the facts used by the two agents.

(ii) The system supports some VCR-like commands such as: pause, forward, back. Construct the set of rules used to handle these commands.

Problem 4. An eight-puzzle consists of a 3×3 square board with eight tiles that can slide horizontally and vertically. The goal state is the one depicted in Figure 7.13(a). Given the board in some state like the one in Figure 7.13(b) the purpose is to move the tiles until the goal state is reached.

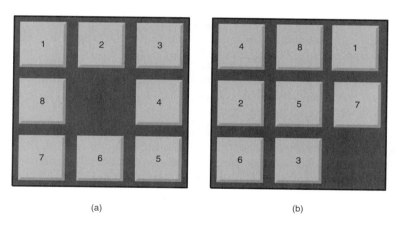

(a)   (b)

Fig. 7.13 An eight-puzzle. (a) The goal state. (b) The current state.

(i) Show that the size of the search space is about 3^{20}; thus, an exhaustive search is not feasible.

Hint: Evaluate the number of steps and the branching factor.

(ii) Show that we have $362, 880$ different states.

(iii) Consider the following function:

$$h = \sum_{i=1}^{8} (\text{distance of tile } i \text{ from its goal position})$$

For example, in the case illustrated in Figure 7.13(b)

$$h = 2 + 2 + 3 + 3 + 2 + 1 + 3 + 2 = 18.$$

Show that h defined above and called *Manhattan distance* is an admissible heuristic function. Recall that an admissible heuristic function never overestimates the cost to reach the goal state.

(iv) Design a heuristic to reach the goal state from the state in Figure 7.13(b).

Problem 5. Define a vocabulary and represent the following sentences in first-order logic:

(i) Only one computer has a read-write CD and a DVD combo.

(ii) The highest speed of an ATM connection is larger than the one of an Ethernet connection.

(iii) Every computer connected to the Internet has at least one network interface.

(iv) Not all computers are connected to the Internet.

(v) No person buys a computer unless the computer has a network interface card.

(vi) Smart hackers can fool some system administrators all the time, they can fool all system administrators some of the time, but they cannot fool all system administrators all the time.

Problem 6. Consider an $n \times m$ two-dimensional torus. In this torus row line i, $1 \leq i \leq n$ is connected to all column lines $j, 1 \leq j \leq m$ and forms a closed loop. Each column line also forms a closed loop.

Each node (i, j) at the intersection of row line i and column line j can route a packet north, south, east, or west. A packet originating in node (i_s, j_s) for the destination (i_d, j_d) travels along the line i_s east or west until it reaches the column j_d on the shortest route. If $j_s < j_d$, then it goes west if $j_d - j_s < \frac{m}{2}$ and east otherwise; if $j_s > j_d$, then it travels east if $j_s - j_d < \frac{m}{2}$ and west otherwise. Once on the right column, it travels north or south to reach row i_d on the shortest route.

(i) Using first-order logic describe the actions taken by a packet when it reaches node (i, j).

(ii) Describe this routing scheme using situation calculus.

Problem 7. Construct an ontology to help the assembly process of a laptop.

Problem 8. Construct an ontology for the QoS in the Internet.

Problem 9. Using inference in first-order logic design a set of rules to detect when a Web server is subject to denial of service attacks.

Problem 10. Give an example from the automobile industry when two abstract subplans cannot be merged into a consistent plan without sharing steps.

REFERENCES

1. R. Fikes and A. Farquhar. *Distributed Repositories of Highly Expressive Reusable Knowledge.* Technical Report 97-02, Knowledge Systems Lab. Stanford University, 1997.

2. E. Friedman-Hill. Jess: the Java Expert System Shell.
   URL http://herzberg.ca.sandia.gov/jess/.

3. J. Giarratano and G. Riley. *Expert Systems: Principles & Programming.* PWS-KENT, 1989.

4. O. Lassila. Web Metadata: A Matter of Semantics. *IEEE Internet Computing,* 2(4):30-37, 1998.

5. N. F. Noy, R. W. Fergerson, and M. A. Musen. The Knowledge Model of Protege-2000: Combining Interoperability and LFlexibility *12th Int. Conf., on Knowledge Engineering and Knowledge Management, Methods, Models and Tools, Lecture Notes in Artificial Intelligence,* volume 1937, pages 17–32, 2000.

6. S. J. Russell and P. Norvig. *Artificial Intelligence. A Modern Approach.* Prentice-Hall, Englewood Cliffs, New Jersey, 1995.

7. P. Spencer. *XML Design and Implementation.* Wrox Press, 1999.

8. W3C World Wide Web Consortium. Resource Description Framework, September 1997.

9. Q. Yang. *Intelligent Planning: A Decomposition and Abstraction Based Approach to Classical Planning.* Springer-Verlag, Heidelberg, 1997.

10. Software Agent Humor http://www.cs.umbc.edu/agent/Topics/Humor, 1999.

8

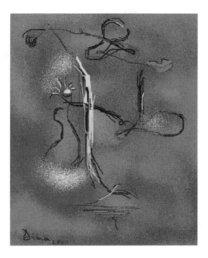

Middleware for Process Coordination: A Case Study

In the previous chapters we provided the theoretical foundations for understanding distributed systems communicating through the Internet and workflow management based on software agents. Chapters 2 and 3 were dedicated to models of communication and computing systems, then in Chapter 4 we presented the Internet. In Chapter 1 we introduced workflows and in Chapter 5 we discussed ubiquitous Internet applications and open systems built around the Internet and outlined the role of middleware for coordination of complex tasks. Chapter 6 was dedicated to process coordination and software agents. We argued that software agents provide promising alternatives for Internet workflow management. Agents can manage resources, act as case managers, brokers, matchmakers, monitor the environment, or serve as enactment engines.

In this chapter we attempt to illustrate the practical application of the concepts, ideas, and design principles presented earlier in the book. We dissect an agent-based framework capable of supporting process coordination written in the past few years. First, we discuss the message-oriented distributed object system, then we introduce the component-based architecture for building agents.

Our thinking and design choices were influenced by existing systems and, whenever possible, we adopted ideas and integrated implementations fitting our agent model. We integrated with relative ease Jess, a Java expert system shell from Sandia National Laboratory [19], and a tuple space, the TSpaces from IBM [27].

At the time of this writing the system consists of about $100,000$ lines of Java code and 700 Java classes grouped into core, agents, and applications packages.

Throughout this chapter we discuss our basic design philosophy, introduce the concepts, and discuss the implementation of various components. Whenever necessary we list the relevant source code or the pseudocode and comment on the functions provided. The reader needs to examine the actual source code to fully understand the system.

8.1 THE CORE

We take the view that an agent is an active mobile object with some level of intelligence. *Active* means that the object has one or more threads of control, *mobile* means that the object may migrate from one site to another, *intelligence* means that the object has some degree of learning, planning, and/or inference abilities. From this definition of agents it follows that we need first to construct an infrastructure for distributed objects and then build an agent framework on top of this infrastructure.

A basic design choice for a distributed object system is the communication paradigm, i.e., a system may use remote method invocation (RMI) or message passing or possibly both. The two paradigms are dual, the same functionality that can be achieved with one of them, can be provided by the other. Systems supporting synchronous communication are based on remote method invocation, while those supporting asynchronous communication typically use message passing.

Several general-purpose distributed-object systems are based on remote method invocation. Implementations of CORBA [39], such as Visibroker [49] from Inprise, Orbix [40] from IONA, Java RMI [45], or Microsoft's DCOM belong to this group.

There are also a few message-oriented distributed systems, such as MSMQ from Microsoft or iBUS [28] from SoftWired. The bond.core package implements a message-oriented distributed object system [8].

This section covers Bond objects, communication, and message handling.

8.1.1 The Objects

A Bond program is a flat collection of Bond objects. A Bond object extends the standard Java object with:

(i) *A unique identifier:* Every Bond object is assigned a unique identifier for the lifetime of the object. An entire collection of Bond objects can be identified by an *alias*.

(ii) *Communication support:* All Bond objects are capable of receiving messages.

(iii) *Registration with a local directory:* Bond objects are registered at the creation time with a local directory. They can be found using either the unique identifier or an alias. Lightweight Bond objects are registered on demand.

(iv) *Serialization and cloning:* All Bond objects are serializable and clonable, while only some Java objects are. The serialization and cloning functions are over-written to accommodate the unique ID of Bond objects.

(v) *Dynamic properties:* Bond objects may have dynamic properties created at run-time, in addition to the regular fields of a Java object.

(vi) *Multiple inheritance:* The Bond system extends the Java object model with multiple inheritance using a preprocessor of Java files.

(vii) *A visual editor:* all Bond objects can be visually edited.

We now discuss basic properties of Bond objects.

8.1.1.1 Bond Identifiers.
Every Bond object has a unique identifier, bondID generated by its constructor as follows:

```
bondID= ''bondID'' + bondIPaddress +
commEnginePort +
     localMillisecondSinceStartOfResident + timeAndDate
```

Here "+" stands for string concatenation, "bondID" is a string, bondIPaddress is the IP address of the host where the Bond system is running, commEnginePort is the port number of the Bond Communication Engine, the next string gives the time in milliseconds since the local Bond Resident was started, and timeAndDate is a string giving the hour, minute, second, day, month and year when the object was created. The resident and the communication engine are discussed in Sections 8.1.1.2 and 8.1.2.7, respectively.

This algorithm is fast and guarantees the uniqueness of the bondID.

The bondID remains the same throughout the lifetime of an object, it is invariant to operations such as: saving and loading the object to/from persistent storage or transferring to/from remote locations.

In Bond we have a *flat namespace*, the bondID does not carry information about the type or role of the object. A flat namespace cannot be used for routing during communication or for classifying objects, a useful feature for directory services. While these difficulties are real, they are inherent to the problem, not to the naming scheme.

A hierarchical naming scheme like IP-addresses cannot be used for a distributed object system supporting mobility because the ID of the object should be the same after migration. However, most Bond objects remain at their creation site; thus, the host information, contained in the bondID, can be used as a way of speeding up the search. In this case, when the object is not found at the resident subfield in its ID, a global directory search is carried out.

Bond is a message-oriented system and each object identified by its unique `bondID` can receive messages. The `say()` method discussed in Section 8.1.3.4 is used to deliver a message to an object.

8.1.1.2 Bond Resident.   A Bond resident, `bondResident`, is a container object hosting all Bond objects located within a given virtual machine. Every Bond resident contains a *local directory*, `bondDir`, implemented as a singleton object [17] and a *communication engine*, `bondCommEngine`, see Section 8.1.2.7.

The constructors for a Bond executable and for a resident are:

```
public class bondExecutable extends bondObject
                            implements Runnable {
  public bondExecutable() {}
  public bondExecutable(boolean reg) { super(reg); }
  public void run(){} }

public class bondResident extends bondExecutable {
  public bondResident() {dir.addAlias("Resident", this);}
}
```

Other objects are loaded dynamically as needed, using dynamic probes presented in Section 8.1.3.3. For example, whenever a message for an object called an Agent Factory arrives, the object is loaded and the message is passed to it. Agent Factories are discussed in Section 8.2.

A resident can be configured as a client, some type of server, e.g., Authentication, Persistent Storage Directory Server, or as host for a number of agents.

The procedure called to initialize the Bond system is:

```
public static void initbond() {
  bondConfiguration.initSysProperties();
  loader = new bondLoader();
  dir = new bondDirectory();
  com = new bondCommunicator();
  conf = new bondConfiguration();
  bondMessage.initMessage();
  return;
}
```

A configuration file specifies the options requested by the user and a resident is configured accordingly. Section 8.1.3.6 addresses this issue in more detail.

8.1.1.3 Local Directory and Aliases.   Bond objects are registered automatically with the local directory at the creation time. Objects loaded from persistent storage and objects arriving from a remote location as a result of a `realize()` operation are registered at their instantiation time. The `realize()` method discussed in more depth in Section 8.1.1.5, allows creation of a local copy of a remote object. Registration with the local directory is a precondition for any object to receive messages.

Lightweight objects are the only exception to the automatic registration rule. There are two classes of lightweight objects: bondShadow, discussed in Section 8.1.1.5, and bondMessage. Messages and shadows have a unique bondID and can be registered with the local directory, if needed.

Registered objects cannot be *freed* in the Java sense because the local directory keeps a pointer to them. Thus, they are not garbage collected until *unregistered*. Unregistering an object removes its ability to receive messages and makes it eligible to be garbage collected by Java. The call dir.unregister(bo) is used to unregister a Bond object bo.

An object can be registered using either its unique bondID or an *alias*. An object may have multiple aliases and multiple objects may have the same alias. Objects with the same alias form an equivalence class and are indistinguishable from one another at some level. The alias mechanism implements the so-called *anycast* addressing abstraction.

For example, within the same resident we may have several agent factories. A user or an agent who needs to create or migrate an agent at/to that site, sends a message with the alias "AgentFactory" as destination object. On receipt of the message, the local directory selects one of the objects in the class at random, and delivers the message to it. In its reply, the selected agent factory responds with its unique bondID. The addressing ambiguity is resolved after the first message exchange and subsequent communication carries the unique identifier of the object.

The alias system supports *load balancing* for servers. If multiple servers are registered under the same alias, an incoming request is delivered to a randomly chosen object, thereby dividing the load among servers. A server can even choose to temporarily unregister itself from the alias if it is overloaded, without affecting its current clients because they communicate with the server using its unique identifier.

Table 8.1 lists *reserved aliases* for standard Bond services.

Table 8.1   Reserved aliases.

Alias	Function
Resident	Container object for all Bond objects at a given site.
AgentFactory	Create, destroy, checkpoint and migrate agents.
PSS	Persistent storage service: save/retrieve objects from storage.
Directory	Directory service: remote access interface for the local directory.
Monitor	Monitoring service.

8.1.1.4 *Serialization and Cloning.* *Serialization* allows an object to be saved in an input/output stream; it *flattens* the object. *Cloning* creates an exact copy of the object.

Java objects can be serialized if they implement the `Serializable` interface. This interface does not implement new methods. Threads are not serializable in Java.

All Bond objects are serializable and can be cloned; `bondObject`, the root of the object hierarchy, implements the `Serializable` interface and reimplements the `clone()` method. A clone of a Bond object is identical with the original object, but has a different `bondID`.

The code to set the `bondID` and to register a new object with the local directory follows:

```
public class bondObject implements Serializable, Cloneable {
 public bondObject() {
    maybeInformDirectory();
    if (bondID != null) { setName(bondID); }
    }
  public bondObject(boolean val) {
    if (val) {
      bondID = dir.getBondID();
      setName(bondID); }
 }
  private void readObject(java.io.ObjectInputStream in)
    throws IOException, ClassNotFoundException {
    in.defaultReadObject();
    if (bondID !=null)   dir.register(this);
 }
   protected void maybeInformDirectory() {
    try {
      bondID = dir.getBondID();
      dir.register(this);
    } catch (NullPointerException e)
    }
```

8.1.1.5 Bond Shadows.
A distributed system needs an abstraction for communication with remote objects. In Voyager [20] this abstraction is called a *proxy*. CORBA [39] and Java Remote Method Invocation, RMI [45] call it a *stub*. In Bond this abstraction is a lightweight object called a *shadow*.

The communication infrastructure is discussed in Section 8.1.2. Here we only provide an informal introductions to terms necessary to understand the concept of a shadow. A resident is a container object; all messages are first delivered to a resident and then delivered to the destination object. Residents communicate with one another using an object called a *communication engine* that transports messages from one resident to another.

To communicate with objects hosted by a `bondResident` we need to know the IP address of the host were the Bond system is running. The communication engine runs at a known port on that host. The pair (`bondIPaddress`, `commEnginePort`) defines a `bondAddress`.

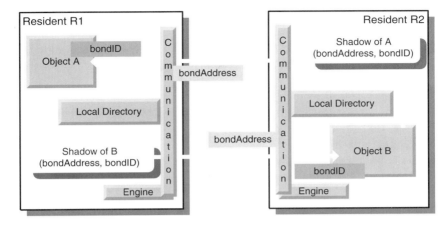

Fig. 8.1 Communication with remote objects. A Bond communication engine runs at a known port on a host identified by an IP address. A bondAddress consists of a pair (bondIPaddress,commEnginePort). In turn, a Bond shadow consists of the pair (bondAddress, bondID). To send a message to a remote object B, object A needs a shadow of B. Once this shadow exists then A sends messages for B to its shadow.

In turn, a shadow of an object A consists of the pair (bondAddress, bondID), where bondAddress allows us to uniquely identify a resident and bondID uniquely identifies the object on that resident, see Figure 8.1.

In Bond there is no distinction between communication with local and with remote objects, a message delivered to the local shadow is guaranteed to reach the remote object. Moreover, the realize() method allows us to create a local copy of a remote object when we have a shadow of the object. The local copy created with the realize() method has the same bondID as the original object.

The constructor for a bondShadow and the realize() method supporting object migration are:

```
/**  Default constructor. Don't register.*/
 public bondShadow() {
     super(false);
 }
/** Create shadow from bondID and address of object*/
 public bondShadow(String remote_bondID,
                                 String rem_address){
     super(false);
     this.remote_bondID= remote_bondID;
     remote_address = new bondIPAddress(rem_address);
 }
/**  Create shadow from an address */
 public bondShadow(String remote_bondID,
```

```
                    bondIPAddress address){
        super(false);
        this.remote_bondID= remote_bondID;
        remote_address = (bondIPAddress)address.clone();
    }
/** Create shadow of a local object */
  public bondShadow(bondObject bo) {
        super(false);
        local = bo;
    }
/** Object migration */
 public bondObject realize() {
        bondID = dir.getBondID();
        dir.register(this);
        bondObject bo = null;
        if (local != null) {
            return local;
        } else {
            bondMessage m =new bondMessage(
              "(tell :content realize)", "PropertyAccess");
            m.setNeedsReply();
            say(m, this);
            m.waitReply(30000);
            return m.bo;  }
    }
```

Figure 8.1 illustrates full-duplex communication between two objects A and B registered with residents R1 and R2 on two different systems. A sends messages for B to the shadow of B on R1 and, in turn, B sends messages to A to the shadow of A on R2.

8.1.1.6 Dynamic Object Properties.
The ability to create on demand new properties/fields of an object is a feature of programming languages such as Lisp or Scheme that allow programmers to handle data whose name or type is not known at compile time. The compilers and linkers for programming languages such as C or C++ usually discard the names of the variables, keeping only their addresses in the compiled code. Java keeps this information in the compiled class files and allows access to it through a mechanism called *reflection*.

Dynamic properties are important for software agents, their functionality makes it difficult to anticipate all the fields of an agent at the instance the agent is created. For efficiency reasons regular Java fields should be used whenever possible, and we should resort to dynamic fields only when the name and/or type of the field is not known at compile time. Dynamic properties have a longer access time than regular Java fields, but for remote objects this difference is masked by the network latency. Compile-time type checking cannot be done for dynamic properties; thus, the programmer looses important type-safety information.

Bond objects implement a common interface with two methods, `get` and `set`, to access static fields and dynamic properties:

`Object get(String name)` returns the value of the field or dynamic property called "name". Numerical values, which are not objects in Java, are first converted to their object counterpart, e.g., an `int` is converted to an `Integer` object. The get function returns `null` when there is no object or field with the given name.

`Object set(String name, Object value)` sets the value of the field or dynamic property called `name` to the value specified by `value`. If there is no field or dynamic property with the given name, a new dynamic property is created. If there is a field with the given name but its type conflicts with the type of the object `value`, a casting exception is thrown.

All dynamic properties are considered to be of type `Object` and any value can be set for them. To delete a dynamic property, the `value` is set to `null`.

The `get` and `set` functions support multilevel access using the familiar dotted notation. Assume that we have a Bond object `foo` with `boo` as a field. `boo` has a `name` field. The `set` and `get` functions applied to `foo` allows us to set the `name` field of its member object to the value "hector" and to retrieve the value:

```
foo.set(''boo.name'', ''hector'')}.
String val =foo.get(''boo.name'')}
```

The multilevel addressing can be done to arbitrary depths. This facility increases the access time due to overhead for parsing the string. Multilevel addressing can be turned off by setting the `useAccess` boolean variable in the Bond configuration object.

The property access subprotocol discussed in Section 8.1.3.5 can be used to access the fields and dynamic properties without making a local copy of a potentially large remote object.

8.1.1.7 *Multiple Inheritance.*   Multiple inheritance is a controversial feature of object-oriented programming languages. Some, such as C++ and Eiffel, support it, whereas others such as Java, Objective C, and Modula-3, do not. Name resolution, repeated inheritance, and more obscure and difficult to read code are some of the problems associated with multiple inheritance.

Sometimes multiple inheritance is necessary because an object may have multiple roles. Even in the base Java classes `InputOutputStream` is a specialization of both `InputStream` and `OutputStream`. There are several examples of multiple inheritance in Bond, for example, `bondMessage` may inherit KQML and XML parser classes.

Java allows *multiple interface inheritance*, but does not implement multiple class inheritance. There are *ad hoc methods* to circumvent the limitations of Java [48]:

(i) *Copy and modify:* copy the code and modify it.

(ii) *Base class modification:* modify the base class to eliminate the need for multiple subclasses.

(iii) *Delegation:* create a member object and a number of wrapper functions that forward the requests to the member object.

The first two techniques require access to the source code and lead to code duplication and poor quality code. Our approach to multiple inheritance is similar to the one of the Jamie system at the University of Virginia [48]; it is based on preprocessing into regular Java code but uses a less elaborate merging approach.

The source code is created in Bond from specially constructed files, with the .bj extension, instead of the regular .java extension, see Figure 8.2. These files may contain variables and methods, but only one of them has the regular class headers. The .bj files are preprocessed by the cpp preprocessor of the GNU C/C++ distributions, to create the Java source code.

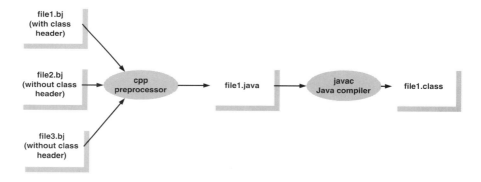

Fig. 8.2   Implementation of multiple inheritance in Bond.

This implementation does not solve the problem of multiple subtyping, nor does it provide name resolution. The names of variables and methods should be disjoint. The method supports *conditional multiple inheritance*, the inheritance changes depending on the configuration of the system.

Only the original .bj files should be modified. The dependency from the .bj files to the Java file is expressed in the makefile of the Bond system, and the Java files are recreated whenever the .bj files are modified.

8.1.1.8 *Visual Editing of Objects*   Bond objects can be visualized and edited. *Object editors* consist of independent dialog boxes and allow us to edit the fields and the dynamic properties of an object, as shown in Figure 8.3. They provide a functionality similar to the *property sheets* and *bean customizers* of the JavaBeans.

Visual objects represent an object and show its state and relationships with other objects as seen in Figure 8.4.

Bond Control			
Kind	Name	Type	Value
Field	bondID	java.lang.String	bondID_9512151178...
Field	address	-	null
Field	values	-	null
Field	name	-	null
Field	mastercopy	java.lang.Boolean	true
Field	resolved	java.lang.Boolean	false
Field	listeners	-	null
Property	Message	java.lang.String	No previous model c...
Property	ErrorMessage	java.lang.String	Unexpected error
Property	ghim.FileName	java.lang.String	Ghim.mdl
Property	STATE.GhimControl	java.lang.String	Inactive
Property	Main.Alias	java.lang.String	Ghim
Property	STATE.GhimVisuals	java.lang.String	SetupGhim
Property	ghimsave.FileName	java.lang.String	Ghim.mdl

☐ **Static fields** ☐ **Constants** ☑ **Fields** ☑ **Dynamic properties**   Refresh

Fig. 8.3 Screen shot of the Bond object editor, displaying the content of the model of the agent.

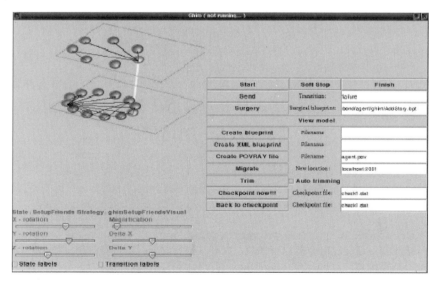

Fig. 8.4 Screen shot of the Bond agent editor. The bullets and lines represent the visual objects attached to Bond objects.

Bond editors objects inherit from the `bondEditor` and are created on demand whenever the `edit()` function of the original object is called. The editor of a Bond object is itself an object attached to the `editor` dynamic property of the original object and removed when the object is destroyed.

The mechanism described below ensures that every object can be edited and allows the user to customize the editor. The Bond editor object is accessed by *name lookup with inheritance based fallback* as follows: given an object of type `a.b.c` the system attempts to create an editor object of type `a.b.cEditor` and if that fails, an object of type `bond.core.editor.cEditor`. If this attempt fails, the system determines the first ancestor of the object and repeats the process recursively. The `bond.core.editor.bondObjectEditor` is invoked as the last resort as the editor for the object, because every object inherits from `bondObject`.

Visual objects inherit from the `bondVisualObject` object and are attached to the `visual` dynamic property of the original object. Visual objects do not have a window of their own, instead they are represented as a graphic widget in the context of an editor presenting multiple objects and relations at the same time. An example is the visual representation of the multiplane finite state machine of the agents shown in Figure 8.4. The states and transitions have attached visual objects displayed on the screen, bullets for the states, lines for transitions. The visual representation reflects the internal state of the object.

8.1.1.9 Bond Loader.
The `bondLoader` allows ordinary Bond objects to be loaded dynamically from the local repository using a search path constructed statically. It also allows loading of a class given the URL of a remote repository. The skeleton of the `bondLoader` code follows.

```
public class bondLoader extends bondObject {
  public Vector defaultpath = null;
  ClassLoader cloader = null;

  public bondLoader() {
   // default loading path
   defaultpath = new Vector();
   defaultpath.addElement("bond.core.");
   defaultpath.addElement("bond.services.");
   defaultpath.addElement("bond.agent.");
   defaultpath.addElement("bond.application.");
   defaultpath.addElement("bond.application.TupleSpace.");
  }
/** Create object "name" with default constructor
    given "searchpath" */
 public Object load(String name, Vector searchpaths) {
     Object o = null;
     Class cl;
     try {
```

```
      if ((cl = loadClass(name, searchpaths)) != null) {
          o = cl.newInstance(); }
      } catch(IllegalAccessException cnfe) { }
        catch(InstantiationException ie) { }
      return o;
  }
/** Load a local class given its "name" */
 public Class loadClass(String name, Vector searchpaths) {
      String completename;
      for(int i=0; i!=searchpaths.size(); i++) {
        try {
          Class cl = Class.forName(makeName
              (name, (String)searchpaths.elementAt(i)));
          return cl;
        } catch(ClassNotFoundException cnfe) {
        } catch(Exception ex) { }
      }
/** Load classes remotely */
  if (cloader == null) {
    String c_repository = System.getProperty
                    ("bond.current.strategy.repository");
    String repository = System.getProperty
                    ("bond.strategy.repository");
    if (c_repository != null && repository != null) {
      try {
        URL urlList[] = {new URL(c_repository),
                                  new URL(repository)};
        cloader = new URLClassLoader(urlList);
      }
      catch (MalformedURLException e) { }
    }
    else if (repository != null) {
      try {
        URL urlList[] = {new URL (repository)};
        cloader = new URLClassLoader(urlList);
      }
      catch (MalformedURLException e) { }
    }
  }
  for (int i = 0; i < searchpaths.size(); i++) {
    try {
        Class cl = Class.forName(makeName(name,
                (String)searchpaths.elementAt(i)),
                    true, cloader);
        return cl;
```

```
      }
      catch (ClassNotFoundException cnfe) { }
      catch(Exception ex) { }
      }
      return null;
    }
}
```

8.1.2 Communication Architecture

The communication infrastructure was designed with several objectives in mind:

(i) Support multiple external message formats for interoperability with other systems.

(ii) Hide the intricacies of message formatting and parsing.

(iii) Support multiple transport mechanisms for different levels of reliability and functionality. Delegate this function to a communication engine.

(iv) Support asynchronous communication and provide abstraction for delayed response. In a wide-area distributed system expect the response to a query or to a request for service to arrive only after a very long delay.

(v) Separate semantic understanding of messages from message delivery.The semantic understanding of messages should be done at the object level, various objects should have different levels of semantic sophistication. Stamp each message with an indicator, allowing the recipient to determine with ease if it understands the message or not.

(vi) Support dynamic collections of semantically related objects.

(vii) Allow every object to receive messages. *Active objects* have a thread of control and can receive messages without any additional complications. *Passive objects* do not have a thread of control, yet there are instances when it would be beneficial to receive messages. For example, the *model of an agent* is a passive object containing the knowledge about the external world. Other agents should be able to send messages and update the model even when the agent is not running and the model is stored by a *persistent storage server*.

The communication architecture is presented in Figure 8.5 where we see the objects involved: the sender, the receiver, a pair of communicators that compose the message and a pair of communication engines that transport a message from one resident to another.

In this section we address the mechanics of message delivery and defer the problem of semantic understanding of messages for Section 8.1.3.1, when we introduce the concept of subprotocols.

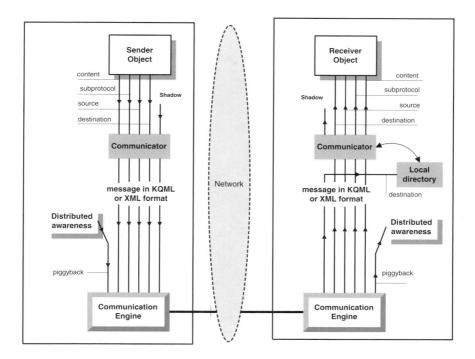

Fig. 8.5 Message delivery in Bond. On the sending side, the `communicator` constructs the message, converts it to external format and passes it to the `communication Engine`. On the receiving side, the `communicator` gets the message from the `communication engine`, converts it to the internal format and delivers it to the destination.

8.1.2.1 *Message Delivery.*

The basic philosophy of the message delivery system is to transport a message for a remote object first to the resident hosting the object and then, using the local directory, to deliver it to the object itself, as shown in Figure 8.6.

Two pairs of internal objects are involved in the communication between a sending and a receiving object: the communicators and the communication engine. The *communicators* are responsible to format the message and convert it from the internal to the desired external format on the sending side and perform a reverse transformation on the receiving side.

The *communication engines* transport a message. The communication engine on the sending side performs a multiplexing function, it may append additional information before delivering the message to its peer on the receiving side. The communication engine on the receiving side performs a demultiplexing function, it removes the additional information and then delivers the message to the communicator. The distributed awareness mechanism discussed in Section 8.1.2.10 relies on piggybacking control information on regular messages. The communicators are discussed in Section 8.1.2.6 and the communication engines in Section 8.1.2.7.

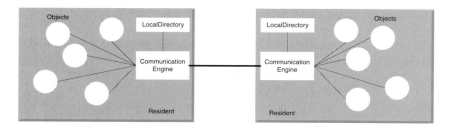

Fig. 8.6 A message is first delivered to a `Resident` and then to an object. Messages are multiplexed by the communication engine on the sending site and demultiplexed by the communication engine on the receiving site.

To construct a message for a remote object, the communicator at the sending side needs:

(i) The contents and the dialect of the message (the subprotocol). They are provided by the sender object.

(ii) The `bondAddres` of the resident and the `bondID` of the object. They are provided by the shadow of the remote object.

On the receiving side, the message is delivered to the communication engine, which uses the local directory to locate the destination object and then sends it to the communicator. Here the message is converted to the internal format and delivered.

8.1.2.2 Internal and External Message Format.
The internal format of the messages is an unordered collection of *name-value* pairs implemented as dynamic properties of the `bondMessage` object . The *name* is a string, while the *value* can be any data type, including user-defined Java objects. There are four groups of *reserved names*, see Table 8.2, derived from the parameters of KQML messages.

1. *Addressing variables:* the source, the destination, and, optionally, the retransmission objects location and their IDs.

2. *Message identifiers:* identify the message, request an answer (`reply-with`) or identify the question to which the current reply is a message (`in-reply-to`).

3. *Semantic identifiers:* identify the context of the message. Bond favors the use of the `subprotocol` variable, but `language` and `ontology` might be used, especially in the case of interoperation with other systems.

4. *Hidden variables:* variables attached to the message object during its lifetime but not delivered at the destination. The hidden variables are removed either by the message thread or by the preemptive probes; this is the case of the `piggyback` variable used by the distributed awareness mechanism [30].

Table 8.2 Reserved names for the internal format of Bond messages.

Reserved name	Description
sender	bondAddress of message sender
destination	bondAddress of message destination
reply-with	Unique identifier that the destination object should use when replying to this message
in-reply-to	Unique identifier in the reply-with variable of a previous message that this message replies to.
subprotocol	The message is part of a subprotocol. If destination object does not understand the subprotocol, it answers sorry.
performative	The speech act of this message, question, answer, notification, etc. as required by KQML specification.
contents	The contents of the message.
piggyback	Data field attached to the message to carry information between two directories or two communication engines.

Most of the parameters in Table 8.2 are added automatically to messages. The process of message annotation is summarized in Figure 8.5.

The internal format of Bond messages relies on the dynamic properties of Bond objects and cannot be used to communicate to other systems; thus, we need an external representation for messages.

There are two external representations for Bond messages: KQML [18] and XML [44]. In both cases there is a one-to-one mapping between the internal and external format. The XMLMessaging variable determines the format of the messages delivered to the network. The parser method of the bondMessage object recognizes the format of a message and delivers it for parsing to either the internal KQML parser or to the external XML, xerces parser.

The system can use KQML and XML format messages simultaneously and it is possible to specify XML or KQML messages on a host-by-host basis; thus, objects may interact with KQML- and XML-based systems simultaneously.

The conversion from internal format to a text-based external format implies a considerable performance penalty, somewhat higher for XML. For slow- and medium-speed networks, this penalty is hidden by the network latency, but for high-speed networks the conversion overhead may have a significant negative performance impact. Whenever interoperability with other systems or readability of messages are not important, the system can be configured to send messages in a serialized version of the internal format.

The KQML composer transforms the internal format of Bond messages to valid KQML statements. The value of the performative variable is set as the performative of the KQML message. If there is no such variable, the tell performative is used. All other variables are set as parameters of the resulting message. If the type of the variable is not String, the variable is Java serialized into a byte buffer and encoded using the Base64 algorithm. Base64 encoded strings are prefixed with the "@@@" escape sequence, to allow the KQML parser to recognize them.

The KQML parser, bondKQMLParser, at the receiving side, parses a KQML message into bondMessage internal format, and decodes the embedded variables. Mapping name/value pairs to/from KQML is highly efficient. The KQML implementation in Bond is limited to syntactic parsing, the semantic interpretation is done by the object, using the internal format.

XML, the extensible markup language [44] is a general-purpose information exchange format. An XML text consists of a *document type definition (DTD)* followed by a series of potentially embedded *elements*. Each element is defined by a starting and an ending tag. A number of parameters can be specified as the name = value format of a starting tag. This feature allows sets of name/value pairs to be mapped into XML format. BondMessage.dtd gives the rules to map Bond messages into XML:

```
<?xml encoding="US-ASCII"?>
 <!ELEMENT message> <!ATTLIST message
        performative CDATA #REQUIRED
        content CDATA #REQUIRED
        sender CDATA #REQUIRED
        destination CDATA #REQUIRED
        subprotocol CDATA #REQUIRED
        reply-with CDATA
        in-reply-to CDATA
>
```

The conversion into XML is done by the composer function of the bondMessage object. XML messages are parsed by an external XML parser. Bond can use any XML parser conforming to the SAX event-oriented API. The performance of parsers varies, currently we use the *Apache-xerces* parser. A full featured XML parser is more complex then a KQML parser; thus, parsing XML messages is less efficient then parsing KQML messages.

8.1.2.3 Synchronous Communication. Message-oriented distributed object systems support both asynchronous and synchronous communication. Systems based on remote method invocation (RMI) favor synchronous communication when the caller blocks until the call returns.

Some systems based on remote method invocation circumvent this limitation and allow remote method invocation without return values; they implement asynchronous method calls as a pair of synchronous method calls without return values.

In Bond all communication primitives are based on the say() function described in Section 8.1.3.4. Synchronous communication is supported by the ask and waitReply() methods. The ask() function automatically tags the message as one that needs a reply, and waits until the reply arrives, or a timeout occurs. The ask() function returns the reply, or null in case of a timeout. The following example illustrates this:

```
bondMessage question = new bondMessage(''(ask-one :
    content get :value i :)'', ''PropertyAccess'');
bondMessage rep = bs.ask(question, this, 10000);
if (rep == null)
    {
    System.err.println(''Timeout of 10s was exceeded'');
    } else {
    System.out.println(''Field i of remote object is''+
        (String)rep.getParameter(''value''));
    }
```

The ask() function blocks only the current thread of the Bond application, all other threads continue to run.

The waitReply() method is an alternative for synchronous communication, allowing the execution of some code between message sending and the reply. The message should be marked as needing a reply and sent using the say() method as in the following example:

```
bondMessage question = new bondMessage(''(ask-one
  :content get :value i :)'', ''PropertyAccess'');
question.needsReply();
bs.say(question, this);
...
code executed before the reply
...
rep = question.waitReply(10000);
```

8.1.2.4 *Asynchronous Communication.* Asynchronous communication is more difficult to implement then synchronous communication, the system must be prepared to accept an incoming message at any time, regardless of its current state. Such an *active message* system is difficult to program, it must treat each message as an interrupt. In case of multiple messages it is difficult to pair the incoming message with the original request.

Bond provides a mechanism to pair incoming messages with the original requests. Messages that require an answer call the needsReply() function that creates a reply-with field in the message and attaches a unique identifier to it.

Before sending a message with a reply-with field, the communicator creates a *message waiting slot* for the sender object. The message waiting slot contains the original message and the unique ID of the reply. When processing incoming messages, the communicator checks the waiting slot table for the unique ID of the message. If the message has a waiting slot, the communicator pairs the reply and question together and delivers them to the on_reply function:

```
public int on_reply(bondMessage message, bondMessage reply)
```

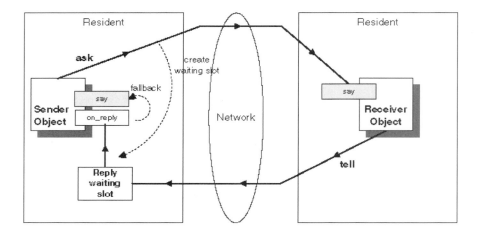

Fig. 8.7 Asynchronous communication. The sender object uses the `ask` performative with `reply-with` field to send an asynchronous message. The communicator creates a *message waiting slot* for the sender object and deposits there a copy of the original message and the unique ID of the reply. Eventually, the receiver object replays using the `tell` performative. When processing incoming messages, the communicator checks the waiting slot table for the unique ID of the message and if a waiting slot exists, the communicator delivers the message to it. If the incoming message has the `on_reply` field set then it is delivered directly, else it is delivered by the `say()` method.

An object can isolate replies to earlier messages, from unexpected messages by catching the message in the `on_reply()` instead of the `say()` method. The `say()` method acts as a fallback for messages even if the object does not implement `on_reply` as shown in Figure 8.7.

8.1.2.5 The Subscribe-Notify Model for Event Handling.
Java objects use the *listeners* abstraction to capture events. An object can *register* itself as a listener for a certain type of events. The object is notified every time the corresponding event occurs, until it decides to *unregister*, see Figure 8.8 (a). The object should implement a Java interface for the type of events it registered. The events are passed as procedure calls to the given interface.

Distributed object systems such as CORBA extend this concept for objects that are not co-located. An *event* service allows an object to register itself as a listener for events generated by a remote object, as shown in Figure 8.8(b).

The *subscribe-notify* model used in Bond is an extension of the Java model for handling remote events in a distributed-object system, see Figure 8.8(c). In this model an object expresses its interest in events associated with remote objects by subscribing to them and it is notified when the events occur.

Throughout this presentation the object subscribing to an event is called a *monitor*, whereas the object generating the event is called a *monitored object*.

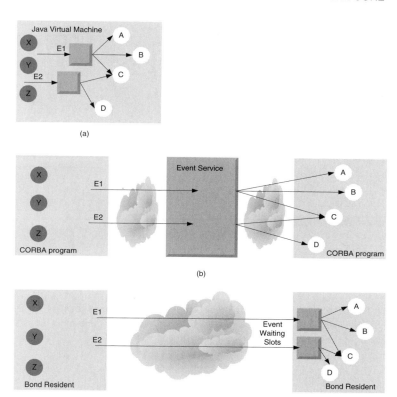

Fig. 8.8 Event notification. Objects X, Y, Z generate events $E1$ and $E2$; objects A, B, C subscribe to event $E1$ and C, D to $E2$. (a) Java solution is confined to objects co-located within the same JVM. (b) CORBA uses an event service. (c) Bond relies on event waiting slots.

In Bond events are generated when a property of a Bond object changes. Thus, even passive objects may generate events. A property of an object stored by a persistent storage server may be changed and the instance the change occurs, an event is generated.

When a Bond object decides to monitor a remote object it sends a message with the *subscribe* performative to that object. Internally, an *event waiting slots* is created automatically by the communicator of the resident hosting the monitor, as shown in Figure 8.9.

The object being monitored sends a message with the `tell` performative every time the corresponding property of the object changes. The monitor matches these messages against the set of event waiting slots. If a match is found, the message is delivered to the object by the `on_event` function. The event waiting slot is automatically removed by the communicator object whenever the monitor sends an `unsubscribe` message.

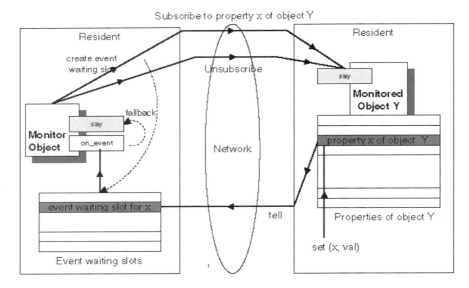

Fig. 8.9 The subscribe-notify event model. An object called a monitor may request to be notified when property x of object Y is modified. When the subscribe message is sent, the communicator of the monitor creates an event waiting slot.

A monitor can separate an event notification message from other types of messages. If the object does not implement the on_event function, the say() function is used as a fallback to deliver the message to the monitor.

The code for the bondListener follows:

```
public class bondListener extends bondObject
                    {publicbondListener() { }
 public void subscribeAsListener(String property,
                          bondObject listener) {
     Vector v;
     if (values == null)
        values = new Hashtable();
     try { v = (Vector)listeners.get(property); }
     catch (NullPointerException e) {v = new Vector();}
     v.addElement(listener);
     values.put(property, v); }
 public void unsubscribeListener(String property,
                          bondObject listener) {
     Vector v = (Vector)values.get(property);
     if (v == null)   return;
     else   v.removeElement(listener); }
 public void notifyListener(String property,
```

```
                                    Object value) {
    Vector v;
    if (values == null)  return;
    if ((v = (Vector)values.get(property)) == null)
        return;
    if (v.size() == 0) return;
    for (Enumeration e = v.elements();
                              e.hasMoreElements();) {
        bondListenerInterface bl =
        (bondListenerInterface)e.nextElement();
        bl.propertyChanged(property); } }
}
```

The set function executed by the object being monitored notifies the monitor when a property subject to monitoring changes:

```
public synchronized Object set(String name, Object value) {
  Object ret = null;
  try {
    if (conf.useAccessors) {
        try {invokeSet(name, value);return value;}
        catch (InvocationTargetException ite2)
        catch (NoSuchMethodException nsme2) }
    try  {
        Field f= getClass().getField(name);
        f.set(this, value);
        ret = value; }
    catch (NoSuchFieldException nf)  {
        if (values==null) values=new Hashtable();
        if (value==null)  {
        values.remove(name);
        return null;      }
        values.put(name,value);
        ret = value;   }
  }
  catch (IllegalAccessException iae1)
  catch (IllegalArgumentException iae2)
  catch (NullPointerException npe)
  if (listeners != null) listeners.notifyListener(name, value);
  return ret;
}
```

Example. Consider an agent that monitors the stock market and maintains several accounts. The portfolio managed by each account consists of many stocks. The owner of the account may request to be notified when the market value of the account goes below a threshold.

The agent queries periodically one of the servers providing market updates and modifies accordingly objects named `account`, one for each customer. This object has a property called `warning`, a boolean variable, with a default value `false`. This value is set to `true` when the condition requesting the user to be notified is met. If the owner of the account has subscribed to this property, she will be notified immediately when this property changes. The `account` object may have multiple properties and the user could subscribe to any, or to all of them.

8.1.2.6 *The Communicator.*

The function of the communicator on the sending site is to compose a message out of its components and to pass the message to the communication engine, see Figure 8.5. It fills in:

(i) the `sender` field with the `bondIPaddress` and the `bondID` of the sender;

(ii) the `destination` field with the `bondIPaddress` and the `bondID` of the destination;

(iii) the `reply-with` field with a newly created identifier, if the message requires a reply;

(iv) the waiting slots with the message or event identifier if waiting slots are needed.

The pseudocode for the sending process of the communicator follows:

```
for(every sent message)
   if (external format)
      transform message in internal format
   endif
   annotate with the sender address
   if (reply needed)
      annotate with a unique reply-with field
      create a reply waiting slot
   endif
   if (performative is subscribe)
      create an event waiting slot
   endif
   if (performative is unsubscribe)
      delete the event waiting slot
   endif
   if (need to send info to destination)
      annotate with the piggyback field
   endif
   pass the message to communicator engine
```

On the receiving side the communicator extracts the components of a message delivered by the communication engine as shown in Figure 8.5. First, the communicator converts the message to internal format, then checks if the message is expected:

(i) searches the *message waiting slots* table to check if the message is a reply to an earlier message and if so, the waiting slot is deleted and the message is delivered to the object paired with the original question;

(ii) searches the *event waiting slots* table to determine an event notification.

Finally, the communicator delivers the message:

- If the destination has a unique bondID, the communicator searches the local directory and delivers the message to the object;

- If the destination is an alias, the communicator picks up at random one of the objects with the given alias and delivers the message to it.

- If the destination object cannot be found, the communicator sends an error message.

The communicator uses a *thread pool* to deliver a message to an object. A thread pool is a collection of threads waiting to be activated. Whenever a message needs to be delivered, the communicator wakes up a thread, passes to the thread the message and a reference to the destination object as parameters, and calls the say function of the destination object in the newly activated thread. After the return of the say function, the thread goes back to the wait state.

This message delivery mechanism decouples the communicator object from the processing of messages at the object level and allows multiple messages to be processed simultaneously. The default size of the thread pool is $nthreads = 10$. If more than $nthreads$ messages need to be processed at the same time, additional threads are created, they deliver the messages and then the thread pool returns to its original size. The pseudocode for message delivery is:

```
for(every incoming message)
   parse message
   remove the piggyback field if any
   if (has in-reply-to field) and
      (in-reply-to field maches a reply waiting slot)
   then
      deliver to object waiting on the reply waiting slot
      delete the reply waiting slot
   else if (performative is tell) and
           (sender maches an event waiting slot)
   then
      deliver to object waiting on the event waiting slot
   else
      lookup the destination object
      if (destination is alias)
         select an object with the alias at random
      else
```

```
        look up the object in local dir
      endif
      if (no object)
         send error message to sender
      wake up a thread in the threadpool
      deliver the message using the thread
   endif
end for
```

8.1.2.7 Communication Engines. A communication engine transports messages from one resident to another. The engine runs at a known port at a host with a given bondIPaddress. The system comes with four interchangeable communication engines:

1. *UDP communication engine* – based on the UDP protocol. Datagrams do not require connection establishment or acknowledgements; thus, the UDP engine is faster then the TCP engine supporting a reliable connection-oriented protocol. Message size is limited to 64 KBytes and there is no guaranteed delivery.

2. *TCP communication engine* – based on the TCP protocol. Its advantage is the unlimited message size and the guaranteed delivery.

3. *Infospheres communication engine* – based on the info.net package from the Infospheres system [14]. Message size is limited to 32 KBytes.

4. *Multicast communication engine* – based on the IP multicast protocol. It is used when the same message must be sent to a number of objects in a virtual object network.

Currently, the system does not support the concurrent use of multiple communication engines.

Each engine has two methods to send, one for messages and another for objects, and one method to receive messages. Before sending an object with the realize() function the object is converted to a string and then it is encoded. The skeleton of the code to send messages and objects follows:

```
public void send(bondShadow bs,bondMessage m) {
  String mes = m.compose();
  try{
    InetAddress targetIP = InetAddress.getByName
                  (bs.remote_address.ipaddress);
    myUDPDaemon.send(targetIP, bs.remote_address.port, mes);}
    catch(UnknownHostException e){e.printStackTrace();}
  }
public void sendObject(bondShadow bs, bondObject bo,
                             String in_reply_to) {
```

```
  bondExternalMessage bm = new bondExternalMessage();
  bm.in_reply_to = in_reply_to;
  bm.bo = bo;
  String m = Base64.Object2String(bm);
  try{
    InetAddress targetIP = InetAddress.getByName
                   (bs.remote_address.ipaddress);
    bondUDPDaemon.send(targetIP, bs.remote_address.port, m);}
    catch(UnknownHostException e){e.printStackTrace();}
  }
```

Each communication engine has one daemon responsible to send and to receive
messages using the specific transport protocol for that engine. The skeleton of the
bondUDPDaemon follows:

```
public class bondUDPDaemon extends bondObject {
  public bondUDPDaemon(int port) throws SocketException {
    super(false);
    udpSocket = new DatagramSocket(port);
    localport = port; }
  public int getLocalPort(){return localport;}
  public void send(InetAddress targetIP,
                   int targetPort, String m) {
    bufOut = m.getBytes();
    udpOutPacket = new DatagramPacket(bufOut,
         bufOut.length, targetIP, targetPort);
    try{udpSocket.send(udpOutPacket);}
    catch(IOException e){}
  }
  public String receive() {
    try{
      udpInPacket = new DatagramPacket(bufIn, 65535);
      udpSocket.receive(udpInPacket);
      InetAddress fromAddress = udpInPacket.getAddress();
      fromHostname = fromAddress.getHostName();
      fromPort = udpInPacket.getPort();
      String mes = new String(udpInPacket.getData(),
                         0, udpInPacket.getLength());
      return mes;}
    catch(IOException e){ return null; }
  }
  public String getFromHostname(){
    return fromHostname; }
  public int getFromPort(){
    return fromPort;}
}
```

8.1.2.8 *Virtual Networks of Objects*. Distributed systems frequently contain groups of objects semantically related to one another such as local directories of various residents; the groups of objects monitored by a single monitor; or the group of sensors connected to a single data collector. These groups may overlap, an object may be a member of multiple groups. The members of a group may receive multicast messages and may be created and destroyed together even though they may be distributed across several residents.

In Bond we have an abstraction called a *virtual network of objects* for a group of semantically related objects. A virtual network of objects consists of the shadows of the objects as shown in Figure 8.10. The `bondVirtualNetwork` object supports primitives for:

   (i) Objects to join and leave a virtual network.

  (ii) Testing if the objects in a virtual network are alive; it automatically partitions the objects into two groups, *live* and *dead*.

 (iii) Multicasting to the objects of the virtual network. If the application has the multicast communication engine installed, the message is transmitted using IP multicast. If the multicast engine is not available, or the location of the objects does not allow IP multicast, the multicast results into a sequence of unicasts.

The system could use virtual networks to connect local directories of residents to a global directory.

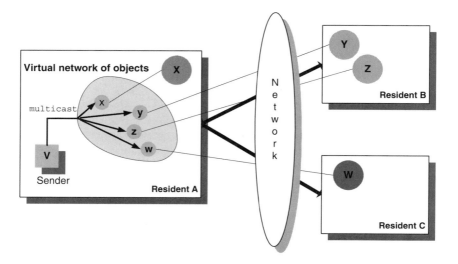

Fig. 8.10 An object V multicasts to a virtual network of objects. The virtual network of objects consists of the shadows x, y, z, w of objects X, Y, Z, W. Each shadow has the `bondAddress` and the `bondID` of the object. Thick lines connecting the residents indicate transport paths through the network.

8.1.2.9 Object Mobility.   The system provides a simple way of moving objects across the network, using the `realize` function applied on shadows. The sequence of operations needed to bring a remote object to the current resident is:

   (i) create a shadow of the remote object (either by knowing its name and location or by using the directory service) and

   (ii) call `realize()` method on the shadow.

The object mobility using the `realize()` function is triggered on the receiving side (*pull mode*) and does not require a cooperating entity on the sending side, see Figure 8.11.

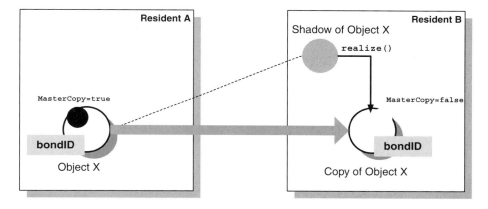

Fig. 8.11   Object mobility. The `realize()` function supports the creation of a local copy of a remote object. The original object and the copy have the same `bondID`, but the original has the `MasterCopy` boolean property set to `true` while the copy has it set to `false` .

A problem raised by the mobility is the *consistency of the copies*. The `realize()` function creates a remote copy of the object, with the same `bondID` as the original, and tags the moved object by setting its `MasterCopy` boolean variable to `false`. If the new object is modified, then two different copies of the same object exist. There are several ways of handling this problem:

   (i) Physically move the object, discard the original object immediately after the move, and make the new object the master copy.

   (ii) Clone the object, assign a new `bondID` to the copy immediately after the move.

   (iii) Synchronize copies of the object to the master copy.

8.1.2.10 Distributed Awareness   Distributed awareness is a passive mechanism for the nodes of a message–passing distributed system to learn about the existence of other nodes without the need to communicate explicitly with them. Passing along information about other objects and residents is appropriately called *gossiping*.

In Bond each resident maintains an *awareness table* and exchanges the information in this table with other residents at the time of regular message exchanges between objects. This mechanism can be turned off at the start-up time.

An entry in the awareness table contains:

(i) `bondAddress` of a resident,

(ii) `lastHeardFrom`, the time when we last heard from the resident, and

(iii) `lastSync` the time when the awareness information was last sent to the resident.

The awareness information is piggybacked onto regular messages exchanged between two residents as shown in Figure 8.5.

8.1.3 Understanding Messages

How do humans understand each other? Try to ask a total stranger the question "How many five-fold axes does an icosahedron have" in Swahili. After a few trials you will realize that in order to communicate with one another, two individuals have to find some common ground; first, they have to speak the same language, then they have to share some common domain knowledge.

How do objects in a distributed system understand each other? A solution is to have some public service where each object deposits a note describing the methods it can perform. CORBA uses such a service called "interface repository."

An open system consists of a continuum of objects ranging from simple objects such as an icon to complex ones such as a server or an agent. Moreover, some objects are created dynamically or may acquire new properties dynamically. The sender of a message expects the receiver to understand and then to react to the message. This expectation places a rather heavy burden on the objects of an open system. In closed systems the semantic gap can be closed, objects may agree to communicate only after some prior agreement as in the case of CORBA.

In Bond we partition the set of messages into "dialects" called subprotocols; two objects may communicate with one another if and only if they implement a common subset of subprotocols. The subprotocols are a close relative to the agent conversations discussed in Chapter 6.

Before delivering a message, the say() method examines the subprotocol field of the message and it only delivers the message if the destination object, one of its ancestors, or a probe attached to the object implements the subprotocol.

In this section we first introduce the concept of a subprotocol, then introduce static subprotocols and subprotocol inheritance in Section 8.1.3.2, followed by a discussion of dynamic subprotocols and probes in Section 8.1.3.3. We examine message delivery and the property access subprotocol implemented by all Bond objects in Sections 8.1.3.4 and 8.1.3.5. We conclude with a presentation of the configuration mechanism in Section 8.1.3.6.

Table 8.3 Subprotocols.

Subprotocol	Function
Property access	Read/write access to properties of a Bond object.
Security	Establish trust relationship among Bond objects.
Monitoring	Monitor an object.
Agent control	Start, stop, and control a remote agent.
Scheduling	Schedule a contract
Persistent Storage	Save/load objects to/from persistent storage
Data Staging	Move files
Registration	Register a resident with the `SystemMonitor` and the `Directory Server`

8.1.3.1 Subprotocols.
The set of Bond messages is partitioned into small, closed subsets of commands necessary to perform a specific task, called *subprotocols*. Each message identifies the subprotocol the message belongs to; thus, an object can decide if it understands the message or not.

Closed means that commands within a subprotocol do not reference commands outside it. The reply is always a member of the same subprotocol with the question. The only exception to these rules are the (`sorry`) and (`error`) performatives, valid replies to messages of any subprotocol.

Every Bond object implements at least the *property access subprotocol*, which allows it to interrogate and set the properties of another object. A typical object implements a number of subprotocols. Table 8.3 lists a subset of Bond generic subprotocols.

If two objects have no knowledge about one another, they interrogate each other's property `SubprotocolsImplemented` and find the subprotocols implemented by the other object . Then they can communicate using the intersection of the two sets, see Figure 8.12.

Some subprotocols are *static*, they are available at the time an object is created; others are *dynamic*, added to an object as needed during the lifetime of the object. Subprotocols can also be created automatically as discussed later in Section 8.1.3.3.

8.1.3.2 Static Subprotocols and Inheritance.
A Bond object inherits the subprotocols implemented by the objects above it in the object hierarchy. The message thread of a resident delivers an incoming message to the `say()` function of the destination object.

If the message is not understood by the `say()` function of the object, it is then passed to the `say()` function of the immediate ancestor in the object hierarchy; this process continues recursively until either an ancestor that implements the subprotocol

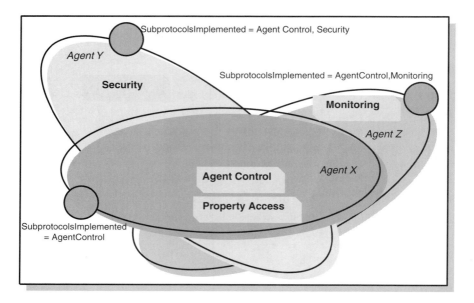

Fig. 8.12 Each Bond object has a property called `SubprotocolsImplemented` that lists the subprotocols implemented by the object. All Bond objects implement the Property Access subprotocol. All agents including X,Y,Z implement the *Agent Control* subprotocol. In addition agent Y implements the *Security* subprotocol, and agent Z the *Monitoring* subprotocol.

of the message is found, or the `say()` function of the `bondObject`, the root of the hierarchy answers (`sorry`).

Figure 8.13 shows two examples of messages delivered to a `bondScheduler` object. This object extends a `bondAgent`, which in turn extends a `bondExecutable`, which in turn extends a `bondObject`.

The scheduler agent understands an agent control message because it inherits the agent control subprotocol from the `bondAgent`. The agent control message is delivered by the `bondAgent.say()` function.

However, the scheduler agent is unable to understand a monitoring message; neither `bondScheduler.say()`, `bondAgent.say`, `bondExecutable.say()`, nor `bondObject.say()` can deliver this message; thus, the reply is (`sorry`). To understand a monitoring message an object must inherit the *monitoring* subprotocol from a `bondScheduler` object.

8.1.3.3 Dynamic Subprotocols and Probes.
Some members of a class of objects may have functions and requirements different from those of the majority of objects in that class. For example, an agent may need to monitor other objects, or may have very strict security requirements. Yet, requiring all agents to understand the monitoring and the security subprotocols imposes an unnecessary overhead for those who do not need to monitor or do not need additional security.

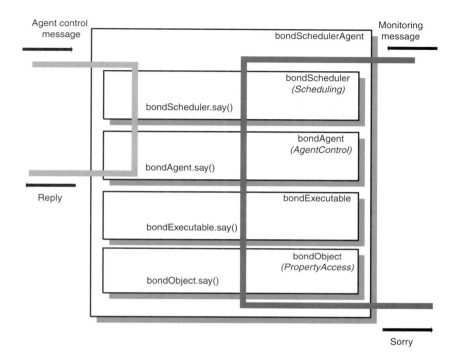

Fig. 8.13 The `bondSchedulerAgent` inherits the subprotocols of his ancestors, `bondScheduler`, `bondAgent`, `bondExecutable`, `bondObject`. The subprotocols implemented by each ancestor are in parenthesis. An agent control message is delivered by the `bondAgent.say()` function. However, the scheduler agent is unable to understand a monitoring message; neither `bondScheduler.say()`, `bondAgent.say()`, `bondExecutable.say()`, nor `bondObject.say()` can deliver this message; thus, the reply is (`sorry`).

In Bond we have specialized objects called *probes* that are attached to a regular Bond object as a dynamic property. The only function of a probe is to understand a subprotocol. A Bond object implements all static protocols on its subtree of the Bond object hierarchy and all subprotocols supported by the probes attached to it after the object was created.

This construction is similar in scope to the Decorator design pattern [17], it extends dynamically the functionality of an object without subclassing. However, the implementation is different; instead of a wrapper which captures the function call, we append dynamically an object.

Another object-oriented structure that allows objects to acquire new functionality after "programming time" is a *mixin* [11]. Mixins are generally implemented as abstract classes, with reserved functions for future functionality. As such, the programmer needs at least a rough idea about the nature of the functionality with which

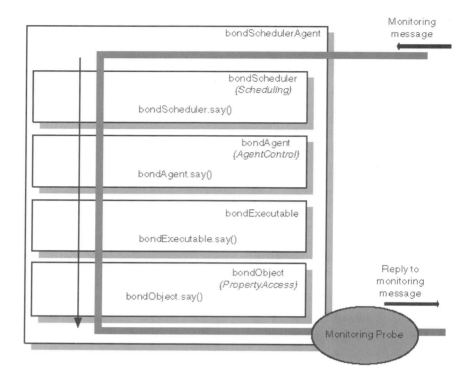

Fig. 8.14   A bondScheduler object extended with a monitoring probe. Now the object understands the monitoring subprotocol and gives a meaningful reply to a monitoring message.

the object may be extended. In our case, the probes offer greater flexibility and add the cost of the time to interpret syntactically and semantically the message.

The implementation of the bondObject guarantees that when an object does not understand a message, its dynamic properties list is searched for a probe that can handle the subprotocol and then deliver the message to the object. If no probe is found, the object replies sorry.

Two commonly used probes are the bondMonitoringProbe, which understands the monitoring subprotocol, and the bondSecurityProbe, which allows an object to understand encrypted messages.

Figure 8.14 shows the same scheduler agent, this time extended with a monitoring probe. The probe implements the monitoring subprotocol. An incoming message in the monitoring subprotocol is passed down the inheritance hierarchy without being delivered to the object. At the bondObject level, we first check that the message does not belong to the property access subprotocol. Then we check the list of dynamic properties and find a probe that understands the monitoring subprotocol. The message is delivered to the probe that produces a meaningful reply.

In our system there are three types of probes:

1. *Regular* - activated after searching the list of the static subprotocols understood by an object, e.g., the monitoring probe.

2. *Preemptive* - activated before searching the list, e.g., the security probe.

3. *Autoprobes* - used to load dynamically a probe at run time.

The skeleton of the code for the bondAutoProbe is listed below. The say function parses the message and identifies the subprotocol, then examines a hash-table of probes and if one is found, the probe is loaded and the message is delivered to it.

```
public class bondAutoProbe extends bondProbe {
  Hashtable lookup;
  public bondAutoProbe(bondObject parent) {
    super(parent);
    lookup = new Hashtable();
    initDefaults();
  }
 public void initDefaults() {
    addAutoLoad("Monitoring","bondMonitoringProbe");
    addAutoLoad("AgentControl","bondAgentFactory");
  }
 public void addAutoLoad(String name, String probename){
    lookup.put(name, probename);
  }
 public boolean implementsSubprotocol(String name) {
   if (lookup.get(name) != null) { return true; }
     return false;
  }


// the say() function is used to receive a message

 public void say(bondMessage m, bondObject sender){
     String name = (String)m.getParameter(":subprotocol");
     String val = (String)lookup.get(name);
     bondProbe p = loader.loadProbe(val);
     p.parent = parent;
     parent.set("AutoProbe_"+name, p);
     p.say(m,sender);
  }
}
```

8.1.3.4 *Message Sending and Delivery.*
Any Bond object can send and receive messages using the say() method.

The say function, defined at the root of the bondObject hierarchy, can be used to receive messages as indicated in the last segment of code above, or to receive a message when it has the following signature:

```
public void say(bondMessage m, bondObject sender) {
  if (sender == null) {
    sender = m.getSender();
  }
  String sp = m.getSubprotocol();
  if( sp != null ){
    if (sp.equals("PropertyAccess")) {
      sphPropertyAccess(m,sender);
      return; }
  }
  else {
    switch (m.performative) {
    case bondMessage.PF_SORRY:
    case bondMessage.PF_ERROR:
    case bondMessage.PF_DENY:
    return;
      default:
      }
  }
  if (values != null) {
    bondAutoProbe ap = null;
    for (Enumeration e = values.elements();
                        e.hasMoreElements();) {
    bondObject o = (bondObject)e.nextElement();
    if (bondProbe.class.isAssignableFrom(o.getClass())
        && o.implementsSubprotocol(sp)) {
      if (o instanceof bondAutoProbe) {
        ap = (bondAutoProbe)o;
      } else {
        o.say(m,sender);
        return; }
    }
    if (ap != null) { ap.say(m,sender);}
    }
}
```

The say() method is overwritten to support specific features for individual classes of objects. The message processing ability of an object is inherited in the object-oriented sense. At the end of the overwritten say() method of an object there is a fallback to the say() function of its immediate ancestor.

8.1.3.5 The Property Access Subprotocol.   The *property access* subprotocol is implemented by every Bond object. This subprotocol is used to read and write properties of another object. Table 8.4 lists the messages in this subprotocol;

Table 8.4 The messages of the property access subprotocol.

Performative	:content	Parameters	Description
ask-one	get	:property *name*	Get value of property *name* of remote object.
achieve	set	:property *name* :value *new_value*	Set value of property *name* of remote object to value *new_value*.
tell	value	:value *value*	Reply to get. *value* is the value of the requested property.
tell	ok		Reply to set. Confirms setting the property.
sorry		:error *error-name* :description *description*	An error occurred.

a message consists of a *performative* indicating the broad meaning of the message, *content*, and parameters.

A message consists of a *performative* indicating the broad meaning of the message, *content*, and parameters. The *performative* gives the broad meaning of the message. For example, ask-one is a question requesting an answer, achieve is an imperative request, tell is the response to a question. The *content* specifies the actual function requested, for example, set, get are used to store and read a property, respectively. The parameters provide command-specific information.

When we set the value of a property, then the *new_value* is either a string, or a BASE64 encoded value, see Chapter 5. In a reply to get the *value* is either a string or a BASE64 encoded value; if there is no such property, *value* is a BASE64 encoded null. A reply to set confirms setting the property and it is sent only if needsReply() was invoked on the set message.

Example. If object X wants to obtain the value of the property w of object Y, it sends the following message:

```
(ask-one :sender X :receiver Y :subprotocol PropertyAccess
         :content get :property w :reply-with zzzz)
```

Assuming that property w of object Y has value 7, then object Y replies with the following message:

```
(tell :sender Y :receiver X :subprotocol PropertyAccess
      :content value :value 7 :in-reply-to zzzz)
```

The property access subprotocol supports the get, set, and realize functions shown below.

```
void sphPropertyAccess(bondMessage m, bondObject sender){
   switch(m.performative) {
   case bondMessage.PF_ASK_ONE:
     if (m.content.equals("get")) {
        Object val = get((String)m.getParameter(":property"));
        bondMessage rep = m.createReply("(tell
           :subprotocol PropertyAccess :content value)");
        rep.setParameter(":value", val);
        sender.say(rep,this);
        return;}
     if (m.content.equals("set")) {
        set((String)m.getParameter(":property"),
                        m.getParameter(":value"));
     if (m.expectsReply()) {
        m.sendReply("(tell :content ok)", this);}
        return;}
   case bondMessage.PF_TELL:
     if (m.content.equals("realize")) {
        com.sendObject((bondShadow)m.getSender(),
        this, (String)m.getParameter(":reply-with"));
        return;}
     if (m.content.equals("ok")) { return;}
     return;
     return;
   }
}
```

8.1.3.6 *Bond Configuration.* At start-up time the system reads a file with the
desired system properties and creates a configuration object, bondConfiguration.
A sample properties file is shown in Figure 8.15.

Most of the system properties in this file are self-explanatory. Here we only
note that agent strategies can be loaded when an agent is activated, or can be deferred until the strategy is actually needed, an option controlled by the setting of the
bond.agentLazyLoading variable.

A bondStategy is a procedure activated when an agent enters a state as described
in Section 8.2. A strategy repository is a database of common strategies. Distributed
awareness, see Section 8.1.2.10, is a feature allowing residents to learn about each
other. Bond agents support several schedulers for their actions, one of them being
round robin (RR).

A microserver is an object that understands the HTTP protocol and is capable of
accessing the properties of an object via a Web browser.

Events can be logged on a file and a resident may request to be monitored by a
running agent. The fault detection features may be activated at the start-up time.

In summary, the bondConfiguration object creates a running environment tailored to the options in the properties file.

```
# The system expects to find this information in:
# Bond/bond/core/properties
bond.debug=false
bond.agentLazyLoading=true
bond.strategy.repository=http://olt.cs.purdue.edu:8001/Bond/
bond.distributedAwareness=false
bond.communicationengine=UDP
bond.UDP.port=2000
bond.TCP.port=2000
bond.scheduler=RR
bond.microserver.enable=false
bond.microserver.port=2099
bond.filelogger = yes
default.monitoring.agent=Agent1+danube.cs.purdue.edu:2000
bond.faultDetection=true
```

Fig. 8.15 A sample properties file.

8.1.4 Security

Security is an important concern for any network environment. The information in transit is vulnerable to attacks. At the same time, the use of resources in different administrative domains introduces issues of trust and consistency between them.

A distributed object system poses new challenges to security mechanisms. For example, *security auditing* should be able to identify correctly the *principal*, the original sender of a request, even after a chain of calls involving multiple objects.

There is also the need of delegation, the propagation of attributes of the principals between components. Delegation allows one component to act on behalf of a principal.

8.1.4.1 Security and Network-Centric Computing. Various applications of network computing have vastly different security requirements and the trade-off between security and performance is application specific. It is infeasible to consider one security model suitable for all applications and all environments.

Additional security challenges posed by network computing are discussed below. The user population and the resource pool are large and dynamic. A user may only be aware of a small fraction of the components involved in a computation.

The relations among components may be rather complex, a component may act both as a server and a client at the same time. Traditional distributed systems use RPC or TCP/IP as their primary communication mechanism. In contrast, a distributed computing environment may use a two-sided communication mechanism such as message passing, streaming protocols, multicast, and/or single-sided get/put operations, as well as RPC. Components may communicate through a variety of mechanisms.

The boundaries of trust are more intricate because of the dynamic characteristic of components. The trust users have in components is threatened when components can be mobile between hosts and new components can be created on the fly. Boundaries of trust are more complex because an activity typically involves multiple domains with different security policies and security models. Computation may be distributed to many more machines than any given user has control over.

Granularity, consistency, scalability, flexibility, heterogeneity, and performance are important aspects of distributed object security. A security design implies trade-offs among these requirements. For example, strong security and good performance are competing requirements. Coarse-grain security is easier to manage than fine-grain.

8.1.4.2 *Security Models.*   Security in a network environment includes authentication and access control. *Authentication* refers to the process of identifying an individual. *Access Control* is the process of granting or denying access to a network based on a two-step process: (1) authentication to ensure that a user is who he/she claims to be, and (2) access control policy, which allows the user access to various resources based on the user's identity.

Some of the authentication models are:

PAP - Password Authentication Protocol. The most basic form of authentication, the user's name and password are transmitted over the network and compared to a table of name-password pairs. Typically, the stored passwords are encrypted.

CHAP - Challenge Handshake Authentication Protocol. The authentication agent, typically a network server, sends the client program a key to encrypt the username and the password.

Kerberos - ticket-based authentication . The authentication server assigns a unique key, called a ticket, to each user that logs on to the network. The ticket is then embedded in every message to identify the sender of the message.

Certificate-based authentication. This model is based on public key cryptography. Each user holds two different keys: public and private. The user can get a certificate that proves the binding between the user and its public key from a third party. The private key is used to generate evidence that can be sent with the certificate to the server side. The server uses the certificate and evidence to verify the identity of the user.

Credential is a secret code that proves the identity of an individual. Authentication models use different credentials:

- username/password in PAP and CHAP,

- user identifier/ticket in ticket-based authentication, and

- user certificate/private key in the certificate-based authentication.

Access control models include a firewall and an access control list (ACL). A firewall grants or denies access based on the IP address of the requester. An access control list specifies the operations a user may perform on each resource.

8.1.4.3 Bond Security.
In Bond we opted for an extensible core object that can support multiple security models and can be added dynamically to an existing object. This philosophy leads to several design principles:

(i) Provide a framework for security, not force an implementation. Bond leaves the decision of choosing the format of credentials, the authentication policy, the access control policy, and so on, to the system developer or the system administrator. Bond security is implemented as an extensible core Bond object called `BondSecurityContext` and a set of well-defined security interfaces.

(ii) Separation of concerns: various aspects of a complex object design, including security, should be separated from one another. In the initial design and implementation phase the creator of an object should only be concerned with functionality. Once the object is fully functional the creator needs to investigate the security requirements and augment the object with the proper security context by including a *probe* called BondSecurityContext. This dynamic property of a Bond object sets up a secure perimeter for the object; it intercepts all incoming and outgoing messages and enforces the security and access control models selected by the creator of the object.

(iii) Support multiple authentication and access control models. This goal is achieved by defining a common interface for different security functions, such as credential, authentication, and access control.

The Bond security framework is based on the concept of *preemptive probe* discussed in Section 8.1.3.3. The preemptive probe is activated before any attempts are made to deliver the message to the object, it intercepts all messages sent to the object.

8.1.4.4 Implementation.
Four components, including a preemptive probe and security interfaces, support the security models implemented in Bond:

1. `BondSecurityContext` is a preemptive probe that establishes a defense perimeter for the object it is attached to, by intercepting incoming and outgoing messages with two methods:

   `incomingMessageProcess()` and

   `outgoingMessageProcess()`.

2. `BondCredentialInterface` - defines the method to access the credential possessed by the current `BondSecurityContext`. This interface provides two groups of methods:

   (i) Methods to respond to authentication request from a remote object. Usually a challenge is contained in the authentication request, and the response is derived from both the challenge and the information provided by the credential. The response is generated differently depending on security models.

(ii) Methods to generate a user identifier and a proof to be embedded in each outgoing message and prove to the receiver the identity of sender. The proof has a different meaning in different security models. In a username/password model the proof can be a password, or an encrypted password; in a ticket based security model, the ticket itself can be a proof; in a certificate–based model, the evidence generated by encrypting a random string with the private key can be an eligible proof.

3. BondAuthenticatorInterface - defines the authentication method for each message received by an object. The developer or the administrator may deploy one of the authentication models mentioned earlier. The only restriction is to adhere to this interface. The authenticateClient() is the only method provided by this security interface. This method returns an authenticated user identifier. This identifier can be used for access control or auditing.

4. BondAccessControlInterface - defines the access control method for each message received by an object. The methods provided by this security interface are initACL() and checkRight() based on the authentication models discussed earlier.

The code below illustrates the implementation of bondSecurityContext that supports authentication and access control in the incomingMessageProcess().

```
bondSecurityContext extends bondProbe {
 private bondCredentials bcs;
 private bondAuthenticatorInterface bau;
 private bondAccessControlInterface bac;
/* incomingMessageProcess is called by the message
   thread on each received message */
 public void incomingMessageProcess(m, sender){
/*1.authenticate message */
  authenticated_user_id
   = bau.authenticateClient(m);
  if( authenticated_user_id == null ){
    sender.say( sorry message );
    return;}
/* 2.enforce access control */
  result = bac.checkRight(authenticated_user_id,m);
  if( result == false){
    sender.say( sorry message ); return;}
/* 3.pass the message to the object */
  parent.say(m, null); }
```

The code also shows several objects that implement the security interfaces defined above.

Table 8.5 Authentication models.

Type	Interface	Authenticator Interface
Name & Pass	`bondPAPCredentail`	`bondPasswordAuthenticator`
CHAP	`bondCHAPCredential`	`bondChallengeAuthenticator`

Table 8.6 Access control models.

Type	Access Control Interface	Required Authenticator
IP	`bondIPAddressAccessControl`	-
ACL	`bondNameBasedAccessControl` `bondRightBasedAccessControl`	`bondChallengeAuth` `bondPasswordAuth`

Table 8.5 lists the authentication models and Table 8.6 lists the access control models implemented in Bond.

All authenticators in Table 8.5 need an authentication server maintaining the usernames and the passwords. If the service provider uses one type of authenticator, the client should use the corresponding credential to make the authentication successful.

Example.

This example illustrates how to construct secure objects. Assume that we have one client, two generic servers, and an authentication server that provides account management and authentication services.

The client `clio` uses an existing account (`uid=hector` and `passwd=hamham`) to access services provided by the two servers:

- `serverA` enforces plain password-based authentication and firewall-based access control.

- `serverB` enforces CHAP-based authentication and name–based access control.

The code below shows how to set up `serverA` as a secure object enforcing plain password-based authentication and firewall-based access control.

```
/* create a new server object*/
  serverA = new server();
/* create a plain-password based authenticator */
 bondPasswordAuthenticator bau  = new
        bondPasswordAuthenticator(baserver);
```

```
/* create a firewall-based access controller AC */
bondIPAddressAccessControl bac = new
                         bondIPAddressAccessControl();
bac.initACL("firewall.acl");
/* create a security context */
bondSecurityContext gatekeeper = new
                         bondSecurityContext(serverA);
/* set the AC and authenticator of context */
 gatekeeper.setAccessControl(bac);
 gatekeeper.setAuthenticator(bau);
/* set the security context into serverA */
 serverA.setSecurityContext(gatekeeper);
```

The format of the access control list firewall.acl is:

```
* Firewall configuration file consisting
* of pairs <hostname><mask>
dragomirna.cs.purdue.edu 255.255.255.0
```

Hosts in the same subnet with the machine dragomirna.cs.purdue.edu can access serverA.

The code below shows how to create a secure object enforcing CHAP-based authentication and name-based access control.

```
/* create a new server object*/
 server serverB= new server();
/* create a CHAP-based authenticator */
 bondChallengeAuthenticator bpau  = new
            bondChallengeAuthenticator(baserver);
/* create name-based AC and initialize it */
 bondNameBasedAccessControl bac = new
                 bondNameBasedAccessControl();
bac.initACL("names.acl");
/* create a security context for serverB */
 bondSecurityContext gatekeeper = new
                 bondSecurityContext(serverB);
/* set the access controller and authenticator */
 gatekeeper.setAccessControl(bac);
 gatekeeper.setAuthenticator(bpau);
/* set security context as dynamic property of serverB*/
 serverB.setSecurityContext(gatekeeper);
```

The format of the access control list file `names.acl` is:

```
*
* Name based ACL, the format of
* this file is as following
* <name> <right1,right2,rightN>
hector persistent-object-read,persistent-object-write
```

This means that user `hector` is allowed to save objects to and reload them from this server.

The parameter, `baserver`, is used to create the authenticators in both cases. This means serverA and serverB share the account information stored by the `baserver`, the authentication server of the domain.

To set up a client as a secure object:

```
/* create a client object */
 client clio = new client();
/* create a security context for client */
 bondSecurityContext bsc = new bondSecurityContext(clio);
/* setup a PAP credential */
 bondPAPCredential bc1 = new bondPAPCredential
      ("hector","ham"); bsc.setCredential(bc1,"serverA");
/* setup a CHAP credential */
 bondCHAPCredential bc2 = new bondPAPCredential
      ("hector","ham"); bsc.setCredential(bc2,"serverB");
/* setup this security context for client */
 clio.setSecurityContext(bsc);
```

Once properly set up, `bsc` adds appropriate credentials to outgoing requests by checking destinations; requests to `serverA` are associated with `bondPAPCredential`, while those to `serverB` are associated with `bondCHAPCredential`.

A scenario involving the interaction between the client and `serverA` is shown in Figure 8.16:

- the client sends requests for service;

- the message is intercepted by the security context of the client and the `username` and the `password` are inserted into the message before forwarding it to `serverA`;

- when the message reaches its destination it is intercepted by the security context of the server, which enforces authentication and access control;

- after validating the `username` and the `password`, the message is passed to `serverA`.

The scenario illustrated in Figure 8.16 is appropriate when the server trusts the identifier and the proof contained in a message. But the identifier and proof may

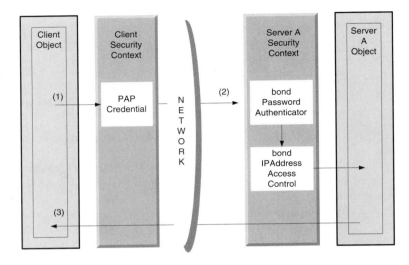

Fig. 8.16 Processing a service request using a PAP model. (1) The original service request from the client. (2) The service request with a username and password added by the client's security context. (3) The response to the service request sent by the client if the security context of the server validates the credentials.

be captured by a malicious third party and used to obtain unauthorized access to the server.

To prevent such attacks, the security context of the server should use a stronger authentication scheme as shown in Figure 8.17.

- the client sends a service request to `serverB`;

- the security context of the client detects that a `bondCHAPCredential` is used and only forwards the message;

- the message is captured by the security context of the server.

- the authenticator of the security context of the server sends a challenge to the credential component of the security context of the client and expects a response derived from both the challenge and information contained in client's credential;

- the authenticator uses the challenge and corresponding response to authenticate the client. If the service request is validated, the server object grants the service.

8.2 THE AGENTS

The `bond.agents` package implements the agent framework. In Section 8.2.1 we discuss the agent model then address the problem of agent control in Section 8.2.2. The agent description language is introduced in Section 8.2.3 and in Section 8.2.4

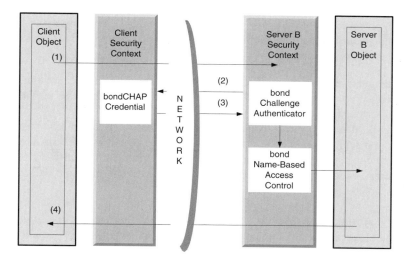

Fig. 8.17   Processing a service request using a CHAP credential. (1) The original service request from the client. (2) A challenge generated by the security context of the server. (3) The response to the challenge. (4) The response to the service request sent when the security context of the server validates the credentials.

we present agent transformations. Extensions to the agent framework are outlined in Section 8.2.5.

8.2.1   The Bond Agent Model

Our agent model was designed with several objectives in mind:

(i) Assemble dynamically an agent from reusable components. Use a description language to specify the structure of an agent.

(ii) Create a supporting environment for an agent. The environment should be open-ended and support societal services.

(iii) Map the agent description into a data structure and feed this data structure to the control unit responsible for coordinating the execution of an agent.

(iv) Support concurrent activities as a defining feature of an agent rather than an afterthought. Agents should be able to respond promptly to external events and, at the same time, carry out multiple tasks previously initiated.

(v) Support changes in the behavior of an agent. Since behavior is determined by structure, support structural mutations of an agent.

(vi) Support a weaker form of agent mobility, allow agents to migrate at discrete instances of time and to specific locations only. Conceive an architecture where the complexity of the agent state periodically reaches a minimum, and exploit this feature to facilitate mobility. Allow agents to migrate only to sites that are part of the environment.

Bond agents are based on a *multiplane agent model*. The agents are described by *functional components* called strategies and by *structural components* provided as a multiplane state machine.

The multiplane structure provides the means to express concurrent agent activities. Each state machine is said to be operating in its own *plane*; thus, the term *multiplane state machine* for our model. Each plane may perform a different task, one may support reasoning or planning functions, another the execution, while a third one is used for bookkeeping.

8.2.1.1 Aspects of Agents.

The behavior of an agent is often *multifaceted*, it consists of several loosely coupled aspects. A full-featured agent may exhibit several facets:

Reasoning. Agents use inference to generate new facts from existing ones using a set of rules.

Visual interface. Most agents present a visual interface and interact with humans: (a) presenting its knowledge, i.e., a part of the model in a visual format, and (b) collect user interface events.

Reactive behavior. Agents react to external events.

Active behavior. Agents perform actions in pursuit of their agenda even without external events.

In most cases, a separation of these facets is possible, and the relative independence of the facets justifies their separate treatment. For example, the various steps taken by an agent to pursue its goal are changes in its active behavior, but these changes may not necessarily lead to a change in its reactive behavior, the look of the user interface, or the reasoning process of the agent.

The multiplane model provides an elegant way to express the multifaceted behavior of an agent, every plane expresses a facet of the behavior of the agent. There are no restrictions on the nature and behavior of planes, so the agent designer can create the structure most suitable to the problem at hand.

However, the independence of facets is relative, significant interdependence existing between them. In the multiplane state machine structure, the interdependence among planes is captured by the fact that all planes share a common model and transitions triggered by one plane are applied to the whole structure, providing a signaling mechanism among planes.

8.2.1.2 Agent Components.

Our agent model consists of four components, state machines or planes, strategies, a model of the world, and an agenda, see Figure 8.18. The terms *state machine* and *plane* are used interchangeably throughout

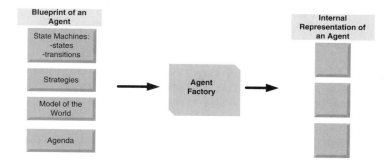

Fig. 8.18 The components of an agent: state machines, strategies, model of the world, and agenda. The object factory takes an agent description, including the four components, and transforms it into an internal agent representation .

this chapter, the first when discussing the agent structure and the second in the context of the functionality of an agent.

Structurally, an agent is a collection of state machines. In turn, each state machine is described by states and transitions among states. Strategies, the functional components of an agent, are specified for each state.

To describe an agent we introduced an agent description language called *Blueprint*. A Blueprint program is interpreted by an *agent factory* object, which creates an internal data structure. In turn, this data structure is used by the agent factory to control the run-time behavior of the agent.

(i) *The State Machine* is defined by a graph with nodes corresponding to states and edges corresponding to transitions among states.

Each state machine has one active node at any given time. The *state of the agent* is defined by a *vector of states* , one state per plane.

A state machine changes its state by performing *transitions*. The transitions are triggered by internal or external *events*. External events are caused by messages. The set of external messages that trigger the transitions of one or more state machine defines the *control subprotocol* of the agent.

(ii) *The Strategies* are the functional components of an agent. Once a state machine enters a state it triggers the excution of the strategy associated with that state. In turn, a strategy consists of a sequence of `actions` executed under the control of a scheduler.

Strategies are written in programming languages such as Java, C, C++, or in interpretative languages such as JPython. They can be specified as executables, Java class files, or be embedded in the blueprint as source programs, to be processed by an existing interpreter. The strategies are discussed in depth in Section 8.2.2.3.

Multiple strategies may be used to handle different events. For example, a strategy in one plane may be used to handle external messages, while another plane handles user interface events.

(iii) *The Model of the World* is an unordered collection of free-formatted items accessed by name, representing all the information an agent has about the environment and itself.

The model can be a knowledge base, an ontology, a pretrained neural network, a collection of meta-objects, handles of external objects, e.g., file handles, sockets, etc., or a heterogeneous collection of all the above. It also contains agent state information.

The model of the world is a Bond object itself, with a set of dynamic properties, one for each component. The model is used by strategies as a shared memory; strategies communicate with each other by storing and retrieving data to/from the model. The naming scheme supports namespaces and allows multiple strategies to reuse variable names without conflicts. Programming languages such as C++ use namespaces to resolve name conflicts.

The model of the world is a passive object, inherits the serializability and mobility properties of Bond objects, and allows migration and checkpointing of Bond agents. The information in the model may be time and location dependent and be meaningless after migration. For example, the string /usr/bin/netscape giving the path information for the executable of a browser is meaningless when an agent migrates from a Linux to a Windows NT system.

(iv) *The Agenda* is an object that defines the goal of the agent. The agenda implements a boolean distance function on the model. The boolean function shows if the agent has accomplished its goal. The agenda acts as a termination condition for the agents, except for agents with a *continuous agenda* where their goal is to maintain the agenda as being satisfied. The distance function may be used by the strategies to choose their actions.

8.2.2 Communication and Control. Agent Internals.

An agent can only exist in a supporting environment provided by a resident. Several objects in this environment control the lifecycle of an agent, see Figure 8.19. The bondAgentFactory, assembles the agent based on its blueprint and generates its *agent control subprotocol (ACS)* and an agent control structure. The *ACS* allows the agent to communicate with other objects. The agent control structure is an internal data structure used by the bondSemanticEngine and the bondActionScheduler to control the run-time behavior of the agent.

The structural and functional components of the agent, the blueprint, and the strategies come from local or from remote repositories. The agent factory assembles an agent based on its blueprint and may also create a modified blueprint if the control agent structure is modified at run-time, as discussed in Section 8.2.2.10.

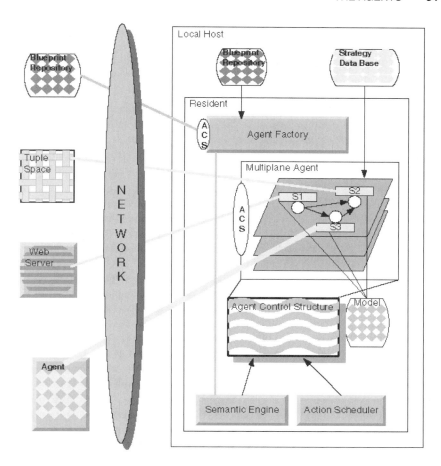

Fig. 8.19 The agent run-time environment. The agent and its *agent control subprotocol* *(ACS)* are created by the `bondAgentFactory`. The structural component of an agent, the *blueprint*, and the functional components, *strategies*, come from local or from the remote repository. The agent has multiple planes, each plane is a state machine. Each state of a state machine has a strategy associated with it. Once created, the `bondActionScheduler` and the `bondSemanticEngine` control the execution of the agent using an internal data structure. Strategies can be loaded dynamically from local repositories ($S2$), from Web servers ($S1$), or may be written in a scripting language and transmitted in a message from another agent ($S3$). Strategies communicate with one another through the model.

Each state of each plane has a strategy associated with it. Strategies may be loaded statically when an agent is created, or dynamically, at the time of a transition to the corresponding state. Strategies may come from the local strategy database, may be downloaded from a Web server, or from the tuple space, or may be provided by the entity requesting the creation of the agent. At the time of this writing, strategies in the JPython scripting language may be included in an agent control message.

All objects, including agents, react to messages by invoking methods implemented by the object. To understand the behavior and functions of an object we examine the two facets of an object: (i) message decoding, and (ii) the actions taken by the object in response to messages described by the methods supported by the object.

In this section we describe the major events in the life of an agent as follows: creation in Section 8.2.2.6; activation in Section 8.2.2.7; checkpointing and restarting in Section 8.2.2.8; migration in Section 8.2.2.9; modification or surgery in Section 8.2.2.10. These events occur in response to messages sent either to the agent factory controlling the agent or to the agent itself. The messages controlling the life cycle of an agent form the agent control subprotocol discussed in Section 8.2.2.1.

8.2.2.1   Agent Control Subprotocol (ACS).

An agent uses a dynamically created ACS to communicate with: the agent factory, the entity controlling the agent, and other objects including agents. The messages of the *ACS* are described in Table 8.7. These messages are used to control checkpoint and restart, modify, and migrate an agent.

The ACS follows the major events in the lifetime of the agent: it is created dynamically when the agent is assembled; disappears when the agent is killed; it is modified when the agent undergoes surgery. The ACS is itself an object and may be distributed to other objects.

The ACS requires actions to be taken by the agent factory or by the agent. The following messages are sent to the agent factory controlling the agent and invoke methods of bondAgentFactory: assemble-agent, checkpoint, modify-agent, migrate-from-here, kill-agent. The agent itself supports methods to communicate with the model getModel, setModel, to report the state, getState, or to provide its subprotocol, learn-subprotocol. The methods supported by bondAgent are discussed in Section 8.2.2.2, the ones supported by bondAgentFactory in Section 8.2.2.4.

8.2.2.2   Agent Communication.

Agents are objects; Bond objects communicate using the say() method.

By default the say() method of an agent supports the delivery of messages in two subprotocols: (1) agent control subprotocol, and (2) the fault detection subprotocols.

In addition, it delivers external messages that may cause transitions of the state machines. An external message is delivered to all state machines.

The say() method falls back on the the say() method of the ancestor as shown by the following segment of code. Here we see the activation of the scheduler at the time an agent is created and at the time of message delivery with the say() method.

The bondAgent has a constructor for an empty agent and methods to start, stop, soft-stop, and kill an agent. The constructor sets up one of the action schedulers and the semantic engine. The round-robin scheduler is the default. Starting and stopping an agent implies starting and stopping the scheduler.

At this time all agents support the fault detection mechanism, see Section 8.2.5.4, initialized at the time an agent is started.

Table 8.7 The messages of the agent control subprotocol. The entities involved are: the *beneficiary*, the *agent*, the *agent factory controlling the agent*, AgF, the *agent factory at a new location*, AgF_{new}.

Message	Parameters	Message function
`assemble-agent`	`:blueprint` `:blueprint-address` `:visual`	Sent to AgF and request to assemble an agent using the blueprint downloaded from blueprint-address. Specify `:visual` if editor window is desired.
`agent-created`	`:bondID` `:bondAddress`	Sent to beneficiary by AgF to confirm creation of agent. Gives bondID and bondAddress.
`start-agent`	`:model :alias`	Sent to agent by beneficiary. Request agent to start or resume execution.
`soft-stop`		Request agent to soft stop.
`checkpoint`	`:bondID` `:checkpoint file`	Sent to AgF. Agent factory soft stops agent `:bondID`, saves its current state to local file `:checkpointfile`, and restarts agent.
`checkback`	`:bondID` `:checkpoint file`	Sent to AgF. Agent factory soft stops the agent, restores its state from local file `:checkpointfile` and restarts agent.
`modify-agent`	`:blueprint` `:blueprint-address`	Sent to AgF. Request to modify the agent. Surgical blueprint embedded in the blueprint or downloaded from blueprint-address.
`migrate-agent`	`:blueprint` `:visual :bondID` `:modelID`	Sent to AF_{new} by AgF. AF_{new} recreates the agent with `:bondID` using the embedded blueprint and realizes the model of agent `:modelID`, from the source site.
`migrate-from-here`	`:bondID` `:remote-address`	Sent to AgF. Initializes migration of agent `:bondID` from source to destination site `:remote-address`.
`migrated`	`:bondID`	Sent to AgF by AgF_{new}. Successful migration. Request AgF delete old copy of agent.
`kill-agent`	`:bondID`	Sent to AgF. If running, agent is soft-stopped and disposed of.
`getModel`	`:property`	Sent to agent. Agent replies with the value of the property property from the model.
`setModel`	`:property` `:value`	Sent to agent. Sets value of the model property `:property` to `:value`
`getState`		Sent to agent. Agent responds with its current state vector.
`learn-subprotocol`		Request agent to generate and send subprotocol object.

```
public bondAgent() {
   model = new bondModel();
   initStrategyPath();
   String schedulerName = System.getProperty
                                    ("bond.scheduler");
   if (schedulerName.equals("MT")) {
     basched = new bondMTActionScheduler(this);}
   else {
     if (!schedulerName.equals("RR")) {
        Log.Debug("Action scheduler invalid, using RR"); }
        basched = new bondRRActionScheduler(this);}
   semantic = new bondStateMachineSemantic(planes, model);
 }
public void say(bondMessage m, bondObject sender)
   try {
     if (m.getSubprotocol().equals("AgentControl")) {
       sphAgentControl(m, sender); return;}
     if (m.getSubprotocol().equals("FaultDetection")){
      sphFaultDetection(m, sender); return;}
     if (genericSPH(m, sender)) {return;}
     if (m.getSubprotocol().equals(sp.getName())) {
        for(Enumeration e=planes.elements();
                         e.hasMoreElements(); ) {
           bondAgentPlane bap = (bondAgentPlane)
                              e.nextElement();
           bap.fsm.say(m,sender);}
     } else {
     super.say(m, sender);}
     }
   catch (NullPointerException e) { }
 }
```

The code for the agent control subprotocol listed below handles the following messages: get-state, start-agent, stop-agent, kill-agent, getModel, setModel

```
public void sphAgentControl(bondMessage m, bondObject sender) {
  if (sender == null) sender = m.getSender();
  if (restricted_control && !sender.equals(beneficiary)){
     sender.say( m.createReply("(deny)"),this); }
  if (m.content.equals("get-state")) {
     String state = "";
     for(Enumeration e=planes.elements();e.hasMoreElements();){
     bondAgentPlane bap = (bondAgentPlane) e.nextElement();
     state += "."+bap.fsm.getState().getName();}
     sender.say( m.createReply("(tell :content state:
                         state "+state+")"),this);}
```

```
        if (m.content.equals("start-agent")) {
            initDropBox();
            populateModel(m.getParameter(":model"));
            String als = (String)m.getParameter(":alias");
            if (als != null) dir.addAlias(als, this);
            initFaultDetection();
            start();
            sender.say( m.createReply("(tell :content ok)"),this);
            return;}
        if (m.content.equals("stop-agent")) {
            softstop = true;
            sender.say( m.createReply("(tell :content ok)"),this);
            return;}
        if (m.content.equals("kill-agent")) {
            kill();
            sender.say( m.createReply("(tell :content ok)"),this);
            return;}
        if (m.content.equals("getModel")) {
            Object val = model.get((String)m.getParameter
                                            (":property"));
            bondMessage rep = m.createReply("(tell :content value)");
            rep.setParameter(":value", val);
            sender.say(rep,this);
            return;}
        if (m.content.equals("setModel")) {
            model.set((String)m.getParameter(":property"),
                                    m.getParameter(":value"));
            if (m.getParameter(":createReply") != null)
                    {m.sendReply("(tell :content ok)", this); }
            return;}
}
```

8.2.2.3 *Strategies.* Strategies are the functional components of an agent. Formally, a strategy is a function that takes as parameters the model of the world and the agenda of the agent and returns actions. A strategy implements three interfaces, `install()`, `action()`, and `unistall()`, see Figure 8.20. When the state machine generates a transition to a state, the thread of control invokes the three methods in this order.

The actions determine the behavior of the agent. Actions are atomic and strategies do not reveal their entire state to the agent or the environment. While a strategy executes, it cannot be interrupted and its state may be rather complex.

A strategy consists of a sequence of actions, in an infinite sequence interrupted only when a transition takes place. An alternative approach is to have *one-shot strategies*, generating only one action, followed by a transition. A strategy is activated as the flow of control requires, or in response to external events.

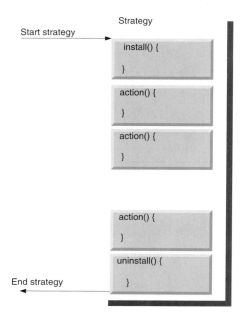

Fig. 8.20 The structure of a strategy.

Messages from remote applications and *user interface events* such as pressed keys and mouse clicks are examples of external events. The strategies are activated by the event-handling mechanism – the Java event system for graphics user interface (GUI) events, the message thread for messages in case of external events, or by an *action scheduler*. Activation using the external messages is characteristic for strategies derived from `bondProbeStrategy`, while activation as a result of user interface events are handled by strategies derived from `bondGuiStrategy`.

The model is used by strategies as a shared memory, strategies communicate with each other by storing and retrieving data to/from the model.

There are two methods `getModel` and `setModel` to read and write data into the model. By default, a strategy accesses only its own namespace, but may address variables outside its namespace by specifying the full name of the variable. The default namespace of a strategy is specified in the blueprint of the agent.

Example. The blueprint statement:

```
add state ExecBrowser with strategy Exec.Start::Browser;
```

means that the `ExecBrowser` strategy uses the namespace `Browser`.

```
String toexec = getModel("commandline");
```

returns the model variable named `Browser.commandline` and

```
setModel("output", commandOutput);
```

writes `commandOutput` into the model variable named `Browser.output` if the methods are invoked by strategies with `Browser` as default namespace.

Only a small fraction of the internal state of a strategy is exposed to the outside world through the model. When the agent enters a new state the strategy associated with that state is activated and may read from the model the current value of model variables. A strategy may deposit results in the model just before completion.

At any given time t the *internal state of an agent* is given by the internal state of all its strategies and the model. The *external state* or the *agent state* is a vector stored in the model describing the state of each state machine.

From the implementation point of view, a strategy is a Java interface with a function called `action()` that performs the actions required when an agent enters a state. The system provides three primitive strategies:

1. `bondGuiStrategy` handles a GUI window. When entered the strategy initializes the user interface and it closes the window on termination.

2. `bondProbeStrategy` automatically installs and uninstalls itself as a probe for a specific subprotocol.

3. `bondDefaultStrategy` is a place holder for a real strategy in case of lazy-loading.

The system supports strategies written in Java, other programming languages wrapped in the Java Native Interface (JNI), and scripting languages such as JPython. The following objects may be used as strategies:

(i) Objects derived from `bondDefaultStrategy`, `bondGUIStrategy` or from `bondProbeStrategy`. This is the method of choice to create Java strategies.

(ii) Objects implementing the `bondStrategy` interface. This method allows us to create strategies that inherit from classes outside the Bond hierarchy.

(iii) External objects with JNI wrappers. Any external object written in a programming language other than Java can be transformed into a Bond strategy using a JNI wrapper. The wrapper must implement the `bondStrategy` interface.

(iv) Embedded languages. The source code of a strategy can be embedded into the blueprint specification of an agent. The code can be in an interpreted language with an existing Java interpreter. We currently support Python, through the JPython interpreter [26], and `Jess`, the Java-based expert system shell [19].

Most of the strategies in the Bond strategy database are grouped together into strategy groups. Table 8.8 lists the most important strategy groups.

8.2.2.4 Agent Factory. The agent factory translates a blueprint agent description into an internal data structure, called agent control structure, and then uses this data structure to control the agent as seen in Figure 8.21. An agent may be altered dynamically as discussed in Section 8.2.2.10 and then the agent factory is able to generate a modified blueprint.

Table 8.8 Strategy groups in the strategy database.

Name	Function of the Strategy Group
Util	Utility, e.g., delay.
Agent	Checkpoint, migration, surgery, termination.
Dialog	Dialog boxes for warnings, messages, and yes/no questions.
Exec	Start, supervise, and control local applications.
RemoteExec	Start, supervise, and manage remote applications.
AgentExec	Start and control agents and groups of agents
FTP	Data migration.
Model	Save, load and merge models.
Scheduler	Metaprogram scheduling algorithms.
Synch	Strategies for agent synchronization.

The sequence of steps taken by the agent factory to create an agent is:

(i) Get the blueprint and the components (states, transitions, strategies).

(ii) Generate the finite state machines and link each state with its corresponding strategy.

(iii) Generate the control subprotocol of the agent.

(iv) Send a copy of the control subprotocol object to the beneficiary and to other objects the agent needs in order to communicate with the controlling authority, be it a user interface or another agent.

The agent factory controls the run time behavior of an agent and uses the action scheduler to transfer control to a new action whenever the current one completes its execution. Once a transition from the current state to the next state takes place, the agent factory is responsible to load the strategy corresponding to the new state.

The strategy loader, looks up a strategy, Foo, in the following order:

(i) Searches the strategy databases for the Java class bondFooStrategy.class.

(ii) Searches the directories specified in the import statements in the blueprint description of the agent. The order of the import statements is important.

(iii) As a last resort, it considers the strategy name a full name of the Java class, i.e., Foo.class and repeats the search in the same order.

After loading the blueprint file, the agent factory parses the script and assembles the agent according to the specification. The initialization of strategies can be done in two modes:

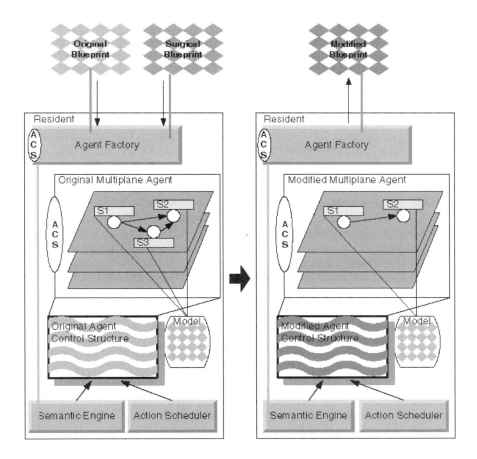

Fig. 8.21   The *Agent Factory* translates a *Blueprint* into an internal control structure and an agent.   When a *Surgical Blueprint* is provided, the agent factory modifies the internal data structure controlling the agent and is able to automatically generate the modified blueprint.

1. *Full-load* mode. The strategies are loaded and instantiated at the time the agent is created by the bondStrategyLoader object.

2. *Lazy-load* mode. None of the strategies are loaded, but they are replaced with a lightweight object called bondLazyLoadingStrategy. Whenever a state is entered, the lazy-loading strategy attached to the state triggers the loading of the real strategy, and replaces itself with the real one.

The bondAgentFactory is an object with the alias "AgentFactory" that implements some of the methods for the agent control subprotocol. These methods are described in the following sections.

The milestones in the life-cycle of an agent are discussed elsewhere: `assemble-agent` in Section 8.2.2.6, `checkpoint` and `checkback` in Section 8.2.2.8, and `migrate-agent`, `migrate-from-here`, and `migrated` in Section 8.2.2.9.

Now we present the code for the agent control subprotocol. Once the content of a message is identified, the corresponding method of the agent factory is invoked.

```
public class bondAgentFactory
  extends bondProbe {
    public bondAgentFactory() {
    dir.addAlias("AgentFactory", this);
  }
 public void say(bondMessage m, bondObject sender) {
    if (genericSPH(m, sender)) { return;}
    super.say(m, sender);}
 public void sphAgentControl(bondMessage m, bondObject sender) {
    if (m.content.equals("assemble-agent")) {
      assembleAgent(m, sender);}
    if (m.content.equals("modify-agent")) {
      modifyAgent(m, sender);}
    if (m.content.equals("migrate-agent")) {
      migrateAgent(m, sender);}
    if (m.content.equals("migrate-from-here")) {
      migrateFromHere(m, sender);}
    if (m.content.equals("migrated")) {
      migrated(m, sender);}
    if (m.content.equals("checkpoint")) {
      checkpoint(m, sender); }
    if (m.content.equals("checkback")) {
      checkback(m, sender);}
    if (m.content.equals("kill")) {
      kill(m, sender);}
}
```

8.2.2.5 Lazy-Loading.
This mode leads to faster startup time. Moreover, agents with a complex structure may never reach some of their states; thus, the corresponding strategies may never be entered. However, the loading process triggered by entering a state will cause delays during the execution; thus, this method is not suitable for agents operating in a real-time environment.

Mobile agents may travel to sites where some of the strategies are not available. In this case, the lazy loading may prevent some load-time errors. When an agent migrates to a new site, each strategy is loaded again when the agent enters the corresponding state. In this case a different strategy, the one available locally, will be loaded instead of the strategy used at the original site. This feature can be used to customize an agent depending on the current host. For example, when an agent migrates to a palmtop computer a different user interface than the one for a desktop may be used.

The lazy-loading strategy differs in scope and implementation from the run-time linking provided by the Java class loader. Java loads classes at their first instantiation and the linker assumes that the class was known at compile time, although it can be cheated into loading classes it has never seen before. This just-in-time loading is especially useful for applets, because it helps in hiding the network latency and provides for a faster startup.

8.2.2.6 Agent Creation.

The agent creation process is triggered when the agent factory receives an `agent-create` message. This message can be: (i) sent by another object, (ii) generated locally by the `RunAgent` object from command line parameters, or, (iii) generated by the user from a local or remote agent control panel. Then the agent factory method `assembleAgent` is invoked.

```
void assembleAgent(bondMessage m, bondObject sender) {
   String visual = (String)m.getParameter(":visual");
   bondAgent ba = interpretFromMessage(m, null);
   if (ba == null) {
     m.sendReply("(error :content BadBlueprint)", this);
     return; };
   String res = (String)m.getParameter(":repository");
   if (res != null)
     System.setProperty
            ("bond.current.strategy.repository", res);
   if (sender instanceof bondShadow) { ba.beneficiary =
                                  (bondShadow)sender;}
   else { }
   if (visual == null) {
     String visualFlag = System.getProperty
                                  ("bond.agent.visual");
     if (visualFlag != null && visualFlag.equals("true"))
        visual = "yes";
     else   visual = "no";
   }
   if (visual.equals("yes")) {ba.edit();}
   bondMessage rep = m.createReply
                      ("(tell :content agent-created)");
   rep.setParameter(":bondID", ba.bondID);
   rep.setParameter(":address",
                   com.localaddress+":"+com.localport);
   if (!(sender instanceof bondShadow)) {
     bondShadow t = new bondShadow(sender);
     t.say(rep, this);}
   else { sender.say(rep,this);}
}
```

The blueprint for the new agent may be provided within the message or may be specified using the `repository` parameter of the message. An agent may be created with or without a visual editor.

The object sending the `agent-create` request to an agent factory is called the *beneficiary* of the agent. There is a special relationship between an agent and its beneficiary. The agent keeps a shadow of its beneficiary and sends notifications regarding important events in its lifetime, such as termination, migration, error conditions.

The agent factory sends the `agent-created` message to the beneficiary after the agent is successfully created. However, the agent is not started immediately after its creation. The beneficiary may initialize the model between creation and the agent start.

The beneficiary may request the agent to reject messages from other objects and communicate exclusively with itself by setting the `beneficiary-only` parameter in the `agent-create` message. This security mechanism is similar to the sandbox security model of Java [21, ?].

The `interpretBlueprint` method of the `bondAgentFactory` invokes a blueprint parser and examines one of the switches of the configuration file to determine if lazy loading is in effect.

```
public bondAgent interpretBlueprint(Reader is,
                                    bondAgent ba) {
  bond.agent.blueprint.syntaxtree.Node root = null;
  blueprintParser parser = new blueprintParser(is);
  if (parser == null) return null;
  try {
    root = parser.BluePrintProgram();}
  catch (ParseException pex) { }
  if (root == null) return null;
  BlueprintInterpreter bp = new BlueprintInterpreter();
  bp.lazyLoad = Boolean.getBoolean("bond.agentLazyLoading");
  bp.ag = ba;
  root.accept(bp);
  return bp.ag;
}
```

The `interpretFromMessage` method of the `bondAgentFactory` determines if the blueprint is supplied with the message and if so, invokes the blueprint parser. This is done by examining the `blueprint-program` parameter.

```
bondAgent interpretFromMessage(bondMessage m,
                               bondAgent ba){
  bondEmbeddedBlueprint blueprint_prog =
    (bondEmbeddedBlueprint)m.getParameter
                        (":blueprint-program");
  if (blueprint_prog != null) {
    return interpretBlueprint(
```

```
                              blueprint_prog.getReader(),ba);}
   String blueprint = (String)m.getParameter (":blueprint");
   if (blueprint != null) {
     return interpretBlueprint(
                          openBlueprint(blueprint), ba);}
   bondEmbeddedBlueprint xml_blueprint_prog =
     (bondEmbeddedBlueprint)m.getParameter
                          (":xml-blueprint-program");
   if (blueprint_prog != null) {
     return interpretXMLBlueprint
                    (xml_blueprint_prog.getReader(),ba);}
   String xml_blueprint =
                 (String)m.getParameter(":xml-blueprint");
   if (xml_blueprint != null) {
     Reader is = openBlueprint(xml_blueprint);
     return interpretXMLBlueprint(is, ba);}
   return null;
}
public Reader openBlueprint(String bpfile) {
   if (bpfile.startsWith("http://")) {
     try{
       URL con = new URL(bpfile);
       return new InputStreamReader(con.openStream());}
     catch (MalformedURLException muex) { }
     catch (IOException ioex) { }
   } else {
     try { return new FileReader(bpfile);}
     catch (FileNotFoundException fnfex) { }
     }
}
```

8.2.2.7 *Agent Activation.*

The start-agent message triggers the activation of the agent. The processing of this message is illustrated by the code presented in Section 8.2.2.2. On receipt of this message:

(i) if the message includes the :model parameter, then the model is initialized by the populateModel function listed below.

(ii) the state vector of the multiplane state machine becomes the initial state specified in the blueprint,

(iii) the current strategies are installed,

(iv) the execution thread is created, and

(v) the *action scheduler* starts to execute actions according to the current strategies.

```
public boolean populateModel(Object mXML) {
  if (mXML == null) return false;
  bondXMLmodel temp = new bondXMLmodel();
  temp.setModel(model);
  if (mXML instanceof bondEmbeddedBlueprint) {
    bondEmbeddedBlueprint model_XML =
                  (bondEmbeddedBlueprint)mXML;
    temp.fromXML(model_XML.getReader());}
  else {
    String model_XML = (String)mXML;
    if (model_XML.startsWith("http://") ||
      model_XML.startsWith("HTTP://") ||
      model_XML.startsWith("file:/") ||
      model_XML.startsWith("FILE:/")) {
        temp.fromXML(model_XML);}
    else { temp.fromXML(new ByteArrayInputStream
                  (model_XML.getBytes()));}
  }
  return true;
}
```

In the default running mode the active strategies of the agent perform actions. These actions are performed in response to:

- action scheduler polling,

- user interactions handled by GUI strategies, and

- external messages handled by probe strategies.

The vector of currently active strategies can be changed as a result of transitions. Transitions are triggered as a result of messages. These messages can be sent either from the current strategies of the agent (*internal transitions*) or from external objects (*external transitions*). The internal transitions form a special group in the blueprint specification, and they represent events that are intrinsically linked to the currently active strategy like success or failure. The agent framework does not allow external objects to trigger internal transitions. External transitions correspond to commands, and they can be triggered both externally or internally.

The execution of Bond agents can be stopped with the stop-agent message. This message instructs the action scheduler to stop the execution of the agents on the next *action boundary*. Thus, a soft stop is not instantaneous, and the time until it occurs depends on the action scheduler (single threaded or multithreaded) and on the granularity of the actions. At a soft stop of an agent the message handling is blocked, so the strategies triggered by messages or user input are blocked too.

8.2.2.8 *Agent Checkpoint and Restart.* In a soft-stopped state, the current status of the agent can be checkpointed. This is done by sending the checkpoint

message to the agent factory. The agent factory will serialize the model of the agent to a file indicated in the :file parameter of the message. The editor window of the agent allows interactive checkpointing.

The reverse operation of checkpointing is the checkback operation, triggered by a checkback message sent to the agent factory. The agent factory performs soft stops on the agent if it is running, restores the model, and reinstalls the state vector to the strategies that were active at the moment when the agent was checkpointed.

The bondAgentFactory has two methods to support checkpointing and restarting an agent. The first method extracts the unique agentid and the name of the checkpoint file. Then it locates the agent and calls the writeObject method. As a result, a copy of the agent model is written into the checkpoint file.

```
void checkpoint(bondMessage m, bondObject sender) {
    String agentid = (String)m.getParameter(":agentid");
    bondAgent ag = (bondAgent)dir.findLocal(agentid);
    if (ag == null) { return;}
    try {
      String checkpointfile = (String)m.getParameter
                                        (":checkpointfile");
      FileOutputStream fs = new FileOutputStream
                                        (checkpointfile);
      ObjectOutputStream outs = new ObjectOutputStream(fs);
      outs.writeObject(ag.model);
      outs.close();
    } catch(IOException ioex) {}
}
void checkback(bondMessage m, bondObject sender) {
    String agentid = (String)m.getParameter(":agentid");
    bondAgent ag = (bondAgent)dir.findLocal(agentid);
    if (ag == null) { return;}
    try {
      String checkpointfile = (String)m.getParameter
                                        (":checkpointfile");
      FileInputStream fs = new FileInputStream
                                        (checkpointfile);
      ObjectInputStream outs = new ObjectInputStream(fs);
      if (ag.running) {
          ag.softStop();
          ag.model = (bondModel)outs.readObject();
          setStatus(ag);
          ag.start();}
      outs.close();}
    catch(IOException ioex) { }
    catch(ClassNotFoundException cnfex) { }
}
```

8.2.2.9 Agent Migration. The system implements *weak migration* of agents; they are allowed to migrate only when all strategies active at the time of the request have completed their execution. At that moment no threads are running, all strategies have completed their execution, and the state of the agent is minimal.

This approach reflects the view that migration is a relatively rare event in the life of agents. It also reflects the difficulties of migrating running Java programs. Java does not support thread migration; thus, to migrate a running Java program all running threads must be stopped, their status saved, and then recreated at the destination site.

To migrate an agent we have to send to the new site its blueprint and model. The blueprint and the model are passive objects, one is an ASCII file and the other a data structure and their serialization is fully supported by Java.

The migration process involves the agent factory controlling the agent, AgF, and the agent factory at the new resident, AgF_{new}; agent migration consists of the following sequence of the events:

(i) The migration process is initiated by a `migrate-agent` message sent to AgF. The message contains the address of AgF_{new} and the `bondID` of the agent.

(ii) AgF soft stops the agent.

(iii) AgF generates the blueprint of the agent using the internal data structure reflecting the current agent state. This structure may be different than the original agent structure. The mapping is done by the `bondAgentToBlueprint` class.

(iv) AgF sends to AgF_{new} the blueprint generated in step (iii), embedded into a `migrate-agent` message.

(v) AgF_{new} reassembles the agent from the blueprint. The new agent is a copy of the old one, but it does not have the model yet.

(vi) AgF_{new} creates a shadow of the model of the original agent, and realizes it. The model is thus transferred to the new host.

(vii) AgF_{new} calls the `relocate()` function on the model.

(viii) AgF_{new} sends to AgF a `migrated` message to report the successful creation of the agent.

(ix) AgF unregisters the old agent and makes it eligible for garbage collection. It also installs a *forwarder* object if the `:forwarder yes` parameter was specified. This object forwards any messages sent to the agent at the old site to its new location.

(x) AgF sends a `start-agent` message to the agent at its the new location.

(xi) AgF sends a `success` message to the originator.

(xii) The beneficiary sends agent control messages to AgF_{new}.

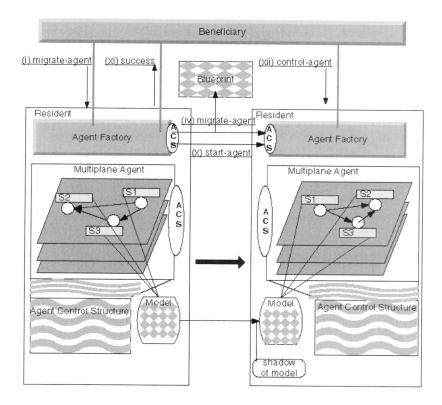

Fig. 8.22 Messages exchanged during agent migration.

A successful migration requires that the information in the model be moved to another site. Information such as descriptors of open files are meaningful only locally. A set of rules must be observed to make the model mobile – for example, keeping all immovable information inside atomic actions. This implies that we should open and close a file inside a single action.

The bondMigrationStrategy allows an agent to trigger its own migration to a new location. The target of the migration process may be specified by a model variable and the decision to initiate the migration can be based on a predefined condition, or may be due to situations detected by other strategies of the agent, possibly from a different plane. An external agent may decide the target location and the time of migration. For example, a controller agent can relocate a set of agents to sites where they are needed. Agent migration can also be done using the user interface, locally from the agent editor, or remotely using the remote agent control panel.

The bondAgentFactory methods for agent migration are presented now.

```
void migrateAgent(bondMessage m, bondObject sender) {
   String agentid = (String)m.getParameter(":agentid");
```

```
     if (sender == null) sender = m.getSender();
     String visual = (String)m.getParameter(":visual");
     bondIPAddress address = ((bondShadow)sender).remote_address;
     bondAgent ba = interpretFromMessage(m, null);
     if (ba == null) {
       m.sendReply("(error :content BadBlueprint)", this);
       return; };
     String modelid = (String)m.getParameter(":modelid");
     bondShadow shModel = new bondShadow(modelid, address);
     ba.model = (bondModel)shModel.realize();
     if (visual==null || visual.equals("yes")) {
       ba.edit(); }
     setStatus(ba);
     ba.start();
     bondMessage rep = new bondMessage("(tell :content
                                 migrated)","AgentControl");
     rep.setParameter(":agentid", agentid);
     sender.say(rep,this);
}
void migrateFromHere(bondMessage m, bondObject sender) {
   // find the local agents
   String agentid = (String)m.getParameter(":agentid");
   bondAgent ag = (bondAgent)dir.findLocal(agentid);
   if (ag == null) {return;}
   String remoteAddress = (String)m.getParameter
                                 (":remote-address");
   ag.softStop();
   bondShadow shFactorynew = new bondShadow("Resident",
                                 remoteAddress);
   bondMessage mes = new bondMessage(
           "(tell :content migrate-agent)","AgentControl");
   bondEmbeddedBlueprint ebp = new bondEmbeddedBlueprint();
   bondAgentToBlueprint a2b = new bondAgentToBlueprint(ag);
   a2b.generate();
   ebp.value = a2b.toString();
   mes.setParameter(":blueprint-program", ebp);
   mes.setParameter(":modelid",ag.model.bondID);
   mes.setParameter(":agentid",ag.bondID);
   shFactorynew.say(mes,this);
}
void migrated(bondMessage m, bondObject sender) {
   String agentid = (String)m.getParameter(":agentid");
   bondAgent ag = (bondAgent)dir.findLocal(agentid);
   if (ag == null) { return;}
   bondEditor ed = (bondEditor)ag.get("Editor");
```

```
   if (ed != null) {ed.close();}
   dir.unregister(ag);
}
```

8.2.2.10 *Agent Surgery.* The dynamic modification of the structural components of an agent is called *agent surgery*. The changes are described by a *surgical
blueprint script*. Surgical scripts act on existing agents, and may contain `delete` and
`replace` operators. The format of surgical blueprint scripts are described in detail
by the Backus Naur form (BNF) syntax specification.

The agent surgery is triggered by the `modify-agent` message sent by an object
to the agent factory controlling the agent. The sequence of actions in this process is:

(i)   A *transition freeze* is installed. The agent continues to execute normally, but
      if a transition occurs the corresponding plane is frozen. The transition will be
      enqueued, and executed when the transition freeze is lifted.

(ii) The agent factory interprets the blueprintblueprint and modifies the multiplane
      state machine accordingly. Two special cases are considered:

      (a) If an entire plane is deleted, the plane is brought first to a *soft stop*, i.e.
           the last action completes.

      (b) If the current node in a plane is deleted, a *failure* message is sent to the
           current plane. If there is no failure transition from the current state, the
           new state will be a null state. This means that the plane is disabled and
           will no longer participate in the generation of actions.

(iii) The transition freeze is lifted, the pending transitions performed, and the mod-
      ified agent continues its existence.

An agent may initiate the surgical operation itself using the `bondAgentSurgery`
strategy. This strategy takes the address of the surgical blueprint script from the
model. The surgery may be initiated by a remote agent or may be triggered by a user
from an agent control panel.

The surgery is useful to build up a sophisticated agent capable of performing
complex actions from a simple generic agent. For example, in a network discovery
application, a simple discovery agent is sent to a remote site by a controller agent. As
the discovery agent learns more about the remote environment, it is upgraded using
a sequence of surgical blueprints sent by the controller agent.

The `modifyAgent` method of the `bondAgent` is listed below.

```
void modifyAgent(bondMessage m, bondObject sender) {
   bondAgent ba = null;
   String agentid = (String)m.getParameter(":agentid");
   ba = (bondAgent)dir.findLocal(agentid);
   if (ba.running) {
     ba.softStop();
```

```
      ba = interpretFromMessage(m, ba);
      ba.start();}
   else { ba = interpretFromMessage(m, ba);}
   if (ba == null) {m.sendReply("(tell
         :content error agent not modified)",this);}
   else {
      m.sendReply("(tell :content agent-modified)",this);}
}
```

8.2.2.11   *Action Scheduler.* The action scheduler transfers control to an action at the time of a transition or at the completion of the current action. The *actions* are the primitives used by a strategy to accomplish its functions. An action notifies the scheduler on completion.

At this time we have two scheduler and both guarantee that actions from the same strategy do not overlap:

1. The bondRRScheduler supports a single-threaded, round-robin scheduling of actions across state machines.

2. The multithreaded action scheduler bondMTScheduler allows multiple actions from different planes to be executed concurrently.

The bondRRScheduler identifies the state of a state machine in one plane and schedules for execution the action associated with the strategy of the current state. When the action finishes, it notifies the scheduler, the state of the plane is updated, and the scheduler moves to the next plane. The process continues, one action at a time.

The scheduler may activate a strategy in response to an event as soon as the current action finishes. For example, a strategy may inform the scheduler that it may not take any action for a specific time and provides the *expected next action* time. This allows the action scheduler to skip the activation of the strategy during the normal Round Robin activation but it will activate the strategy once the timeout expires. This scheduling strategy assumes that a strategy is decomposed into a set of short actions.

The bondMTScheduler iterates over the set of planes, in each plane it identifies the current state, starts up a new thread, and then waits to be interrupted by a notification from any of the threads currently running actions. When a thread is started, it identifies the state and the strategy and runs the code of the action. When the action terminates, it notifies the scheduler.

```
/* Run a strategy in the context of this thread */
public void run() {
   setRunning(true);
   boolean firstTime = true;
   while ((ba.agenda == null) ||
```

```
                !ba.agenda.satisfiedBy(ba.model)) {
            bondStrategy strat =
                    ap.fsm.getState().getStrategy();
            if (softstop) { sched.decr(); return;}
            if (strat != null) {
                strat.action(ba.model, ba.agenda);}
            if (!firstTime) {
                try { sleep(500);}
                catch (InterruptedException e) {}
            }
            firstTime = false;
        }
        setRunning(false);
    }
    /** Start thread */
    public void start() {
        softstop = false;
        AgentThread = new Thread(this);
        AgentThread.start();
    }
    /** Main agent loop */
    public synchronized void run () {
        if (ToKill) { ba.kill();   return;}
        for (Iterator i = ba.planes.iterator(); i.hasNext(); ) {
            bondAgentPlane ap = (bondAgentPlane)i.next();
            bondFiniteStateMachine fsm = ap.fsm;
            fsm.setState(fsm.getState());
            PlaneThread thr = new PlaneThread(this, ap);
            synchronized (threads) { threads.put(fsm, thr);}
            thr.start();
        }
        count = threads.size();
        while (count > 0) {
            try { wait(); }
            catch (InterruptedException e) { }
        }
        for (Enumeration e=ba.planes.elements();
                                        e.hasMoreElements(); ) {
            bondAgentPlane ap = ((bondAgentPlane)e.nextElement());
            bondStrategy strat = ap.fsm.getState().getStrategy();
            if (strat != null) { strat.uninstall();}
        }
    }
}
}
```

8.2.2.12 Semantic Engine. A semantic engine controls the transition from one state to another in a state machine or a collection of state machines. Multiple execution semantics are possible and a system may have several semantic engine objects.

In our system semantic engines can be changed without the need to recompile the agents. At the time of this writing, we have only a default semantic engine but more sophisticated semantic engines could support:

Conditional transitions. The conditions should be specified as metadata attached to the multiplane state machine structure.

Buffering of events. A semantic engine could buffer events, and apply them at a later time.

Actions associated with transitions. The default semantic can be extended allowing actions executed whenever the transition is triggered.

Synchronization rules among planes.

The statecharts model as described in Harel et al. [24] uses conditional transitions and actions associated with transitions.

The default semantic engine in Bond has the following attributes:

(i) it supports only unconditional transitions;

(ii) the actions are associated with the strategies of the state machines; once a state machine enters a certain state, the strategy associated with that state is activated;

(iii) executes the transitions immediately on receiving the corresponding events. The default semantic engine discards the events if they do not correspond to a valid transition at the instant they arrive.

The operation of the default semantics engine is summarized by the following pseudocode:

```
forall (incoming message m)
  if message is transitionAll t
    forall (planes p)
      if transition t exist from current state on plane p
        call uninstall on current strategy
        change state to the endpoint of transition t
        call install on current strategy
      else
        ignore
      endif
    discard message
  else if message is transition t on plane p1
```

```
    if plane p1 exists
       if transition t exist from current state on plane p1
          call uninstall on current strategy
          change state to the endpoint of transition t
          call install on current strategy
       endif
    endif
    discard message
  endif
endfor
```

8.2.3   Agent Description

A Bond agent can be assembled out of components. In this section we present the *Blueprint* agent description language, discuss the initialization of model variables, and give an example of a simple agent.

8.2.3.1   *The Blueprint.*   We use an agent description language called *Blueprint* to specify the structural components and to initialize the model of an agent. The BNF syntax of Blueprint is presented elsewhere [8]. A blueprint is designed by a programmer and can also be generated by the AgentFactory object, see Section 8.2.2.4. A blueprint agent description is a text file, it can be easily transported over the network, embedded in a message, or downloaded from Web servers.

The agent description starts with import statements. The create agent and end create declarations mark the beginning and the end of the agent description. An agent description consists of several planes. Whenever a statement such as plane foo is encountered, the agent factory searches the component databases for a plane named foo and creates a new plane if the search fails. If the search is successful the plane is opened and subsequent declarations may add new components to the existing structure.

Plane descriptions consist of description of states, as well as internal and external transitions. The statement:

add state StateName with strategy StrategyName;

declares a state called StateName with a strategy named StrategyName.

State declarations may contain variable initializations. For example, to initialize variable commandline with value netscape we use the following statement:

```
add state StateName with strategy StrategyName::NS
  model {
  commandline = ''netscape'';
  };
```

In this example the strategy has a namespace (NS), see Section 8.2.2.3 for a discussion of namespaces.

Internal and external transitions are declared separately. We can declare transitions one at a time, indicating the source and the destination state as well as the label of the event triggering the transition, `from Source to Destination on Event;`.

The *chain declaration* of transitions is used to specify a sequence of transitions on the same event. For example, instead of:

```
{
  from S1 to S2 on success;
  from S2 to S3 on success;
  from S3 to Sfinal on success;}
}
```

we can write

```
from S1 to S2 to S3 to Sfinal on success;
```

When transitions converge from multiple states to the same state, on the same event, instead of:

```
{
from S1 to ErrorHandler on failure;
from S2 to ErrorHandler on failure;
from S3 to ErrorHandler on failure;
}
```

we can write

```
on failure from S1,S2,S3 to ErrorHandler;
```

8.2.3.2 *Initializing Model Variables.*

The blueprint can be used to initialize model variables. The model variable initialization is usually done after the agent description. This code is executed only once, when the agent is created. Blueprint recognizes three primitive variable types: strings, integers, and doubles. The initialization has a syntax similar to Java. For example, we can write:

```
model {
  stringValue = ''Hello world!'';
  intValue = 1;
  doubleValue = 5.6;
}
```

We can also initialize the standard Java `Vector` and `Hashtable` types. The restriction is that the elements in both cases must be types accepted by blueprint (i.e., strings, integers, floats, vectors or hash-tables). The keys of the hash-table must be strings.

The syntax is:

```
model {
 vectorValue = [1, 2.5, ''String''];
 hashtableValue = {First =''One'',Second=2,Third=3.0};
}
```

Complex structures can be created using multiply embedded vectors and hash-tables:

```
model {
   complexStructure = { Name = ''Bond'',
          Type = ''AgentSystem'',
          Version = 2,
          Developers = [''boloni'', ''junkk'']
       }
}
```

We cannot initialize user-defined variables because their type may not be known to the agent factory.

8.2.3.3 *Example.* Now we present a simple agent which displays the "Hello World" message, waits for user confirmation, then exits. The blueprint of this agent can be found in the `blueprint` directory in the Bond distribution:

```
import bond.agent.strategydb;
create agent HelloWorld
plane Main
  add state Message with strategy Dialog.OkDialog
    model {
      Message="Hello, world!";
    };
  add state Exit with strategy Agent.Kill;

  internal transitions {
    from Message to Exit on success;
  }
end plane;
end create.
```

The first line `import bond.agent.strategydb;` specifies the path used by the agent to load its strategies. Then, we describe the structure of a new agent called `HelloWorld` with only one plane, `Main`. The state machine in that plane consists of:

(i) Two states, one called `Message` with a strategy called `Dialog.OkDialog`, the other `Exit` with strategy `Agent.Kill`. The dot notation indicates that we are looking for a strategy called `OkDialog` from a *strategy group* called `Dialog`.

This strategy displays a message box with a label and single button labeled Ok. The text of the label is read from the model, from a variable called Message. The strategy succeeds if the "Ok" button is pressed.

(ii) One internal transition between the two states.

The following commands start the agent editor and load the agent:
```
RunAgent blueprint/HelloWorld.bpt  – on Linux
java RunAgent blueprint/HelloWorld.bpt  – on Windows.
```
To start the agent directly:
```
RunAgent -novisual blueprint/HelloWorld.bpt.
```

In these examples we assume that we are in the Bond directory, otherwise we have to specify the full paths.

8.2.4   Agent Transformations

A significant part of the interagent communication can be described as *control*: the behavior of the *controlled* agent is changed as a result of an action of a *controller* agent. The behavior of the agent is described by the state vector, and it can be changed by transitions, which alter one or more states of the state vector.

One way to trigger transitions is by sending a message. Figure 8.23 illustrates the case when agent A desires to change the behavior of agent B by changing a strategy on the first plane of the agent. A sends to B a message labeled with a transition name. The transition is performed in a plane if a match between an existing transition and the one in the message can be found.

Agents often cooperate to achieve certain goals. Cooperation requires knowledge sharing. In our structure this means that a segment of the model of one agent is copied to the model of another one. Information sharing is a very complex topic, we have to determine what part of the model will be shared, the identities of the agents, the confidence level in the shared knowledge, and so on.

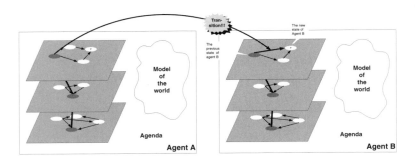

Fig. 8.23 Agent A desires to change the behavior of agent B by changing a strategy on the first plane. It sends a message labeled with a transition name. The transition is performed on all planes of agent B where a match between an existing transition and the one in the message can be found. In this example we see only a match in the first plane.

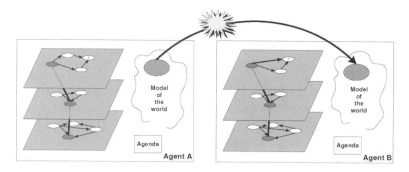

Fig. 8.24 Interagent cooperation using knowledge sharing. Agent A pushes part of its model into the model of agent B.

Our system contains support for information sharing at the communication layer level, and contains various mechanisms to enforce security for interagent cooperation [22, 23]. Figure 8.24 presents an example of cooperation through knowledge sharing using the push mode. Agent A pushes part of its model to the model of agent B.

Joining and *splitting* are two useful operations facilitated by the multiplane agent model. When joining two agents, the new agent contains the planes of the two agents and the model of the resulting agent is created by merging the models of the two agents. We may separate the two models through the use of namespaces.

When splitting an agent, we obtain two agents and the union of their planes gives us the set of planes of the original agent. The two agents need not be disjoint, some planes may be replicated. Both agents inherit the full model of the original agent.

There are five cases when joining or splitting agents is useful:

1. Joining control agents from several sources to provide a unified control,

2. Joining agents to reduce the memory footprint by eliminating replicated planes,

3. Joining agents to speed up communication,

4. Migrating only part of an agent,

5. Splitting to apply different priorities to parts of the agent.

Another useful operation is *trimming*. The state machines describing the planes of an agent may contain states and transitions unreachable from the current state. These states may represent execution branches not chosen for the current run, or states already traversed and not to be entered again. The semantics of the agent does not allow some states to be entered again, e.g., the initialization code of an agent is entered only once.

Trimming is recommended before agent migration or checkpointing to limit the amount of data transferred in case of migration or stored in case of checkpointing. Run-time trimming reduces the memory footprint of an agent. Trimming is built into current agent migration code.

Determining the components to be trimmed is a problem in itself and requires reachability analysis. The Sethi-Ullman algorithm for reusing temporary variables from the theory of compiler construction [42] may be used to identify components that are no longer reachable.

8.2.5 Agent Extensions

Technologies for wide-area applications are continually evolving and an important design objective for any type of middleware is to be *open-ended*. Thus, a major concern in the design of the system described in this chapter is to integrate with ease new functions and to interoperate with systems developed independently.

In this section we discuss three important extensions of the system. The objectives of these extensions are to:

1. improve the mobility of agents and their ability to communicate with one another and coordinate their actions;

2. support fault detection and fault information dissemination in a federation of agents;

3. support inference by integrating an expert system shell.

So far, we discussed only one aspect of agent mobility: the blueprint and the model are text files that can be transported with ease to a new location. Knowing the structure and the state of the agent, the agent factory at the new site may reassemble and restart the agent.

Yet, to be functional, the agent at the new site needs access to the strategies associated with the states of each plane of the agent. An agent may also need access to a blueprint to perform surgery to adapt to changes in the new environment. Thus we need a societal service, a persistent storage server with a built-in access control mechanism where strategies and blueprints can be available for agents in need of sharing them.

Another problem is communication between strategies in the same plane or in different planes of an agent, and, by extension, communication between strategies of two different agents. Until recently the only mechanism available for strategies to communicate with one another was through the model of the agent. Yet, no methods supporting access control and concurrency control have been discussed yet; we had the choice of implementing a tuple space, a mailbox where items can be deposited and then retrieved, or to integrate someone else's implementation.

The solution to both problems came in the form of a software developed at IBM Research called T Spaces [46]. The integration of tuplespace with the agent system is discussed in Section 8.2.5.1 and an application for synchronization of a group of Web monitoring and benchmarking agents is presented in Section 8.3.2.

Oftentimes, agents have to work together to achieve a common goal. For example, a federation of agents with different functions may be involved in monitoring and control of a Web server. The failure of any agent in the federation may either affect the functionality or the quality of the system. In Section 8.2.5.4 we discuss an extension to the system that allows agents in a federation to monitor each other and once a fault is detected to take corrective actions.

An orthogonal problem to mobility and fault tolerance is the intelligent agent behavior. As mentioned in Chapter 7, intelligence is necessary to guarantee autonomous behavior and has several dimensions: inference, learning, and planning. Inference provides agents with the ability to derive new facts from a set of existing facts and a set of inference rules.

For example an agent may be dispatched to a new site and be required to install new software on that site. We do have the choice of a complex agent capable of working with any operating system, any hardware and software configuration, or we may send a simple agent capable to discover basic facts about the site and then report them to a more sophisticated beneficiary that can use the facts to build a surgery blueprint to transform the original agent into a functional one. Again, we had the choice to implement our own inference engine or to integrate an existing one. In Section 8.2.5.5 we discuss the integration of the Jess expert system shell [19] into our agent system and present an application to an adaptive MPEG server.

8.2.5.1 *Tuplespaces.*   The *Tuplespace* concept was originally proposed by Carriero and Gelernter as part of the Linda coordination language [12, 13]. A Tuplespace is a globally shared, associatively addressed memory space that is organized as a bag of tuples.

In Chapter 6 we discussed the advantages of shared data spaces for process coordination in an open system and the use of tuplespaces. Now we review some of the concepts introduced earlier in the context of the agent system scrutinized in this chapter.

Recall from Chapter 6 that tuplespaces extend message-passing systems with a simple persistent data repository that features associative addressing. They provide a powerful mechanism for interprocess communication and synchronization: a producer process generates a tuple and places it into the tuplespace; a consumer process requests the tuple from the space.

A *tuple* is a vector of typed values, or fields. *Templates/antituples* are used to associatively address tuples via matching. A template is similar to a tuple, but some fields in the vector may be replaced by typed place holders called *formal fields*.

A formal field in a template is said to match a tuple field if they have the same type. If the template field is not formal, both fields must also have the same value. A template matches a tuple if they have an equal number of fields and each template field matches the corresponding tuple field.

Tuplespaces have several distinctive features:

(i) Communication is fully anonymous, the creator of a tuple does not need to have any knowledge about the future use of that tuple.

(ii) Time-disjoint processes are able to communicate seamlessly.

(iii) An associative addressing scheme allows processes to communicate regardless of machine or platform boundaries.

The combination of Java and tuplespace is pursued by projects such as Jada [16], JavaSpaces [50], and T Spaces [27, 46] . Jada is a Linda implementation used to provide basic coordination for PageSpace [15], a high-level coordination system.

JavaSpaces, currently under development at Sun Microsystems, is designed to provide "distributed persistence" and aid in the implementation of distributed algorithms. The system allows arbitrary Java classes to be communicated as tuples and made persistent through tuplespace. Transactions are provided for tuplespace integrity, and a facility for notifying a process when a tuple is written to a tuplespace is provided instead of the standard blocking read and take operations. JavaSpaces provides a simple transactional data repository and communication mechanism.

Tuplespace security is a major concern, as pointed out in Chapter 6.

8.2.5.2 T Spaces. T Spaces is a software system developed at IBM Research and available as freeware. The system is written in Java; it provides group communication services, database services, URL-based file transfer services, and event notification services.

The basic T Spaces tuple operations are: write, take, and read.

The write method stores its tuple argument in a tuplespace. The take and read methods are nonblocking operations, each uses a tuple template argument that is matched against the tuples in a tuplespace.

The take method removes and returns the first matching tuple in the tuplespace, whereas the read returns a copy of the matched tuple, leaving the tuplespace unchanged. If no match is found, take and read each return the Java type null and leave the space unchanged.

Blocking versions of these methods are supported. If no match is found, the following two methods block until a matching tuple is written by another process:

1. waittotake
2. waittoread.

T Spaces also extends the standard tuplespace API with the operations scan, consumingscan, and count. The scan and consumingscan methods are multiset versions of read and take, respectively, and return a "tuple of tuples" that matches the template argument. The count method returns an integer count of the matching tuples. Figure 8.25 shows a T Space server and the methods it supports.

In T Spaces a tuple matches the template when all of the following conditions hold:

(i) The tuple and template have the same number of fields.

(ii) Each of the fields of the tuple is an instance of the type of the corresponding field of the template.

(iii) For each nonformal field of the template, the value of the field matches the value of the corresponding tuple field.

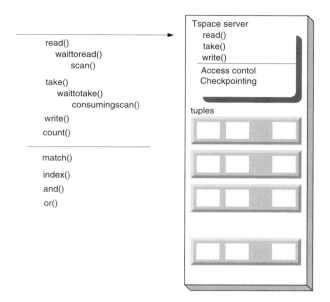

Fig. 8.25 A T Spaces server and the methods it supports.

T Spaces also provide several types of queries: Match, Index, And, and Or queries. A Match query performs structural or object compatibility matching, whereas an Index query performs a named-field query. And and Or queries can be used to combine these other queries and build complex query trees.

A T Spaces server is controlled by a configuration file, tspaces.cfg, that specifies a wide range of parameters for the server such as:

- the port number the server listens to,

- a checkpoint file and the time interval between checkpointing the T Spaces server,

- time intervals to check for deadlocked threads and for expired tuples,

- access control parameters; if access checking is enabled, add/delete users or groups, access control lists.

8.2.5.3 *Agent Communication Using T Spaces.* A *T Space* server can be used for interagent communication. The shared tuple space can also be used as a repository for agent descriptions, or *Blueprints*. Last but not least, a *T Space* could play the role of a strategy database; agents may load dynamically strategies from a *T Space* server.

The bondTupleSpaceEnabledStrategy allows agents to communicate with one another via a T Spaces server. Moreover, strategies of different state machines of an agent can communicate with one another using tuplespaces provided that they extend the bondTupleSpaceEnabledStrategy.

This strategy extends the bondDefaultStrategy. Its install() action reads from the model the location of the T Space server and a string giving the tuple space name and sets up the tuple space.

```
import com.ibm.tspaces.*;
import bond.agent.*;
import bond.agent.interfaces.*;
import java.io.*;
public class bondTupleSpaceEnabledStrategy extends
                                bondDefaultStrategy {
  protected TupleSpace space, save;
  boolean inited = false;

  public void install(bondFiniteStateMachine fsm) {
    super.install(fsm);
    if (!inited) {
      String host = (String)getModel("TupleServer");
      String sname = (String)getModel("SpaceName");
      if (host == null || sname == null) {
              inited = true; return;}
      inited = setTupleSpace(host, sname);
    }
  }
  public boolean setTupleSpace(String host, String sname) {
    try {
      space = new TupleSpace(sname, host);
      return true;
    }
    catch (TupleSpaceException e) {return false;}
    catch (Exception e) { return false;}
  }
}
```

The code for the actual blocking methods to take an item from the tuple space without leaving a copy, to read an item and leave the copy in the tuple space, and to write an item into the tuple spaces is shown below. These methods are wrappers for the methods supplied by the com.ibm.tspaces package: waitToTake, waitToRead, and write.

```
public Object getFromTupleSpace(String host,
        String sname, String s)throws Exception {
  if (!setTupleSpace(host, sname)) return null;
  return getFromTupleSpace(s);
}
```

```
public Object getFromTupleSpace(String s)
                                throws Exception {
  Tuple msg = space.waitToTake(s, new
                    Field(Serializable.class));
  return (Object)msg.getField(1).getValue();
}
public Object copyFromTupleSpace(String host,
      String sname, String s)throws Exception {
  if (!setTupleSpace(host, sname)) return null;
  return copyFromTupleSpace(s);
}
public Object copyFromTupleSpace(String s)
  throws Exception {
  Tuple msg = space.waitToRead(s, new
                    Field(Serializable.class));
  return (Object)msg.getField(1).getValue();
}
public boolean putIntoTupleSpace(String host, String
  sname, String s, Serializable o) throws Exception {
  if (!setTupleSpace(host, sname)) return false;
  return putIntoTupleSpace(s, o);
}
public boolean putIntoTupleSpace(String s,
              Serializable o)throws Exception{
    space.write(s, o);
    return true;
}
```

8.2.5.4   *Fault Detection and Fault Information Dissemination.* There are many instances when the failure of a single agent may have adverse consequences for the a system based on software agents. Very often agents have to coordinate their activities or monitor an environment and the failure of a single agent may compromise the mission of the entire federation.

Consider for example a group of agents monitoring the sensors of a critical installation such as a nuclear power plant. The failure of an agent may result in the inability of the system to detect an emergency, such as a high level of radiation escaping from the reactor core, or the fact that the temperature of the coolant is in a dangerous zone.

Recall that agents have built-in capabilities to monitor each other. Yet, this capability does not allow an agent to detect the failure of an agent simply because the subscription mode is based on an agent actively generating events. Failure detection is a deliberate activity that requires additional communication among the agents.

Adding fault detection and fault information dissemination mechanisms was facilitated by the structure of the agents presented earlier. To minimize the number of messages exchanged among agents and the overhead for monitoring we had to construct optimal monitoring topologies.

We say that a monitoring topology is optimal iff each agent is monitored by a minimal number of agents and, in turn, it monitors the smallest possible number of agents. A *ring* provides the best monitoring topology; agent i is monitored by one other agent, its predecessor in the ring, predecessor(i) and, in turn, monitors only one other agent, its successor in the ring, successor(i).

Once we detect the failure of an agent we have to disseminate this information to all agents in the federation using an optimal *dissemination topology* that minimizes the number of messages.

We now provide details of the algorithm and the data structures used for fault detection and fault information dissemination .

Status table is a data structure containing fault–status information maintained by each agent. Let N be the total number of agents in a federation; some of them are faulty, others are fault–free. Consider an agent A, with aid_A, monitoring an agent B, with aid_B, and being monitored by C, with aid_C. The status table maintained by agent A contains the following data:

A list of event-status counters for every other agent in the federation. $status[aid_i]$ is a nonnegative integer value for the most recent "fail" or "join" event regarding agent i with aid_i. If $status[aid_i]$ is odd, then agent i is faulty, if $status[aid_i]$ is even, agent i is fault-free.

The event-status counter provides information about the ordering of the events because it is incremented by one after each "fail" or "join" event regarding B, detected by A. When B joins the federation and requests to be monitored by A, the counter is set to $status[aid_B] = 0$. When A detects a "fail" event of B, it increments the counter; thus, $status[aid_B] = 1$. When it detects a "join" event then it increments again, $status[aid_B] = 2$, and so on.

Recall that A monitors only one agent B and learns about failures detected by other agents through dissemination. In addition to "fail" events generated during monitoring, an agent may generate a "fail" event during the dissemination process when the contact agent fails to acknowledge a dissemination message.

A counter is only modified by an agent that has detected the occurrence of an event.

Monitoring keeps the aid of the agent that it is monitoring.

Monitored_By keeps the aid of the agent that is monitoring this agent.

The messages exchanged during the fault-detection and dissemination are:

test-msg and fine are a monitoring message sent by agent A to agent B it monitors, and a reply of B to A. Agent A expects the reply within a certain time interval. If the reply fails to materialize within that interval, a time-out occurs and A detects a "fail" event.

info-msg and received are a propagation message and an acknowledgment to the propagation. A propagation message contains: (i) the aid of the agent that generated the event, (ii) the value of the event status counter, (iii) the list of agent aid's the information should be forwarded to, and (iv) the list of the rest agents. The propagation continues until the forwarding list becomes empty. Unless the acknowledgment is received by the agent sending the message within a well–defined interval, a time-out occurs and it is considered as the "fail" event.

request-monitoring , I-will-monitor-you and I-am-busy. A new agent B sends a request-monitoring message to an agent A of the federation it knows about. Agent A may respond I-am-busy or I-will-monitor-you.

request-join , I-will-monitor-you and I-am-busy are a monitoring request message from a new or repaired agent and two possible replies: accept or deny. The reply messages also contain the list of fault-free agents to give the joining agent a hint about the current members of the federation.

you-are-orphan is a message to force a reconfiguration of the ring-monitoring topology when a new agent joins the federation. If agent A currently monitoring agent B receives a monitoring request from a new agent C and realizes that the ring topology forces it to accept to monitor C instead of B, then it sends a you-are-orphan message to B.

Example. A has $aid_A = 10$, B has $aid_B = 20$. A new agent C with $aid_C = 15$ joins the federation and then the ring topology requires the new agent to be inserted between A and B and the monitoring relations be changed from $A \Rightarrow B$ to $A \Rightarrow C \Rightarrow B$.

The pseudocode of the algorithm consists of a set of processes: *message_handler*, *info_handler*, *info_disseminator*, *monitor_searcher*. These processes run in parallel on separate execution threads and sometimes create instances of another processes.

Message Handler receives all the algorithm messages. On receipt of a message, this process handles it or dispatches it to other processes.

```
process MESSAGE_HANDLER() {
1 while (TRUE) {
2  receive message from agent i;
3   switch (type of message)
4    case TEST-MSG:
5 send FINE to agent i
6    case INFO-MSG:
7 process__INFO_HANDLER(message, agent i)
8    case REQUEST-MONITORING:
9    if (procedure__Can_Monitor(agent i)) {
10     process__FAULT_MONITOR(agent i)
11     send I-WILL-MONITOR-YOU to agent i }
12    else
13     send I-AM-BUSY to agent i
14    case REQUEST-JOIN:
15    if (procedure__Can_Monitor(agent i)) {
16     process__FAULT_MONITOR(agent i)
17     send I-WILL-MONITOR-YOU to agent i
```

```
18    if (status[agent i] exists)
19        status[agent i]++; /* set as fault free */
20    else
21        add status[agent i] = 0; /* add initialized one */
22    process__INFO_DISSEMINATOR(agent i) }
23    else
24    send I-AM-BUSY to agent i
25  case YOU-ARE-ORPHAN:
26    set Monitored_By to null
27    process__MONITOR_LOCATOR() }}

procedure boolean Can_Monitor(agent requester) {
1  if (Monitoring== null)
2    return true;
3  cur_id = the id of the agent that it monitors
4  req_id = the id of agent requester
5  my_id = the id of this agent
6  if (my_id < cur_id)
7    if (my_id < req_id && req_id < curr_id)
8      return true /* accept request */
9  else if (my_id > cur_id) {
10   if ((my_id > req_id && req_id < cur_id) ||
                                    (req_id > my_id)) {
11     return true /* accept request */
12 return false /* deny request */
```

When the message handler receives a request to monitor or join, it decides whether to accept or deny the request after checking its current monitoring state; if it does not monitor any agent, it accepts the request after verifying that the ring topology is satisfied. Otherwise, it compares the aid of the requesting agent with its own and with that of the agent it currently monitors and then makes a decision subject to the condition that the ring topology is satisfied, see the procedure *Can_Monitor()*.

Fault Monitor monitors one agent by periodic polling. Once detecting a failure event, it starts a info_disseminator process to propagate the event to other fault–free agents.

```
process FAULT_MONITOR(agent i) {
1  if (Monitoring != null) /*monitoring other agent */
2    stop monitoring;
3  Monitoring = agent i;   /* set new monitoring target */
4  while (NOT STOPPED) {
5    send TEST-MSG to agent i
6    timed-wait FINE from agent i
7    if (time-out)
8      status[agent i]++; /* set as faulty */
```

```
9      process__INFO_DISSEMINATOR(agent i)
10      Monitoring = null;
11      exit /* stop monitoring */
12   wait for monitoring INTERVAL 13 }
14 if (STOPPED) {          /*forced to reconfigure */
15   send YOU-ARE-ORPHAN to agent agent i
16   timed-wait FINE from agent i
17   if (time-out)
18     process__INFO_DISSEMINATOR(agent i)
19     status[agent i]++; }}/*set as faulty */
```

The timeout period for a reply message (*fine*) takes into account both message processing and network latency times. Once an agent detects a "fail" event, it increments its local status counter of the faulty agent by one to indicate a faulty agent.

Info Disseminator initiates the event dissemination. It constructs a binary dissemination tree based on the snapshot of the current fault–free agents.

```
process INFO_DISSEMINATOR(agent i) {
1  for all status[agent k] { /* collects all fault-free agents */
2    if (status[agent k] ==even)
3      Array fault-free[] += agent k }
4  procedure__SPLIT_AND_SEND(agent i, fault-free)

procedure SPLIT_AND_SEND(agent event, list) {
1  N = size of list[]
2  Array list_1[] = list[0..N/2-1]   /* group 1*/
3  agent x = random one of list_1[] /* contact agent of group 1 */
4  Array list_2[] = list[N/2+1..N-1] /* group 2*/
5  agent y = random one of list_2[] /* contact agent of group 2 */
6  process__SPREAD_INFO(agent event, agent x, list_1)
7  process__SPREAD_INFO(agent event, agent y, list_2)}

process SPREAD_INFO(agent event, agent receiver, list) {
1 INFO-MSG = (event, list)
2  send INFO-MSG to agent receiver
3 timed-wait RECEIVED from agen receiver
4  if (time-out) {
5 status[agent receiver]++; /* set as faulty */
6 process__INFO_DISSEMINATOR(agent receiver)
7    if (list != null) {
8      agent another_receiver = list[0];
9      list = list[] - another_receiver;
10     process__SPREAD_INFO(agent event,
                 agent another_receiver, list)}}}
```

The procedure SPLIT_AND_SEND() splits the current list of fault-free agents into two groups and selects randomly two contact agents from each group. The timeout for the acknowledgment message (*received*) includes the time to tolerate the faults of the receiver agents during dissemination.

Info Handler handles the event messages propagated from other agents. After updating its local status table, it forwards the message to the next level of agents.

```
process INFO_HANDLER(message, agent sender) {
1   if (more recent status[agent k] than local) {
2     update local status[agent k]
3     if (I am orphan)
4       process__MONITOR_LOCATOR();
5   }
6   else if (older status[agent k]) {
7     send RECEIVED to agent sender;
8     return;}
9   list[] = message.getList();
10  if (list != null)
11    procedure__SPLIT_AND_SEND(agent k, list)};
12  if (the monitored agent is not in the dissemination list)
13    forward the message to the monitored agent
14  if (propagation ends)
15    send acknowledgment
```

After updating the local status table of an agent, the info handler checks whether the value of $status[Monitored\_By]$ is odd; if so, it attempts to find another monitor. The acknowledgment is sent after the propagation to next-level contact agents is completed, to avoid the case that leads to inconsistent status tables. In line 11 and 12, the agent checks whether the agent that it is monitoring receives the message. If not, it forwards the message to the monitored agent.

Monitor Locator attempts to locate a fault-free agent able to monitor this agent. This process is initiated either when this agent joins a federation for the first time, or when it finds itself to be an orphan.

```
process MONITOR_LOCATOR() {
1   while (Monitored-By == null) {
2   for all status[agent k] {
3       if status[agent k] == even
4         Array fault-free[] += agent k }
5     agent target = procedure__CALCULATE_MONITOR(fault-free[]);
6     if (a new joining or repaired agent) {
7       send REQUEST-JOIN to agent target
8       timed-wait reply from agent target
9       if (time-out)
10          continue /* try another agent */
11        else {
12          update local status table
```

```
13          if (reply == I-WILL-MONITOR-YOU) {
14             Monitored-By = agent target
15             exit }
16          else { /* I-AM-BUSY */
17             continue }}}
18     else { /* fault-free orphan agent */
19       send REQUEST-MONITORING to agent target
20       timed-wait reply from agent target
21       if (time-out) {
22             status[agent target]++; /* set as faulty */
23             process__INFO_DISSEMINATOR(agent target)
24          continue; }
25       else {
26          Monitored-By = agent target
27          exit }}}}
```

```
procedure int CALCULATE_MONITOR(array agents[]) {
1   N = size of agents[]
2   sort(agents[]) /* sort agents[] in ascending order */
    /* get index of current agent */
3   index i = binarySearch(my_agent_ID, agents[])
4   if (i == 0)
5       return the ID of agents[N-1]
        /* the largest ID agent should monitor */
6   else
7       return the ID of agents[i-1]}
```

The CALCULATE_MONITOR() procedure determines the aid of the agent to which a request message is sent. It consists of three steps: (1) sort the current list of fault–free agents in increasing order; (2) find the position of the intended recipient in the sorted list; and (3) select the aid of the agent preceding it.

8.2.5.5   *Integrating an Inference Engine.*

In this section we discuss the integration of an inference engine, Jess [19], in our agent system and in Section 8.3.1 we analyze in depth the application of inference for an adaptive video service.

The generic architecture of an expert system is presented in Figure 8.26. Its components are:

(i) Knowledge acquisition subsystem responsible for collecting new facts.

(ii) Knowledge base, the store for factual and heuristic knowledge.

(iii) Inference engine, provides the inference mechanisms to manipulate symbolic information and knowledge.

(iv) An explanation system.

(v) A user interface.

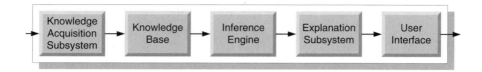

Fig. 8.26   The architecture of an expert system.

An expert system shell consists only of an inference engine and a user interface.

Jess is a rule-based expert system shell written in Java. It applies continuously a set of if-then statements, the *rules* to a set of data, the *facts* in the knowledge base). An example of a rule, from the Jess programming manual is:

```
(defrule library-rule-1
  (book (name ?X) (status late) (borrower ?Y))
  (borrower (name ?Y) (address ?Z))
=>
  (send-late-notice ?X ?Y ?Z))
```

This rule says that if a book at a library is overdue a notification should be sent to the borrower. The facts here are the name and status of the book and the name and address of the borrower.

A typical expert system has a fixed set of rules while the knowledge base changes continuously. The obvious implementation of an inference engine would be to keep a list of rules and continuously cycle through the list, checking each one's *left-hand-side (LHS)* against the knowledge base and executing the *right-hand-side (RHS)* of any rules that apply.

In the Rete algorithm [19], the past test results are remembered across iterations of the rule loop. Only new facts are tested against any rule LHS. The computational complexity per iteration is linear in the size of the fact base.

Inference in Bond.   All Bond strategies using inference extend the strategy called bondInferenceEngine. The code listed below shows the definition of the inference engine object and the execution of Jess commands.

```
import jess.*;
import bond.core.*;
import java.io.*;
public class bondInferenceEngine extends bondObject {
  public  Rete infegn;
  private StringBuffer kbase;
  public bondInferenceEngine() {
      infegn = new Rete();
      infegn.addUserpackage(new jess.ReflectFunctions());
      infegn.addUserpackage(new jess.StringFunctions());
```

```
    }
    public boolean executeCmd(String cmd) {
       try { infegn.executeCommand(cmd); return true;}
       catch (JessException e) {return false;}
    }
    public void run(int n) {
       try { infegn.run(n); }
       catch (JessException rexp) { }
    }
}
```

The Jess package provides a set of methods to add and retract facts to/from the knowledge base, assertString(fact) and retractString(fact), to clear and reset the inference engine, clear() and reset(), to load facts into the knowledge base, parse(), to load rules, append(), to show the facts ppFacts(). Below we see the wrappers for these methods.

```
    public boolean insert_fact(String fact) {
       try {infegn.assertString(fact);}
       catch (JessException rexp) { return false;}
       return true;
    }
    public boolean remove_fact(String fact) {
       try {infegn.retractString(fact);}
       catch (JessException rexp) { return false;}
       return true;
    }
    public boolean clear_infegn() {
       try { infegn.clear();return true;}
       catch (JessException rexp) { return false;}
    }
    public boolean reset_infegn() {
       try { infegn.reset(); return true;}
       catch (JessException rexp) { return false;}
    }
    public boolean load_kbase(StringBuffer kbase) {
       if (kbase == null)  return false;
       this.kbase = kbase;
       StringReader sr = new StringReader(kbase.toString());
       Jesp jesp = new Jesp(sr, infegn);
        try {jesp.parse(false);}
       catch (JessException rexp) { return false;}
       return true;
    }
    public void loadRulefromFile(String fname) {
       try {
```

```
            RandomAccessFile f = new RandomAccessFile(fname, "r");
            StringBuffer s = new StringBuffer("");
            String str;
            while ( (str = f.readLine()) != null)
                s = s.append(str+"\n");
            if (!load_kbase(s)) {}
        }
        catch (FileNotFoundException e) {}
        catch (IOException e) {}
    }
    public boolean insertObject(String tmpltname, Object o) {
        try {
            Funcall f = new Funcall("definstance", this.infegn);
            f.add(new Value(tmpltname, RU.ATOM));
            f.add(new Value(o));
            f.execute(this.infegn.getGlobalContext());
        }
        catch (Exception e) { return false;}
        return true;
    }
    public String show_facts() {return infegn.ppFacts();}
```

8.3 APPLICATIONS OF THE FRAMEWORK

Now we discuss in depth two applications of the system presented in this chapter and
survey two others. The first example illustrates the design and implementation of an
adaptive video service where a server agent uses an inference engine to select the data
streaming mode based on feedback from a client agent. Network congestion as well
as limitations of the CPU cycles available at client and/or server sites are detected and
stored as facts in a knowledge base. The server agent uses a set of rules to transmit a
compressed video stream in the normal mode, to reserve communication bandwidth
and/or CPU cycles at the client and server sites, or, if reservations fail, to drop frames
or to transmit decoded frames if there is enough communication bandwidth but the
client is unable to decode the frames at the desired rate.

The second application presents a Web-monitoring and benchmarking service. A
federation of monitoring agents install the benchmarking software on a set of client
systems and then generate the requested workload. The monitoring agents work in
lock step, the synchronization is provided by a tuplespace server.

8.3.1 Adaptive Video Service

We now discuss an application of inference to support server reconfiguration and
resource reservations for a video service [31, 53].

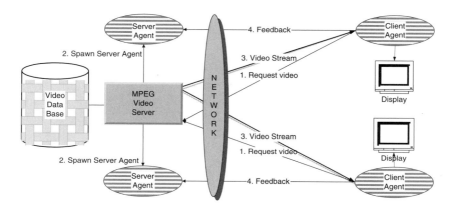

Fig. 8.27 The adaptive system consists of an MPEG server and server-client agent pairs supporting video streaming and display functions, respectively. A server agent adapts to changing traffic and load conditions using a set of rules. The sequence of events: (1) A client agent sends a request to the video server; (2) The video server spawns a server agent ; (3) The video server starts delivering the video stream; (4) The client agent provides feedback.

The architecture of the adaptive MPEG system is shown in Figure 8.27. In response to a request from a client, the MPEG video server spawns an MPEG server agent which delivers and controls the video streaming. The MPEG client agent displays the video stream, monitors its reception, and provides feedback regarding desired and attained quality of service at the client side. The server agent responds by reconfiguring video streaming and reserving communication bandwidth and/or CPU cycles according to a set of rules. An inference engine, a component of the server agent, controls the adaptation mechanism. A native bandwidth scheduler and a CPU scheduler in Solaris 2.5.1 support QoS reservation as described in [53].

Two communication channels exist between a client and its peer on the server side: a channel for data streaming and a control channel for streaming commands and feedback from client to server as shown in Figure 8.27. We use UDP for video streaming with one frame per UDP packet. The packets arriving out of order are rearranged.

The *profile* of a video file is the data rate corresponding to a frame rate. Table 8.9 shows the profile of one of the video files we used for testing.

8.3.1.1 Server Agent.

A partial description of the blueprint for the server agent follows. The agent has two planes, one for delivering the video stream and one to control the data-streaming mode, see Figure 8.28.

We only show the plane responsible for data streaming. As in other examples the error handling states are omitted. The two planes communicate with each other through the model.

The descriptions of the state machine for MPEG transmission (the data-streaming plane) of the server agent follows:

Table 8.9 Profile of a sample application.

Frame Rate (frames/sec).	Transmission Rate (bps))
5	4000
10	7000
15	10000
20	13000
25	16000
30	20000

```
import bond.application.MPEG;
create agent MPEGserver
plane MPEGtransmit
 add state Init with strategy
   bondMPEGServerStrategyGroup.InitDataChannel;
 add state NormalMode with strategy
   bondMPEGServerStrategyGroup.TransVideoStream;
 add state DecodeMode with strategy
   bondMPEGServerStrategyGroup.TransPixelData;
 add state Drop&DecodeMode with strategy
   bondMPEGServerStrategyGroup.TransPixelDataWithDropping;

external transitions {
   from NormalMode to DecodeMode on gotoTransPixelData;
   from NormalNode to DropMode on gotoTransDroppedPixelData;
   from DecodeMode to NormalMode on
              goFromTransPixelDataToTransVideoStream;
   from DropMode to NormalMode on
         goFromTransDroppedPixelDataToTransVideoStream;
}

 internal transitions {
   from Init to NormalMode on gotoTransVideoStream;
 }
 model {
   FILENAME = "bond/application/MPEG/Blazer.mpg";
   ALTFILENAME = "bond/application/MPEG/red.mpg";
 }
 end plane;
 plane MPEGcontrol
  .....
 end plane
 end create.
```

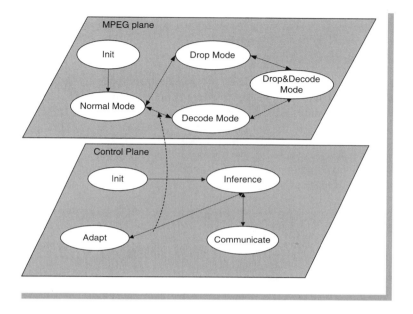

Fig. 8.28 The MPEG server agent has two planes.

The server agent shown in in Figure 8.28 supports four streaming modes:

Normal Mode. The MPEG server reads the video stream from the video Database or from a local file and transmits it to a client. The MPEG client decodes the video stream and displays the frames. Decoding the video stream is a CPU-intensive operation.

Drop Mode. The MPEG server partially decodes the video stream to identify the frame types and drops certain type of frames. The server selects the frames that affect the least the video quality, for example, the P-type. This data-streaming mode is suitable when the amount of bandwidth available is low.

Decode Mode. The MPEG server transmits decoded frames. Thus, this data-streaming mode is suitable for clients running on systems with CPU-intensive programs, but connected via high-bandwidth networks.

Drop and Decode Mode. This data-streaming mode is the combination of the previous two modes. It is suitable for overloaded clients connected with moderate bandwidth.

At the start of each transmission the server agent is in *normal mode* and as the network traffic and CPU load on the server and client change, the server agent reacts by selecting one of the other modes.

8.3.1.2 The Facts and the Rules. The following *facts* are stored in the knowledge base:

(i) `Transmission rate` in *bps* as measured by the server.

(ii) `Packet loss rate`. We detect lost packets by comparing the frame numbers on the client side. The packet loss rate is not the same as the frame loss rate, because P-frames and B-frames are dependent on I-frames. If an I-frame is lost, the depending frames are considered to be lost.

(iii) `Interframe time`. The interframe time shows the time elapsed at the client side between two displayed frames. I and P frames are larger than B frames; thus, the number of operations and the time to decode them is larger.

(iv) `Receiving rate`. The client determines this rate using the information about packet sizes. This rate is affected by network congestion.

The *rules* for the resource reservation and reconfiguration are:

(i) `Bandwidth Reservation Rule`. The objective of this rule is to reduce the packet loss rate by reserving bandwidth when the network is congested. The profile also has the maximum packet loss rate allowed to maintain a certain frame rate. We determine if the network is congested by comparing the `(packet-loss-rate)` with the `(maximum-loss-rate)` and, if so, we reserve the bandwidth necessary to achieve the `(desired-frame-rate)`. The rule is:

```
(packet-loss-rate ?lr)
(desired-frame-rate ?fr)
(maximum-loss-rate ?mr)
(test (> ?lr ?mr))
=>
(reserve-bandwidth ?fr)
```

After this rule fires, the strategy of the *adapt* state in the control plane looks up the profile of the video transmission to determine the necessary bandwidth and passes the information to the bandwidth reservation interface.

(ii) `CPU Reservation Rule`. This rule fires when a CPU-intensive program running either at the server or the client affects the server transmission rate, or the interframe time at the client. The transmission rate of the server is compared with the profile and the interframe time is compared to the desired interframe time. This rule is repeatedly fired, and raises the reservation level gradually, until the desired rate is achieved. The rules are:

```
(transmit-rate ?tr)
(required-transmmit-rate ?rtr)
```

```
(test (< ?tr ?rtr))
=>
(increase-cpu-reservation)

(inter-frame-time ?ft)
(required-inter-frame-time ?rifr)
(test (< ?rifr ?ft))
=>
(increase-cpu-reservation)
```

(iii) Drop Rule. This rule fires when either the bandwidth or CPU reservation fails. In this rule new facts are added to the knowledge base:

(bandwidth-reservation-failed),

(cpu-reservation-failed).

```
(bandwidth-reservation-failed)
=>
(trigger-drop-mode)

(cpu-reservation-failed)
=>
(trigger-drop-mode)
```

We now present the actual facts and rules used by the server agent. At first, we see the definition of different rates measured by the server or reported by its peer client. Then there are several rules to maintain the facts in the knowledge base. Each measurement carries a time stamp and the fact corresponding to an older measurement is retracted. We only show one of these maintenannce rules.

```
;; Target frame rate the server wants to reach
 (deftemplate current-server-frame-rate
   (slot timestamp)(slot rate))
;; Actual frame rate measured
 (deftemplate actual-server-frame-rate
   (slot timestamp)(slot rate))
;; Server transmission rate
 (deftemplate transmit-rate-bytes-per-sec
   (slot timestamp)(slot interval) (slot rate))
;; Current mode of operation
 (deftemplate tcurrentmode
   (slot stime) (slot mode))
;; Client receiving rate
 (deftemplate receiving-rate-bytes-per-sec
   (slot timestamp)(slot interval)(slot rate))
```

```
;; Frame loss rate reported by client
 (deftemplate frame-loss-rate-frames-per-sec
   (slot timestamp) (slot interval) (slot rate))
;; Display rate reported by client
 (deftemplate display-rate-frames-per-sec
   (slot timestamp)(slot interval)(slot rate))

(assert (minimum-frame-rate 20.0))

;; Server actual frame rate maintenance rule
 (defrule actual-rate-maintenance
   (declare (salience 100))
   ?ar1 <- (actual-server-frame-rate (timestamp ?ts1))
   ?ar2 <- (actual-server-frame-rate (timestamp ?ts2))
   (test (< ?ts1 ?ts2))
   =>
   (retract ?ar1))
;; Server transmission rate maintenance rule
 .........
;; Current mode maintenance rule
 .........
;; Receiving rate maintenance rule
 .........
;; Frame loss rate maintenance rule
 .........
;; Display rate maintenance rule
 .........
;; Server rate maintenance rule
 .........

;; Decrease server frame rate rule
(defrule decrease-server-frame-rate
   (tcurrentmode (mode normal))
   (current-server-frame-rate (rate ?r))
   (actual-server-frame-rate (rate ?r1))
   (display-rate-frames-per-sec (rate ?r2))
   (test (< (/ ?r2 ?r1)(/ 90 100)))
   =>
   (printout t "Decrease server frame rate to
       " (- ?r 1) ": current display rate--> " ?r 2 crlf)
   (if (< 2 ?r) then
    (call (fetch MODEL) setModelFloat "frameRate"(- ?r 1))
   else
    (call (fetch MODEL) setModelFloat "frameRate" 1.0)))
;; Increase server frame rate rule
```

```
(defrule increase-server-frame-rate
   (tcurrentmode (mode normal))
   (current-server-frame-rate (rate ?r))
   (actual-server-frame-rate (rate ?r1))
   (display-rate-frames-per-sec (rate ?r2))
   (minimum-frame-rate ?mr)
   (test (< ?r2 ?mr))
   (test (>= (/ ?r2 ?r1) (/ 90 100)))
   =>
   (printout t "Increase frame rate to " (+ ?r 2)  "
               : current display rate--> " ?r2 crlf)
   (call (fetch MODEL) setModelFloat "frameRate" (+ ?r 2)))
;; Measurement rule
 (defrule measurement(tcurrentmode (mode normal))
   (actual-server-frame-rate (timestamp ?ar))
   (display-rate-frames-per-sec (rate ?r) (timestamp ?t))
   (minimum-frame-rate ?mr)
   (test (<= ?r ?mr))
   (not (under-minimum-frame-rate))
   =>
   (assert (under-minimum-frame-rate)) ; flag
   (assert (under-minimum-frame-rate-since ?ar)))
;; Reset mode rule
 (defrule reset
   (tcurrentmode (mode normal))
   (display-rate-frames-per-sec (rate ?r) (timestamp ?t))
   (minimum-frame-rate ?mr)
   (test (> ?r ?mr))
   ?x<-(under-minimum-frame-rate)
   ?y<-(under-minimum-frame-rate-since ?k)
   =>
   (retract ?x)
   (retract ?y))
;; Test if under minimum frame rate rule
 (defrule under-minimum-rate
   (tcurrentmode (mode normal))
   (display-rate-frames-per-sec (rate ?r) (timestamp ?t))
   (minimum-frame-rate ?mr)
   (test (<= ?r ?mr))
   ?x<-(under-minimum-frame-rate)
   ?y<-(under-minimum-frame-rate-since ?ts)
   (test (> (- (* (time) 1000) ?ts) 30000)) ;
            under-minimum-rate continues over 30 sec.
   =>
   (printout t "**To Drop>>" crlf)
```

```
    (retract ?x)
    (retract ?y)
    (call (new bond.application.MPEG.MPEGAdaptation)
                adapt Normal Drop (fetch MODEL)))
;; Go back to normal rule
 (defrule go-back-to-normal
    (tcurrentmode (mode drop) (stime ?st))
    (actual-server-frame-rate (timestamp ?ts))
    (test (> (- ?ts ?st) 30000)) ; retry after 30 sec.
    =>
    (printout t "**To Normal>>" crlf)
    (call (new bond.application.MPEG.MPEGAdaptation)
                adapt Drop Normal (fetch MODEL)))


 (deffunction
  fetch-from-model (?a) ;;  (call (fetch MODEL) getModel ?a))
```

8.3.1.3 *Strategies.* The bondMPEGStrategyGroup object provides the strategies associated with the states of the server agent. Here we only show the strategies
for the *init* and *normal mode* states in the *MPEG plane*. The intialization strategy
identifies the thread handling a new connection to the video server and writes this
information in the model. Then it causes a transition to the *normal mode* state. The
strategy associated with the normal transmission mode in its install() function
first reads from the model the name of the video file to be transmitted and the name of
the coordinator, then initiates the transmission of the UDP stream, and finally writes
into the model the name of the current state.

```
public bondMPEGServerStrategyGroup(String name) {
super(name);
// 1. The strategy for the INIT state of the server
strat = new bondDefaultStrategy() {
  OutputStream os = null;
  boolean errorFlag = false;
  public void install(bondFiniteStateMachine fsm) {
    super.install(fsm); }
  public long action(bondModel m, bondAgenda a) {
    setModel("MPEGServerThreadGroup",
      new ThreadGroup("MPEGServerThreadGroup"));
    if (!errorFlag)
      transition("gotoTransVideoStream");
    else
      transition("gotoError"); return 1000L;}
};
addStrategy("InitDataChannel", strat);
```

```
// 2. The strategy for the Normal Mode
strat = new bondDefaultStrategy() {
  UDPTransmitter ut;
  public void install(bondFiniteStateMachine fsm) {
    super.install(fsm);
    ut = new UDPTransmitter(this, (String)getModel("FILENAME"));
    setModel("UDPTransmitter", ut);
    bondCoordinator bc = (bondCoordinator)getModel("COORDINATOR");
    bc.insert_fact("(tcurrentmode (mode normal)
          (stime "+System.currentTimeMillis()+" ))");
  }
  public long action(bondModel m, bondAgenda a) {
    return 10000L; }
  public void uninstall() {
    ut.stop();
    dir.unregister(ut);
    ut = null;
  }
  public String getDescription() {
            return "Transmit video stream";}
};
addStrategy("TransVideoStream", strat);
```

8.3.1.4 *Client Agent.*

The run method of the MpegDisplay object used to display data on the client side is listed below. It reads from the input the data stream and uses the display function of a Java MPEG player to display a frame with a given sequence number and a given type. Periodically, it sends to the server agent a report with a time stamp, the interval between two consecutive measurements, and the display rate.

```
public void run() {
  String mpegserver =(String)bds.getModel("mpegserver");
  int port = ((Integer)bds.getModel("portnumber")).intValue();
  try {
   Socket s = createSocket(mpegserver, port, port);
   ois = new ObjectInputStream(new BufferedInputStream
                                    (s.getInputStream()));
  }
  catch (StreamCorruptedException sce) { }
  catch (IOException ioe) { }
  mpd = new MPEG_Play_Decoding((JFrame)bds.
                                  getModel("DisplayFrame"));
  while (!finish) {
   try {
```

```
ap = (AnotherPacket)ois.readObject();
if (first) {
    Runnable r = new Runnable() {
      public void run() {
        mpd.set_dim(ap.width, ap.height, ap.ori_w, ap.ori_h);}
    };
    SwingUtilities.invokeAndWait(r);
    first = false;
    mpd.display(ap.picture, ap.num, ap.type);
    long t1 = System.currentTimeMillis();
     if ((t1-lastDisplayMeasureTime) >
                           DisplayRateMeasureInterval) {
      double rate = ((num_of_frames+1)*1000)
                             /(t1-lastDisplayMeasureTime);
      fm.sendFeedback("(display-rate-frames-per-sec "+
                  "(timestamp "+t1+" )"+"(interval+"
        DisplayRateMeasureInterval+")"+"(rate "+rate+"))");
      num_of_frames = 0;
      lastDisplayMeasureTime = t1;
      }
      else {num_of_frames++;}
      catch (EOFException eofe) {}
      catch (IOException ioe) { }
      catch (ClassNotFoundException cnfe) { }
      catch (Exception e) {}
  }
 }
}
```

The client agent measures the display rate, the frame loss rate, and the actual data rate and provides feedback to its peer server agent that changes its streaming mode accordingly. Our adaptation strategy is based on the observation that the bottleneck can be any of the three resources along the end-to-end streaming path, the server CPU, the network, and/or the client CPU.

The system identifies the bottleneck as follows:

- if the server transmission rate is below a minimum rate, then the CPU on the server side is a bottleneck;

- if the packet loss rate measured as the difference between the sender frame rate and the receiver frame rate, is high, then the network is the bottleneck;

- if the interframe display time at the client exceeds a threshold and the network is not congested, then the CPU on the client side is the bottleneck.

8.3.1.5 Experiments. In this section we present measurements for the MPEG application with and without resource reservation. In this experiment the server runs on an Ultra Sparc-1 machine with 128 MBytes memory, under Solaris 2.5.1. The client runs on a Pentium II 300 MHz, with 128 MBytes memory system under Solaris 2.5.1. To simulate increased traffic load a communication-intensive program generates a burst of UDP packets. To simulate the CPU load, a CPU-intensive program is used.

The first experiment shows the effect of bandwidth reservation, see Figure 8.29. On the server side, in addition to the MPEG application, we start a communication-intensive program. The traffic generated by this application affects the video traffic and we study the effect of this interference. Without reservation a large percentage of video packets are lost. Once sufficient bandwidth to support the desired frame rate is reserved, the number of lost packets is noticeably reduced, even under the heavy network traffic.

The second experiment shows the effect of CPU reservations, see Figure 8.30. We run three CPU-intensive processes to compete with the MPEG process. The experiment is performed first without CPU reservation, and then with reservation. The results show the effect of the CPU reservation on the interframe time. We start the CPU-intensive processes while the client displays frame 120 and then stop it around frame 230.

8.3.2 Web Server Monitoring and Benchmarking

In this section we present a monitoring and benchmarking system as an example of coordination of Web-based activities. The system is described in detail in [29]

This section is organized as follows: first, we formulate the problem, then we survey a tool capable of generating synthetic workloads, then we describe the architecture of our system and discuss its advantages.

8.3.2.1 Introduction. The widespread use of Web servers for business-oriented activities requires some form of QoS guarantees; short-term unavailability of services and large variations of the response time may have a severe negative economic impact. Yet, providing QoS guarantees is a complex problem with multiple facets. One of them is the ability to continually monitor a Web server and subject it periodically to realistic benchmarks.

Web monitoring and benchmarking require several entities distributed over a wide-area network to work together. Given that the number of clients of a Web server is very large, multiple client machines are often required to generate a realistic workload. Multiple monitoring points scattered throughout the network are necessary to simulate user actions.

Several commercial Web monitoring service companies exist today [25, 35]. Generally, they provide a static service, the locations of the clients and the workload they generate are fixed and rarely emulate the behavior of real-life clients. The next generation Web monitoring services are expected to address the problem of client mobility and of accuracy of benchmarking.

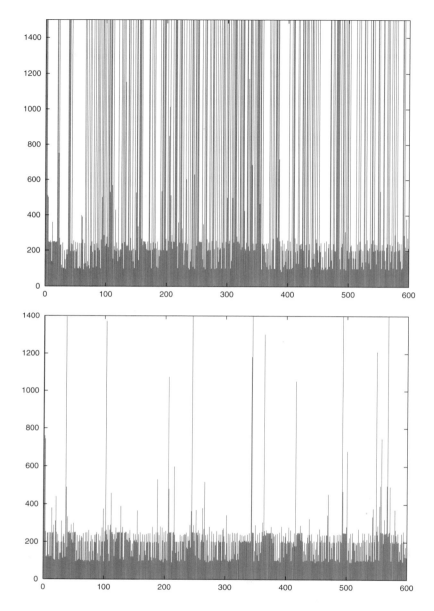

Fig. 8.29 The effect of the bandwidth reservation. The graph shows the interframe times measured at the client site, with the frame number on the horizontal axis and time in milliseconds on the vertical axis. The interframe time for lost frames is set to the maximum value, $60,000$ milliseconds; thus, lost frames appear as vertical lines in the graph. Without reservation a large percentage of video packets are lost, as shown in the upper graph. Once sufficient bandwidth to support the desired frame rate is reserved, the number of lost packets is noticeably reduced, even under the heavy network traffic, see lower graph.

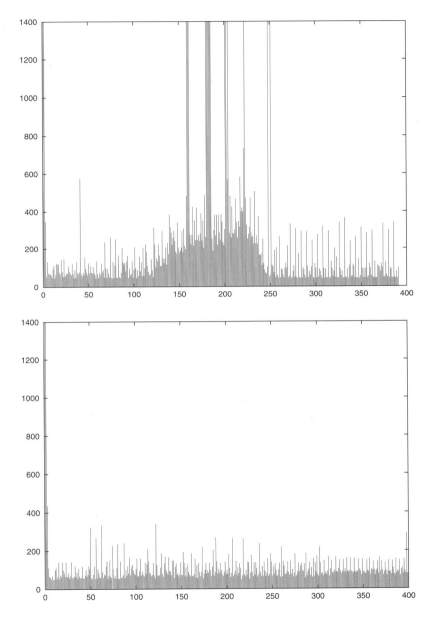

Fig. 8.30 The effect of CPU reservation. The graphs show the interframe time for individual frames at the client side when the MPEG display process competes with another CPU-intensive process. In the upper graph, the CPU-intensive process is started while the client is running and then stopped. In the lower graph, the CPU-intensive program does not affect the client's ability to process the MPEG frames due to CPU reservation. The frame numbers appear on the horizontal axis.

The functionality of existing benchmark suites and monitoring tools can be extended using mobile agent technology. Mobile agents have several advantages over the existing techniques:

(i) *Software installation:* Once a mobile agent is deployed at a site it can download the software tools for benchmarking and measurements, compile, and install them without human intervention.

(ii) *Complex tasks:* The mobile agents supervising data collection and analysis can perform their task autonomously and assist in performing complex measurements and data analysis tasks that require inference and/or planning.

(iii) *Coordination:* The agents can coordinate the measurements performed by multiple tools. They can provide coordination primitives for data collection and analysis, such as barrier–synchronization [29] and event notification.

(iv) *Efficient data analysis:* A large volume of data can be processed by dispatching mobile agents to the data site rather than moving the data. In addition, the mobile agents can migrate among network nodes to process the measurement data, which are distributed over a set of client machines.

8.3.2.2 *Surge – a Workload Generator for Web Servers.*   Several tools to generate synthetic workloads are available:

- HTTPerf [38] uses multiple processes to generate HTTP requests at a fixed rate, a situation rarely encountered in the real world.

- SpecWeb [43] is a Web benchmark software developed by industry and university researchers. It measures the maximum simultaneous number of connections that a Web server can sustain.

- WebStone [37] and WebBench [52] provide similar benchmark softwares and directions.

- TPC Benchmark W (TPC-W) [47] is a benchmark specification to test the transactional functionality of Web servers for electronic commerce.

Surge [1] is a software system that generates realistic Web workloads based on six empirical statistics: server file size distribution, request size distribution, relative file popularity, embedded file references, temporal locality of reference, and user think times.

The architecture of this tool separates the problem of creating the workload from the methodology for benchmarking. Surge consists of three components: *workload data generator*, *client request generator*, and *server file generator*.

The workload data generator creates workload datasets that specify the file size distribution; the request sequence; the number of embedded files in each requested file; and the sequence of user think times.

The client request generator is a multithreaded process, each thread simulating one user. The client request generator makes HTTP requests as specified in the dataset. Multiple client request generators on different machines can be used in one benchmark.

The server file generator creates a set of files matching the file size distribution of the dataset. The files are placed into a document subtree of a tested Web server. Both the server file generator and the client request generator rely on the generated datasets to perform their tasks.

8.3.2.3 *Web Benchmarking Agents.*

The Web benchmarking procedure consists of four steps: software installation, workload dataset generation, request generation, and analysis of measurements. At each step multiple *monitoring agents* perform the tasks required by that step. The control agent on the server site installs the software system to generate the files used in the benchmarking process and then activates the client. The monitoring and the control agent are supervised by a *coordinator agent*.

The flow of control in the benchmarking process is described in Figure 8.31. The benchmarking process is initiated when the beneficiary, in this case the individual conducting the benchmarking experiment, uses the visual interface to send an `assemble-agent` message to the agent factory running on the system hosting the coordinator.

This message contains the address of the blueprint repository and the path of the blueprint for the coordinator agent. This blueprint is presented later in this section.

The agent factory uses the blueprint to assemble the coordinator agent. When the agent assembly is completed, the agent factory sends an `agent-created` message to the beneficiary and provides the *bondID* of the agent. Next, the beneficiary sends a `start-agent` message for the agent identified by the *bondID* to the resident at `coordinatorIPaddress:2000`. This message includes the model of the agent.

The model is an XML description of the information needed by the coordinator to create and control monitoring agents for each Web client as well as the control agent for the Web server. The model description consists of six vectors, four for the monitoring agents on the client side and two for the control agent on the server side. Each client vector is named after the corresponding benchmarking step and consists of three hash-tables, one for each client. Each hash-table provides a pair name and value for three strings identifying the host, the path on that host to the blueprint for the monitoring agent, and the path to the model. There are two vectors for the control agent on the server side. The agent has to install the file generation software and then activate it.

```
<?xml version="1.0"?> <Model>
 <! Install SURGE on Web clients >
 <Vector name="SoftwareInst.Agents">
 <Hashtable>
 <String name="RemoteAddress">c1Host:2000</String>
 <String name="Blueprint">c1Bpt/SoftInst.bpt</String>
 <String name="Model">c1Mod/workloadclient.xml</String>
```

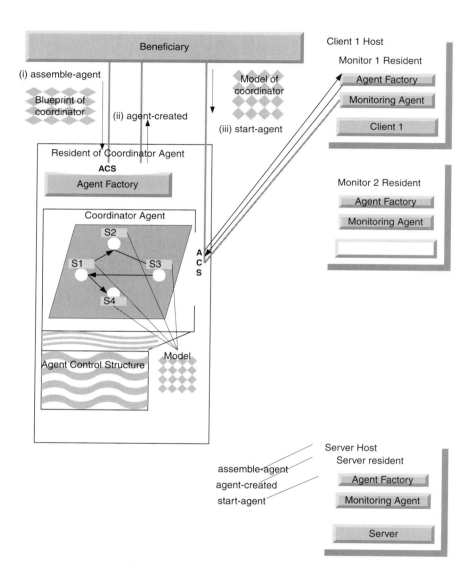

Fig. 8.31 Agent-based Web benchmarking system. The beneficiary triggers the assembly and the startup of the coordinator agent. The blueprint and the model of the coordinator agent are supplied by the beneficiary in the `assemble-agent` and `startup-agent` messages. Once started, the coordinator uses information in its model to start up the three monitoring agents on sites where the clients are located as well as the control agent on the Web server site.

```
    </Hashtable>
    ..........
    </Vector>


<! Generate workload data; client-side command execution>
 <Vector name="WorkloadGenCmdExec.Agents">
 <Hashtable>
 <String name="RemoteAddress">c1Host:2000</String>
 <String name="Blueprint">c1Bpt/WorkloadGenCmdExec.bpt</String>
 <String name="Model">c1Model/WorkloadGenCmdExec.xml</String>
 </Hashtable>
       ........
    </Vector>


<! SURGE workload generation>
 <Vector name="StartGeneration.Agents">
 <Hashtable>
 <String name="RemoteAddress">c1Host:2000</String>
     <String name="Blueprint">c1Bpt/WorkloadGen.bpt</String>
     <String name="Model">c1Mod/WorkloadGen.xml</String>
     ......
   </Hashtable>
   </Vector>


<! SURGE data analysis>
 <Vector name="Analysis.Agents">
 <Hashtable>
 <String name="RemoteAddress">c1Host:2000</String>
     <String name="Blueprint">c1Bpt/loganal.bpt</String>
     <String name="Model">c1Mod/loganal.xml</String>
     ......
   </Hashtable>
   </Vector>


 <! Install file generator software on Web server>
 <Vector name="WebFileSoftInst.Agents">
 <Hashtable>
 <String name="RemoteAddress">sHost:2000</String>
 <String name="Blueprint">sBlpt/SoftInst.bpt</String>
 <String name="Model">sModel/workloadfile.xml</String>
 </Hashtable>
 </Vector>
 <Integer name="WebFileSoftInst.Interval">1000</Integer>


<! Server-side Command execution>
```

```
<Vector name="WorkloadGenCmdExecServer.Agents">
<Hashtable>
<String name="RemoteAddress">sHost:2000</String>
<String name="Blueprint">sBpt/WorkloadGenCmdExec.bpt</String>
<String name="Model">sMod/WorkloadGenCmdExecServer.xml</String>
</Hashtable>
</Vector>
</Model>
```

The blueprint for the coordination agent consists of one plane only. In this plane there are four groups of states each corresponding to one benchmarking step at the client site and two groups corresponding to the software installation and activation at the server site. We only discuss the client section of the blueprint for the coordinator agent. Recall that a monitoring agent goes through four steps:

1. Install the Surge tools on the client machine.

2. Use the Surge tools to generate the workload description files to be used by the client processes.

3. Start up client processes that generate the HTTP requests.

4. Start up the data analysis tools.

For each of the four steps described the coordinator uses the information provided by its model to create and control each monitoring agent. The coordinator model gives: (a) the host; (b) the path to the blueprint, and (c) the path to the model for each agent. Figure 8.32 shows that the coordinator goes through the following four states in each step:

1. Locate the hosts where the agents are expected to run.

2. Request the respective agent factories to assemble each agent using the blueprint.

3. Start up each agent using the information in the model

4. Wait until all agents in the group have completed their execution.

The bondMultiAgentDeployStrategy uses different namespaces:
::SoftwareInst to install Surge and
::StartGeneration for measurements.

A partial blueprint for the coordinator agent consisting of only two steps, installation of the Surge and generation of HTTP requests follows.

```
import bond.agent.strategydb;
importbond.agent.strategydb.barrier;
create agent WebCoordinationAgent
plane Control
```

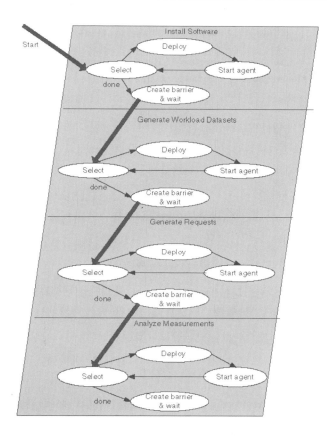

Fig. 8.32 A representation of the blueprint of the coordinator agent restricted to the client-side agents. It shows the states and transitions among them, where the states are grouped to form workflows corresponding to the four steps of the Web benchmark.

```
// instal Surge
add state SoftwareInst with strategy
     bondMultiAgentDeployStrategy::SoftwareInst;
add state Deploy with strategy
    bondAgentExecStrategyGroup.CreateAgent;
add state Start with strategy
        bondAgentExecStrategyGroup.StartAgent;
add state FirstBarrier with strategy
    bondBarrierWaitStrategy::FirstBarrier;
// measurements
add state StartGeneration with strategy
     bondMultiAgentDeployStrategy::StartGeneration;
add state DeployForGeneration with strategy
```

```
                bondAgentExecStrategyGroup.CreateAgent;
add state StartForGeneration with strategy
                bondAgentExecStrategyGroup.StartAgent;
add state GenerationBarrier with strategy
        bondBarrierWaitStrategy::GenerationBarrier;

internal transitions {
// Install SURGE
    from SoftwareInst to Deploy on success;
    from Deploy to Start on success;
    from Start to SoftwareInst on success;
    from SoftwareInst to FirstBarrier on next;
    from FirstBarrier to WebFileSoftInst on success;
// Generate HTTP requests
    from StartGeneration to DeployForGeneration on success;
    from DeployForGeneration to StartForGeneration on success;
    from StartForGeneration to StartGeneration on success;
    from StartGeneration to GenerationBarrier on next;
    from GenerationBarrier to GenerationSuccess on success;
}
end plane;
end create.
```

When the coordinator agent initiates a step, it creates a barrier in the tuplespace then starts up a set of monitoring agents that have identical tasks, see Figure 8.33. Each monitoring agent is assigned the tasks required for that step. After finishing a task a monitoring agent deposits a token in the tuplespace. When the specified number of tokens is collected, the control agent is notified and it proceeds to the next step.

During the software installation step, a monitoring agent downloads from a Web server the Surge tools, currently the C language version, and then compiles them using the C compiler and the libraries. Even though Java agents are platform-independent the agents require that the platforms have preinstalled compilers and libraries to install the benchmarking software. Currently, we are able to run the Surge tools only on Linux-based systems, because Surge-requiring thread libraries are unavailable on other systems.

In the workload dataset generation step, a monitoring agent executes a list of command-line programs with parameters specifying the number of files, maximum number of file references, as required by Surge [1].

During the request generation and data analysis steps, a monitoring agent invokes Linux processes, which handle actual HTTP requests and data processing, and the agent waits until the processes finish. The monitoring agent checks the correct completion of the Linux processes by comparing the output strings with expected ones. We use Perl-written scripts to process the measurement data for efficiency and ease of use.

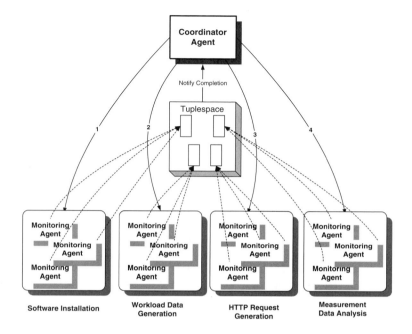

Fig. 8.33 Coordination of monitoring agents in the agent-based Web benchmarking system. The coordinator agent supervises a group of three monitoring agents and leads them through each step. All monitoring agents in the group have to complete a step before the next one is initiated. The barrier-synchronization is implemented by a tuplespace.

We now examine the bondMultiAgentDeployStrategy. Its function is to get from the model of the coordinator a vector containing the list of agents and then to go through this list and identify the host where the agent is expected to run, the path to the blueprint of the agent, and the alias of the agent.

```
public class bondMultiAgentDeployStrategy
extends bondDefaultStrategy {
  boolean first = true;
  int index = 0;
  Vector agents;
  long interval;
public long action(bondModel m, bondAgenda ba) {
 if (first) {
     agents = (Vector)getFromModel("Agents");
     first = false; }
 if (index < agents.size()) {
     try {Thread.currentThread().sleep(interval);}
     catch(InterruptedException e) { }
     Object o = agents.elementAt(index++);
```

```
            if (o instanceof Vector) {
               Vector v = (Vector)o;
               putIntoModel("RemoteAddress", v.elementAt(0));
               putIntoModel("Blueprint",
                                "blueprint/"+v.elementAt(1));
               putIntoModel("Alias", "Agent"+index);
               transition("success"); return 01;}
            else if (o instanceof Hashtable) {
               Hashtable h = (Hashtable)o;
               if (h.containsKey("RemoteAddress")) {
                      putIntoModel("RemoteAddress", h.get
                            ("RemoteAddress"), false);}
               else {transition("fail"); return 01;}
               if (h.containsKey("Blueprint")) {
                  putIntoModel("Blueprint",
                            h.get("Blueprint"), false);}
               else { transition("fail"); return 01;}
               if (h.containsKey("Model")) {
                putIntoModel("Model", h.get("Model"), false);}
               if (h.containsKey("Alias")) {
                  putIntoModel("Alias", h.get("Alias"), false);}
               transition("success"); return 01;}
      }
      transition("next");return 01;}
 }


 public class bondBarrierWaitStrategy extends
                    bondBarrierEnabledStrategy {
    private Object blocker = new Object();
    private bondBarrier barrier;
    final static long WAITTIME = 30000;
    public long action(bondModel m, bondAgenda ba) {
      // create barrier
      String bn = (String)getFromModel("BarrierName");
      String sa = (String)getFromModel("SpaceAddress");
      String sn = (String)getFromModel("SpaceName");
      int numToken = ((Integer)getFromModel
                            ("NumToken")).intValue();
      try {
        if (!createBarrier(bn, sa, sn, numToken, null,
          true)) { transition("fail");return 01; } }
      catch (TupleSpaceException e) {
        transition("fail");
        return 01; }
      // wait until wake-up from callback
```

```
while (true) {
  try { synchronized (blocker) {
      blocker.wait(WAITTIME); } }
  catch (InterruptedException e) { }
  // compare number of token
  if (barrier != null) {
if (barrier.goalReached()) {
  barrier = null;
  break;
}
else { barrier = null;}
  }
}

// make transition
transition("success");
return 01;
}
```

At each step, failures are monitored by the distributed adaptive fault detection algorithm described in [29]; failures of worker agents during benchmarking may lead to incomplete workload generation or loss of measurement data. The workers and the coordinator form a ring monitoring topology at each step. The monitoring topology is initialized at each step with a new set of worker agents. The coordinator agent is the initial contact point providing a current list of fault-free agents and it is responsible for fault recovery in the case of failure detection.

8.3.3 Agent-Based Workflow Management

Agent-based workflow management is motivated by deficiencies of existing workflow management systems (WFMS) in the area of flexibility and adaptability to change.

In some WFMS implementations agents enhance the functionality of existing WFMS and act as personal assistants performing actions on behalf of the workflow participants. In other systems the agents facilitate the interactions with other participants or act as the workflow enactment engine.

We propose an agent–based WFMS architecture in which software agents perform the core task of workflow enactment [41]. We concentrate on the use of agents as *case managers*: autonomous entities overlooking the processing of single units of work.

Our assumption is that an agent-based implementation is more capable of dealing with dynamic workflows and with complex processing requirements where many parameters influence the routing decisions and require some inferential capabilities. We also believe that the software engineering of workflow management systems is critical and instead of creating monolithic systems we should assemble them out of components and attempt to reuse the components.

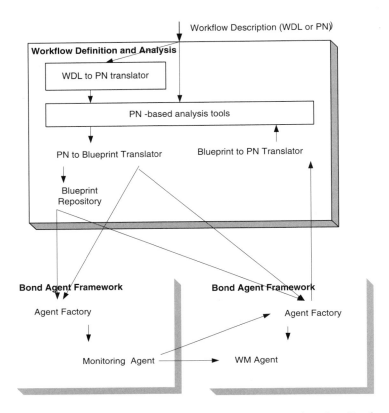

Fig. 8.34   The architecture of the workflow management system based on Bond agents.

Figure 8.34 illustrates the definition and execution of a workflow in Bond. The workflow management agent originally created from a static description can be modified based on the information provided by the monitoring agent.

Several workflows may be created as a result of mutations suffered by the original workflow. Once the new blueprint is created dynamically, it goes through the analysis procedure and only then can it be stored in the blueprint repository. The distinction between the monitoring agent and the workflow management agent is blurred; if necessary, they can be merged together into a single agent.

We use Petri nets as an unambiguous language for specifying the workflow definition and provide a mechanism for enacting a large class of Petri net-based workflow definitions on the Bond finite state machine. For interoperatbility reasons we also supply a translator based upon an industry standard [51] to our internal representation.

8.3.4   Other Applications

To test the limitations and the flexibility of our system, we developed several other applications of Bond agents ranging from a resources discovery agent to a network

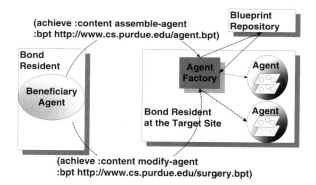

Fig. 8.35 The dynamic deployment and modification of monitoring agents. The Beneficiary agent sends either a blueprint (solid line) or a surgery script (dotted line) to an agent factory to deploy a monitoring agent or to modify an existing one. The agent factory assembles it with local strategies or ones from a remote blueprint repository

of partial differential equation (PDE) solver agents. We overview some of these applications.

8.3.4.1 *Resource Discovery.*

The Bond agents for resource discovery and monitoring have distinct advantages over statically configured monitors, which have to be redesigned and programmed if they are deployed to other heterogeneous nodes. Moreover, the local monitors should be preinstalled. The dynamic composability and surgery of the Bond agents make it possible to deploy monitoring agents on the fly with strategies compatible with target nodes, and modify them on demand either to perform other tasks or to operate on other heterogeneous resources.

We developed an agent-based resource discovery and monitoring system shown in Figure 8.35. Agents running at individual nodes learn about the existence of other agents by using the *distributed awareness* mechanism described in Section 8.1.2.10. Each node maintains information regarding the locations of other nodes it has communicated with over a period of time. The nodes periodically exchange this information among themselves [30].

Whenever an agent, a *beneficiary agent*, needs detailed information about individual components of other nodes, it uses the distributed awareness information to identify a target node, then creates a blueprint of a monitoring agent capable of probing and reporting the required information on the target node, and sends the blueprint to an agent factory of it. The agent factory assembles the monitoring agent and launches it to work. A blueprint repository, which is either local or remote, stores a set of strategies. By sending a surgery script, the beneficiary agent can modify the agents as desired.

This solution is scalable and suitable for heterogeneous environments where the architecture and the hardware resources of individual nodes differ, the services provided by the system are diverse, the bandwidth and the latency of the communication links cover a broad range. However, the amount of resources used by agents might be larger than those required by other monitoring systems.

8.3.4.2 A Network of PDE Solver Agents.   PDE solvers are legacy programs developed over the years and used in virtually all areas of science and engineering. More recently very large applications have stretched the limits of existing systems.

Such applications require solving either one problem on a very large domain, or solving multiple PDSs for multiple physics problems when we are interested is several physical problems. For example, an impact code may attempt to solve mechanical and thermal equations. The obvious solution is to use a network of PDE solvers and decompose the domain into a set of subdomains and assign each subdomain to one solver. This becomes a coordination problem and software agents simplify the problem and reduce the amount of effort to solve it.

Data parallelism is a common approach to reduce the computing time and to improve the quality of the solution for data-intensive applications. Often the algorithm for processing each data segment is rather complex and the effort to partition the data, to determine the optimal number of data segments, to combine the partial results, to adapt to a specific computing environment and to user requirements must be delegated to another program. Mixing control and management functions with the computational algorithm leads in such cases to brittle and complex software. We developed a network of PDE solver agents and discussed its application for modeling propagation and scattering of acoustic waves in the ocean.

Agents with inference abilities coordinate the execution and mediate the conflicts while solving PDEs. Three types of agents are involved: one PDECoordinator agent, several PDESolver and PDEMediator agents. The PDECoordinator is responsible for the control of the entire application, a PDEMediator arbitrates between the two solvers sharing a boundary between two domains, and a PDESolver is a wrapper for the legacy application. Thus, we were able to identify with relative ease the functions expected from each agent and write new strategies in Java. The actual design and implementation of the network of PDE solving agents took less than one month. Thus, the main advantage of the solution we propose is a drastic reduction of the development time from several months to a few weeks.

8.4 FURTHER READING

Various components of the system are described in detail in the Ph.D. dissertations of Ladislau Bölöni [2] and Kyungkoo Jun [29]. The first, covers the distributed object system and the agent framework and the second presents extensions to the system and applications.

An overview of the system is presented in [5] and more details can be found in [9]. The subprotocols are discussed in [4], security aspects are presented in [22, 23]. The agent model is presented in [6, 7] and the surgery in [8].

Applications of the system are presented as follows: multimedia applications in [31, 53], resource discovery in [30], the workflow management system in [41], the network of PDE solvers in [10], applications to problem solving environments in [33], monitoring of web servers in [29]. An algorithm for fault detection and fault information dissemination can be found in [29].

Tuplespaces are presented in several papers related to Linda [12, 13], Javaspaces [50], Pagespace [15], Jada [16], T Spaces [27, 46].

A number of Java-based agent or distributed object systems are presented in [20, 49]. The Java expert system shell, Jess is discussed in [19]. Java security is surveyed in [21]. Excellent references for mixins and design patterns are [11] and [17].

There is a vast literature on Web monitoring [1, 25, 35, 37, 38, 43, 47].

A discussion of biological metaphors applied to the design on complex systems can be found in [3, 34]. Reference [32] discusses applications of mobile agents for process coordination on information grids.

8.5 EXERCISES AND PROBLEMS

Problem 1. Download the Bond system and install it on your system. Locate the strategy repository and identify the function of each strategy.

Problem 2. Locate the code of the "GHIM", the ghost on your machine, and experiment with it on two or more systems.

Problem 3. Create a set of primitives for synchronization among different tasks, based on the T Spaces server.

Problem 4. Create a strategy repository using the T Spaces server.

Problem 5. Create a persistent storage server using the T Spaces server.

Problem 6. Modify the communication between strategies to use a T Spaces server as a model.

Problem 7. Identify the code for preemptive probes and the methods supporting authentication and access control. Design an authentication server and test theses methods.

Problem 8. Construct a new semantic engine based on the semantics of statecharts [24] and integrate it into the system.

Problem 9. Construct a priority-based action scheduler and integrate it into the system.

Problem 10. Locate a Web server providing real-time or near real-time stock quotes. Construct an agent capable of connecting to a server and gathering information about a set of stocks.

(i) The agent should first contact the user to create a portfolio, a set of stocks to watch, and a set of significant events. A significant event could be that one of the indices (Dow or Nasdaq) has a sharp increase or drop; the total value of the portfolio has exceeded predefined low or high watermarks; the value of one of the stocks in the portfolio has exceeded predefined low or high watermarks; the value of one of the stocks in the watch list has exceeded predefined low or high watermarks. The actions taken in case of a significant event are: send Email to the owner, get in touch with the stock trading company and buy or sell stocks.

(ii) Periodically the agent should contact the server and check all the stocks in the portfolio and in the watch list then determine if a significant event has occurred and if so take the appropriate actions.

Problem 11. Locate the code supporting fault detection and experiment with it in a federation of 10 agents. Extend the code with a recovery mechanism to be activated when an agent failure has been detected.

Problem 12. Write a translator from the workflow definition language into a Petri net language. Then translate this Petri net language into a blueprint.

Problem 13. Create an agent capable of controling a distributed simulation environment.

REFERENCES

1. P. Barford and M. Crovella. Generating Representative Web Workloads for Network and Server Performance Evaluation. In *Proc. SIGMETRICS 98, Performance Evaluation Review*, 26(1):151-160, 1998.

2. L. Bölöni. Contributions to Distributed Objects and Network Agents Ph.D. Thesis, Purdue University, 2000.

3. L. Bölöni, R. Hao, K. Jun, and D. C. Marinescu. Structural Biology Metaphors Applied to the Design of a Distributed Object System. In *Proc. Workshop on Biologically Inspired Solutions to Parallel Processing Problems. IPPS-SPDP Proceedings, Lecture Notes in Computer Science*, volume 1586, pages 275–283. Springer–Verlag, Heidelberg, 1999.

4. L. Bölöni, R. Hao, K. K. Jun, and D. C. Marinescu. An Object-Oriented Approach for Semantic Understanding of Messages in a Distributed Object System. In *Proc. Int. Conf. on Software Engineering Applied to Networking and Parallel/Distributed Computing, Rheims*, pages 157–164. ACIS Press, Pleasant, Michigan, 2000.

5. L. Bölöni, K. Jun, K. Palacz, R. Sion, and D. C. Marinescu. The Bond Agent System and Applications. In *Proc. 2nd Int. Symp. on Agent Systems and*

Applications and 4th Int. Symp. on Mobile Agents (ASA/MA 2000), Lecture Notes in Computer Science, volume 1882, pages 99–112. Springer–Verlag, Heidelberg, 2000.

6. L. Bölöni and D. C. Marinescu. A Component Agent Model – from Theory to Implementation. In *Proc. Second Intl. Symp. From Agent Theory to Agent Implementation*, pages 633–639. Austrian Society of Cybernetic Studies, 2000.

7. L. Bölöni and D. C. Marinescu. A Multi-plane Agent Model. In *Autonomous Agents, Agents 2000*, pages 80–81. ACM Press, New York, 2000.

8. L. Bölöni and D. C. Marinescu. Agent Surgery: The Case for Mutable Agents. In *Proc. Workshop Biologically Inspired Solutions to Parallel Processing Problems*, volume 1800 of *LNCS*, pages 578–585. Springer–Verlag, Heidelberg, 2000.

9. L. Bölöni and D. C. Marinescu. An Object-Oriented Framework for Building Collaborative Network Agents. In H.N. Teodorescu, D. Mlynek, A. Kandel, and H.-J. Zimmerman, editors, *Intelligent Systems and Interfaces*, Int. Series in Intelligent Technologies, chapter 3, pages 31–64. Kluwer Publising House, Norwell, Mass., 2000.

10. L. Bölöni, D. C. Marinescu, P. Tsompanopoulou J.R. Rice, and E.A. Vavalis. Agent-Based Networks for Scientific Simulation and Modeling. *Concurrency Practice and Experience*, 12(9):845–861, 2000.

11. G. Bracha and W. Cook. Mixin-Based Inheritance. In Norman Meyrowitz, editor, *Proceedings of the Conference on Object-Oriented Programming: Systems, Languages, and Applications / Proceedings of the European Conference on Object-Oriented Programming*, pages 303–311. ACM Press, New York, 1990.

12. N. Carriero and D. Gelernter. Linda in Context. *Comm. of the ACM*, 32(4):444–458, 1989.

13. N. Carriero, D. Gelernter, and J. Leichter. Distributed Data Structures in Linda. *ACM Trans. on Programming Languages and Systems*, 8(1), Jan 1986.

14. K. M. Chandy, J. Kiniry, A. Rifkin, and D. Zimmerman. Infosphere Infrastructure User's Guide. URL http://www.infospheres.caltech.edu, January 1998.

15. P. Ciancarini, A. Knoche, R. Tolksdorf, and F. Vitali. PageSpace: An Architecture to Coordinate Distributed Applications on the Web. *Computer Networks and ISDN Systems*, 28(7-11):941–952, 1996.

16. P. Ciancarini and D. Rossi. Jada – Coordination and Communication for Java Agents. In J. Vitek and C. Tschudin, editors, *Mobile Object Systems: Towards the Programmable Internet, Lecture Notes in Computer Science*, volume 1222, pages 213–228. Springer–Verlag, Heidelberg, 1997.

17. E.Grama, R. Helm, R. Johnson, and J. Vlissides. *Design Patterns: Elements of Reusable Object-Oriented Software*. Addison Wesley, Reading, Mass., 1995.

18. T. Finin, R. Fritzon, D. McKay, and R. McEntire. KQML – A Language and Protocol for Knowledge and Information Exchange. In *Proc. 13th Int. Workshop on Distributed Artificial Intelligence*, pages 126–136, Seattle, Washington, 1994.

19. E. Friedman-Hill. Jess, the Java Expert System Shell. Technical Report SAND98-8206, Sandia National Laboratories, 1999.

20. G. Glass. ObjectSpace Voyager — The Agent ORB for Java. *Lecture Notes in Computer Science*, volume 1368, pages 38–47, Springer–Verlag, Heidelberg, 1998.

21. L. Gong. Java Security Architecture (JDK 1.2). Technical Report, JavaSoft, July 1997.

22. R. Hao, L. Bölöni, K. Jun, and D. C. Marinescu. An Aspect-Oriented Approach to Distributed Object Security. In *Proc. Fourth IEEE Symp. Computers and Communication, ISCC99*, pages 23–31. IEEE Press, Piscataway, New Jersey, 1999.

23. R. Hao, K. Jun, and D. C. Marinescu. Bond System Security and Access Control Models. In *Proc. IASTED Conference on Parallel and Distributed Computing*, pages 520–524. Acta Press, Calgary, Canada, 1998.

24. D. Harel, A. Pnueli, J. P. Schmidt, and R. Sherman. On the Formal Semantics of State Charts. In *Proc. 2nd Symp. on Logic in Computer Science (LICS 87)*, pages 54–64. IEEE Computer Society Press, Piscataway, Los Alamitos, California, 1987.

25. Holistix. Holistix. URL http://www.holistix.net.

26. J Hugunin. Python and java: The best of both worlds. In *Proc. 6th Int. Python Conf.*, San Jose, California, October 1997.

27. Ibm. TSpaces: Intelligent Connectionware. www.almaden.ibm.com.

28. Ibus. URL http://www.softwired-inc.ch .

29. K Jun. Monitoring and Control of Networked Systems with Mobile Agents: Algorithms and Applications. Ph.D. Thesis., Purdue University, 2001.

30. K. Jun, L. Bölöni, K. Palacz, and D. C. Marinescu. Agent–Based Resource Discovery. In *Proc. Heterogeneous Computing Workshop 2000*, pages 43–52. IEEE Press, Piscataway, N.J., 2000.

31. K. Jun, L. Bölöni, D. Yau, and D. C. Marinescu. Intelligent QoS Support for an Adaptive Video Service. In *Proc. IRMA 2000 - Challenges of Information Technology Management in the 21st Century*, pages 1096–1098. Idea Group Publishers, Hershey, Penn., 2000.

32. D. C. Marinescu. Reflections on Qualitative Attributes of Mobile Agents for Computational, Data, and Service Grids. *Proc. 1st IEEE/ACM Int. Symp. on Cluster Computing and the Grid 2001*, pages 442-449, IEEE Press, Piscataway, New Jersey, 2001.

33. D. C. Marinescu and L. Bölöni. A Component-Based Architecture for Problem Solving Environments. *Mathematics and Computers in Simulation*, pages 279–293, 2001.

34. D. C. Marinescu and L. Bölöni. Biological Metaphors in the Design of Complex Software Systems, *Journal of Future Computer Systems*. 17:345–360, 2001.

35. Service Metrics. Service Metrics. URL http://www.servicemetrics.com.

36. Sun Microsystems. Java Developer Connection. http://java.sun.com.

37. Mindcraft. WebStone 2.5. URL http://www.mindcraft.com/webstone/.

38. D. Mosberger and T. Jin. httperf: A Tool for Measuring Web Server Performance. In *Proceedings of Internet Server Performance Workshop*, pages 59–67, 1998.

39. OMG. *The Common Object Request Broker : Architecture and Specification. Revision 2.3*. TC Document 99-10-07, October 1999.

40. Orbix. URL http://www.iona.com/.

41. K. Palacz and D. C. Marinescu. An Agent-Based Workflow Management System. In *Proc. AAAI Spring Symp. Workshop "Bringing Knowledge to Business Processes"*, pages 119–127. AAAI Press, Menlo Park, California, 2000.

42. R. Sethi and J. D. Ullman. The Generation of Optimal Code for Arithmetic Expressions. *Journal of the ACM*, 4(17):715–728, 1970.

43. SPECweb99. The Standard Performance Evaluation Corporation. SPECweb99. URL http://www.specbench.org/osg/web99/.

44. Simon St. Laurent. *XML: a primer*, second edition. IDG Books, San Mateo, California, 1999.

45. Sun Microsystems. Java RMI.

46. L. Tobin, M. Steve, and W. Peter. T Spaces: The Next Wave. *IBM System Journal*, 37(3):454–474, 1998.

47. tpc. TPC Benchmark W (TPC-W). URL http://www.tpc.org/wspec.html.

48. J. Viega, P. Reynolds, W. Tutt, and R. Behrends. Multiple Inheritance in Class Based Languages. Technical Report, University of Virginia, 1998.

49. Visibroker. URL http://www.borland.com/visibroker/ .

50. J. Waldo. JavaSpace Specification - 1.0. Technical Report, Sun Microsystems, March 1998.

51. Workflow Management Coalition. Interface 1: Process Definition Interchange Process Model, 11, 1998. WfMC TC-1016-P v7.04.

52. WebBench. URL http://www.zdnet.com.

53. D. Yau, K. Jun, and D. C. Marinescu. Middleware QoS Agents and Native Kernel Schedulers for Adaptive Multimedia Services and Cluster Servers. In *Proc. Real-Time System Symp. 99.* IEEE Press, Piscataway, New Jersey, 1999.

Glossary

ACID   The initials of four properties of database transactions: atomicity, consistency, isolation, and durability.

action   Component of a strategy; the code executed when a Bond agent enters a state consists. This code consists of one or more actions.

action scheduler   Component of the Bond system responsible to activate actions.

acknowledgment   Abbreviated ACK, sent by the receiver to confirm that data transmission was successful.

adaptability   Attribute of a system, ability to use feedback from the environment and tailor its actions accordingly.

additive increase multiplicative decrease   Abbreviated AIMD, a congestion control strategy used by the TCP transport protocol to adjust its window to the network traffic.

addressing   In networking, the mechanisms to identify the recipient of a message.

address resolution protocol   Abbreviated ARP, protocol in the Internet suite used to establish a correspondence between logical, or IP addresses and physical, or hardware addresses.

address space   In networking, the set of network addresses; in operating systems, the set of all addresses referenced by a process.

Advanced Research Projects Agency   Abbreviated ARPA, research organization of the Department of Defense, responsible for funding the development of ARPANET, the precursor of the Internet. Also known as DARPA, Defense Advanced Research Projects Agency.

agenda   Component of a Bond agent describing the goal.

agent   Short for software agent, a computer program exhibiting some level of autonomy, intelligence, and mobility.

agent communication language   Abbreviated ACL, language used by software agents to communicate. ACLs support knowledge-level communication between intelligent agents. KQML and FIPA ACL are examples of ACLs.

agent factory   Component of the Bond agent system responsible for assembling an agent from its description and for controling its run-time behavior.

agent life cycle   Milestones in the life of an agent; creation, activation, migration, suspension, termination.

agent migration   The process of moving an agent from one site to another. The agent identity is preserved during this process.

aggregation of states   Reducing the size of the state space of a process by replacing a set of equivalent states with a single state.

Agreement   Related to fault-tolerant broadcast. If a correct process delivers a message m, then all correct processes deliver m.

Akamai   Company providing content delivery services in the Internet. See also content delivery service.

alias   Generic name for an object. In Bond objects such as the `agent factory` do not have a unique `bondId` but a generic name. In programming languages aliasing allows a variable or constant to be referenced using multiple names.

Aloha   Multiple access algorithm; introduced by Abramson to connect several campuses of the University of Hawaii using packet radio networks.

alphabet   A set of symbols; input alphabet, the set of symbols accepted as input by a communication channel; output alphabet, the set of symbols delivered by a communication channel; example, the binary alphabet consists of only two symbols, 0 and 1.

anycast   Addressing scheme when the members of a group are partitioned into equivalence classes and a message is delivered to only one member of an equivalence class.

applet   Java code downloaded from a remote site and executed on the local system.

application programming interface   Abbreviated API, the interface available to application programs to access system functions; for example, the *socket* API in Berkeley Unix.

architecture neutral   Typically refers to an interpretative system such as Java when bytecode can be executed on any system regardless its instruction level architecture and operating system, as long as an interpreter runs on that system; JVM is the Java interpreter.

area   Component of a routing domain, set of routers that share all routing information with one another.

ARPANET   The precursor of the Internet, a network funded by ARPA.

ASCII   Format for binary representation or encoding of text.

asymmetric choice Petri net   A net where two transitions may share only a subset of their input places.

asymmetric data service line   Abbreviated ADSL, access network supporting high-speed connection to individual homes.

asynchronous system   Distributed system where no upper bound on the communication delay among components exists.

asynchronous traffic   Traffic with no timing constraints.

asynchronous transmission mode   Abbreviated ATM, connection-oriented transmission technology based on transmission of 53 byte packets, called *cells* through virtual circuits.

automatic repeat request   Abbreviated ARQ, strategy to request retransmission of a packet after a certain time or after detecting bit errors in a packet.

autonomous system   Abbreviated AS, networks and routers under the same administrative authority and using the same intradomain routing protocols.

autonomy   attribute of an agent, ability to direct itself to achieve a goal.

available bit rate   Abbreviated ABR, service model for ATM networks. Allows a source to increase or decrease the transmission rate based on the feedback from network routers. See also constant bit rate, unspecified bit rate, and variable bit rate.

backbone   A network that has connections to all other networks or network segments.

backlogged node   In Aloha, a node that has experienced a collision and has to retramsmit a packet. See Aloha.

bag   Multiset of symbols from an alphabet.

bandwidth   A measure of the capacity of a communication channel. Typically given in bits per second, *bps*, or multiples of it, *Kbps, Mbps, Gbps*.

behavioral properties   Properties of a Petri net that are related to the dynamic behavior of the net; reachability, boundedness, liveness, reversibility, persistance, synchronic distance, and fairness. See also structural properties

belief-desire-intention   Abbreviated BDI, theoretical model of agent behavior.

benchmark   Method to evaluate a service or a device based on a set of standard tests.

Berkeley Unix   Version of the Unix system developed at University of California at Berkely. The system included support for networking.

best-effort   A service model for a communication network when delivery of messages is attempted but it is not guaranteed. The current Internet is based on the best effort service model.

big endian   Method of representation of bytes or characters in a computer word when the most significant byte is to the right. Contrast with little endian.

binary alphabet   An alphabet with only two symbols usually denoted as 0 and 1.

binary exponential backoff   Algorithm to resolve a collision in case of multiple access channels. The nodes involved in a collision retransmit with decreasing probability after successive collisions.

binary symmetric channel   Abstraction used in Iinformation theory; a noiseless binary symmetric channel maps a 0 at the input into a 0 at the output and a 1 into a 1; a noisy symmetric channel maps a 0 into a 1, and a 1 into a 0 with probability p; an input symbol is mapped into its itself with probability $1 - p$.

bipartite graph   A graph with two classes of nodes; arcs always connect a node in one class with one or more nodes in the other class.

block code   A code where a group of information symbols is encoded into a fixed length code word by adding a set of parity check or redundancy symbols.

Blueprint   Language for agent description. Also the description of an agent.

border gateway protocol   Abbreviated BGP, an inter-domain routing protocol allowing autonomous systems to exchange information on how to reach various networks.

boundness   Property of a Petri net when the maximum number of tokens in a place is limited.

branching bisimulation   Method of study of transition systems based on partitioning of states into equivalence classes.

bridge   A switch that forwards link-level frames from one physical network to another.

broadcast   Addressing scheme when a message is delivered to all members of a group; see also Byzantine agreement and reliable broadcast.

browser   A Web client. Has a standard GUI and uses HTTP to access a Web server.

buffer acceptance   Algorithms used for traffic control with one or with multiple classes of traffic; see also random early detection and random early detection with in and out.

bytecode   A Java compiler generates bytecode for a Java Virtual Machine rather than machine code. This feature is common to other interpreted programming and scripting languages.

Byzantine failure   Components can exhibit arbitrary and malicious behavior, possibly involving collusion with other components.

Byzantine agreement   Known also as terminating reliable broadcast. Similar to reliable broadcast except that it has the additional property that correct processes also deliver a message. See also reliable broadcast.

calculus of communicating systems   Abbreviated CCS, observational process model due to Milner.

carrier sense multiple access with collision detection   Abbreviated as CSMA/CD, multiple access algorithm used by Ethernet-based LANs. The sender senses the common media before sending a packet and stops immediately if it detects a collision.

causal order   Related to fault-tolerant Bbroadcast, if the broadcasts of a message m precedes the broadcasts of a message m', then no correct process delivers m' unless it has previously delivered m.

cause-effect relationship   Binary relation between two events with several properties: (a) it is transitive; (b) for local events can be derived from the local history; (c) for communication events a send causes the receive.

cell   An ATM packet; 53 byte-long with a 5-byte header and 48-byte payload.

certificate   A document containing the public key of an entity, signed by an authorized party.

channel   Also communication channel, an abstraction for the process-to-process connection.

channel capacity   Maximum data rate through a communication channel. Shannon's theorem gives the channel capacity for a noisy channel in terms of the signal-to-noise ratio and the bandwidth of the noiseless channel.

channel latency   The time it takes a message to be transmitted and to propagate through the channel from the sender to the receiver.

channel sharing   Communication when a number of nodes are connected to the same communication channel.

checksum   An error detection method. The sender of a message typically performs a one's complement sum over all the bytes of a protocol data unit and appends it to the message. The receiver recomputes the sum and compares it with the one in the protocol data unit and decides that there is no error if the two agree.

ciphertext   Plaintext encoded with a secret key.

circuit switching   Networking technique when a switch physically connected an input line with an output line. Used by some interconnection networks. It was also used by the old phone system. See also packet switching, message switching, and virtual circuit.

clairvoyant scheduler   An ideal scheduler capable of constructing schedules subject to the stated objectives; able to predict the future requests and the behavior of resources it needs to allocate to them; a dynamic scheduler is optimal if it can find a schedule if the clairvoyant scheduler does.

class   Related to object-oriented programming; collection of data and methods that operate on that data.

class A,B,C,D, Internet address   Internet addresses for different types of networks; e.g., a network with a class C address may have up to 256 nodes.

classless interdomain routing   Abbreviated CIDR, Internet addressing based on the aggregation of a block of contiguous class C addresses into a single network address.

classloader   Component of the Java run-time environment responsible for dynamic loading of classes.

client   An entity requesting service in a distributed system.

Clips   Expert system designed at NASA/Johnson Space Center.

clock rate   Of a microprocessor; all operations are controlled by a clock and their duration is measure in terms of the number of clock cycles needed for completion; a 1 GHz processor is capable of executing 10^9 operations if each one of them requires one clock cycle.

cloning   In object-oriented programming; copying the data from one object into another object.

code   In coding theory; the set of all valid code words; the code is known to sender and receiver; if the message received is not a code word, then the receiver decides that an error has occurred. See also code word.

code on demand   Form of virtual mobility when an Internet host loads code from a remote code repository and links it to a local application; see also virtual mobility, mobile agent, and remote evaluation.

code word   An n-tuple constructed by adding r parity check bits to m information symbols to support error correction, error detection, or both.

coding theory   Study of error correcting and error detecting codes.

collision   In multiple access channels; occurs when more than one node connected to a shared communication channel attempts to transmit at the same time.

collision domain   networks interconnected to form a shared communication channel; e.g., all LANs connected to a hub share the same collision domain.

collision-free   Multiple access algorithms to schedule transmissions through a shared communication channel to avoid collisions. Such scheduled access allows only one node to transmit at any given time, e.g., a token ring.

collision resolution   Algorithms for scheduling transmissions of nodes involved in a collision in the context of multiple-access communication.

common object request broker architecture   Abbreviated CORBA, software architecture developed by OMG to support interopereability across multiple platforms. See also Object Management Group.

communicating sequential processes   Abbreviated CSP, observational model of concurrency due to Hoare.

communication engine   Component of the Bond system responsible for transporting a message from one resident to another; the system supports TCP-based, UDP-based and multicast communication engines.

complex instruction set computer   Abbreviated CISC, computer architecture supporting a large set of instructions. See also reduced instruction set computers.

compression   Encoding a data stream to reduce its redundancy and the amount of data transferred. Used for audio and video streams.

computational grid   Infrastructure allowing users to access a network of autonomous systems in a transparent and seamless manner and carry out computations requiring resources unavailable on any single system. See also grid, service grid, and data grid.

concurrent events   Events that are not related by a causal relationship.

concurrent system   A system where multiple activities happen at the same time.

congestion   State of a network when there are too many packets injected into a store-and-forward network and routers start dropping packets due to insufficient channel capacity and buffer space.

congestion control   Ensemble of network management strategies and techniques to avoid network congestion.

congestion control window   Used by the congestion control mechanism of the transport protocols such as TCP to limit the number of segments sent and unacknowledged by the receiver.

connectionless communication   Communication model where messages are exchanged without the need to establish a connection; for example, the user datagram protocol is an Intenet transport protocol for connectionless communication.

connection-oriented communication   Communication model requiring the establishment of a connection, prior to the exchange of any message; for example, the transport control protocol is an Internet transport protocol for connection-oriented communication.

consistent cut   A cut closed under the precedence relationship. See also cut.

constant bit rate   Abbreviated CBR. ATM service model that allows transmission at a constant rate; see also available bit rate, unspecified bit rate, and variable bit rate.

constrained routing   Routing subject to additive, concave, or multiplicative constraints; e.g., route a flow to guarantee a minimum bandwidth on all links crossed by the flow.

content delivery service   A network service that replicates the actual content delivered by several content providers; servers placed at strategically located points in the network help reduce the network traffic, improve the response time, and make the system more scalable. Akamai provides content delivery services in the Internet.

content language   Language used in interagent communication to transmit the actual information; agent communication languages allow agents to specify the contents language used in a particular exchange.

content provider   Internet service providing the information available through a service such as the Web; for example, `cnn.com` is a content provider. See also content delivery service.

context switch   Mechanism used by the kernel of an operating system to stop the execution of one process and activate another one.

controlled load   A service class available in the Internet integrated services architecture.

control structure   A data structure produced by the `agent factory` from the agent description and used to control the run-time behavior of an agent.

conversion   In signal processing; transformation of a signal from an analog to a digital format or vice versa.

cookies Items stored by a Web server on the client side; a Web server uses the HTTP protocol to build a distributed database used, for example, to track the user's interest; it is a questionable practice because it violates user's privacy.

coordination model Abstraction for the mechanisms and policies used for coordination.

core router A router located at the core of the the the Internet.

coverable marking A marking M of a Petri net is coverable if there is a marking M' such that $M'(p) \geq M(p)$ for every place p.

credential Information item used to verify the identity of a party in secure communication.

cut A subset of the local history of all processes in a system.

cyclic redundancy check Abbreviated CRC, error detecting code; the parity check symbols are computed over the characters of the message and are then appended to the packet by the networking hardware.

data encryption standard Abbreviated DES, algorithm for data encryption based on a 64-bit key.

datagram The basic transmission unit in the Internet; contains the information necessary to ensure its delivery to destination.

data grid Infrastructure allowing a large user population to access data repositories; for example, the nuclear research facility at CERN in Geneva attempts to build a data grid to support high-energy physics experiments. See also grid, computational grid, and service grid.

deadline Time to complete an action, such as transmission of a data packet.

deadlock Synchronization anomaly in concurrent processing; all threads of control stop waiting for one another; for example, one thread has exclusive control on resource A and needs B, while a second thread has resource B and needs A.

dead transition In a Petri net a dead transition is one that can ever fire.

decoding The process of restoring encoded data to its original format.

decompression The process of restoring compressed data to its original format in case of lossless compression, or to a format very close to the original one in case of lossy compression.

decryption The process of recovering encrypted data; the reverse of encryption.

demodulation Extracting information from a carrier.

dependability analysis Study of system availability, maintainability, reliability, and safety.

dial-up Network access method when a user connects to a service provider using a phone line.

differentiated services Architecture to provide QoS guarantees supporting assured forwarding, or expedited forwarding. See also Integrated Services.

digital subscriber line Abbreviated DSL, standard for high-speed communication over twisted pairs.

discrete cosine transform   Abbreviated DCT, transformation method used by the JPEG compression.

discrete Fourier transform   Abbreviated DFT, transformation method used in signal processing.

directory   A data structure containing information about the entities in a system. In Bond, a primitive object containing the bondId of all objects of a resident.

dispatcher   Component of a system whose task is to activate other components; in Bond, the dispatcher is part of the scheduler and its function is to select the next strategy to be executed.

distance vector algorithm   Abbreviated DV, routing algorithm due to Bellman and Ford, when routers share routing information only with their immediate neighbors.

distributed awareness   Mechanism used in Bond to acquire information regarding the agents in a federation.

distributed component object model   Abbreviated DCOM, software component architecture from Microsoft.

distributed snapshot   Algorithm to construct consistent cuts and allow checkpointing of concurrent systems.

distributed system   Collection of n sequential processes and a network implementing unidirectional communication channels among them; see also channel and process.

distribution   Function characterizing the probability that a random variable takes a value in its range; for example, in the case of uniform distribution the random variable takes all values in its range with equal probability.

document object model   Abbreviated DOM, a platform- and language-neutral interface that will allow programs and scripts to dynamically access and update the content, structure, and style of documents; supported by W3C.

domain   Context in the hierarchical DNS namespace, or a region of the Internet treated as a single entity in hierarchical routing.

domain name services   Abbreviated DNS, distributed database service used to map host names into IP addresses; for example `arthur.cs.purdue.edu` has two IP addresses: `128.10.9.1` and `128.10.2.1`.

dynamic host reconfiguration protocol   Abbreviated DHCP, protocol used to dynamically assign IP addresses to computers.

dynamic language   Programming language that supports dynamic loading of components; for example, Java allows classes to be loaded and instantiated at any time.

edge router   A router connecting a LAN or another type of access network to the Internet.

enabled transition   A transition whose input places are populated with tokens.

encapsulation/decapsulation   Technique used by the protocols in a protocol stack; on the sending side, each protocol layer treats the entire structure coming from its upper layer as data and adds to it its own header containing control information such as sequence number, identification of its peer; decapsulation is the inverse operation, removal of the header by the peer protocol on the receiving side.

entropy Measure of uncertainty in a system.

environment Generic term describing the set of entities an agent may have to interact with.

ergodic process Stochastic process when time averages and set averages are identical.

error-correcting code Code allowing the receiver to reconstruct the code word sent, in the presence of transmission errors.

error-detecting code Code allowing the receiver to detect transmission errors.

error recovery Actions taken by a system to reach its normal operating mode after a failure.

Ethernet Local area network. Uses the CSMA/CD channel sharing algorithm. Introduced by Boggs and Metcalfe in 1970s. The 10-Mbps Ethernet was very popular in the 1980s; nowadays 100-Mpbs and even 1-Gbps Ethernets are available.

event A change in the state of a process.

event-handling mechanisms Actions taken in response to an event.

exhaustive service Policy used by the server with vacation model; once the server visits a queue, all customers in that queue are served. See also gated service policy, semigated service policy, and k-limited service policy.

explicit congestion notification Abbreviated ECN, technique used by the edge routers to communicate congestion information to the hosts.

Extended Markup Language Abbreviated XML, a document description language.

fabric of a switch The component of a switch that actually connects inputs with outputs and moves a packet from an input to an output line.

fail-silent A system that either delivers correct results or no result at all.

failstop system A system that fails by stopping and remains in that state; all other systems are able to detect the failure of the system.

fairness Property of a system to treat the users of all resources of the system in an equitable manner.

fast retransmit Strategy used by TCP to avoid timeouts in the presence of lost packets; after receiving three consecutive duplicate acknowledgments for the same segment, TCP retransmits the following segment.

fault The manifestation of an error experienced by a system.

fiber distributed data interface Abbreviated as FDDI, 100-Mbps token ring supporting synchronous and asynchronous traffic.

file transfer protocol Abbreviated FTP, application layer protocol in the Internet protocol stack used for transferring files between two computers.

first in first out order   Abbreviated FIFO and related to fault-tolerant broadcast. If a process broadcasts a message m before it broadcasts a message m', then no correct process delivers m' unless it has previously delivered m.

firing of a transition of a Petri net   The process of transporting the tokens from the places in preset of the transition to the places in its postset.

firewall   Network security mechanism when a switch filters packets based on their IP addresses.

first come first served   Abbreviated FCFS, scheduling algorithm when customers are served in the order they arrive.

flat namespace   An unstructured namespace where there is no relationship among names; for example, from the hardware address of a network interface one cannot draw any conclusions regarding the location of the host where the interface is; as opposed to a hierarchical namespace.

flooding   Routing algorithm where a node sends all packets to every node connected to it with the exception of the one from which it has received the message.

flow   Traffic sharing some common characteristics; for example, the traffic between a pair of nodes.

flow control   Mechanism used by a receiver to throttle down the sender.

flow control window   Used by the flow control mechanism built in the data link, transport, or application layer protocols to limit the number of frames, respectively, segments sent and unacknowledged by the receiver.

flow relation   Arc in a bipartite graph connecting places with transitions or transitions to places.

flowspec   Mechanism used by RSVP to specify the bandwidth and delay requirements of a flow to the network.

forward error correction   Abbreviated FEC, error correction for data streams (audio or video) when retransmission is not an option due to timing constraints.

forwarding   Routers forward packets arriving on an input link to one of the output links the router is connected to.

forwarding table   Sometimes called routing table; used by routers to forward packets; for each destination address the router determines the output link the packet should be sent over.

Foundation for Intelligent Physical Agents   Abbreviated FIPA, a non-profit organization producing standards for interoperability of heterogeneous software agents.

fragmentation and reassembly   In networking: the process of splitting a PDU into smaller units; for example, a datagram may be fragmented when entering a network with a small MTU; the opposite of fragmentation is reassembly. In memory management: creating unusably small blocks of free space as a result of allocation and deallocation of variable length blocks of memory.

frame   In networking, the transport layer PDU; in multimedia communication, a transfer data unit in a video stream.

free-choice Petri net   A Petri net with the property that if two transitions share an input place they must share all places in their presets.

Free Software Foundation   Abbreviated FSF, non-profit corporation that seeks to promote free software and eliminate restrictions for copying, redistribution, understanding, and modification of the software.

frequency   Characteristic of a period signal, the number of cycles per unit of time; measured in Hertz, Hz, a unit named after the great German physicist Hertz; multiples of this unit are 1 KHz, $1,000$ cycles/second, 1 MHz, 10^6 cycles/second, 1 Ghz, 10^9 cycles/second.

gang scheduling   Also called coscheduling; scheduling of a process group, a set of processes that communicate to one another; thus the scheduler needs to make sure that all are running at the same time.

gated service   Policy used by the sever with vacation model; once the server visits a queue, all customers in that queue that were present when the server arrived are served but not those that arrived while the server is processing the queue. See also exhaustive service policy, semigated service policy, and k-limited service policy.

gateway   Router connecting two different networks.

genetic algorithms   Algorithms used to solve optimization problems; based on the idea of investigating the effect of slight mutations of the environment on an objective function.

global predicate evaluation   Abbreviated GPE, the objective is to establish the truth of a Boolean expression whose variables refer to the global state; fundamental problem in distributed systems, many other problems reduce to GPE.

global state   The union of states of individual processes in a distributed system.

goal-directed behavior   Agents take actions towards achieving their goals.

goal test function   Used in planning to determine if the goal has been achieved.

gossiping algorithms   Algorithms to spread information about the state of a system, or about the topology of a network.

graphics interchange format   Abbreviated GIF, a format widely used for image archiving.

graphics user interface   Abbreviated GUI, visual interface for interacting with a computer program.

gratuitous ARP   Mechanism used in mobile communication; a home agent informs the other hosts in the home network that all packets for the mobile host should be sent to him instead, by issuing an ARP request to associate his own hardware address with the IP address of the mobile host.

grid   Computing infrastructure allowing a very large user population to share global services in the Internet; analogous to a power grid; see also computational, data, and service grids.

Hamming bound   The minimum number of parity check bits necessary to construct a code with a certain error correction capability, e.g., a code capable to correct all single-bit errors.

Hamming distance   The number of positions where two code words differ.

hardware address   Also called physical address. The address of the network interface of a host; it is used by the data link layer protocol to deliver IP packets; there is a one-to-one correspondence between the IP address and the hardware address.

header   Control structure added to a PDU by a protocol on the sending side and removed from the PDU by the peer protocol layer; contains information such as source, destination, sequence number, flags; examples IP header, TCP header, UDP header, HTTP header, and so on. See also encapsulation/decapsulation.

helper applications   Applications necessary to process a response from a server; for example, the Ghostview visualization program or the Acrobat Reader are helper applications used to display Postscript and PDF files, respectively, included in an HTTP response or sent by Email.

heterogeneous system   A distributed system were individual computers are dissimilar; for example some are based on the SPARC architecture and run Solaris, others are based on thy Intel architecture and run different flavors of Windows.

hierarchical namespace   A structured namespace where the name provides some indication about the properties of the object; for example, the IP address of a host gives an indication of the network the host is connected to.

hierarchical routing   Routing exploiting the hierarchical structure of the IP namespace; a packet is first delivered to the destination network and then to a host in that network.

high-level Petri nets   Abbreviated HLPNs, Petri nets populated with multiple types of tokens, where firing of a transition can be expressed as conditions relating these types of tokens.

home address   The IP address of a mobile host in its home network, the network were the host is registered.

home network   The network were a mobile host is registered.

homogeneous system   A distributed system were individual computers have common characteristics; for example, computers based on the Intel architecture and running Linux. See also Intel architecture, Linux.

Horn clause   A sentence in propositional logic when holding of all conditions implies the conclusion.

host   Computer connected to one or more networks via network interfaces.

host mobility   Also physical mobility. The ability of a computer connected to the Internet via a wireless communication channel to change its location in time. See also virtual mobility.

Huffman algorithm   Algorithm used for data compression, encodes the most frequent strings in the input text into the shortest codes.

hybrid fiber coaxial cable   Abbreviated HFC, high-speed access network promoted by cable companies.

hypertext markup language   Abbreviated HTML, language used to describe Web pages.

hypertext transport protocol   Abbreviated HTTP, application level protocol used by the Web.

incidence matrix   Matrix describing the structural properties of a Petri net; given a net with n transitions and m places the incidence matrix $F = [f_{i,j}]$ is an integer matrix with $f_{i,j} = w(i,j) - w(j,i)$; $w(i,j)$ is the weight of the flow relation from transition t_i to its output place p_j and $w(j,i)$ is the weight of the arc from the input place p_j to transition t_i; see also flow relation and structural properties.

inference   The process of establishing new facts given a set of rules and a set of facts.

information symbols   The symbols carrying information in a code word. See also parity check symbols, the ones used for increasing the redundancy of a message.

inference engine   A computer program that uses a matching algorithm such as Rete to infer a set of new facts from a set of facts and rules.

inheritance   In the context of object-oriented programming; an object inherits data and methods from its class.

inhibitor arc   A flow relation in a Petri net that prohibits a transition to fire when a token is present in an input place connected to the transition by the inhibitor arc.

Institute for Electrical and Electronics Engineers   Abbreviated IEEE, professional society; defines network standards such as the one for Local Area Network, IEEE 802.

integrated services data networks   Abbreviated ISDN, digital service combining voice and data connections, offered by telephone carriers.

integrity   Related to fault-tolerant broadcast, for any message m, every correct process delivers m at most once and only if m was previously broadcast by send(m); in the context of network security, a service that ensures that a received message is identical to the one sent.

Intel architecture   Abbreviated IA, microprocessor architecture with a complex instruction set (CISC) promoted by Intel Corporation; the Pentium microprocessors belong to the IA family.

interdomain routing   Routing among different domains; BGP is an example of interdomain routing protocol; see also domain and intradomain routing.

Interface Definition Language   Abbreviated IDL, description language used in CORBA to provide information about the methods of a class.

interface repository   CORBA service; allows clients and servers to store and retrieve IDL descriptions of interfaces.

interference   In analog and digital communication; undesirable interaction between two communication channels, the signal on one channel is affected by the signal on the other channel.

internet   Or internetwork, collection of packet-switched networks interconnected by routers.

Internet   Global network based on the Internet architecture; world-wide interconnection of computer networks based on the TCP/IP protocol suite.

Internet Activity Board   Abbreviated IAB, a body overseeing the development of standards, protocols, and recommendations for the Internet.

Internet address   Or logical address, unique address identifying a network and a host in that network; used to deliver packets to a destination host in the Internet.

Internet caching protocol   Abbreviated ICP, protocol used by the Web for cashing.

Internet control message protocol   Abbreviated ICMP, protocol in the Internet suite allowing hosts to exchange control information. A host may report an error in processing an IP datagram using ICMP.

Internet protocol   Abbreviated IP, network protocol responsible for delivery of datagrams in the Internet; provides connectionless delivery; two versions IPv4 based on 32-bit IP addresses and IPv6 based on 128-bit IP addresses.

Internet service provider   Abbreviated ISP, provider of Internet connectivity for individual users or to organization.

interrupt   An event generated by hardware or software that tells the operating system to stop its current activity, identify the cause of the interrupt, and take the corresponding course of action.

intradomain routing   Routing within a single domain. See also domain and inter-domain routing.

IP security   Abbreviated as IPSEC, an architecture for authentication, privacy, and integrity in the Internet.

Jada   A shared data space for Java.

Java   According to Sun Microsystems Java is a simple, object-oriented, distributed, interpreted, robust, secure, architecure neutral, portable, high-performance, multithreaded, and dynamic programming language.

Java Beans   Java component architecture; allows components built with Java to be used in graphical programming environments.

Java expert system shell   Abbreviated JESS, expert system shell developed at Sandia National Laboratory. Written in Java, JESS is closely related to an earlier system called Clips.

Java native interface   Abbreviate JNI, standard programming interface for writing Java native methods and embedding the Java virtual machine into native applications.

Java virtual machine   Abbreviated JVM, an interpreter for the Java bytecode generated by a Java compiler; the interpreter regards bytes as instructions, identifies the type of each instruction, and it executes them.

JavaRMI   Java remote method invocation, remote procedure call protocol for Java.

JavaSpaces   Java-based tuplespace product offered by Sun Microsystems.

Jini   Distributed computing environment based on Java, from Sun Microsysytems.

jitter   Variation in the delay experienced by the packets of an audio or video stream when crossing the network. Jitter has a negative impact on the quality of an audio connection.

Joint Photographic Experts Group Abbreviated as JPEG. Used to denote a compression algorithm and a format for transmission of still images.

Kerberos Authentication system developed at MIT in which a trusted party is used by two entities to authenticate each other.

key distribution Mechanism for distribution of cryptographic keys, in particular of public keys.

k-limited service Scheduling policy used in the sever with vacation model; once the server visits a queue at most k customers in that queue are served. See also exhaustive, gated, and semigated policies.

knowledge acquisition The process of gathering domain-specific knowledge.

knowledge base A set of representations of facts about the world; each fact is represented by a *sentence*.

knowledge engineer An individual trained in representation but not an expert in a particular domain; she interacts with the domain experts to become educated in that domain through a process called knowledge acquisition; her role is to investigate what concepts are important and to create a formal representation of the objects and relationships in that domain.

knowledge engineering The process of building a knowledge base.

Knowledge Interchange Format Abbreviated KIF, content language based on first-order logic and set theory developed at Stanford as a result of the knowledge-sharing effort of DARPA.

Knowledge Query and Manipulation Language Abbreviated KQML, agent communication language developed as a result of the knowledge-sharing effort of DARPA.

knowledge representation language Language to represent the sentences in a knowledge base.

latency The time needed for an activity to complete.

laxity Interval of time left until the expiration of a deadline; for example, shortest-laxity-first scheduling strategies schedule real-time tasks based on their laxity.

layered communication architecture Decomposition of the communication functions into layers that have well-defined interfaces and functionality and communicate only according to well-defined patterns among themselves; for example a layer communicates only with the one above and below.

leasing Strategy to avoid wasting of resources when entities they are allocated to fail before releasing them; the resource is released unless the lease is renewed periodically.

least-cost path A path such that the sum of the costs associated with the links crossed traversing the path is minimal.

light-weight object In Bond, an object that does not have a bondId, for example, a message.

link Physical connection between two nodes of a network.

link state   Abbreviated LS, routing algorithm due to Djikstra; routers need complete information about the network topology.

Linux   Unix-like operating system; the Linux kernel was developed in 1991 by Linus Torvalis. The Linux systems and applications developed for it have contributed to the advancement of open source movement.

little endian   Method of representation of bytes or characters in a computer word when the most significant byte is to the left; contrast with big endian.

liveness   Informally, a property of a system saying that eventually something "good" will happen, the system will reach a good state, for some definition of what a "good" state means; for example, for a sequential program liveness means that the program will terminate; testing for violation of liveness properties require looking at infinite executions.

load balancing   The process of distributing evenly the load placed on the compute nodes of a distributed system.

local area network   Abbreviated LAN, network technologies supporting communication limited to a geographic area of up to a few Kilometers; Ethernet, FDDI are examples of LAN technologies. Typically uses a shared communication channel.

lossless compression   Data compression when no information is lost; several techniques such as run length encoding, or Huffmann encoding result in lossless compression.

lossy compresion   Data compression when some of the information lost cannot be recovered, but the information loss is deemed tolerable; JPEG and MPEG allow different levels of compression for different image, audio, or video quality.

Manchester   Encoding scheme; transmits the exclusive-OR of the clock and the NRZ-encoded data.

marking of a Petri net   Disposition of tokens in the places of the net; determines the state of the system modeled by the net.

Markov chain   Memoryless stochastic process; the next state the system could get into does not depend on the past history, it is only determined by the current state of the system

maximum likelihood decoding   Decoding strategy when a received n-tuple is decoded into the code word to minimize the probability of errors.

maximum transmission unit   Abbreviated MTU, the largest packet size accepted by a network.

media access control   Abbreviated MAC, algorithms used for access control for shared communication channels.

message authorization code   Abbreviated MAC, a message digest with an associated key.

message digest version 5   Abbreviated MD5, checksum algorithm used to verify that the contents of a message has not been altered.

message passing   Widely used communication paradigm in distributed systems; dual to remote method invocation.

message switching   Networking technique when entire messages are sent through a store-and-forward network; impractical because the size of a message can be very large. See also circuit switching and packet switching.

metadata   Data used to describe the format of data.

metropolitan area network   Abbreviated MAN, high-speed networking techniques used for transmission capable of covering a metropolitan area. See also LAN and WAN.

middleware   Software supporting societal services in a wide-area distributed system.

mobile agent   Form of virtual mobility when an Internet host stops a process, sends the data, the code, and the state of a running process to another host and the process resumes execution at the remote location.

mobility   Ability to move a host or code within the Internet. See also physical and virtual mobility.

model   Abstraction of a system retaining the most relevant aspects of the system.

modulation   Inscribing information on a physical signal carrier. See also demodulation.

Moving Picture Experts Group   Abbreviated MPEG; typically referring to a format and an algorithm for video stream compression.

MPEG Layer 3   Abbreviated as MP3, audio compression standard.

multicast   Addressing scheme supporting the delivery of a message to a set of recipients from a list.

multicast backbone   Abbreviated MBone, logical network superimposed over the Internet, consisting of multicast-enhanced routers that use tunneling to transport multicast messages or streams.

multimedia communication   Communication involving transmission of text, audio streams, images, and video streams.

multiple access   Communication paradigm allowing a number of stations to share a communication channel. See also Ethernet, Aloha.

multiplexing   Combining several information or signal streams into one; for example, on the sending side the IP layer multiplexes TCP, UDP, and other packet streams into one.

multiprotocol label switching   Abbreviated MPLS, technique to implement IP routers on ATM switches.

multipurpose Internet mail extensions   Abbreviated MIME, set of specifications to convert binary data such as images into ASCII text and send it by Email.

multithreaded language   A programming language that supports multiple threads of execution.

multithreaded server   A server that supports multiple threads of control, usually one per client process.

name resolution   Determining the IP address knowing the host name. See also domain name services.

name server   Server used by domain name services.

network file system   Abbreviated NFS, distributed file system from Sun Microsystems.

network layer   An abstraction for a set of functions expected from a network.

non-preemptive scheduling   Policy that prevents a scheduler from forcing a principal to relinquish control over a resource; for example, once the transmission of a packet has begun, the transmission cannot be interrupted and a higher priority packet sent instead.

Nyquist theorem   Gives the minimum sampling rate for analog to digital conversion.

n-tuple   Vector with n components. Each component is a symbol from an input alphabet; for example, a binary 4-tuple is a vector with four components, each one being either 0 or 1.

Object Management Group   Abbreviated OMG, organization formed in 1989 to create a component-based software marketplace, by introduction of standardized object software.

object request broker   Abbreviated ORB, component of the CORBA system, effectively a software bus.

ontology   A particular theory of the nature of being; used to decide on a vocabulary of predicates, functions, and constants for knowledge representation.

open knowledge base connectivity   Abbreviated OKBC, an emerging standard for knowledge representation.

open source   Movement to distribute freely the source code of systems and applications. The roots of the movement can be traced back to Richard Stallman's launching of the GNU project in 1983, aimed at creating free Unix-like operating systems. See also Free Software Foundation.

Open Software Foundation   Abbreviated OSF, consortium of computer vendors who have defined standards for distributed computing.

open system   A system whose components are free to join and leave the system at any time.

open systems interconnection   Abbreviated OSI, the seven layer model developed by the International Standards Organization, ISO.

open shortest path first   Abbreviated OSPF, routing protocol based on the Link State algorithm.

optimal scheduling algorithm for dynamic scheduling   A scheduler that can produce a schedule when a clairvoyant one does.

packet   Data unit sent over a packet-switched network; a message is cut into packets and transmitted through the network.

packet switching   Networking technique based on splitting a message into pieces of a maximum size, packets, and individual routing of the packets through a store-and-forward network towards their destination. See also message switching and circuit switching.

parity check symbols   Symbols added to a message to increase the redundancy and support error correcting and/or error detecting capabilities of a code.

peer   Protocol at the same layer on a node we communicate with; network architectures are based on peer-to-peer communication.

peer-to-peer communication   Layered communication model when the sending layer adds to a data unit control information for its peer on the receiving side.

peer-to-peer architecture   Architectural model supporting interoperability of distributed systems; also, consortium of companies supporting this architecture.

persistence of a Petri net   A Petri net is persistent if for any two enabled transitions, the firing of one will not disable the other.

persistence of a database transaction   A database transaction is persistent if once committed its effects cannot re reversed.

persistent storage   Storage where information can be preserved and retrieved after very long periods of time, the opposite of volatile storage.

Petri nets   Bipartite graphs introduced by Karl Adam Petri in 1962 to model the behavior of concurrent systems.

place   Type of node of a Petri net used to model conditions. See also transition.

plain old telephone system   Abbreviated POTS, the phone system based on analog signal transmission and circuit switching.

plaintext   Text to be encoded to preserve confidentiality. See also ciphertext.

platform   Refers to the hardware, the operating system, or both; for example, Linux platform is a system running Linux, Intel platform is a system based on the Intel architecture; the concept was extended to cover higher level environments, e.g., Java platform, a system capable to run Java.

point-to-point protocol   Abbreviated PPP, data-link layer protocol used to connect computers over dial-up lines.

polymorphic function   Function accepting input arguments of different types, where the actual processing and the results are determined by the type of the input.

port   The point where a host attaches to the network; the unique identification of a socket given the transport protocol; the connection to input and output links on a switch.

portable data format   Abbreviated PDF, widely used format to archive text and images.

Postscript   Page description language from Adobe.

postset of a transition/place in a Petri net   The set of places/transitions connected with arcs originating from a transition/place.

preemptive scheduling   Scheduling policy that allows the scheduler to interrupt the execution of the current process and give control to another process; in general, the ability to force a principal to relinquish control over a resource.

preset of a transition/place in a Petri net   The set of places/transitions connected with arcs terminating on a transition/place.

process   Abstraction for a computer activity.

promiscuous mode   The mode when a network interface connected to a broadcast communication channel receives all frames transmitted rather than those carrying its own hardware address.

protocol   A communication discipline, a set of rules followed by all the parties involved in a communication act.

protocol data unit   Abbreviated PDU, a data unit exchanged between peer protocol layers. For example, in case of the transport layer protocols the peers exchange TDUs, transport data layer units, also called frames.

protocol stack   Set of protocols corresponding to the layers of a networking architecture; for example, the IP protocol stack includes IP at the network layer, TCP and UDP at the transport layer, and a variety of application protocols such as FTP, HTTP, RTP, RTCP.

public key cryptography   Communicating entities have both a *private* and a *public* key. A secure message is sent to an entity E by encrypting it with E's *public key*; E decrypts the message with its own *private key*.

quality of service   Abbreviated QoS, performance guarantees covering the bandwidth, delay, and jitter provided by a network architecture.

quantization   The process of transforming a continuous-amplitude set of samples into a set of discrete values; if we have n bits per sample, we can distinguish between 2^n quantization levels. Quantization and sampling are necessary for analog to digital conversion.

quantization noise   Noise introduced by the quantization process; the limited number of quantization levels limits our ability to express exactly the amplitude of the analog signal.

qubit   Quantum bit.

random early detection   Abbreviated RED, mechanisms allowing the routers to anticipate network congestion and drop packets before they run out of resources; the hosts using TCP react to this by decreasing their congestion windows.

random early detection with in and out   Abbreviated RIO, packet drop policy based on random early detection supporting two classes of service, `in` and `out`; the probability of dropping the In packets is lower than the one for the Out packets when the network is congested.

random variable   A real-valued variable associated with an experiment.

reachability analysis of a system   Finding all the states that can be reached given the current state of the system.

real-time streaming protocol   Abbreviated RTSP, protocol used for client-server coordination in multimedia streaming.

real-time system   A system when individual tasks have deadlines.

real-time transport control protocol   Abbreviated RTCP, control protocol for the real-time transport protocol.

real-time transport protocol   Abbreviated RTP, end-to-end protocol used for multimedia communication.

reduced instruction set computer   Abbreviated RISC, computer architecture supporting a minimal set of instructions. See also complex instruction set computers.

reliable broadcast   Form of broadcast with two properties, validity and uniform integrity.

remote evaluation   Form of virtual mobility when a host sends data and code to another host and initiates remote execution there.

remote procedure call   Abbreviated RPC, transport protocol used by client-server applications; often synchronous, the client blocks waiting for a response; more recently asynchronous RPCs are supported.

repeater   Device that propagates signals from one network segment to another; repeaters forward signals; bridges forward data link layer units called frames; routers forward network layer data units, packets.

request for comments   Abbreviated RFC. Internet reports containing protocol specifications, algorithms, or other technical data.

resource   Generic term for facilities offered by a system and needed for the completion of a task; in the context of the Web, a file stored on a Web server.

resource description framework   Abbreviated RDF, lightweight ontology system to support the exchange of knowledge on the Web.

resource reservation protocol   Abbreviated RSVP, protocol using the soft state to reserve resources along a path between the receiver and the sender.

Rete   Pattern matching algorithm used by many inference engines.

reversibility   Property of a system guaranteeing that one can always get back to the original state.

router   Switch connecting several networks to one another.

routing   The process of computing routs and constructing forwarding tables used by routers to forward incoming packets on the output links they are connected to; sometimes the term routing covers construction of routing (forwarding) tables as well as packet forwarding.

routing information protocol   Abbreviated RIP, an intradomain routing protocol first introduced in Berkely Unix.

RSA   Public key encryption algorithm named after its inventors, Rivest, Shamir, and Adleman.

safety   Informally, a safety property of a system means that the system remains in a "good" state, for some definition of what a "good" state means; mutual exclusion is an example of a safety property of a concurrent system; a violation of safety can be observed in finite time.

sampling   The process of converting a continuous-time signal into a set of discrete samples; used in analog to digital conversion.

sampling theorem   Due to Nyquist; to allow the reconstruction of a continuous-time signal from a set of discrete samples, the sampling frequency should be at least twice the largest frequency in the spectrum of the signal; for example, the sampling frequency for voice communication is 8000 samples per second, because the highest frequency in the spectrum of voice communication is 4000 Hz.

scheduler Component of a system that decides who controls a resource at a given time; for example, a CPU scheduler gives control over the CPU to a process for a specified time slot, then stops the process and picks up the next process ready to run from a list and allocates the CPU to it.

scheduling algorithm Method to control the allocation of shared resources.

scheduling policy Algorithm to decide the order in which the customers are served; examples of scheduling policies are: FIFO, LIFO, priority-based. Also in case of a server with vacation the decision regarding the number of customers served; see server with vacation.

secure socket layer Abbreviated SSL, protocol layer above TCP supporting authentication and encryption.

semantic engine Component of the Bond system that controls the transition from one state of a state machine to another state.

semigated service policy Used by the sever with vacation model; once the server visits a queue, it serves customers in that queue until the number of customers left is one less than the number when the server arrived. See also exhaustive service policy, gated service policy, and k-limited service policy.

sensor Device capable of collecting information about the environment; for example, a camera collects visual information, a microphone collects audio information, a motion detector collects motion information.

server Provider of service in a distributed system.

server with vacation Service model when a server visits multiple queues, serves customers from that queue, and then proceeds to the next queue; useful for modeling token passing systems.

service grid Infrastructure allowing a large community of users to share services offered by autonomous service providers connected at the edge of the Internet.

shaper Component of a traffic control system that delays flows that do not follow the contracts.

shell Command interpreter; allows a user to interact with the operating system; examples are the C-shell and the Bourne shell for Unix.

signaling The process of transmitting control information; in-band signaling, the control information is embedded into the data stream; out-of-band signaling a separate communication channel is used to transmit control information.

simple mail transfer protocol Abbreviated SMTP, the Internet mail protocol.

simulated annealing Optimization technique based on a thermodynamics analogy.

sliding window Window mechanism supporting flow control and congestion control; the sequence numbers of the segments the sender is allowed to send and the receiver is able to accept, advances in time as acknowledgments from the receiver arrive. See also window, congestion control window, and flow control window.

slow start   Component of the congestion control mechanism implemented by TCP; a timeout signals a congested network and then the congestion window size is decreased following the AIMD algorithm.

societal services   Services provided to the entire user community in a wide-area distributed system, such as directory services, event services, and persistent storage services.

socket   An abstraction for the end point of a communication channel. First introduced in Berkeley Unix; a socket exposes the API for network communication primitives to user processes.

soft state   Mechanism used in conjunction with resource leasing by RSVP and distributed systems such as Jini for resource reservation. A resource is only leased and released if the lease is not renewed; in contrast with hard state when, once allocated, the resource has to be explicitly deallocated.

software agent   Computer program exhibiting some level of autonomy, intelligence, and mobility.

software composition   The goal of component-based architecture, building more complex programs from simple components.

Solaris   Operating system from Sun Microsystems.

source routing   Algorithm when the source of the packet decides the path the packet will follow.

stochastic high-level Petri net   Abbreviated SHLPN, extension of high-level Petri nets with an exponentially distributed random variable associated to a transition.

stochastic Petri net   Abbreviated SPN, a Petri net where there is an exponentially distributed random variable associated with a transition, the time from the instance the transition is enabled and the instance it fires.

stochastic process   An indexed collection of random variables X_t for $t \in T$ where T is a non-empty set. All random variables have the same associated probability space.

stop and wait   Reliable but very inefficient data link protocol.

strategy   Component of a Bond agent; once an agent enters a state, the strategy associated with that state is activated.

strongly typed language   A programming language that allows for extensive compile-time checking for potential type-mismatch problems.

structural properties of Petri nets   Properties related to the topology of the net and reflected by the incidence matrix and the invariants.

subprotocol   Closed set of messages exchanged by two Bond agents; based on the idea of conversations.

switch   A device with multiple inputs and outputs capable to connect any input to any output.

synchronic distance   A metric closely related to the mutual dependence between two events in a condition/event system.

synchronous optical network   Abbreviated SONET, standard for digital data transmission over fiber optics networks; based on clock framing.

synchronous system   System where the communication delay between any two nodes is bounded.

synchronous traffic   Traffic with timing constrains.

TELNET   Remote access protocol in the Internet protocol suite.

thrashing   Undesirable state of a computer system when frequent context switching prevents the completion of any task.

thread   Or light-weight process; abstraction for a dispatchable unit of work. Multiple threads may share the same address space.

threat to a causal link in planning   A step that can nullify that link; the step γ is a positive threat if its inclusion between α and β would make step α useless;

throughput   A quantitative measure of results produced by an entity; for example; the throughput of a network is given in number of packets or bytes delivered per unit of time, the throughput of a computer system is the number of jobs completed per unit of time, and so on.

timeout   Event generated when the interval allowed for completion of a task expires; for example, once a TCP segment is sent a timeout related to the round trip time is set; the segment is retransmitted if the timeout expires.

timestamp   Indication of the time of an action recorded on a transaction or a message; if the clocks of the sender and receiver are synchronized then the timestamp will provide an indication of the communication time.

time to live   Abbreviated TTL, a measure of the time a datagram is allowed to travel in the Internet. Usually given in number of hops.

token   In Petri nets, entities flowing through the bipartite graph.

token bucket   Abstraction used for traffic control; a token bucket is capable to describe not only the average resource needs but also the bursty behavior. Tokens accumulate at a given rate into a bucket and are consumed for every byte of data transmitted; once the bucket is empty, the flow must stop transmitting; a bursty flow may use all the tokens in the bucket in a very short period of time.

total order   Related to fault-tolerant broadcast, if correct processes p and q both deliver messages m and m', then p delivers m before m' if and only if q delivers m before m'.

trace   Collections of past events; the history of a system can be used to replay its behavior to detect the cause of an error or to study the behavior of a modified version of the system.

transition   Type of nodes of a Petri net used to model events or actions.

transport control protocol   Abbreviated TCP, connection-oriented transport protocol in the Internet protocol suite, providing reliable, in-order, segment delivery.

transport protocol   A communication protocol connecting two processes. Addresses end-to-end issues in communication. TCP and UDP are Internet transport protocols.

trimming   Transformation of a Bond agent; states unreachable from the current state are eliminated.

tunneling   Creating an express path between two communicating entities by encapsulating a message; for example, in case of mobile IP, a tunnel is established between the home and the foreign agent. Also IP multicast packets are encapsulated into IP unicast packets and tunneled between routers implementing the multicast protocol.

unicast   Addressing scheme when a PDU is sent to a unique destination.

uniform integrity   Related to fault-tolerant broadcast, for any message m process q recives m at most once from process p and only if p has previously sent m to q.

uniform resource identifier   Abbreviated URI, the mechanism used to identify a resource in the Internet. An URL is an example of URI.

uniform resource locator   Abbreviated URL, a string used to identify a resource on a host in the Internet; it is obtained by concatenating a string identifying the resource and the name of the host; for example, "http://bond.cs.purdue.edu" identifies the system aliased to "bond" on the HTTP server running at port 80 on the host named "cs.purdue.edu".

unspecified bit rate   Abbreviated UBR; ATM service model corresponding to best-effort service. See also available bit rate, constant bit rate, and variable bit rate.

user datagram protocol   Abbreviated UDP; an unreliable, connectionless transport protocol in the Internet protocol suite.

validity   Related to fault-tolerant broadcast, if a correct process broadcast message m then all correct processes eventually deliver m.

variable bit rate   Abbreviated VBR; ATM service model for applications whose bandwidth requirements vary in time, such as compressed video. See also available bit rate, constant bit rate, and unspecified bit rate.

virtual circuit   Networking abstraction for connection-oriented communication, when all packets exchanged between the same source-destination pairs follow the same path in the network. Contrast with datagram networks when packets exchanged between the same source-destination pairs follow different routes.

virtual mobility   Type of Internet mobility when code, data, and/or process state is transferred from one host to another in the Internet. Contrast to physical mobility when a host moves around the Internet. See also code on demand, remote evaluation, and mobile agent.

weighted fair queuing   Abbreviated WFQ, a queuing discipline allowing consumers to be allocated different fractions of the capacity of a shared resource.

weight of an arc in a Petri net $w(i,j)$, the weight of the flow relation from transition t_i to its output place p_j, $w(i,j)$ represents the number of tokens added to the output place p_j when transition t_i fires. $w(k,m)$, the weight of the arc from the input place p_k to transition t_m, $w(k,m)$ represents the tokens removed from the input place p_k when transition t_m fires.

wide area network   Abbreviated WAN, network technique for interconnecting systems spanning a large geographic area.

window   In communication, abstraction used to limit the number of messages exchanged between a sender and a receiver; in graphics, user interfaces, a graphics object connected to a process.

workflow   Coordinated execution of multiple tasks or activities.

Workflow Description Language   Language for process description proposed by the Workflow Management Coalition.

Workflow Management Coalition   Organization of vendors, users, and researchers in the worflow area.

World Wide Web   Abbreviated WWW, ubiquitous Internet application based on the HTTP protocol for client-server communication and HTML, a description language for Web resources; also referred to as the Web.

World Wide Web Consortium   Abbreviated W3C, non-profit organization whose charter is to develop interoperable technologies (specifications, guidelines, software, and tools) to lead the Web to its full potential as a forum for information, commerce, communication, and collective understanding.

Index